WORLD CHRONOLOGY
OF
MUSIC HISTORY

Dayot, Armand – La Renaissance en France de Charles VIII a Louis XIII Paris: Flammarion, 1910 –   *Abraham Bosse (1602-76) Paris*

World Chronology
of
Music History

VOLUME **II**

1594 - 1684

Compiled and Edited by

Paul E. Eisler

Foreword by Fritz Kramer

1973 OCEANA PUBLICATIONS, INC./Dobbs Ferry, New York

Library of Congress Cataloging in Publication Data (revised):

Eisler, Paul E.   1919-
  World chronology of music history.

    CONTENTS: v. 1. 30,000 B.C. - 1594 A.D. v. 2. 1594 - 1684.
    1. Music — Chronology.   I. Title.
ML161.E4   780'.9   72-4354
ISBN 0-379-16080-3
    0-379-16082-X (v. 2)

Manufactured in the United States of America.

To my beloved wife, Edith
and
to my earlier chronology
Judith
Paul III
Karen
and
Peter
with deepest affection

FOREWORD

The average music student, leaving school to enter life and embark on a career of his own, supposedly has a solid foundation of knowledge of the history of Eastern and Western music, both ancient and modern, and of the various musical styles and the ways to perform them. There is little doubt, however, that the sheer quantity of the material absorbed during the years of study is so overwhelming that for the young practicing musician it will take years for him to achieve true order and logic in his vision of historic perspective. There are also many professional musicians who pick up at random whatever they know about the different periods and styles of music, and the state of even their accumulated knowledge is deplorable.

The *World Chronology of Music History* is a concise survey of the art of music, especially its forms, its styles, the development of different theories, the ups and downs of music throughout the centuries and, of course, individual composers. Included, of necessity, are important highlights of what happened in other arts, what locations acquired transitory importance at any given time, and which crowned heads, emperors and kings and princes, and which theoreticians made their names known as relevant to music.

The importance of this particular *Chronology* lies in its comprehensiveness. Not only does it list the aforementioned items; it also gives literally thousands of examples of performances, premieres and — last but not least — performers. It is a gigantic undertaking. When it is complete, roughly 32,000 years of human evolution and culture will have been covered, starting with the Paleolithic Age and ending with electronic music.

Upon completion of the entire set (anticipated extent: 8-10 volumes) there will, of necessity, be added a separate index volume containing an alphabetical listing of the persons, works and events discussed in the *Chronology*.

The use of the book ought to be described. If a reader wants information about a specific time period, he will find this time period covered in chronological sequence. Should a reader wish to obtain information about a personage whom he cannot locate as to the exact time in which he lived, he may find his name listed in the Index, together with the pertinent page in the volume. The first volume, covering the ages up to the latter part of the 16th Century, will, for instance, have more to say about the Renaissance period than, let's say, about the 9th Century, the century whose only towering personage was Charlemagne, the initiator of certain chant codifications and founder of the first music schools to teach strictly Western music.

From about the middle of the 16th Century on, the material is so abundant as to require a year-by-year coverage. Let us, for example, take the year 1590. What knowledge opens up on the first Madrigal opera, on Mr. Byrd, on the "Liber Secundum Sacrarum Cantionum," on the Council of Brunswick, the popularity of lute music, the painter Zuccari, *young* Monteverdi's doings, and the violin makers in Brescia! And after having read up on the multiple facts of the year 1590, we may proceed to pages and pages of happenings in 1591, and so on. In quoting examples, the standard practice has been followed of referring to major collections of published music.

Reading about music or listening to lectures about music without listening to the music itself is definitely a profitless undertaking. It is the music itself that matters above anything else. Our author, therefore, has taken special pains to emphasize the importance of certain works by various composers which are not to be overlooked. Parallel with the emphasis on masterworks run entries of the pertinent periods in general, such as Classical Antiquity, the Middle Ages (including the Gothic centuries), the Renaissance (as far as Vol. I covers) composers up to the heavenly heights of Byrd, Orlando di Lasso, Palestrina and Victoria.

Now, *to understand music it is also necessary to have some knowledge of the forces which have conditioned the various epochs during their growth.* Music can be grasped in its very depth only if coordinated with the sum total of the art of its time of origin, with literature, painting, sculpture and architecture. The *Chronology* offers assistance even above and beyond these features by also keeping close watch over the war-and-peace-makers of different time periods, their most cunning counsellors, their most eminent philosophers.

Fritz Kramer

INTRODUCTION

The problems described in the introduction to Volume I have continued in this volume and have been handled in much the same manner. The great increase in material has, however, brought with it new areas that require some degree of explanation.

As in all historical research, continued progress reveals mistakes created either by inaccurate information or by further and more successful investigation into material uncovered through careful searching. No better example can be provided than the discovery in the last few years that Jeremiah Clarke was indeed the composer of one of the most celebrated trumpet voluntaries previously attributed to Henry Purcell. Similarly many composers' deaths previously given by year, or even by approximate year, move to a more definite category such as an exact month and date or a definite year. In cases such as this the second volume herewith may provide a more accurate date of death than that given as a death reference in the first volume. As mentioned in the introduction to the first volume, where evidence is insufficient, or where there is disagreement between major sources the different dates are given but cross-referenced as much as possible. The index volumes will carry all entries to eliminate oversight.

What may appear to be double entries are actually separate listings under different categories. For example, an opera may or may not be written the same year as it is published or produced, and so the work will appear under both categories. Briefly then, every effort has been made to make these volumes all inclusive and to accommodate the reader interested in specific areas of information.

As the magnitude of this project continues to mount, needless to say I have found it necessary to avail myself of more assistance. In addition to those mentioned in the first introduction the following have contributed greatly to this volume: Lee-Alison Blum, Alecia Gillman, Bradford Wray Hill, Erica Kaplan, Markie Trottenberg and Diane Volpe. Many thanks to them all for extra effort.

Paul E. Eisler

1595

(January 1) Henry Lawes was baptized. (Conceivably this could have been exactly one year later.)

(January 18) Thomas Farnaby's will carried this date. He was the father of Giles Farnaby.

(January 23) Richard Nicolson was appointed organist and instructor of the choristers at Magdalen College, Oxford. (Conceivably this could have been exactly one year later.)

(January 25) John Johnson's widow, Alice, was granted a lease in reversion for fifty years at Cranbourne Manor, Dorset as well as other lands. This was in consideration of her husband's services.

(February 5) An attempt to stab Orazio Vecchi was made.

(March 3) A letter was found in the Este records bearing this date and written by Giacomo Alsise, a horn-maker from Padua. In it he stated "I have let Messer Alessandro see and hear . . . one of my quill instruments (da penna), of new invention, that with two unisons (due mani di corde) forms three changes of sound."

(March 30) Marenzio dedicated his sixth book of madrigals to Margherita Gonzaga.

(April 5) John Wilson, English lutenist, violist, singer and composer, was born (died 1674, February 22).

(May 24) Camillo Lambardi was permitted to perform his own (cont.) music. Prior to this he could only perform music by the organists Stella and de Macque.

(May 26) St. Philip Romolo de' Neri, priest and music lover of noble birth, died at Rome (born 1515, July 21).

(June 18) Adultery by Girolamo Vecchi's wife brought on a domestic scandel. He was Orazio Vecchi's brother.

(July 13) Dowland went to Italy to study with Marenzio who had written to him from Rome.

(July 15) Byrd strengthened his position by securing a Crown lease for Stondon Place for the lifetime of his son Christopher and daughters Elizabeth and Rachel.

(October 1) Nathaniel Giles was appointed clerk, organist, and master of the choristers at St. George's Chapel, Windsor.

(October 20) Marenzio wrote to Don Diego de Campo.

(October 26) William Gibbons, English musician and composer, was buried at Holy Trinity.

(November 19) Huberto Waelrant, Flemish theorist, died at Antwerp (born c.1517).

(March) Nathaniel Patrick, English organist and composer, died (birthdate unknown).

(April) Orazio Vecchi was punished for non-residence at Correggio by deprivation of his canonry.

(May) Leonard de Hodemont,

Netherlandish composer, was
sent to the University of
Louvain to finish his education
following his studies at the
Liège choir school.

(May) Leading the Compagnia di
San Gimigniano, Orazio Vecchi
made a pilgrimage to Loreto that
he later described in his
"Breve compendio del
pellegrinaccio di Loreto."

(September and October)
Marenzio was host for two
months to John Dowland, who was
then about 32 years of age.
The latter came to Rome express-
ly to study with him.

(October) William Gibbons,
English musician, died at
Cambridge (born c.1540).

(November) Dowland sent a long
autobiographical letter to Sir
Robert Cecil, who had helped
him obtain a license to travel
in Europe. The letter was
written at Nürnberg.

Thoinot Arbeau, French writer
on dance forms, died (born
1519).

John Johnson, English lutenist
and composer, died (born
c.1540).

Francesco Manelli, Italian
singer and composer, was born
at Tivoli (died 1667,
September).

Johann Nauwach, German composer,
was born in the territory of
Brandenburg (date of death
unknown).

Torquato Tasso, Italian poet,
died (born 1544).

Domenico Allegri was a choir
-boy at San Luigi de' Francesi
in Rome at this time.

Giovanni Bassano was maestro of
music at the seminary of St.
Mark's at this time.

Bathe entered the novitiate of
Tournai. (This conceivably
might have taken place a year
later.)

The Records of the Archdeaconry
of Essex, at Chelmsford, showed
that during Byrd's residence at
Stondon he and his family were
regularly presented as recusants.
The first such entry was in
this year.

Byrd took over tenancy of
Malepardus Farm.

William Byrd obtained a crown
lease on his property.

Dennis Lolly continued to live
at Stondon Place and paid rent
to Byrd.

Demantius lived at Leipzig at
this time and his publications
appeared through 1650.

Dowland entered his name under-
neath a short canon in Johannes
Cellarius' "Album Amicorum."

Dowland "not being able to
dissemble the great content he
had found in the profered
amity of the most famous Luca
Marenzio," thought the mere
word of their correspondence
would add to the chance of his
own works being well received.

Andreas Düben was cantor at
St. Thomas in Leipzig.

Johann Fischer was organist of

Morungen in the district of
Königsberg, as well as at
Angerburg from this year on.

Tommaso Graziani became maestro
di cappella at Ravenna.

Marenzio returned to Rome.

Shortly after Dowland's depar-
ture Marenzio apparently took
a long journey in spite of his
delicate condition. He went to
Cracow, where with other
Italian composers he represented
Italian music at the court of
Sigismund III Bathory.

Marenzio is said to have been
appointed to the Papal Chapel.

George Marson entered Trinity
College, Cambridge.

Massaini became maestro di
cappella at Cremona.

Monteverdi accompanied Vincenzo
on his campaign in Hungary.

Monteverdi married Claudia
Cattaneo, a singer at the ducal
court in Mantua.

Nicholas Morgan, countertenor
and Gentleman of the Chapel
Royal, entered the Jesuit
College at Saint-Omer.

Thomas Morris arrived in Rome.

Antonio Mortaro, Italian composer and monk, entered the
Minorite monastery at Brescia.

Francis Pilkington was awarded
the Bachelor of Music degree
from Oxford.

Costanzo Porta was appointed to
the church of St. Antonio for

(cont.) the second time and
remained there until his death.

Arthur Scarlett was named
Sargeant-Trumpeter of the Royal
Household.

Johann Stobaeus, German composer,
was sent to Königsberg for further education.

Wilbye became resident musician
at Hengrave Hall.

Ludovico Zacconi was appointed
Kapellmeister at the Court of
the Pfalzgraf Wilhelm, Duke of
Bavaria. He moved to Munich at
the Duke's invitation.

Flandrius Arnoldus' "Sacrae
Cantiones" for 4 voices was
published by Gardano of Venice.

Banchieri's instrumental work
"I canzoni alla francese a 4
voci per sonar" appeared.

Banchieri's "Concerti
ecclesiastici" contained music
for double chorus, and was one
of the oldest prints containing
an organ part.

Banchieri's "spartitura" appeared this year.

Thomas Bassandine printed an
edition of the Psalms at
Edinburgh.

Calvisius' gospels for the year
appeared (also in 1599).

Campian produced a volume of
Latin epigrams and elegiacs
under the title "Poemata." It
was reprinted in 1619.

A book of Castro's motets for
six voices was published at
Antwerp.

1595(cont.)

Cavalieri's "Il Giuoco della Cieca" was performed before the Archduke Ferdinand.

Henry Charteris printed an edition of the Psalms at Edinburgh.

De Christo's "Liber Passionum" was printed in Lisbon.

Clinio's "Christi Domini Passiones 3,4, et 6 v." appeared at Venice.

Cortellini's Psalms were published by Vincenti starting at this time.

Giovanni Croce's "Triaca musicale" appeared.

Count Alfonso Fontanelli's first madrigal book was published at Ferrara. The signatures on the collections showed his name although it was an "anonymous" work.

Giovanni Gabrieli's Intonazioni e ricercari per l'organo was published for a second time.

Gastoldi's third book of three-voiced canzonette was published.

Gesualdo's third book of five part madrigals was published.

Adam Gumpeltzhaimer's "Contrapunctus" was published.

Adam Gumpelzhaimer wrote "Compendium musicae latinum-germanicum" at Augsburg. Fétis maintained that at least twelve editions were published.

Marenzio's concern for melodic expression was evident in the Guarini lament, "Cruda

(cont.) Amarilli," in the seventh book of madrigals for five voices published this year.

Marenzio's "Completorium et Antiphonae 6 vols." appeared. They have since been lost.

Marenzio's "Il 1° libro delle Villanelle a 3" was reprinted by Vincenti at Venice.

Marenzio's "Il 3° libro de Madrigali a 5" was reprinted by Gardano at Venice.

Marenzio's 5° libro de Madrigali a 6" was reprinted twice by Gardano and Scotto.

Marenzio's "Il 6° libro de Madrigali a 6" was published by Gardano at Venice.

Marenzio's "Il 7° libro de Madrigali a 5" was published by Gardano at Venice.

Roger Michael's works included a "Te Deum laudamus . . . sex vocibus compositum" written this year.

Gian Montella's first book of five part madrigals was published.

Thomas Morley's "The First Booke of Balletts to five voyces" was published. It also appeared in an Italian edition published in London. It was an imitation of Gastoldi.

Thomas Morley's "The First Book of Canzonets to Two Voyces" appeared. It was included in Vol. I of "The English Madrigal School."

Jacopo Moro published a book of

psalms.

Mosto's only book of madrigals for six voices published in Venice this year was composed during his first years in Transylvania, and dedicated to Prince Sigismund.

Collections of laude sung by Neri's congregation and by others were printed during his lifetime and long after his death this year.

Joannes Nucius published his second book of motets for five and six voices at Prague. It was titled "Cantiones sacrae . . . "

Palestrina's Mass #49 "Illumina oculos meos" was published this year.

Palestrina's "Liber Septimus . . . Missae Quinque" appeared in a second edition.

Peeter Philips' "Le Rossignol" and "Galliarda" appeared.

Rore's six-part "Hodie Christus natus est" was included in the "Sacrae Cantiones" published this year.

"Sacrae Litaniae variae" was published at Antwerp.

Da Salò wrote a second book of canzonets.

François Sale's "Sacrarum cantionum omnis generis instrumentis musicis et vivae voci accommodatorum . . . " was published at Prague.

Matthias de Sayre's "Liber primus motetorum quinque

(cont.) vocum . . . " was published at Prague.

Jan-Jacob van Turnhout, Flemish composer, published a set of madrigals for five voices.

Usper's "Ricercari et arie francesi" for four voices appeared.

Orazio Vecchi's Selva di varie ricreazioni was published.

Verovio's "Lodi della Musica a 3 voci" appeared.

The first of Viadana's psalms appeared at this time.

Eisik Walich of Worms collected one of the earliest known books of Jewish-German folk poetry from this time on.

The Dresden catalog of "musicalia" showed almost complete predominance by Italian musicians.

The Maurizianum was established by Landgrave Moritz of Hessen.

A passage from "La Nobilita di Milano" of this year read as follows: "Hannibal Rosso was worthy of praise, since he was the first to modernise clavichords into the shape in which we now see them . . . "

The eponymous pavan must have been known in Germany by this time.

Archduke Ferdinand of Tyrol died (birthdate unknown).

Edward Winslow, one of the founders of New England, was born (died 1655).

1595(cont.)

John Milton was apprenticed to James Colbron, a member of the Scriveners' Company.

George Peele's "The Old Wives Tale" was published.

Shakespeare's "Richard II" was completed.

Sir Philip Sidney's "Defense of Poesy" was published.

Edmund Spenser's "Epithalamium" and "Amoretti" were published.

(to 1596) Shakespeare's "Merchant of Venice" was completed during this period.

(to 1597) Johann Vom Enda (de Fine) was court organist at Cassel and participated in the approval of the organ at Groningen during this period.

(to 1598) Marenzio must have become quite familiar with the poetry of Livio Celiano, since a number of his texts were included in the former's eighth book of madrigals.

(to 1599) Monteverdi had to accompany the Duke on his campaigns in Hungary and Flanders during these years. These efforts were on behalf of Emperor Rudolph II.

(to 1599) Da Salò was maestro di cappella of the great church at Salò during these years.

(to 1600) Spanish painting: El Greco painted "Resurrection" (9' x 4'2") during this period.

(to 1605) Giovanni Croce da Chioggia was the favorite mu-(cont.) sician of the doge, Marino Grimani during these years.

(to 1608) Luca Bati was maestro di cappella at San Lorenzo in Florence during these years.

(to 1611) Gesualdo wrote several madrigal books during these years.

(to 1612) Pujol was "maestro de capilla" at the Cathedral of El Pilar at Saragossa during these years.

c.1595

Antonio Cifra, Italian composer, born in Rome (died 1629, October 2).

Noé Faignient, Flemish composer, was born in Antwerp (date of death unknown).

Richard Farnaby, English composer and son of Giles Farnaby, was born (date of death unknown).

Biagio Marini, an Italian composer, may have been born.

Walter Porter, English tenor and composer, was born (died 1659, November).

Marco Scacchi, Italian conductor and composer, was born in Rome (date of death unknown).

Annibale Stabile, Italian composer, died (born c.1540).

Francesco Turin, Italian composer, was born in Prague (died 1656).

Giovanni Bardi, Count of Vernio and a Florentine noble, lived at this time and Doni attributes to

him the first concept of the
opera. The first conferences
and performances of the kind
were held at his home by the
Florentine "Camerata," Vicenzo
Galilei, Caccini, Strozzi,
Corsi, Peri, and Rinuccini.
Bard himself wrote the texts for
several of the early experimental works in the new idiom.

Most of Byrd's important keyboard pieces were completed by
this time.

John Holmes was organist of
Winchester Cathedral.

Monteverdi, until he reached
forty, wrote canzonette and
madrigals only and worked in
the area of aristocratic chamber
music.

A manuscript dating from this
time was said to have contained
twenty two ricercari by
"Gianetto Palestina," (a cor-
ruption of the composer's name
which occurred elsewhere during
this period).

Magister Záviš' compositions
were still performed in Hussite
churches, in Czech.

The chromatic harp developed at
this time.

The regal at the Musée of the
Conservatoire at Paris supposedly dated from this time
and used a compass of four
octaves.

The founders of the new instrumental schools gave as much
care to their viols as their
predecessors had given to their
voice parts.

Musical typography underwent no
radical change from its first
invention up to this time.

It became evident by this time
that poetry had become so closely
allied to music in the drama
that a school could hardly have
one of these arts as a discipline
without including the others.

Secco recitative was invented by
the "Camerata" during this time.

Spanish soprani were in great
demand at this time.

The more common characteristics
of the Chorale and Volkslied
were the use of the melody or
cantus firmus in the tenor with
the key or mode treated diatoni-
cally and one note given to every
syllable.

Songs in the Czech language had
become so popular that, in spite
of their banning by the Council
of Basle, the Catholic clergy
re-introduced them at this time.

The effects of the great changes
in vocal music at this time were
probably more evident in France
and Belgium than elsewhere.

At this time music fell into two
categories, "pathetic" and
"pastoral."

Around this time the court of
Transylvania and the cathedral
of the residence in Gyulafeh-
érvár (Alba Julia) were renowned
for their organ music.

French Renaissance painting:
Antoine Caron, "Melchizedek
investing Abraham."

Italian Renaissance painting:
Annibale Carracci, Fishing

c.1595(cont.)
(53 1/2" x 99 5/8").

(to 1613) Bartholomäus Gese was
cantor at Frankfort an der Oder
during this period.

(to 1670) The Teatro Tron di San
Cassiano was opened as the first
public opera-house. A Roman
company performed in B. Ferrari's
"Andromeda" with music by F.
Manelli. The opera-house func-
tioned until 1670.

(until 17th Century) A "basso
seguente," a bass that doubles
the lowest voice of a polyphonic
composition, was a technique
traceable to 1595 that continued
far into the 17th century. It
was not, however, a genuine
basso continuo.

(to c.1750) From this time on,
the mass gradually became shorter. In many parts of Southern
Germany, the Latin order of service was entirely omitted, but
in other areas such as Leipzig
it was retained until well into
the 18th century.

1596
(January 5) Henry Lawes,
English composer and son of
William Lawes, was born at
Dinton, Wiltshire (died 1662,
October 21).

(January 8) Peter Philips' "Il
primo libro de' madrigali a sei
voci" was printed at Antwerp by
Phalese. It was dedicated to
Signor Alessandro di Giunta.

(February 23) Antoine
Francisque, French lutenist and
composer, married Marguerite
Bonhour (Behour) in Cambrai.

(March 31) René Descartes,

(cont.) French philosopher, was
born at La Haye-Descartes, Indre
-et-Loire (died 1650, February
11).

(May 6) Giaches de Wert,
Netherlandish composer, died at
Mantua and was buried in the
ducal chapel of St. Barbara
(born 1535). Certain sources
claim his date of death as May
23rd.

(September 3) Nicolo Amati, the
great violin-maker, was born at
Cremona (died 1684).

(September 4) Sir Constantin
Huygens, Dutch poet and musician,
was born at the Hague (died 1687
March 28).

(November 3) Lady Gresham, the
widow of Sir Thomas Gresham,
English financier, died in
London (birthdate unknown).

(November 30) Lord Maier, Mayor
of London, was discharged by
Queen Elizabeth.

(December 6) A list of East's
musical publications was recorded
in the Stationers' Registers on
this date.

(February) Richard Nicolson was
awarded the degree of Bachelor
of Music by Oxford University.

(February) In a typical two-week
period at this time the Admiral's
men presented ten plays on twelve
acting days. Two of them were
repeated and one was a new work.

(March) Donato's appointment as
"maestro di cappella" at St.
Mark's was renewed.

(August) Cifra remained at the
chapel of San Luigi de'

1596(cont.)
Francesi, Rome until this date at least.

(October) Vecchi was appointed chapel-master at Modena cathedral. Two years later he received the same position in the court, however, he also had to act as music-master for the ducal family, and also had to furnish music for solemn and festival occastions, grand masquerades, and other major events. Vecchi succeeded Guido Ferrari.

Valentin Geuck, German choir singer and composer, died (born 1570).

Philippe Rogier, mass and motet composer, died in Spain (born c.1562).

Benjamin Schütz, younger brother of Heinrich, was born (died 1666).

Hugh Sempill, Scottish mathematician and occasional writer on music, was born in Craigevar (died 1654, September 20).

Gregorio Allegri finished as a boy chorister at the church of San Luigi dei Francesi in Rome under G. Bernardino. He also had belonged to the school founded by G. Maria.

Dr. Joseph Avenarius came from Zeitz and enrolled for the winter semester at Leipzig University.

Valerio Bona was "maestro di cappella" at Mondovi, San Francesco, Milan.

Borchgrevinck had been given a subordinate organist's post at

(cont.) Copenhagen by this time.

William Brade left Copenhagen and returned to Berlin for a period of three years.

Richard Browne and John Webster visited Cassel in the retenue of the Earl of Lincoln.

On the queen's recommendation, Dr. John Bull was appointed the first Music Professor at Gresham College. The previous requirement that lectures on theory be given in Latin was waived, since he was unable to speak the language.

Robert Fludd was awarded the degree of Bachelor of Arts from St. John's College, Oxford.

Gesualdo left Ferrara for Florence at the end of the year as Ferrara's musical splendor waned. He left his wife and child behind for a short time.

Orlando Gibbons was a chorister at King's College. He was twelve years of age.

Nathaniel Giles was organist and master of the choristers at the Chapel Royal.

Francisco Guerrero described his pilgrimage to the Holy Land in his travel-book "Viaje de Jerúsalem."

Dennis Lolly served as church warden of Stondon.

Prince Tsai-Yu, Chou dynasty, found an exact formula for equal temperament and left valuable works on Chinese musical history and theory. He recognized the seven-tone scale while measuring a bronze flute.

1596(cont.)

Viadana entered the Franciscan
order.

Friedrich Weissersee was rector
at Madeburg town school.

Since Wert had died Monteverdi
was obliged to give way to
Pallavicino and see him appointed choirmaster in Mantua.

Many of Agazzari's publications
appeared in Antwerp, Frankfort,
Milan, Rome and Venice (also
1600, 1602, 1607 and 1608).

Ippolito Baccusi's "Hippolyti
Baccusi, Eccl. Cath. Veronae
musicae magistri, missae tres,
tum vivâ voce tum omni instrumentorum genere cantatu accommo-
datissimae, cum octo vocibus,
Anadino, Venice, 1596."

William Barley published a
transcription in "A new Booke of
Tabliture" for bandora, lute
and orpharion.

Giovanni Biffi dedicated his
first book of canzonettas for
six voices to Moritz at
Nürnberg.

Joachim a Burgk's "Crepundia"
appeared.

Calvisius' music, both original
and edited, comprised "Harmonia
cantionum, a M. Luthero . . .
compositarum" published in
Leipzig.

Campian issued three songs.

A book of Castro's motets was
published at Cologne.

Fabio Costantini's compositions
included motets for two, three
and four voices, issued in

(cont.) Rome.

Croce's "Il primo libro de
madrigali a 5 voci" was reprinted (also 1607, 1615).

Croce's madrigal comedy "Triaca
musicale" was reprinted (also
1607).

Croce's "Messe a 5 voci" and
"Messe a 8 voci" appeared.

Croce's "Salmi che si cantano a
terza" appeared.

Music by Francis Cutting, for
lute, bandora and orpharion was
included in Barley's "A New
Booke of Tabliture."

Thomas Cutting's Galliard
(probably for guitar) appeared.

The "Orchésographie (Davies) was
reprinted at Langres.

Some of Dowland's compositions
were included in Barley's collection.

Dowland issued a first volume of
lute pieces.

Johannes Eccard composed
"Crepundia sacra" that were published at Mühlhausen on this
date and 1577.

Eccard's "XX Odae sacrae . . . ."
was published (see also 1626).

Vincenzo Gallo published a Mass
in Rome.

Gastoldi's "Balletti a 5 per
cantare, suonare, e ballare"
was published in Antwerp.

Gesualdo's improvisatory pieces
were published.

1596(cont.)

The fourth book of five-part madrigals by Gesualdo was published at Ferrara.

Hans Leonhard Hassler's "Concentus ecclesiastici" was published at Augsburg.

Hans Leo Hassler's "Neüe teütsche Gesang nach art der welschen Madrigalien und Canzonetten," twenty-four pieces for four to eight voices, was published (dedicated to Moritz).

Kirbye's "Madrigals" was published by East.

Krzysztof, Krainski published "Katechizm z naukami i piesnami" ("Catechism with Lessons & Songs").

Leone Leoni wrote "Penitenza," a book of spiritual madrigals.

Macque's first book of motets for five, six and eight voices appeared.

Marenzio's "Il 1° libro de Madrigali a 6" was reprinted by Scotto at Venice.

Marenzio's "Il 2° libro de Madrigali a 6" was reprinted by Scotto at Venice.

Marenzio's "Il 4° libro delle Villanelle a 3" was reprinted by Gardano at Venice.

One of Marenzio's madrigals appeared in "Madrigalia otto voci" published by Phalèse at Antwerp.

Three of Marenzio's madrigals were included in "Paradiso Musicale" published by Phalèse at Antwerp.

One of Marenzio's madrigals was included in "Vittoria Amorosa" published by Vincenti at Venice.

First publication of Palestrina's Mass #50 "Ave Maria."

Phalese's "Madrigali a otto voci de diversi eccellenti et famosi autori" was published at Antwerp. Two Madrigals for eight voices by Philips were included.

Phalese's "Paradiso musicale di madrigali et cazoni a cinque voci" was published at Antwerp. Two of Philips' madrigals were included.

Peter Philips, a rather prolific composer of madrigals, published two sets for six voices and one for eight at Antwerp (see also 1598 and 1603).

The third volume of Tripartiti operis officiorum missalium by Francois Sale was published.

Bartolomeo Sorte's masses were published.

Andreas Spaeth's "Paraphrase of the Psalms" appeared at Heidelberg.

Striggio's "Il terzo libro de madrigali a cinque voci" was published.

Striggio's "Il quattro libro de madrigali a cinque voci" was published.

Vecchi published a book of Psalms.

A volume of litanies by several authors was published at Munich by Georgius Victorinus. It was titled "Thesaurus litaniarium."

1596(cont.)

The first part of Zacconi's "Prattica di musica . . . " was reprinted at Venice.

A "private" (roofed-in) theatre was opened at Blackfriars and leased to a company of Chapel Royal children.

The court at Cöthen adopted the Reformed (Calvinistic) Church.

A source reported that "Dafne" was presented at Jacopo Corsi's home. The music was by Caccini and Peri, poetry by Rinnucini.

The first performance of Guarini's "Pastor Fido" took place in Ronciglione.

Musicians from Coburg, Danzig, Dresden and Torgau were brought to Nürnberg for the coronation and wedding ceremonies of Christian IV. Trumpets were also imported.

The Gröningen Congress of Organists in Germany took place.

Martin Opitz, German poet, was born at Landau (died 1639). His birth is sometimes given as 1597.

Shakespeare's son Hamnet died.

James Shirley, writer of numbers of school plays, or masques, set to music by Edward Coleman, was born (died 1666).

John Donne went on an expedition to Cadiz with the Earl of Essex.

Edmund Spenser returned to London.

Edmund Spenser published three books of "The Faerie Queene" as

(cont.) well as the "Prothalamium," which was written to celebrate the marriage of the two daughters of the Earl of Worcester.

Cortona, Italian architect, was born (died 1669).

Dutch painter, Jan van Goyen, was born (died 1656).

Michael Romanov, Russian ruler, was born (died 1645).

(to 1597) Shakespeare's "Taming of the Shrew" was written at this time.

(and 1597) Striggio's last three madrigal books were published by his son Alessandro Striggio the Younger.

(to 1597) Viadana's "Concerti Ecclesiastici" for few vocal parts and figured bass was published in Rome during these years.

(to 1598) Marenzio was at the court of King Sigismund III in Poland (Cracow).

(and 1598) Madrigals by Antonio Bicci were found scattered among the works of Stefano Venturi.

(to 1599) A number of masses by Croce, from this period, indicated that he was the chief exponent of the Missa brevis in Italy.

(to 1599) John Farmer was organist at Christ Church.

(to 1600) Jean Le Febure, French composer, was Kapellmeister to Cardinal Andreas of Austria at Constance.

1596(cont.)
(to 1601) Morley lived at St.
Helen's parish, Bishopsgate
during these years.

(to 1601) Pallavicino was
choirmaster at Mantua.

(to 1603) Giovanni Ferretti is
supposed to have been choirmaster at the Santa Casa in
Loreto.

(to 1604) Nathanial Tomkins was
a chorister at Magdalen College,
Oxford.

(to 1631) Engelmann published
vocal music.

c.1596
Zygmunt Lauxmin, Polish musician,
was born (date of death unknown).

Heinrich Scheidemann, German
organist and composer, was born
in Hamburg (died 1663).

Bernhard Schmid the Elder, in-
tabulator and dance composer,
died (born c.1520).

Gabriel Vogtländer, German musician and poet, born at
Reideberg (died 1643, February
22/23).

Croce's "Sette Sonetti
penitentiali" appeared.

Christoph Demantius was cantor
at Zittau.

Monteverdi's friend Viadana,
later to be maestro di cappella
at Mantua Cathedral, composed
his first "Concerti
Ecclesiastici." One or various
singing voices were treated as
soloists and were accompanied
by a moving instrumental bass
(mostly unfigured).

Thomas Tomkins became organist
of Worcester Cathedral.

French Renaissance painting:
Anonymous. La Belle Gabrielle
And La Marechale De Balagny.

1597
(February 26) Vecchi visited
Venice to supervise the printing
of his works. He returns from
the trip accompanied by Count
Alvise Montecucoli.

(March 31) The Queen's State
Papers contained an interesting
entry bearing this date. The
item granted Robert Holland,
Hugh Holland's cousin, the
Welsh poet friend of
Shakespeare and Bull, a lease
in reversion for fifty years
"of messuages and lands in the
counties of York, Surrey,
Lancaster, Anglesey and Derby at
a rent of   10 8s. 4d. without
Fine, in consideration of the
services of John Bull, organist
of the Chapel."

(April 15) William Shelley died,
his widow then made a claim that
Stondon Place belonged to her as
part of her marriage and that it
had been wrongly taken and
should be restored to her.

(May 20) Vecchi's "Amphiparnaso"
was printed for the second time.

(July 7) At the consecration of
the church of St. Michael, a
sacred play was given by students in the place in front of
the church. Victorinus composed
the music for the production.

(July 22) Virgilio Mazzocchi,
Italian composer, was born at
Veia, near Civita Castellana
(died 1646, October 3).

1597(cont.)

(August 1) Vecchi's "Convito musicale" appeared.

(October 6) Bull delivered his first music lecture at the opening Gresham College.

(November 23) An extract from the Aberdeen Burgh recorded as faithfully transcribed by the editors of the Spalding Club publications stated that "The maister of the sang schoole sall serve bayth the Kirkis in uptacking of the psalmes theirin."

(June) When William Hunnis died, Nathaniel Giles was appointed gentleman and master of the children of the Chapel Royal.

(July) "Jesuitenspiele" (mysteries) were presented at the Court of Munich on a large scale; one such at this time when in addition to the principal actors, there were nine hundred chorus singers, three hundred devils who with Lucifer were driven into the flames of Hell by St. Michael.

(September) Friedrich Lindner, German composer, died at Nürnberg (born c.1540).

(December) Duke Alfonso II died in Italy (birthdate unknown).

(December) Cristofano Malvezzi, Italian composer, died (born 1547, July).

Alfonso II's death marked the end of the court of Ferrara, the cultural center of the late Renaissance in Italy.

Elias Ammerbach, a German composer of the "Coloristic"

(cont.) school, died (born c.1530).

Joannes Albertus Bannius, author on musical subjects, was born (died 1644).

Pietro Busto (Busti), Italian singer, died at Byulafehérvár (birthdate unknown).

Benedetto Ferrari, musician and composer, was born at Reggio (died 1681). He was director of the first Roman company to visit Venice.

Denis Gaultier, French lutenist, was born, probably in Marseilles (died 1672, January).

Eleuterio Guazzi, Italian musician, was born in Parma (died 1622, May). A source gives his birthdate as February 22.

Biagio Marini, Italian violinist and composer, possibly a pupil of Monteverdi's, was born at Brescia (died 1665, March 20).

Pierre de Nyert, who rejuvenated the dying popularity of the "air de cour," was born (date of death unknown).

Luigi Rossi, the major Roman opera composer, was born (died 1653).

Francesco Rovigo, a prominent composer in the court of the Duke of Mantua, died (birthdate unknown).

Cyriakus Schneegass, German chorale composer, died (born 1546).

Abdias Treu, author on music, was born (died 1669).

Georg Weber, a cantor at
Weissenfels, died (birthdate
unknown).

A small group of Men in the
arts - all disciples of the
Renaissance - met in Florence at
Count Giovanni Bardi's house
with the avowed goal of reviving
the style of musical declamation
supposedly used in Greek tragedy.
This was the group referred to
before as the Florentine
"Camerata."

Byrd agreed to permit Dennis
Lolly to continue his residence
in Stondon Place till the end of
his lease this year.

The list of payments mad to John
Chappington for an organ he
built this year for Magdalen
College, Oxford, showed that the
practice of painting the front
pipes was sometimes observed
during that period.

Heinrich Colander retired from
his position of organist at
Schwabach to become burgomaster.

C. Conradus was court musician
at Lemgo, in Lippe-Detmold, of
Count Simon of Lippe.

Diruta was organist of Chioggia
Cathedral. In his "Transilvano"
he criticized organists who
"lose half the harmony" because
they "strike the keys and raise
their hands."

John Dowland returned to England
where he was awarded the
Bachelor of Music degree from
Cambridge University.

Johannes Eccard moved the melody
to the treble in Luther's "Ein'
feste Burg."

Georg Fugger invited Gabrieli to
his wedding in Augsburg, but the
latter did not attend.

Alessandro Grandi became maestro
di cappella to the Accademia
della morte at Ferrara.

Landgrave Moritz tried unsuccessfully to get Hassler to leave
his position with Octavian Fugger
at Augsburg and become his assistant Kapellmeister.

Richard Jones joined the Earl of
Pembroke's men.

Benedetto Pallavicino was ap-
pointed to the position of
Maestro di cappella to the Duke
Vincenzo I Gonzaga a year after
Wert's death.

Peri's Dafne was performed during the Carnival this year, in
Jacopo Corsi's palazzo in
Florence, before Ferdinand,
grand-duke of Tuscany. Peri
himself played the part of
Apollo.

Enrico Radesca became organist
at the cathedral in Turin.

Rinuccini revised Peri's "Dafne."

Schütz married Moritz the
Learned's sister.

The dedication of the "Fidi
Amanti" showed that Torelli had
lived in Padua as a music teacher
in the home of Francesco Rosini
from this date forward.

Ludovico Viadana was in Rome on
or before this date.

Caccini reset Rinuccini's
"Dafne." This was probably the
first opera libretto of the
year.

Caignet's "Airs de Court" in
four, five, six and eight parts,
was published in Paris.

Three Chansons by Caignet were
in a collection published this
year.

Calvisius' "Harmonia cantionum,
a M. Luthero . . . compositarum"
was published at Leipzig.

Capilupi's "Canzonette" for
three voices was published in
Venice.

Vecchi included sixteen pieces
by Capilupi in his book of seven
part canzonets. The latter was
a pupil of his.

Cavaccio's "Canzoni francesci a
quatro" was published at Venice.

Cavaccio's "Madrigali a 5 voci,
lib. 5" was published at Venice.

"The English Madrigal School"
Vol. XXXVI contained madrigal
writings of William Holborne.

Robert Cooper, an English composer, was praised by Morley
"Plaine and Easie Introduction."

Several of Croce's works appeared in Morley's collection of
Italian canzonets this year.

Croce's "Motettia quattro voci"
appeared.

Croce's "Vespertina omnium
Solemnitatum Psalmodia octonis
vocibus" appeared.

Dering's "Cantiones sacrae sex
(? quinque) vocum cum basso
continuo ad organum" was published at Antwerp.

The first use of a thoroughbass
appeared in a work by English
composer, Richard Dering, whose
set of "Cantiones Sacrae" was
published at Antwerp this year.
A figured bass was used.

Diruta's "Il Transilvano Dialogo
sopra il vero modo di sonar
organi & istromenti da penna"
was published in Venice.

The difference between harpsichord and organ playing was
described in Diruta's "Il
Transilvano . . ."

Donato's "Se pur ti guardo"
"Livre VII des chansons a 4
parties" was published at
Antwerp (See also 1613, 1620 and
1636).

Dowland's "The First Booke of
Songes or Ayres of foure parts
with Tablature for the Lute.
So made that all the partes together, or either of them severally may be song to the Lute,
Orpherian, or Viol de gambo" was
published by Peter Short. Subsequent volumes appeared in 1600,
1603, and 1612.

The collection "Le Rossignol
musical" published by Phalese
contained a piece by Du Caurroy.

Dufon's eight-part motet "Omnes
de Sabat venient" was performed
in the royal chapel at Madrid.

East published "Musica
Transalpina" in a second edition.

Eccard's "Echo nuptialis
magnifico . . ." appeared.

Eccard's "Der erste Theil 5
-Stimmiger geistlicher Lieder"
in four volumes was published
at Königsberg.

Eccard's fifty-five "Songs of the Chorale" (Lieder auf den Choral) appeared.

Comparatively few of G. Gabrieli's works appeared in print during his lifetime. Most notable was Part I of the "Sacrae Symphoniae" which contained vocal and instrumental compositions for six to sixteen voices. It was published at Venice and proved to be a model for the species.

Gabrieli's "Jubilate Deo" for eight voices appeared.

Gabrieli dedicates his "Sinfoniae sacrae" Vol. II to Marcus Fugger's four sons.

G. Gabrieli wrote a sonata pian e forte for two groups of instruments with alternation of forte and piano to indicate light and shade.

A Kyrie, Gloria, Sanctus and Benedictus by G. Gabrieli were included in a publication. They apparently belonged to a single mass.

Giovanni Pietro Gallo's book of five-voice madrigals appeared.

Twenty selections by Jhan Gero were included in a collection of madrigals for three voices published by Gardano.

Gardano published Vecchi's "L'Amfiparnaso."

Gastoldi's "Balletti a cinque voci, con li suore versi per cantare, suonare et ballare." appeared.

Gastoldi's "Viver lieto voglio"

(cont.) and "A lieta vita" were adopted as Hymn tunes by Lindemann. He used the texts "Jesu, wollst uns weisen" and "In dir ist Freude."

Bartholomäus Gese published his "Hymni scholastici . . ." for four voices.

Hassler's "Cantiones novae" appeared.

The English "ayre" drew on the "air de cour." The great popularity of the "ayre" was proven by many English editions, either in the original French as by Tessier this year or in translation as by Hilton in "French Court-Ayres with their ditties Englished," published in 1629.

"The Cittharn Schoole, by Antony Holborne, Gentleman, and servant to her most excellent Majestie." was published by Short. It included thirty-three compositions for solo cittern and twenty-five other selections.

East published George Kirbye's "The First Set of Madrigals to 4, 5, and 6 Voyces" dedicated to the two daughters of Sir Robert Jermin, Knt., whom the composer termed his "very good maister," and containing 24 madrigals.

Madrigals for four voices
1. Lo, here my heart I leave.
2. Alas, what hope of speeding?
3. What can I do, my dearest?
4. Woe am I, my heart dies.
5. Farewell! my love.
6. Sleep now, my muse.

Madrigals for five voices
7. Ah, sweet, alas, when

1597(cont.)
first I saw.
8. Mourn now, my soul.
9. Sound out, my voice.
10. She that my plaints.
11. What! shall I part thus?
12. Sorrow consumes me.
13. O heavens! what shall I do.
14. Why should I love?
15. Sweet love, O cease thy flying.
16. That muse which sung.
17. See what a maze of error.
18. If pity reign with beauty.

Madrigals for six voices
19. Ah! cruel hateful fortune!
20. I love, alas, yet am I not loved.
21. Must I part, O my jewel?
22. Up then, Melpomene.
23. Why wail we thus?
24. Sleep now, my muse.

A collection of airs de cour was made by Adrien le Roy.

Luzzaschi's madrigals were composed before the death of Duke Alfonso II.

Macque's madrigal books for five voices appeared (see also 1587, 1599 and 1613).

Five sets of madrigals were printed in England.

Marenzio's "Il 2⁰ libro delle Canzonette alla Napoletana a 3" was reprinted by Vincenti at Venice.

One madrigal by Marenzio appeared in "Canzonette a quattro voci," published by Vincenti at Venice.

Five madrigals by Marenzio were

(cont.) included in "Fiori del Giardino" published by Kauffmann at Nürnberg.

Three madrigals by Marenzio were included in "Musica Transalpina," The Second Book, published by East at London.

Two madrigals by Marenzio were included in "Il Vago Alboreto," published by Phalese at Antwerp.

Marenzio's "Il 3⁰ libro delle Villanelle a 3," was reprinted by Gardano at Rome.

Many selections in Monteverdi's Fourth Book of Madrigals were composed prior to this date. This was indicated by the preface.

No ayres were published before this date. An arrangement of fifteen of Morley's "canzonets a 5" was published this year by Short in addition to the Dowland book.

Morley published "Canzonets or little short songs to four voices." These were selected from the best Italian authors and two were by Morley himself.

Morley published "Canzonets or Little Short Aers to five and sixe voices."

Morley published a third and fourth volume of Canzonets.

Thomas Morley's "Plaine and easie Introduction to Practicall Musicke" was published at London by Short. It provides a table, which showed the various kinds of proportion then in general use. Morley went on to say, "there were within these 200 years" (and therefore in 1400)

18

"but four (notes) known or used of the musicians, those were the Long, Breve, Semibreve and Minim." He further stated, "If a white note, wh they called blacke voyd, happened amongst blacke full, it was diminished of halfe the value, so that a minime was but a crotchet, and a semibriefe a minime."

Morley protested against transposing music written in the chiavette from the pitch-level of the actual notation. He also described an interesting relationship of a "vertuous contention" between Alfonso Ferrabosco and W. Byrd in making each to the number of 40 parts upon the plainsong of Miserere, "without malice, envie, or backbiting," "each making other censor of that which they had done." He further referred to Byrd as "never without reverence to be named of the musicians." Morley made use of bars and parts presented in rectangular arrangement, each part facing outwards as the book is placed open on the table. He quoted a passage from Dunstable's motet "Nesciens virgo mater virum," in which he had divided the middle of the work "Angelorum" by a pause two Long rests in length, as an example of "one of the greatest absurdities which I have seene committed in the dittying of musick."

Twenty-eight "intradas a 5 and a 6" by Alexander Orologio were published at Dresden. The pieces were probably intended for zinks and trombones. The composer was himself a zink player.

Pietro Pace's Opus I, a book of five-voiced madrigals appeared.

Patrick's "Songs of Sundry Natures" was published by East.

Jacopo Peri's operas "Dafne" and "Dante" appeared.

Biagio Pesciolini was only styled canon at Prato in Tuscany.

A toccata by Quagliati was included in Diruta's "Il Transilvano," I.

Francois Sale's "Missa super exultandi tempus est" was published in Prague.

"Seven Sobs of a Sorrowfull Soule for Sin" was published in London.

John Skene publishes his "De Verborum Significatione."

Soriano published only two volumes of madrigals up to this time, after which he turned to sacred music.

A book of motets by Soriano was published.

Striggio's book "Il quinto libro de madrigali a 5 voci" was published.

Charles Tessier's "Le Premier Libre de chansons et airs de court, tout en francais qu'en italien et un gascon à 4 et 5 parties" was printed in London by Este.

Dutch composer Jan Tollius published 2 collections of five-part motets and one of six-part madrigals.

The famous madrigal comedy,

19

1597(cont.)

L'Amfiparnaso, by Vecchi, was published at Venice.

Vecchi's "Canzonette a 3 voci" was published, the first volume was in part by Capi-Lupi).
Vecchi made the transition from Marenzio's villanelle to monody.

One of Vecchi's major madrigal collections, "Convito musicale," was published.

Vecchi's Motets, and Sacrae Cantiones appeared at these dates (see also 1590 and 1604).

One of Venturi's madrigals was included in Younge's "Musica transalpina."

Verdonck's "Le feu couvert" from the Rossignol musical was characterized by lively syncopation.

Este published Weelkes set of "Madrigals to 3, 4, 5 and 6 Voyces" which he described in the dedication as "the first fruicts of my barren ground." (see also 1598 & 1600). Weelkes was only twenty-one years old at the time.

Wilbye's first set of madrigals was printed and revealed a subtle stylist working within a rather restrained idiom.

The madrigal "Dolorosi martir" became popular in England due to Yonge's excellent translation.

Este published Yonge's "Musica Transalpina" Vol. II, containing 24 madrigals, six by Ferrabosco, three each by Marenzio, Croce & Quintiani and two each by Eremita, Nanini, Venturi, Feliciani and Bicci.

(cont.) (see also 1588).

Yonge's second collection of madrigals included two original sets of major importance, one by Weelkes, and the other by Kirbye.

From this date on, a number of collections containing pieces specifically for broken consorts appeared in England.

The school of lutenists began to expand with John Dowland.

At this time the Modal Sign was usually placed after the Clef, similar to Time Signature in modern music. Innumerable varieties were found in music of different periods. Even this early Morley bitterly lamented the absence of a rule for universal application.

Peri's "Dafne" was first performed in Corsi's house.

The first piece of music in which "Violino" occurred was a double quartet in church style, published this year.

Jean Laet, a well known printer, died (birthdate unknown).

Francis Bacon published his Essays.

Thomas Deloney, in "Jack of Newberry" and "The Gentle Craft" told realistic stories about cloth workers and shoemakers of his own time.

Ben Jonson was established in London as a playwright as well as actor with the Admiral's Men.

Shakespeare bought the largest place in Stratford.

Shakespeare's "Henry IV" part
I and Romeo and Juliet were
completed.

William Shelley, whose estate
was to be in legal involvement,
died without issue (birthdate
unknown).

Pieter Jansz Saenredam, French
painter, was born (died 1665).

Justus Suttermans, Flemish
painter, was born (died 1681).

The "Enciclopedia italiana"
named as its founder the famous architect G.B. Aleotti
detto d'Argenta. The date of
its founding was 1597. (Some
sources say 1600).

Italian painting: Michelangelo
da Caravaggio, St. Matthew and
the Angel.

(to 1600) The Monodic School
flourished in Florence during
these years.

(to 1602) The Florentine Opera
Festivals occurred during these
years.

(to 1603) "William Byrd, alias
Borne," who figured frequently
in the diaries of Henslowe and
Alleyn in connection with the
Admiral's Company at the Rose
Theatre, may possibly be iden-
tified with the composer.

(to 1603) Viadana's "100
Concerti ecclesiastici" appeared during this period.

(to 1604) Demantius was cantor
at Zittau during these years.

(to 1611) Giovanni Battista
Gnocchi, Italian composer, pub-

(cont.) lished various masses,
litanies, sacred songs and
motets during these years.

(to c.1613) Florence and Mantua,
greatly encouraged by the
Gonzagas and the Medicis respectively, were the centers of opera.

(to 1614) Paul Kauffmann, German
music publisher, printed a number of collective volumes during
these years.

(to 1615) Instrumental works
such as "sonate" or "ricercari"
of the G. Gabrieli type or
"battaglie" of A. Gabrieli and
Annibale Padovano, or even other
original works for the organ and
keyboard instruments have not
survived. Frescobaldi's,
Merulo's and Schütz' works have
suffered the same fate.

(to 1617) Robert Jones, Welsh
musician, was active during
these years.

c.1597
Tullio Cima, Italian singer and
composer, was born at
Ronciglione near Rome (date of
death unknown).

Giovanni Pietro Gallo, Italian
composer, was living in Bari at
this date.

Italian painting: Caravaggio,
Calling of St. Matthew. S.
Luigi dei Francesi, Rome. An
example of luminism.

Fernando de las Infantas returned to Spain.

Singing received great impulse
with the creation of opera.

The history of opera started
with the performance of

21

c.1597(cont.)
Rinuccini's "Dafne" in Florence.

1598

(April 9) Johann Crüger, German composer, was born at Gross -Breese near Guben, Prussia (died 1662, February 23).

(June 27) The earliest mention of the Pianoforte appears in records of the Este family in letters from a musical instrument maker named Paliarino, bearing this date. Another was dated December 31, 1598, and both were addressed to Alfonso II, Duke of Modena.

(August 20) Landgrage Moritz of Hessen spent the night with Schütz' parents. When he heard the youngster sing Grace he begged his parents to enter their son in the Mauritzianum.

(September 24) A volume of eight -part madrigals by Peter Philips dedicated to Sir William Stanley was published by Phalese.

(October 10) Gery (de) Ghersem became assistant maestro de capella at Philip II's chapel.

(October 20) Marenzio signed and dedicated a work to D. Ferrante Gonzaga in Venice.

(November 11) Dowland was appointed court lutenist to King Christian IV of Denmark. He received a high salary.

Robert Dowland was born before his father left England to settle in Denmark in this year (date of death unknown).

Giovanni Dragoni, a madrigal composer and pupil of Palestrina, died at Rome (born 1540).

Giovanni Battista dalla Gostera, Italian composer, died in Genoa (birthdate unknown).

Hieronymus Moors, Flemish organ builder and organist, died at Schwerin (born 1519, Antwerp).

Banchieri studied with Gioseffo Guami in Lucca.

By this time Byrd had obtained a lease for three lives of Stondon Place from the crown. The property was an estate in Essex, which had been taken from William Shelley, who was committed to the Fleet for taking part in an alleged Popish plot.

After Philip II's death Cerone remained in the service of Philip III.

Correa was appointed organist at the church of San Salvador.

Dallam made a "Turkish Organ" (the earliest known musical clock). It was a gift to the Sultan of Turkey.

Gastoldi had taken orders and was addressed as "Monsignore" in a collection of compositions on texts by Grillo which contained almost nothing but pieces by ecclesiastics.

Willem Janszoon Lossy (son of Sweelinck's teacher) arrived at Amsterdam.

Marson was awarded the Bachelor of Music by Trinity College, Cambridge.

Thomas Morley was granted a patent for the exclusive printing of music books for twenty -one years. He printed the works of William Barley, Thomas

22

Este, Peter Short, John Windet, and several others, during the terms of this arrangment. The previous rights had been held by Tallis and Byrd.

Antonio Mortaro was at the Franciscan monastery at Milan.

Mateo Romero became maestro at the Madrid royal chapel. He directed the Flemish choir, Capilla Flamenca and was a pupil of Philip Rogier.

Christoph Schubardt, the singer, merited comment as a composer who was a member of the Schütz circle in Cassel.

When he was thirteen Schütz was taken into the service of Landgraf Moritz of Hesse-Cassel.

Scipione Stella, Italian organist and composer, entered the monastery of San Paolo Maggiore at Naples.

Adriaan Valerius, a Dutch historian, lawyer, musician and poet, married Elizabeth Bowwens.

Banchieri's "La Pazzia senile, raggionamenti vaghi e dilettevole, composti e dati in luce colla musica a tre voci" was published at Venice. The work was the composer's first madrigal comedy.

Banchieri's "La Saviezza Giovanile" appeared.

Dowland's fame received attention in Barnfield's sonnet "To his friend Maister R.L., in praise of Musique and Poetrie."

Robert Barret's "The Theorike &

(cont.) Practice of Moderne Warres . . ." was published in London.

Giovanni Bassano, a Venetian singer, used a madrigal from Rore's fourth book as an example of pseudomonodic elaboration of a tenor part for his text book on ornamentation.

Luca Bati's two madrigal books appeared (See also 1594).

The tenth volume of Adam Berg's "Patrocinium musices" was published.

Biffi's "Madrigali a cinque voci, con duoi Soprani" appeared.

Caraccio's "Canzonette a tre" was published at Venice.

Cavendish's ayres fused textual and musical rhythms with great skill.

Croce's "Canzonette a 4 voci" was reprinted (See also 1604).

Croce's "Nove pensieri musicali a 5 voci" (Book III of madrigals) was reprinted.

Donato's "Oime ch' il mio languire" "Madrigali de' diversi a 4 voci. Raccolta da G.M. Radino." appeared.

Dowland contributed several eulogistic verses to Farnaby's "Canzonets."

Dulichius' "Fasciculus novus continens Dicta insigniora ex evangeliis . . . " was published.

Eccard composes "Preussische Festlieder, 5, 6, 7, 8 Stimmen."

The Eisleben Gesangbuch was published.

Short published Farnaby's
"Canzonets to foure voyces, with
a song of eight parts." There
were commendatory verses prefixed by Alison, Dowland,
Holborne and Holland.

Gabriele Fattorini published his
first book of madrigals.

Giovanni Pietro Flaccomio edited
"Le risa a vicenda, vaghi e
dilettevoli madrigali a 5 voci
di diversi autori."

Giacomo Franco's "Habiti e feste"
was written.

A book of madrigals by Giulio
Cesare Gabussi appeared.

Giovanni Battista Galeno,
Italian singer and composer,
wrote a book of seven-voiced
madrigals.

Josephus Gallus, Flemish composer, wrote his "Sacri operis
musici alternis modulis
concinendi, lib.I."

Five bicinia by Gastoldi appeared.

A collection, "Pietosi affetti,"
containing settings of poems by
Padre Don Angelo Grillo, prior
of San Giuliano at Genoa, included "Monsig. Gio. Mattheo Asola"
and "Monsig. Gio. Giacomo
Gastoldi" on the list of
"diversi Reverendit Eccellen-
tissimi Autori."

Guarini's "Pastor Fido" was
performed at the court of Mantua.

Guarini wrote numerous madri-

(cont.) gals which were set to
music long before their publication this year. They were with
his sonnets and canzoni which
musicians certainly passed on
from one to the other.

Krystof Harant composed his
motet in six parts "Qui
confidunt in Domino" in
Jerusalem.

Haultin, at La Rochelle, printed
the "Dodecacorde," twelve psalms
written according to Glareanus'
twelve church modes.

"The English Madrigal School"
Vol. XXXVI contained madrigal
writings of Michael Cavendish
(See also 1597, 1604).

The volume of the "Patrocinium
Musices" from this year contained six masses, the last one
being the "Missa pro defunctis,"
the last important publication
of Lassus' works.

Luzzaschi produced a collection
of "motets a 5" at Ferrara.

Marenzio's "Il 8o libro de
Madrigali a 5" was published by
Gardano at Venice. It was ded-
icated to Ferrante Gonzaga of
Guastalla.

One of Marenzio's madrigals was
included in Morley's "Madrigals
to five voyces," published by
East at London.

Two of Marenzio's motets were
included in "Sacrae symphoniae,
diversorum excellentissimorum
authorum," published by
Kauffmann at Nürnberg.

Edward Blancks was ranked among
the "famous English musicians"
of the time by Francis Meres in

1598(cont.)
his "Palladis Tamia Wits
Treasury," published this year.

Merulo's "Toccate . . . Lib.I"
appeared.

Filippo da Monte dedicated his
nineteenth madrigal book, published this year, to Don
Geronimo di Ghevara.

Morley composed Ballets, popular
dance-like songs, this year.

Morley's "Madrigals" and
"Canzonets" published this year.

Morley's "Madrigals to five
voyces selected out of the best
approved Italian authors" was
published this year by Este.
It contained two English madrigals by Philips.

Nanino's "Madrigali, a 5 voci,"
Lib. I. was published at Venice
this year (See also 1579 and
1588).

A great number of simple dance
tunes were preserved in the
books by Augustus Nörmiger.

Nörmiger, court organist at
Dresden, wrote his tablature
for Duchess Sophia of Saxony
this year.

Palestrina's second volume of
masses was printed by Gardano
at Venice.

Peter Philips, a rather prolific
composer of madrigals, published
two sets for six voices and one
for eight at Antwerp (See also
1596 and 1603).

Giovanni Maria Radino's
"Madrigals de diversi a 4 voci
raccolti di Gio. Maria Radino

(cont.) . . ." was published at
Venice this year.

Sale's "Dialogismus 8 vocum de
amore Christi sponsi ergo
ecclesiam" was published at
Prague.

Sale's "In natalem Domini Jesu
Christi" was published at
Munich.

Sale's "Oratorio ad B.V. Mariam'
was published at Prague.

Francisco Soto de Langa's "Il
quinto libre delle laudi
spirituali . . ." was published.

The dedications of Torelli's
madrigals were signed at Padua.

Some of Torelli's verses were
set to music by his nephew at
this date.

Orfeo Vecchi published a book of
five-part masses.

Orfeo Vecchi's "Motetti di Orfeo
Vecchi Maestro di Cappella di
S. Maria della Scala e d'altri
eccellentiss. Musici" appeared.

Orfeo Vecchi published a book of
the complete Psalms.

One of Venturi's madrigals was
included in Morley's collection
of this year.

Weelkes' "Balletts and Madrigals
to five voyces," which included
"On the plains fairy trains,"
exaggerated the tendencies of
Morley's Balletts. One was for
six voices. Weelkes spoke of
his years being "unripened" in
the dedication.

Este published Weelkes' set of
"Madrigals to 3, 4, 5 and 6

1598(cont.)

Voyces," which he described in the dedication as "the first fruicts of my barren ground." (See also 1597 and 1600). Weelkes was only twenty-one years old at the time.

Wilbye, the leading English madrigal writer, wrote his "The First Set of English Madrigals to 3, 4, 5 and 6 voices," which contained thirty compositions. The popular "Flora gave me fairest flowers," and "Lady, when I behold" were included. The publisher was Este.

Robert Barret's "The Theorike and Practice of Modern Warres" mentioned the office of Drum -Major.

Florio defines the term contral-to or alto as applying to "a counter treble in musicke."

The word Tucket was derived from the Italian Toccata, which Florio in "A Worlde of Wordes" translated as "a touch, a touching."

Popular secular songs were set to sacred words, especially "Innsbruck, ich muss dich lassen."

Trumpet books by the German trumpeters, Heinrich Lubeck and Magnus Thomsen showed that in-fluence in part came from Königsberg, and also in part from Nürnberg.

The League was terminated by the submission of Mercoeur.

The Polish dance, described as such, appeared early in Nörmiger's collection.

A document bearing this date and quoted by Pedrell gave full de-tails of the contract entered into between Victoria and a printing-house at Madrid for the publication of his book of 1600 which was to be dedicated to King Philip III.

Maillard was commissioned to have the Cathedral processional reprinted by Plantin at Antwerp.

John Rose was making "chests" of viols.

Ludwig Hembold, a German reli-gious poet, died (born 1532).

George Peele, Elizabethan poet, died (born c.1558).

Francis Beaumont left Pembroke College, Oxford at this time when his father died.

Michael Drayton's "England's Heroical Epistles" was written.

Ben Johnson turns to a more classical comedy form and writes "The Silent Woman" and "Volpone" as well as the tragedies "Catiline" and "Sejamus."

Ben Jonson was imprisoned for killing another actor in a duel; and during the same year he achieved instantaneous success with "Every Man in his Humour."

Shakespeare acted in Jonson's "Every Man in his Humour."

Shakespeare's "Henry IV" Part II was completed.

Shakespeare's "Merry Wives of Windsor" was completed.

Edmund Spenser's castle in Ireland was burned during a

1598(cont.)
rebellion.

King Charles VIII of France
died (birthdate unknown).

King Philip II of Spain died.
He had reigned since 1556.

Cornelis Pruenen, treasurer and
later sheriff of Antwerp, died
(birthdate unknown).

Paul Hentzner, a Bradenburg
jurist, described his impression
of the theatres on his recent
London visit.

Gianlorenzo Bernini, Italian
painter, was born (died 1680).

Longhena, Italian architect,
was born (died 1682).

Mansart, French architect, was
born (died 1666).

Francisco de Zurbaran, Spanish
painter of monastic life, was
born (died 1662).

(to 1599) Bassano composed motets a 5-12 with "bassi per
l'organo" during these years.

(and 1599) Peter Philipps'
"Madrigali a otto voci" appeared
during these years.

(to 1600) Several of Caspar
Hassler's vocal pieces were
found in "Symphoniae sacrae"
published at Nürnberg during
this period.

(to 1601) Francesco Guami was
maestro di cappella at Lucca for
this period.

(to 1604) John Cowden's six madrigals were published in collective volumes at Venice.

(to 1605) The reign of Czar
Boris Goounov over Russia.

(to 1606) Dowland remained at
the court of King Christian IV
of Denmark during these years.

(to 1606) John Farrant was organist at the Salisbury Cathedral
during this period.

(to 1606) Pedals were known as
cloves in England at this time.

(to 1607) Edward Gibbons, son of
William Gibbons and brother of
Orlando, was at Exeter during
these years.

(to 1609) Wilbye's madrigals for
four and five voices appeared
during this time.

(to 1611) Chapman's "Iliad" was
written during this period.

(to 1611) Valentin Haussman's
works appeared between these
dates and consisted of collections of German secular songs
for four to eight voices.

(to 1622) G.P. Cima's collections of motets, "ricercari" and
"concerti ecclesiastici" were
published at Milan.

c.1598
Antonio Maria Abbatini, Italian
composer, was born at Tiferno
(died 1680).

Cavalier poet Thomas Carew was
born (died 1639).

René de Mel, a French madrigalist, died (born c.1554).

Hans Ruckers or his son was in
charge of the organs at St.
Bavon.

27

c.1598
Weelkes was organist of
Winchester College.

Italian painting: Caravaggio,
St. Matthew (rejected version).

Spanish painting: El Greco,
Portrait of the Cardinal
Inquisitor Don Fernando Nino De
Guevara.

1599
(January 16) Edmund Spenser, the
poet, died London (born 1552).

(January 23) John Case, medical
doctor and music theorist, died
(birthdate unknown). Some
sources place his death on the
same day one year later.

(March 18) Giles Farnaby's son,
Joy, was christened at St.
Mary le Bow.

(March 23) Thomas Selle,
German composer, was born in
Zörbig, Saxony (died 1663, July
2).

(April 7) Ruggiero Giovanelli
became a member of the Sistine
Choir.

(May 10) Three months before
Marenzio's death he dedicated
his ninth and last madrigal
book to Duke Vincenzo Gonzaga,
who had requested some of
Marenzio's music a few months
before.

(June 9) Before starting on his
journey to Flanders with the
Duke, Monteverdi sent his wife
Claudia, who was pregnant, to
Cremona to stay with his father,
Baldesar.

(August 15) Ancina addressed
himself to Girolama Colonna,

(cont.) Duchess of Monteleone
in Rome in his dedication
"Tempio armonico," one of the
most important works in the
early history of the oratorio.

(August 20) Schütz was brought
to the Landgrave by his father.

(August 22) Luca Marenzio,
major Italian composer, died at
the Villa Medici in Pincio
(born 1553).

(October 16) Jacob Regnart,
Netherlandish singer-composer,
died at Vienna (born c.1540).
Some sources list him as dying
at Prague in 1600.

(November 8) Francisco Guerrero,
Spanish composer, died in
Seville (born 1527, May, or
1528).

(December 5) Verdonck wrote a
cantata for six voices to celebrate the entry of the Archduke
Albert and Archduchess Isabella
into Antwerp.

(July) François Sale,
Netherlands singer and composer, died in Prague (birthdate
unknown).

(August) Byrd's son,
Christopher, was mentioned in
Lord Salisbury's papers as
". . . a gunmaker, a man both
very religious and very well
acquainted with ordinance matters, having been trained up in
the tower."

Walentyn Adamecki, Polish
violist, was born at
Wawelnica (died 1653).

Antonio Carreira, Italian musician, died of the plague
(born c.1525).

1599(cont.)

John Hilton, II, English composer, was born at Oxford (died 1657, March).

Pedro Pimentel, Portuguese organist and composer, died (birthdate unknown).

Thomas Selle, one of C.P.E. Bach's predecessors as cantor in Hamburg, was born (died 1663). See March 23.

Nathaniel Tomkins, English organist, was born at Worcester (died 1681, October 20).

Aichinger went to Rome for two years to study.

According to Rimbault, Thomas Bateson became organist at Chester Cathedral.

Prince Andrew Bathori, who played virginal, died (birthdate unknown).

Borchgrevinck went to Venice with his pupil, Pederson, where both studied with G. Gabrieli.

William Brade returned to Copenhagen where he remained until 1606.

John Dowland's skill as a lutenist was proclaimed in one of the sonnets of Shakespeare's "Passionate Pilgrim," published this year. The sonnet had previously been included in a work by Richard Barnfield.

The position of Surintendant de la Musique du Roi was created for Du Caurroy.

Eccard was made kapellmeister to the Margrave of Brandenburg at Königsberg.

Flecha the Younger became abbot at the Monastery of La Portella (Catalonia). He had returned from Italy to spend the rest of his life in Spain.

Ruggiero Giovanelli was appointed singer at the Papal Chapel. He had been maestro at St. Peters up to this time.

Tommaso Graziani became maestro di cappella for the Concordia Cathedral, Milan.

Guarini entered the service of the Grand Duke of Florence the year after the surrender of Ferrara to the papal Curia and the cultural collapse of the city.

Francesco Lambardi, first a sopranello and then a tenor in the Santa Casa dell' Annunziata at Naples, became organist at the royal chapel.

Macque became choirmaster of the Royal Chapel.

Marenzio returned to Mantua.

George Marson succeeded George Juxon as organist and master of the choristers at Canterbury Cathedral. He also was married there the same year.

Monteverdi accompanied Duke Vincenzo I on a journey to Flanders. While there he met French musicians and heard much French dance music.

Daniel Norcome, the lutenist, was appointed to Court of King Christian IV in Copenhagen.

King Christian IV sent five musicians, including the composer Mogens Pederson, to Italy to study with G. Gabrieli.

Pederson went to Venich with Borchgrevinck.

John Reason was listed as a recusant at St. Margaret's Westminster.

Gasparo da Salô purchased a house in Brescia.

Paul Sartorius was organist to the Archduke Maximilian of Austria.

Schein became a chorister at the court chapel in Dresden.

Schütz was admitted as a chorister at the chapel of the Landgrave Moritz of Hesse -Cassel. He left Weissenfels to go to Marburg.

William Smyth was a minor canon at Durham Cathedral until this date.

Soriano was Maestro di cappella at St. John Lateran.

Johann Stobaeus, the German composer, became a student of Eccard at Königsberg.

Michale Thoma was a native of Weiden but studied at Leipzig University during the summer semester this year.

C.T. Walliser taught at the Academy of Strasbourg and was music director in two churches.

Orazio Vecchi journeyed to Rome with the new Cardinal, Alessandro d'Este.

Verdonck, in the preface to his collection of chansons deplored

(cont.) the decline of music in his country.

Richard Allison published his settings of "The Psalmes of David in Meter." The book was printed by William Barley.

The last of the 16th-century lauda collections, "Tempio armonico," was composed by Padre Giovenale Ancina, a disciple of Neri's.

Banchieri's stage work "Il donativo di quattro asinissimi personaggi" appeared.

Banchieri's sacred vocal work "Missa solenne" for eight voices was published.

Antoine Barbe's treatise "Exemplaire des douze tons de la musique, et de leur nature" was published at Antwerp.

Twenty-five fantasies for lute by Giovanni Battista dalla Gostena were published posthumously.

John Bennet's "Madrigalls to Foure Voyces" were published by Barley. They were referred to as "his first works."

Erhard Bodenschatz' Magnificat appeared.

Bottrigari's dialogue "Il desiderio, overo de' concerti di varij strumenti musicali" was published. The author used the pseudonym of Alemanno Benelli. It was originally published in 1594 at Venice and reprinted under his own name this year. Artusi issued it in 1601 under that of Melone.

Calvisius' "Bicinia 70" was

issued.

A book of canzonets in organ tablature in French style was published at Venice.

Capilupi's first book of madrigals appeared.

Caraccio's "Madrigali a 5 voci, lib. 6" was published at Venice.

A three-part mass by Castro was published at Cologne.

Cavendish composed a set of "Ayres for four Voyces" published this year.

Croce's "Messe a 5 and 6 voci appeared.

Croce's "Motetti a quattro voci" was reprinted (See also 1605 and 1611).

Croce's "Motetti a 8, libro primo" was reprinted (See also 1603, 1607 and 1615).

Croce's "Septem Psalmi poenitentiales" was published at Nürnberg.

A "London Cries" by Dering was entered on the Stationers' Register this year but no proof is available that the work was actually published.

Donato's "Di B.D. Maestro di capella della serenissima signoria di Venetia in San Marco . . ." appeared.

A sonnet by Dowland was included in Allison's "Psalms."

Dulichius' "Novum opus musicum duarum partium . . ." was published at Leipzig (See also

Eccard's "Viertzig deutsche christliche Liedlein L. Helmboldi . . ." was published by A. Hantzsch.

The "Editio Plantiniana" of the Gradual was published at Antwerp.

John Farmer's "First Set of English Madrigals to Foure Voyces" was published by Barley.

Ruggiero Giovannelli's fifth book of madrigals was published.

Hassler published eight masses for four to eight voices dedicated to his patron, Octavian Fugger.

Anthony Holborne's "Pavans, Galliards, Almains and other short Aeirs" was published by Barley.

Holborne's "Cittharn Schoole" was published.

Holborne, a lutemaker, published a consort "for Viols, Violins, or other Musicall Winde Instruments" under the title "My selfe."

The "Verborgen Musica" by Lechner appeared.

Sir William Leighton composed verses as a prefix to Allison's "Psalms."

Macque's madrigal books for five voices appeared (See also 1587, 1597 and 1613).

Marenzio's "Il 9º libro de Madrigali a 5" was published at Venice by Gardano.

Three of Marenzio's madrigals

arranged for lute were included in "Terzi, Il secondo libro de intavolatura" published at Venice by Vincenti.

Two of Marenzio's madrigals were included in "Bargnani, Canzonette Arie et Madrigali" published by Amadino at Venice.

One of Marenzio's motets was included in "Motetti et Salmi a otto voci" published by Vincenti at Venice.

One of Marenzio's pieces was included in "Tempio Armonico" published by Mutii at Rome.

Mathias Mercker wrote a manuscript of "Christ Gottes und Mariae Sohn" for five voices. It was copied this year.

Simone Molinaro's tablature written this year contained passamezzi.

A lute-book by Simone Molinaro was published at Venice.

Monteverdi's Fifth Book of Madrigals was printed.

Jacopo Mori published a book "Officium et missa defunctorum, 8v."

Morley's "The first booke of Consort Lessons . . ." was published by Barley. Some of them were used by or composed for jigg companies. They were written for six instruments, two viols and four plucked: treble lute, pandora, citterne, bass-viol, flute, and treble viol.

Giovanni Bernardino Nanino's "Madrigali a 5 voci, Lib. II" was published at Venice.

The third book of canzonets by V. Neriti de Salo appeared.

Philipp Nicolai published "Freudenspiegel des ewigen Lebens" at Frankfort. Included in it were words and tunes of the two well known chorales "Wachet auf, ruft uns die Stimme" and "Wie schön leucht' uns der Morgenstern." Bach used them in two church cantatas.

Asprillio Pacelli's book of psalms and motets for four voices was published at Rome.

Palestrina's late works "Aeterna Christi munera" and "Iste confessor" were found with the piece composed on the madrigal "Nasce la gioja mia" in his ninth book published this year.

Palestrina's "Missarum . . . Liber Octavus" was published by Tiberius de Argentis.

This year saw the first publication of Palestrina's Masses:

51. Quem dicunt homines
52. Dum esset summus pontifex
53. O admirabile commercium
54. Memor esto
55. Dum complerentur
56. Sacer dotes Domini
57. Ave Regina coelorum
58. Veni sponsa Christi
59. Vestiva i colli
60. Sine nomine
61. In te Domine speravi
62. Te Deum laudamus

Morley's "Consort Lessons" included a Pavan and Galliard by Peter Philips.

Philips' 8 part madrigals were

reprinted.

Praetorius' "Opus musicum" Vol. I, "Cantiones sacrae de praecipuis festis totius anni" was dedicated to the chief parishioners of St. James's, Hamburg.

Erich van der Putten's "Pallas modulata" was published at Milan.

Two sacred songs by Quagliati were included in Ancina's "Tempio armonico."

The "Auferstehungshistorie" (Resurrection History) of Nikolaus Rosthius appeared.

A keyboard book, inscribed "Suzanne van Soldt, 1599" on its cover, has been largely ignored by Continental scholars because of its apparent English repertory. English historians, on the other hand, have passed it by because of its Dutch associations.

Peter Short published Cavendish's Ayres.

Giovanni Antonio Terzi, Italian lutenist, published "Il secondo libro Intavolatura . . ." It consisted of arrangements of folksongs for from one to four lutes. He used complicated rhythms and unusually contrapuntal texture. The collection contained canzoni, motets, etc. by various French and Italian authors. It was published at Venice.

Vecchi's "Canzonette a 3 voci" was published. The first volume was in part by Capi-Lupi. Vecchi made the transition from

(cont.) Marenzio's villanelle to monody.

Five books of "Poésies françaises de divers autheurs . . . . à 5 parties avec une chanson a 10 voix" presumably by Verdonck appeared.

Collections such as Allison's Psalter gave ensemble players a much more important supporting role.

Lanfranco and Bottrigaro said that the lira da braccio was unfretted, although an illustration in Praetorius showed frets.

The church at the site where St. Cecilia was executed in Rome was repaired and refurbished and a monument to the saint was erected.

The cult of St. Cecilia was formed when her corpse was discovered in the catacombs this year.

The date of the first recognition of a seventh sound in addition to the six already included in the hexachord was problematical. Burmeister this year mentioned the additional note as "nota adventitia" which indicated that the note had not yet come into general use. The subject was brought into question by van der Putten in his "Pallas modulata."

A troupe stopping at Münster this year was described as having brought "vielle verschieden instrumente, dar sie uf speleten, als luten, zittern, fiolen, pipen und dergelichen . . . ."

Oliver Cromwell, English statesman, was born (died 1658).

Venice was referred to as the "Paradise of Delights" by the German traveller Paul Heussner.

Marlowe contributed to the vogue of narrative poetry in "Hero and Leander." Two cantos were left on his death and were completed by George Chapman this year.

Peele's "David and Bethsabe" was published.

Shakespeare was granted a coat of arms by the College of Heralds.

Shakespeare's "Henry V" was completed.

Shakespeare's "Much Ado about Nothing" was completed.

The Italian architect Francesco Borromini was born (died 1667).

Anthony van Dyck, Flemish painter, was born (died 1641).

Diego Velazquez, Spanish painter, was born (died 1660).

Thomas Dallam travelled to Constantinople with the mechanical clock-organ for the Grand Turk.

(to 1600) Philipp Dulichius composed gospels for the year.

(to 1600) Hans Nielsen studied at Venice with G. Gabriele during these years.

(to 1600) Shakespeare's "As You Like It" was written during this period.

(to 1601) O.T. de Argentis edited Palestrina's eighth through thirteenth books of masses.

(to 1601) John Maynard, English lutenist and composer, was in the service of King Christian IV of Denmark in Copenhagen.

(to 1601) Shakespeare's "Julius Caesar" was completed during this period.

(to 1603) Tommaso Pecci's "Canzonette" for 3 voices were composed during this time.

(to 1608) William Cobbold was organist of Norwich Cathedral throughout these years.

(or 1610) Affonso Vaz da Costa, Portuguese composer, died at Avila. There is some question as to whether he died during this year or 1610. He was born at Lisbon.

(to 1611) Thomas Bateson was appointed organist of Chester Cathedral and held the position throughout this period.

(to 1614) John Bennet was active during these years.

(to 1614) Macque served as maestro of the Viceroyal Chapel for this period.

(to 1614) The development of the English madrigal was an anachronism. From the time of Marenzio's death until after 1614 and the publication of Monteverdi's Sesto Libro, the madrigal on the continent was very much outmoded.

(to 1614) Morley, Rosseter and Leighton wrote music for a broken consort of lute, pandora, cittern, treble and bass viols, and bass recorder during these years.

(to 1618, 1622 to 1625) Some of

1599(cont.)
Praetorius' works were first
published separately and later
(1622 to 1625) at his expense
in an enlarged complete edition
in five volumes.

(to 1622) Mathias Mercker, Dutch
instrumentalist and composer,
was organist at St. Nicholas
Church at Strasbourg.

(and 1624) Twelve books with
Latin and German texts, as well
as some single numbers, were
published at these dates.

(to 1628) Magalhães was the
principal instructor of Estévão
Lopes Morago, Spanish choirmaster of the Cathedral of Viseu
(northeast of Coimbra) during
these years.

(to 1629) Robert du Buisson was
organist at St. Gervais throughout this period.

c.1599
Piotr Elert, Polish violinist
and composer, was born (died
1653).

John Lawes, lay-vicar of
Westminster Abbey and brother
of Henry Lawes, was born in
Salisbury (died 1655, January).

Palestrina published his third
volume of masses.

17th Century
The change in style involved
many composers and musical personages of whom little was
known but who were active at
the turn of the century. They
are listed hereunder, alphabet-
ically.

Jacopo Abbatis (De Abbatis,
Abbates), an Italian composer.

Innocenzio di Alberti, a mu-
sician in the service of
Alfonso, Duke of Ferrara.
Caterina Alessandro, an
Italian composer.
Edward Allde, an English
printer.
Richard Allison, an English
composer.
Michele Angelo Amadei, an
Italian composer.
Simon Amorosius, a Polish
composer.
Miguel de Arizo, a Spanish
singer and composer.
Flandrius Arnoldus (or
Flandrus), a Flemish composer.
Giovanni Bacilieri
(Bacilerius), an Italian com-
poser.
Ballard, a French lutenist.
Juan Barahona de Esquivel,
a Spanish composer.
Bartolomeo ("detto il
Pesarino) Barbarino, an Italian
composer.
George Barcroft, an English
organist and composer.
William Barley, an English
music printer.
The Baroni family, Italian
musicians.
Girolamo Barte I, an Italian
composer, born at Arezzo.
John Bartlet (Bartlett), an
English lutenist and composer.
Bassano (Basson, de Basson),
an Italian family of musicians.
Lodovico Bellanda, an
Italian composer.
Dionisio Bellante, an Italian
composer.
Francesco Bellazzi (Belatius),
an Italian composer.
Domenico Belli, an Italian
composer.
Gioseffo Belloni, an Italian
composer.
Pietro Benedetti, an Italian
composer.
John Bennet, an English com-
poser.

17th Century(cont.)

Gaetano Berenstadt, an Italian bass.

Elway Bevin, a Welsh theorist, organist and composer.

Pietro Antonio Bianchi (Bianco, Blanchis), Italian composer.

Edward Blancks, an English composer.

Giovanni Battista Bonometti, an Italian tenor.

Nicolo Borboni, an Italian composer.

Bernardino Borlasca, an Italian composer.

Giovanni Battista Bovicelli, an Italian Franciscan monk and singer.

Thomas Boyes, an English composer.

Johannes Brassicanus (Brassianus), an Austrian composer.

Antonio Brunelli, an Italian organist, theorist and composer.

Domenico Brunetti, an Italian organist and composer.

Giovanni Brunetti, an Italian composer.

John Buchan (Bughen), a Scottish musician.

Vincenzio Calestani, an Italian composer.

Floriano Canali (Canale), an Italian or Flemish organist and composer.

Michel Angelo Cancineo, an Italian composer.

Alessandro Capece, an Italian composer, born in Teramo, Abruzzi.

Fabrizio Caroso, an Italian dancing master.

Girolamo Casati ("detto Filago"), an Italian composer.

Ludovico Casali, an Italian organist and composer.

Dario Castello, an Italian composer.

Giovanni Ceresini, an

(cont.) Italian composer.

Bartolomeo (Count) Cesana, an Italian composer.

The Champion, family of French musicians.

Chevalier, a French violist and composer.

Giovanni Paolo Cima, an Italian organist and composer.

Giovanni Antonio Cirullo, an Italian composer.

Claudio Cocchi, an Italian composer.

William Corkine, an English composer and possibly lutenist.

Pierre Cornet, a Netherlandish organist and composer.

Camillo Cortellini, an Italian composer.

Benjamin Cosyn, an English organist and composer.

Cesare Crivellati, an Italian amateur musician.

Domenico Crivellati, an Italian amateur musician.

Francis (or Thomas) Cutting, an English lutenist and composer. This conceivably could be two different men.

Baltazar Dankwart, a Polish violin maker.

Adrian Denss, a German music printer.

The Dentice family of Italian musicians.

Jean Desquesnes, a Netherlandish composer.

Agostino Diruta, an Italian composer.

Francesco Dognazzi, an Italian composer.

John Earsden, an English composer.

Martyr Edwarde, an English composer.

Muzio (Mutio) Effrem, an Italian composer.

Georg Engelmann, a German organist and composer.

Francesco Eredi (Heredi), an Italian composer.

John Heath, an English composer. His name occurred in Clifford's Collection (2nd ed. 1664), but only as the composer of an anthem, of which the text was given. A Magnificat and Nunc Dimitis as well as a seven part verse anthem by Heath are in the R.C.M.

Mercurio Jacovelli, an Italian composer who published a book of "Canzonette" for four voices.

Daniel Lagkhner, an Austrian organist and composer. He was born in Marchpurg, Styria.

Manoel Leitão de Avilez, a Portuguest composer.

Henry Lichfild, an English composer.

Guglielmo Lipparino, an Italian composer.

John Lisley, an English composer.

Romano Micheli, an Italian composer who was born and died at Rome.

Giulio Cesare Monteverdi, an Italian composer and organist, brother of Claudio, born at Cremona.

Antonio Naldi, an Italian musician, who was chamber musician to the Duke of Tuscany at the end of the 16th and beginning of the 17th centuries. According to Arteaga, he was the inventor of the theorbo.

Romulo Naldi, an Italian composer, priest and knight at St. Peter's in Rome. He composed a book of madrigals for five voices and a book of motets for double chorus, both were published at Venice.

Stefano Nascimbeni, an Italian composer of choral music, born in Mantua.

Johann Nauwach, a German secular composer, served the Elector of Saxony at Torgau as

(cont.) a musician. He was one of the first to succumb to the influence of new Italian monody.

Alexis Neander, a German motet composer, born at Kolberg.

Marc' Antonio Negri, an Italian composer, born at Verona.

Cesare (detto il Trombone) Negri, an Italian dancer and ballet master at the court of Milan.

Pomponio Nenna, an Italian composer, born at Bari.

Filippo Nicoletti, an Italian composer, born at Ferrara.

Hans Nielsen, a Danish lutenist and composer.

The Norcome (Norcombe), family of English musicians.

Thomas Oldfield, an English composer.

Giuseppe Olivieri, an Italian sacred and secular composer.

Camillo Orlandi, an Italian pastoral composer.

Alessandro Orologio, two Italian musicians who worked at two different German courts; one was a cornetist and one was a violinist.

Stephan Otto, a German composer, born in Saxony.

Valerius Otto, a German organist and composer, born at Leipzig.

Pietro Paolo Paciotti, an Italian composer, born and died at Rome.

Marcin Paligonius (Paligoniusz), a Polish composer.

Nicola Parma, Italian composer, born at Mantua.

Francesco Pasquali, an Italian composer, born at Cosenza.

Serafino Patta, an Italian musician.

Edward Pearce, an English composer.

Desiderio Pecci, an Italian composer, probably a younger brother of Tomaso, born at Siena.

Vincenzo Pellegrini, an Italian composer, born at Pesaro.

Biagio Pesciolini, an Italian composer.

Paul Peuerl, an Austrian organ builder, organist and composer.

José Peyro, a Spanish composer.

Giovanni Picchi, an Italian organist and composer.

Giovanni Piccioni, an Italian organist and composer, born at Rimini.

Giulio Sano Pietro del Negro (Negri), an Italian composer of noble birth, born at Milan.

Cristoforo Piochi, an Italian composer.

Ercole Porta, an Italian organist and composer.

Isaac Posch, an Austrian (possibly German) organist and composer.

Pellegrino Possenti, an Italian composer.

Robert Ramsey, an English composer.

Francesco Rasi, Italian singer and composer, born of a noble family in Arezzo.

Andreas Reinhard, a German organist and theorist.

Lewis Richard, an English composer, Master of the Queen's Music under Elizabeth and organist of Magdalen College.

Pedro Rimonte, a Spanish composer, born at Saragossa. He was taken from Spain by the Infanta Isabella at the time of her marriage to Archduke Albert, Governor of the Netherlands.

Thomas Robinson, an English lutenist and composer.

Giovanni Battista Rossi, an (cont.) Italian composer, born at Genoa.

Johann Kaspar Nikolaus Rosth, a German composer, born at Weimar. He studied theology and music at Torgau.

Pawel Roszkowicz, a Polish instrumentalist and member of the Royal band at Warsaw.

Niccolo Rubini, an Italian cornetist and composer.

Standish, an English family of organists.

Giovanni Stefani, an Italian musician.

Giovanni Battista Stefanini, an Italian composer.

Francesco Stivori, an Italian organist and composer.

Alessandro Striggio II, Italian instrumentalist and librettist, son of Alessandro Striggio.

Nicholas Strogers, an English organist and composer.

Simon Stubbs, an English composer.

Robert Tailour, an English composer.

Giovanni Antonio Terzi, an Italian lutenist and composer.

Pietro Paolo Torre, an Italian organist and composer.

Vito Trasuntino, an Italian harpsichord maker, born and died at Venice.

Flaminio Tresti, an Italian organist and composer.

Antonio Troilo, an Italian composer.

Edmund Tucker, an English composer.

Usper (Francesco Sponga), an Italian organist and composer.

Fulgentio Valesi, an Italian composer.

Thomas Vautor, an English composer.

Stefano Venturi del Nibbio, an Italian composer, born and died at Venice.

Michel Angelo Verovio

17th Century(cont.)
(Michelangelo del Violino), an
Italian violinist.

Simone Verovio, an Italian
music printer and publisher.

Gasparo Villani, an Italian
organist and composer.

Giacomo Vincenti, an Italian
music publisher and printer.

The Air A Boire, a French drink-
ing song in a convivial style,
was very popular. It was sung
in parts.

The Ballett, a vocal composition
of this time, was light in
character and in the madrigal
style, most often in its
English form, with a "Fa la"
burden. It could be either
sung or danced. "These pieces,"
according to Morley, were "commonly called Fa las."

The Bergamasca was an Italian
dance, founded on one of the
harmonic grounds which were a
major feature of the music of
the time, both frivolous and
serious.

Broken Consort was an English
term of the period applied to
teams of instruments, or music
written for them. String and
wind instruments were mixed in
this form.

The Canzone was an instrumental
form at the turn of the century.

Albinoni and Torelli composed
the earliest concertos for solo
violin and orchestra.

Consort was the English term for
a group of instruments playing
concerted music. The term was
used either for the music or
its performance.

Counter was an English term
used to describe improvised
variations on a given tune.

The Cushion Dance was common
among all social classes.

The Napoletana was a light song
for several voices. It was similar to the villanella and was
cultivated especially at Naples.

The Passamezzo was a formal
dance and variant of the pavan.
It was common throughout
Europe.

Walther's and Scandello's
Passions were examples of the
type of scenic Passion produced
by Protestant and Roman
Catholic musicians.

The Verset was a type of organ
interlude used in the Roman
Catholic church.

The Villanella was an unaccompanied part song, light and
rustic in character and popular
ar this time.

Ornaments in use at the turn of
the century:

A small letter was used for
the modern natural ($\natural$).

An ornament sign of the period "𝄌" was used to signify a
mordent, half-shake, ascending
slide, or possibly a trill.

The sign for Tremelo or trill
(trillo) was "t."

Another sign for trills or
tremolo was "tr" or even "tri."

A double rising stroke across
the stem was used if there was
one trill, half-shake, or mordent, "≠."

English virginalists made extensive use of a small number

of specific ornaments.

Pioneers of the Italian "nuove musiche" had definite views on vocal embellishment.

Both the "chitarrone" and the arch-lute were used in Italy.

Clavichords during this period had a range of three and one -half octaves.

The Crumhorn, a woodwind instrument, was sounded by an enclosed double reed.

Curtall was the English name for bassoon.

The dolcian was frequently mentioned on the Continent during this period.

The Domra was a Russian lute with a long neck in use at this time.

The origin of the "musette," which was apparently the prototype of the bellows bagpipe, was not known with certainty, however, the instrument was in an advanced state by this time.

Organs of this time had Barpfeife, a soft reed stop which sounded a growling tone.

In Germany strange qualities were obtained from the use of Regal stops.

The term, "pair of organs," has always been a difficult one as to its true meaning.

The Ottavino keyboard instrument with jacks was sometimes called the "octavina." It was used alone or placed on top of (cont.) a virginal or harpsichord for use as a second manual.

The pipe and tabor remained popular and widespread, since it was economical and provided a one man band for dances.

The rackett, now obsolete, was a woodwind instrument, using a double reed and popular in France and Germany. It was quite possibly a type of bassoon.

The recorder was known in France as "la flûte à neuf trous" since the movable footjoint had not yet been introduced. Makers provided for the needs of both right- and left-handed players by duplicating the lowest hole. The hole not being used was stopped with wax to leave the normal eight holes to function.

The Amati family lived at Cremona and worked at their special craft of violin making for over a hundred years.

Records of royal courts prior to this date showed that groups of instrumentalists were employed in regular service. They were to provide music for worship and entertainment as well as for ceremonial occasions.

P. Philips lived in the Netherlands.

The status of Persian music of this period was obvious in the graphic arts as noted by European travellers such as Barbaro, Chardin, Dontarini, Du Mans, Poullet and Raphael.

Accademia was the name given an institution of a type which flourished in Italy at this time. The schools were founded

17th Century(cont.)
for the promotion and progress of the arts, literature and science.

Bologna had four societies for public instruction in music.

Church performances continued to be more common.

The Middle Ages of music were extended by the Czech Reformation movement.

The sacred drama underwent great development at Palermo, however, the peculiar effect of the Renaissance on Sicily removed practically all trace of the pastoral drama.

There was little opportunity for individuality of style within the narrow limits of the harmonic range at this time.

Italy remained the most influential musical nation of Europe for one hundred and fifty years.

Madrid during Scarlatti's time was still a town more typically Spanish than it is today.

German pietists under Johannes Kelpius settle near Philadelphia. They used hautboys (oboes), kettledrume, posaunen (trombones), and viols (stringed instruments) and also had an organ they had procured from Germany.

The cathedral at Puebla was the most active musical center in New Spain, more so even than Mexico City cathedral.

The ducal palace at Parma was visited by the most noted instrumentalists and singers and

(cont.) music by Monteverdi and Ferrari as well as many others was performed there.

The polyphonic music of this time, especially in England, was barred only when in score, and even then not necessarily in regular metrical units.

The dot of division disappeared during this and the next century.

Up to this time Durezza was used as the Italian word meaning discord.

By the time of the "Bahjat al -rúh" there were twenty-four rhythmic modes (usúl) in Persian music.

Ruggiero, an Italian hamonic ground, was in wide use at this time.

Musicians were restricted as to the number of key signatures at their disposal up to this time.

The Persian, Safí al-Dín 'Abd al-Mu'min, who died in 1294, regularized the systematist theory which Parry called "the most perfect ever devised" and this had ruled together with the simpler Pythagorean system until this time.

Music engraving was introduced during this period.

Plantin established the Flemish printing plant.

The study of mathematical proportions shed light on the theory and the practice of music after the works by Greek writers on music were translated and studied in Italy.

41

17th Century(cont.)
Four members of the Corelli
family were good poets.

The composers listed below were
to be active in this century.
Little is known about the greater
portion of the group:

Jan Accoltuhus, a Polish
hymn composer.
Hendrick Aertsens (Aertssens),
a Flemish ecclesiastic and mu-
sician.
Mario Agatea, an Italian
motet composer.
Paul (Johann) Agricola,
German composer and kapell-
meister.
Wolfgang Christoph Agricola,
German sacred composer.
Sebastian Aguilera de
Heredia, a Spanish composer and
monk.
Gottfried Aich, a German
composer who was canon and sub
-prior of the monastery at
Weissenau.
Samuel Akeroyde, an English
composer and Musician in
Ordinary to James II, William
and Mary and William III.
Bartolommeo Albrici, an
Italian organist and composer.
Giulio d'Alessandri, an
Italian sacred composer.
Giovanni Battista Aloisi
(Alovisio, Alovisius, Aloysius),
an Italian composer and friar.
Charles d'Ambleville, a
French composer and Jesuit.
Arne, an English air composer,
not to be confused with Thomas
A. Arne.
Giovanni Giacomo Arrigoni,
an Italian composer and court
organist to Emperor Ferdinand
II and III at Vienna.
Gracián Babán, a Spanish
composer and maestro de capilla.
Scipione Bargaglia, an
Italian composer, probably born

(cont.) and died at Naples.
Rev. John Barnard, an
English ecclesiastic and musical
editor.
Francesco Maria Bazzani, an
Italian opera composer.
Diedrich Becker, a German
organist, violist and composer.
Angelo Berardi, an Italian
composer and maestro di capella,
born near Urbino.
John Birchensha (or
Birkenshaw), a Welsh (?) violist
and music theorist who spend
much of his life in Ireland.
Isaac Blackwell, an English
ayre composer.
Giovanni Battista Borri, an
Italian sacred composer who
worked at Bologna.
Giovanni Battista Brevi, an
Italian composer and maestro di
capella.
Estevão de Brito, a
Portuguese composer and choir-
master.
Luis Brizeño, a Spanish
guitarist and composer.
William Bull, an English
trumpeter and brass-instrument
maker.
Lelio Calista (Colista), an
Italian composer whose work was
popular in England.
Carlo Caproli (called Carlo
del Violino), an Italian compos-
er, probably a pupil of Rossi,
born in Rome.
John Carr, an English music
publisher, died in London.
Richard Carr, an English mu-
sic publisher, born and died at
London.
Thomaso Cecchini of Verona,
Italian musician who spent his
entire life in Dalmatia.
Remigio Cesti, an Italian
composer and organist.
John Cobb, an English organ-
ist and composer.
Johann Georg Conradi, a
German composer and conductor.

17th Century(cont.)

William Cranford, an English singer and composer.

Dallam (Dalham, Dallans or Dallum), family of organ builders.

Jan Dankwart, a Polish violin maker.

Thomas Deane, an English organist and composer.

Derrick, an English sacred composer.

Luigi Dionigi, an Italian theorist, born at Poli.

Antonio Draghi, probably the mos prolific of all 17th-century composers, at least as far as dramatic works were concerned, born in Rimini and died in Vienna.

Jacques Duponchel, a Flemish organist and composer, probably born at Douai and died at Osimo.

Thomas Eisenhut, a German theorist and composer.

Sebastian Erthel, a German composer and monk.

Antonio Dal Gaudio, an Italian opera composer, probably born at Rome.

George Alexander Hack, a German composer and court musician at Munich.

Jean Florent (Nicolas) A' Kempis, a Flemish composer and organist.

Jan Liliys, a Polish choirmaster to the bishipric at Wlcclawek.

Maria Francesa Nascimbeni, an Italian composer and pupil of Scipione Lazarini, born in Ancona.

Massimiliano Neri, an Italian organist and composer.

Johann Michael Nicolai, a German chamber music composer.

Van Noordt, a family of several well-known Dutch musicians.

William Norris, an English Protestant church composer.

Angelo Notari (Notary or Notario), an Italian musician and composer, died at London.

Jakob Jerzy Nowakowski, a Polish composer whose "Planctus de Passione Domini" for four parts is his only surviving work.

David Oberndörffer, a German instrumentalist and compiler of instrumental collections.

Cornelis Thymans Padbrué (Padbrouck or Padbruck), Dutch singing teacher.

Juan de Padilla, the most prolific Mexican composer, was a contrapuntist who followed Victoria's practice of writing parody masses on his own motets.

Giovanni Maria Pagliardi, an Italian composer and conductor, born in Florence.

Henry Palmer, an English sacred composer.

Robert Palmer, an English sacred composer of whom very little is known.

Domenico Del Pane, an Italian male soprano singer and composer, probably born at Rome.

Ghizzolo Steffano Pasino, an Italian composer, born at Brescia.

Andrzej Paszkiewicz, a Polish composer and monk.

Perrine, a French lutenist and possibly a composer.

Francesco Petrobelli, an Italian composer, born at Bologna.

Diego Pizarro, a Spanish composer and author.

Jan Podbielski, Polish organ composer.

Stanislaw Podolski, a Polish composer of a concerto "Levita Laurentius," for S.S.A.T.B., two violins, viola, bassoon and organ.

Primrose, an English suite composer.

William Pysing (Pising) an English Protestant church composer.

Sisto Reina, an Italian organist and sacred composer.

Francesco Rossi, an Italian opera composer, born in Bari.

Jean Rousseau, a French violist and composer, pupil of Saint-Colombe, born and died at Paris.

Hyacinthus (Jacek) Różycki, a Polish composer and pupil of either Scacchi or Pękiel.

The Ruckers family in Antwerp, builders of the finest harpsichords.

Lucas Ruiz de Ribayaz, a Spanish guitarist.

Staggins, an English family of musicians, oboists and violinists (James, Issac, Charles, Nicholas).

Samuel Stokrocki, a Polish organist and composer.

Barbara Strozzi, an Italian singer and composer.

Jan Strzyzewski, a Polish composer.

Antonio Francesco Tenaglia, an Italian opera composer.

Biagio Tomasi, an Italian organist and composer.

Giovanni Battista Vacchelli, an Italian composer, organist and friar.

Elia Vannini, an Italian composer and maestro di capella.

Simone Vesi, an Italian composer.

Johann Vierdanck, a German organist and composer.

Vuillaume, a French family of violin makers.

The Arietto family (Simone, Francesco, Simone II), were prominent Italian violinists.

Baltzar was an exceptional violinist who used the entire (cont.) fingerboard.

Pietro Benedetti was most renowned first as a theologian, but also like other musical amateurs of the time, turned to composing in the new monodic style.

In Germany, John Bull was frequently listed as "Johannes Bull."

G. Caccini's reputation lasted considerably longer in various countries than that of most of his countrymen. His popularity exceeded that of Caccini.

The older branch of the Cavendish family became extinct.

Marcantonio Cesti led the typical life of a conductor of his time.

Evléyá Chelebí named ten or more of the many types and sizes of the náy.

Coperario represented the spearhead of the development of the English fantasy for viols. This resulted in unchallenged supremacy for the English in this field.

According to Riehl, Corelli was the link between two musical epochs, the first being 17th century counterpoint and the second the melodic freedom of the 18th century.

The great collection of sacred and secular compositions that survived in the Uppsala Library was made by Gustaf Düben the elder.

Probably the greatest figure in keyboard music of this period

17th Century(cont.)
was Frescobaldi, a predecessor
of D. Scarlatti's at St. Peter's
in Rome.

Gigault, the French organist,
arranged it so that frequent
cadences enabled the player to
fit neatly into all but the most
awkward liturgical lacunae.

King John IV of Portugal was
noted as the author of the
"Defensa de la musica moderna."
He also was the collector of one
of the most valuable music li-
braries of the time. Unfortun-
ately the collection was later
destroyed by fire.

Occasionally Scarlatti imitated
violinistic figurations in a
manner common among keyboard
composers from this time forward.

The Florentine Scarlattis had
been in Portugal.

Alessandro Scarlatti retained
certain facets of Venetian
opera.

Heinrich Schütz was felt by
most to be the greatest musician
in Germany during this period.

William Smegergill (Caesar) was
an English composer of some
reputation.

Giovan Battista Vitali founded
the Bolognese instrumental
school. Corelli found it in
good order and flourishing.

Zahn enumerated more than four
hundred fifty hymn-books published during the century.

A translation of Aelred's "De
abusa musices" by William
Prynne was published and later

(cont.) reprinted in Gerbert,
Vol. I.

Anerio published adaptations of
works by Palestrina, including
the "Pope Marcellus" Mass.
These appeared in several editions during the century.

The last music for the vihuela
was a manuscript by Antonio de
Santa Cruz which contained
passacaglias and other pieces.

A "Concerto a 4" for posthorn
and strings was composed by
Baer.

Significant collections of
Cathedral Music were made by
Barnard.

Campion's "New Way of Making
Fowre Parts in Counterpoint"
was reprinted on several occasions.

Carissimi's "Jephthah" was one
of the most satisfactory works
of its kind during the period.

Numerous chorale melodies were
added to the repertoire of
traditional tunes by Crüger.
He set the texts of Paul
Gerhardt, the only German poet
capable of approaching Luther's
cogent language and religious
fervor.

Deering's "Cries of London and
Country Cries." appeared.

A large minority of descriptive
names appeared in "La
Rhétorique des Dieux" by
Gaultier. The book was a large
collection of lute music done
for Anne de Chambre, a talented
amateur lutenist.

A setting of "Greensleeves" was

found in a manuscript for virginal.

The "air de cour" represented a
large portion of the literature
published by Le Roy and Ballard.
It was distributed throughout
Europe.

The Mystery of Elche as we
know it today was the 17th century version of an earlier
play.

Diego Pizarro compiled a manuscript volume of secular vocal
music, "Libro de tonos humanos."
It has been preserved in Madrid.

"Rory Dall's Port" (i.e. Blind
Rory or Roderick's composition)
was associated with the blind
harpist of this period.

The carol "Schlaf, mein
kindelein" appeared.

F.L. Schubert, "Die Tanzmusik,"
included an example of the
"Canarie" in 6/8 time.

The Skene Manuscript included a
"Port Ballangowne."

Information about the pitch of
English organs at this time
was included in Tomkin's
"Musica Deo Sacra" by Ouseley.
He in turn called the attention
of A.J. Ellis to it for inclu-
sion in his "History of Musical
Pitch."

The first flowering of Austrian
music began when the Habsburgs
acted as patrons of music and
themselves took an active part
in the development of music.

England was active in musical
development during this century,

(cont.) however, political and
aesthetic conflicts acted to
some degree as deterrents.

Italian influence was strong on
English music during these
years.

Music in England was for the
most part of a very cheerful
nature.

There was little evidence as to
how extensively English music
was embellished.

The Restoration's most important
musical style was the anthem.
The conflict between the royalists and the parliamentarians
(Tories and Whigs) was apparent
in these compositions.

Birthday Odes (musical settings
of odes) by English court poets
were written to celebrate birth-
days of royal personages.

English church music in part-
books all but disappeared and
were replaced by printed books
and scores. Religious fanatics
were active in this process.

Villancicos de Navidad dominated
the field, and as a result the
English carol became a predominantly religious song associated with Christmas.

Act-Tune was an old English
word for a musical interlude
between the acts of a play.
Incidental music was performed
while the curtain was down.

In England the arts of engraving
and etching for pictorial purposes attained a fine degree of
perfection.

The "ballet de cour" went

17th Century(cont.)
through various stages that
closely paralleled the development of the English court
masque.

The "Country Dance" was an
English dance very popular during this period.

Pavans enjoyed great popularity
in England during this century.

Some pavans and galliards with
elaborately varied repeats were
included in the manuscript collections of English virginal
music. They were exceedingly
virtuoistic and in this sense
unrivalled.

The tempo of Baroque dances were
different from one period to
another as well as from one
place to another. A good example was the slow continental
saraband as opposed to the rapid
English saraband.

Dot-Way was an English system of
notation for recorders at this
time.

Driving was an English term for
syncopation.

Change-Ringing was developed in
England during this period.

The "genre" piece for harpsichord could be traced back to
the English virginalists. It
spread to lute and keyboard music during these years.

English music for keyboard instruments did not equal the
great tradition of the virginalists.

The English school of lutenist
song-writers flourished at this

(cont.) time.

In England the resources for
variation in organ accompaniment
were increased when Father Smith
and Renatus Harris introduced a
few new stops hitherto unknown
in England. An additional short
manual organ called the Echo was
added as well.

The recorder stop became popular
in England.

English pavans for three, four,
five and six viols were not
virtuoistic pieces but rather
chamber music, quiet, serene and
emotional in quality. Alfonso
Ferrabosco II's "Dovehouse Pavan"
and "Four-Note Pavan" were never
excelled.

The origins of quartet, elements
other than the preclassical
trio, appeared starting with the
consorts and fantasias for viols
which were abundant in England.

England had excellent composers
writing for the violin.

The violoncello was already in
use in England at this time.

The Trumpet Marine was used in
France.

France had many composers writing
for plucked string instruments.

The French Basse-Contre was a
bowed string instrument of the
violin family. It became obsolete after this century.

The French haute-contre was a
bowed string instrument of the
violin family, now obsolete.
Its range was upward from "a"
below middle "c."

17th Century(cont.)

The Sordino or Kit, an old bowed string instrument, was used in France at this time.

The standard of violin playing in France as well as England was high. Virtuosity was not, however, a great feature.

The French saraband was slow, the English very fast at this time.

Carissimi's influence through Charpentier and Dumont was strongly felt in the French motet.

The French Tragédie Lyrique was an opera with a serious libretto but not necessarily a tragic story.

All music of France was ultimately under the patronage of King Louis XIV. Ballets played an important role at the courts of Henry IV, Louis XIII and Louis XIV.

German musicianship was attempting to combine the older style of pure vocal music with the newer style of instrumental accompaniment. Greater freedom of harmonic modulation was an important facet of the technique.

German composers were less successful in writing good new melodies than in arranging existent ones to the satisfaction of current tastes.

The change that occurred in German hymnody was most obvious in the melodic lines.

Combining improvisatory and fugal styles was successfully (cont.) executed by many German organ composers of the period.

Italian melodic style became prevalent in Germany.

The German Nachtanz (tripla) had a time signature of three.

The Cornettino gained great favor in Germany.

In Germany, the organ was not used in support of congregational singing until this time.

Organists of Germany developed a great school of organ music which culminated in J.S. Bach, based mainly on extemporization.

Passions known as "Affektenlehre" developed in Germany.

Protestant Holland was growing stronger and its art was approaching maturity as evidenced in the work of Brouwer, Hals and van Ostade.

Hungary inherited the material for its religious folk music but other than that had to initiate its own monophonic song literature as well as dance music.

Italian musical art spread throughout Europe.

Italy, although it possessed an unusual number of gifted musicians, lacked good spoken drama. The gap, however, was filled by the development of opera.

The strophic bass was a device used mainly in Italian cantatas of the period.

The remarkable resemblance between an Italian dulcimer and a

17th Century(cont.)
modern Georgian "santir" has been noted by Carl Engel.

The five-course guitar music of Italy was of great importance.

Italian composers moved the accent from wind instruments to stringed instruments.

Violin makers had their first great period.

Italian librettists combined the comic, the grotesque, and the sensational into supposedly serious drama.

In Persia the use of the harp in Persian music had to be defended.

A Peruvian codex of the period, one of the few musical documents of the time that survived in the Western Hemisphere, contained some part-music written in a popular Spanish style.

Polish dances (precursors of the polonaise and mazurka) were popular until the beginning of the 19th Century.

The Polonaise, a stately Polish dance, was the most characteristic of all the national dances of Poland. The French dance which was current even in its own country dated back to this time. During this period three French princesses in succession became consorts to Polish kings. French customs and the French language were used at the Polish court.

The earliest example of the follia was Spanish in origin. This bass was known in Italy as well.

From the beginning of this century it was the custom to credit the Spanish with the origin of the follia. They were called "folies d'Espagne." A number of lexicographers and classical Spanish writers defined the follia as a "Portuguese dance."

Combinations of music and drama, as were found in Sanchez de Badajoz, Cervantes, and Lope, brought on the zarzuela, a Spanish national theatrical form which was established by the renowned poet, Calderón.

Spanish drama had considerable influence on Italian opera.

The Spanish domination of Naples accented the more serious aspects of Neapolitan tradition.

The Polska, a Swedish folk dance of Polish origin, made its way to Sweden in late 16th Century and was danced only by the peasantry throughout this period.

At this time of Evlíyá Chelebí, Turkey had only ten "chang" players.

Foreign composers in large numbers came to London throughout the century.

In Paris, Ballard and Le Roy printed Lully's works.

Two theatres arose in Parma. One was large and had an amphitheatre, the other was small and called "Il Teatrino."

Rome was an important center of opera and cantatas and had a strong influence on sacred music at this time.

17th Century(cont.)
Conservative Roman counterpoint was less important than the style of the "colossal Baroque."

Venice was a leading musical city during these years.

The Venetian school had its most characteristic expression in vocal and instrumental polyphony. This was centered at St. Mark's as well as in the opera-houses.

There were as many as four opera houses in Venice all playing at the same time. Commoners sat in the pit, gentility rented the loges.

The "furlana" was danced at the Viennese court.

Baroque dance music consisted of dances that had survived from the renaissance. New dances were added as the century continued.

Stylized dance music was important not only for its own sake but also because of the extent to which dance rhythms were used in other music, both instrumental and vocal.

The "Amener" was a form of branle included in many dance suites for orchestra.

The ballet was always accompanied, usually by an orchestra but occasionally vocally.

The name "corante" denoted two entirely different dances.

In this century the corrente which followed a balletto used the latter's theme with a more relaxed rhythm. This was not to

(cont.) be construed as a simple variation.

The courante was popular and it reached its height of popularity under King Louis XIV.

References to the cushion dance appeared in many books.

The follia was probably fast originally but became a slow and stately dance somewhat like the chaconne or sarabande and frequently performed by a solo dancer.

No branded instruments by makers of this century survived.

The Aeolian harp appeared during this period.

The archlute was used with the chitarrone and violone (bass viol). They played the lowest part in instrumental music and accompaniments often combined with the clavicembalo in order to support recitative.

A family of five varieties of bassoon existed.

The Chalumeau was made in soprano, alto, tenor and bass sizes.

For a short time a plectrum or quill was used on the cittern instead of the fingers.

The "cornemuse," a second drone which rested on the player's shoulder, was added. The instrument sounded one octabe below the small drone.

The terms "Double" and "Single" were applied to the curtall (bassoon) and sackbut (trombone).

17th Century(cont.)

The "Dessus" was a bowed string instrument in the violin family which is now obsolete.

Drums and fifes became very popular during this period.

The one-piece two keyed dulzian gave place to the jointed three keyed bassoon at sometime during this century.

Flutes occasionally replaced oboes during these years.

Individually plucked notes were introduced on the guitar.

The word harpsichord did not appear before this century.

Cardinal Ottoboni owned fourteen harpsichords, eight of which were constructed "d'ottava stesa" (with the full range of keys), not the short octave in the bass that was common at this time.

Keyboard collections arranged according to the series of modes went back to the Renaissance but could be found throughout these years.

The art of fingering for keyboard instruments did not exist at the start of this century.

The lira da braccio, a bowed instrument very popular during the Renaissance, was discarded during this period.

The lira da gamba, a bass form of the lira da braccio but more elaborate, was discarded during this century.

Double reeds (oboes, bassoon) were used in almost all (cont.) orchestras which included wind instruments.

Certain scores of the period used tenor oboe.

The fingering of the oboe always showed considerable subtlety in the matter of enharmonic variants and of trills. These were found before the end of the century and demonstrated the artistic completeness of the oboe at its earliest stage of development.

Composers wrote considerable organ music.

Organ verses interpreted the cantus firmus with a great deal of freedom.

Playford's "Introduction to the Skill of Musick" described the "Poliphant" as an excellent instrument somewhat like a lute. According to an illustration given by Randle Holme, it had from twenty-five to forty strings and resembled the later harp -lute.

Orchestras used a pair of trumpets and a pair of kettledrums as a special feature for martial sounds. The same combination was also employed for religious music of great exhaltation.

The trombone was occasionally used in opera.

The consort of viols was replaced by the consort of violins in what seemed to be a sound decision.

The name "viola da braccio" gradually was used only for the original instrument (the alto of the group).

17th Century(cont.)

The six-stringed viola da gamba was the established solo, chamber and orchestral bass of the period. It was a very popular instrument and easier to handle than the heavier cello.

The gradual progress in harmonic thinking in the diatonic key system came during this century.

Notation of this period would have been utterly unintelligible to a 14th Century musician.

Notation differed in detail but not in principle from a 20th Century score.

The present-day convention that an accidental holds good to the end of a measure became accepted during this century.

"Adagio" was not as slow a tempo as it became a century later.

Barring in homophonic music though still somewhat erratic moved toward its ultimate goal of establishing the meter. Use of bar-lines became quite general during this century.

Most music began to be written and heard in measures, definite patterns of strong and weak beats.

The consistent use of the double -bar probably dated from this period.

Breaking was the name given to the practice of varying a theme by use of diminution and/or the use of passing tones.

The breve corresponded to a double wholenote; the semibreve to a wholenote; the minim (once (cont.) a diamond with cauda), to a halfnote; the semiminim, to a quarternote; the fusa (once a black diamond with a cauda and flag) to an eighth-note; etc.

The use of words and abbreviations to indicate dynamics became rather frequent during this period.

The pause or "fermata" came into use in its modern sense of a hold.

Among the early Italian composers of sonatas the feeling for modality had almost disappeared and was replace by the major-minor concept. Early examples included the works of Biagio, Marini, Cazzati, and many others.

The art of temporary modulation was fairly common in experimental chromaticism of this century. However, a coordinated scheme of tonality based on the assumption of equal temperament did not yet exist.

The three leading national styles developed three different systems of ornamentation.

During this century long appoggiaturas were current.

Composers showed stepwise appoggiaturas under various names.

In this century the dotted slide was neglected.

17Th Century English authorities by "shaking" meant a trill of any length or a mordent of any length.

17th Century(cont.)
During the 17th Century the groppo (turn) gradually acquired immense prominence.

Special signs for ornaments in keyboard and lute music appeared with increasing frequency.

Throughout the 17th Century "white" forms for C & Q remained in use in France and Italy, particularly for triple time.

The Double Relish compound ornament was used in England in place of the continental double cadence.

Ornaments used by Edward Bevin were in a table of ornaments of virginal music books.

D'Anglebert called this an irregular turn sign " ⌇ ."

D'Anglebert used an inverted comma after a note to indicated a mordent " ⸜ ."

D'Anglebert's sign for the trill had a turned ending "〰⌒ ."

D'Anglebert's sign " 〰⌒ " was a veriant of the 17th and 18th Century French sign for a trill with turned end "〰, ."

Chambonnières used the lower appoggiatura sign " + ."

Chambonnières used the mordent sign "⫽〰."

Chambonnières called this sign an irregular turn " ⌇ ."

The 17th Century English sign " ＼ " before a note indicated a falling note of anticipation (cadent).

The 17th Century English sign for an upper appoggiatura was " ⸲ ."

The 17th Century English sign of a double comma was indicated by a descending slide sign " ⸲⸝ ."

The 17th Century English sign for a prepared long mordent was " ⁄⸫ ."

The 17th Century English sign for a single relish (brief trill with turned ending) was "∴ ."

The 17th Century English sign for a double relish ornament was "⦂∵ " also "∷\\ ∴ ."

The 17th Century English sign for an ascending slide was " ┼ ."

The English 17th century ornament sign used by Edward Bevin for an ascending slide was " ⋰ ."

The 17th Century English sign used by Edward Bevin for an ascending slide leading to a trill was " ⫢ ."

The 17th Century English springer sign was " ⁄ " between and above the notes.

The 17th Century English sign for an ascending trill with or without turned termination was " ⧺ ."

The 17th Century English ornament " • " indicated a vibrato or tremolo.

The 17th Century French sign for an arpeggio was " ⁄ " through the stem. It was before

53

17th Century(cont.)
the stem when used by Marais.

The 17th Century French sign for an ascending arpeggio was " { " before the chord.

The 17th Century French sign for an ascending arpeggio was " { ."

The 17th century French sign for a mordent was " ⩘ ."

The 17th Century French and German trill sign was " ⩗ ."

This sign " ⩗⩗ " was used in varying ways: by French and German composers - trill; by Loulie - double mordent; Purcell and Locke(?) - appoggiatura, prepared lower mordent; L'Affilard - prepared trill; Th. Muffat - ascending trill; Mace - vibrato; L'Affilard - tremolo.

Loulié used this sign for a "triple mordent" " ⩗⩗ V ."

Mace used this " ⩗⩗ " as a vibrato sign.

L. Mozart used this as a mordent sign " ∾ ;" English, French, German - the ubiquitous sign from 17th Century to pre-send day was the correct usage. Spohr following Mozard calls it a "mordent."

Th. Muffat and J.G. Walther used as an upper appoggiatura sign " \ " before the note; Purcell and Türke - falling note of anticipation (cadent); Türk - descending slide.

Th. Muffat used this sign

(cont.) for an ascending trill " ⩗⩗ ."

G. Muffat used "tm" for a trill lasting the full length of a note.

The term "baroco" originally had a derogatory meaning that clearly indicated the scorn with which earlier generations viewed the period.

Carols were treated in polyphonic style.

Considered to be poetic literature, the chorale survived the Thirty Years' War.

Several writers on military subjects described the functions of a drum-major.

The natural expansion of music served as an important stimulus to the development of music itself and its increasing relative importance in the cultural world.

Extemporization played a large part in the two forms most characteristic in this century, the opera and the sonata.

The music of the Italian peninsula crossed the Alps all through this period.

The century marked the beginning of orchestral development.

The comic element in opera continued until late in the century.

The word opus first appeared during this period.

Protestantism passed through a "scholastic" period of rigid orthodoxy. Violent quarrels with the Calvinists and later with the Pietists dealt primarily with dogma.

Avison referred to baroque contrapuntists as "the Ancients."

The manner of performance of Gesualdo's late madrigals is not known.

The more elaborate of L. Mozart's violin bowings should not be used, especially not in performance of music of this century.

The conservative "stile antico" and the progressive "stile moderno" were opposed in church music.

The polychoric style was cultivated in Italy by composers whose works have not been published.

The "basso continuo" was gradually applied to all kinds of music.

The canti continued on into this century.

Auvergne was the center of the carols of Natalis Cordat.

Ancient Gregorian chants for the psalms and canticles were used not only immediately after the Reformation, but well into this century.

Dialogue was a type of composition for two voices representing two people or images.

A lilliburlero was a party tune, attributed to H. Purcell.

Ther terms passacaglia and chaconne were used indiscriminately.

Vocal polyphony in instrumental music stemmed from this period and essentially from Italy.

Recitative was a term used to describe a declamatory melody supported by simple accompaniment. A solo voice was used most but an instrumental piece, such as an organ piece with the tune played on a solo stop, was possible.

The sonata for solo instrument, with or without a figured bass, was rare for almost the entire century.

This age has been called "the age of the variation" because the principle of variation was used in so many of the instrumental forms of the period.

A fairly large number of plans for musical cryptography were devised.

Publications of music was very difficult and extremely expensive. It could only be achieved through the patronage of a member of the nobility.

Azione Teatrale was a term for an opera or a musical festival play.

Bolognese musical academies flourished continuously. Their goal was to patronize and guide the study of music.

The principal theatre of Brussels, the Théâtre de la Monnaie, was named from an "atelier monétaire" which had occupied the site in this century.

This was one of the major periods in the history of philoso-

17th Century(cont.)
phy and science.

John Donne led a group of young "Metaphysical" poets in London.

At the start of the century "non-migratory" artists appeared in Haarlem, Dordrecht, Delft and Amsterdam. Previously, Netherlandish artists had felt it necessary to go to Italy to study. Now they began to realize themselves within their native habitat.

In their stillifes, as in their genre paintings, Dutch artists linked up again with the "primitives" of the 15th Century both in quality of execution and in sobriety and aptness of the feeling.

Indian architecture: Madura, Great Temple, Gopuram, c.200' high.

Japanese architecture: Nikko, Toshogu Shrine, Yomeimon Gate.

Islamic architecture: Taj Mahal (at Agra) 186' x '86' x 187' high).

1600

(January 23) John Case, English physician and musical theorist, died (birthdate unknown).

(February 27) John Milton, the poet, was admitted to the freedom of the Scrivener's Company.

(April 4) Adam Zacharias Puschmann, German mastersinger, died at Breslau (born 1532).

(April 10) Giulio Cesare Stradivari, an early member of the famous family, married Doralice Milani.

(July 20) Simon Ives, English organist and composer, born in Ware, was baptized (died London 1662, July 1).

(October 6) Rinuccini's "Euridice" with music by Peri was first performed at the Pitti Palace in Florence, on the occasion of the marriage of Maria de' Medici and King Henry IV of France. (One source gives the date as October 16).

(October 6) Venturi, Luca Bati and Pietro Strozzi bought shares in Caccini's opera "Il rapimento di Cefalo" produced this date at Florence.

(October 9) Caccini's "Il rapimento di Cefalo" was produced at the Palazzo Vecchio.

(November 13) Elizabeth Gibbons, Orlando's sister, married James Dyer at Holy Trinity.

(February) John Milton, the poet, married Sarah Jeffrey and settled in Bread Street.

(October) Peri's libretto for "Euridice" was printed with a dedication to Marie de' Medici.

(December) Thomasine Hopper's Agnes was baptized at Holy Trinity. Thomasine was the daughter of William Gibbons and sister of Orlando.

Francesco Bazzini, Italian organist, theorbist and composer, was born at Lovere, Brescia (died Bergamo, 1660, April 15).

Jachet van Berchem, Flemish contrapuntalist, died (born 1536).

Giles Farnaby, English composer,

died (born c.1560).

Claude La Jeune, court composer to the King of France, died at Paris (born 1528).

Adam Puschmann, a pupil of Hans Sachs and a composer of Meistersinger songs, died (born 1532).

Hieronymus Schultheiss, father of the organist Benedict, was born (died 1669).

Anerio became "maestro di cappella" at St. John Lateran.

Some time after this date Arnoldus worked at Nassau-Dillingen.

Banchieri certainly knew Vecchi as proved by his "Studio dilettevole" written this year.

At the time of his marriage this year Bataille still described himself as a clerk, but eventually became a full-time lutenist.

Bodenschatz became Cantor at Schulpforta.

Borchgrevinck returned to Denmark and was appointed first court organist.

Caccini used the term basso continuato or basso seguente in the preface to his "Euridice."

Caccini and Peri set to music the pastoral-mythological drama "Euridice" by Rinuccini.

G. Caccini stopped writing for the stage after this year.

Emilio dei Cavalieri provided

(cont.) no special instructions in his "Rappresentazione di anima e di corpo," however, he expected the conductor to score it for instruments, just as organ music left the registration to the performing organist. This was so nothing interfered with the special conditions of the church instrument.

When the Chapel Royal was re-established this year E. Coleman was appointed one of the gentlemen.

Dowland received an extra payment of 600 dalers from King Christian IV of Denmark.

T. Easte described himself as "The Assigne of Thomas Morley."

Nathaniel Giles, Master of the Chapel Royal at this time, organized another company of child actors, leased Blackfriars, and, in partnership with Ben Jonson, competed with other London acting companies.

Marcin Groblicz was appointed violin maker to the court of King Sigismond III.

Hassler was appointed director of the town band at Augsburg. He soon was bored and regotiated with the Nürnberg authorities to return there.

Wincenty Lilius went to Poland where he became a member of the royal orchestra at Cracow.

Morley's last compositions were lute ayres.

The success of Peri's opera was so great that he was asked to provide a greater work "Euridice" for the festivities at the mar-

1600(cont.)

riage of King Henry IV of France and Marie de' Medici. The libretto was to be by Rinuccini.

Walter Porter, the son of Henry Porter, Mus.B. Oxon. became a chorister at Westminster Abbey.

Pujol was ordained a priest.

Stobaeus, the German composer, attended the University at Königsberg.

Orazio Vecchi, the composer and poet, accompanied Cardinal Alesandro d'Este to Rome.

Verso was at Palermo at the contest between Raval and Falcone in the spring of this year.

Weelkes first employed the phrase "apt for voices or viols" this year in connection with madrigals.

Adriaensen published a new edition of "Pratum musicum."

Artusi's "L'Artusi, ovvero Delle imperfettioni della musica moderna," in two parts attacked Monteverdi's use of unprepared sevenths and ninths. It was published and later reprinted in 1600.

Banchieri's secular vocal work "Canzonets, 4 v.," five books, was released sometime before this date.

Banchieri's secular vocal work, "Canzonets, 3 v.," two books, were published after this date.

Banchieri's "Metamorfosi musicale" was written.

Bathe's "A Brief Introduction to the Skill of Song" was published by East at London.

Giulio Belli's "Cantiones sacrae" for four to twelve voices appeared.

Caccini published "Euridice" at Florence. It was dedicated to Giovanni Bardi.

Caccini's treatise "Nuove musiche" was published.

S. Calvisius' "De origine et progressu musices" a music history was published.

Calvisius' "Exercitationes musicae duae" was published at Leipzig.

Canali's "Canzioni da sonare a quattro et otto voci di D. Floriano Canale de Brescia organista . . . " was published.

At Venice Caroso's dance manual "Il Ballarino" was reissued in an enlarged edition, titled "La Nobilta di dame." The book contained directions for dancing the passamezzo. The book was dedicated to the Duke and Duchess of Parma and Piacenza.

Emilio de' Cavalieri's morality play with music "La rappresentazione di anima e di corpo" was published at Rome.

Donato's "Più potente a più forte;" "Vergin Dea ch' il Ciel' adora;" "Vergine dolc'e pia." Arascione's "Nuove laudi ariose a 4 voci" were published at Rome.

Donato's "Veni domine" (a 6). "Sacrarum symphoniarum

1600(cont.)

continuatio div. excell. authorum." were published at Nürnberg.

Dowland's "First Book of Ayres" was reprinted in a second edition.

Some of John Dowland's compositions for lute were included in a collection by Rude, "Flores Musicae."

Dowland's "Second Booke of Songs or Ayres, of 2. 4. and 5. parts" was published by East.

Eccard's "Gebetlein umb ein gnediges glückseliges . . . " appeared.

Eccard's "Nachdem die Sonn' beschlossen" from the "Gebetlein" appeared.

Erbach's first book of his "Modi sacri seu cantus musici vocibus 4, 5, 6, 7, 8 et pluribus, ad omne genus instrumenti musici accommodatis" was published at Augsburg.

Eredi published a book of madrigals.

An important collection of lute music, "The Trésor d'Orphée" by Antoine Francisque, was published. It was dedicated to Prince de Condé.

Gabriele Fattorini composed his "Sacri concerti a 2 voci" at Venice.

Flemish composer, Francois Gallet's "Sacrae Cantiones" was reprinted in a second edition.

Giovanni Pietro Gallo wrote a book of motets for five to

(cont.) eight voices.

Bartholomäus Gese published his "Psalmodia choralis . . . ."

Jacob Hassler published a collection of Italian madrigals for six voices.

Robert Jones' five books of lute songs as follows were published. "The First Booke of Songs and Ayers of foure parts with Tableture for the Lute So made that all the parts together or either of them severally may be song to the Lute, Orpherian or Viol de Gamba."

Lassus' "Prophetiae Sibyllarum" was published.

Morley's "The First Book of Ayers or Little Songs; to sing and play to the Lute and the Bass Viole" was published by Barley. This was his only book of ayres and included the famous "It was a lover and his lass."

Morley's "The First Booke of Ballets to five voyces" was issued in a second edition.

Morley's "Madrigals to Foure Voyces" was issued in a second edition with two additional madrigals included.

The first publication of Palestrina's Masses:

68. Descendit angelus
69. Regina coeli
70. Quando lieta sperai
71. Octavi toni (Festum nunc celebre)
72. Alma Redemptoris

Pallavicino published his sixth book of madrigals for five voices.

1600(cont.)

Pallavicino's madrigal "Dolce, grave e acuti" was composed.

Peri's "Euridice" was published in Florence and dedicated to Marie de' Medici.

Porta's skill in contrapuntal writing was demonstrated in his motet for four voices, "Vobis datum est," printed at the end of Artusi's "Delle imperfettioni della moderna musica."

Salomone Rossi's Book I for five voices was composed.

J. Rudenius' "Flores musicae" a collection of lute pieces was published.

Paul Sartorius wrote a set of madrigals for five voices.

Cornelis Schuyt's "Il primo libro de madrigali a 5 voci" was published by Jan Moretus.

Caroso da sermoneta's "La Nobiltà di dame" was published in Venice.

Three motets by Ventury were included in Caspar Hassler's collection "Symphoniae sacrae" published this year.

A collection of Victoria's works was published at Madrid.

The following works by Victoria appeared:

   Canticles:
     "Magnificat primi toni"
     "Magnificat sexti toni"
     "Nunc dimittis"

   Hymns:
     "Ad coenam Agni providi"
     "Ad preces nostras"

(cont.)

   "Aurea luce"
   "Ave, maris stella"
   "Conditor alme siderum"
   "Christe, Redemptor omnium" (two settings)
   "Decus egregie Paule"
   "Deus, tuorum militum"
   "Exultet coelum laudibus"
   "Hojus obtentu Deus"
   "Hostis Herodes impie"
   "Iste confessor"
   "Jesu corona virginum"
   "Jesu dulcis memoria"
   "Jesu nostra redemptio"
   "Lauda Mater Ecclesia"
   "Lucis Creator optime"
   "O lux beata Trinitas"
   "Pange lingua"
   "Petrus beatus"
   "Quicumque Christum quaritis"
   "Quodcum que vinclis"
   "Rex gloriose Martyrum"
   "Salvete, flores Martyrum"
   "Sanctorum meritis"
   "Te Deum"
   "Tibi, Christe, splendor Patris"
   "Tristes erant Apostoli"
   "Urbs beata"
   "Ut queant laxis"
   "Veni Creator Spiritus"
   "Vexilla Regis prodeunt"

Two settings of the Magnificat by Victoria, antiphonal choruses and organ, were published. One was Primi toni for two, the other Sexti toni for three choruses of four voices each.

   Masses:
     "Alma redemptoris"
     "Ave Regina"
     "Laetatus"
     "Pro victoria" (based on Jannequin's "La Guerre")

   Sequences:
     "Veni Sancte Spiritus"

Thomas Weelkes' "Madrigals of five parts" with viols was published by East.

Weelkes "Madrigals of six parts" with viols was published by East.

Three of Yonge's madrigals were included in England's Helicon.

Henry Youll composed music for Ben Johnson's "Cynthia Revells"

The importance of the chorus increased as the name "ballet aux chansons" indicated. Ballets danced to singing were, however, less common in France than in England or Italy at this time.

From this time on all music became subject to the rigidity of regularly recurring bar-lines, each followed by a strong beat.

The English low comedy plays were brought to the Netherlands and Germany after this date. They could hardly be called operas since the numerous verses were sung to a few popular ballad tunes.

G. Gabrieli's later works, probably composed after this date, brought a revolutionary spirit to all aspects of composition, the treatment of dissonance, the melodic design and rhythmic flow, and even the attitude toward the words, as well as the disposition of instrumental and vocal parts.

Giovanni Gabrieli had assumed the musical style in which two or more choirs sang antiphonally.

Shortly after this date composers began to develop a definite independent instrumental technique.

In England the masque's influence showed in such plays as Twelfth Night. The play included songs and catches and a love-sick Duke who was pursued by the sound of music.

This date is generally considered to be that of the birth of monody or accompanied solo song in Italy.

The recitative had developed into a form not only of speech but of all the passions, moods, and characters that speech expressed.

The recitative style as exemplified in "Euridice" made a great impression on audiences of this time.

The Renaissance started a flood of discussion in prefaces and pamphlets where music and especially the monodic revolution associated with Florentine opera came in for considerable attention.

This year was mistaken by many as the beginning of the musical Renaissance.

Three complete opera scores of primary importance came from this year.

Reading from a score was a rare procedure before this date.

Long pieces with religious texts, chorus, soloists, and orchestras were called villancicos.

The earliest opera from which the music has survived is "Euridice," one composed by Peri and the other version by Caccini.

Caccini's "Euridice" contained many embellishments and ornaments.

Cavalieri's "Rappresentatione di anima e di corpo" was first performed in the oratory of the monastery of San Girolamo at Rome. This was one of Neri's oratories.

A Roman oratory congregation, Santa Maria in Vallicella, performed the spiritual drama, "La rappresentazione di anima e di corpo." The test was by Laura Guidiccioni.

Peri's "Dafne" was never published but the libretto appeared at this time and in 1604.

"Euridice," by Rinuccini and Peri, was performed at Florence this year. Caccini succeeded in getting some of his music included in it according to the preface to Peri's score, released in 1601. The first performance was in Corsi's house.

The lute started to lose importance in Italy.

The Poliphant (Polyphon) was a wire-string instrument evolved from many forms current at this time. Daniel Farrant, son of the organist of St. George's Chapel, Windsor, and afterwards one of the court musicians to James I and Charles I, developed the instrument.

The English expression "taborer" quite possibly denoted a player (cont.) of the pipe and tabor, as it did later on. An example was Kemp's "Nine Daies Wonder," which gave an account of how the famous actor morris-danced to Norwich accompanied by his "taberer" Thomas Slye.

There was a brief time when lyra viols were fitted with sympathetic strings.

Paris had a standing theater at this time.

Prior to this time the use of two dots, one above the other, showed that the preceding note was nine units long. A symbol of this sort was needed for the transcription of early music.

Sweelinck shows "Tirate" (passing notes) in his chromatic Fantasia, "Toccata IV."

Richard Hooker, an Elizabethan writer, died (born 1554).

King Charles I of England, House of Stuart, was born (died 1649).

The drama of the period reached height with Hamlet, Othello, King Lear, and Macbeth.

For the Jubilee this year, 3,000,000 pilgrims thronged to Rome. Among them were painters from every nation who had come for a few weeks, but stayed many years.

Le Lorrain Claude Gelee, French painter, was born (died 1682).

Baroque architecture: Rome, "Sta Suzanna" by Maderna.

(to 1602) Verso was at Venice during these years.

(to 1602) Weelkes was organist at the College at Windsor for these years.

(to 1603) Anerio was maestro di cappella at St. John Lateran for this period.

(to 1603) Banchieri's secular vocal canzonets, "Il studio dilettevole a 3 voci nuovamente con vaghi argomenti e spasse voli intermedii fioriti dal Amfiparnaso comedia musical dell' Horatio Vecchi" was published at Milan. (Cologne, 1603)

(to 1603) Dowland's Songs with lute during these years included: "Flow, My Tears," "I Saw My Lady Weep," "Say, Love," "Sorrow, Sorrow, Stay," and "Weep You No More, Sad Fountains."

(to 1603) Fynes Moryson, who wrote the "Itinerary," was in Ireland during this period.

(to 1607) Jean Le Febure, French 17th-Century composer, was Kapellmeister at Mainz Cathedral during these years.

(to 1608) Rubens, the Flemish painter, studied in Italy and was especially influenced by Titian.

(to 1610) More lute ayre folios were published in England than madrigal books during this period.

(to 1612) Zacharias Füllsack, German instrumentalist and editor, was lutenist and trombonist at the Hamburg Council chapel at this time.

(to 1612) Five collections of

(cont.) songs and duets by Jones appeared.

(to c.1620) Vincenzo Galilei, music theorist, died (birthdate unknown).

(to 1625) A dance arrived from the West Indies or Mexico, the "chaconne." It was "licentious in character" and enjoyed popularity in Spain during this period.

(to c.1640) During this period, a number of semidramatic dialogues on sacred themes were produced.

(to c.1650) The continuo madrigal flourished throughout this period.

(to c.1650) Settings of sacred texts in monodic or in concerto style became common during these years.

(to c.1650) A certain descrepancy between intention and form was detectable in much of the music of this period.

(to c.1650) The sphere of Italian influence that enveloped Germany in these years was followed by a period of French influence. The combination of these stimuli presented unique problems to German music.

(to c.1650) In England, the most important chamber works in the literature of the viol were produced during these years.

(to c.1650) During this period instrumental music gradually became equal, in quantity and content, to vocal music.

(to c.1650) Much Italian vocal

1600(cont.)

chamber music was published in collections of arias, dialogues, duets, madrigals, etc.

(to c.1650) English composers of this time wrote many songs with continuo accompaniment. They were used in connection with the court masques.

(to c.1650) The Cancionero by the scribe Claudio de la Sablonara appeared.

(to c.1650) "Romances y letras de a tres vozes," a manuscript from this period, has been pre-served at Madrid.

(to c.1650) A work titled "Il Primo, Secundo e Terzo libro della chitarra spagnola" was published. The composer's name was L'Academico Caliginoso detto Il Furioso," which has been indicated by Gaspar Sanz in his book to be the pseudonym of the Italian guitarist Foscarini.

(to c.1650) The Italian compan-ies of both the Accesi and the Fedeli were in great demand in France during these years.

(to c.1650) France was inspired by the austere fervor of Pascal and his Jansenist adherents at Port-Royal. Philippe de Champaigne was the group's re-cognised painter. He was of Flemish origin and associated with Poussin, he personified the spirituality that illumina-ted the most direct kind of truth.

(to 1660). This period, in England, was one of fading se-cular preoccupation, (a legacy of the Renaissance) as well as (cont.) incipient religious concern and conflict, which had its beginnings in the Reforma-tion. England was under Puritanical rule.

(to 1750) The dates generally assigned to the Baroque period of music. This was also a period of absolute governments in Europe.

(to c.1900) The conception of a tonal system of major and minor became firmly entrenched after 1600 and remained until the end of this period.

(to present) Orthochronic Notation has been used through-out this period.

c.1600

Caspar Bach II (2nd generation of the Bach family) was born (date of death unknown).

Diego del Castillo, a Spanish organist and composer, died at Madrid (birthdate unknown).

Andrezej Chyliński, a Polish composer, was born (date of death unknown).

Manoel Correa, a Portuguese composer, was born at Lisbon (died 1653, August 1).

Doisi de Velasco, a Portuguese guitar player, was born (date of death unknown).

Michael Düben, a Swedish musi-cian, died at Lützen (b.c.1536).

Thomas Elsbeth, a German compos-er, was born at Neustadt, Franconia (date of death un-known).

R . . . Florido (first name

unknown), an Italian bass and composer, was born in Barbarano, Lombardy (died sometime after 1672).

The French lute composer Denis Gaultier was born. He restored polyphonic structure to lute music (died 1672). See 1597.

Michel Angelo Grancini, an Italian organist and composer, was born (died c.1669).

Hendrik Liberti, a Dutch organist and composer, was born in Groningen (date of death unknown).

Franciszek Lilius, a Polish composer born in Cracow (died 1657). The family was of Italian origin.

Biagio Marini, a violinist, native of Brescia, was born (died 1655, March 20).

Jan Matelart, a French lutenist and and composer, was born (date of death unknown).

Tarquinio Merula, an Italian composer, was born (date of death unknown).

Adam Václav Michna, a Czech composer and poet, was born at Jindřichův, Hradec, Bohemia (died 1676).

Martino Pesenti, an Italian composer, was born in Venice (died c.1647).

Jakob Regnart, a Netherlandish song composer, died (born c.1543). He was active at several German courts.

Michel Angelo Rossi, an

(cont.) Italian composer, was born at Rome. He was an organ pupil of Frescobaldi (died c.1660).

Pietro Paolo Sabbatini, an Italian composer, was born at Rome (died c.1660).

Giovanni Felice Sances, an Italian tenor and composer, was born in Rome (died 1679, November 24).

"Camerata" was the collective name by which the group of musicians working together at Florence was known. Jacopo Corsi as well as Count Bardi, served as a patron.

"The Accademia degli Intrepida" of Ferrara was founded.

A group of ground basses appeared at this time under the name of "ciacona" (chaconne) or "passacaglia."

The fundamental change from intervallic to chordal harmony and from prepared to unprepared dissonance took place around this time.

The new monodic style was soon brought to Dalmatia.

An example of the monopoly music-paper, stamped T.E. was in Thomas Hunt's autograph of his service.

The Nuove musiche movement started at this date.

The Nuove musiche period was an important point in the history of music. It marked the start of opera, oratorio, the cantata and the Baroque period itself.

c.1600(cont.)

Oratorio at this time designated
a locality.

The addition of organ accompaniments to Gregorian Melodies,
and even the substitution and/or
use of the organ in place of
voices was officially sanctioned.

Several modern organ builders
have revived the German type
organ of this period.
Praetorius described it in the
second volume of his "Syntagma."

Instrumental music tended to
lead an existence independent of
vocal polyphony prior to this
date.

With polyphony eliminated, composers were at last able to adhere to humanistic claims without restrictions.

"Stile rappresentativo" has
been considered the most important turning point in the history of music.

Historians at one time dated the
beginning of the musical
Renaissance at this time when
opera first made its appearance.

The musical interrelationship
of European countries at the
time of the Renaissance was well
illustrated in a manuscript collection made in Leyden and known
as "the Thysius Lute-Book" after
its owner. The probable compiler and first owner was a
Rotterdam minister named Adriaan
Joriszoon Smout.

Jacopo Abbatis became a member
of the royal band in Warsaw.

Maschera, Banchieri and G.
Gabrieli wrote canzoni and

(cont.) sinfonie for quartet or
double quartet in a style inspired by the old "a cappella"
choirs.

Luca Bati became chapel master
at the Cathedral in Florence.

Matteo Bente finished working as
a contemporary of Giovanni Paolo
Maggini's. He had been with him
for thirty years.

Charles, son of Mathurin
Couperin, was a tradesman in the
town of Chaumes. He was also
organist at the parish church
and the Benedictine abbey in
Chaumes. He was the grandfather
of Couperin "le Grand."

Mathurin Couperin, great grandfather of Francois, "le Grand"
was a village lawyer at Beauvoir,
in Brie. He was succeeded by
his son, Denis.

Erbach became organist to the
Fuggers at Augsburg.

Daniel Farrant invented the
"stump," an obsolete English
cittern type instrument. No
specimen survived.

Gabriele Fattorini, Italian composer, was maestro di cappella
at the church of Santa Maria
delle Carceri in Venice.

G. Gabrieli and Hassler were
apparently the most favored composers in Sweden at this time.

Valentin Haussmann, composer,
was active at this time.

Rinuccini and Caccini encouraged
the development of musical elements rather than literary ones
in French ballet.

Verso was at Venice at this
time.

Banchieri's Secular vocal work,
Canzonets, three volumes, four
books (I, "Hora prima di
recreatione"; IV, "Metamorfosi
musicale") were completed by
this time.

Adam Berg published music at
Munich up to this time.

A piece by Bevin was included
in Benjamin Cosyn's Virginal
Book.

"Cruda Amarilli" achieved notor-
iety through the vitriolic
criticism it provoked in
"L'Artusi overo delle
imperfettione della moderna
musica."

A lute piece of this period by
"Fr. Cutting" was found in
Cambridge University Library
and others by "F.C." or
"Cutting" as well.

Lute music by "Frauncis
Cuttinge" (and similar spellings)
was published.

Hassler's two collections of
songs in 4, 5, 6, and 8 parts
based on Italian models, were
published at Nürnberg (see also
1596).

Music between the acts was common at the Rose and Blackfriars,
sometimes also dance music and
even dancing.

The "aria" of Monteverde and
his contemporaries was almost
exactly like their "musica
parlante," a very slight im-
provement on the "plain-song"
of the middle ages.

Romulo Naldi composed a book of
motets for double chorus which
was published at Venice.

Opera as an art form was created
in Florence and Mantua about
this time, however, actually
republican Venice freed the new
art of the shackles that had
made it an exclusively aristocratic privilege.

Caldéron, the poet who wrote
"El jardín de Falerina" for
which José Peyro wrote the incidental music, was born (died
1681).

Bartlomiei Groicki, a Polish
lawyer and songbook editor, died
in Cracow (born c.1519).

Claude Lorrain, a French painter
who exerted a lasting influence
on European art, was born (died
1682).

William Prynne, a Puritan writer,
was born (died 1669).

Salomon van Ruisdael, a Dutch
painter, was born (died 1670).

Renaissance architecture:
Stairs at Seven oaks, Knole Park,
22 feet wide.

1601
(January 31) Jaques Champion de
Chambonnières, was the grandson
of Thomas Champion and son of
Jacques Champion, "sieur de la
Chapelle" and of Anne Chartriot,
the daughter of Robert Chartriot,
"sieur de Chambonnières." The
latter two were married on this
date.

(May 6) Benedetto Pallavicino,
Cremonese composer, died at
Mantua (born c.1560).

1601(cont.)

(May 26) Costanzo Porta, Italian madrigalist and pupil of Willaert, died at Padua (born 1530).

(November 22) Ann Dyer was baptized. She was the daughter of Elizabeth and James Dyer. Elizabeth, in turn, was the daughter of William Gibbons.

(November 28) Monteverdi wrote to the Duke of Mantua and requested the position of director of music in the Mantuan court since Pallavicino had died.

(December 31) Jan (Brant) Brandt, Polish composer, died at Lwow (born 1551).

(January) G. Caccini's setting of "Euridice" was printed shortly before Peri's, almost certainly in January.

Francesco Guami, Italian trombonist and composer, died at Lucca (born c.1544).

Leonhart Schröter, a Lutheran composer, died (born 1532).

Delphin Strungk, a German composer and organist, was born (died 1694). He was organist at St. Martin's, Braunschweig.

Johan Agricola was professor at the Augustinianum at Erfurt.

Micheal Altenburg, German clergyman and musician, studied theology at Halle.

Valerio Bona was "maestro di cappella" at the Cathedral Monti Regali at this time.

On a trip for his health, Bull traveled in France, Germany and (cont.) the Netherlands. He was greatly admired and Queen Elizabeth ordered him home in fear that some foreign court might engage him. When he returned he remained closeted with the Queen for some time.

Byrd's son Thomas was appointed deputy to Dr. John Bull in his musical offices, including the Gresham professorship.

Caccini, in the preface to "Nuove musiche," demanded "a certain noble contempt of song in order to speak, as it were, through music."

Caccini in "Nuove musiche" condemned "those who do not well understand what it is to sing passionately."

Campanus was a professor at Prague University from this date forward.

Scipio Cerreto described Horatio da Parma as a Neapolitan viol player.

In his will, drawn this year, Diomedes bequeathed his lutenist 1000 zlotys.

John Dowland was sent to England to purchase musical instruments amounting to 300 dalers. While there, he was decorated and presented with the King's portrait.

M. East was invited to contribute to "The Triumphes of Oriana."

Alfonso Fontanelli, an Italian madrigal composer, was sentenced to death for the murder of his second wife's lover. He was later reprieved.

1601(cont.)

Melchior Franck, the German
composer, was living at
Augsburg.

Tommaso Graziani became maestro
di cappella at Porto Gruaro,
Lombardy.

Hassler was appointed organist
of Our Lady's Church
(Frauenkviche) and director of
the town band at Nürnberg.

Paul Homberger became a cantor
and teacher at Venice. He composed "Psalmodia vespertinae"
and a large number of occasional
songs, both in parts and for
solo voices.

John Maynard, with his colleague
Daniel Norcombe, left Denmark
suddenly and fled to Venice by
way of Germany and Hungary.
They were pursued by emissaries
of the Danish King.

Monteverdi became a conductor
at the ducal court of Mantua.

Jacob Paix finished his engagement as organist at Launigen.
He had assumed the position in
1575.

Porta was director of the chapel
of the Cappella Antoniana until
this year when he died.

Quagliati was organist at Santa
Maria Maggiore at Rome from
this date forward.

Philip Rosseter described
Campian's music and poetry as
"superfluous blossoms of his
deeper studies." Rosseter was
referring to the study of medicine.

Henry Sandam was the court

(cont.) dancing-master at
Copenhagen.

Floris Corneliszoon Schuyt was
organist at St. Peter's Church
in Leyden until this date when
he retired. He had held the
post since 1585.

Cornelis Floriszoon Schuyt succeeded his father as organist
at St. Peter's, Leyden.

Stobaeus was bass singer at the
ducal chapel in Königsberg.

Verdonck entered the service of
Jean de Cordes, governor of
Wichelen and of Cherscamp.

Agricola's "Motetae Novae pro
praecipuis in anno festis
decantandae" was published.

Blasius Ammon's "Introitus
dominicales per totum annum,"
for four voices, was published
at Vienna.

Banchieri's literary work,
"Cartella, overo Regole
utilissime a quelli che
desideranno imparare il canto
figurato" appeared.

The records in "The Chapter Acts
of Christ Church Cathedral,
Vol. I, showed this item, "Payd
unto Mr. Bateson for ye new
organ booke belonging to o'r
Quier xl[s]."

John Bennet's "All creatures
now are merry minded" was No.4
of "The Triumphes of Oriana."

Caccini's and Peri's published
versions of Euridice both appeared. They are the two earliest surviving complete operas.

In the preface to Caccini's

"Nuove musiche" in his description of contemporary ornamentation, he takes for granted the "inequality" in the equipment of singers.

Campian's first musical publication, "A Booke of Ayres, Set foorth to be song to the Lute Orpherian and Base Violl" appeared. Rosseter was the co-author.

Canali's "Canzonette a tre voci di D. Floriano Canale da Bressa organista . . ." appeared.

Richard Carlton's "Madrigals to Five voyces" was published. On the title page there was purported to be the following: "printed by Thomas Morley dwelling in Little Saint Helen's."

Scipione Ceretto's "Della Prattica Musica vocale e strumentale" was written.

Cerreto wrote concerning the lira da gamba, its technique and its music.

A madrigal "With wreaths of rose and laurel" by Cobbold was included in "The Triumphes of Oriana."

Croce's canzonette for three and four voices appeared at this date (See also 1588).

Croce's "Sacrae catniones a 5 voci" was published (See also 1605).

Christoph Demantius' "Sieben und siebentzig newe auszerlesene liebliche, zierliche, polnischer und teutscher Art Täntze" appeared.

Anselmo Facio, Italian composer, published a book of six-voice madrigals in Venice.

Fattorini published a second book of motets, for eight voices.

Gese published a collection of "Geistliche Lieder."

Girolamo Giacobbi published a volume of motets for six voices.

Gumpeltzhaimer's "Sacrorum concentuum" (Vol. I) was published.

Haus C. Haiden wrote words and music for a book of four-part dance songs for voices and instruments.

Hassler's "Lustgarten neuer Teutscher Gesang" appeared. It included thirty-two songs for four to eight voices, mostly of the ballett and gagliarda type, with eleven instrumental intradas for six parts. The tune "Mein Gemut ist mir verwirret" in simple five-part harmony was included.

Hassler dedicated his second collection of motets, "Sacri concentus" for five to twelve parts and including forty-eight compositions to the Nürnberg Senate.

Jacob Hassler published a collection of church works including magnificats, a mass, and other works.

H.C. Heyden's two books of four-part dance songs for voices or instruments was published (See also 1614).

A five-part madrigal, "Fair Oriana, Beauty's Queen" by John

Hilton I was included in "The Triumphes of Oriana."

Joachim van den Hove's "Florida sive cantiones" with voice parts and lute accompaniment was published at Utrecht.

East published Jones's "1st book of Ayres."

East published "The Triumphes of Oriana."

Jones' "The Second Booke of Songes and Ayres, Set ont to the Lute, the base Violl the playne way, or the Base by tableture after the leero fashion" was published.

A six-part madrigal by Edward Johnson, "Come, blessed bynd," was included in the "Triumphes of Oriana."

Kirbye wrote a six-part madrigal which was included in "The Triumphes of Oriana."

Krzesichleb's Psalm Book containing a large number of anthems, hymns, and religious songs, was reprinted (See also 1603, 1620, 1640 and 1646).

Lisley's six-part madrigal, "Faire Citharea presents hir dares" was included in "The Triumphes of Oriana."

Luzzaschi's book published this year provided the only specimen of written accompaniments for keyboard during this period.

Luzzaschi's "Madrigale per cantare e sonare . . ." for one to three voices appeared. It was composed in conservative style and was an example of the

(cont.) trend toward composition for few-voices.

Geo. Marson's five part madrigal "The nymphs and shepherds danced lavoltas" was included in "The Triumphes of Oriana."

John Milton's madrigal "Fair Oriana in the morn" for six voices was included in "The Triumphes of Oriana."

The Triumphes of Oriana, published this year, included works by twenty-nine English composers. The compositions honored Queen Elizabeth.

The complete acceptance of the Italian style in England was evidenced by the publication of "The Triumphes of Oriana." It was an ambitious anthology patterned after "Il Trionfo di Dori," but in this case in honor of Queen Elizabeth.

Two of Morley's madrigals were included in "The Triumphes of Oriana."

Moritz published a Lutheran "Gesangbuch" with tunes only. Twenty-four of them were composed by Moritz.

John Mundy's five-part madrigal "Lightly She whipped o'er the dales" was included in "The Triumphes of Oriana."

Nicholson's five-part madrigal "Sing Shepherds All" was included in "The Triumphes of Oriana."

Norcome's madrigal "With angel's face and brightness" was included in "The Triumphes of Oriana."

Pacelli's one book of madrigals for four voices was published at Venice.

Paciotti's book of motets for five voices was published at Rome.

This year marked the first publication of Palestrina's Masses:

73. Regina coeli
74. O Rex gloriae
75. Ascendo ad Patrem
76. Qual è il più grand' amor
77. Tu es Patrus
78. Viri Galilei
79. Laudate Dominum
80. Hodie Christus natus est
81. Fratres enim ego accepi

"Euridice" by Peri appeared at Florence as "Le Musiche . . . sopra L'Euridice . . ." (dedication dated February 6, 1600, i.e. 1601, new style).

Peri's "Euridice" was published and became the first opera of which the music has been preserved complete.

A six-part madrigal by Phillips was included in the "Ghirlanda di madrigali" published by Phalese at Antwerp.

Quagliati's book of ricercari and toccate appeared.

Rosseter's "A Booke of Ayres" co-authored with Campian was published.

Rosseter's songs were similar to Jones'.

Paul Sartorius wrote "Neue teutsche Lidelein."

Paul Sartorius composed his "Sonetti spirituali" for six voices.

The second book of madrigals by Soriano was published.

Francesco Stivori finished his six books of sacred songs ("Sacrae cantiones") for five to eight voices. He had started the project in 1579.

Thomas published "The Triumphes of Oriana."

Lute books by Thysius van den Hove containing English dances and fantasies were published this year (See also 1612).

Orfeo Vecchi published seven penetential Psalms in six volumes.

A six part madrigal by Weelkes was included in "The Triumphes of Oriana."

Caccini's "Nuove musiche" contained examples of altered time (tempo rubato), and passing tones called "cascata doppia" and "cascate per raccore il fiato." Considerable space was given to vocal embellishments.

Italian musicians sang and played Mass on the field the day following the battle in which they were captured by General Basta.

When King Christian IV's youngest brother, Hans, left for Russia to marry the Czar's daughter his entourage included eighteen musicians.

King Louis XIII of France (House of Bourbon) was born (died 1643).

1601(cont.)
Tristan L'Hermìte, poet and
writer, was born (died 1655).

Thomas Nash, Elizabethan poet,
died (born 1567).

J. Kepler became chief mathematician to Emperor Rudolph II.

Parliamentary protests against
Elizabeth raged.

By this time the Puritan movement was to have become powerful
enough to attack the Queen
openly in Parliament.

Alonso Cano, chief architect of
Granada Cathedral and court
painter to Philip IV, was born
(died 1667).

Dutch artist Simon Ulieger was
born (died 1653).

(to 1602) F. Weissensee was
pastor at Altenweddingen during
these years.

(to 1603) Giulio Belli was master of music at Montagnana,
Osimo, Ravenna for this period.

(to 1604) Gregorio Allegri sang
as a tenor at the festivals
held in San Luigi during these
years.

(to 1604) Melchior Franck's
melodiae sacrae for three to
twelve voices was composed
during these years.

(to 1605) Rinuccini and Caccini
were working at Florence to
create the "dramma per musica"
during this period.

(to 1607) Banchieri was organist
of the church of Santa Maria in
Regola at Imola for this period

(cont.) of years.

(to 1608) Philipp Nicolai,
erstwhile musician, was the
first pastor of the Church of
St. Catherine at Hamburg during
these years.

(to 1609) Orazio Scaletta, composer, lived at Crema during
this time.

(to 1611) Johann Agricola composed three collections of motetts during these years. They
were published at Nürnberg.

(to 1628) Daniel Lagkhner composed motets for four to eight
voices as well as other church
music. He also wrote secular
songs.

c.1601
Caccini's "Nuove musiche" was
published in Florence. It included canzonette.

Carlton's "Calm was the air" for
five voices was included in
"The Triumphes of Oriana."

Kepler had begun a translation
of the "Harmonic" which he
abandoned at about this time.

Francesco Stivori, Italian composer, retired from his position
as town organist at Montagnana.

Giovanni Maria Trabaci, organist
and composer, became organist at
the royal chapel in Naples.

Wilbye published "The Lady
Oriana" for Morley's "The
Triumph of Oriana."

1602
(February 14) Pier Francesco
Caletti-Bruni, referred to as
Cavalli the name of the Venetian

73

patrician who oversaw his education, was born at Cremona (died
1676, January 14).

(March 11) Emilio del Cavalieri,
Italian composer, died at Rome
(born c.1550).

(March 17) William Gibbons'
widow's will executed on this
date had a codicil dated April
11, 1603. The witnesses were
James Deyer, her son-in-law,
and Orlando Gibbons, her son.
There is a question as to the
possibility of the will being
exactly one year later.

(May 2) Athanasius Kircher,
German scholar and musical theo-
rist, was born at Geisa near
Fulda (died 1680, November 28).

(May 28) Maillard was given
Anselme Barbet's position as
precentor at the Cathedral.

(July 13) Weelkes was awarded
the degree of Bachelor of Music
at Oxford, New College.

(October 1) Hernando de Cabezón,
keyboard player and composer,
died at Valladolid (born 1541).

(October 7) Morley was succeeded
by George Woodson at the Chapel
Royal.

(November 16) João Alvares Frovo
(Frouvo), Portuguese writer on
music theory, was born in
Lisbon (died 1682, January 29).

(November 17) It was recorded
in the Chapter Acts of Christ
Church Cathedral Vol.I "For a
little Deske for Mr. Bateson his
organ book vis."

(December 5) Caccini's "Euridice"

(cont.) was performed at
Palazzo Pitti in Florence.

(May) Fontanelli became major
-domo to Cardinal Alessandro
d'Este.

Johannes Bach, Arnstadt musician
and son of Caspar, member of the
second generation of Bachs, was
born (died 1632).

Hans Jensen Buxtehude, Danish
organist, was born at Odesloe
(died 1674, January 22).

Jacques Champion de
Chambonnières, French harpsichordist and composer, was born
(died c.1672 or 1670).

Robert Dallam, English organ
builder, was born at Lancaster
(died 1665, May 31).

Joan Gibbons was born before
this date. She was the daughter
of Edward and Jane Gibbons (died
1627).

Anthony Holborne, English dance
composer, died (born c.1570).

John Holmes, English organist
and composer, died at Winchester
(birthdate unknown).

Athanasius Kircher, German poly-
historian who wrote Musurgia
Universalis, was born (See
May 2). His writings included
some on the Aeolian harp.

William Lawes, English composer,
was born at Salisbury (died
1645).

Andreas Raselius, German composer, died (born c.1563).

Ancina was appointed Bishop of
Saluzzo.

Barbarino served Monsignor Giuliano della Rovere as "musico" until this date.

Barbarino became organist at Pesaro Cathedral.

Jean Baptiste Besard, French lutenist and composer, married in Besancon, his birthplace.

Samuel Besler was cantor at Breslau from this date forward.

Caccini titled his collection of canzonets and madrigals "Nuove Musiche."

Elsbeth was at Coburg.

Erbach succeeded Hassler as town organist at Augsburg.

Melchior Franck, German composer, lived in Nürnberg at this time.

Marco da Gagliano became music instructor for the younger priests at San Lorenzo.

Orlando Gibbons composed music, for a fee, for King's College at Cambridge.

The Widow of William Gibbons (father of Orlando) mentioned Gibbons' niece in her will.

Hassler returned to Nürnberg as chief Kapellmeister of the town.

Giovanni Maggini was working at Brescia as an apprentice under Gasparo da Salo at this time.

Antonio Mortaro was organist at the Cathedral of Novara at this date.

Daniel Norcome, the lutenist, became a minor canon of St. George's Chapel, Windsor.

Daniel Norcome, the violist, was in service of the archduke at Brussels.

Pietro Pace was maestro at the Cathedral of Pesaro. He was also in the service of Giuliano della Rovere, a member of the ruling house of Urbino.

G. Piccioni was organist at Orvieto Cathedral until this date.

Pilkington was mentioned for the first time in the Chester Cathedral treasurer's books at Midsummer of this year as a singing-man or conductor, as Pilkington called himself, a "chaunter."

Stobaeus was appointed cantor at the cathedral and school in Königsberg.

Vulpius became cantor at Weimar.

Anerio's "Madrigali" for six voices, book II, was published.

Anerio's "Responsorii per la Settimana Santa" for four voices appeared.

Anerio's "Sacri hymni e cantica" for eight voices, book II, appeared.

Most of Giovanni Bassano's music published up to this date was instrumental and included "capricci," "fantasies," "ricercari," and organ arrangements of madrigals, chansons and motets.

Lodovico Bellanda wrote a book

of madrigals for 5 voices, Vol.
I, this year.

Bottrigari's "Il Melone" for
2 parts was published at Venice.

Caccini in the preface to the
Nuove Musiche maintained that
he had yielded to a noble disdain of melody, "una nobile
sprezzatura del canto."

The earliest surviving compositions in the Florentine monodic
style, several songs by Caccini,
were published at Florence and
titled "Le nuove musiche." The
dedication bore the date February 1, 1601.

Calvisius' "Compendium musicae
practicae . . ." was published
in a second edition.

Campian's "Observations on the
Art of English Poesie" appeared.

Campion's treatise on quantita-
tive meter (in English) made his
interest in Baïf and the Pléiade
even more obvious.

Canali's "Sacrae Cantiones - 5
voc." was published by Vincenti
at Venice.

A book of masses by Borgo, composed at this time, was discovered.

An enlarged edition of Gabriele
Fattorini's "sacri concerti a
2 voci" was published.

Frank wrote his "contrapuncti
compositi" for four voices.

Franck composed his "Farrago"
for six voices.

Franck's "musikalische

(cont.) Bergreyen" for four
voices was written this year.

A collection by Franck was published.

Marco da Gagliano's first book
of "Madrigali a cinque voci"
was published.

The title of the "Venusgarten"
by Valentin Haussmann published
this year included the words:
Darinnen hundert ausserlesene
gantz liebliche mehrteils
polnische Täntze." In the preface he required the improvisa-
tion of a "tripla" in the Polish
"manner."

Michael Herrer, German composer,
wrote "Canticum gloriosae
deiparae V.M. 6v." It was probably the same as "Magnificat
6v." (Augsburg, 1604); and three
motets in collective volumes.

Krzysztof Kraiński's "Kancyonal
abo Piesni duchowne" (Cantionale
or Devotional Songs) was published.

Leone Leioni's madrigals were
included in Torchi's "L'arte
musicale in Italia."

Leone Leoni finished five books
of madrigals this year. He had
started the works in 1588.

Alfonso Lobo's "Liber primus
missarum" was published.

Duarte Lobo's "Opuscula:
Natalitiae noctis responsoria"
was published by Jan Moretus.

Publication of Caccini's "Nuove
Musiche" brought on many similar
collections. One of these was
"Megli" published this year.

1602(cont.)

R. Michael composed "Hochzeitsgesang" for six voices (manuscript).

The Middleburg Psalter had three tunes appointed to twenty-two Psalms.

Negri increased the repertoire of practical dance music by adding his "Le gratie d'amore." It was a collection of ancient tunes.

G. Oristagno at Palermo wrote a book of "Responsoria Nativitatis et Epiphaniae Domini" for four voices.

Pieces from this date by Philips were included in "The Fitzwilliam Virginal Book" (See also 1603 and 1605).

Posthumous publications or Porta's works included the four-part "Hymnodia sacra totius per anni circulum." Forty-four selections were found.

H. Praetorius' "Opus musicum," Vol. II, "Magnificat octo vocum super octo tonos consuetos cum motetis" was dedicated to Landgrave Mortiz of Hesse.

Erich van der Putten's "Musathena" (originally "Pallas modulata") was published at Hanover.

Sartorius wrote a set of motets for six to twelve voices.

Orfeo Vecchi published a book of five-part masses this year.

Lodovico Grossi da Viadana's work Cento Concerti "Ecclesiastici a 1, 2, 3, 4,Voci (cont.) con il Basso Continuo per Sonar nell' Organo" was published at Venice. It was important because it contained concerted music accompanied by a "following bass." They were not truly monodies but only appeared to be. The collection was an important early step in Baroque music, however.

Vulpius' "Cantiones sacrae 8 vocibus" was published at Jena.

C.T. Walliser published his "Teutsche Psalmer."

The continuo madrigal developed simultaneously with monody. Rossi's collection of this year made this evident.

The inventory of King Philip II of Spain mentioned cornetts.

Caccini's "Euridice" was performed at Florence but not revived again.

Not only opera but monodies also started with Caccini's "Nuove Musiche" this year.

Cardinal Mazarin, Richelieu's eventual successor, was born (died 1661).

Shakespeare's Hamlet was completed.

Philippe de Champagne (Champaigne), French painter, was born (died 1674).

Frans Snyders, Flemish stillife and animal specialist, became a master at Antwerp this year.

French sculpture: "Calvary." Anonymous sculpture of granite at Plougastel, Brittany.

1602(cont.)

(to 1603) Stefano Felis, an Italian composer, was canon at St. Nicolas, Bari, during these years.

(and 1603) The "Mundum Books" showed that Orlando Gibbons was paid special fees by King's College at Cambridge "pro musica" "in festo Dominae Reginae" and for the feast of the Purification. The fee was not for music composed, but rather for providing musical performances.

(to 1604) Lute books by Cesare Negri were published during these years.

(to 1604) Hans Nielsen studied with G. Gabrieli at Venice during these years.

(to 1605) Francesco Stivori, Italian organist and composer, was in the service of the Archduke Ferdinand of Austria during this period.

(to 1605) Zangius was deputy organist at St. Mary's, Danzig for these years.

(to 1606) Agazzari was "maestro di cappella" at the German College in Rome during this period.

(to 1609) Several of Domenico Maria Megli's books of monodies were published during these years.

(to 1609) S. Orlandi wrote five books of madrigals during this span of years.

(to 1610) English Renaissance Arch: Burton Agnes (137' wide).

(to 1612) Jacob Hassler was

(cont.) Kammer-Organist to the imperial court in Prague during these ten years.

(to 1620) Pierre Guedron's "Airs de cour avec la tablature de luth" were published during these years.

(to 1622) Leone Leoni composed "sacri fiori," four books of motets, during this period.

(to 1623) Weelkes became organist at Chichester Cathedral, and remained in the position until his death.

(to 1631) Benedikt Faber, a German composer, was a teacher and singer at Coburg during this period.

(to 1637) Works by D. Lobo including four books of Masses, Motets and Magnificats, were published at Antwerp.

c.1602

Teodoro Clinio, an Italian composer, died at Treviso. He was probably born at Venice.

Marco Scacchi, an Italian composer, was born in Rome (date of death unknown).

Campian first referred to himself as a "Doctor of Physic" at this time.

1603

(March 1) Monteverdi's dedication letter to his fourth book of madrigals bore this date.

(March 24) Queen Elizabeth of England died (born 1533).

(March 30) Jan P. Sweelinck wrote a letter to the Burgomasters and Aldermen of

1603(cont.)
Amsterdam concerning his presen-
tation to them of some psalms
that he had set to music.

(April 11) The codicil to
William Gibbons' widow's will
was executed on this date (See
1602, March 17).

(April 19) William Gibbons'
widow died at Cambridge and was
buried at Holy Trinity on this
date.

(April 21) William Gibbons'
widow's will proved on this date
by Ellis, her son and sole executor in the Cambridge
Archidiaconal Court.

(May 14) Ellis Gibbons' will was
completed on this date.

(May 14) Ellis Gibbons, second
son of William and Mary, died
on this date (born 1573).

(July 4) Philippe da Monte,
Netherlandish composer, died at
Prague on this date (born 1521).

(November 10) Philips published
a second book of madrigals for
six voices at Antwerp. It was
dedicated to the Archduke and
Archduchess.

(March) Empress Maria died and
Victoria composed a Requiem
Mass in respect for her memory.

Melchior Bach, Arnstadt musician and son of Caspar I and a
member of the second generation
of the Bach family, was born
(died 1634).

Giulio Cesare Barbetta, Italian
lute composer, died (born 1569).

Cornelius Conradus, Dutch organ-

(cont.) ist, singer and composer,
died at Lemgo, Lippe-Detmold
(born 1557).

Baldassare Donato (Donati),
Italian organist, singer and
composer, died at Venice
(birthdate unknown). He was
maestro di capella at St. Mark's
at the time.

Jean de (Johannes a) Fosses
(Fossa), Flemish composer, died
at Munich (birthdate unknown).

Thomas Morley, English organist,
theorist and composer, died at
London (born 1557). He made
several settings of Shakespeare's
songs from the plays.

Sophonias Päminger, writer on
music, died (born 1526).

Agazzari was appointed Maestro
di Cappella at the German
College at the church of S.
Apollinaris prior to this date
and subsequently at the
Seminario Romano.

Anerio completed his tenure as
"maestro di cappella" at St.
John Lateran.

Sebastián Aguilera de Heredia
was appointed organist of the
old cathedral (La Seo) at
Saragossa.

Artusi published a defense of
his criticisms of Monteverdi.

Thomas Bateson's son, Thomas,
was baptized.

Bodenschatz became pastor at
Rehausen.

Thomas Boyes was awarded the
Bachelor of Music degree at
Oxford.

1603(cont.)

Benedict Browne became Sargeant -Trumpeter of the Royal Household.

Cecchino was "maestro di cappella" at Spalato (Split) in Dalmatia, a Venetian possession, from this date forward.

Cerone returned to Italy.

Coelho went to Lisbon and entered the Chapel Royal where he stayed for twenty years. He held the position of Capellão e Tangedor de Tecla de Sua Magestade ("Chaplain and Player on Keyboard Instruments to His Majesty").

Croce succeeded Donato as maestro di cappella at St. Mark's.

The Warsaw Conservatory owns a violin made by Dankwart with an identification in Polish. It reads as follows: "Baltazar Dankwart we Wilnie 1603, Jego Król. Mości sluga" (Baltazar Dankwart at Wilno, 1603, His Majesty's servant.).

Donato's activity as a composer of secular music was all in his early years.

Dowland was back in England.

Ann Dyer, daughter of Elizabeth and James Dyer, inherited £20 under the will of her uncle, Ellis Gibbons. Elizabeth was the daughter of William Gibbons.

Edward Gibbons was described in his brother Ellis' will as "of Acton." Presumably this was the village of Acton in Middlesex, but no record has revealed what he was doing

(cont.) there. Conceivably the phrase meant he owned property there.

Ferdinando Gibbons, son of William and Mary Gibbons, certainly born before 1583, was living at this time.

Orlando Gibbons composed music, for a fee, for King's College in Cambridge (See also 1602).

The first "King's drum-major" was William Gosson who was drummer in ordinary from this date forward.

Sir William Leighton wrote a poem in Praise of James I. It was titled "Vertue Triumphant."

Monteverdi had not published anything since 1592 although he had been composing.

An Alessandro Orologio, a cornett player and composer, was elected vice-Kapellmeister at Dresden.

An Alessandro Orologio, a composer and violinist, was Kapellmeister at the court chapel of Emperor Rudolf in Prague.

A. Pacelli accepted an invitation from the King of Poland (Sigismund III) to preside over the royal chapel in Warsaw. He remained there till his death.

Pederson stayed in Venice till this time when he was appointed a singer in the royal chapel at Copenhagen. He returned there at once.

Juan Ginés Perez was credited with the composition of some of the music sung at the annual performance of the "Mystery of

Elche," a religious drama based on the death and assumption of the Virgin Mary. It has been presented annually in Spain since this date.

Corneille (Cornelis) Phalèse, of the Flemish music publishing family, still lived at Antwerp.

Anne Phalèse, baptized on this date, died young.

Johann Hermann Schein attended the "Gymnasium" at Scholpforta.

Soriano became director of the choir at St. Peter's.

Johann Stadlmayer, a German composer, described himself as a musician in the service of the Archbishop of Salzburg.

English composer Robert Stone's name was included among the gentlemen who received an allowance for mourning livery for the funeral of Queen Elizabeth.

Thomas Strutius, German organist and composer, was organist at Stargard at this time.

"Be strong and of good faith" an anthem by Tomkins was used at King James coronation.

Vincenzo Ugolini, an Italian composer, was appointed maestro di cappella of Santa Maria Maggiore, Rome at this time.

Matthew White, English organist and composer, was a gentleman of the Chapel Royal at this time.

Aichinger's works, published in a collection of this year, showed influence from the

(cont.) Venetian school.

Anerio's "Canzonette" for four voices was reprinted this year.

Artusi's "L'Artusi, ovvero delle imperfettioni della musica moderna" was reprinted at this time.

Banchieri's "Fantasia in Eco movendo un Registro" of this year was in aba form with a coda.

A fantasia by Banchieri composed this year has the form abab.

Banchieri's instrumental work "I canzoni alla francese a 4 voci per sonar" appeared (See also 1595).

Banchieri's stage work "Trattenimenti in villa" appeared.

Giulio Cesare Barbetta published four books of lute tablature from 1569 to this date.

East published Bateson's "First book of Madrigals" at this time.

Gioseffo Belloni wrote masses for five voices, Op. 1. The first edition appeared this year (See also 1611).

Besardus' lute book of this year included English dances and fantasies.

A variation of the tune "Monicha" was composed by Besard. It was arrange for lute and voice.

Jean Baptiste Bésard's "Thesaurus Harmonicus Divini Laurencini Romani . . ." was published by Greuenbruch at Cologne this year.

1603(cont.)

The first edition of Part I of Bodenschatz' "Florilegium Portense" was printed by Lamberg at Leipzig.

Byrd and Ferrabosco's forty different settings for the plain-song "Miserere" were printed under the title of "Medulla Musicke."

Calvisius' "Tricinia . . ." was published at Leipzig.

Canali's "Sacrae cantiones sex vocibus concinendae tum viva voce, tum instrumentis cuiusuis generis cantatu accommodissimae, . . . " appeared.

Capilupi's book of motets was composed.

Besard's "Thesaurus harmonicus" included four compositions attributed to Diomedes Cato.

"Breve et facile maniera" a book by Conforti was reprinted at Rome. It had previously appeared in 1593.

Croce's "Devotissime lamentationi" appeared.

Croce's "Li sette sonetti penitentiali" was published at Venice.

Croce's "Motetti a 8, libro primo" was reprinted (See also 1599, 1607 and 1615).

Two books of Desquesnes' madrigals for five voices were published, one this year and one in 1594.

Besard's Thesaurus of this year included eight pieces, six of

(cont.) which were villanellas, by Albert (Adalbert, Wojciech) Dlugoraj, who was lutenist to King Stephen Báthori. The former was a musician who hurt his reputation by disloyalty to one of his patrons.

Works by Dowland were included in Besard's "Thesaurus harmonicus."

Dowland's "Third and last Booke of Songs or Ayres" was published by Morley. It was the last book published under Morley's patent.

East may have printed the "Medulla Musicke" but no copy has survived to prove this fact although some sources claim it to be true.

Alfonso Fontanelli's first book of madrigals was reprinted at Venice with an introduction by Orazio Vecchi.

Franck published several dance collection.

Franck composed his "Opusculum etticher newer und alter Reuter Liedlein" for four voices.

Franck composed the "Neue Paduanen, Galliarden . . . ."

Antoine Galli, a Flemish composer, published his "Thesaurus harmonicus."

Bartholomäus Gese published a collection of "Geistliche Lieder" this year.

Carlo Gesualdo's first, second and third books of five-part madrigals were reprinted.

Gesualdo's "Sacrae Cantiones" for five voices (Vo. I) was

published.

Gesualdo's "Sacred Cantiones" for six and seven voices, (Vol.I) was published.

Johann Groh's "Sechsvnddressig neue liebliche und zierliche intraden" was published.

Valentin Haussmann published "Rest von polnischen und andern Täntzen" this year.

"Le Printemps," a collection of measured chansons by Le Jeune, was published by Ballard.

Duarte Lobo's "Officium defunctorum" was published at this time.

Karel Luython's "Sacrae Cantiones" was published this year.

"The Raid of Kilchrist" has been attributed to Macdonald of Glengarry's piper. He composed and performed this pibroch (bagpipe variations) this year.

R. Michael's works this year included "Introitus dominicorum" for four and five voices published at Leipzig.

Da Monte published his ninth book of madrigals for six voices.

Monteverdi's "Il quatro libro de madrigali a 5 voci" was first issued this year.

"The Triumphs of Oriana," edited by Morley, madrigals in honour of Queen Elizabeth, was published this year.

Compositions by Philips were (cont.) included in "The Fitzwilliam Virginal Book." (See also 1602 and 1605).

Philips' second book of madrigals for six voices was published by Phalese at Antwerp and dedicated to the Archduke and Archduchess.

Peter Philips, a rather prolific composer of madrigals, published two sets for six voices and one for eight at AntwerP (See also 1596 and 1598).

East published Thomas Robinson's "Schoole of Musicke." It was actually a method book for lute, orpharion, pandora and bass viol.

Johann Stadlmayer, the German composer, published his "Magnificat" this year.

Giovanni Maria Trabaci published a work described in the title as including" Ricercate, Canzone francesi, Capricci, Canti fermi, Gagliarde, Partite diverse, Toccate di durezze e ligature, Consonanze stravaganti, opere tutte da sonare a 4 v., Lib.I."

Orfeo Vecchi published "Cantiones Sacrae" for six voices this year at Antwerp.

Vernizzi's motets for five to ten voices with an organ part for the double-chorus, Vol.I. appeared this year.

Victoria referred to his six -boice "Officium defunctorum," written for the funeral of the Empress Maria, as his "swan song."

A French lute tablature from

this year was executed by
Johannes Wolf, Schrifttafeln.

In Caccini's "Nuove Musiche"
passing notes were called
"cascata doppia" and cascata
per raccore il fiato."

In Conforti's "Maniera" passing
notes were referred to as
"groppo di sopra," "di sotto,"
and "mezzo groppo."

Starting at this time a continuo
part appeared in most new
Italian publications.

The "Mystery of Elche" was revived this year and it has been
performed annually since them.

When King James I ascended the
English throne this year there
were two drummers and two fifers
in the Court ensemble.

After the union between England
and Scotland this year, King
James' interest in his distant
chapel diminished and only a
minimal staff was maintained.

Florio's Montaigne was published. It was an English
translation of the essays of the
French writer Montaigne made by
Florio.

Caravaggio, the Baroque painter,
was thrown into prison in Rome.
He was a violent personality
who made enemies and was involved in brawls and duels.

British painting: Portrait of
Henry Frederick, Prince of Wales
and Sir John Harrington, by an
anonymous artist (79 1/2" by
58").

(to 1604) Banchieri's stage

(cont.) work "Il zabaione
musicale" was written during
this year.

(to 1604) Dowland stayed in
England during this winter, and
possibly another year.

(to 1604) Vulpius published his
"Cantiones sacrae" for five,
six and eight voices at Jena.

(to 1605) Pedro Ruimonte was
maestro músico de camera at the
archducal court at Brussels,
during these yars.

(to 1608) Short's publishing
business was taken over by
Humphrey Lowndes during these
years.

(to 1609) Croce, after Donato's
death, became maestro di cappella and remained in that pos-
iton until his own death in
1609.

(to 1613) Matthias de Sayve
(II.) was a singer in the imperial chapel in Vienna during
these years.

(to c.1616) Johann Staden was
in the service of the Margrave
Christian Ernst of Kulmbach and
Bayreuth as court organist for
this period.

(to 1625) Orlando Gibbons held
the position of Organist of his
Majesties Chapel Royal from
this date to his death (1625).

(to 1625) The reign of King
James I, House of Stuart, over
England and Great Britain.

(to 1639) Franck was Kapellmeister to the Duke of Coburg
during this period.

1603(cont.)
(to 1649) The "Masque," similar
to the French Court ballet,
flourished during these years
in England.

c.1603
Denis Gaultier, lute composer
and cousin of Jacques Gaultier,
was born (died 1672). See 1597.

Randolph Jewett, Irish or
English organist and composer,
was born at Dublin or Chester
(died 1675, July 3).

Jacob Moors, Flemish organ
builder and organist, brother
of Hieronymus, born at Antwerp,
died after this date (birthdate
unknown).

Jan Tollius, a Dutch composer,
died at Copenhagen (born c.1550).

Don Marco Uccellini, famous
violinist and composer who was
attached to the service of the
court at Moderna, was born
(died 1680).

Orfeo Vecchi, Italian composer,
died at Milan (born c.1540).

William Leighton was knighted.

Vincenzo Pellegrini was a canon
at Pesaro at this time.

Illustrations of members of the
Chapel Royal taking part in
Queen Elizabeth's funeral pro-
cession have been preserved.

(to 1648) Vernizzi was organist
of San Petronio at Bologna for
this period of time.

1604
(January 16) Loreto Vittori, a
màle soprano and composer, was
born at Spoleta (died 1670).

(February 10) Cyriak
Spangenberg, German theorist and
composer, died at Strasbourg
(born 1528, January 17).

(March 1) Edmund Hooper was
sworn in as a Gentleman of the
Chapel Royal.

(March 19) King John IV of
Portugal was born at Villa-Vicosa
(died 1656, November 6).

(April 2) Dowland's "Lacrymae,
or Seven Teares, figured in
seven passionate Pavans" was
entered at Stationers' Hall.

(May 1) Peerson's earliest known
work was performed at Highgate.
It was a setting of Ben Jonson's
"See O see who comes here a
-maying" from "The Penates," a
masque performed "for the King
and Queen's entertainment."

(May 4) Claudio Merulo, Italian
organist and composer, died at
Parma (born 1523 or 1533, April).

(May 10) George Marson was ordained a deacon and priest at
London and appointed a minor
canon of Canterbury. This was
in addition to his position as
organist.

(July 8) Heinrich Albert, German
poet, organist and composer, was
born at Lobenstein, Voigtland,
Saxony (died 1651, October 6).

(July 14) John Daniel was awarded
the degree of Bachelor of Music
at Christ Church, Oxford.

(Midsummer) Robert Johnson, II
was appointed King's musician
on the lute.

(August 31) Giovenale
(Giovanni) Ancina, an Italian

85

cleric, poet and composer, died
at Saluzzo (born 1545, October
19).

(September 7) Lucas Osiander,
German theologian and musician,
died at Stuttgart (born 1534,
December 16).

(October 7) Capilupi succeeded
Orazio Vecchi as "maestro di
cappella" at Modena Cathedral.

(October 27) Vincenzo Gallo was
appointed maestro di cappella at
the church of the royal palace.

(November 15) Davis Mell,
English violinist, was born at
Wilton near Salisbury (date of
death unknown).

(November 26) Johannes Bach,
the eldest of the sons of
Johannes Bach, was born at
Wechmar (died 1673, May 13).
He was director of the town mu-
sicians and organist at Prediger
-Kirche, Erfurt.

(November 27) Alfonso Ferrabosco
was given twenty pounds in
English currency in order to
buy two viols for Henry, Prince
of Wales. He was appointed music master to the Prince.

(December 7) Ambrosius Reiner,
a German organist and composer
who composed masses, psalms,
litanies, odes, and sacred
songs, was born at Altdorf
(died 1672, July 5).

(December 15) Lodovico Balbi,
Italian composer, died at
Venice before this date (birth-
date unknown).

(October) Orazio Vecchi, com-
poser-poet, was dismissed from

(cont.) his position as maestro
di cappella at Modena for continuing to teach music to the
nuns against specific orders
from the Bishop.

(December) Alfonso Ferrabosco
was given a life pension of fifty
pounds a year in return for his
service as music master to Henry,
Prince of Wales.

(December) Monteverdi sent a
recently completed ballet to the
Duke of Mantua, by whose com-
mision he had composed it. The
letter revealed that Monteverdi
was ill at the time.

Heinrich Albert, a German song
composer, was born (died 1651).
He was a cousin of Schütz.

Johann Bach, son of Johannes and
grandson of Veit (3rd generation
of the Bach family), was born
(died 1673). See November 26.

Jacopo Corsi, Italian amateur
musician and patron, died at
Florence (born c.1560).

Mateo Flecha the Younger,
Spanish madrigalist, died at
Solsona, Lerida (born c.1520).

Francesco Foggia, an Italian
composer, was born in Rome (died
1688, January 8).

King John IV composed music himself and defended Palestrina in
print. He assembled a remarkable library (died 1656).

Claudio Merulo, organist at St.
Mark's, who died this year at
Parma, was noted for initiating
the "toccata" style (born 1523 or
1533, April).

Lucas Osiander, a German preacher

1604(cont.)
and composer, died (born 1534).

Giovanni Pasta, Italian musician
-poet, was born at Milan (died
1664).

Orfeo Vecchi's death was given
at this time by a respected
source. Most give it as c.1603.

Lorenzo Allegri was an important
musician at the Florentine court
of the Medici under Grand Dukes
Ferdinand I and Cosimo II. He
served from this date until almost the time of his death.

Registers of Ely indicated that
Ralph Amner was elected a lay
-clerk there in this year.

William Bathe was appointed
Spiritual Director of the Irish
College at Lisbon.

La Cecchina (Caccini) accompanied her father on a visit to
France.

Clavijo del Castillo was professor of music at the
University of Salamanca until
this date. He started in 1594.

John Cooper was in Italy prior
to this date and adopted the
name Giovanni Coperario, which
he retained after he returned
home.

Demantius became cantor at
Freiberg.

Eccard succeeded Riccio as
"Kapellmeister" at Königsberg.

Andrea Falconieri became lutenist to the Duke of Parma.

Gery (de) Ghersem became master
of music at the court in

(cont.) Brussells.

Orlando Gibbons appointed organist of the Chapel Royal at this
time.

Hassler received permission from
the Nürnberg Senate to retire to
Ulm. He married there and settled for a time. Emperor
Rudolph honored him and he now
received an appointment as Hof
-Diener und Kammer-Organist at
the imperial court in Prague.

Nicholas Lanier was esteemed as
the musician for the flutes.

Giovanni Maria Nanino became
director of the Sistine Chapel.

An example of the "Canarie" appeared in a quartet by Negri.

M. Praetorius entered the service of the Duke of Brunswick
as organist. He later became
his "Kapellmeister" and secretary.

Sweelinck (1st town musician of
Haarlem) went to Antwerp to buy
a harpsichord on order of the
magistracy of Amsterdam.

Ugolini, the composer, became
ill with a condition that remained for the rest of his life.

Orazio Vecchi was discharged as
director of the singers at the
cathedral in Modena by the
bishop. The parishioners strongly protested the act.

Simone Verovio worked in Rome
from 1586 until this date.

E. Widmann was Kapellmeister to
Count Hohenlohe at Weickersheim.

Amorosius' eight-part motet,

"Cantabant sancti canticum," was included in "Melodiae sacrae" published this year at Cracow.

Artusi's "Impresa del molto R. M. Gioseffo Zarlino" appeared.

Este printed Bateson's "The first set of English Madrigals to 3, 4, 5, and 6 voices. Newly composed by Thomas Bateson, practicioner in the Art of Musicke, and Organist of the Cathedral Church of Christ in the Citie of Chester, 1604. 4 to."

Lodovico Bellanda wrote "Sacrae cantiones, 3, 4 et 5 vocibus" this year.

Giulio Belli's Psalms for six voices appeared.

Gioseffo Belloni composed "Psalms and vespers, 5 v., Op. 2."

Five of Bennet's hymn-tunes were included in Barley's Psalter published sometime between this year and 1614.

The fifth volume of Besard's "Mercurius gallobelgicus" was printed.

Campanus composed his "Psalmi poenitentiales."

Blas de Castro was mentioned by Lupe de Vega in many poems and plays, for example, "El peregrino en su patria," written this year.

Croce's "Mascharate piacevole et ridicolose" was reprinted.

East published Michael East's "1st set of Madrigals."

Erbach's second book of "Modi sacri seu cantus musici vocibus 4, 5, 6, 7, 8 et pluribus, . . ." was published.

Fattorini's second book of madrigals was published.

Johann Fischer, organist, completed his compilation of 150 motets by 16th-century composers. He initiated the project in 1594.

Fontanelli's second book of madrigals was published.

A second enlarged edition of Fattorini's "Sacri concerti a 2 voci" was published.

Marco da Gagliano's "Il secondo libro de madrigali" was published.

A lute-book by Gastoldi was published.

Gesualdo's second book of five-part madrigals was reprinted for the second time.

Gesualdo's fourth book of five-voice madrigals was reprinted.

Vincenzo de Grandis composed a motet, probably at Rome.

Windet published Thomas Greaves work titled: "Songs of Sundrie Kindes; first Aires to be sung to the Lute and Base Violl. Next, Songs of Sadnesse, for the Viols and Voyces. Lastly, madrigalles for five Voyces."

Johann Groh's "Dreissig neue ausserlesene Padovane und Galliard . . ." was published.

Haussman composed an entrata, a somewhat pompous piece for four to six instruments written in a note-against-note style.

J. H. Kapsborger published the first of his four books of "Intavolatura di Chitarrone."

Kepler's "Astronomiae pars optica" was published and re-vealed a discovery in the law of refraction.

Bernhard Klingenstern's "Rosetum Marianum . . ." was published.

K. Kranski's "Cantionale or Devotional Songs" made such a great impression that in the next twenty-two years six edi-tions appeared, the last one this year.

Lassus' sons, Rudolph and Ferdinand, published a collec-tion of 516 motets, in from two to twelve parts, composed by their father. Some had previ-ously been published and others newly printed from manuscripts. The work was published at Munich and bore the title, "Magnus opus musicum."

"Magnum opus musicum" was pub-lished by Henrici at Monaco.

Giovanni Battista Leonetti's madrigals for six voices were included in Orazio Scarletta's "Affettuosi affetti."

Wincenty Lilius published a col-lection, "Melodiae sacrae." It contained motets by various composers, both Polish and for-eign, predominantly Italian.

In a collection "Melodiae Sacrae" published this year by Lilius an eight-part motet, "Ego sum pater bonus," by "De

(cont.) Abbatis" was included.

Karel Luython's "Lamentationes" was published.

Luzzasco Luzzaschi published seven books of madrigals from 1575 to this date.

The organ accompaniment of the chorale was already present in the Hamburg "Melodeien -Gesangsbuch" published this year.

R. Michael's "Hochzeitlied" for Johann Georg of Saxony and Sybilla Elizabeth of Württemberg was composed for two choruses of four voices. It appeared in manuscript only.

R. Michael's "Carmen nuptiale" for Johann Georg of Saxony and Sybilla Elizabeth of Württemberg was composed for twelve voices. It appeared in manuscript only.

Jacopo Moro composed and pub-lished two books of "Concerti ecclesiastici" for one to eight voices.

Navarro at Mexico City published "Liber in quo quatour passiones Christi Domini continentur." It included monodic settins of the four Passion narratives, a set of lamentations and the prayer of Jeremy. The work was in plainsong and was one of the earliest publications on the North American continent.

Cesare Negri wrote "Nuove inventioni di balli" which con-tains a description of La Volta, a popular court dance of the period. The tunes were ancient.

Filippo Nicoletti's "villanelle" for three parts appeared.

G. Otto published his "Opus musicum divinum" in three books, of motets for five to eight voices on Latin texts from the Gospel for every Sunday and festival and other occasions in the church year, at Cassel.

Annibale Padovano's "Toccate e Ricercari" published posthumously this year was printed in organ score.

Peri's "Dafne" had never been published, but the libretto appeared this year as well as in 1600.

The second edition of Philips' "Il primo libro de madrigali a sei voci" was released at Antwerp.

T. East published Pilkington's "1st book of Songs or Ayres."

H. Praetorius was well represented in the "Hamburger Melodeyen-Gesangbuch" of this year.

J. Praetorius was a major contributor to the "Hamburger Melodeyen-Gesangbuch."

"Adoremus te, Christe" by Josquin Des Pres appeared.

"In Hora ultima" by Josquin Des Pres was composed.

The "Rosetum Marianum" was published.

Lambert de Sayve composed a set of twenty-four four-part "Teutsche Liedlein" in the style of canzonette. The work was published this year at Vienna.

The eight-part canon by

(cont.) Andrzej Staniczewski, "Beata es Virgo Maria," was published by V. Lilius under the name of Andreae Stanicze. It was included in the collection "Melodiae Sacrae."

Charles Tessier's "Airs et vilanelles français, italiens, espagnols, suices et turcgs, mis en musique à 3, 4 et 5 parties" was printed in Paris this year.

Usper published a book of Madrigals for five voices this year.

Orazio Vecchi published his opera "Le veghe di Siena" this year.

Orfeo Vecchi's "A Scielta" appeared.

Vernizzi's "Armonia ecclesiasticorum" Op. 2 was written.

More of Viadana's psalms appeared at this time (See also 1595 and 1612).

Vulpius published his "Kirchengesänge und geistliche Lieder D. Lutheri und Anderer mit 4 und 5 Stimmen" at Leipzig at this time.

Two other editions of "The Whole Book of Psalms, with their wonted tunes, in four parts." were printed by Este (See also 1594).

"Ballets de la Chienne," a ballet preceded by "overtures" with the "Lullian coupe" : slow (2/2) : fast (3/2) with repeated changes was produced.

The baroque masque established itself in the masque "Proteus"

and Daniel's "Vision of Twelve
Goddesses" this year.

Isabella Andreini, Italian actress, died in France. Her
memory was honored throughout
Europe (born 1562).

Della Porta, Italian architect,
died (born 1537).

Italian architecture: The Dome
of St. Peter's was completed.
Originally designed by
Michelangelo, it was completed
by Della Porta (c.140' diameter).

(to 1605) Caccini was at the
court of King Henri IV at this
time.

(to 1605) Franck wrote his
"Deutshe weltliche Gesänge und
Täntze" for four to eight voices
during these years.

(to 1608) John Adson was in the
service of the Duke of Lorraine
during this period.

(to 1608) William Burt, a cornettis, was in the service of
the Duke of Lorraine for this
period.

(to 1612) Johann Groh was organist at the electoral school of
St. Affran at Meissen, Saxony
during these years.

(to 1614) Farnaby's music was
included in "The whole Booke of
Psalmes" issued by Barley during
these years.

(August 18 to 1628) Girolamo
Giacobbi was maestro di cappella
of San Petronio, Bologna for
this period of time.

c.1604

Johannes Wanning, Dutch contrapuntist and composer, died at
Danzig (birthdate unknown).

Priuli was a musician in the
chapel of the Archduke Ferdinand
at Graz at this time.

The first organ in what is now
the United States was apparently
in the Mission at San Felipe,
New Mexico at this time.

(to 1614) Spanish painting: El
Greco, "View of Toledo" (47 3/4"
by 42 3/4").

1605

(February 19) Orazio Vecchi,
composer and poet, died at
Modena (born 1550).

(March 21) Orlando Gibbons, at
twenty-one years of age, became
organist at the Chapel Royal.

(April 18) Carissimi was baptized.

(April 19) Orazio Benevoli, an
Italian composer, was born at
Rome (died 1672, June 17).

(May 4) Dowland's name appeared
in the accounts of Trinity
College, Dublin.

(June 3) Hawkins maintained that
on Tallis' recommendation Elway
Bevin was admitted a gentleman
extraordinary of the Chapel
Royal on June 3, 1589. This
was an error, he was not admitted
until this date, by which time
Tallis had been dead almost
twenty years.

(September 27) Jane Farnaby,
mother of composer Giles
Farnaby, was buried at Waltham
St. Lawrence.

1605(cont.)

(October 5) Antoine Francisque,
French lutenist and composer,
was buried in Paris.

(October 14) Dulichius'
"Hymenaeus VII vocum in
solemnia nuptiarum . . .
Christopheri Albini . . ." was
published.

(October 16) Charles d'Assoucy,
French poet, musician and adventurer, was born at Paris
(died 1677, October 29).

(November 18) Dulichius'
"Hymenaeus VII vocum solemnibus
nuptiarum . . . Guilhelmi
Simonis . . ." was released on
this date.

(November 20) Christian
Ameyden, Netherlandish tenor and
composer, died at Rome (born
c.1534).

(December 12) Alexandre de
Aquiar, Portuguese poet and
lutenist, died near Talavera
(birthdate unknown).

(December 16) Manuel Mendès,
Portuguese composer, died at
Evora (birthdate unknown).
His students included Duarte
Lôbo.

(March) The following was recorded in "The Chapter Acts of
Christ Church Cathedral" Vol.I,
"To Mr Bateson for mending ye
organs when they were removed
iiijs xd."

(March) Antonio Bertali, an
Italian composer, was born at
Verona (died 1669, April 1).

Orazio Benevoli, Italian composer, was born (died 1672).
See April 19.

Jean de Cambefort, composer of
"ballet de cour," was born (died
1661).

Giacomo Carissimi, a major
Italian composer, was born at
Marino near Rome (died 1674,
January 12). He was a noted
church organist at Sant'
Apollinare in Rome. Pitoni
gave his birthdate as 1604.

Antoine Francisque, French lutenist and theorist, died at Paris
(born c.1570).

Bonifazio Graziani, an Italian
composer, was born at Marino
(died 1664, June 15).

Arthur Phillips, an English
organist and composer, was born
at Winchester (died 1695, March
27).

Jakób Polak, a Polish lutenist
and composer, died at Paris
(born c.1545). He was also
known as "Polanais."

Pierre Thierry, a French organ
builder, was born (died 1665,
September 16).

Barbarino left Pesaro Cathedral
to become a musician to the
Bishop of Padua.

Bateson's daughter, Jane, was
baptized.

Juan Bautista Comes was musical
director at the Colegio del
Patriarca, Valencia at this
time.

Blas de Castro was musician as
well as usher to King Philip
III at this time.

Robert Fludd (Flud) was awarded
the degrees of Bachelor of

Medicine and Doctor of Medicine
this year.

Fontanelli was "gentleman resident" to the Duke of Modena at
Rome.

Gery (de) Ghersem became master
of music at the Oratory of
Albert and Isabella.

Hans Haiden, the inventor of a
bowed clavier instrument, wrote
an essay concerning it.

Sir William Leighton was probably a relative of the Thomas
Leighton whom F. Pilkington
commemorated in an elegy in his
first work which was produced
this year.

Simone Molinaro succeeded his
uncle and teacher, G.B. dalla
Gostena, as maestro di cappella
at the Genoa Cathedral. They
were both madrigalists.

Monteverdi referred to the op-
posing Baroque styles as "prima
prattica" and "seconda prattica."
In his fifth book of madrigals
he announced that he did not
adhere to the "prima prattica"
but rather to the "seconda
prattica." He opened his fifth
book with a contested madrigal.

Nicholas Morgan, an English
singer, was ordained a Jesuit
priest.

Moritz adopted Calvinism and
the extremist view that nothing
but words of the Scripture in
the vernacular should be sung
in churches.

Nanino wrote a four-part canon
for each when Clement VIII and
Leo XI both died this year.

Alexis Neander was musical
director at the College of St.
Kilian, Würzburg at this time.

Filippo Nicoletti was Maestro
di cappella at church of San
Lorenzo in Damaso, Rome at this
time.

Pilkington's single volume of
ayres included polyphonically
conceived works in the madrigal
tradition.

John Price I's name first appeared in the Stuttgart court
records this year.

Lamberd de Sayve wrote a motet
for the wedding of Sigismund III
Vasa of Poland and Constance of
Austria which took place this
year.

Samuel Scheidt went to
Amsterdam to study with Sweelinck.

Lorenzo Vecchi, an Italian composer, was mansionarius and
maestro di cappella at San
Petronio in Bologna.

William Wigthorpe was awarded
the degree of Bachelor of Music
by New College, Oxford.

Giacomo Alberici's "Catalogo
breve degl" illustri venetiani
was published at Bologna this
year. It provided details
about thirteen Venetian musicians of the 16th century.

Lodovico Balbi's Masses and
Motets including a "Te Deum"
for eight voices was published.

Banchieri's stage work, "La
barta da Venezia per Padova,"
with a libretto by Guarini (also
called "La nuova mescolanza")
was published this year and in

1623.

Banchieri in "La barta di
Venezia . . ." paid tribute to
Radesca by using the phrase
"imitatione di Radesca."

Banchieri's most important
theoretical work was probably
"L'organo suonarino" published
by Amadino at Venice this
year. The author drew on
Cavazzoni for his description
of the organ-Mass.

Belli's "Compieta, falsi
bordoni, litanie, e motetti"
for eight voices was issued
this year and for 4, 5, and 6
voices (3 books) in 1607.

Belloni wrote psalms and other
sacred pieces for five voices,
Op. 4, this year.

Bodenschatz' "Psalterium
Davidis" for four voices was
published at Leipzig.

Borchgrevinck's five-part madrigals, Book I, was published
by Heinrich Waldkirch at
Copenhagen.

Byrd's first set of "Gradualia"
was published by East for Lord
Northampton and Lord Petre of
Writtle (See also 1607).

Calì's "I° libro di ricercari
a due voci" was published by
Amadino at Venice this year.

The Carol, "Joseph, lieber
Joseph mein," appeared.

A revised and enlarged edition
of Caroso's "Il Ballarino" was
published under the title "La
Nobilta di Dame."

An example of the entrada was
provided by Colerus of the North
German School.

Croce's "Magnificat omnium
tonorum" was composed.

Croce's motets were published by
Giacomo Vicenti at Venice. They
were in part books, inferior in
execution to earlier examples.

Croce's "Motettia 8 voci, libro
secondo" was published and reprinted in 1609.

Croce's "Motetti a quatro voci"
was reprinted (See also 1599 and
1611).

Croce's "Sacrae cantiones a 5
voci" was reprinted (See also
1601).

Dowland wrote "Lachrymae, or
Seaven Teares, Figured in Seaven
Passionate Pavans for lute,
viols, and violins." Both Byrd
and Farnaby made versions of the
work for virginal.

Amante Franzoni's first book of
"Fioretti musicali" was published.

Marco da Gagliano's "Il terzo
libro de' madrigali" was published.

Francesco Genvino, an Italian
composer, wrote his second book
of madrigals.

Bartholomäus Gese published a
collection of "Geistliche
Lieder" this year.

Johann Heyden's "Commentatio de
musicale instrumento . . ." in
which he described a bowed keyboard instrument, the archicembalo, which he had invented

1605(cont.)

was published. It was reprinted in 1610.

Hume's "The First Part of Ayres, French, Polish, and others together, some in Tabliture and some in Pricke-Song . . ." was published by Windet.

Jones' "Ultimam Vale, with a triplicity of Musicke, where of the first part is for the lute, the Voyce, and the Viols Degambo . . ." was published.

The "Nervi d'Orfeo," published at Leyden this year, was significant because of its eight Italian madrigals by Le Jeune.

Two madrigals by Philips were included in "Nervi d'Orfeo."

Lobo's Cantica B.M.V. vulgo Magnificat was published by Moretus.

John Marston's "The Wonder of Women," a play with incidental instrumental music, was published.

G.C. Martinengo's book of madrigals for four, five and six voices was published.

One book of masses, motets and a magnificat appeared as late as this year.

Monteverdi's "Il quinto libro de madrigali a 5 voci, col basso cont per il clavicembano, chitarrone ad altro simile istrumento; fatto particolarmente per li sei ultimi & per li altri a beneplacito" was published.

By this date Monteverdi's madrigal books III, IV and V were

(cont.) published and had established his fame as a composer of progressive and harmonically inventive madrigals.

Monteverdi's Fifth Book of Madrigals began with an open letter to Artusi.

Nanino's "Madrigali," Lib. II was reprinted (See also 1580, 1582, 1587).

Nicoletti's madrigals for two voices appeared in a second edition.

Pallavicino's "Sacrae Dei Laudes" was published, posthumously.

Compositions by Philips were included in "The Fitzwilliam Virginal Book" (See also 1602 and 1603).

Two madrigals by Philips were included in "Nervi d'Orfeo" published at Leyden.

Pilkington's "First Booke of Songs and Ayres . . ." in two volumes appeared.

Porta's "Psalmodia vespertina cum 4 canticis B.V." a 8 was published posthumously.

The "Nervi d'Orfeo," composed by Cornelis Schuyt or his father Floris, was published at Leyden.

By this date Francesco Stivori had composed six books of madrigals. He started the series in 1583.

The ricercari by Palazotto Tagliavia were included in G.B. Cali's "Iº libro di ricercari a 2 voci" published this year at Venice.

A collection of Victoria's works was published at Madrid.

Victoria's Requiem Mass, written in honor of the Empress Maria, was published.

Victoria's Missa: Pro Defunctis was composed.

Victoria's "Officium defunctorum" was published at Madrid and dedicated to the Princess Margaret.

Victoria's Responsory: "Libera me" was compososed.

Victoria's "Taedet animam" appeared.

Victoria's Motet: "Versa est in luctum" appeared.

Vulpius published "Canticum B.V. Mariae 4, 5, 6, et pluribus vocibus" at Jena.

Banchieri's publication had parts which the organist played at mass.

Croce's Requiem Mass was performed at the funeral of the doge.

A specimen of the dulzian bearing this date and made at Frankfort has survived at Vienna.

The "Masque of Blackners" was produced. Ferrabosco contributed some songs to the work.

In England, figuration was particularly idiomatic to the keyboard. A transcription by Philips of a Lassus chanson done this year provided the best example.

John Bolt became a secular (cont.) priest at Douai.

Théodore de Bèze (Beza), a poet who translated the psalter, died (born 1519).

Sir Thomas Browne, a physician and author, was born (died 1682).

Sir Francis Bacon's "Advancement of Learning" was written.

Count Ridolfo Campeggi's play "Filarmindo" was first published.

The collaboration of Ben Jonson with the architect Inigo Jones ("Masque of Blackness") started this year.

Ben Jonson completed "Twelfth Night" this year.

In Rowley's play "When You See Me You Know Me," written this year, King Edward VI spoke to Christopher Tye.

Adriaen Brouwer, a Flemish painter, was born (died 1688).

German architecture: Peller House, Nürnberg (in Renaissance style).

(to 1605) The Papal reign of Leo XI (born at Florence).

(to 1605) The reign of Czar Theodore II over Russia.

(to 1606) The eldest Dallam, Thomas, built a "double" organ for King's College, Cambridge during these two years.

(to 1606) The reign of Czar Demetrius I over Russia.

(to 1606) Alexis Neander's four books of motets for four to

1605(cont.)
twenty-four voices were published in Frankfort during these
years.

(to 1609) The King of Denmark
sent Pederson back to Venice to
study under G. Gabrieli at the
former's expense during this
period.

(to 1610) Solomon de Caus was
engineer to the Archduke Albert
and Archduchess Isabella at
Brussels.

(to 1613) Gibbons' Fantasias,
for three viols were composed
during this period.

(to 1617) Enrico Radesco put
out five books of "Madrigali
canzonette et arie." (Vol. I
was published this year and
reprinted in 1612 and 1616; II
and III were published between
1605 and 1610, but the first
editions were lost; both were
reprinted in 1616; IV was published in 1610 and reprinted in
1616; and V was published in
1617).   These books included
many Spanish songs, dances,
dance-songs and occassional
pieces.

(to 1621) The Papal reign of
Paul V (born in Rome).

(to 1624) Francesco Manelli was
a singer at Tivoli Cathedral
during this period.

(to 1624) Giovanni Domenico
Rognone-Taegio, an organist and
composer, published organ canzonas in 1605, two books of
madrigals in 1619 and a Requiem
in 1624.

(to 1630) Vincenzo de Grandis
was a singer in the papal chapel

(cont.) in Rome throughout these
years.

c.1605
Johann ("Noricus") Agricola,
German composer, died at Erfurt
(born c.1580).

Adam Gobiatus, a Polish composer,
was born (died c.1651).

Michel de LaGuerre, a French
organist and composer, was born
(died 1679, November 13).

Girolamo Bartei was general of
the Augustinian Order of monks
in Rome at this time.

Campian ranked highly in the
school of English song writers
which flourished at the beginning of this century.

Chevalier's name appeared as a
composer of ballets.

Cifra was appointed musical
director of the Roman Seminary.

Fetis and Mandel put Della
Porta's birth at the beginning
of this century.

"Canzonette a 3 voci dell'
affettuoso lib 5°" was engraved
by Camillo Ghini of Siena at
this time.

Early in the century Monteverdi
was installed as Martinengo's
successor at St. Mark's.

Ellis quoted Praetorius' interesting link between instrumental
pitches used in Germany and
England at the beginning of the
century.

With the abrupt change of musical style and outlook Victoria's
compositions shared in the gen-

97

c.1605(cont.)

eral oblivion to which vocal polyphonic works sank.

The steady flow of English comedians and violists to Germany at the beginning of the century brought orchestral dance music to the Continent where it developed at a rapid pace.

No collections of music for "Spanish" guitar appeared until the beginning of this century.

Instrumental ensemble music came to the fore in Germany at the beginning of the century.

Performances of opera and ballet were organized at the Brussels Court from the beginning of the century.

Many part-songs were written, quite different from those of the preceding century. Their musical interest appeared in one voice, generally the upper, while the other parts were subordinated.

The construction of sonata form revealed that the most elaborate of the works were found in dances at the beginning of the century.

At the beginning of the century verse anthems (anthems with solo sections) far outnumbered full anthems.

Until the beginning of this century accidentals occurring during a composition were often not marked. Singers or players were assumed to be sufficiently musical to supply them themselves.

At the beginning of the century

(cont.) treatises on "diminution" and ornamentation, vocal or instrumental, were more numerous than during the middle and late baroque periods.

Dresden had an active musical life starting at this time.

Prague's musical life flourished at this period.

Adriaen Brouwer, a Netherlandish painter, was born (died 1688).

Italian painting: Caravaggio, "David with the Head of Goliath."

(to 1622) Benjamin Cosyn's Virginal Book was written during these years.

1606

(February 1) Guillaume Costeley, French organist and composer, died at Evreux (born 1531).

(February 24) John Dowland was dismissed from royal service at the Danish court and returned to England.

(May 9) Edmund Hooper was appointed organist at Westminster Abbey.

(July 1) John Chappington, an English organ builder, died at Winchester (birthdate unknown).

(December 1) John Shepherd was sworn in a Gentleman of the Chapel Royal.

(December 15) Bull was admitted "into the freedom of the Merchant Taylors' Company by service, having been bound apprentice to Thomas Earl of Sussex, who was free of the Company."

(December 21) A. Scarlatti's

1606(cont.)
"Clearco In Negroponte" was
published at Naples.

(December 31) Bull's name was
included in a list of persons to
whom King James I ordered "gold
chains, plates or medals" given.

(December) Christoph Schultze,
German composer, was born in
Sorau (died 1683, August 28).

Robert Ballard, the French
printer, died (birthdate
unknown).

William Child, an English organ-
ist and composer, was born at
Bristol (died 1697, March 23).
His teacher was Elway Bevin.

Leonhard Lechner, German instrumentalist and composer, died at
Stuttgart (born 1553). He
studied with Lassus at Munich.

Tommaso Pecci, an Italian composer, died (birthdate unknown).

Jakob Reiner, who wrote Latin
texts for Passion music, died
(birthdate unknown).

Domenico Allegri received his
first appointment. He was made
a choirmaster at the Collegiata
di Santa Maria.

Richard Allison's patron was
apparently Sir John Scudamore,
to whom he dedicated his collection of part-songs entitled
"An Houres Recreation in
Musicke, apt for Instruments and
Voyces," composed this year.

Anerio lived in Rome at least up
to this date.

One of John Baldwin's most important contributions was a

(cont.) manuscript book evidently
kept for his own use and written
by him on various occasions up
to this year. It included ex-
tracts and some complete works
by a variety of composers who
would otherwise have remained
unknown.

William Bathe went to Salamanca.
He was there "professed" in
1612.

Brunelli was organist and
"maestro di cappella" at San
Miniato, Tuscany.

Gabriel Diaz was purported to be
assistant choirmaster at the
royal chapel in Madrid.

When Dowland finally returned to
England permanently this year
he found that "simple Cantors,
or vocal singers" and "professors
of the lute" found his music
"after the old manner."

Dowland once more lived in
Fetter Lane.

M. East was awarded the Bachelor
of Music degree by Cambridge.

Gibbons was awarded the Bachelor
of Music degree by Cambridge.

The simple settings by the organist Mareschall from Basle had
the melody in the top voice.

A primitive tablature by
Montesardo replaced the tradition of polyphonic "punteado"
playing by chordal strumming,
the "rasgueado" playing, which
made it possible for amateurs
to play a continuo or the latest
dance hit with little instruction.

Nielsen was studying with G.

99

1606(cont.)
Gabrieli at Venice at this time.

"The Red Lion," the house where
Phalese had published books, was
sold, although Phalese's lease
lasted another two years.

Quagliati's "Carro" was performed on a Carnival car at
Rome.

Schütz left for Venice to study
with G. Gabrieli.

John Tomkins was appointed organist at Kings' College, Cambridge
this year.

Vito Trasuntino made an enharmonic archicembalo (a large
harpsichord) for Camillo Gonzago,
Count of Novellara.

Adriaan Valerius, historian,
lawyer, musician and poet, established himself at Veere as a
notary this year.

Agazzari's pastoral drama
"Eumelio" was performed by a
group of his students at the
Seminario Romano. It was published this year by Amadino at
Venice. The work continued the
line of allegorical plays with
incidental music.

Agazzari's third volume of
"Motetti" was published this
year by Zanetti at Rome.

Allison's collection of part
-songs "An Howres Recreation in
Musicke, apt for Instruments
and Voyces" was published this
year by Windet.

Anerio's "Responsoria" for four
voices appeared.

Masses, motets, and a volume

(cont.) of "Ecclesiastici
concentus" with organ or other
instruments by Balbi were published this year.

Bartlett's "A Booke of Ayres"
was published this year by
Windet.

Barbarino's first secular book
was published.

Belloni wrote six volumes of
masses and motets, Op. 5 this
year.

Bodenschatz' "Florilegium
hymnorum" for four voices was
published at Leipzig.

Borchgrevinck's five part madrigals, Book II, was published
at Copenhagen.

Domenico Brunetti composed
"L'Euterpe," a book of madrigals,
canzonets and other selections
this year.

Brunetti's "Euterpe" included a
very early example of a chamber
duet.

Brunelli's treatise "Regole
utilissime per li scholari che
desiderano imparare a cantare,
sopra la pratica della musica,
con la dichiarazione de' tempi,
proporzioni e altri accidenti"
was written at this time.

Capilupi's "Canzonette" for
three voices was published in a
German edition (See also 1597).

G.P. Cima's "Partito de Ricercari
& Canzoni alla Francese" appeared.

Coperario published his "Funderal
Teares for the Death of the Right
Honorable the Earle of

Devonshire . . ."

Danyel's ayres fused textual and musical rhythms with great skill (See also Cavendish, 1598).

John Danyel's "Chromatic Tunes" appeared.

Adams published John Danyel's "Songs for the Lute, Viol and Voice."

Diomedes wrote religious songs set to words by Father S. Grochowski. They were published at Cracow this year.

Donato's "Deh Pastorale" "Leggiadre nimphe a 3 voci alla napoletana" was published this year by Gardano.

Dowland's first book of ayres was reprinted for the second time.

The third edition of Dowland's "First Booke of Songes" was printed by Lownes this year.

Dowland released a translation of the "Micrologus" by Ornithoparcus at London.

Windet published M. Easts "Second Set of Madrigals" this year.

Erbach's third book of "Modi sacri seu cantus musici vocibus 4, 5, 6, 7, 8 et pluribus, . . ." was published.

Ferrabosco wrote "Hymenaei" for one of Ben Jonson's masques.

Ford's collection of ayres appeared this year.

Melchior Franck wrote a second "Farrago" for four voices.

Marco da Gagliano's first book of "madrigali a cinque voci" was published for the second time.

Marco da Gagliano's "Il quarto libro de' madrigali" was published.

Ruggiero Giovannelli's sixth book of madrigals was published.

Johann Groh's "Bettler Mantel . . . ." was published.

Le Jeune's "Pseaumes en vers mezurez mis en musique" released this year included a few examples in Latin as well as the main portion in French.

Jones' "A Musicall Dreame, Or the Fourth Book of Ayres, ..." was published.

Mareschall published Ambrosius Lobwasser's German versified translation of the Psalter with the original French tunes as they were in Goudimel. However, the melody was in the soprano. Some additional German hymns and tunes were included.

In Marston's "Sophonisba" released this year "the cornets & organs" played for the first act.

T. Merricocke's three-part motet "Gloria laus et honor" was included in the Commonplace Book by John Baldwin, completed on this date and started in 1581.

Montesardo's "Nuova inventione d'intavolatura per sonare i balletti sopra la chitarra spagnuola senza numeri e note" was published at Florence. He was credited with the invention

of the new guitar tablature
"without numbers and notes" for
many years.

Morley's second edition of
"Canzonets Or Little Short Songs
to Three" was printed with four
additional canzonets.

Nielsen's collection of madrigals under the italianized name
Giovanni Fonteio, "Il primo
libro de madrigali a cinque
voci" was published by A. Gardano
at Venice.

The third book of motets by
Nicola Parma appeared.

A book of masses by Patta was
released this year.

Pierre Phalese reprinted
Pallavicino's first book of
madrigals for six voices and
wrote as the dedication
"Benedetto Pallavicino di felice
memoria."

José de Puente published a book
of madrigals at Naples.

Quagliati's "Carro di fedelta
d'amore" was staged entirely on
wheels, on a vehicle modeled
after the Thespian cart.

Johann Staden published a collection of secular songs and
instrumental dances. The songs
were for four to five voices
with an appendix of instrumental
dances.

Antonio Troilo composed four
five-part instrumental canzoni
this year.

Vernizzi's "Angelici concentus"
Op. 3 was published (See also
1611 and 1631).

Agazzari's Eumelio was performed
this year.

The "Masque of Hymen" was produced including songs composed
by Ferrabosco.

The Phalèse music publishing
house was sold.

During a Carnival in Rome five
masked performers enacted a
play set to music by Paolo
Quagliati. As it was performed
the cart was driven from street
to street. It provided an example of lyric drama of the
period.

An act of Parliament guaranteed
the status of the Chapel Royal
in Scotland as a musical institution.

The old building of the Chapel
Royal at Stirling in Scotland
was torn down and a new chapel
was built to replace it.

Pierre Corneille, neo-classical
French tragedian, was born
(died 1684).

William Davenant, English poet,
was born (died 1668).

John Lyly, English writer and
special master of prose, died
(born 1554).

Sir Edmund Waller, English poet,
instrumental in the development
of the heroic couplet as a verse
form, was born (died 1687).

Jonson's masque, "Hymenaei" was
performed this year.

Shakespeare's Macbeth was probably completed this year.

Harmensz van Rijn Rembrandt,

1606(cont.)
monumental Dutch painter, was
born (died 1669).

King James IV founded the
Scottish Parliament of this year
as well as that of 1594.

Sir George Villiers, father of
Buckingham, died (birthdate
unknown).

(to 1608) Mortaro was back in
Brescia during these years. He
wrote masses, motets, sacred
songs, four books of "Fiamello
amoroso" for three voices, an
organ "Canzon" and other pieces
in collected volumes.

(to 1608) Nielsen was a student
of Richard Howett, English lutenist, at Wolfenbüttel during
these years.

(to 1608) Quagliati was in the
service of Cardinal Odoardo
Farnese during this period.

(to 1609) William Brade was in
the service of the Duke of
Holstein-Gottorf at Gottorf
during these years.

(to 1609) Michael Herrer collected and edited an important
set of works by Italian composers, published in three
books during this period.

(to 1610) Thomas Elsbeth, a
German composer, was at
Liegnitz during these years.

(to 1610) Haussman edited (with
German texts) fifty-one of
Marenzio's villanelle, also
four volumes of Vecchi's canzonets for three and four
voices, Gastoldi's "Tricinia"
and Morley's first book of
ballets. His other works inclu-

(cont.) ded instrumental dances
for four and five parts
(intradas, paduans, galliards)
and a few sacred compositions.
This project embraced this period of years.

(to 1610) The reign of Czar
Basil IV Shuiski over Russia
(died 1612).

(to 1626) St. Peter's Church in
Rome, originally planned as a
circular, symmetrical structure
fifty years earlier, was given
a long nave during this period
and thus became the largest
church in the world.

(to 1626) Roman architecture:
Maderna's design for the nave
of St. Peter's at Rome (total
interior length - 710').

(to 1627) Humfrey Lownes, the
elder, printed several musical
works during these years.

c.1606
Tomaso Pecci, an Italian composer, probably elder brother of
Desiderio, died at Siena (born
c.1576).

Adams (or his widow) published
two editions of Gibbons'
"Fantazies of III parts" at the
Bell in St. Paul's. An earlier
edition had been published this
year, without any indication of
either printer or publisher.

Agazzari was maestro di cappella
at the Seminario Romano from
this date (at the very latest)
forward.

It was probably about this time
or after 1621 that Anerio's period of service as musician at
the court of King Sigismund III
of Poland started. The date

c.1606(cont.)
previously considered to be accurate was 1609.

Caravaggio, Italian Baroque painter, was in Rome from 1590 until this date. His presence there provided stimulus leading to the birth of an important artistic movement, the "tenebrosi" or Luminists. Some of the greatest European artists of the century belonged to this group.

Gibbons married Elizabeth, daughter of John Patten, at this time.

(to 1610) Gibbons' "Fantazies of III. Parts" appeared.

(to 1616) (George) Leopold Fuhrmann, a German lutenist, engraver and bookseller, worked at Nürnberg during these years.

(to c.1625) Daniel Farrant, English violist and composer, son of Richard Farrant, was one of the King's musicians during this period.

1607
(January 28) Cesare de Judice, an Italian composer, was born at Palermo (died 1680, September 13).

(February 24) Monteverdi's opera "La Favola d'Orfeo," librettist Alessandro Striggio II, was produced probably at Mantua.

(March 8) Johann Rist, German poet and musician, was born at Ottensen near Hamburg (died 1667, August 31). He founded the Hamburg song-school and awoke the interest of many of the song composers of the period.

(March 11) Giovanni Maria Nanini, Italian composer, founder of a public music school, first ever of its kind in Rome founded by an Italian, died at Rome (born 1543 or 1545).

(June 2) James Gibbons, son of Orlando and Elizabeth Gibbons, was baptised.

(June 4) James Gibbons, son of Orlando and Elizabeth Gibbons, died in infancy.

(July 14) According to Oxford University registers Orlando Gibbons was awarded the Master of Arts Degree. A Joseph Foster suggested that "M.A." might be a clerical error for "B. Mus." the date of which corresponds.

(July 16) When King James and Prince Henry dined at the Merchant Taylors' Hall, Bull acted as an entertainer.

(July 17) Bull and Nathaniel Giles were admitted to the livery of the Merchant Taylors' Company.

(August 10) Alvaro de los Ríos was appointed músico de cámara to the Queen Doña Margherita.

(September 10) Monteverdi's wife, Claudia (Cattaneo), died and left two infant sons (birthdate unknown).

(September 11) Luzzasco Luzzaschi the Italian organist and composer died (born 1545). He was a student of Rore and himself taught Belli and Frescobaldi.

(September 21) Francesco Bianciardi's "Short Rules to play from a (figured) Bass on any kind of Instrument" was

104

1607(cont.)
published by Zucchi at this time subsequent to Biancinardi's death.

(October 24) William Gibbons (son of Edward Gibbons) was baptised according to Bristol Cathedral records.

(December 20) Bull resigned his professorship at Gresham. The position was tenable only by single men.

(December 22) Bull obtained a marriage licence for himself and Elizabeth Walter from the Bishop of London.

(June) Marco da Gagliano founded the Accademia degl' Elevati at Florence.

Paul Gerhardt, principal hymnist of the century, was born (died 1676).

Georg Philipp Harsdörffer, a poet and one of a small group of musicians and music-loving men of letters involved in the creation of German music drama, was born (died 1658).

Christian Keimann, a hymn composer, was born (died 1662).

Gian Domenico Montella, an Italian lutenist and composer, died (born 1570).

Johann Rist, a pioneer of the German song, was born (See March 8).

Sigmund Gottlieb Staden (or Theophil Staden), a German organist and composer and son of Johann Staden, was born (died 1655, July 30).

Aichinger was the first to publish a printed continuo score. It was issued this year.

Banchieri inaugurated a new organ at Monte Oliveto.

Girolamo Bartei was "maestro di cappella" at the Cathedral of Volterra.

Giovanni Bassano became "capo de' concerti" at St. Mark's.

Thomas Bateson's daughter, Sarah, was baptized.

Belli went to Padua.

Bonini was living at the abbey of Ripoli near Florence at this time.

In the preface to his second book of Gradualia, Byrd described his feelings about the deaths of many of his students.

Ceresini was "Accademico Etereo" at this time.

Thomas Clayton, a Doctor of Medicine, was appointed professor of music at Gresham College.

Croce suffered from gout and so was given a deputy to assist him this year.

A Thomas Cutting, lutenist, was in the employ of Lady Arabella Stuart.

Marco da Gagliano visited Mantua at the invitation of Prince Francesco.

Apparently Edward Gibbons (brother of Orlando) was already working at Bristol Cathedral in some unofficial capacity earlier than this date.

Klingenstein was the first to imitate the conservative continuo writing of Viadana.

Marson became rector of St. Mary Magdalene, Canterbury.

Two "chitarroni" were used in the performance of Monteverdi's "Orfeo."

Monteverdi's first opera, Orfeo, was completed when the composer was forty this year.

V. Otto was organist at the Lutheran church in Prague.

John Patten, father-in-law of Orlando Gibbons, was Keeper of the King's Closet at this time.

A letter by Peri from this date exists.

Johann Schein attended the University of Leipzig this year.

Alessandro Striggio II acquired a reputation as librettist for Monteverdi's "Orfeo" produced this year.

Thomas Tomkins was awarded the Bachelor of Music degree by Magdalene College, Oxford.

Agazzari's "Del sonare sopra'l basso con tutti li stromenti e dell'uso loro nel conserto" was published at Siena. It was one of the most important early instrumental methods printed.

Anerio's "Canzonette" for four voices was reprinted this year.

Anerio published a collection

(cont.) of galliards for harpsichord and lute at this date.

Artusi's "Considerazioni musicali" appeared.

A "new and corrected edition" of Asola's "Canto firmo sopra messe, binni, et altre cose ecclesiastiche" was issued.

Giovanni Bacilieri's "Lamentationes, Benedictus et Evangelia" for five voices, Op. 1 was published by Gardano.

Banchieri's sacred vocal work "Ecclesiastice sinfonie" for four voices was completed.

Banchieri's "La Prudenza giovenile" appeared.

Banchieri's "Sinfoni d'Istromenti senza voci" of this year was composed in aba form.

Banchieri's stage work, "Il virtuoso ridotto tra signori e donne," also referred to as "La prudenza giovanile" and "La saviezza giovanile" appeared this year and in 1628.

Barbarino's second secular book was published.

Barbarino's song "S'ergano al cielo" appeared.

Bartei published a set of "Responsoria" for four equal voices.

Lodovico Bellanda wrote twenty-five songs this year.

Belli's "Compieta, falsi bordoni, litanie, e motetti" was issued for four, five and six voices (3 books) this year.

1607(cont.)
"Thesaurus Harmonicus" was
written by Jean Baptiste Bésard
at this time.

Bodenschatz' Psalter (without
title) appeared.

Bonini's "Madrigali e canzonette
spirituali" for solo voice was
published. It was reprinted a
year later.

A Pavan by Borchgrevinck was
included in Füllsack's collection published this year at
Hamburg.

Borchgrevinck's Nine Psalms for
four voices was published at
Copenhagen this year.

Nine pavans and galliards for
five parts by Brade were inclu-
ded in the collections edited
by his colleagues, Füllsack and
Hildebrandi in "Ausserlesene
Paduanen . . . Erster Theil"
(Hamburg, 1607) and
"Ausserlesene Paduanen . . .
Ander Theil" (Hamburg, 1609).

Byrd's second book of "Gradualia"
was published by East.

Byrd wrote the text "St. John"
for Passion music.

Caignet composed fifty Psalms
for three to eight voices.

Campian composed songs for a
masque produced at the marriage
of Sir James Hay this year.

Ceresini's first book of madrigals appeared.

"Passagi" a book by G.L.
Conforti on ornaments was published at Venice.

Croce's "Madrigali a 5 et 6"
(vol. 4) was published at
Venice this year.

Croce's "Motetti a 8, libro
primo" was reprinted (See also
1599, 1603 and 1615).

East published Croce's "Musica
Sacra" at this time.

Dognazzi's "Secondo libro di
fioretti musicali" appeared.

Dowland's viol pieces were included in Füllsack's
"Auserlesener Paduanen . . .
erster Theil" published this
year.

Dulichius' "Prima pars
Centuriae octonum et septenum
vocum harmonias sacras laudibus
sanctissime triados consecrates
continentis accurata diligentia
adornata . . ." Part I was published.

Thomas Ford published Vol. I of
his "Musicke of Sundrie Kindes."

A song of Ford's, "Since first
I saw your face" was published
this year.

Amante Franzoni's second book
of "Fioretti musicali" Book II
was published by Dognazzi at
Venice.

Füllsack's "Auserlesene
Paduanen" was published at
Hamburg this year. It was one
of the most popular dance collections of its time and music
by Danish, Dutch, and English
composers accounted for the
majority of the collection.

Gagliano's "Officium defunctorum
quatuor paribus vocibus
concinendum, una cum aliquibus

1607(cont.)
funebribus modulationibus" was
published at this time.

Vincenzo Gallo's "Salmi del Re
David" was published at Palermo
this year.

Gastoldi's "Salmi intieri che
nelle solennita dell'ano al
Vespro si canta" was published
during this year.

Bartholomäus Gese published a
collection of "Geistliche Lieder"
at this time.

Carlo Gesualdo's first book of
five-part madrigals was reprinted
for the second time.

Carlo Gesualdo's second book of
five-part madrigals was reprinted for the third time.

Hassler published his "Psalmen
und christliche Gesäng mit vier
stimmen auf die melodien
fugweis componvit." It included
fifty-two of thirty well-known
chorale melodies in elaborate
motet form. Hassler stated that
they were "composed fugue-wise"
or in the style of Praetorius.

Tobias Hume published his
"Captaine Hume's Poetical
Musicke principally made for 2
bass-viols, yet so contrived
that it may be plaied eight
severall waies upon sundry
instruments with much facilitie
. . ."

Windet Jones published his
"1st set of Madrigals of 3, 4,
5, 6, 7 & 8 Parts, for Viols
& Voices or for Voices alone; or
as you please."

The following madrigals by
Robert Jones have survived:

(cont.)
1. Thine eyes so bright
2. She only is the pride
3. When I behold her eyes
4. But let her look in mine
5. Love, if a God thou art
6. O! I do love
   above for three voices
7. Sing, merry birds
8. I come, sweet birds
9. Cock-a-doodle-doo
10. Shrill-sounding bird
    above for four voices
13. Come, doleful owl
14 Sweet, when Thou singest
    above for five voices
22. Your presence breeds my
    anguish
    above for six voices
25. Are lovers full of fire?
26. The more I burn
    above for seven and
    eight voices

Francesco Lambardi's first set
of "Villanelle" for three to
five voices was published this
year at Naples.

Lobo's "Liber processionum et
stationum Ecclesiae
Olyssiponenss" was published
this year.

Michael's wedding music for
Johann Georg of Saxony and
Magdalena Sybille, eight volumes
in manuscript, appeared.

Montella's last book of five
-part madrigals was published
this year posthumously.

Monteverdi's "Scherzo musicale"
included earlier canzonettas
that reflected renaissance tradition, as well as many continuo
songs, mostly for two voices.
His later madrigal books also
contained similar works.

Monteverdi's "Musical tolta da

1607(cont.)
i madrigali di Claudio
Monteverdi" (spiritual parodies
of secular madrigals) was published by A. Coppini.

The libretto for Monteverdi's
"La favola d'Orfeo" by Striggio
(II) was issued at Mantua.

Monteverdi's "Orfeo" was actually
published, probably at Mantua.

Monteverdi's "Scherzi musicali
a 3 voci . . ." was published
this year.

Giulio Cesare Monteverdi's
(brother of Claudio) madrigal
"Occhi vidi d'amore (a 3 voci
col basso continuo)" was included
in the collection "I nuovi
fioretti musicali a 3 voci
d'Amante Franzoni" published
this year at Venice.

Giulio Cesare Monteverdi edited
Claudio Monteverdi's "Scherzi
musicali a 3 voci" and was
author of "Dichiarazione della
lettera stampata nel quinto
libro de suoi madrigali" this
year.

Giulio Monteverdi's works included Scherzi "Deh chi tase" and
"Sidpiegate quance" included in
C. Monteverdi's "Scherzi
musicali" published this year
at Venice.

G. Negro composed "Gl'amorosi
pensieri. canzonette, villanelle
et arie napolitane a 3 voci
. . ." (three books).

P. Nenna's set of "Responsoria
for Matins of Christmas & Holy
Week" a 4 appeared.

A pavan and galliard for five
instruments by Philips was

(cont.) included in Füllsack's
"Ausserlesene Paduanen und
Galliarden" published at
Hamburg this year.

One of the most important
chorale books of the baroque
period, Praetorius, "Musae
Sioniae" V-VIII, appeared this
year.

A few organ pieces by Quagliati
were included in Schmid's
"Tabulaturbuch" this year.

Enrica Radesca published a collection of psalms, motets, falsi
bordoni, etc. at Milan.

The trio sonata, classic medium
of baroque chamber music, was
brought to the fore in
"Sinfonie e Galiarde" by
Salomone Rossi Ebreo, published
this year.

Crescenzo Salzilli's book of
five-part madrigals was published and dedicated to the
Prince of Rocca Romana.

The younger Schmid's organ
tablature published this year
included mainly Italian works
by Andrea and Giovanni Gabrieli,
Marenzio and Rore, as well as
works by Aichinger, Erbach, and
Hassler.

Donato Antonio Spano composed
"Madrigaletti ariosi, e
vilanelli" for four voices. He
was guided by Jean de Macque at
Venice.

Antonio Troilo wrote a
Magnificat included in G.B.
Biondi's "Salmi intieri" of
this year.

Verovio issued an instrumental
publication which included

sixteen gagliarde by Anerio,
intabulated both for cembalo and
lute.

East published Youll's
"Canzonets" this year.

Prior to this date at least ten
books containing music were
printed in America. This year,
that of the founding of
Jamestown, showed substantial
activity in the recognition of
music's position in the early
church.

Ballets des Sénateurs were produced. It was a ballet with an
overture of the "Lullian coupe"
type.

Campian's masque "Lord Hay" was
produced at Whitehall on
Twelfth Night in honor of Sir
James Hay's marriage.

Easte's Psalter was favored by
settlers at Jamestown, Virginia
this year.

At the festival on the occasion
of the marriage of Francesco
Gonzaga and Margherita, Infanta
of Savay, Monteverdi's "Arianna"
and Gagliano's "Dafne" were performed.

Monteverdi's "Orfeo" provided
the earliest example of trumpet
music, a five-part fanfare
opening. The opera opens with
a short prelude (nine measures)
called a toccata and repeated
three times. It served as a
forerunner to the overture.
The opera used a mixed group of
instruments.

After the establishment of opera
in Florence, Mantua took over
with the performance of

(cont.) Monteverdi's "Orfeo" at
the "Accademia degli Invaghiti."

"La Favola D'Orfeo," Monteverdi's
five-act opera with libretto by
Alessandro Striggio II, was
produced at the Mantuan court
this year.

The great success of "Orfeo,"
which made its composer immediately famous, had a great influence on subsequent operas,
especially Gagliano's "Dafne"
and Belli's "Orfeo Dolente."

King James was received by the
Merchant Taylors' Company in its
hall.

The first permanent British
settlement was established at
Jamestown, Virginia by the
London Company.

Sir Edward Dyer, Elizabethan
poet, died (born c.1550).

Heywood's play The Rape of
Lucrece was written.

Madeleine de Scudéry, French
novelist, was born (died 1701).

(January to 1607, February)
Girolamo Frescobaldi was organist at the church of Santa
Maria in Trastevere, Rome during
these months.

(to 1608) Dufon again had to
leave Madrid to visit his home
during this period.

(June to 1608, June) Frescobaldi
lived in the Netherlands during
these years.

(to 1608) Monteverdi composed
"Arianna" and "I Ballo dell'
Ingrate," both were composed for
the festivities planned for

1607(cont.)
Prince Francesco's marriage.
The composer was, however, involved in other works during
these years.

(to 1609) Cirullo lived at
Andria for these two years.

(to 1610) Michael Praetorius'
"Musae Sioniae" was published
during this period.

(to 1615) All Bonini's known
music dated from some time during these years.

(to 1625) Niccolo Rubini was
cornet player at the Modena
court chapel during these
years.

(to 1627) The twenty years after
Monteverdi's "Orfeo" showed
little progress in opera.

(to 1635) Patrick Davidson was
master of the Aberdeen sang
school during these years.

(to 1642) Monteverdi wrote all
seven of his full-length operas
during this period.

c.1607
Francesco Bianciardi, Italian
organist, composer and theorist,
died at Siena (born c.1572).

Thomas Cutting served as lutenist to King Christian IV of
Denmark at this time.

Orlando Gibbons married
Elizabeth, daughter of John
Patten of Westminster.

Daniel Lagkhner, Austrian organist and composer, was organist
to Count Losenstein at Losdorf.

Editions of the Sternhold

(cont.) -Hopkins Psalter, up to
this date, included "An
introduction to Learn to Sing."

Mathieu Le Nain, a French
painter, was born after this
time (died 1677).

1608
(January 20) Peri wrote a letter
explaining that he was too busy
with Carnival preparations to
visit Cardinal Ferdinando
Gonzaga at Mantua.

(March 9) Caterina Martinelli,
a noted singer, died at Mantua
(birthdate unknown).

(June 2) Guarini's comedy "La
idropica" was performed at
Mantua. It included a prologue
composed by Monteverdi.

(June 4) Monteverdi's "Il ballo
delle ingrate," written with
Rinuccini, was produced at
Mantua.

(July 4) Eccard was called to
Berlin to become "Kappellmeister"
to the Elector of Brandenburg,
Joachim Friedrich.

(July 18) The Elector of
Brandenburg, Joachim Friedrich,
died (birthdate unknown).

(September 11) Johann Sigismund,
in a letter bearing this date,
confirmed Eccard's appointment
as "Kapellmeister."

(October 26) Philipp Nicolai,
German theologian and musician,
died at Hamburg (born 1556,
August 10).

(October 27) Mrs. William Shelley
presented a petition to Lord
Salisbury listing eight points
of grievance against Byrd in a

1608(cont.)

property dispute.

(November 1) Frescobaldi was
appointed organist at St. Peter's
in Rome.

(December 2) Monteverdi wrote a
letter to Annibale Chieppo, an
important administrator at the
Mantuan court. In it he asked
for aid in obtaining a favorable
release from his duties by the
Duke. The composer complained
that he was severely overworked
and underpayed. The letter also
contained a vivid description
of the composer's poor state of
health.

(March) John Hilton, I, an
English organist and composer,
died at Cambridge (birthdate
unknown).

(May) Marco da Gagliano left
Mantua with a gift of 200 scudi
from Prince Francesco.

(May) Monteverdi's "L'Arianna"
written with Rinuccini was
produced at Mantua.

(November) Marco da Gagliano
became maestro di cappella at
San Lorenzo in Florence, succeeding Luca Bati.

Ludovico Balbi, a polyphonic
composer and student of Porta,
died (born c.1545 or c.1550).
Presumably he and Luigi Balbi
were the same person.

Luca Bati, an Italian composer,
died at Florence (birthdate
unknown).

Philipp Nikolai, hymn composer,
died (born 1556).

Francis Tregian, father of

(cont.) Francis Tregian jr, musician, died in exile at Lisbon
(birthdate unknown).

Anerio had returned to Rome.

At Christ Church two payments
showed that the treasurer and
Bateson were straightening out
their accounts in preparation
for the latter's departure from
Chester for Ireland.

Bodenschatz became pastor at
Gross-Osterhausen.

Bonini moved to Santa Trinita
monastery at Florence.

William Brade joined the
Hamburg municipal band.

John Buchan, Scottish musician,
was still Master of the New
Kirk at Glasgow.

Byrd engaged in a minor lawsuit
with Robert Jackson concerning
a lease in Gloucestershire.

Cerone was transferred to the
Royal Chapel at Naples.

Cobbold became a "singing-man"
at Norwich Cathedral.

Eccard moved to Berlin.

A canon often appeared in Juan
de Esquivel's mass written this
year.

Gagliano used an enlarged version of "Dafne" for his opera.
During the period when he was
working on the composition he
was deputized by Peri.

Hassler was appointed organist
to the electoral college at
Dresden and became chamber organist and music librarian to

1608(cont.)
the Elector of Saxony.

William Inglott became organist at Norwich Cathedral.

John Jordan, a "music-player from London" lived at Leyden at this time.

Ascanio Mio, an Italian composer, was maestro di cappella at the church of San Giacomo degli Spagnuoli at Naples.

Montesardo by this time had become maestro de cappella at the Cathedral of Fano in the Romagna.

Monteverdi's "Arianna" has been lost except for the celebrated "lamento." The latter selection became a model for many composers.

Santi Orlandi, who had become maestro di cappella to Cardinal Ferdinando Gonzaga at Florence, was appointed temporary maestro at the ducal court of Mantua this year.

Pacelli's "Sacre cantiones" showed a style of polychoric music, greatly in favor at Warsaw as well as elsewhere.

A letter written by Peri this year has been preserved.

Peri's opera "Tetide" was sent to Mantua but was not produced. The libretto was by Cini.

Phalèse's lease was up on the building of his music publishing firm, however, he bought the "Coperen Pot" on the same street and changed its name to "De Koning David." This location remained the seat of the firm until it ceased publishing.

Marie Phalèse, the daughter of Corneille, married Pierre Willems at this time.

Lambert de Sayve started in the service of Archduke Matthias, King of Bohemia and Hungary.

Pompeo Signorucci was maestro di cappella at Pisa Cathedral.

Giovanni Battista Stefanini, the composer, was maestro di cappella of the church of Santa Maria della Scala, in Milan.

William Stonard, an English organist and composer, was awarded the Bachelor of Music degree by Oxford and was required to compose an eight-part choral hymn.

John Tomkins, organist and composer, was awarded the Bachelor of Music degree by Kings' College, Cambridge.

Verso taught at San Domenico convent.

Many of Agazzari's publications appeared in Venice.

Anerio published "Madrigali" for five to eight voices this year.

Costanzo Antegnati wrote an important treatise, "L'arte organica."

A book of Arnoldus' madrigals was published at Dilligen. It was combined with a Mass, titled "Si fortuna favet."

Banchieri's stage work "Il festino nella sera del giovedi grasso avanti cena" appeared this year.

Weelkes' "Ayeres or Phantasticke Spirites" was published by Barley this year.

Several masses for eight voices by Bartei appeared.

The first of six books of "Airs de différents autheurs mis en tablature de luth par Gabriel Bataille" was published by Ballard.

Giulio Belli's book of masses for four to eight voices was completed.

Bodenschatz' "Harmonia angelica," a collection of Luther's hymns, appeared.

Bonini composed his "Canzonette affettuose" for four parts to be used at the wedding of the prospective new Grand Duke Cosimo II of Tuscany.

Bonini's "Madrigali e can-zonette spirituali" for solo voice was reprinted (See also 1607).

Antonio Braccino da Todi (possibly actually Giovanni Artusi) wrote his discourse: "Discorso secondo musicale di Antonio Braccino da Todi per la dichiaratione della lettera posta ne Scherzi musicali del Sig. Claudio Monteverdi" this year.

Cancineo's second book of motets for five voices ap-peared.

Capilupi's second book of madrigals was written.

Cerreto's "Dell' arbore

(cont.) musicale" appeared at this time.

Three madrigals by Cerre were included in one of the reprints of Arcadelt's madrigals.

Chiabrera's libretto "Il rapimento di cefalo" was trans-lated into French at this time.

Croce's "Septem Psalmi poenitentiales" were given an English text and published as "Musica sacra" by East this year at London.

Francesco Crotti, a monk from Ferrara, published his "Concerti Ecclesiastici" at this time.

Demantius' "Conviviorum deliciae" appeared.

Part II of Diruta's "Il Transilvano" appeared.

The fourth edition of Dowland's "First Booke of Songes" was printed.

Dulichius' "Prima pars Centuriae octonum et septenum vocum harmonias sacras laudibus sanctissime triados consecrates continentis accurata diligentia adornata . . ." Part II was published.

Ottavio Durante published his "Arie devote," a collection of sacred arias.

Eccard's "Geistliche Lieder," including some five-part chorales, was published by Pfeilschmidt.

A third and enlarged edition of Fattorini's "Sacri concerti a 2 voci" was published at this time.

"The Masque of Beauty" by Ferrabosco was composed to one of Ben Jonson's masques.

Ferrabosco composed his "The masque for Lord Haddington's Marriage." It was based on one of Ben Jonson's masques.

Franck composed his first "Geistliche Gesänge und melodien" for five to eight voices.

Franck wrote his "Newes Echo" for eight voices.

Franck wrote his "Newe musikalische Intraden" for six voices.

Franck wrote his Psalm CXXI for five voices.

Dognazzi published Franzoni's five-part madrigals this year.

Four early canzoni by G. Gabrieli for four parts were included in a collection of miscellaneous works by various composers printed this year.

Marco da Gagliano's opera "Dafne" was published at this time. In the preface the composer paid tribute to Peri.

Gagliano's "Il quinto libro de' madrigali" was published at this date.

At this time Girolamo Giacobbi wrote four intermezzi for Campeggi's play "Filarmindo."

Guarini's comic opera L'Idropica was compiled at this time.

Hassler's "Kirchengesänge, Psalmen und geistliche Lieder (cont.) auf die gemeinen Melodien mit vier Stimmen simplicitor gesetzt" appeared. It included seventy settings of chorale melodies in simple note-against-note counterpoint, as for congregational singing. This was one of the major publications of the Baroque period.

Jones' "Ultimatum Vale, or Third Booke" was published.

Leone Leoni wrote his "Sacrae cantiones" at this time.

Ascanio Mio composed five books of madrigals, however, all have been lost except the third and fifth volume.

Montesardo published several volumes of sacred songs for one to eight voices.

Monteverdi's ballet, "Ballo delle Ingrate," scored for a string ensemble, was completed.

Monteverdi's second book of five-part music was reprinted in Tradate, Milan.

Monteverdi's "Scherzi" was published this year.

Giulio Monteverdi collaborated with his brother, Gastoldi, Gagliano, S. Rossi and Paolo Biat in the composition of the music for Guarini's play "L'idropica." He composed the music for its fourth interlude.

A second edition of Morley's "A Plaine and Easie Introduction to Practicall Musicke" reprinted this year included eight compositions by Morley, principally motets.

Negri's "Affetti amorosi" for

three voices was completed and dedicated to Giacomo and Andrea Morosini, members of an illustrious Venetian family.

The Nürnberg hymn-book of this year was printed.

Pacelli's "Sacre cantiones" for five to twenty voices was published at Venice.

Pederson's "Madrigali a cinque voci, libro primo" was published by Gardano at Venice.

Peri's "Euridice" was reprinted at Venice.

Quagliati made a unique but unsuccessful attempt to bridge the gap from madrigal to monodic literature by composing hybrid madrigals. These could be performed as continuo madrigals or as monodies. They were published this year.

One selection by Quagliati was included in Myller's "Teutsche Villanellen" this year.

Georg Quitschreiber's Jena collection was an important hymn book of this time.

A book by Rasi was published this year.

The Raveri collection, published at Venice this year, included a composition for sixteen trombones.

Rinuccini's libretto for Monteverdi's "Arianna" was issued in Mantua this year.

Francesco Rosi published his first solo songs, "Vaghezze di musica." Most of the songs

(cont.) were written for solo voice and many had texts by the composer. He also issued a volume of poetry this year.

Donato Antonio Spano composed (still under the supervision of Jean de Macque at Naples) "I lib. de madrigali" for five voices.

Johann Stadlmayr, a German composer, published a "Magnificat" this year.

Antonio Troilo wrote "Sinfonie, Scherzi . . . a 2 voci" to sing and play on any instruments. It appeared this year.

Orfeo Vecchi published his "Cantiones Sacrae" for five voices this year at Antwerp.

Vulpius published his first edition of wedding hymns with Latin words.

Weelkes published his "Ayeres or Phantasticke Spirites" for three voices this year.

Weelkes wrote a set of verses in memory of Thomas Morley.

Henry Youll's "Canzonets to three voices" was published.

"Ballet de la Comédie," a ballet with a "Lullian coupe" overture, was produced this year in France.

At the Teatro della Sala, Rudolfo Campeggi, a musician to the Counts of Doccia and the poet Girolamo Giacobbi, moved the early music-drama from Florence by producing their "Aurora ingannata" this year.

The "Masque of Beauty" to which

1608(cont.)
Ferrabosco contributed some songs was produced this year.

"The Masque at Lord Haddington's Marriage" to which Ferrabosco contributed some songs was produced this year.

The favola "Idropica," by Gastoldi, Claudio and Giulio Monteverdi, Salomone Rossi, Monco and Paolo Biat, was performed this year at Mantua.

A report from this year remarked that when Monteverdi's opera "Arianna" was being performed at the court of Mantua, "many" shed tears on hearing the heroine lament for Theseus, who had deserted her.

At an opera festival in Mantua, two of Monteverdi's operas, and one ballet, were produced. The performances brought the composer considerable renown.

Gagliano composed a second version of Rinuccini's "Dafne." It was written for the court of Mantua and performed this year.

Thomas Fuller, English writer, was born (died 1661).

John Milton, renowned English political and religious author and poet, was born (died 1674).

Prince Francesco, heir to the Gonzaga succession, married the Infanta Margherita of Savoy.

Thomas Sackville, Elizabethan poet and writer, died (born 1536).

Giovanni Bologna, Italian sculptor, died (born 1529).

Jean de Boulogne, Flemish sculptor, died (born 1529). (He was also known as Giovanni Bologna).

Italian painting: Caravaggio, Portrait of Alof de Wignacourt" (oil on canvas 76 3/4" x 52 3/4").

Spanish painting: El Greco completed his painting "View of Toledo" (a storm scene, town in symbolic form and city of the imagination).

(to 1609) Antonelli was "maestro di cappella" of St. John Lateran in Rome at this time.

(to 1609) Cifra was musical director at the German College in Rome during thse years.

(to 1609) Vincenzo Liberti published two books of madrigals for five voices during these years.

(April to 1610, October) Thomas Cutting was in the service of King Christian IV in Copenhagen at a salary of 300 daler per annum for this period.

(to 1611) John Bolt was organist in Brussels during these years.

(to 1611) Nicholas Morgan held the position of organist at the convent of Benedictine nuns in Brussels during these years.

(to 1613) Gabriel Bataille's "Airs mis en tablature de luth" were published during this period.

(to 1614) Giovanni Battista Stefanini was maestro di cappella of Turin Cathedral during this period.

1608(cont.)

(to 1617) Except for a setting
for one to six voices of a text
by Ferdinando Saracinelli,
Allegri's "Primo libro delle
musiche" consists of eight sets
of dances for five or six un-
specified instruments and a
continuo, taken from "balli"
performed at court during these
years.

(to 1618) During these years
eight books of "Airs de
differents autheurs," a collection of melodies to which
the French court-lutenist,
Gabriel Bataille, had supplied
lute accompaniments, were published at Paris.

(to 1620) Pierre Guédron wrote
many ballets for the court of
King Louis XIII during this
period.

(to 1625) Giovanni Ghizzolo's
compositions were published
during these years.

(to 1625) Antonio Gualteri was
maestro di cappella at the
church and college of Monselice,
Lombardy for this period of
years.

(to 1630) Thomas Bateson was
organist of Christ Church during
these years.

(to 1643) Girolamo Frescobaldi
was organist at St. Peters during this entire period.

c.1608

Quagliati was organist at Santa
Maria Maggiore in Rome at this
time.

Fernando de las Infantas, a
Spanish priest, died (born
1534).

(January) A performance of
Gagliano's "Dafne" took place
at Mantua in this month and
probably this year.

Samuel Scheidt became organist
at the Moritzkirche in Halle at
this time.

Schütz enrolled at the University
of Marburg at this time.

1609

(January 17) East died prior to
this date, when his successor,
Thomas Snodham, took over his
"copyrights."

(January 25) The "deliberazioni"
of the Church of the
Annunciation at Naples on this
date mentioned Cerone.

(January 26) Gagliano was made
canon at San Lorenzo in Florence.

(January 31) Andrew Blackhall
(Blakhall, Blakehall), a
Scottish musician, died at
Inveresk, Musselburgh (born
1516).

(March 9) Michal Gomólka,
Polish conductor and instrumentalist, died at Jazlowiec
(born 1564).

(March 24 and April 5) Thomas
Bateson appeared as "Vicar
Choral of the Cathedral of the
Holy and undivided Trinity,
Dublin" on March 24th. On April
5th he was described as "Vicar
and organist of this church."

(March 25) Exeter Chapter*
"decreed a patente to be made to
Mr. Gibbons (Edward) Bachelor
of Musicke of xx^{li} per annum so
longe to continue as he shall
teach the choristers and
secondaries of this church in

1609(cont.)
instrumentall musicke."
(*Exeter Cathedral Chapter Act
Book, No. 3553 pos. 11-12).

(April 14) Gasparo da Salò, an
Italian violin maker, died at
Brescia (born 1542). He made
the first true violin.

(May 15) Giovanni Croce (Joanne
a Cruce Clodiensis), the
Italian composer, died at Venice
(born c.1557). Many of his
works were published posthumously.

(August 7) Eustache Du Caurroy,
French contrapuntist composer,
died at Paris (born 1549).

(August 8) A dispensation was
granted to Edward Gibbons and
he was admitted a Pries Vicar by
the College of Vicars Choral of
Exeter.

(August 22) Martinengo was
elected as successor to Croce
at St. Mark's, Venice as maestro
di cappella.

(August 22) Monteverdi's music
for "La favola d'Orfeo" was
published at Venice.

(August 24) Monteverdi wrote a
letter to Alessandro Striggio,
the poet.

(September 10) Monteverdi wrote
a letter to Allessandro Striggio
in which he discussed the merits
and deficiencies of Galeazzo
Sirena, a composer and organist.

(September 12) Agostinho da
Cruz was a regular canon at the
community of Santa Cruz at
Coimbra. He acquired his habit
on this date.

(October 1) Giovanni Matteo
Asola, Italian composer, died
at Venice (birthdate unknown).

(October 28) Cifra had left
Rome to become choirmaster of
the Santa Casa, Loreto.

(January) Cerone became a priest
and tenor singer at the church
of the Annunciation at Naples.

(January) Thomas East, English
musical typographer, publisher,
and composer, died at London
(birthdate unknown).

(February) Peri's balletto
"L'imperiale" and the ballo
"Cortesia" with text by
Salvadori appeared.

(July) Anerio was appointed
"maestro di cappella" at Verona
Cathedral.

Ippolito Baccusi, an Italian
composer, died at Verona
(birthdate unknown).

Jan Brebos, a Flemish organ
builder, died at Madrid
(birthdate unknown).

Paul Flemming, a hymn composer,
was born (died 1640).

Giovanni Giacomo Gastoldi,
Italian madrigalist, died (born
c.1545 or c.1560). Some sources
give his date of death as 1622.

João Soares Rebello, a
Portuguese composer, was born at
Carninha. He was a fellow-stu-
dent of Prince John (later King
John IV) and was choirmaster at
court when John was king. He
received his titles and honours
from the King (died 1661,
November 16).

Mrs. William Shelley, who from
1595 had been involved in property disputes with Byrd, died
(birthdate unknown).

Henry Ainsworth had amicable
relations with the company which
settled in Leyden this year.
The group formed the nucleus of
the band of Pilgrims who arrived
in Plymouth in 1620.

Anerio returned to Rome at the
end of this year.

Ralph Amner was succeeded as
lay-clerk at Ely by Michael
East.

Banchieri returned to his former
position of organist at the
church of Santa Maria in Regola
at Imola at this time.

At this time Pietro Antonio
Bianchi was canon of San
Salvator at Venice.

Domenico Brunetti was organist
at Bologna Cathedral at this
time.

Girolamo Casati was organist of
the Cathedral at Novara at this
time.

G.P. Cima was organist at Milan
Cathedral this year.

G. Diruta was organist of
Agobbio (Gubbio) Cathedral.
He either held the position
through 1612 or returned at the
latter date. Evidence is not
clear on the facts.

T. East described himself as
"The Assigne of William Barley"
at this time.

Robert Fludd (Flud) was made a

(cont.) Fellow of the College of
Physicians at this juncture.

Edward Gibbons was appointed
"priest-vicar" at Exeter
Cathedral this year.

Wincenty Lilius moved to Warsaw
with the court. He remained a
member of the Royal Chapel.

Monteverdi used the "violino
piccolo" in the orchestral
score for "Orfeo."

Prior to this date M. Peerson
married Amy, the widow of
William Wiles, and they lived at
Stoke Newington that year.

M. Pederson lived in Copenhagen
from this date forward except
for the period from 1611 to
1614.

A music teacher, Cristobal de
Quinoñes, was brought from
Spain for the purpose of in-
structing Indians who showed
response to the sound of strings,
woodwinds, and percussion. They
eventually became members of an
orchestra.

Mateo Romera succeeded Rogier,
his teacher, and was ordained a
priest.

Schütz went to Venice to study
with G. Gabrieli.

Thomas Snodham becan to work
this year as a music printer.

Ugolini, the composer, went to
Benevento as maestro di cappella
of the cathedral this year.

Viadana was appointed "maestro"
at Concordia this year.

Agazzari's fourth book of his

"Sacrae Cantiones" was published this year at Rome.

Caterina Alessandra published a book of motets, Op. 2, this year at Milan.

Anerio published a book of motets for one to eight voices this year.

Lodovico Balbi's "Completorium" for twelve voices was published this year.

Banchieri's "La Cartella," a book on ornamentation, was published this year at Venice.

Banchieri, an early admirer of Monteverdi, mentioned the latter favorably in this year's edition of his "Conclusioni del suono dell' organo," published at Bologna.

Banchieri's sacred vocal work "Gemelli armonici," twenty-one motets, appeared.

Banchieri's literary work, "Sul canto figurato, fermo o contrappunto," was completed this year.

Barbarino's first secular book was reprinted at this time.

William Barley published Robinson's "Ne Citharen Lessons" as well as "Pammelia" by Ravenscroft.

A book of motets for two voices by Bartei appeared.

Heinrich Baryphonus wrote "Isagoge musica," published this year at Magdeburg.

Pietro Antonio Bianchi's "Sacri (cont.) concentus" for eight voices appeared.

Bonini's "Madrigali e motetti" for solo voice and his motets for three voices were completed this year.

Borlasca's "Scherzi musicali ecclesiastici sopra la cantica a 3 voci" was composed at this time.

Brade's first published collection "Newe ausserlesene Paduanen . . ." for five parts was published this year at Hamburg.

Domenico Brunetti this year composed "Vari concentus," a collection of pieces for the church.

Charles Butler was the author of "The Feminine Monarchie, or a Treatise concerning the Bees" published this year at Oxford (Also 1619 and 1634).

Blas de Castro appeared in the "Jerusalén conquistada" this year.

This date marked one of the earliest printed collections of catches.

Du Caurroy's "Preces ecclesiasticae" was published this year at Paris.

"Curiosidad es del cantollano" was referred to as being by Cerone "Madrid, 1709." Almost assuredly this was an error and should have been 1609.

Cerone's treatise "Le regole piu necessarie per l'introducttione del canto fermo" was published this year at

1609(cont.)
Naples.

Vincenti published Cortellini's Masses this year.

Croce's "Motetti a quatro voci" was reprinted this year and in 1611.

Croce's "Motettia 8 voci, libro secondo" was reprinted this year.

Diruta's "seconda parte del Transilvano" appeared.

Donato's "Motetto a 5 voci" "Florilegium sac. cant." was published this year at Antwerp.

Dulichius' "Fasciculus novus continens Dicta insigniora ex evangeliis . . ." was published in a second edition this year (See 1598).

Dulichius' "Novum opus musicum duarum partium . . ." was reprinted at Leipzig this year (See also 1599).

Eccard's "Dreyssig geistliche Lieder . . ." was reprinted this year at Erfurt (See 1594 and 1626).

Ferrabosco this year published two volumes of music: a book of "Ayres," dedicated to Prince Henry and consisting of twenty-eight songs with lute and bass viol accompaniment, and a book of "Lessons for 1, 2, and 3 Viols," dedicated to the Earl of Southampton.

Ferrabosco's "Ayres" was published and included many of his songs for masques.

Ferrabosco's song "Like hermit poor" was published this year.

Ferrabosco wrote "The Masque of Queens" to one of Ben Jonson's masques.

Fontanelli's second book of madrigals was reprinted at this time.

The dance collections of Füllsack-Hildebrand were published in north-west Germany this year as well as in 1607.

Girolamo Giacobbi published a group of psalms at this time.

India and Peri's "Varie Musiche" was published this year.

Jones' "A Musicall Dreame or Fourth Booke" was issued at this time.

Luython's "Lib. I Missarum" was published this year.

Mathias Mercker composed a book of pavans, galliards, etc., in five parts this year.

The score of Monteverdi's La favola d'Orfeo was published at Venice.

Morley's First Booke of Balletts to 5 voyces was reprinted this year in a German translation at Nürnberg.

Several of Morley's canzonets and balletts were reprinted this year in editions by Staricius.

Two book of motets for five to six voices by Nucius, "Cantiones sacrae . . .," were published at Liegritz this year.

Adams this year published "Andreas Ornithoparcus His Micrologus or Introduction: containing the Art of Singing."

1609(cont.)

"Andreas Ornithoparcus his Micrologus . . . digested into foure books . . . by John Dowland" was published at this time at London.

Patta's "basso generale per l'organo" appeared.

In a letter bearing this date M. Peerson was said to have "composed many lessons for the virginals, which is his principle instrument." The only four which have survived are the four included in the "Fitzwilliam Virginal Book."

Peri was important in early chamber monody which stemmed from Caccini's "Nuove Musiche" on the strength of his "Le varie musiche" for one to three parts and continuo, his only published work other than Euridice.

Three motets by Philips were included in Books II and III of M. Herrerius' "Hortulus musicalis," published this year at Munich.

Philips' "1580" pavan was printed in the tablature in Robinson's "New Citharen Lessons" published at London this year.

E. Porta's "Giardino di spirituali concerti" for two to four voices appeared.

Adams this year published Ravenscroft's Deuteromelia pieces entitled K.H. (King Henry's) Mirth, or Freeman's Songs and, despite the late date, this material may be authentic and, in part, even date back as far as the reign (cont.) of King Henry VII. It was called the "Second part of Musicke's Melodie, or Melodious Musick of Pleasant Roundelaies. K.H. Mirth . . . and such delightful catches."

Ravencroft's "Pammelia: Musicke's Miscellanie or mixed varietie of Pleasant Roundelayes and delightful Catches of 3, 4, 5, 6, 7, 8, 9, 10 parts in one. . . ." was published this year.

Serafino Razzi issued an additional collection of laude this year.

Thomas Robinson this year published at London his "Newe Citharen Lessons, which is an excellent tutor for the cittern."

Rocco Rodio's "Regole di musica" appeared.

Rosseter's "Lessons for Consort: Made by sundry Excellent Authors" was issued this year.

Schein's "Venus-Kränzlein mit allerley lieblichen und schönen Blumen gezieret und gewunden . . . ." was published at this time at Leipzig.

A book of masses by Soriano was published this year.

Johann Staden this year published a collection of secular songs and instrumental dances, in songs for four and five voices, and appendix of instrumental dances.

Reprints of Viadana's "Ecclesiastic Concertos" appeared at this time.

Vulpius published "Ein schön

1609(cont.)

geistlich Gesangbuch" this year at Jena.

M. Vulpius published his second edition of wedding hymns to Latin texts this year.

Wilbye published his "second set of English madrigals" this year and revealed a subtle and re-strained style (See also 1597).

Zangius "Aulicus" appeared at Prague.

In a masque this year Jonson introduced the "antimasque," at which acrobats, buffouns, and "country dances" were in contrast with the preceding elegance, either by lack or by poking fun at it.

With Jonson's "Masque of Queens" this year antimasques which stressed burleque and comedy made their initial appearance.

The "Masque of Queens," to which Ferrabosco contributed some songs, was produced.

In Monteverdi's "Orfeo," the demisemiquavers in Act III probably represent a trill.

Queen Anne of Denmark obtained her own company of Revels this year and the warrant stated: "Whereas the Queene our dearest wife, hath for her pleasure and recreation appointed her seruavntes Robert Daborne, William Shakespeare, Nathaniel Field and Edward Kirkham to provide and bring upp a con-ventient nomber of children who shall be called the Children of her Maiesties Revelles . . . within the Blacke Fryers in our cittie of London and els where

(cont.) within our realme of England . . . and them to exercise in the qualitie of playing, according to our pleasure: provided allwayes that noe playes, etc., shall be by them presented, but such playes etc., as have received the aprobacion and allowance of our Maister of the Rovelles For the tyme being."

The Jesuit Father, Ignatius, became Pope Paul V this year.

Kepler's "Astronomia nova" was published this year and con-tained "Kepler's laws."

Sir John Suckling, the English poet, was born (died 1642).

Michael Drayton's "Legend of Thomas Cromwell" was printed this year.

Annibale Carracci, an Italian artist, died (born 1560).

F. Zuccari, an Italian architect, died (born c.1530).

Rubens, the Flemish painter, married Isabella Brandt, a lady from a good family.

Spanish architecture: Santa Fe, Governor's Palace (400' long).

Domenico Allegri was choirmaster at Santa Maria Maggiore during these years until his death.

(to 1610, February 8) Robert Allison, a gentleman of the Chapel Royal for twenty years, sold his place to Humphry Bache at this time.

(to 1611) The largest collection of popular vocal music of this time was preserved in

1609(cont.)

Ravenscroft's three printed catch books: Pammelia Deuteromelia and Melismata collected during these years.

(to 1612) Isabella Girardeau, an Italian soprano, sang second soprano parts at the Queen's Theatre in the Haymarket, London for this period of time.

(to 1612) E. Porta was the organist at the collegiate church of San Giovanni at Persiceto, near Bologna during this period.

(to 1612) G. Gabrieli at Venice received Schütz as one of his pupils during the last three years of his life.

(to 1621) The period of the reign of Grand Duke Cosimo II, when Peri along with Gagliano was the leading musician of Florence even including Caccini.

(to 1622) The Bologna Liceo Musicale had copies of editions of G. Diruta's "Seconda parte del Transilvano" bearing thse dates.

(to 1624) P. Nenna published eight books of madrigals in various editions during these years.

(to c.1639) Lipparino wrote eight and nine-part masses during this period.

c.1609

Henric Van Utrecht, Corneliszoon, Dutch organist and composer, died (birthdate unknown). He composed "Parnassus Musicus" for five instruments, published at Hamburg in 1625.

Anerio served at the court of King Sigismund III of Poland at this time.

Orlando Gibbons' "Fantazies of three parts for viols" appeared.

1610

(January 4) Robert Jones, the lutenist and composer, Philip Rosseter, Philip Kingham and Ralph Reene were granted a patent to assemble and train a school of children in London to be called the "Children of the Revels to the Queene within Whitefryars."

(February 8) A Robert Allison, probably a relative of Richard's, sold his place as a Gentleman of the Chapel Royal to Humphry Bache.

(March 9) Philips was appointed to a canonry at the collegiate church of Saint-Vincent at Soignies. The position was vacant because of the death of Claude Carlier.

(March 25) The dedication of Diruta's "Seconda parte del Transilvano" carried this date.

(April 26) Giacomo Alberici, an Italian ecclesiastic, died at Rome (birthdate unknown).

(May 24) Joachim Burck (Burgk) (actually Joachim Moller von Burck), a German organist and composer, died at Mühlhausen (born 1546). See also 1616.

(July 15) Pierre Maillard's treatise "Les Tons, ou discours sur les modes de musique et les tons d'église et de la distinction entre iceux" appeared.

(July 24) Dufon asked to be

125

allowed to return home because of infirmity.

(December 9) Baldassare Ferri, an Italian male soprano, was born in Perugia (died 1680, September 8).

(December 18) Charles Du Cange, a French musical scholar, was born at Amiens (died 1688, October 23).

(December 28) According to a letter from Monteverdi, Caccini also played the lute, guitar and harpsichord.

(September) Monteverdi's "Sanctissimi Viriginis Missa senis vocibus ad Ecclesiarum choros as Vesperae pluribus decantandae cum nonnullis concentibus" was published at Venice.

(October) L. de Hodemont received an extra payment for taking care of and possibly playing the carillon, at St. Lambert's Cathedral, at Liege.

Adam Berg, the German music printer, died at Munich (birthdate unknown).

Pierre Bourdelot, Abbot of Massay Abbey in the Char Department, France, was born (died 1685, February 9). He assembled material for an history of music.

Henri de Thier Du Mont, walloon organist and composer, was born at Villers - l'Évêque near Liège (died 1684, May 8).

Michel Lambert, composer and father-in-law of Lully, was born (died 1695 or 1696).

Jan Moretus, the successor to the Flemish printer, Plentin (his son-in-law), died (born 1543).

Paolo Virchi, Italian lutenist, composer and famous chitarrone player at the courts of Modena and Ferrara, died (birthdate unknown).

John Amner became organist and master of the choristers at Ely Cathedral succeeding George Barcroft. He held the position until his death.

Anerio served at the Cathedral of Verona this year.

A petition, presented by Raimundo Ballestra to the Austrian Archduke Ferdinand, requested funds to assist in the publication of a collection that included "some reservata." The request was granted. (The date may have been in 1611, January).

John Bartlet was awarded the Bachelor of Music degree by Oxford.

Borlasca was a musician at the Munich court chapel at this time.

Antonio Brunelli was "maestro" at Prato Cathedral this year.

The long dispute over Stondon Place was ended by the death of Mrs. Shelley this year. Shortly after this Byrd bought the property outright from John Shelley.

Cerone became a tenor in the Neapolitan royal chapel this year.

When Richard Dering applied for the degree of Bachelor of Music from Christ Church, Oxford this year he stated that he had been studying music for ten years.

Alessandro Grandi became maestro di cappella at San Spirito, Ferrara this year.

Mendes' pupil, Lobo, tried to get some of his teacher's works printed. He wrote to the manager of Planten's printing house at Antwerp, but was rejected.

Romano Micheli was a clerico at this time.

Monteverdi received a letter from Abbot Angelo Grillo, thanking him for setting one of his pieces to music.

The younger Pierre Phalèse' daughter Barbara married Jean de Vos this year.

Philips became canon at Soignies at this time.

Crescenzo Salzilli was lutenist at the church of the Annunziata in Naples. His salary was 5 ducats per month.

René Savoye of Paris had an instrument from this year which, if considered to be a piano-forte, would antedate Cristofori's invention by a hundred years.

Johann Stadlmayer, German composer, was at this time "Kapellmeister" to Archduke Maximilian of Austria, probably at Innsbruck.

Rev. John Taverner became a professor of music at Gresham College during this year.

Gasparao Villani was organist at Piacenza Cathedral at this time.

The "Ballet d'Alcina" was composed this year.

Alstedt's "Scientiarum omnium Encyclopaedia" appeared.

Giovanni Bacilieri composed "Vesperae" for eight voices, Op. 2, published this year by Gardano.

Banchieri's literary work, "La cartella utile agli figliuoli et principarti che desideranno con facilità imparare sicuramente il canto figurato," was written by this time.

Banchieri's sacred vocal work "Vezzo de perle musicali" was composed this year.

Barbarino's motets were published this year and in 1612.

Barbarino's third secular book was published this year and a copy has survived in the British Museum.

Daniell Batchelar's "Almaine" (probably for guitar) appeared.

"The Maids Tragedy" by Beaumont and Fletcher, a play with incidental music, was produced this year.

Bellanda wrote twenty-three songs, Vol. II this year.

Brunelli's treatise "Regole e dichiarazioni di alcuni contrappunti doppii utili alli studiosi" was completed at this time.

Two songs by Caccini were included in Dowland's "A Musicall

Banquet" published this year at London.

This date was given by one source for the publication of Campian's first and second books of airs.

Giovanni Francesco Capello, a Veronese, published his "Lamentations" this year.

Du Caurroy's "Fantaisies" was published this year at Paris.

Du Caurroy's "Meslanges de musique" was published this year by Pierre Ballard, Robert's son and successor at Paris.

A collection of ayres by Champion appeared this year.

Corkine published his "Ayres to Sing and Play to the Lute and Basse Violl. . . ." this year.

Croce's "Nove lamentationi" appeared this year.

Croce's "Sacrae cantilene concertate" was published this year and reprinted in 1612 and 1613.

Three of John Dowland's songs were included in a collection edited by his son Robert this year.

Some of John Dowland's works were included in T. Simpson's "Opusculum" of this year.

Adams this year published "A Musicall Banquet" edited by Robert Dowland, John's son.

Compositions by Diomedes were included in R. Dowland's "Varieties of Lute-lessons"

(cont.) published this year.

Adams published Robert Dowland's "Varietie of Lute Lessons," a collection of lute pieces prefaced by "Necessarie Observations Belonging to the Lute, and Lute-playing," a translation from Besard's "Isagoge in artem testudinariam," followed by "Other Necessary Observations belonging to the Lute, by Iohn Douland, Batcheler of Musicke."

Dulichius "Prima pars Centuriae octonum et septenum vocum harmonias sacras laudibus sanctissime triados consecrates continentis accurata diligentia adornata . . ." Part III was published.

East's "The madrigals in his third and fourth books" was issued this year and in 1618.

M. East published his third set of books, "Pastorals, Neapolitans, Anthems, Madrigals, and Fantasies" this year.

Eccard's "Honorabile est inter omnes" appeared at this time.

Franck wrote his "Flores musicales" for four to eight voices this year.

Franck wrote his "Musikalische Fröhlichkeit" for four to eight voices at this time.

Gese published his "Cantiones sacrae Chorales" for four to six voices this year.

Alessandro Grandi's first book of motets (for two to eight voices) was published this year. It was the first of six books.

Karel Guillet's "Vingt-quatre
Fantasies à quatre parties
disposées suivant l'ordre des
douze modes" was published this
year by Ballard.

Johann Heyden's "Commentateo de
musicale instrumento . . ." in
which he described a bowed keyboard instrument, the archicembalo, which he had invented,
was reprinted this year.

Jones' "The Muses Gardin for
Delights, or the Fifth Booke"
was issued at this time.

J.H. Kapsberger published the
first of his four Villanelle
for voices, with chitarrone accompaniment at this time.

Macque's madrigal books for four
voices appeared at this date
(see also 1586).

Two motets by Martinengo were
included in Croce's "Nove
lamentioni" published this year.

Matthias Mason's invention of
three frets for the lute was
mentioned in Dowland's
"Varietie of Lute Lessons" published this year.

"Mélanges de la musique," a
collection of pieces and carols,
was published at Paris at this
time.

Thomas Mencken wrote texts for
St. Matthew and St. John in
German at this time.

R. Micheli's "Psalmi ad officium
vesperarum musicis notis
expressi et ternis vocibus
decantandi. Una cum parte
organica" Vol. I was published
at Rome this year by J.B.

(cont.) Roblectum.

Johann Möller composed a six
-part "Vater unser" this year.

Monteverdi's first publication
of church music was this year.
The first volume included both
prima and seconda prattica music. The book was released at
Mantua.

Monteverdi's Mass for six parts
printed this year was based on
Gombert's "In illo tempore
loquente Jesu."

Monteverdi's "Vespers" was published this year.

A variation of the air "Monicha"
was written by Pario for voice
at this time.

Praetorius' "Musae Sioniae" appeared.

Thomas Simpson's "Oposculum
newer Pavanen" for five parts
was published this year at
Frankfort.

Soriano's 110 canons on "Ave
maris stella" was published this
year.

Staden this year published a
collection of secular songs and
instrumental dances, songs for
four and five voices and an
appendix of instrumental
dances.

Stadlmayr published his "Missae
8 voices, cum duplici basso ad
organum" this year.

Gregorio Turini's "Teutsche
Liedar" was published this
year.

Villani's "litanies" was published this year.

Villani published his "Missa, Psalmi and Vesperas et Motecta" at this time.

Vulpius published his first edition of "Musicae Compendium" at this time.

Vulpius published his "Opusculum novum" this year.

C.T. Walliser published his "Hexastichon" at this time.

During the reign of King Henri IV of Navarre ending at this time more than eighty court ballets were produced.

The dramatically inclined "ballet comique" re-established itself with the production of Ballet D'Alcine.

Compeggi and Giacobbi produced "Andromeda" at the Teatro della Sala this year.

Arnold Dolmetsch has described a pianoforte from this date, of Dutch origin, in the collection of René Savoye of Paris. He said it had a simple form of Viennese action with no dampers.

In Dowland's "Musical Banquet" the difference in style between ayre and monody was obvious since English ayres were included with Spanish and Italian monodies.

The Masque "Love freed from Ignorance and Folly" to which Ferrabosco had contributed some songs was produced this year.

Gagliano's opera "Dafne" was performed at the Carnival in

(cont.) Florence this year.

Girolamo Giacobbi's opera "Andromeda" with libretto by Count Ridolfo Campeggi was produced this year at Bologna.

The musical baroque began in France after the death of King Henri this year.

True monody forced its way into sacred music only after this date.

Sung "recitative," which contained an element of heightened dramatic tension, was introduced at France from this date forward.

Michelangelo Merisi, known as Caravaggio, an Italian painter, died (born 1573).

Pierre Mignard, a French painter, was born (died 1695).

Adriaen van Ostade, a Dutch painter, was born (died 1684).

David Teniers, the younger, a Flemish painter and the founder of the Antwerp Academy, was born (died 1690).

(October to 1612, November) In Prince Henry's account during this period was an entry of £ · 35 paid to John Bull "for sundry sortes of musicke bookes."

(to 1613) Belli served as tutor in church music to the young clerics at the church of San Lorenzo. He succeeded Gagliano in this position.

(to 1613) William Brade left Hamburg to serve Count Ernst of Bückeburg during this period.

(to 1613) Giovanni Ghizzolo, an Italian composer, probably lived in Milan during these years.

(to 1613) A "Time of Troubles" reigned in Russia during these years.

(to 1615) Edward Allde worked in London and printed a few musical works during these years.

(to 1615) Raffaello Rontani was employed as a musician in the service of Don Antonio Medici at Florence at this time. The latter was a natural son of Grand Duke Francis I and Bianca Capello.

(to 1616) Adriana Basile, one of the most famous singers of her time, was in the service of the Gonzagas at Mantua during these years.

(to 1620) Simon Besler was a cantor at Stiegau for this period.

(to 1621) During this period a new form, incorporating dance, song, spectacle, pantomime and gesture, was created and flourished under the leadership of Constable de Luynes, whose death ended the life of this form. It was referred to as "ballet mélodramatique."

(to 1624) Francesco Roanone -Taegio, born in Milan, composed fauxbourdons, madrigals, masses, motets, "correntie gagliarde, aggiunta dello scolare di violino, selva di warii passaggi," etc. during these years.

(to 1625) Thomas Tomkins, Sr. was Precentor at St. Mary's

(cont.) during this period.

(to 1643) The reign of King Louis XIII (House of Bourbon) over France.

c.1610

Sebastien Le Camus, a French composer, was born (died 1677).

Fabritio Caroso, a dancing master of Sermoneta, died (born 1535).

Wolfgang Ebner, a German organist and composer, was born at Augsburg (died 1665, February 12).

Marcin Groblicz, a Polish violin maker, died (born c.1555).

Cesario Gussago, an Italian organist and composer, was born in Ostia, a province of Rome (deathdate unknown).

Michel Lambert, a French lutenist and singer, was born in Vivionne, Poitou (died 1696, June 29).

Alfonso Lobo, a Spanish composer, died (born c.1555).

Edward Lowe, an English organist and composer, was born (died 1682, July 11).

Juan Navarro, a Mexican composer, died (born c.1550).

Juan de Padilla, a Spanish -Mexican composer, was born at Zamora (died 1673, December).

Marco Uccellini, an Italian composer, was born at Modena (date of death unknown).

Steffano Bernardi's work provided a general idea of the

c.1610(cont.)
musical taste of this period.

William Brade, and Thomas
Simpson, were two of the most
important figures among
Englishmen working in Germany
at this time.

Carlo Farina, an Italian violinist, was active at this time.

The works of Ivan Lukačić and
Tomaso Cecchini, who lived near
each other, (one at Split and
one at Hvar) represented the
peak of musical activity in
Dalmatia during this period.

The early 17th-Century scientist
and theorist, Marin Mersenne,
noted that the composer Jacques
Mauduit saved certain works of
Baïf and Le Jeune during the
fighting at Paris at this time.

Like John Bull, who was also a
refugee at Antwerp, Philips apparently was personally acquainted with Sweelinck at this
time.

John Price I was one of the
many instrumentalists who settled in Germany at this time.

Byrd's Masses for three and
four voices were printed at
this time.

Coperario's "Rules How to
Compose" appeared at this time.

Gibbons' "Cutin copper" was
published as a novelty about
this time.

A set of nine fantasias for
three parts comprised Gibbons'
first published work. It was
the earliest music to be engraved on copper in England,

(cont.) antedating Parthenia by
about a year.

Manuscripts in a collection of
five-part fantasies for viols,
and included two pavans by John
"Ockeover" ("Oker"). Single
parts of anthems by "Oker" composed at this time were preserved.

Scheidt's "Tabulatura Nova" of
this time ended the old Nordic
style and associated music with
the new baroque of Italy and
Germany.

"The Winter's Tale" was published in Ireland at this time.
It was a treatise of sorts concerned at least partially with
Irish dances.

The popularity of the aria grew
from this time on.

One important type of ostinato
bass that appeared early in the
century was a "chaconne" or
"passacaglio" bass.

The Chitarrone was the favourite
instrument used for accompaniment to the voice in the new
monodic style of this period.

"Concertato" style developed and
became widespread during this
period.

English musicians were greatly
in demand at this time.

All that existed in France at
this time, other than dances, of
instrumental ensemble music was
fantaisies, preserved in a small
number of early part-books.

It was not until this time that
any quantity of German music
for viols was composed.

c.1610(cont.)
Instrumental music became very
popular in England at this time.

Collections of monodies published at this time achieved
unity by keeping the same bass
for every stanza while the melody of the solo part for each
repetition of the base pattern
was varied.

Monody infiltrated all music,
both secular and sacred, during
this period.

During this period Monteverdi's
"stile concitato" contributed
to the constantly growing language of music.

The title "musico da camera"
described a position held by a
musician in a noble household
at this time.

English organ books of this period showed the preference for
"ad libitum" organ accompaniment
over polyphonic choral music in
English churches.

Popular bass forms of the period
were the "romanesca," the
"ruggiero" and the "passamezzo
moderno."

This period was remarkable for
the production of German suites
of dances for instrumental
groups.

Vocal chamber music at this
time appeared in many forms and
styles. It combined elements
of the concerto, madrigals,
monody, dance songs, national
idioms, and dramatic recitative,
as well as the bel canto aria.

Vocal music was still the
primary interest among com-

(cont.) posers in this period.

The final form of bar-line was
not yet established at this
time.

"Musica ficta" should not be
ignored in comparing the suita-
bility of diatonic and chromatic
embellishments in music of this
time.

In Italy at this time " γ "
stood for "Groppo," often in
the form of trill.

Starting at this time sharp key
-signatures were found in
practical as distinct from theoretical use, first occuring in
instrumental music, and years
later in vocal music.

The organ of the time was fitted
with a "skakinge stoppe"
(tremulant) by Dallam. It was
used at King's College Chapel,
Cambridge.

French architecture: Place des
Vosges, Paris.

Spanish painting: El Greco,
"Laocöon."

(to 1611) Jacques Cordier was a
dancer and choreographer in
England and involved in the
production of court masques
during these years.

1611
(January 1) The Masque being
aristocratic, was generally
intended to honor a particular
occasion. The "Oberon" produced
on New Year's Day was a gift to
Prince Henry.

(January 6) It was determined
that Andrea Falconieri would be
paid six scudi a month to play

133

1611(cont.)

the lute for the Duke of Parma during the latter's meals. He was to receive retroactive wages back to December of the past year.

(January 30) Matthew White was admitted as a perpetual Vicar-choral of Wells Cathedral on this date.

(March 12 and 13) Peter Philips' name appeared as organist at the royal chapel at Brussels where he served at the funeral of the Archduchess Marie of Austria.

(March 14) Anerio became "maestro di cappella" at the Seminario Romano on this date.

(June 22) On this day Monteverdi wrote to Cardinal Ferdinando Gonzaga to express his gratitude for receiving the Cardinal's two madrigals. He also took the opportunity to request a pension for his son.

(July 17) Marin Mersenne entered upon his novitiate as a Minorite.

(August 27) Tomás Luis de Victoria, Spanish composer, died at Madrid (born 1540). At the time of his death he was chaplain to the Infanta Margaret and organist at the convent.

(December 12 and 13) Philips' name appeared on this date as organist at the royal chapel at Brussels, in receipt of "10 aunes de drap, au prix de six livres l'aune" for services rendered at the funeral of the Archduchess Marie of Austria.

(June) Thomas Cutting was back in England, almost surely in the service of Prince Henry.

(July) Simon Lohet, a Belgian organist and composer, died at Stuttgart (birthdate unknown).

(Autumn) Johann Eccard, a Protestant church composer, died at Berlin (born 1523 or 1533).

(December) Pierre Cornet was mentioned in the list of expenses incurred by the funeral of the Queen of Spain.

Andrea Amati of Cremona, violin builder whose style was developed from da Salo, died (born 1535).

Leonora (Eleonora) Baroni, a singer, instrumentalist and composer, was born at Mantua (date of death unknown).

Thomas Brewer, an English composer, was born at London (date of death unknown).

Gioseffo Guami, an Italian organist and composer, died at Lucca (born c.1540).

Johannes Olearius, a hymn composer, was born (died 1684).

Edward Smyth, an English organist and composer, died at Durham (birthdate unknown).

Chu Tsai-yii, a Chinese author of a compendium of music, died (born 1536).

An entry in the register at Cremonda bearing this date recorded the burial of Andrea Amati's second wife.

Felice Anerio was at this time a composer to the papal chapel.

Anerio served as prefect at the Roman Seminary of Jesuits at

this time.

Banchieri mentioned the "Arpsicordo Leutato" along with his own invention, the arptarrone.

Belli returned to Imola at this time.

Pietro Benedetti was admitted with the name of "l'Invaghito" to the Florentine "Accademia degli Elevati," founded by Gagliano.

A volume of canons bearing Elway Bevin's autograph and this date has been preserved.

John Bolt went to Louvain where he remained as organist at St. Monica's convent until his death.

Valerio Bona was a musician at San Francesco, Brescia at this time.

Bonometti was a singer at Milan Cathedral at this date.

Steffano Bernardi was at this time appointed director of cathedral music at Verona.

Bull was in the service of Prince Henry at this time and his name was listed first on the roll of the prince's musicians. He received a salary of 40 per annum.

Calvisius was offered the chair of mathematics at Wittenberg this year.

Pierre Cornet became a canon at the collegiate church of Saint -Vincent at Soignies this year.

Cotgrave this year defined "Kit" (a tiny violin, either boat -shaped or in a narrowed, normal shape) as "a small gitterne."

Gabriel Diaz composed the Requiem for Dona Margarita of Austria this year and then re- signed his position.

Thomas Ford was a musician to Prince Henry at this time, with a salary of £ 30 per annum.

Franzoni was maestro di cappella at Forli Cathedral at this time.

Gabussi finished his term of service as maestro di cappella at the Cathedral of Milan at this time. He had assumed the posi- tion in 1582.

"A prelute upon ye Organ as was then usuall before ye Anthem by Mr. Edward Gibbons, Costos of ye College of Preist-vicars of Exeter 1611" has been preserved.

Gibbons presented a petition to Lord Salisbury, Lord High Treasurer, on this date. It concerned a lease of certain duchy lands without fine.

Gibbons received a large grant from the king and queen as a mark of royal favor.

At this time sixty years of age, Francisco Guerrero set forth on a pilgrimage to Palestine. An account of the journey was later published at Alcala bearing the title "El viage de Jerusalem que hizo Francisco Guerrero."

A fine bass viol, formerly in the possession of Canon Galpin and labelled "Henrie Jaye in Southwarke. 1611," confirmed a later opionion by Mace (1676)

that Jaye had been an outstanding
instrument maker of the time.

Robert Johnson II's name appeared on the Audit Office
Declared Accounts this year as
one of Prince Henry's musicians.

Two duets from Negri's book were
dedicated to Giacomo and Andrea
Morosini, members of one of the
most renowned Venetian families.

Negri's sonatas were actually
only ritornellas or toccatas.

Hans Nielsen was lutenist at
the royal chapel in Copenhagen
until this year when he was
dismissed. He then went to
Heidelberg to study at the
University.

V. Otto was a musician at the
court of Prince Lictenberg this
year.

Parma was maestro di cappella
in Pavia at Novara Cathedral at
this time.

Pederson and three colleagues
went to England this year to
study music.

A letter of Peri's written this
year has been preserved.

Entry of payment in the town
accounts indicated that Philips
and his colleagues took part in
the Easter services this year.

This year Philips was summoned
to Mechlin, with several of his
colleagues of the archducal
chapel, to report on a new organ
erected in the church of Saint
-Rombaud.

John Shelley was created a

(cont.) baronet at this time.

At this time, Spencer, one of
the best-known jigg comedians,
had nineteen actors and sixteen
musicians in his troupe. The
large number was not, however,
typical.

Biagio Tomasi was organist at
Comacchio this year.

Jiří Třanovský, Bohemian-Slovak
humanist, theologian and hymnologist, probably went to Bohemia
this year.

Fulgentio Valesi referred to
himself this year as "Monache
San Ambrosiana."

A document bearing this date
indicated that in 1578 Victoria
had received the appointment of
chaplain to the widowed Empress
Maria, daughter of King Charles
V.

Caspar Vincentius explicitly referred to transposition down a
fourth or a fifth, of selections
in which the lowest part is
notated in tenor clef, as possible to "anyone at his pleasure."

Humphrey Withey was a chorister
at this time.

John Adson's "Courtly Masquing
Ayres composed to 5 and 6 parts
for Violins, Consorts and
Cornets" was published this
year.

Alstedt's "Elementale
Mathematicum" was published at
Frankfort this year.

Anerio this year published a
book of motets which included
some litanies and antiphons.

Anerio published his "Ricreatione armonica" for one and two parts this year.

Robert Ballard, a lute-player to Marie de' Medici, wrote a lute tablature which was published this year.

Banchieri invented an instrument which he called the "arpichitarrone." It was described in the second edition of "L'organo suonarino" published this year.

Barbarino's second secular book was reprinted at this time.

William Bathe's "Janua linguarum" was published this year at Salamanca.

Bellanda and Benedetti published a book of monodies at this time.

Gioseffo Belloni wrote masses for five voices, Op. 1. The first edition appeared in 1603 and the second at this date.

Pietro Benedetti issued at least four books of "Musiche," the first this year.

A common ground for motets existed in the "stile antico." This was disseminated in German by two important collections, the "Promptuarium" by Schadeus published this year, and the "Florilegium Portense" by Bodenschatz published in 1603.

Borlasca's "Canzonette a 3 voci" appeared at this time.

Byrd's carol "This day Christ was born," a definite example of key structure, was composed at this time.

With the exception of two "Fantazias" included in the set of Byrd's vocal works published this year, compositions for strings were in manuscript in single parts.

Byrd published his third and last volume of madrigals this year.

Byrd's "Psalms, Songs and Sonnets" was published this year by Thomas Snodham at London.

A second printing of Byrd's "Psalms, Songs, and Sonnets" occurred this year.

Calvisius' "Exercitatio musicae tertia" was published this year.

Two compositions "Floriani Canali" for six parts were included in the collection "Promptuarii musici, sacras harmonias sive motetas v. vi. vii. et viii. vocum" published by Schadaeus this year.

Cavaccio's Requiem was published this year at Milan.

Croce's "Motetti a quattro voci" was reprinted (See also 1599 and 1605).

Croce's "Musica Sacra" with English text was reprinted by East at London this year (See 1608).

Dulichius' "Dictum Psalmi; 30. Stettini." appeared at this time and was probably published.

Draud's "Bibliotheca classica" was published at this time and reprinted in 1625.

The chorale motets of 1597 and the "Preussische Festlieder" by

Eccard were posthumously published.

Ferrabosco wrote "Love freed
from Ignorance" to one of Ben
Jonson's masques produced this
year.

Giovanni Pietro Flaccomio's "Il
Libro de' madrigali a 3 voci
col basso continuo" and a "Liber
primus in duos distincti choros"
were both published by Gardano
at Venice this year.

Florio published his "New World
of Words" this year.

Amante Franzoni wrote his
"Concerti ecclesiastici" at this
time.

Franck wrote his second
"Geistliche Gesänge und melodien"
for five to eight voices at this
time.

Franck wrote his "Sechs deutsche
Konzerte" for eight voices at
this time.

Franck wrote his "Tricinia nova"
this year.

Gese published his "Missae ad
imitationem Orlandi et aliorum"
for five voices this year.

Carlo Gesualdo's madrigals for
five voices, "Moro Lasso al mio
duolo" and "Resta di darmi
voia" appeared this year.

Gesualdo's third book of five
-voice madrigals was reprinted
this year for the second time.

Gesualdo's fourth book of five
-voice madrigals was reprinted
this year for the second time.

Gesualdo's fifth and sixth
books of five-part madrigals
were published at this time.

Johann Groh's "Sechsvnddreissig
neue liebliche und zierliche
Intraden" was re-published this
year.

Andro Hart at Edinboro printed
an edition of the Psalms at this
time.

Jones' fifth and last volume
"The Muses Gardin for Delights,
Or the fift Booke of Ayres onely
for the Lute, the Base-vyoll &
the Voyce" was published this
year.

Leone Leoni's motets were included in the "Promptuarium" by
Schadaeus" published this year.

John Maynard's "The XII Wonders
of the World" was published this
year by Snodham at London.

Johann Möller wrote German motets for five to eight voices
at this time.

Giulio Monteverdi's opera "Il
rapimento de Proserpina" with
libretto by Ercole Marigliani
was performed at Casale
Monferrato this year and presumably since lost.

The second edition of Morley's
"The First Booke of Consort
Lessons, made by divers exquisite
Authors for 6 Instruments" was
issued this year.

Negri's "Affetti amorosi" for
one, two and five voices with
numerous sinfonie and sonate for
two violins and continuo was
published this year.

Otto's collection from this

year was comprised of music "in the English style."

Ten motets for six to eight voices by Pacelli were included in the "Promptuarium" by Schadaeus published this year.

The "Parthenia" or the "Maydenhead" was titled "the first musicke that ever was printed for the Virginalls." It included thirty-one compositions by Byrd, Bull, and Gibbons. Its sequel was called "Parthenia Dinviolata."

Patta's "basso generale per l'organo" was reprinted this year.

A song by Peri was included in Benedetti's book published this year. The song was from "Ninfe di Senna."

The first variation suites appeared in the "Neue Paduan" by the Styrian organist Paul Peurl published this year. The same melodic material was presented with four different rhythmic aspects.

Peter Philipp's "Melodia Olympica di diversi Excellentissimi Musici a IV, V, VI et VIII voci" was published in 1591 and this year.

Two of Philips' eight part "Cantiones sacrae" were included in Schadaeus' "Promptuarium musicum" published at Strasbourg this year.

A portrait of Josquin was reproduced as a woodcut in Opmeer's "Opus Chronographicum" which appeared this year.

Quagliati's "Carro di fedelta d'amore" for five voices, melody instruments and continuo was completed this year.

Ravencroft's "Melismata: Musicall Phansies fitting the court, citie, and countrey Humours" was published this year by Adams.

A second book of madrigals by Crescenzo Salzilli was published this year.

Lambert de Sayve composed a motet for the wedding of Matthew of Austria and Anna of Styria this year.

A set of twenty-four four-part "Teutsche Liedlein" in the canzonette style, written by de Sayve, was reprinted by Michael Praetorius this year.

Abraham Schadäus' "Promptuarii musici" was published at Strasbourg at this time.

Heinrich Schütz's "Il primo libro de madrigali de Henrico Sagitario Alemanno" was published in Venice this year. It was dedicated to his patron Landgrave Moritz. The last selection was a flattering poem set for eight voices. The work was an apprentice piece.

Cornelis Schuyt's "Madrigali nuptiali a 6 voci" was published this year.

Thomas Simpson's "Pavanen, Volten und Galliarden . . ." was published at Frankfort this year.

The second edition of Turberville's "The Noble Arte of Venerie or Hunting" was issued this year.

Fulgentio Valesi published "canons of Various Kinds in 2 canti fermi in the 1st mode for 3-6 voc." this year at Milan.

Vernizzi's "Angelici concentus" Op. 3 was published (See also 1606 and 1631).

Gasparo Villani's "Ad Deum opt. max. ad Deiparamque Virginem . . ." was published this year.

C.T. Walliser published his "Musicae figuralis praecepta brevia" for two to six voices this year.

Mikolaj Zieleński composed his "Adoramus te Christie" at this time.

Banchieri in the second edition of "L'organo suonarino" pre-scribed six different tempo markings: adagio, allegro, veloce, presto, piu presto, prestissimo.

Robert Johnson II set the younger Ferrabosco's songs to the lute for Ben Jonson's masque "Love freed from Ignorance & Folly" produced this year.

Jonson's masque "Love Freed from Ignorance & Folly" was performed at this time and well received.

Jonson's masque "Oberon" was performed this year.

Peri's "Mascherata di Ninfe di Senna" was performed with Francesca Caccini and Lorenzo Allegri.

The new King James version of the Bible was published. It combined both imagination and plain, clear diction.

Shakespeare began to cater to popular taste for the sensational and melodramatic in "A Winter's Tale" completed this year.

Herman Hals, a Dutch painter, was born (died 1669).

Willem van de Velde I, a Dutch painter, was born (died 1693).

English architecture: Hatfield House (125' wide; long gallery - 160' long).

Italian architecture: Maderna completes "Acqua Paola" (95' 9" wide).

Japanese architecture: Nagoya, Castle.

(to 1614) M. Pederson was in Endland during these years.

(to 1614) Rubens painted "Descent from the Cross" during this period (13'10" x 10'1").

(to 1615) Richard Betson, a foundationer of the King's School during these years, may have been an older son of Thomas Bateson.

(to 1616) John Farrant was or-ganist at the Salisbury Cathedral during these years.

(to 1617) Adam Michna, except for a short interruption, studied at the Jesuit College of Jindřichův Hradec during these years.

(to 1620) Thomas Adams was established at the Bell, St.

1611(cont.)
Paul's Churchyard for this period.

(September 1 to 1622, April 7) Pietro Pace was organist at the Santa Casa, Loreto during these years. At the same time Antonio Cifra was the maestro di cappella.

(to 1623) G.N. Mezzagorri published a large number of sacri concerti, masses, madrigals, motets, etc. during these years.

(to 1631) Vincenzo Pellegrini was maestro di capella at Milan Cathedral during these years.

c.1611
(Dom) Pierre - Benoit de Jumilhac, a French theorist, was born at Château Saint-Jean Lig

Tomasz Szadek, a Polish composer and ecclesiastic, died (born 1550).

Nicholas Zieleński was organist at Gniezno at this time. He published a volume of "Offertoria" for one to eight voices with organ score at Venice.

1612
(April 26) In a letter to Sir M. Hicks, Bull requested that his son's name be inserted instead of his own in a patent bearing this date.

(June 8) Hans Leo Hassler (Hasler), organist and composer and brother of Kaspar Hassler, died at Frankfort (born 1564, October 25 or 26).

(July 31) Claudio and Giulio

(cont.) Monteverdi were ignominiously discharged by Francesco Gonzaga, who had succeeded his father, Vincenzo.

(August 3) S. Orlandi succeeded Monteverdi as maestro at the ducal court of Mantua this year.

(August 21) Giovanni Gabrieli, Andrea's nephew and a major Italian organist and composer, died at Venice (born 1557).

(September 24) Johann Lippius, an Alsatian theorist, died en route to Speyer (born at Strasbourg 1585, June 25).

(September 30) Ercole Bottrigari, an Italian aristocrat and author on music, died at Bologna (born 1531, August 24).

(October 28) Dowland was appointed one of the King's Musicians as a lute-player.

(December 12) A "Florian Canale, Bresciano" wrote a medical treatise titled "Sei secreti universali" published this year at Venice. The dedication was signed "Da Brescia, Florian Canale" and bore this date.

(December 27) Frederic, Elector Palatine, and Princess Elizabeth, daughter of James I, became engaged. "Parthenia" was dedicated to the couple.

(February) Duke Vincenzo I, of Mantua, died (birthdate unknown).

(October) R. Carlton was presented by Thomas Thursby to assume the incumbency of Bawsey cum Glosthorp in Norfolk.

(December) Duke Francesco II,

1612(cont.)
successor to Vincenzo I at
Mantua, died of smallpox (birthdate unknown).

Giovanni Battista Ala, an
Italian organist and composer,
died (born 1580).

Count Giovanni Bardi, a noble
patron of music and head of the
Florentine Camerata, died (born
1534).

Isaac de Benserade, a ballet
composer, was born (died 1691).

Girolamo Diruto, an Italian instrumental composer, died (born
1557).

Andreas Hammerschmidt, Austro
-Bohemian organist and composer,
was born at Brüx, Bohemia (died
1675, November 8).

Juan Gine Pérez, a Spanish composer, died at Orihuela (born
1548).

Thomas Bateson's son John, aged
twenty, was rector of Kiljarran
in the diocese of Ferns at this
time.

The first graduate in music at
Trinity College was probably
Thomas Bateson this year. He
was awarded the Bachelor of
Music degree.

William Bathe was at Salamanca.
He was there "professed" this
year.

Borlasca was vice-"Kapellmeister"
in the Munich court chapel at
this time.

Francesca Caccini married the
composer Giovanni Battista
Signorini some time prior to

(cont.) this date.

T. Cima was a choirboy at the
Lateran Chapel in Rome until
this time.

Thomas Cutting joined the King's
orchestra at London this year.

At the time of Prince Henry's
death this year Thomas Cutting
was one of the musicians listed
as receiving mourning livery.

At this date a Mr. Deering was
in Italy in the service of Sir
John Harrington. This may well
have been the composer Richard
Dering.

Donati was probably organist of
Pesaro Cathedral prior to this
date.

Donati was organist at Urbino
Cathedral at this time.

John Dowland served as lutenist
to Lord Walden and later became
one of the six lutenists at the
court of King Charles I.

In the preface to his last work,
"A Pilgrimes Solace," published
this year, John Dowland was
described as lutenist to Lord
Walden.

Alfonso Ferrabosco II became
music master to the future King
Charles I at the time of Prince
Henry's death.

Daniel Friderici at this time
moved from Eisleben to Rostock
in Mecklenburg.

Gibbons, whose single secular
collection of this year was
misnamed Madrigals and Motetts,
developed a "rich and unique
personal idiom within the gen-

eral scope of the accompanied
solo song."

King James at this time displayed
a new outlook toward the Chapel
Royal in Scotland.

Adam Jarzebeki was appointed
violinist at the court of the
Elector Johann Sigismund in
Berlin this year.

This year Hassler accompanied
the Elector of Saxony, Johann
Georg I, to Frankfort where the
imperial election was to be
held. While there he died.

Pietro Maria Marsolo was maestro
di cappella at Ferrara at this
time. He published five madrigals and three books of motets.

Giovanni Nicolo Mezzogorri was
vicar and maestro di cappella
at Comacchio Cathedral at this
time.

When Duke Vincenzo died this
year, Monteverdi's release from
the position of maestro della
musica was granted and he visited
Milan and Cremona. He then
took the opportunity to look for
a better position. He became
choirmaster and conductor at St.
Mark's in Venice.

Giulio Monteverdi was organist
at Castelleone after this date.

Negri was appointed vice maestro
di cappella at St. Mark's,
Venice this year.

Anne Phalèse, daughter of
Corneille of the Flemish music
publishing house, died at
Antwerp (birthdate unknown).

Robert Phalèse, a lawyer and

(cont.) son of Corneille (of the
Flemish music publishing family),
was at Antwerp.

Gerard Philipp, who may have a
connection with P. Philips, at
this time succeeded Salomon de
Caus as engineer to the Archduke
Albert and the Archduchess
Isabella at Brussels.

Francis Pilkington became a
minor canon this year.

Francis Pilkington wrote the
preface (September 25, "from my
own mansion in the monastery")
of his Madrigal book of 1614.

Zacharias Pilkington, probably
a son of Francis Pilkington, was
a chorister at Chester for several years, ending this year.

De Sayve became Master of the
Imperial Chapel, in Hungary at
this time.

The contrabass trombone in A
was made with a double slide by
Jobst Schnitzer at Nürnberg this
year.

Heinrich Schütz remained in
Venice until the death of
Gabrieli this year.

Viadana went to the Cathedral of
Fano this year.

Zangius was kapellmeister at the
court in Berlin at this time.

Another English verse translation of the psalter was prepared
by Henry Ainsworth and published
this year at Amsterdam. It had
melodies only and was for the
use of English "Separatists"
who had settled there.

Henry Ainsworth's collection of

psalms published at Amsterdam appeared in an American edition as "The Book of Psalms."

In Banchieri's "Moderna armonia" the marking "a cori" indicated the modern "orchestral rein-forcement of one part by a great number of players. The technique however was not in general use at this time.

Banchieri's "Moderna armonia di canzoni alla francese, Op. XXVI" for organ with and without other instruments was issued at this time.

Barbarino's motets were published this year (See also 1610).

Thomas Bateson's "Have I found her?" was set this year by Z. Pilkington of Chester with whom Bateson was well acquainted.

S. Besler wrote German texts for all four Evangelists to be used for Passion music.

Calvisius' "Biciniorum libri duo . . ." was reprinted at Leipzig. It had originally been issued in 1590.

Calvisius' "Musicae artis praecepta . . ." was published this year at Leipzig.

Campian's first and second books of airs could not have been pub-lished prior to this year since the death of Prince Henry is mentioned in the volumes.

Rimbault gave this date as that of publication for Campian's third and fourth books of airs.

Cecchino's "Amorosi concetti" was published this year.

William Corkine's "Second Booke of Ayres" appeared this year.

Fabio Costantini's "Shirlandetta amorosa" was published this year at Orvieto.

Croce's "Sacrae cantilene concertate" was reprinted this year (See also 1610 and 1613).

Compositions by Diomedes were included in J. van den Hove's "Delitiae musicae" issued at this time.

Donati's "Ignatii Donati Ecclesiae Metropolitanae Urbin Musicae Praefecti sacri concentus 1, 2, 3, 4 & 5 vocibus, una cum parte organica . . ." appeared at this time.

John Dowland's "A Pilgrime's Solace" was published this year in two volumes, including "Three Songs" published originally in Robert Dowland's "A Musicall Banquet" (1610).

One of John Dowland's finest songs "Go nightly cares" from "A Pilgrimes Solace" was set in deepest melancholy.

Some of John Dowland's composi-tions were included in a collec-tion by van den Hove published this year.

Dulichius' "Prima pars Centuriae octonum et septenum vocum harmonias sacras laudibus sanctissime triados consecrates continentis accurata diligentia adornata . . ." Part IV was published.

Juan Barahona de Esquivel's motets were published this year at Salamanca. A second part comprised of hymns, magnificats, etc. was published in 1613. They were for four to eight voices.

Franck wrote his "Suspiria musica" for four voices at this time.

Francesco Genvino composed his third book of madrigals at this time.

Gibbons' "Madrigals and Motets of five parts" appeared this year. They are all in English and not definitely ecclesiastical in character.

Goudimel's setting of traditional melodies, most commonly used, were expanded by Landgrave Moritz of Hessen this year.

Johann Groh's "Dreissig neue ausserlesene Padovane und Galliard . . ." was reprinted this year.

Hassler's original "Sacri concentus" was enlarged to fifty-six compositions with the further addition of three instrumental pieces titled "Ricercari" and "Canzoni" for forty eight parts.

Several lute collections by van den Hove, among them his "Delitiae musicae" were brought out this year at Utrecht.

Van den Hove's lute books were reprinted this year (See also 1601).

Robert Johnson wrote "Full Fathom five" and "Where the bee sucks" for "The Tempest," a particularly fine masque of this time.

J. C. Kapsberger's "Lib. 1 di aria passeggiate" appeared at this time at Rome.

Kapsberger's "Lib. 1 di motetti passeggiati" appeared at Rome this year.

P. P. Melii published a book of theorbo music this year.

Johann Möller wrote two books of pavans, galliards etc. for five instruments this year.

Montesardo this year published volumes of sacred songs for one to eight voices and also "I lieti giome di Napoli," which included 56 arias and madrigals for solo voices in which he used the new monodic style, dance-like songs, villanelle, etc. for two and three voices, and "puzzel" canons.

Monteverdi's "Lamento d'Erminia" with words by T. Tasso was issued this year.

Moritz reprinted his "Gesangbuch" this year. He provided all the tunes with his own four-part harmony.

Morley's "Canzonets" with German translation were published at this time at Cassel.

It is not until this year or the next that Parthenia was published in England according to a highly respected source.

"Parthenia" was one of the earliest English music books printed from engraved plates.

The neglectful manner in which Dowland was treated in England was alluded to by Henry Peacham in his "Minerva Britanna" of this year.

Peter Philips' first set of "Cantiones sacrae" for five voices was published by Phalèse at Antwerp this year. A second set for double chorus was issued a year later.

Praetorius' "Terpsichore" was published at Wolfenbüttel this year. It erroneously derived the minuet from the branle de Poiton.

Quagliati's motets and psalms for twelve voices appeared this year.

Ramsey wrote "What teares, deere Prince," apparently for the death of Henry, the Prince of Wales, this year.

Rasi's "Musica di camera e chiesa" was published this year.

A motet was composed by Lambert de Sayve at this time for the coronation of Matthew as emperor.

More of Viadana's psalms appeared at this time (See also 1595 and 1604). The psalms were polychoral.

Villani's five eight-part masses were published at this time.

Vernizzi's "Coelestium applausus" Op. 4 appeared this year.

Michael Vredman published a book this year on violin and cittern playing at Antwerp.

Vulpius published a book of "Deutsche songtëgliche evangelietee Sprüche" for the whole year at this time.

Plymouth - a small company of settlers - preferred the Ainsworth psalter, "The Booke of Psalmes: Englished both in Prose and Metre," published at Amsterdam this year, partly because they knew the Dutch and French tunes with their variety of meters, and tunes that were unfamiliar to the Puritans.

The Middlesex J.P.s issued an order banning jiggs throughout the country because they had become so notoriously rowdy.

A special place, a "music room," was reserved for Theatre musicians at the Swan Theatre at this time.

The scoring was noticeably reduced in Sweelinck's "Rimes françoises et italiennes" issued this year.

Scipione Bargagli, a Sienese academician, died (born 1540).

Archbishop Wolf Dietrich was in power in Salzburg up to this date. He had assumed power in 1587.

Emperor Rudolph II's power during the Counter-Reformation ended at this time.

Pierre Mignard, a French painter, was born (died 1695).

Le Vau, a French architect, was born (died 1670).

(to 1613) "The Earl of Salisbury" by William Byrd was included in the "Parthenia."

(to 1613) "The Earl of Salisbury," a pavane for virginal by Gibbons, was included in "Parthenia."

1612(cont.)

(to 1613) De Sayve published a set of 141 motets during these years.

(to 1614) Dutch painting: Rubens, "Descent From The Cross."

(to 1615) Randolph Jewett was a chorister at Chester during these years.

(to 1618) Thomas Pilkington, brother of Zacharias, was a chorister at Chester throughout this period.

(May 3 to 1620) Giovanni Domenico Pullaschi was a singer at the papal chapel for this period.

(and 1625) Copies of the 1612 and 1625 editions of G. Diruta's "Il Transilvano" have been preserved.

(to 1626) Pujol was "maestro de capilla" at Barcelona during these years.

(to 1640, August 3) Nicholas Morgan was organist at the convent of Augustinian nuns during this period which terminated with his death.

c.1612

Johann Lyttich, a German composer, died (birthdate unknown).

William Hale's fame as an illustrator rested on his engraved music, some of the earlies produced in England. His work appeared in "Parthenia."

Monteverdi's musical services at the ducal court of Mantua ended. He had been there since c.1590.

1613

(February 14) Bull wrote an anthem to the words of the Benediction, beginning with "God the Father, God the Son" for the marriage on this date of Princess Elizabeth, daughter of King James I, and the Prince Palatine.

(February 20) Coperario composed music to "The Masque of the Inner Temple and Graye's Inn" performed at Whitehall on this date.

(April 19) Christoph Bach, court and town musician at Arnstadt and second surviving son of Johannes Bach, was born at Wechmar (died 1661, September 12). He was the grandson of Veit and a member of the third generation of the family.

(June 9) Christaan van (Crétien de) Placker, a Flemish musician, was born at Poperinghe on this date (died 1691, January 20).

(July 2) Robert Stone, an English composer, died at London (born 1516).

(July 8) M. Peerson was awarded the Bachelor of Music degree at Lincoln College, Oxford on this day.

(August 5) Alice Gibbons, daughter of Orlando, was baptized on this date.

(August 18) Giovanni Maria Artusi, Italian scholar and composer, died at Bologna (born c.1540).

(September 8) (Don) Carlo Gesualdo, Prince of Venosa and a major composer, died at Naples (born c.1560).

1613(cont.)

(September 13) Gesualdo's wife wrote to her brother on this date telling him of her husband's death, five days earlier.

(October 12) Monteverdi wrote to Alessandro Striggio to describe his recent ordeal when he was robbed while enroute to Venice.

(October 22) Johann Heyden, organist and instrument maker, was buried.

(December 26) Three songs by Coperario were included in the masque performed at Whitehall on St. Stephen's Night this year.

(Spring) Schütz returned to Germany from Venice.

(May) John Amner was awarded the Bachelor of Music degree by Oxford.

(August) Monteverdi was appointed maestro at St. Mark's in Venice.

(October) Johann Heyden (or "Hans The Elder"), an organist and instrument maker, died at Nürnberg (born 1536, January 19).

Prince Sigismund Báthori, a Polish lutenist, died (born c.1571).

William Brade's son Hieronymus, was born (date of death unknown).

Bartholomäus Gese, a German composer, died at Frankfort (born c.1555).

Duke Heinrich Julius of Brunswick, a dramatist, died (born 1564).

Guilio Cesare Martinengo, an Italian composer, died at Venice (birthdate unknown).

Lorenzo Penna, an Italian composer, was born (died 1693, October 20).

Gaspard Poussin, a painter of harpsichord cases, was born (died 1675).

Anerio was Maestro at the Lateran until this date.

The last trace of Belli was found at this date at Imola.

Bonini was appointed organist of the cathedral of San Mercuriale at Forli prior to this date. He held the position for about twenty years.

Brade returned to Hamburg to direct the municipal band.

John Bull left England without permission and went to Brussels where he was employed as organist to Archduke Albert. The English ambassador claimed that Bull had left to avoid deserved punishment for certain crimes. He was employed prior to Michaelmas and became friendly with Sweelinck.

Cerone provided definite directions for tuning the Lira da Braccio.

J. B. Comes was musical director at Valencia Cathedral at this time.

Dallam built an organ for Worcester Cathedral at this time.

Both John and Robert Dowland's names appeared on a list of musicians paid for performing in Chapman's "Masque of the Middle Temple" and "Lincoln's Inn" at Whitehall.

Gagliano became music instructor to the younger priests of San Lorenzo at Florence.

William Hole worked on music engraving at this time.

Welsh master ap Huw was a musician to King James I at this time.

Johann Jeep was Kapellmeister to Count Hohenlohe at Weickersheim from this date until at least 1640. He composed a book of psalms and several books of secular songs during his lifetime.

Nicholas Lanier was representative of the broad culture encouraged and practiced by the Stuarts. At this time he sang in the "Squires' Masque" and set one of the songs to music.

Marin Mersenne received full orders following a course of theology and Hebrew at Paris.

Monteverdi served first as a string player and singer at the court of Mantua and from this date until his death he held position of highest prestige in Italy, that of chapel master at St. Mark's in Venice. He succeeded Croce in this position.

Schein became Kapellmeister at Weimar at this time.

Schütz visited Dresden this year.

Jiří Třanovský, the hymnologist, moved to Moravia at this time

(cont.) and became rector of Holesov school.

Flaminio Tresti was organist at San Pietro di Bergolio, in Alessandria at this time.

Nicolas Vallet, the French lutenist, settled in Amsterdam this year.

Matthew White this year became Gospeller in London, replacing Robert Stone.

Wilbye was granted a lease on some excellent pasture land. The proceeds from this made him a wealthy property owner.

The eighth part of Alstedt's "Methodus admirandorum mathematicorum" published this year treated music to a considerable extent.

Anerio published his "Antifoni e sacri concerti" for one to three voices this year.

Banchieri's secular vocal work "Duo in contrappunto sopra Ut, Re, Mi, Fa" was issued at this time.

Banchieri's motet "Ego Domino," in "Libro III di nuovi pensieri ecclesiastici" published this year, revealed dynamic directions "f" and "p" for the first time.

Banchieri's "Moderna prattica musicale" was published this year at Venice.

Banchieri's sacred vocal work "Salmi festivi" for four voices was completed this year.

Bellanda wrote "Sacre laudi," twenty-three songs, this year.

1613(cont.)

Pietro Benedetti issued at least four books of "Musiche," the second this year.

Bonini's "Lamento d'Arianna . . . in stile recitativo" (in twenty sections) was issued.

Boschetti's book of madrigals for five voices appeared at this time.

Brunelli's "Varii esercizii" for one and two voices or cornetts, German flutes and violins, was completed at this time.

Brunelli's three secular books of "Scherzi, arie, madrigali . . ." for one to five voices was published this year and in 1614 and 1616.

Caccini's "Fuggilotio musicale . . . madrigali, sonetti, arie, canzoni & scherzi, per cantare nel chitarrone, clavicembalo o altro instumento" was issued in a second edition at Venice at this time.

Campian's treatise "A New Way of making Fowre parts in Counterpoint, by a most familiar and infallible Rule" was completed at this time.

Campian composed songs for a masque for an entertainment in honour of Queen Anne produced at Caversham House by Lord Knollys this year.

Campian composed songs for a Masque to be presented at the marriage of Robert, Earl of Somerset, this year.

Campian composed songs for a masque to be presented at the marriage of Princess Elizabeth.

Campian this year wrote the words for a set of "Songs of Mourning Bewailing the untimely death of Prince Henry."

Cardoso's "Magnificats" for five voices were published this year at Lisbon.

Cerone wrote his 1160-page "El Melopeo y Maestro" (The Art of Music and Instructor), published this year at Naples. The text was in Spanish and the work codified the Palestrinian style. It was in two volumes and dealt primarily with ornamentation.

Cesana this year published a volume of songs for one, two and three voices.

William Cranford wrote a "Passion" on the death of Prince Henry" this year.

Croce's "Sacrae cantilene concertate" was reprinted this year (See also 1610 and 1612).

Christoph Demantius' "Fasciculus chorodiarum" appeared at this time.

Donato's "Beati eritis cum maledixerint" (a 5). Promptuarii musici" was published this year by Schadaeus.

Donato's "Se pur ti guardo" "Livre VII des chansons a 4 parties" was reprinted at Antwerp (See also 1597, 1620 and 1636).

Dowland's first book of ayres was reprinted this year for the third, fourth and fifth time.

Franck wrote his "Viridarium musicum" for five to ten voices this year.

1613(cont.)

The Austro-Hungarian march "The March of the Musketeers" by Friedland was published at this time.

Gese published his "Opus novum continens Missas, Introitus" for four to nine voices this year. It included a St. Mathew's Passion for six voices.

Gesualdo's compositions were included in a single volume of madrigals published at Genoa, in parts (1585) and in score this year.

A volume was published this year including Gesualdo's six books of five-part madrigals in score form.

Giacobbi this year wrote some new intermezzi, "Proserpina rapita," for Campeggi's play "Filarmindo."

Orlando Gibbons composed "Blessed are they" for the wedding of Lord Somerset and Lady Essex held this year.

Orazio Giaccio's first book of three-part canzonette, "Armoniose voci," was published at this time.

A book of motets for two to eight voices by A. Grandi was published this year. This was the second of six books.

Heinrich Hartmann this year and in 1617 composed two books of sacred songs for five to ten voices, as well as masses and motets.

Hassler's five-part "Mein gmüth ist mir verwirret" this year had the superius revised (cont.) with a religious text, "Herzlich thut mich verlangen." It was later used by Bach, with Paul Gerhardt's words, O Haupt voll Blut und Wunden," in the St. Matthew Passion. The Hassler work was published by Görlitz.

"Valet will ich dir geben," a hymn by Valerius Herbergen, the Lutheran pastor at Fraustadt, was composed this year.

One of Herbst's most important compositions, "Theatrum Amoris," was published this year at Nürnberg. It included twelve German madrigals for five voices and two Latin texts for six.

Nicholas Lanier was joined by several others in composing music for Campian's masque for the marriage of Robert Car, Earl of Somerset, and Lady Frances Howard.

Leone Leoni wrote "Psalmodia" at this time.

Henry Lichfild, English composer, published a book of five-part madrigals this year.

Macque's madrigal books for five voices appeared (See also 1587, 1597 and 1599).

Michael's music for the birth of Prince Johann Georg of Saxony, son of Elector Johann Georg, Dresden, was composed this year.

Molinaro edited Gesualdo's six books of five-part madrigals published in score thus providing a link between the two composers by use of striking modulations.

Composers frequently revised their early works by adding a continuo to modernize them. Monteverdi did this when his fourth book was reprinted this year.

Jacopo Moro this year published a book of "Concerti ecclesiastici" for one to four voices.

Negri's First Book of Psalms for seven voices, Opus 3 appeared at this time.

G. Negro's "Grazie ed Affetti di musica moderna a 1, 2 e 3 voci . . .," Opus 5 in two books, was published.

Notari's "Prime musiche" was printed this year by William Hale in an elegantly prepared folio.

Angelo Notari's "Prime musiche nuove" (miscellany of music for 1, 2, 3 voices), partially in the monodic style, was completed at this time.

A theoretical work by Nucius titled "Musices poeticae sive de compositione cantus" appeared at this time.

Secular solo madrigals by Pietro Pace were published this year at Venice.

Patta's "basso generale per l'organo" was reprinted at this time.

An Angelo Patti printed a "Lyrical Plaint of the Virgin Mary Over the Face of the Dead Christ" this year.

A book of songs for five voices (cont.) by Peuerl was issued at this time.

Philips' collection of "Cantione sacrae" for eight voices was published by Phalèse at this time and dedicated to St. Peter.

The first edition of Philips' "Gemmulae sacrae binus et ternis vocibus cum basso continuo ad organum" was published at this time by Phalèse at Antwerp.

Francis Pilkington's "First set of Madrigals" was published this year.

Porta's "Vaga ghirlanda di soavi et adorati fiori musicali" for one to five voices was published at this time.

Vernizzi's "Concerto ossia mottetto" was included in Banchieri's "Nuovi pensieri" published this year.

Vulpius published a St. Matthew's passion this year. He wrote the text.

Walliser published his "Sacrae modulationes" at this time.

John Ward published his "First set of English Madrigals" to three to six parts this year.

A masque by Campian was performed at Whitehall on St. Stephen's Night. The occasion was the marriage of the Earl of Somerset and Lady Frances Howard.

A masque by Campian was performed at the Banqueting House in Whitehall on the occasion of the marriage of Frederick, the elector palatine, to Princess Elizabeth.

1613(cont.)
Campian's masque "The Lords" was produced this year.

The earliest appearance of the term "double organ" applied to a combination of a great and a positive organ (chair) recorded at Worcester Cathedral this year.

The English madrigal started a long decline at the turn of the century. After this year the printed output fell off sharply as well.

"Single" and "Double" as applied to harpsichord as well as organs denoted one-manual or two-manual instruments from this time forward.

André Le Nôtre, a designer of gardens, was born (died 1700).

William Browne's "Brittania's Pastorals: Vo. I" was completed this year.

Richard Crashaw, a religious poet, was born (died 1649).

Jeremy Taylor, chaplain to King Charles I and master of "sacred rhetoric," was born (died 1667).

Sir Francis Bacon became attorney-general this year.

George Wither's "Abuses Stript and Whipt" appeared at this time.

Gerard Dou, a Dutch painter, was born (died 1675).

Perrault, a French architect, was born (died 1688).

(to 1614) Abraham Schade was cantor at Torgau during these

(cont.) years.

(to 1615) Giovanni Ghizzolo was choirmaster to the Prince of Correggio during this period.

(to 1615) Johann Klemm continued his musical education under Christian Erbach at Augsburg at this time.

(to 1617) Capece was "maestro di cappella" at the cathedral of rieti during these years.

(to 1619) P. Pace published nine volumes of motets during these years.

(to 1620) Anerio served as maestro di cappella at Santa Maria dei Monti in Rome for these years.

(to 1620) Anerio was musician to the distinguished Roman family of Giacomo Avila during these years.

(and 1621) Belli's set of "Concerti ecclesiastici" for two and three voices and organ appeared between these dates.

(October 11 to 1621, July) Eleuterio Guazzi was a soprano at the ducal cappella della steccata at Parma for these eight years.

(to 1624) Franck wrote his "Gemmulae evangeliorum musicae" for four voices during these years.

(to 1627) Artus Auxcousteaux was "haute-contre" (counter -tenor) for over thirteen years in the chapel of King Louis XIII.

(to 1628) Cecchino's sacred

1613(cont.)
works during these years included six known books of masses,
motets, psalms, etc. for at
least two voices, and mostly for
five and eight voices.

(to 1630) Fétis mentioned thir-
teen masses for four voices by
Jean Bournonville printed by
Ballard during these years.

(to 1633) Later publications of
Philips' selections containing
sacred works for two and three
parts as well as some for solo
with basso continuo, and a set
of Litanies to the Blessed
Virgin, for four to nine voices,
appeared during this period.

(to 1643) These years embraced
Monteverdi's appointment as
maestro di cappella at St.
Mark's in Venice. He retained
the position until his death.

(to 1643) Monteverdi wrote two
four-part masses in the old
style during this period.

c.1613
Jean Baptiste Boesset (Seigneur
de Dehault), a French composer,
was born (died 1685, December
27).

Estevão de Christo, a
Portuguese composer, died at
Thomas (birthdate unknown).

Thomas Mace, an English writer
on music, was born (died
c.1709).

Byrd, Bull, Gibbons, all contributed to "Parthenia . . ."
published this year and reprinted in 1646, 1651, 1655,
and possibly 1659.

Campian's First and Second

(cont.) Books of Airs were issued at this time.

The first music printed in
England from plates was either
"Parthenia" or Gibbon's
"Fantazies of III Parts" for
viols.

A. Notari, "Prime musiche nuove
a una, due, e tre voci . . .
Intagliate da Guglielmo Hole"
was published at this time at
London.

One of the earliest surviving
harp tunes, the "Robert ap Huw
Manuscript," partly copied from
a manuscript by William Penllyn,
was published this year.

M. Peerson probably became
Master of Choristers at St.
Paul's Cathedral in London at
this time and remained there
until his death.

(to 1614) Heinrich Scheidemann
went to Amsterdam to study with
Sweelinck during these years.

(and c.1617) Campion's works
included songs for five masques
and four other volumes of ayres.
Two of them were probably published this year and the other
two in c.1617.

1614
(January 2) Gagliano was made a
Protonotario Apostolico of San
Lorenzo in Florence on this
date.

(April 13) Richard Farnaby, composer and son of Giles Farnaby,
married Elizabeth Sendye at St.
Peter Westcheap in London on
this date.

(June 17) William Bathe, Irish
music scholar, died at Madrid

1614(cont.)
(born 1564, April 2).

(June 24) Walter Rowe I, violist
and composer, entered the service of the Elector of
Brandenburg. He may not have
accepted the appointment at
once, since he was still in
Hamburg in August of this year.

(September 10) Philipp
Friedrich Buchner, a German
composer, was born at Wertheim,
Franconia (died 1669, March 23).

(September 27) Felice Anerio,
an Italian composer, died at
Rome (born c.1560 or 1564).

(February) Lambert de Sayve,
Netherlands singer and composer,
died at Prague (born 1549).

(May) Benjamin Rogers, an
English organist and composer,
was born in Windsor (died 1698,
June). He was a chorister at
St. George's Chapel, Windsor.

(September) Giovanni de Macque,
Flemish composer, died at
Naples (born c.1552).

Maria Magdalena, wife of
Christoph Bach, of the third
generation of the Bach family,
was born (died 1661).

Amadio Freddi, an Italian composer, was born at Padua (date
of death unknown).

Bernhard Klingenstein, a German
sacred composer, died (born
1545).

Franz Tunder, a notable organist
and cantata composer, was born
at Lübeck (died 1667, November
5). He was Buxtehude's father
-in-law.

Arizo was listed as an alto in
the royal chapel at Madrid at
this time.

The Bolognese Accademia de'
Floridi was founded by Banchieri
at this time (See also 1615).

Adriano Banchieri was extremely
active in the musical life of
Bologna at this time.

Barbarino at this time referred
to the "tanti anni" for which
he had served the Duke of
Urbino.

From this time forward, W.
Barley, the printer, apparently
ceased his activity in that
trade.

Adrian Batten went to London
this year having been appointed
vicar-choral of Westminster
Abbey.

Valerio Bona was prefect at San
Fermo Maggiore, Verona at this
time.

William Brade became violist and
musician to the Duke of Holstein
during this year.

From this year on Brunelli's
principal occupation was to
serve the grand dukes of
Tuscany as "maestro di cappella"
of Santo Stefano at Pisa.

Capece was "organista supplente"
at the Cathedral of Rieti from
this time on.

Cecchino moved to a position
similar to that of "maestro" at
Lesina.

Fabio Costantini was at the
Cathedral of Orvieto at this
time.

1614(cont.)

Henning Dedekind was a preacher
at the School of Langensalza,
Thuringia at this time.

Dognazzi was only a serving musician at this time.

Andrea Falconieri suddenly left
his position at Parma and probably went to Mantua.

Gery (de) Ghersem became a
canon of Tournai this year.

Nathaniel Giles this year wrote
a poem, a tribute to a fellow
musician, praising Ravenscroft's
"Briefe Discourse."

Robert Hole worked at music
engraving at this time.

Gregorio Howett, a Netherlandish
lutenist and composer, one of
the great lutenists of his time,
was discharged from the Duke of
Brunswick's service.

Francesco Milleville, an
Italian composer, became maestro
di cappella at Volterra
Cathedral at this time.

Olthoff retired this year from
active work.

Francis Pilkington became a
minor canon at Chester Cathedral
this year.

Ravenscroft spoke warmly of his
pupil, E. Pearces, as a choir
master and composer for the
lute and other instruments. He
included a hunting-song for
four voices and a song for
voice and three instruments in
his "Briefe Discourse."

Pedro Ruimonte at this time
received money to return to

(cont.) Spain.

Claudio Saracini dedicated a
song to the Duchess of Brunswick
this year.

Schütz was invited to supervise
the music for the christening of
the son of the Elector Johann
Georg of Saxony at this time.

Stefanini was maestro di cappella
at the church of the Madonna
della Consolatione, Rome at this
time.

Trabaci this year succeeded de
Macque as maestro di cappella
at Naples.

Ugolini was in the service of
Cardinal Arigoni in Rome this
year.

Giovanni Valentini was court
organist to the Archduke
Ferdinand at Graz at this time.

Matthew White resigned his position as Gospeller.

E. Widmann was preceptor and
cantor at the school of
Rotenburg at this time.

Anerio published masses for four
to six voices this year.

The Editio Medicea was printed
this year. It was the work of
Anerio and Suriano.

According to Pitoni, a pastoral
drama, titled "Eumelio," has
been credited to Agazzari. It
was surely performed at Amelia
and printed by Domenico
Domenici at Roncilione this year
(Allacci, "Dramaturgia"), but
no author was credited with
either the music or the libretto.

1614(cont.)

A madrigal for solo voice and continuo by Lorenzo Allegri was included in Brunelli's "Scherzi, arie, canzonette e madrigali" published this year at Venice.

The "Ballet des Argonautes" was composed this year.

Banchieri wrote his "Cartella musicale nel canto figurato, fermo & contrapunto . . . novamente in questa terza impressione ridotta dell'antica alla moderna pratica" this year and it was published at Venice.

Banchieri's "Cartellina del canto fermo gregoriano," a literary work, appeared.

Banchieri's secular vocal work "Due ripieni in applauso musicale, 8v" was composed this year.

Banchieri's stage work "Tirsi, Filli e Clori" was completed at this time.

Banchieri's sixth book "Tirsi Filli e Clori" was published at this time.

Barbarino's fourth secular book was published this year.

Brade's "Newe ausserlesene Paduanen . . ." for six parts was published this year at Hamburg.

Brunelli's three secular books of "Scherzi, arie, madrigali . . ." for one to five voices was published this year and in 1613 and 1616.

An impressive occasional piece for solo voice with ritornello, to a text by Ferdinando

(cont.) Saracinelli, was included in Brunelli's "Scherzi, arie, canzonette e Madrigali" for one to three parts.

Four short anthems by Byrd were included in Leighton's "Tears or Lamentations of a Sorrowfull Soule," a collection published this year.

Caccini's ballet "Il ballo delle zigane," an unpublished work, was completed this year.

Caccini's "Nuove musiche e nuova maniera di scriverle" was published this year at Florence.

Several compositions by Caccini were included in Brunelli's "Scherzi, arie, canzonette e madrigali."

Cifra's "Scherzi ed arie" appeared this year.

Coperario contributed two anthems to Leighton's "Teares or Lamentations of a Sorrowfull Soule."

Fabio Costantini published "Selectae cantiones excellentissimorum auctorum" this year at Rome.

Dognazzi's "Primo libro di varii concenti" appeared at this time.

John Dowland contributed two compositions to Leighton's "Teares" as well as some commendatory verses to Ravenscroft's "Briefe Discourse."

Two short anthems by Thomas Ford were included in Leighton's "Teares."

Melchior Franck wrote his

"Recreationes musicae," for four
and five voices this year.

"Follias" were included in
Frescobaldi's "partite" of this
year.

Girolamo Frescobaldi's "Tocate
. . . e partite d'intavolatura"
was published at this time.

Adam Gumpeltzhaimer's "Sacrorum
concentum" Vol. II was published this year.

Gagliano's "Missa et sacrae
cantiones, sex decantandae
vocibus . . ." was published at
this time.

Gagliano this year wrote the
music for the ballet "Scherzi e
balli di giovanette montanine."

Francesco Genvino wrote his
fifth book of madrigals this
year.

Carlo Gesualdo's fifth book of
five-part madrigals was reprinted at this time.

Madrigals for five voices by
Gibbons appeared:

   "Dainty, Fine Bird"
   "How Art Thou Thrall'd"
   "The Silver Swan"
   "What Is Our Life"

Gibbons' "O Lord increase my
faith" was included in
Leighton's "Teares."

Grandi's book of motets for five
voices was published at Ferrara
this year.

A book of motets for two to
eight voices by Grandi was published. It was the third of

(cont.) six books.

Hans C. Haiden this year wrote
the words and music for a book
of four-part dance-songs for
voices and instruments.

Andro Hart printed an edition of
the Psalms this year at
Edinboro.

Bartholomaeus Helder this year
wrote "Cymbalum genethiacum,"
New Year and Christmas songs for
four to six voices.

Haiden's two books of four-part
dance songs for voices or instruments were reprinted (See
also 1601).

Robert Hole this year engraved
a companion col. to William
Hole's "Parthenia In-Violata,"
an oblong quarto containing
twenty duets for virginal and
viol.

Two of E. Hooper's pieces were
included in Leighton's "Teares."

Jones' "Sing Joyfully" and three
anthems were included in
Leighton's "Teares."

Leighton's "Teares" included R.
Johnson II's "Yeelde unto God"
and a five-part "Save me, O
Lord."

The anthems by Robert Kindersley
were included in Leighton's
"Teares."

Francesco Lambardi's second set
of "Villanelle" for three to
five voices was published this
year.

Sir William Leighton published
his "The Teares or Lamentations
of a Sorrowful Soule" at this

time. It was comprised of fifty-four psalms and hymns.

Lichfild's book of Madrigals was dedicated to Lady Cheyney who died this year.

Lipparino wrote madrigals for five voices at this time.

P. P. Melii published a book of theorbo music at this date.

Monteverdi's Balletto "Della bellezza" was issued this year.

Monteverdi's "Lamendo d'Arianna" (Rinuccini) was first issued this year at Venice.

Monteverdi's fourth book of Madrigals included a setting of a love-letter with hardly a dividing line between spoken word and sung word.

Monteverdi published his sixth book of madrigals this year.

Two of Negro's books, Opus 8, "Grazie ed affetti di musica moderna a 1, 2 e 3 voci" appeared at this time.

Ambros praised highly a motet by Pacelli for eight voices "Factum est silentium." It was included in Constantini's collection.

"Parthenia Inviolata," a companion work to the "Parthenia," was issued this year.

Patta's volume of spiritual madrigals and motets with text by Grillo appeared at this time.

Peerson contributed a laudatory poem to Ravenscroft's "A Brief Discourse" as well as three

(cont.) unaccompanied motets to Leighton's "Teares."

F. Pilkington's "First set of Madrigals & Pastorals of 3, 4 & 5 parts. . . ." was issued this year.

F. Pilkington contributed a "song" or anthem in four parts, "Hidden O Lorde;" and another in five parts, "High, Mighty God," to Leighton's "Teares."

Part I of M. Praetorius' Vol. I was published at Wolfenbüttel at this time.

Adams published "A Briefe Discourse" by Thomas Ravenscroft this year.

Edward Allde printed Thomas Ravenscroft's "A Briefe Discourse" this year.

Ravenscroft's "The English Lawyer" was an adaptation of a Latin comedy, "Ignoramus," written this year by George Ruggle.

Pedro Ruimonte's madrigals to Spainish texts and his madrigals published this year were "the only examples of the later chromatic madrigals with Spanish words."

The first book of madrigals and airs by Claudio Saracini was published at this time.

Saracini published his "Le Musiche" this year. Two solo pieces for the theorbo were included in the book.

Erasmus de Sayre's "Melodie spirituale . . . a tre voc . . ." was published this year.

Stadlmayr's "Magnificat. Symphoniae variae secundum varios modos musicos, aliae octonis, una 12 voc., cum basso continuo." was published this year.

Usper's "Messa e salmi" was published at this time.

Vulpius published a book of "Deutsche sontägliche evangelische Sprüche" for the for the whole year at this date.

Vulpius published his third edition of wedding hymns to Latin words at this time.

C.T. Walliser this year published his chief work, "Ecclesiodae."

Weelkes contributed two pieces to Leighton's "Teares."

Wilbye composed two short hymns or anthems for Leighton's "Teares."

Campian's masque, "The Squires" was produced this year.

Frescobaldi in the preface to his Toccatas issued this year gave a number of stylistic instructions. He wrote on broken chords; he prescribed "inequality" in the toccatas; he defined a "partita" as a series of variations; he demanded an (unwritten) pause on the last note of a passage; he said, "You must not divide the trill exactly note for note, but merely try to make it rapid;" and he directed the players not to stick to one steady tempo but quite to the contrary to change it within the same composition (cont.) according to the character of the music.

Only in the works of Gesualdo did the madrigal go through a crisis.

Nicholas Lanier's work for the marriage of Robert Carr and Lady Frances Howard was performed at Whitehall on St. Stephen's Night this year or 1613.

"The Masque of the Flowers," arranged by the Gentlemen of Gray's Inn for Twelfth Night, was in honour of the wedding of the Lady Frances Howard with the Earl of Somerset.

John Wilson's "The Maske of the Flowers" was produced at Whitehall this year.

William Browne's "The Shepherd's Pipe" was completed this year.

John Milton's "Thou God of might" for four parts (printed by Burney), "O Lord behold" for five, "O had I wings" for five (printed by Hawkins) and "If that a sinner's sighs" for five were included in Leighton's "Teares."

Some poems by Thomas Watson were inserted in "England's Helicon" this year.

John Webster's "The Duchess of Malfi" was first performed at London this year.

Domenikos Theotokopoulos (El Greco), renowned painter, died this year (born 1541).

Jacob van Loo, a French painter, was born (died 1670). His best known work was "Concert."

1614(cont.)

(to 1615) Michele Angelo Amadei published two books of motets at Venice during these years.

(to 1615) Bartholomaeus Helder, German composer, studied Theology and became schoolmaster at Friemar near Gotha during this period.

(to 1619) Richard Browne was vicar, organist and master of the choristers at Wells Cathedral during these years.

(to 1620) Andreas Düben (the elder) was a pupil of Sweelinck in Amsterdam during this period.

(to 1620) Praetorius' "Syntagma musicum" was written during these years.

(to 1626) The son of a poulterer, Thomas Brewer was educated at Christ's Hospital during these years when he was apprenticed to Thos. Warner.

(to 1632) Orazio Giaccio was in the service of the Annunziata church at Naples at various times during this period.

(to 1638) John Wilbye's musical output apparently suffered as a result of his agricultural inter- ests, since from this year until his death (1638) he published no music.

(to 1644) Richard Hutchinson was organist at Durham Cathedral during this entire period.

(to 1647) Macque's pupil, Trabaci served as maestro of the Viceroyal Chapel during these years.

(to 1668) John Heath's name ap- peared in the Rochester Cathedral Treasurer's Book as organist there as early as 1614 and as late as 1668.

(to 1672) Schütz worked at the court at Dresden during this long period.

c.1614

Robert Hole's "Parthenia In -violata. Or Mayden-Musicke for the Virginalls and Bass-Viol Selected . . . by Robert Hole." was published by John Pyper at London this year.

Usper was organist of the Church of San Salvatore at Venice at this time.

(to 1615) Antonelli was "maestro di cappella" at the Cathedral of Benevento at this time.

1615

(January 16) Guillaume Dumanoir, I, French violinist and composer, was born at Paris (date of death unknown).

(January 20) Giovanni Maggini, Italian violin maker, married Maddalena Anna Forrestio on this date.

(January 29) On this date Archbishop Abbot issued a man- date to the Dean and Chapter of Exeter to appoint "Master Edward Gibbons Mus Bac, Costos of the College of Vicars Chorel" to be Succentor.

(February 24) Caccini's "Ballo delle zingare" was issued on this date.

(March 27) William Heyther was a lay vicar at Westminster Abbey and on this date was sworn a Gentleman of the Chapel Royal.

161

1615(cont.)

(May 31) A further grant was issued at this date to Jones and three partners, to erect a new playhouse for the Children of the Revels on the site of the house occupied by Jones near Puddle Wharf in Blackfriars.

(August 22) Christopher Gibbons, son of Orlando and an English composer in his own right, was baptized at St. Margaret's Westminster on this date.

(September 16) Heinrich Bach, youngest of Johannes, grandson of Veit, and of the third generation of the Bach family, was born (died 1692, July 10). He eventually became organist at Arnstadt and married Eva Hoffman.

(November 21) Monteverdi wrote to Alessandro Striggio on this date to respond to a commission to write a ballet, and also to send a work he had completed.

(November 24) Seth Calvisius, the German musician, astronomer and chronologer, died at Leipzig (born 1556, February 21).

(December 12) Andrea Falconieri wrote to the Duke of Mantua on this date and sent some of his compositions to him.

(August) Melchior Vulpius, German composer, died at Weimar (born c.1560).

(November) Schein became cantor at St. Thomas's School in Leipzig at this time.

Hans Bach, violinist and one of the first members of the Bach family, died (born 1555).

John Baldwin, an English singer and composer, died at London (birthdate unknown).

John Bennet, an English composer, died (born c.1570).

Byrd's eldest son Christopher died prior to this date.

Carlo Caprolli, Italian opera composer, was born (died 1685).

Cato Diomedes, an Italian lutenist and composer, died sometime after this date (born c.1570).

Christopher Gibbons, English composer, was born at London (died 1676, October 20).

Edward Allde's address was given on Amner's Sacred Hymns, published this year as "dwelling neere Christ-Church."

In all probability Allison was identical with M. Anglus Aloyson. His work was obviously known in Germany, since Fuhrmann included a pavan under that name in a lute-book published this year.

Banchieri founded the Accademia de' Floridi at Bologna this year according to a respected sourse (See also 1614).

Giovanni Bassano was director of music at St. Mark's Venice at this time.

The first degree in music at the University of Dublin was awarded to Thomas Bateson, the madrigal composer, this year.

According to Fétis, Antoine Boesset became "intendant" of the queen's music at this time.

Bonometti moved to Archduke Ferdinand's Court at Graz this year.

Bournonville was at the collegiate church at Saint-Quentin at this time.

The English composer, Caesar, actually William Smegergill, was a chorister at Ely under Amner at this time.

At St. Thomas School in Leipzig, Calvisius had served as cantor since 1594.

Solomon de Caus's organ as described in his "Les Raisons des forces mouvontes" was "bellows-blown," although they were depressed and elevated by the action of a water-wheel.

Dallam (probably Thomas) was engaged to repair the organ at Magdalen College, Oxford this year as well as in 1632 and 1637.

A definite stylistic change was obvious in Gabrieli's later works, printed posthumously this year.

Edward Gibbons was appointed and installed as succentor at Exeter Cathedral at this time.

Gibbons this year received from the King "2 severall bonds one of one hundred pounds & the other of fyfty pounds . . . "for & in consideration of the good and faythfull service heretofore done unto ourselves by Orlando Gibbons our organist & for divers other good causes & consideracons us thereunto movinge . . ." This item appeared in Domestic State Papers, James I, Sign Manuals Vol. V38.

Monteverdi's ballets, intermezzi, operas, religious dramas, and stage works appeared starting this year.

Marie Phalèse married E. de Mayer this year.

Enrico Radesca became well-known at Venice for the dedication this year of his madrigals for five and eight voices.

Publisher Ricciardo Amadino worked on his own account after 1586 and until this year.

Johann Schop at this time entered the court band at Wolfenbüttel.

Schütz took a position at the electoral chapel in Dresden at this time.

Hugh Sempill joined the Society of Jesus at Toledo this year.

Biagio Tomasi was organist at Comacchio at this time.

Jiří Třanovský became rector at Valašské Meziříčí school this year.

Jane Vaux, widow of John Vaux, was at this time a tenant (as a copyholder of the manor of Kennington) of an apartment located near the Thames.

Viadana lived at Piacenza from this date forward.

L. Woodson became organist at Eton college this year.

John Amner this year printed his "Sacred Hymns of 3, 4, 5 and 6 parts, for Voices and Vyols." They were dedicated to his "singular good lord and maister," the Earl of Bath.

1615(cont.)

Banchieri's literary work, "La cartellina musicale che in documenti facili ridotti dall' antico allo istilo moderno introduce i principanti a sicuro possesso del canto figurato Op. XXX Va" appeared this year.

Banchieri's literary work, "Prima parte del primo libro al direttorio monastico di canto fermo" was completed at this time.

Heinrich Baryphonus' "Pleiades musicae" was published this year at Halberstadt.

Steffano Bernardi's manual "Porta musicale per la quale il principiante con facile brevita all' acquisto dell perfette regole del contrapunto vien introdotto" was published this year at Verona.

Bodenschatz' "Bicinia XC" appeared at this time.

Bonini's "Affetti spirituali" for two parts appeared at this time.

Bonini's "Sirena celesta" motets for one to three voices was completed at this time.

Bonometti's anthology of 16th-century church music, "Parnassus musicus Ferdinandaeus," was published this year at Venice.

Brassicanus this year wrote "Similia Davidica . . ." for four voices.

Calvisius' "Der 150. Psalm für 12 Stimmen . . ." was published this year at Leipzig.

Salomon de Caus' "Les Raisons des forces mouvantes avec diverses machine . . ." was published this year at Frankfort.

Cortellini's Litanies were published this year by Vincenti at Venice.

Fuhrmann's "Testudo Gallo-Germanica" issued this year included compositions by Diomedes.

Diruta's "Il Transilvano" was published this year by Vincenti at Venice. It also was issued in 1625 and possibly 1626.

Some of Dowland's works were included in Fuhrmann's "Testudo Gallo-Germanica."

A lute piece by Robert Dowland was included in Fuhrmann's "Testudo Gallo-Germanica."

A fourth and enlarged edition of Fattorini's "Sacri concerti a 2 voci" was published this year.

Franck this year composed his "Deliciae amoris" for six voices.

Franck this year wrote his "Threnodiae Davidicae" for six voices.

Frescobaldi's "Ricercari e canzoni francesi" was published this year at Rome.

Frescobaldi's "Toccate . . . e partite d'intavolatura" was published for the second time this year.

(Georg) Leopold Fuhrmann's lute-book "Testudo Gallo-Germanica" was published at Nürnberg this year. It contained English dances and fantasies.

G. Gabrieli's "Canzoni et Sonate" was published at Venice. The works were for three to twenty-two voices.

G. Gabrieli published his second book of "Sacrae symphoniae" at this time. The book was for voices and instruments.

Gagliano wrote the music for "Ballo di donne turche insieme con i loro consorti di schiavi fatti liberi" this year.

Gagliano's "Musiche a una, due e tre voci" was published at this time. About one half of the selections were duets.

Gese published his theoretical work, "Synopsis musicae practicae," this year.

Girolamo Giacobbi this year wrote the music to Silvestro Branchi's "Amor prigioniero."

Giacobbi published some litanies this year.

Ruggiero Giovannelli at this time published the second volume of his new edition of the "Graduale."

Grandi's "Madrigali concertati" for two to four voices (bk. I) was published at Venice this year.

Georg Gruber, a Nürnberg merchant and music-lover, published "Reliquiae sacrorum concentuum Giovan Gabrielis, Johann-Leonis Haslori, utriusque praestantissimi musici . . . . ." in honor of G. Gabrieli and Hassler. It included many unpublished compositions by both men for four to eighteen voices.

Andro Hart printed an edition of the Psalms this year at Edinboro.

D'India's "Musiche a due voci" was published at this time.

A lute collection of this year, "Secretum musarum," was published at Amsterdam by Nicolas Vallet. It contains mostly preludes and fantasies, but also some dances and a few transcribed chansons, including Le Jeune's "Quand on arrestera."

Leoni wrote "Aurea carona" concerti this year.

T. Marula's "Canzoni a 4 per stromenti, lib. 1" was published this year at Venice.

Micheli's "Musica vaga et artificiosa continente motetti con oblighi, e canoni diversi, etc. Di D.R.M. rom. Venetia, Giacomo Vincenti" appeared in a folio edition this year.

Micheli's "Salmi per i vesperi a tre voci in concerto da cantarsi in diversi modi . . . con il basso cont. per l'organo. Libro secondo. Opera terza" was published in a quarto this year at Venice.

Monteverdi's "Cantate Domino" for "2 canti o tenori" and continuo was included in G.B. Bonometti's collection published this year.

Monteverdi's "Orfeo," his first opera, was printed this year for the second time (Venice). This was an unusual occurence.

J.A. Westrup's performing edition of Monteverdi's "Orfeo" was made from this year's publication. The Oxford University

Opera Club came into existence
as a result of a performance
from this edition.

De Caus in his "Institution
harmonique" included some instrumental trios by Philips
"où les natures de la premiere,
troisiesme, & cinquiesme mode
sont très bien observées." The
composer's name "Pietri Filippi"
was given only for the "Trio de
la premiere mode," but context
showed all three were his work.

De Caus' "Les Raisons des forces
nouvantes" published at Frankfort
this year contained part of a
fantasy by Philips (for a barrel
-organ turned by water) on
Alessandro Striggio's five-part
madrigal "Chi fara fed' al
ciel."

A second edition of Philips'
second book of eight madrigals
for six voices was printed at
Antwerp this year.

Some of Jakób Polak's composi-
tions for lute were included in
Fuhrmann's "Testudo Gallo
-Germanica."

Part II of M. Praetorius' Vol.
I was published at Wittenberg
this year.

Praetorius greatly favord the
continuo. His "Syntagma
musicum" was an invaluable
source of information concerning
early baroque music.

Praetorius' "Syntagma musicum"
in three volumes was completed
this year.

Schein's "Cymbalum Sionium sive
Cantiones Sacrae 5, 6, 8, 10 et
12 vocum" was published at

(cont.) Leipzig at this time.
In it he paid a tribute to
Venice.

F. Severi's "Salmi passeggiate"
was published this year at Rome.

This year at London Snodham pub-
lished Tailour's book of "Sacred
Hyms," including fifty selected
Psalms of David and others.

Trabaci published his "Ricercate
et altri varii Capricci con 100
versi sopra liotti finali
ecclesiastici" this year at
Naples. In the book a partita
referred to a series of variations.

Ugolini composed two books of
five-part madrigals this year.

Vallet's "Secretum Musarum" was
originally published this year.
The volume was in tablature.

A pastoral "Le Triomphe de
Bacchus" produced in France used
music.

John Denham, an English poet,
was born (died 1669).

Middleton's play "The Witch" was
completed this year.

George Wither's "The Shepherd's
Hunting" appeared at this time.

(to 1616) Frescobaldi's "Second
Book of Pieces for Organ and
Cenbalo" was published during
these years.

(to 1618) Pierre Guédron's "Airs
de cour à 4 et à 5 parties" in
four books was published during
these years.

(to 1620) M. Praetorius'
"Syntagma musicum" was published

1615(cont.)
in three volumes during these
years. The second and third
volumes have often been reprinted in modern times.

(to 1620) The Skene lute manuscripts were compiled during
these years.

(to 1620) French architecture:
De Brosse, Luxembourg garden
front, Paris (c.300' wide).

(to 1628, or 1634 to 1643) A.
Nizankowski was a student of
Frescobaldi in Italy and afterwards for three years organist
at the Church of St. Maria sopra
la Minerva in Rome.

(to 1630) Schein was cantor at
Leipzig during this period.

(to 1633) F. Pasquali composed
three books of madrigals and
several books of sacred and
secular songs in one to five
parts during these years.

(to 1636) Francesco Lombardi was
first organist at the royal
chapel during this period.

c.1615
Marco Bigongiari, an Italian
composer, was born at Lucca
(died 1686, March 20).

Jacopo Peri of the Florentine
camerata and important in early
opera composition, died at
Florence (born 1561, August 20).
There is no general agreement
as to Peri's date of death.
It's given also as 1633, August
12).

Dirk Pieterszon Pers, a Dutch
musical collector and editor,
was born at Amsterdam (date of
death unknown).

Brassicanus at this time was
cantor at the school in Linz and
greatly furthered the cause of
Protestant church music.

The decline of the consort of
viols from this time elsewhere
and from the late 17th-Century
in England was the result of
great changes in musical style
and purpose which were characteristic of the period.

Islamic painting: Portrait of
Janangir ($1\frac{1}{2}$" x $1\frac{1}{2}$").

(to 1618) Dutch painting: Rubens,
"Toilet of Venus."

1616
(January 5) Porter became a
Gentleman of the Chapel Royal
without pay.

(March 6) Malachias Siebenhaar,
a German composer, was born in
Creibitz (died 1685, January 6).

(March 29) Johann Erasmus
Kindermann, a German organist,
and composer, was born at
Nürnberg (died 1655, April 14).
He was a pupil of Staden and
Carissimi and the first German
composer to use Italian dramatic
dialogue for comedy.

(April 23) William Shakespeare
died (born 1564, April 26). He
was buried in the church at
Stratford-on-Avon.

(May 11) Thomas Vautor on this
date was dispensed for not hearing lectures of the "praelector
musicae" at Oxford.

(May 19) Johann Jacob Froberger,
German organist and composer,
was born in Stuttgart (died
1667, May 7). He was a pupil of
Frescobaldi and the first im-

1616(cont.)
portant composer for the harpsichord.

(June 12) Cornelis Floriszoon
Schuyt, Dutch organist and composer, was buried at Leyden on
this date.

(July 2) John Hutchinson, son of
Richard, was baptised at Durham.
He was an English organist at
Southwell Minster (date of death
unknown).

(July 4) Thomas Vautor was
awarded the Bachelor of Music
degree by Lincoln College on
this day.

(August 13) Geminiano Capilupi,
an Italian composer, died at
Modena (birthdate unknown).

(September 14) F. Pilkington
became "Curate of St. Bridgets,"
Chester on this date.

(November 23) John Wallis, an
English Mathematician, was born
at Ashford, Kent (died 1703,
October 28).

(December 9) Monteverdi on this
date wrote a letter to
Alessandro Striggio concerning
Monteverdi's consideration of a
libretto "Nozzi di Tetide." He
planned to set it to music for
the wedding of Duke Ferdinando
da Gonzaga. Monteverdi did not
like the libretto and maintained
that it offered no opportunity
for development of human characters or passions.

(December 19) Monteverdi wrote
to Alessandro Striggio a second
time, still displaying a dislike
for his recently-received libretto and asking for further
instructions. At this time

(cont.) Monteverdi had just finished a mass for Christmas Eve
at St. Mark's (See also December
9).

(February) Gagliano this year
wrote the music to a "favola" by
Andrea Salvadori titled "La
liberazione di Tirreno e d'Arnea
autori del sangue toscano."

(February) Ferdinando Gonzaga
married Caterina de' Medici on
this date.

(April) Monteverdi's "Tirsi e
Clori" with libretto by Striggio
appeared at Mantua.

(June) Cornelis Floriszoon
Schuyt, Dutch organist and composer, died at Leyden (born
1557).

(December) Monteverdi in a letter written at this time stated
that "Arianna affected people
because she was a woman, and
Orpheus because he was simply a
man."

Eva (Hoffmann) Bach, wife of
Heinrich Bach of the third generation of the family, was born
(died 1679).

Sir Henry Franshawe, a music
lover and patron, died (born
1569).

William Holder, an English
clergyman and composer, was born
at Nottinghamshire (died 1697,
January 24).

Aleksander Wladyslaw Leszczyński,
a Polish composer, was born (died
1680, September 24).

Joachim von Burgk Möller
(Müller), who wrote the earliest
motet Passion in German vernacu-

lar in 1568, died according to one source. Another gave the date of death as 1610, May 24 (born 1546).

Thomas Adams completed his stay in London at the White Lion, St. Paul's Churchyard. He had been there since 1591.

A painting by Denis van Alsloot bearing this date showed a group of musicians in a religious procession.

Anerio did not become a priest until this year.

Fabio Costantini was at the Basilica Santa Maria at Tivoli this year.

Gabriel Diaz appeared at Lerma.

Donati was "maestro di cappella" of the Arciconfraternitae e Accademia dello Spirito Santo at Ferrara this year and in 1619.

In the dedication of his Psalm CL of this year Elsbeth complained about his poverty.

Fontanelli repeatedly requested a leave from services to the Estensi in order to retire to Rome.

Hans C. Haiden was discharged from his position as organist of St. Sebald's Church at Nürnberg this year.

J. Herbst became Kapellmeister at Butzbach, Hesse at this time.

Micheli was maestro di cappella at the Church of Concordia at Modena at this time.

John Parsons was this year ap-

(cont.) pointed one of the parish clerks and organist at St. Margaret's, Westminster.

G. Piccioni this year referred to himself as maestro di cappella at Monte Fiaschone (province of Rome).

Jan Polak, a Polish composer, was appointed Kapellmesiter for the band of the Margrave of Brandenburg this year.

Roffaello Rontani moved to Rome to become maestro di cappella at San Giovanni de' Fiorentini and capo de concerto to the Sforza family. He remained there until his death.

Erasmus de Sayve was awarded the title of "Burgraf" of Vienna at this time.

Staden returned to Nürnberg this year and was appointed organist, first at the St. Lorenz Church and shortly afterwards at the more important St. Sebald Church. He remained in the latter position until his death.

John Wanless was organist of Lincoln Cathedral at this time.

Marcello Albano's "Madrigali a 5 voci" and "Il 1° libro di canzioni e madrigaletti a 3 ed a 4 voci" were both published this year at Naples.

A book of motets by Ardemanio was published at this time.

Banchieri's literary work, "Progressi politici e christiani di S. S. Francesca Romana," was completed at this time.

Barbarino's fifth secular book was published this year.

Belli's book of "Arie . . . per sonarsi con il chitarrone" for one and two voices, was published this year by Amadino at Venice.

The first of Boschetti's two sets of "Cantiones sacrae" appeared this year (See also 1620).

Boschetti's favola "Strali d'amore" was presented at Viterbo at this time.

Brunelli's three secular books of "Scherzi, arie, madrigali . . ." for one to five voices was published this year and in 1613 and 1614.

Caccini's unpublished ballet "Rinaldo innamorato" was composed.

Orlandi in his publication of arias this year showed another way of setting a poem selected for illustration by Calestani.

Calvisius' "Schwanengesang" for eight voices was completed this year.

Cecchino's "Amorosi concetti" was published at this time.

Three madrigals by Cirullo were included in Phalese's "Il helicone" issued this year.

Coperario's anthem "O Lord, how do my woes increase" was included in Myriell's "Tristitiae Remedium" this year.

Some of Cutting's lute music was included in the Pickering lutebook of this year.

Debolecki's "Benedictiomensae cum gratiarum actione a quinque v. facta" was published this

(cont.) year at Torun.

Donati's "Motetti a 5 voci in concerto con due sorti di letanie della Beata Vergine & nel fine alcuni canoni . . ." appeared at this time.

Falconieri's first book of vilanelle, for one to three voices with guitar accompaniment, was published at Rome this year. It was dedicated to Cardinal de' Medici.

Franck wrote his "Geistlicher musikalischer Lustgarten" for four to nine voices at this time.

Gagliano and Falconieri both published monodies this year.

Ortensio Gentile, an Italian composer, published his "Il I lib. de madrigali a 5 voci . . ." this year.

One of the three sets of part-books which included Gibbons' "London Cry" was in the possession of Thomas Myriell and dated this year.

Gesualdo's first book of five-part madrigals was reprinted this year for the third time.

Gesualdo's second book of five-part madrigals was reprinted for the fourth time.

Gesualdo's sixth book of five-part madrigals was reprinted this year.

A book of motets for two to eight voices by A. Grandi was published this year. It was the fourth of six books.

Alessandro Gualteri wrote motets for one to four voices at this

time.

An example of an entrada, a rather pompous piece for four to six instruments written in note-against-note style, was composed by Hagius of the North German School this year.

A volume of music, edited by Hagius, was published at this time.

Pedro Heredia's motet "Anima mea" for four voices was included in Fabio Constantini's "Selectae cantiones" published this year at Bologna. It had previously been published in 1610 at Rome.

Hans Christoph Heyden after succeeding Paul Lautensach as organist of St. Sebald Church at Nürnberg was discharged this year.

This year several settings of the Genevan Psalter were published. They were composed by Le Jeune.

J.H. Kapsberger published the second of his four books of "Intavolatura di chitarrone" at this time.

J.H. Kapsberger this year published the second and third of his four "Villanelle" for voices with chitarrone accompaniment.

One of Robert Kindersky's anthems was also included in Myriell's "Tristitiae remedium" of this year.

Francesco Lambardi had his third set of "Villanelle" for three to five voices published this year. The volume also included some

(cont.) solo songs with continuo.

Samuel Mareschall published at Basel "Psalmen Davids" including hymns by Luther and others with the melodies moved to the treble.

Pietro Paolo Melii's fourth "Intavolatura di liuto attiorbato" was composed this year at Vienna. It may have been published but this fact is not definitely established.

Micheli's "Compieta a sei voci con tre tenor concertata all' uso moderno con il basso continuo per l'organo di D.R.M. rom. maestro di cappella nella cathedrale di Concordia Venetia" was published this year.

A piece by E. Hooper was included in Thomas Myriell's "Tristitiae remedium."

Thomas Myriell's "Tristitiae remedium" was published this year.

G. Negro's "Musica ecclesiastica concertata alla moderna a 2, 3 3 voci" Opus 9 appeared at this time.

Camillo Orlandi's collection of "Arie a 3, 2 et voce sola" was published this year at Venice. It was considered to be an uninteresting work.

Peri in collaboration with Paolo Francesino produced a ballo a cavallo with a text by A. Ricci.

Peri's intermedio, "La speranza giudata da Mercurio;" and the festa "La guerra d'amore" (with Pagol Grati and Giovanni Battista Signorini) were produced this year.

Philips' "Deliciae sacrae binis et ternis vocibus, cum basso continuo ad organum" appeared this year.

A second edition of Philips' "Gemmulae sacrae binis et ternis vocibus cum basso continuo ad organum" was issued by Phalése this year.

Jean Veruliet of Valenciennes this year issued a small volume of short motets or hymns titled "Les Rosignols spirituels. Liguez en duo dont les meilleurs accords, nommément le Bas, relevent du Seigneur Pierre Philippes, Organiste de leurs Altezes Serenissimes." This book was an arrangement of pop-ular melodies adapted to sacred texts by Philips.

Jane Pickering's Book of English lute music appeared.

H. Praetorius' "Opus Musicum," Vol. III "Liber missarum" was dedicated to a group of Hamburg patricians, patrons of the com-poser.

Bartholomaeus Praetorius was credited as the composer of "Newe liebliche Paduanen, und Galliarden, mit 5 Stimmen," pub-lished this year at Berlin.

Crescenzo Salzilli's second and third of three books of three -part "canzonette" were pub-lished this year. They were titled "La sirena" and "Amarille."

A book of psalms and motets by Soriano was published at this time.

A sacred work by Staden,

(cont.) "Harmoniae sacrae pro festis praecipuis" for four to eight voices, was composed this year.

Stadlmayr published "Missae 12 voc., cum triplici basso continuo" this year.

Two anthems by Simon Stubbs, "Father of Love" and "Have mercy," were included in Myriell's "Tristitiae remedium" of this year.

Fulgentio Valesi wrote two vocal pieces, "Vias tuas," and "Alta immensa" for Lucino's "Concerti" issued this year.

Nicolas Vaelet's "Le Second Livre de tablature de luth" was published this year.

Several of Verdonck's works had appeared in various collections published by Phalèse and others up to this year.

Jean Veruliet of Valenciennes published a volume of short motets by Philips titled "Les Rossignols spirituels." They were dedicated to Charles de Pas, Abbot of Saint-Armand.

Victorinus' "Siren coelestis" was published this year. An English edition appeared in 1638.

The first volume of madrigals by Filippo Vitali appeared at this time.

Belli's "Il pianto d'Orfeo" or "Orfeo dolente" consisted of five scenes which were performed as intermezzi between the acts of Tasso's "Aminta" at the Palazzo Gherardesca, Florence (the seat of the Rinaldi family)

1616(cont.)
in the Carnival this year.

Peri's "Euridice" was revived at Bologna.

The most famous Czech society was founded this year and named "Collegium Musicum."

Instrumental music was often used for supernatural effects as in the quarto of Marlowe's "Dr. Faustus" of this year. Music accompanied the ascent of the angel into heaven.

Francis Beaumont, the Elizabethan poet and playwright, died (born c.1584). He wrote "Love Lies Bleeding."

William Browne's "Brittania's Pastoral's" Vol. II was published this year. Vol. III was not published until the 19th -Century.

Cervantes, the Spanish author, died (born 1547).

Andreas Gryphius, the most notable secular lyric poet of the German baroque, was born (died 1664).

Robert Herrick, a Cavalier poet, was awarded a degree by Trinity College this year.

William Shakespeare, greatest figure in English drama, died (born 1564). See also April 3.

Francois Quesnel, a French painter, died (born c.1544).

(to 1617) Van Dyck joined the Rubens studio at this time.

(to 1617) Karel Guillet was municipal councillor of Bruges

(cont.) at this period.

(to 1619) Vincenzo Ugolini composed four books of one to four part motets with continuo during these years.

(to 1620) Ugolini was at the French church of Saint-Louis at Rome during this period.

(to 1621) Dutch painting: Rubens, "Lion Hunt."

(to 1622) Engelmann published five books of courantes, galliards, and pavans during these years.

(to 1624) Elsbeth was at Jauer, Silesia during these years.

(to 1637) Robert Fludd (Flud) wrote many and various philosophical treatises during this period.

c.1616
Henry Cooke, an English bass singer, choir trainer and composer, was born at Lichfield (died 1672, July 13).

Sir William Leighton, English musical editor and amateur composer, died (birthdate unknown).

Engelmann studied at Leipzig at this time.

Nicholas Strogers, organist and composer, contributed a galliard to Jane Pickering's lute-book this year.

1617
(January 6) Monteverdi on this date wrote to Alessandro Striggio realizing that the libretto under discussion was not for a whole opera, but rather for an "intermezzo" to be performed

1617(cont.)
between acts of a larger work.

(January 20) Monteverdi wrote to Alessandro Striggio accepting the possibility of a commission in honor of the Duke of Mantua's marriage.

(January 27 and February 1) Porter, on the death of Peter Wright (January 27), was sworn a Gentleman of the Chapel Royal on February 1.

(February 22) Nicholas Lanier's music for "Lovers made Men" was performed on this date and introduced "stilo recitativo" to England.

(March 9) Weelkes composed the anthem "Deliver us O' Lord" on this day.

(May 1) Johann Woltz had been Heilbronn's organist and church administrator for forty years.

(June 12) Pierre Bonhomme, a Netherlandish priest, singer and composer, died at Liege (birthdate unknown).

(August 31) Alessandro Grandi was appointed a singer at St. Mark's in Venice on this date.

(February) Hans Christoph Haiden, German organist and composer, died (born 1572, February 14).

(March) S. Orlandi produced his opera, "Gli amori d'Aci e di Galatea" at Mantua.

Barbarino died shortly after this date (birthdate unknown).

Coryate, a Venetian writer on music, died (born 1577).

Giovanni Pietro Flaccomio, an Italian composer, died at Turin (birthdate unknown).

Kaspar Förster, a German singer and composer, was born at Danzig (died 1673, March 1).

Sir William Leighton, who died prior to this date, was among the contributors of verse to Allison's psalter of 1599.

Guillaume Nevers, a French organist, theorist and harpsichord composer, was born at Melun (died 1714).

Jakob Paix, a German organist and composer, probably of French -Netherlandish origin, died after this date at Augsburg (born 1550).

Antonio Pinheiro, a pupil of Guerrero's and director of music at the chapel of the Dukes of Braganza, died (birthdate unknown).

Gabriel Bataille was appointed master of the Queen's music this year.

Borlasca was court "Kapellmeister" at the Munich court chapel at this time.

Bull was appointed organist at Antwerp Cathedral at this time.

Cavalli this year became a singer in the choir at St. Mark's under Monteverdi.

Dallam this year built a double organ for the Chapel Royal Holyrood, Edinboro.

Richard Deering (Dering) was organist at the convent of English nuns in Brussels this year and perhaps even earlier.

It was discovered from the title
-page of his first work, published this year, that A. Diruta
was a nephew of Girolamo Diruta
and a pupil of his.

Effrem was at the court of Mantua
at this time.

Amante Franzoni was maestro di
cappella at Santa Barbara,
Mantua at this date.

Daniel Friderici became cantor
at the St. Marien-Kirche this
year.

Jacques Gaultier, the French
lutenist, went to England this
year.

Ferdinando II Gonzaga married
Caterina de'Medici at this time.

Tommaso Graziani was maestro di
cappella at several churches in
Milan at this time.

It was apparent that King James,
having so long enjoyed the music
of his English Chapel Royal, was
anxious to have something similar
in Scotland.

Giovanni Battista Leonetti was
organist of the church of Sant'
Agostino at Crema at this time.

B. Marini was employed this year
as a violinist at Venice.

Claudio Merulo's nephew this
year presented "an organ for the
most part by the hand of the most
excellent musician, Claudio
Merulo of Correggio, uncle of the
donor" to a confraternity at
Parma.

The abbey in Himmelwitz where J.
Nucius served as abbot burnt
down this year.

Jacob Paix was organist at
Neuberg until this year when he
died.

Abraham Schade retired in
Bautzen at this time.

Thomas Simpson at this time was
employed at the court of the
Count of Holstein-Schaumburg.

Hans Ulrich Steigleder, an organist and composer, was appointed
"Stifts-Organist" at Stuttgart.
He served also at this time as
musician generally to the court
of Württenberg.

Tomkins took a lease on a house
this year.

Giovanni Battista Ala composed
canzonets, madrigals and operas
published at Milan this year and
in 1625.

Domenico Allegri's "Modi quos
expositis in choris" was published this year at Rome.

Anerio this year published
"Diporti musicali" and "Selva
armonica" for one to four voices.

Anerio this year published a
book of motets for one to eight
voices.

Baccusi's "Regulae spiritualis
melodiae, seu Liber spiritualium
cantionus" was published at
Antwerp this year.

Composers at this time often
made the lute arrangements
themselves, as can be seen in
the typical title "Airs de
différents auteurs mis en

tablature de luth par eux
-mesmes." This collection was
published this year by Ballard.

Barbarino's sixth secular book
was published this year.

Girolamo Belli's ninth book of
five-part madrigals was published this year at Venice.

Pietro Benedetti issued at least
four books of "Musiche," the
last this year.

Besard's last two works on the
lute, "Novus partus, sive
concertationes musicae diodena
trium . . ." and "Isagoge in
artem testudinariam . . ." were
published this year at Augsburg.

A printed collection including
Besardus' "Novus partus sive
concertationes musicae"
(Augsburg, 1617) and Tritonius'
"Harmonie" (Augsburg, 1507) was
preserved at Strassbourg,
Germany.

An early dramatic type of
"ballet de cour," "La
Délivrance de Renaud," composed
by several musicians, including
Boesset and Guédron, appeared
this year.

Brade's "Newe ausserlesene
liebliche Branden . . ." for
five parts was published this
year at Hamburg.

A duet by Brunelli was included
in Calestani's "Madrigali et
arie" this year.

Brunelli's "Sacra cantica" for
one to four voices appeared at
this time.

Besides the freely conceived

(cont.) ground basses of the
chamber cantata, some traditional
bass melodies going back to the
Renaissance served as the basis
for vocal and instrumental
variations or provided the harmonic foundation for improvised
singing of popular poetry called
"ottave rime." This technique
was described in Calestani's
"Modo di cantar ottave" written
this year.

Calestani this year published an
extremely attractive collection
of "Madrigali ed arie" at Venice.

Calvisius' "Der Psalter Davids
. . ." was published this year
at Leipzig.

Cardoso wrote a flattering introduction for Coelho's "Flores
de musica" this year.

Cecchino's "Madrigali e
canzonette a 3 v. et basso continuo" appeared at this time.

Ceresini's first book of motets
was completed this year.

Cortellini's masses were published at this time by Vincenti.

Daser's organ piece "Nova
Musices . . ." was published
this year at Woltz.

Dering's "Cantiones sacrae" for
five voices was published at
Antwerp at this time.

A. Diruta's "Sacrae Cantiones
. . ." appeared this year.

Besard's "Novus partus sive
concertationes musicae" of this
year included among other pieces
for lutes a version of Dowland's
"Lachrime" for three lutes, an
unusual combination.

Effrem participated in the composition of "La Maddalena."

This year Ferrabosco II and Lanier set an entire masque by Ben Jonson to music in "stile recitativo." This work might well be called the first English opera.

(Don) Giacomo Fornaci's "Amorosi respiri musicali" for one to three voices was published this year.

Franzoni's third book of "Fioretti musicali" was published at this time.

Gagliano's "Il sesto libro de madrigali a cinque voci" was published this year.

Carlo Gesualdo's second book of five voice madrigals was reprinted this year for the fifth time.

Giacobbi composed his opera "Il Reno sacrificante" this year. The libretto was by Campeggi.

Gibbons composed "Great King of Gods" at this time.

Giovanni Battista Grillo's "Sacri Concentus ac Symphoniae" was published this year.

Heinrich Hartmann this year composed two books of sacred songs for five to ten voices, as well as masses and motets (See also 1613).

Johann Heller, a German composer, at this time wrote "Sacer concentus musicus," containing five masses, motets, psalms, etc. Two sonatas and two pieces from this same year

(cont.) have also been preserved.

Instrumental pieces by Johnson II were included in Brade's "Newe ausserlesene Branden . . ." published in Hamburg or Lübeck this year.

Kapsberger's "Capricci a due stromenti," for lute and theorbo, appeared at this time.

Nicholas Lanieri (with Ferrabosco II) composed music this year to Ben Jonson's masque "Lovers Made Men."

Marini's sonata "La Gardan" provided an early example of "instrumental monody." It was composed at this time.

Marini's concerted instrumental music, opus 1, "Affetti musicali . . . symfonie, canzone, sonate, balletti, arie, brandi, gagliarde e corenti a 1, 2, 3," was published this year at Venice. It included sonatas for two violins, the first one ever for one violin and accompaniment and also trio sonatas.

Francesco Milleville composed his concerto "Fantasia alla Francese" for instruments this year.

Monteverdi's "Andromeda" with libretto by Ercole Marigliani was issued this year at Mantua.

A fragment of Monteverdi's "La Maddalena" (libretto by Andreini) was published by Gardano at Venice.

Monteverdi's "Le nozze di Peleo e di Tetide" with text by Scipione Agnelli was published at Mantua this year.

1617(cont.)

G. Olivieri's "La Turca Armoniosa," two and three voiced madrigals to his own text, appeared at this time.

Only the second book of P. Pace's "Scherzi et arie spirituali concertate" for one to seven parts survived. The work was published this year at Venice.

D. Pecci's book of madrigals appeared at this time.

Vincenzo Pellegrini wrote instrumental pieces in three and four parts included in Lucino and Lomazzo's "Seconda aggiunta alli concerti" of this year.

Compositions for lute by Polak were included in Besard's "Novus Partus give concertationes musicae."

Quagliati's "Affetti amorosi spirituali" for one to three voices was completed this year.

Enrico Radesca di Foggia's "Quinto Libro delle canzonette, Madrigali et Arie, a tre, a una, et a due voci" was published this year at Venice.

Schein's "Banchetto Musicale, neuer anmuthige Padouanen, Gagliarden, Courenten un Allemanden a 5 auf allerley Instrumenten . . ." was published this year at Leipzig. The variation suite assumed its classic form in this work with each of the five dances having the same melodic theme as well as being in the same key. The suites included pavans, galliards, courantes, allemandes, and triplas or Nachtänze in triple time.

Schein composed an entrada, a pompous piece for four to six instruments written in note-against-note style.

A rare piece of music, set specifically for krumhorns, Schein's "Paduana a 4 Krumhorn," was issued this year at Leipzig.

Simpson's "Pavanen, Volten und Galliarden" was reprinted at this time.

Palazzotto Tagliavia this year published a book of Madrigals for five voices at Naples.

Vitali's "Musiche a due, tre, e sei voci" was published this year at Florence by Zanoki Pignoni.

Woltz's "Tabulatura nova" was published at this time. It contained motets, canzonets and fugues.

At this time Campeggi and Giacobbi produced "Il Reno sacrificante" at the Teatro della Sala.

Nicholas Lanier sang the "Masque presented at the House of Lord Hayes" for the entertainment of the French Ambassador. Lanier also ordered and made both the scene and the music.

Slurs occured as early as in Marini's publications of this year.

Peri, with Gagliano, wrote "La liberazione di Tirreno ed Astrea" this year.

Isaac Posch, a composer of variation suites, this year observed thematic unity less consistently than Schein.

1617(cont.)

The first mention of recitative appeared in Ben Jonson's "Vision of Delight," a charming masque produced this year.

"Lovers made Men" prompted Jonson to state, " . . . the whole Maske was sung (after the Italian manner) Stylo recitativo."

Evaristo Baschenis, an Italian painter, was born (died 1677). He painted groups of beautiful musical instruments in the spirit of Caravaggio.

Blondel, a French architect, was born (died 1686).

Eustache Lesueur, a French painter who exerted a lasting influence on European art, was born (died 1655).

Bartolomé Esteban Murillo, a Spanish painter, was born (died 1682).

Gerard Terborch, a Dutch painter, was born (died 1681).

Emanuel de Witte, a Dutch painter, was born (died 1692).

(to c.1620) Paul Schaeffer was a town musician in Gera during these years.

(to 1621) After Orazio Gentileschi had left Rome for the Marches of these years to Genoa, Paris, and finally London, the more conservative elements of his art gradually gained the upper hand.

(to 1622) Spanish painting: Velasquez, "Old Woman Cooking Eggs."

(to 1623) Jan Hommel built an organ at Olkusz during these years.

(to 1624) It is not known where Capece lived, but since he referred to himself as "Romano," even though not born in Rome, he may well have lived there during these years.

(to 1624) Robert Fludd (Flud)'s "Utriusque cosmi majoris, scilicet et minoris metaphysica, physica atque technica historia" was printed at Oppenheim during this period.

(to 1625) Vernizzi during these years wrote five "azioni drammatiche," the first interludes performed at Bologna.

(to 1626) Paul Schaeffer wrote eight volumes of sacred and secular music during this period.

(to 1635) English architecture: Inigo Jones, Greenwich, Queen's House (116' x 116' x 43' high).

(to 1639) Francesco Milleville during these years composed masses for three to eight voices, psalms, litanies, concerti spirituali, sacre gemine, concertos for one to four voices with continuo, as well as seven books of motets for two to six voices.

(and 1640) Valdrighi reported finding the term piano e forte in letters and inventories of records of the d'Este family as early as 1598. There were two instruments, "l'instromento Piane e Forto con l'horggano disotto, un altro istromento di due registri et il Piane e Fortte." These terms were found in documents of both the

179

previously mentioned years.

(to 1642) Boesset's nine books of "Airs de cour" in four and five parts were published by Ballard during these years.

(to 1647) Jacques Gaultier, the French lutenist, was court lutenist at London during this period.

(to 1655) The great variety of Marini's published compositions of these years reflected the transition from imitation of vocal music to genuine instrumental forms.

(to 1672) Schütz served for these fifty-five years as music director to the elector of Saxony at Dresden.

c.1617

Pomponio Nenna, Italian composer and Gesualdo's teacher, died (born c.1555).

Jakob Paix, German organist and composer, died at Augsburg (born 1550)See alternate entry, 1617.

Campian's third and fourth books of ayres contained a reference to the Overbury Plot, and therefore could not have been published before Sir Thomas Monson's innocence was established this year.

Campion's works included songs for five masques and four other volumes of ayres. Two of them were probably published in c.1613 and the other two in this year.

Francesco Cavalli and Alessandro Grandi were appointed singers at St. Mark's at this time.

1618

(March 9) Belli wrote the music for Jacopo Cicognini's "Andromeda" performed at the Palazzo Gherardesca, Florence on this date.

(April 21) Monteverdi submitted the music for "Andromeda" to Striggio. The opera has not survived.

(April 28) Rubens on this date wrote a letter to Sir Dudley Carleton, specifying which of a group of works he had personally painted and where were dome by his collaborators.

(June 12) C. Huygens wrote a letter on this date in which he spoke of his enjoyment of the concerts at Monsieur Biondi's.

(July 21) Monteverdi wrote Striggio and sent him more completed portions of "Andromeda."

(October 6) Ann Gibbons, daughter of Orlando, was baptized on this date.

(December 10) Giulio Caccini, Italian singer and composer, was buried on this date.

(December 24) Giacomo Vincenti, the music printer, worked until this date, when he was succeeded by Alessandro Vincenti.

(May) Anerio at this time arranged for the publication of Puliaschi's "Gemma musicale" which contained arias, madrigals and sonnets for solo voices.

(July) Arnold de Sayve, Netherlandish singer, died at Vienna (birthdate unknown).

(August) Kaspar Hassler, organ-

1618(cont.)
ist and eldest of Isaac's three
sons, died (born 1562, August).

(December) Giulio Caccini,
Italian singer and composer,
died at Florence (born c.1546).

The Spanish composer Juan
Cererols was born (died 1676).

Marcantonio Cesti (Pietro
Antonio), Italian composer, was
born at Arezzo according to a
respected source (died 1669,
October). Other sources have
given his date of birth as
1623, August 5.

Solomon Eccles, musician and
shoemaker, was born (died at
London 1683, February 11).

John Farrant, the English organist, died at Salisbury (born
1575).

Johann Franck, a German hymn-
writer, was born (died 1677).

Krzysztof Kraiński, Polish ecclesiastic and musician, died
(birthdate unknown).

Georgius Otto, German composer
and teacher of Schütz, died
(born 1544 or c.1550).

Borchgrevinck was promoted to
chapel master at the court of
King Charles IV at Denmark. He
held this position until his
death.

Bournonville was at Abbeville
at this time.

William Brade was at Halle and
from there went to Güstrow as
Director of Music.

L. Casali was at this time or-

(cont.) ganist at Scandiano,
Modena.

Fabio Costantini was at Orvieto
this year.

Dowland's name at this date still
appeared in the accounts as that
of second musician for the lutes.

On order of Ranuccio Farnese, a
theatre holding three thousand
people was built at Parma by G.
B. Aleotti of Argenta.

Ghizzolo became choirmaster at
Ravenna Cathedral this year.

This year Grandi became director
of singing at the Venetian seminary, succeeding Gaspare
Lucadello.

Jan Hommel built an organ in the
Mariacki Church at Cracow this
year.

C. Huygens, soon after the completion of his studies this year
at Leyden University, went to
London for the first time.

M. Pederson was appointed vice
-director of the royal chapel
at Denmark at this time.

Peri was appointed camerlengo
generale at Florence this year.

Posch was organist at Laibach at
this time.

Praetorius gave a slightly different setting than Cerone had
for the tuning of the Lira da
Braccio, however, still at the
same pitch.

Praetorius at this time referred
to the established violin as the
Polish "Geige."

1618(cont.)

Pedro Ruimonte was in Brussels at this time.

Stefanini was maestro di capella this year at Modena Cathedral.

The year Robert Tailour was "one of Prince His Highnes Musicians."

Ala this year wrote several madrigals, "Concerti ecclesiastici," issued at Milan (See also 1621 and 1628).

Lorenzo Allegri's "Primo libro delle musiche" published this year at Venice was an important source of music written for court entertainments at Florence in the early part of the century.

Four of the groups of dances which Allegri published this year were written for "balli" whose music music is attributed by the contemporary court diarist Cesare Tinghi to "Lorenzo" or "Lorenzino todesco del liuto," it might well be assumed that both names were actually Lorenzo Allegri.

Aguilera's "Canticum beatissimae Virginis Deiparae Mariae 8 modis seu tonis compositum" for four through eight voices was published at Caesaraugustae (Saragossa) this year by Cabarte.

Anerio published a book of motets for one to eight voices.

Ardemanio's "Falsobordoni" was published this year.

Farces were included in Ayrer's collection published this year.

Some "concerti" and "ricercari"

(cont.) for two voices by Bartei appeared at this time.

Bateson's "Second Set of Madrigals" appeared at this time.

The second edition of Part i of Bodenschatz' "Florilegium Portense" was published this year.

Borboni is known as a composer only by a volume of "Musicali concenti" of this year.

Boschetti published his "Strali d'amore" this year and included in the same volume some canzonets, madrigals, etc. for one to three voices and continuo. The works include considerable embellishments and show Caccini's influence.

Caccini's "Primo libro delle musiche a una e due voci" was printed at Florence this year.

Campanus' "Sacrarum odarum libri duo" appeared at this time.

The first edition of Ceresini's "Messa et salmi" for five voices, Opus 3, was issued this year.

Fabio Colonna this year published a description of Trasuntino's Archicembalum with drawings of an enharmonic keyboard.

Fabio Costantini published another set of motets this year by different composers.

Croce's "Il primo libro de madrigali a 6 voci" was reprinted at this time.

Debolecki's "Completorium

Romanum quinis vocibus
decantandum una cum basso
continuo pro organo, opus
tertium" was this year published by Giacomo Vincenti at
Venice.

Dering's "Cantica sacra" for six
voices was published at Antwerp
this year.

Descartes in his "Compendium
Musicae" of this year recognized
the true nature of syncopation.

A. Diruta's "Davidis exultantis
cantica" appeared at this time.

Donati's "Concerti ecclesiastici
a 1, 2, 3, & 4 . . ." appeared
this year.

Donati's Motetti concertati a 5
& 6 voci con dialoghi, salm e
letanie della B.V. e con il
basso continuo per l'organo
. . ." appeared this year.

John Earsden and George Mason
wrote the music for "Ayres that
were sung and played at
Brougham Castle . . . in the
King's Entertainment" this year.
The words were written by
Campian and published with the
music at this time.

M. East published his fifth set
of books this year.

East's "The madrigals in his
third and fourth books" were
issued in this year and in 1610.

"Armoniose voci," Orazio
Giaccio's first book of three
-part canzonette, was reprinted
this year.

"Laberinto amoroso," Orazio
Giaccio's third book of three

(cont.) -part canzonette, was
published at this time.

Girolamo Giacobbi this year
published a collection of
motets.

Gibbons wrote the anthem
"Behold thou hast made" for the
funeral of Anthony Maxey, Dean
of Windsor.

Francesco Lambardi's second set
of "Villanelle" for three to
five voices was reprinted at
this time.

Marini's concerted instrumental
music Op. 2 "Madrigale et
symfonie, a 1, 2, 3, 4, 5" was
published this year at Venice.

George Mason composed and pub-
lished with John Earsden, "The
Ayres that were sung & played
at Brougham Castle in
Westmerland, in the King's
Entertainment, given by the Rt.
Hon the Earl of Cumberland &
his Rt. Noble son, the Lord
Clifford."

Michel's "Lettera di R.M. rom.
alli . . . sig eccellentiss,
musici della cappella d. N.S.
ed altri musici eromani miei
Patroni osservandissimi" was
published by Vincenti at Venice
this year and included a canon
in twelve parts.

Milanuzii's "Messe concertate"
for four parts was published at
Venice this year.

A second edition of "Pammelia"
was published this year by
Snodham at London. The work
was a collection of catches,
canons and rounds.

M. Praetorius wrote "De

1618(cont.)
Organographia" at this time.

Praetorius' "Syntagma musicum" was published this year at Wolfenbüttel. Evidence was included in the work to the effect that the bellows-blown bagpipe was already in use in France.

Puliti wrote songs for a solo voice with bass this year.

Barnaby Rich referred to fifers as "wry-necked musicians" in his "Aphorisms" written at this time.

Schein's "Opella nova, erster theil Geistlicher concerten mit 3, 4 und 5 Stimmen zusampt dem General-Bass auf jetzo gebräuchliche italienische Invention componirt" was published at Leipzig. It was a major event in the development of the chorale "concertato."

Schütz' concerto in two parts was published this year.

Schütz' "Die Worte Jesus Syrach: Wohl dem, der ein tugendsam Weib hat" was published this year.

Staden this year published a collection of dances - pavans, galliards, courantes, etc.

Stadlmayr this year published "Cantici Mariani septies variati cum 12 voc. cum triplici bass. org."

Steffani's "Affetti amorosi" were reprinted this year by Chilesotti, in "Biblioteca di raritá musicali III."

Valentini published a book of madrigals at this time.

Vallet's "Secretum Musarum" was published this year under the title of "Paradisus musicus testudinis."

Two of Verdina's motets and two canzoni for three voices were included in Giacomo Vincenti's "Lilia sacra" published at this time.

Vitali's "Musiche a una e due voci, libro secondo" was published by G.B. Robletti this year at Rome.

Jacob Vredman this year published a treatise "Isagoge musicae."

Erasmus Widmann published a dance collection at this time.

Maini this year mentiond scordatura in his "Sonata Seconda per il violino."

Marston's "Masque of Montebankes" was produced this year.

M. Praetorius mentioned scordatura (mis-tuning) in his "De Organographia" published this year.

The most decided stimulus for the progress of opera in Germany came from Italy. This can be established as early as this year at Salzburg.

Abraham Cowley, English essayist, poet, and prose writer, was born (died 1667).

Richard Lovelace, English Cavalier poet, was born (died 1658).

Isaac Voss, an English scholar, was born at Leyden (died 1689, February 21).

1618(cont.)

Gerhard J. Voss was a professor
of rhetoric at Leyden at this
time.

Sir Walter Raleigh, English
poet, soldier and statesman,
died (born c.1552). He was
executed by order of King James
I for alleged treason.

The "Thirty Years War" began
this year in Germany.

Sir Peter Lely, an English
painter, was born (died 1680).

Frans Pourbus, a Flemish painter,
became a French citizen. He
was a painter for King Henry IV.

(to 1619) Allegri published two
volumes of "Concertini" printed
by Soldi of Rome at this time.

(to 1619) Karel Guillet was
"hoofdman" (chief) at Bruges
during these years.

(to 1619) Part I of M.
Praetorius' Vol. II and Vol.
III were published during these
years at Wolfenbüttel.

(to 1619) Johann Schop was a
violinist at the Danish court
during these years.

(to 1619) The "Secretum musarum"
reappeared in a two-volume
French edition at this time.
The second half included works
for several lutes.

(to 1619) Vallet's lutebooks
issued during these years contained English dances and fantasies.

(to 1625) Thomas Simpson was
active at the court of King
Christian IV of Denmark during

(cont.) these years.

(to 1628) Francesco Bellazzi's
known works, which appeared
during these years, included
books of masses, motets, psalms,
etc.   The sixth book was numbered
opus 8.

(to 1632) Melchior Borchgrevinck
was director of music at King
Charles IV's chapel in Denmark
for this period.

(to 1633) Monteverdi's six
"lettere amorose" were published
during these years.

(to 1648) The weakened musical
culture of Germany was over-
whelmed by the catastrophe of
the Thirty Years War, however,
ultimately a wealth of musical
life developed and grew.

(to 1660) European wars during
these years resulted in the
downfall of the Hapsburgs and
Spain as a power. Meanwhile,
France and England became major
powers on the continent.

c.1618

Fernando de Almeida, a
Portuguese composer, was born
at Lisbon (died 1660, March 21).

Jacob Hassler, organist, composer and brother of Hans Leo,
died (born 1565, December 17/18).

N. Zangius, German organist and
composer, died (birthdate unknown).

Dutch painting: Rubens, "Rape
of the Daughters of Leucippus"
(7'3" x 6'10").

1619

(February 1) A signed receipt
for £·10 as a quarter's salary

1619(cont.)
to Orlando Gibbons as one of "his highnes musicions" carried this date.

(February 11) Caccini's "La fiera" was performed on this day.

(March 8) Veit Bach, Hungarian baker, and one of the first of the Bach family, died at Wechmar (born c.1550 or 1560). He was probably the father of Lips Bach.

(June 1) Stefano Landi on this date referred to himself as maestro di cappella to Marco Cornaro, bishop of Padua, in a dedication on the score of his opera "La morte d'Orfeo."

(June 11) Orlando Gibbons wrote "O all true faithful hearts" for a thanksgiving service held at Paul's Cross on this date to pray for the King's recovery from illness.

(July 18) Matthew White on this day received a share in the grant of the surveyorship of lands belonging to vicaries and rectories in England, Wales.

(September 19) Domenico Balli and his wife were engaged as musicians at the Medici court at this time.

(September 25) Gagliano and Peri's opera "Lo sposalizio di medoro et Angelica" was performed at the Pitti palace on this date.

(September 25) Francisco Soto de Langa, Spanish pianist, singer and composer, died at Rome (born 1534). He was Dean of the Pope's Chapel at the

(cont.) time of his death.

(October 19) Alessandro Ghivizzani succeeded Frediano Durelli as musical director of the municipal chapel of Lucca at this time.

(October 26) On the death of Henri Jamar at this time, Hodement became his successor as chapel master at St. Lambert's Cathedral, Liège.

(October 29) Musical education was widespread in Amsterdam at this time and intensive as well. An example of this was evidenced by indentures signed on this date binding a boy of eight years of age as an apprentice for five years to learn to play "viole, bas en de tenor" at the end of which term he would receive as presents "de bas en de viole."

(December 26) Filippo Vitali began writing "L'Aretusa" on this day.

(July) Bertolotti was probably correct in stating that Dognazzi became maestro at this time through the death of Orlando Sante.

(July) Sante Orlandi, an Italian composer, died at Mantua (birthdate unknown).

(October) Nicholas Yonge, English singer and musical editor, died (birthdate unknown).

Nicol Bach, an Arnstadt musician, son of Caspar and a member of the second generation of the Bach family, was born (died 1637).

Wendel Bach, a farmer, son of Lips, grandson of Veit, and a

member of the third generation
of the Bach family, was born
(died 1682, December 18).

William Birnie, Dean and Master
of the Chapel Royal at Scotland,
died (born 1563).

Valerio Bona died sometime after
this date (born c.1560).

Giovanni Caraccio, an Italian
madrigal composer, died (born
1555).

Heinrich (Enricus) Dedekind, a
German composer, died probably
at Lüneburg (birthdate unknown).

Sir Christopher Hatton, a
friend of Orlando and cousin of
Lord Chancellor Hatton, who was
Orlando's patron, died (birthdate unknown).

José Marin, Spanish tenor singer
and composer, was born at Madrid
(died 1699, March 17).

Muhammad, born Jalál Ridhavi,
at this time defended the use of
the harp in Persian music.

Jacobus van Noordt, probably a
brother of Anthony van Noordt,
was born (died 1679). He was
organist at the Oude Kerk in
Amsterdam and served on a committee for examining the organ
restoration by B.B. Duischot in
the Nieuwe Kerk.

The wife of Pierre (the younger)
Phalèse died at this time
(birthdate unknown).

Johann Rosenmüller, a German
composer, was born (See c.1619).

Christoph Runge, a German composer, was born (died 1681).

Francis Tregian, English musician, died at London (born
c.1574).

Matthias Weckmann, a German organist and composer, was born
at Oppershausen (died 1674,
February 24).

Bonometti's name appeared in the
records of the court at Vienna
this year as a singer.

Boschetti was probably choirmaster at the Roman Seminary
this year.

J.B. Comes was at this time
vice-master of the King's choir
of the Royal Chapel in Madrid.

Donati was "maestro di cappella"
of the Arciconfraternitae
Accademia dello Spirito Santo at
Ferrara this year and in 1616.

An autograph preserved in the
"Album Amicorum" of Johann
Cellarius of Nürnberg, who died
at this time, written toward the
end of the 16th-Century revealed
the name "Doland" which undoubt-
edly referred to Dowland.

Lute music grew in stature with
Gaultier, known as "le vieux,"
who served at the English court
from this time forward.

This year Gibbons succeeded
Walter Earle as one of the
"musicians for the virginalles
to attend in his highnes privie
chamber."

J. Herbst became Kapellmeister
at Darmstadt this year.

Adam Jarzebski this year became
a member of the royal orchestra
at Warsaw, where he remained
until his death.

1619(cont.)

Lipparino was an Augustinian
monk and maestro di cappella at
Como Cathedral at this time.

Tobias Michael became Kapellmeister at Sondershausen this
year.

Georg Otto was Kapellmeister at
Cassel until this date. He had
been tutor to Moritz and the
latter showed considerable talent for composition and ultimately became a patron of musicians.
Otto was at Cassel from 1588 to
this time.

The earliest reference to the
tenor bassoon was found in
Praetorius' writings of this
year.

The deeper "fagotti" were termed
"Doppel Fagott" by Praetorius at
this time.

Praetorius provided the earliest
detailed account of the "Fagotte"
or "Dolzianen" in his writings
of this year.

M. Praetorius examined the
Halberstadt organ as it had been
reconstructed in 1495 and he
recorded the dimensions of the
largest pipe in his "Syntagma
Musicum."

Praetorius this year mentioned
that trumpets were sometimes
made coiled "like a posthorn."

Praetorius stated this year that
the theorbo had single strings
while the double-necked lute or
theorbo-lute had them in pairs.

From this date until his death
Priuli was Kapellmeister" to the
Emperor Ferdinand II.

Hans Schreiber, "Kammermusikus"
of the electoral court in Berlin,
was said to be making a large
"Fagot Contra" this year.

Schütz first scored for two
bassoons this year. He scored
for three in 1621 and five in
1625.

Schütz married Magdalen Wildeck
this year.

John Tomkins went to London at
this time and became organist at
St. Paul's Cathedral in London.

Verdina went to Vienna prior to
this date.

Zacconi returned to Venice this
year to complete his theoretical
works.

Paolo Agostini's two volumes of
Psalms for four and eight voices
were published this year by Soldi
at Rome.

Anerio published his "La bella
Clori armonica" for one to three
voices this year.

Anerio published two books of
motets for one to eight voices
this year. One was called
"Ghirlanda di Sacre Rose."

Anerio's "Teatro armonico
spirituale" for five to eight
voices of this year consisted of
diaglogue laude, which used
chorus, soloists, and instruments, and made an important
contribution to the development
of the oratorio.

Giovanni Bacilieri's "Totum
defunctorum officium" for five
voices, opus 3, was published
this year by Bartolomeo Magni.

Banchieri's sacred vocal work "Sacra harmonia a 4" appeared this year.

Brade's "Mélodieuses Paduanes, . . ." was published this year at Antwerp.

Brunelli's twelve "concertato psalms" appeared at this time.

Charles Butler was the author of "The Feminine Monarchie; or a treatise concerning Bees" reprinted this year at Oxford (also 1609 and 1634).

Caccini this year wrote music for the younger Michelangelo's comedy "La fiera."

Campian produced a volume of Latin egigrams and elegiacs under the title "Poemata." It was published in 1595 and reprinted this year.

Cifra published a large number of masses this year.

Dering's "Cantiones Sacra" for five voices was published this year at Antwerp.

Two Polish dances for lute composed this year by Dlugoraj appeared in a lute tablature at the Stadtbibliothek in Leipzig.

Donati's "Concerti ecclesiastici . . . Opera IV . . ." appeared at this time.

Donati's "O Maria, dilecta mea" for three voices was completed at this time.

Donati's "Quae est ista" for two voices was composed this year.

Donati's "Sacrae et divinae cantiones, 2 & 3 voc., ad organus decantandae" appeared at this time.

M. East published his fourth set of books this year.

Two volumes of "Musiche" by Falconieri were published at Florence and Venice this year.

Alfonso Fontanelli's second book of madrigals was reprinted for the second time this year.

Amante Franzoni wrote his vesper psalms for six to eight voices at this time.

Gesualdo's third and fourth books of five-voice madrigals were reprinted for the third time this year.

A collection of Masses by Ghizzolo were published this year at Venice. They were composed "parte a cappella, parte da concerto," and were one of the earliest examples of the deliberate juxtaposition of the two styles.

Francesco Giuliani published his "Sacri concerti a 1-4 voci op. 1" this year.

Francesco Gonzaga, a member of the ruling family, published some canzonets and arias at this time.

Alessandro Grandi's "Celesti fiori-concerti a 2-4" was published this year.

The "Ballet de Tancrède" was written by Guédron at this time.

Gumpeltzhaimer's Psalm II for

eight voices was published this
year.

J. Kepler's "De harmonice mundi"
was published this year at
Augsburg. The entire Bk.III
(sixteen chapters) was devoted
to music.

Stefano Landi's madrigals for
four and five voices were published this year.

Rudolph Lassus this year published a collection of one hundred Magnificats composed by
his father.

Melanuzii's "Psalms" for two
voices was published this year
at Venice.

Monteverdi's "Concerto Settino
libro de madrigali a 1, 2, 3, 4
& 6 voci, con altri generi de
canti" was first published this
year.

Monteverdi published two of his
"lettere amorose" at this time.

The music to Monteverdi's opera
"Tirsi e Clori" was first issued
at this time.

Morley's second edition of "The
First Booke of Canzonets to two
voyces" was issued this year.

Psalms which used Horatian
meters were set to music by
Statius Olthoff and published
this year and in 1585.

A book of psalms by Patta was
completed at this time.

Peri's "Lo sposalizio di
Medoro et Angelica" was completed at this time.

Della Porta's collection of
"Villanelle a 1, 2, 3 5 voci,
accommodate per qualsivoglio
stromento" were published by
Robletti this year at Rome.

In Praetorius' "Polyhymnia
caduceatrix" of this year he
applied the continuo to the
Venetian style.

M. Praetorius published his
"Syntagma musicum" Vol. II this
year at Wolfenbüttel. It was
titled "Organographia." Volume
III was issued later this same
year and dealt with ornaments.

Schütz' "Psalmen Davids . . ."
was published this year at
Dresden. The works were polychoral.

Schütz' setting of Psalm
CXXXIII was published at Leipzig
this year.

Sweelinck's vocal works, particularly four books of psalms in
a metrical French translation by
Marot and Beza, were still written in renaissance style; only
the "Cantiones sacrae" of this
year employed continuo.

Usper published his "La Battaglia"
this year.

Vallet's "Vingt et un Pseasumes
de David; accomode pour chanter
et pour du luth ensemble" appeared this year.

Thomas Vautor published his "The
First Set: Beeing Songs of
diuers Ayres and Natures, of
Five and Sixe parts: Apt for
Vyols and Voyces" at this time.

Antonio Il Verso this year published his fourteenth book of
five-part madrigals at Palermo.

1619(cont.)

Zacconi's "Prattica de musica . . ." (second part) was published this year.

Campra's ballet "Trancrede dans la foret enchantee" was produced this year.

Palestrina and other composers connected with the counter-reformation composed laude in a simply polyphonic style. The dialogue laude, however, by Anerio in his "Teatro Armonico Spirituale" of this year have even a polyphonic "testo."

Praetorius this year showed an upper mordent under the name of "tremulus ascendens" and a lower mordent as "tremulus descendens."

Praetorius described "suitable pitch" as A = 424 cycles per second; S = 2·4 (the interval, expressed in equal tempered semitones, to one place of decimals, between each A and the one he took for his zero.

Praetorius, a contemporary of Caccini, showed an ascending slide in dotted or more than dotted form disliked by Caccini.

Praetorius included the springer in his category of accenti.

Soriano's "Passione" was produced this year at Rome.

Jean Baptiste Colbert, Mazarin's successor as chief minister, was born (died 1683). He went down in history for his establishment of manufacturing industries, granting them state aid and tariff laws, but meanwhile imposing strick legal regulations on them governing the quality and price of manufactured pro-

(cont.) ducts.

Archduke Ferdinand became emperor of Rome this year.

Thomas Campion, English poet, died (birthdate unknown).

Samuel Daniel, an English essayist and historian, died (born 1562).

Charles Le Brun, a French painter and creator of the French Academy, was born (died 1690).

Nicholas Hillyarde, a British painter, died (born c. 1547).

(to 1620) Barnaba Milleville, Franco-Italian composer, was maestro di cappella of Chioggia Cathedral during these years.

(to 1621) English architecture: Jones, London, Banqueting House (120' long x 75' high).

(and 1622) Thomas Vautor and Thomas Tomkins showed considerable originality in calling their single publications of these years, respectively, Songs rather than "madrigals." This was to indicate the rather strange mixture contained in the books.

(to 1633) John Oker was organist at Wells Cathedral during these years.

(to 1637) Emperor Ferdinand II led the Catholic forces during this period.

(to 1653) Archbishop Paris, Count Ladron, was in power at Salzburg during these years.

(to 1657) Giovanni Giacomo Arrigoni served for these years

as court organist at Vienna under
Emperors Ferdinand II and III.

(to 1672) Knowledge of Schütz music relied almost entirely on
his sacred compositions during
these years.

c.1619
Roger Micheal, a Flemish singer
and composer, died at Dresden
(born c.1550).

Johann Rosenmüller, German composer, born in Pelnitz, Vogtland,
Saxony (died 1684, September
10 or 11). See 1619 & 1620.

Carlo Milanuzii, an Augustinian
monk, was organist to his order
at Perugio at this time.

1620
(January 9) Johann Weishmann, a
German organist and composer,
was born at Wolgast, Pomerania
(died 1652, July 24).

(January 9) Monteverdi wrote to
Alessandro Striggio, complaining
that he did not have sufficient
time to do a good job composing
"Andromeda."

(February 1) Monteverdi wrote
to Striggio in acknowledgement
of the latter's instructions
regarding "Apollo."

(February 8) The date of the
first performance of Vitali's
"L'Aretusa," using two harpsichords, two theorbos, two
violins, one lute and one viola
da gamba.

(March 1) Thomas Campian
(Campion), English poet and composer, died at London (born
1567, February 12).

(March 8 and October 21) According to his letters to the younger
Striggio on these dates
Monteverdi apparently had a high
opinion of Dognazzi.

(March 13) Monteverdi wrote to
Striggio, refusing the offer to
return to the Mantuan court, and
scorning the treatment he had
received in the past.

(March 25) Joannes Nucius (Nux,
Nucis), German theorist, died at
Himmelwitz, Silesia (born
c.1556). He survived the partial
rebuilding of the burned abbey
house where he had been abbot at
Himmelwitz.

(May 10) Monteverdi wrote to
Alessandro Striggio once more.

(June 27) François Farinel, first
of a family of Italian violinists,
married Anne Chapaty on this date.

(August) Karel Luython,
Netherlandish composer, died
(born c.1556).

(October 10) Lips Bach, son of
Veit and member of the second
generation of the Bach family,
died at Wechmar (birthdate unknown). Forkel gave his date of
death as September 21 of this
year.

(November 17) Alessandro Grandi
became vice maestro di cappella
at St. Mark's in Venice on this
date.

(February) The Chapter Act-Books
recorded payments to Bull of the
sums of 12 "livres d'Artois"
(florins) on this date as well
as in 1623, February.

(September) A complaint was made
against Henry Eveseed, a Yeoman

of the Vestry, for drunkeness
and physical assault on Orlando
Gibbons at this time.

Thomas Adams, an English bookseller and publisher, died at
London (birthdate unknown).

Antonio de Belem, a Portuguese
composer, was born at Evora
(died 1700).

Jean Danican, a brother of
Michel, who served in music of
the Grande Écurie and played
fife, crumhorn, trumpet, marine
and oboe, was born (died 1679).

Thomas Mencken, who composed
German texts for Passion music,
died (born 1550).

Abbé Pierre Perrin, who helped
establish the Académie Royale de
Musique and create French opera,
was born (died 1675). See 1625.

Johann Rosenmüller, a German
composer of Chamber Sonatas,
was born (died 1684). He was a
conductor at Wolfenbüttel and a
rival of Lully. See 1619 & c.1619.

Pietro Ziani, an Italian organist and composer, was born at
Venice (died 1684, February 12).

A number of young students on
their way to musical and theological careers were put in the
care of Filippo Albini at Turin
before this year. The latter
gradually achieving prominence
as a musician.

In his chorale intradas this
year Michael Altenburg added a
chorale melody to the instrumental ensembles "so that every-
body could join in."

Caspar Bach, I this year left
Gotha for the city of Arnstadt.

Banchieri this year became abbot
of the church of Santa Maria in
Regola at Imola according to one
source. Another source placed
him this year as abbot of San
Michele.

Among Italian violinists Marini
excelled at writing entire
suites with the same melodic
material presented with four
different rhythmical aspects
(see "Il Priulino" of this year,
in Torchi, VII). Bassani and
Vitali were to use the same
technique later.

Bevin this year was referred to
as "organist of ye Cathedral at
Bristol."

Boesset at this time was sec-
retary-in-ordinary of the King's
"chambre."

By this time Boschetti had be-
come director of music at the
Benedictine hospital Saxia ad
S. Spiritus in Rome.

Bournonville was at Amiens
Cathedral at this time.

Brade this year went to
Copenhagen and remained there
for two years.

Brunetti was "maestro di
cappella" at Bologna Cathedral
this year.

Bull was living in a house ad-
joining the south door of the
cathedral at Antwerp at this
time.

Richard Dering was still at
Brussels this year.

Leandro Gallerano was organist of the church of San Francesco at Brescia this year.

Orazio Giaccio retired to the monastery of San Pietro a Maiella this year.

Santino Girelli was living as a composer at Brescia at this time.

Alessandro Grandi was "maestro di cappella" at St. Mark's from this time forward.

Alessandro Gualtere was maestro di cappella at the church of Santa Maria at Verona this year.

Robert Johnson II was named as one of the musicians who were to provide music for the proposed amphitheatre in London this year.

The Lämmerhirt family, which later married into the Bach family (Hedwig to Johann), set-tled this year at Erfurt, after leaving East Germany.

Stefano Landi returned to Rome from Padua this year.

As an example of the elaborate forms of certain dances at this time, the best was the courante "avogadrina" by Biagio Marini as included in "L'arte musicale in Italia" by Torchi, VII, 3.

Marini was director of music at the Church of Sant' Eufemia at Brescia this year.

Monteverdi visited Banchieri at Monte Oliveto at this time.

Negri remained at St. Mark's until this year when he was succeeded by Alessandro Grandi,

(cont.) the composer of an early cantate.

Orgas went to Poland at this time and was appointed chorus master of the Cathedral choir at Cracow.

At this time Peerson wrote songs for one or two soloists with short chorus and accompanied by instruments.

G. Picchi was organist at the church Della Casa Grande, at Venice at this time.

Praetorius in his "Theatrum Qustrumentorum" of this year illustrated keys for the thumbs both on large shawms and on bassoon types.

Edward Rabar settle this year at Edinboro as a printer. This was the first date known concerning his life.

Thomas Tomkins was made a Gentleman of the Chapel Royal this year.

Paolo Agostini's two volumes of Magnificats for one, two, and three voices appeared at this time.

Michael Altenburg's "Erster Teil newer lieblich und zierlicher Intraden" was published this year. The work was for violins, lutes, organs, etc.

Anerio published his "Salmi da vespro" at this time.

The farce "The Singing Simpkin" was translated into German ("Pickelherring in the Box) this year. Similar farces were con-tained in Ayrer's collection of 1618 and in the "Liebeskampf"

of 1630. This collection provided a large repertory of popular theatre based on English
models.

Banchieri's sacred vocal work
"Messe e motetti concertati" was
issued this year.

Heinrich Baryphonus'
"Institutiones musico
-theoreticae" was published this
year at Leipzig.

Coelho's "Flores de musica para
o instrumento de tecla e harpa"
was published this year by
Craesbeeck at Lisbon.

G. A. Colonna's "Intavolatura
di chitarra alla spagnuola" was
published this year.

Dering's "Canzonette" a 4 and
"Canzonette" a 3 were published
this year at Antwerp.

Donato's "Se pur ti guardo"
"Livre VII des chansons a 4
parties" was reprinted at
Antwerp (See also 1597, 1613 and
1636).

Gagliano's "Il sesto libro de
madrigali a cinque voci" was
published this year for the
second time.

Glaccio's "Armoniose voci," his
first book of three-part
canzonette, was reprinted this
year for the second time.

Santini Girelli's first book of
psalms was published this year.

Grandi's "Cantade et arie" was
reprinted at Venice this year.
The date of the first publication was unknown. It was one
of the earliest true examples

(cont.) of Strophic bass.

The name cantata first appeared
in Alessandro Grandi's "Cantade
a voce sola" of this year.

Alessandro Gualteri composed
masses for eight voices at this
time.

Bartholomaeus Helder wrote
"Cymbalum Davidicum," sacred
songs mostly taken from the
Psalms of David in five, six and
eight parts. He also composed
a number of sacred and secular
songs in various collective volumes. One song was the well
-known "Das alto Jahr vergangen
ist."

Herbst's "Meletemata sacra,"
twenty for three voices and one
for six voices was published
this year at Nürnberg.

Krzesichleb's Psalm Book containing a large number of
anthems, hymns and religious
songs was reprinted (See also
1601, 1603, 1640 and 1646).

Both Landi's and Grandi's
"Cantade ed Arie" were published
this year.

Marini's opus 3, "Arie, Madrigali
et corente a 1, 2, 3" was published this year at Venice.

Giulio Monteverdi was appointed
maestro di cappella at the
Cathedral of Salo (Lago di Garda)
at this time.

G. Monteverdi's "Affetti musici
- ne quali si contengono
motetti a 1, 2, 3, 4, et 6 voci,
per concertarli nel basso per
l'organo" was published this
year at Venice. The book contained twenty-five compositons.

C. Monteverdi's "Cantate Domino" for SSATTB and continuo was included in Giulio Cesare Banchi's Vol. I published this year.

C. Monteverdi's "Christe adoramus te" for SSATB and "Domine ne in furore" for SSATTB with continuo were included in G.C. Bianchi's "Motetti" Vol. I published this year.

C. Monteverdi's "Fugge, fugge anima mea" for two voices, violin and continuo and his "Obeatae viae" for SS and continuo were included in D. Lauro Calvo's collection published this year.

C. Monteverdi's "Lamento d'Apollo" with text by Striggio was issued this year.

G. Negro's "Canti academici a 2-6 voci, op. 11" appeared this year.

A volume of music, edited by Oberndörffer was published this year.

Pederson's "Pratum spirituale" was published this year by H. Waldkirch at Copenhagen.

Martin Peerson's "Private Musicke . . ." published this year suggested the use of virginals to accompany voices for the first time.

Peurl's "Pavanes, Intrade, Danses et gaillardes" was published this year.

Picchi's "Intavolatura di balli d'arpicordo" was issued this year at Venice.

Porta's "Sacro convito musicale (cont.) ornato di varie et diverse vivande spirituali" for one to six voices appeared at this time.

Part II of M. Praetorius' Vol. II was published this year.

Praetorius' "Sciagraphia" was published at this time.

M. Praetorius' Appendix, "Theatrum instrumentorum, seu sciagraphia, Michaëlis Praetorii C" was published this year at Wolfenbüttel.

Quagliati's motets and dialogues for four to eight voices were composed this year and in 1627.

Giovanni Battista Riccio's Sacred Concerto, "Jubilent omnes" appeared at this time.

R. Rognoni's "Selva di varij passagi" was composed at this time.

The second and third books of madrigals and airs by Saracini were published this year.

Claudio Saracini published his "La Seconde Musiche" this year and dedicated it to Monteverdi. Saracini was an outstanding monodist.

Scheidt's "Cantiones sacrae octo vocum" was published this year at Hamburg. The book was an important contribution to chorale motet literature.

Palezzotto Tagliavia's book of Madrigals for five voices was published this year at Palermo.

Vincenzo Ugolini composed two books of eight-part psalms at this time.

1620(cont.)

Vallet's "Piété Royal" was published this year.

A collection of motets by A.
Vincenti and several other composers was published at this
time.

Filippo Vitali this year published his opera "L Aretusa" and
dedicated it to Cardinal
Borghese. It marked one of the
first appearances of a lyrical
drama at Rome.

"Musiche a una, due e tre voci
per cantare nel cimbalo in
altri stromenti simili con
l'alfaketo per la chiterra un
quelle piu a proposito perfale
stromento" book three by Vitali
was published this year at
Rome.

Zoilo published his madrigals
for five voices this year at
Venice.

The Ainsworth Psalter was
brought to America by the
Pilgrims at this time.

The dramatic ballet had survived for a few decades in
France, but this time all pre-
tence of a unified plot was
abandoned, and the ballet reverted simply to a diversified
spectacle to provide amusement
at the court.

A new form, ballet à ontrées,
emerged in France. It consisted
of récits, dialogue portions
spoken by non-dancing actors,
entrees, the actual acts of the
ballet, and vers, actually narrative passages describing the
characters in the entrees.

The baroque style was fully

(cont.) established after this
date.

After this year the bow started
to lose more of its convexity,
especially the violin bow, although a quite considerable
curve was still a desideratum in
the viol group because of its
chordal demands.

Prior to this date, the term
"cantata" was applied only to
arias in the form of strophic
variations.

Canzonas by Merulo, Banchieri,
Mayone, Trabaci, and Cifra, published before this date, tended
to be polythematic and those of
Frescobaldi actually followed
the same trend at first.

The dolcian was a primitive
bassoon depicted and described
by Praetorius this year.

Besides the musical academies at
Bologna there were proper
schools of music in this year and
later in 1647 and 1700.

In all of Europe except Italy,
a certain amount of keyboard and
consort music was found in this
year and the next few years
printed in open score, each with
a stave of its own.

European lute and keyboard tab-
latures up to this time included
one or more settings of "passing
measures" and "quadro" pavans.
This practice had started in
1560.

After this date Italy, concerned
with form, experienced a mild
classical reaction in architecture and painting. Music did
not lag behind in this case as
it usually did.

197

1620(cont.)

Peri's opera "Adone," written this year for Mantua, was probably never performed.

After the emergence of opera in Northern Italy the leadership in the field moved to Rome, and then nearly twenty years later to Venice.

The first traces of the sonata were at this time. Certain important composers such as Marini, Neri, and T. Merula established its structure.

At the battle, "am weissen Berg" during the "Thirty Years War" the defeat of the Protestants destroyed all national culture in Bohemia.

King Gustaf Adolf of Sweden married a Brandenburgian princess who reorganized the Royal Chapel at Stockholm to follow the German fashion of this time.

A settlement was started at Plymouth, Massachusetts by a refugee group of Separatists from English Separatists who wished to abolish the national (Anglican) Church of England.

Silvio Fiorillo, a Neopolitan actor and the first to portray Pulcinella, died (born c.1570).

Sir Francis Bacon's "Novum Organum" was written this year.

Sir Francis Bacon at this time was accused by Parliament of bribe acceptance.

Israel Naǧgara, a great Palestinian poet, died (born 1550).

Albert Cuyp, a Netherlandish (cont.) painter, was born (died 1691).

Roger Pratt, an English architect, was born (died 1685).

Pierre Puget, a French sculptor, was born (died 1694).

Van Dyck paid a brief first visit to England.

A contract between Rubens and the Antwerp Jesuits (forty paintings for the church) was concluded this year. It provided for the master's designs to be executed by Van Dyck and other pupils who were unnamed.

(to 1621) During these years Altenburg's "Christliche liebliche und andächtige neue Kirchenund Hausgesänge" for six to nine voices was published in three volumes at Erfurt.

(to 1621) John Stanley was violist at Copenhagen during these years.

(to 1622) Diruta was "maestro di cappella" and organist at Asolo at this time.

(to 1622) Karel Guillet was a sheriff at Bruges during these years.

(to 1625) French painting: Valentin de Boullonge, "The Tavern."

(to c.1630) When Thomas Adams died in 1620 his business (sales and publishing) was carried on by his widow for these few years.

(to 1630) The cantata, a shorter and more lyrical version of the oratorio, slowly emerged at this time as a third form of monodic singing.

(to 1630) The canzonetta was abandoned during these years.

(to 1630) Gibbons' "Fantazies of III Parts" was reprinted during these years.

(to 1638) Landi's five books of arias for one and two voices were published during this period.

(to 1640) Lazaro Valvasensi's church music, psalms and motets were published during these years.

(to c.1643) During these years Jan Strzyzewski, a Polish composer, was a member of the royal chapel at Warsaw.

c.1620

Costanzo Antegnati, a noted Italian organist from Brescia, died (born 1557).

Catarina Baroni, a singer, harpist and poetess, died after this date (birthdate unknown).

Ercole Bernabei, an Italian composer, was born at Caprarola (died 1687, December 6).

Maurizio Cazzati, an Italian composer, was born at Guastalla (died 1677). He was an important and influential instrumental composer.

Francisque Corbett, an Italian guitar player, was born at Pavia (died 1681, March).

Alfonso Ferrabosco III was born at Greenwich (died before 1660). He was a violist and wind player.

Thomas Mancinus (actually Mencken), a German composer, died at Wolfenbüttel (born 1550).

Although it is assumed that Negri died in 1620, Venice State Archives list him among "Notaries of the Venetian State" from 1611 to 1621.

Jean Philidor, a member of the French family of musicians née Danican (the name Philidor was bestowed on them by Louis XIII), was born (died 1679). He was a fifer, crumhorn, trumpet and drum player as well as a dance music composer.

François Roberday, a French organist and composer, was born at Paris (died c.1690). Not much of his organ music survived, but what did was of high quality.

Antonio Sartorio, an Italian composer, was born at Venice (date of death unknown). He wrote opera in the heroic style of Monteverdi and Cavalli.

The ayre continued to flourish during this period.

Andre Maugars, a French violinist, spent four years in England playing the viol at the court of King James I.

Jacob Rayman settled in London to become "the father of violin making in England.

At this time a French artist, Richard, the first who substituted small slips of cloth in place of the quill for producing sound on the harpsichord was active.

Scheidt became Kapellmesiter to Christian Wilhelm, Margrave of

1620(cont.)
Brandenburg, at this time.

A sergeant-major Kennedy composed a corranto that has been preserved.

After this time the issue of printed music books in England (except versions of the Psalms) seemed to diminish.

The Rowallan manuscript volume of vocal music was compiled at this time.

"Benjamin Cosyn's Virginal Book" including compositions by Bull, Cosyns, Gibbons, and others, appeared at this time.

The "FitzWilliams Virginal Booke" of this year included:

    Forty-four works by Bull
    Seventy-two works by Byrd
    Fifty-three works by Farnaby
    Two works by Gibbons
    Nine works by Morley
    Ninetween works by Philips
    Two works by Tallis

Dutch painting: Jacob Jordaens, "The Four Evangelists" (oil on canvas, 52½" x 46½ ").

Dutch painting: Rubens, "Helena Fourment" (30½" x 21").

1621
(January 5) P. Philips exchanged his canonry of Soignies with Jérôme van den Berghe for a perpetual chaplainship in the church of Saint-Germain at Tirlemont.

(February 15) Micheal Praetorius, musical scholar and composer, died at Wolfenbüttel (born 1571, February 15). He was born Schulz or Schulze and

(cont.) was one of the major organizers of Protestant church music.

(March 16) Georg Neumark, a German poet and musician, was born at Mühlhausen, Thuringia (died 1681, July 8).

(March 28) Mathias Albani (Alban), an Austrian violin maker, was born at Kaltern, near Bozen (died 1712, February 7).

(March 28) Heinrich Schwemmer, a German singer and composer, was born in Franconia (died 1696, May 26).

(April 19) Mary Gibbons, daughter of Orlando, was baptized on this date.

(April 29) Pietro Pace's music for intermezzi, "L'Ilarocosmo, overo Il mondo lieto," was written for the marriage of Federico Feltrio della Rovere and Claudia de Medici. It was performed at Urbino at this time.

(June 21) Krystof Harant, a Czech nobleman, warrior, writer and accomplished composer, died at Prague (born 1564).

(July 14) Edmond Hooper, an English organist and composer, died at London (born c.1553).

(July 14) Jacob Stainer, the patriarch of Austrian violin makers, was born at Absam near Hall (died 1683).

(October 16) Jan Peterszoon Sweelinck, Dutch organist and composer, died at Amsterdam (born 1562, May). He was a disciple of Andrea Gabrieli.

(October 21) Alessandro Vincenti

1621(cont.)

dedicated the first book of
Nenna's four-part madrigals to
Alessandro Grandi.

(December 7) John Parsons was
appointed organist and master of
the choristers of Westminster
Abbey òn this day.

(August) Antonio Verso II, an
Italian composer, died at
Polermo (born c.1565). The
month of death is not an absolute certainty.

(September) Jacob Vredman, a
Flemish musician, died at
Leeuwarden (born c.1563).

(December) William Inglott,
English organist and composer
at Norwich Cathedral, died at
Norwich (born 1544).

Pierre Guédron, French choral
madrigal composer, died (born
1565). He worked in the medium
of "ballet de cour." See 1625.

Christof Harant of Polžic and
Bezdruzic, composer and author,
died (See June 21).

Constable de Luynes, who had
been in charge of the creation
and life of the "ballet
mélodramatique," died (birthdate
unknown).

Georg Neumark, German hymn composer, was born (died 1681).

Ottavio Rinuccini, Italian writer active in the field of opera
librettos, died (born 1562).

Francesco Soriano, Italian com-
poser, born at Suriano
(Viterbo), died (born 1549).
He studied under Zoilo, Roy, G.
B. Montanari, G.M. Nanino, and

(cont.) Palestrina.

Matthias Weckmann, a North
-German organ composer, was born
(died 1674).

Filippo Albini, who was deputized
from this date forward for
Sigismondo d'India, was absent
from the court for long period
during which he composed "balli,"
"melodrammi," and other works.

Campanus was rector of Prague
University at this time.

Blas de Castro still held the
post of usher to the King at
this time.

William Cranford was represented
in the Ravenscroft Psalter this
year.

Gabriel Diaz appeared in Granada
this year.

A. Düben (the elder) went to
Stockholm at this time.

This year Alfonso Fontanelli
took holy orders and was received
into the Convento de' Padri della
Chiesa Nuova in Rome.

Alessandro Ghivizzani was appointed chapel master at Parma
at this time.

Adam Gumpeltzhaimer was cantor
at St. Anna, Augsburg up to this
year. He had started in the position in 1581.

Edmund Hooper was employed by
Ravenscroft this year to harmon-
ize tunes for his Psalter.

This year Adam Janecki became a
substitute at the Chapel of
Raratists, and later became one
of the nine Chaplain-singers.

Romano Micheli was placed at
Aquileia for awhile this year.

Peter Philips this year became
canon at Tirlemont.

Crescenzo Salzilli's salary at
the church of the Annunziata in
Naples was increased from five
to six ducates per month at this
time.

Paul Schaeffer was a town musician in Breslau this year.

Johann Schop became director of
Council Music at Hamburg this
year.

Dirck Janszoon Sweelinck succeeded his father as organist at
the Old Church in Amsterdam at
this time.

Thomas Tomkins this year was
appointed one of the organists
of the Chapel Royal and became
a member.

Usper this year became deputy
to Grills, the organist at St.
Mark's in Venice.

Adson's "Courtly Masquing Ayres
composed to 5 and 6 parts for
Violins, Consorts and Cornets"
was reprinted this year.

Allegri published two volumes
of "Motetti" this year. They
were printed by Soldi of Rome.

Anerio at this time published
"I lieti scherzi" for one to
four parts.

Belli's set of "Concerti ecclesiastici" for two and three
voices and organ appeared at
this date and 1613.

Five hymn tunes by John Bennet
were reprinted in Ravenscroft's
Psalter this year.

Samuel Besler's Passion according
to St. John was published this
year by Baumann at Breslau.

Some of Edward Blanck's music
was included in Ravenscroft's
Psalter of this year.

Erhard Bodenschatz' "Florilegium
Portense" appeared at this time.

Part II of Bodenschatz'
"Florilegium Portense" was issued
at this time.

Antoine Boesset's "Ballet du
soleil" was completed at this
date.

Brade's "Newe lustige Volten
. . ." for five voices was published this year at Berlin.

Brunetti composed his "Canticum
deiparae virginis" Opus 3 at
this time.

Works by F. Caccini were included
in Costantini's "Ghirlandetta
amorosa" published this year at
Orvieto.

Capilupi's "Concerti
ecclesiastici" was completed at
this time.

Castaldi's "Capricci a due
stromenti, cioe tiorba e
tiorbino" was published this
year at Venice.

Blas de Castro appeared in "La
Filomena" of this year, in the
Epistle titled "The Garden of
Lope de Vega."

Cerreto's "L'Amarillide," a
madrigal book, was completed

1621(cont.)

this year.

Cifra published a large number of masses this year.

The following works by Donati appeared this year:

"Benedicat nos Deus," for
three voices

"Exultavit cor meum" for two
voices

"Filiae Sion exultate" for
two voices

"Gaudebunt labia mea" for
two voices

"Hodie spiritus sanctus" for
three voices

"O dulcissime Domine" for
three voices

"Quando natus es" for two
voices

"Symbolae diversorum
musicorum 2, 3, 4 and 5
voc. cantandae"

Some of Dowland's works were included this year in Simpson's "Taffel-Consort."

A famous handwritten Fitzwilliam Virginal Book preserved at Cambridge, England could not have been copied prior to this date.

Franck wrote his "Teutsches musikalisches fröhliches Konvivium" for four to eight voices at this time.

A book of motets with sinfonias by A. Grandi was published this year. It was the first of three books.

Vincenzo de Grandis wrote his "Sacrae cantiones" for two to five voices this year at Rome.

Otto S. Harnisch wrote the text

(cont.) in German for a "St. John's" Passion composed this year.

D'India published two of his laments at this time.

A paduan by Edward Johnson was included in Simpson's "Taffel Consort."

Some instrumental pieces by Robert Johnson II were included in Simpson's "Taffel Consort" printed this year at Hamburg.

Leone Leoni's motets were included in the "Florilegium" published this year.

Hendrik Liberti this year published a book of "Cantiones sacrae."

Lobo's "Liber I" was printed this year by B. Moretus.

Lobo's "Liber missarum" was published at this time.

Philip Massinger's The Maid of Honour appeared at this time.

Micheli's "Certezza d'artificii musicali, non piu fatte, contenuli nelli dieci obliglie della messa a dieci voci; con la riposta all'apposizione, fatta dal Sig. A. Centonelli, Musico in Roma, sopra la quantita di essi obblighi, Dato in luce da R.M. rom. Beneficiato nella metropoli di Aquileia. Venetia Benfadino" quarto bore this date.

Micheli's "Copia di letters con manoscritta mandata dal Sig. A Centonelli musico in Roma a me R.M., ecc., con da risposta fattagli nelle presente stampe, . . . was published (quarto) this year by Bonfadino at Venice.

Micheli's "Madrigali a sei voci
in canone, con la resolutione
delle parti, nel quale per mezzo
de gli accidenti l'armonia
discende un' tuono e de poi
ascende il tuono qia disceso,
potendosi anco cantare per i
suoi riversi, come li musici
periti saniro, studio curioso
non piu veduto. Con un avviso
a lutti li Sig. musici di Roma.
Dato in luce da R.M. rom.
Beneficiato nella metropoli
d'Aquileia, Roma. Soldi" bore
this date.

Monteverdi's seventh book of
madrigals was published this
year.

Two previously published settings
of tunes by Morley and one
hitherto unpublished setting
were included in Ravencroft's
"Psalter" this year.

Nenna's first book of madrigals
for four voices was published
this year. Milanuzii had added
a continuo part to the book.

Three motets for eight voices
by Pacelli were included in
Bodenschatz' "Florilegium" of
this year.

Peerson's four-part setting of
the metrical psalm-tune
"Southwell" was included in
Ravenscroft's "Whole Booke of
Psalmes."

A second edition of "Les
Rosignols spirituels. Liguez
en duo, dont les meilleurs
accords, nommément le Bas,
releuent du Seigneur Pierre
Philippes, Organiste de leurs
Altezes Serenissimes" was issued

(cont.) this year by Veruliet.

A third edition of Philips'
"Gemmulae sacrae binis et ternis
vocibus cum basso continuo ad
organum" was published this year
by Phalese.

A short instrumental "aria a 4"
by Philips was included in
Simpson's "Taffel-Consort" published at Hamburg.

The Psalters of Prys, containing
some of the earliest Welsh
psalm-tunes were published at
this time.

Puliaschi this year was represented by one solo song in
Costantini's "Ghirlandetta
amorosa."

A dialogue for three voices by
Quagliati was included in
"Ghirlandetta amorosa" edited by
Costantini this year.

A collection of songs for one
and two voices by Roman composers, "Giardino musicale," was
dedicated to Quagliati at this
time.

Thomas Ravenscroft's Whole Book
of Psalms of this year like
Este's offered four-voices settings by the finest English composers. It was an important
addition to the list of psalters
and contained one hundred har-
monizations, forty-eight of
which were by Ravenscroft himself.

A third book of madrigals by
Crescenzo Salzilli was published
at this time.

Scheidt brought out works at
this time quite similar to those
in Schein's "Banchetto musicale."

1621(cont.)

Scheidt's "Ludi musici" was published this year.

Scheidt's "Paduanna, Galliarda . . ." was published at this time.

At this time the first part of Schein's "Musica Boscareccia, Waldliederlein auf Italien -Villanellische Invention . . ." was published.

Schütz' "Syncharma Musicum tribus Choris adornatum . . ." was published in Breslau this year.

Schütz first scored for two bassoons in 1619. He scored for three in this year and five in 1625.

Simpson's dance collections of 1611 were reprinted this year (See 1611).

Thomas Simpson's "Taffel-Consort Erster Theil" was published at Hamburg this year.

Staden this year composed "Harmoniarum sacrarum continuato" for one to twelve voices.

Simon Stubbs contributed several settings to Ravenscroft's "Whole Book of Psalms."

T. Thomkins' Dunfermlin and Worcester (psalm tunes) were published this year.

Turini's "Madrigali a 1, 2, & 3 con sonate a 2 & 3" was published at this time.

This was the date of the "Dalway" harp, made by Donal O'Dermody and Sir John Fitz Gerald of Cloyne, County Cork.

(cont.) Fragments that have been preserved justify the assumption that the instrument had a scale of fifty-two.

A chitarrone preserved at London bears the inscription "Andrew Taus in Siena, 1621."

Jonson's masque "The Gipsies Metamorphosed" was produced this year.

Jonson's masque "News from the New World discovered in the Moon" was performed at this time.

Jean de la Fontaine, French author, was born this year (died 1695).

Andrew Marvell, poet, politician and author of "The Garden" and "To His Coy Mistress," was born this year (died 1678).

John Donne this year was appointed Dean of St. Paul's by King James I.

"The Anatomy of Melancholy" by Robert Burton was published at London this year.

Two psalm tunes (one of them twice) by John Milton were included in Ravenscroft's "Psalter."

Marie de Medici this year summoned Rubens to decorate the gallery of Luxembourg Palace. This was the last great commission obtained by a foreigner in France.

Rubens advised Van Dyck to go to Italy where he studied Titian's work and stayed for six years.

1621(cont.)
Italian painting: Guercino,
"Burial of St. Petronilla"
(23'7" x 13'10").

Dutch painting: Hendrik
Terbrugghen, "The Flute Player."

Dutch painting: Cornelis De Vos,
"Portrait of the Artist and His
Family."

(to 1622) The first part of
Scheidt's sacred concertos was
published during this year.

(to 1623) Borlasca was again
vice-"Kapellmeister" at Munich
during this period.

(to 1623) The Papal reign of St.
Gregory XV, born at Bologna.

(to 1623) Under Pope Gregory XV
during these years Quagliati
was made Protonotary Apostolic
and Secret Chamberlain to the
Pope.

(to 1626) Henry Dumont received
his education at this time at
the collegiate Church of Notre
Dame.

(to 1628) Numberous airs by
Boesset were included in the
eight books of "Airs de cour de
différents auteurs" published
during these years by Ballard.

(to 1628) The few-voiced
"concertato" style with obliga-
tory continuo made its appearance in Schein's three-voiced
"Musica boscareccia" of this
period.

(to 1632) A number of airs by
Boesset were included in the
"Airs de cour mis en tablature
de luth," of which the tenth
book was composed by Boesset and

(cont.) published by Ballard
during these years.

(to 1634) Darby Scott during
these years was court harpist at
Copenhagen.

(to 1640) Dutch painting: Rubens,
"Landing of Marie de Médicis at
Marseilles" (c.12'11 1/8" by
9'8 1/8").

(to 1644) Castello's two books
of sonatas were published at
Venice during this period.

c.1621
(to 1622) The FitzWilliam book,
the largest known viginal book
of the period, was assembled at
this time.

(to 1622) Dutch painting: Van
Dyck, "Self portrait."

1622
(February 10) Caccini collaborated with Gagliano in "Il
martirio di Sant' Agata" first
performed on this date at the
Congregazione di San Giorgi at
Florence. Jacopo Cicognini
wrote the text.

(February 11) Alfonso Fontanelli,
Italian madrigal composer, died
at Rome (born 1557, February 15).

(February 20) John Patten's will
carried this date. His son-in
-law Orlando Gibbons was the
sole executor and residuary
legatee. There was a bequest of
£ 200 to Orlando's children.

(March 12) At the funeral rites
for Archduke Albert on this date
Peter Philips walked in the procession at the head of the
"Chapellains de la Chapelle de
la Cour."

1622(cont.)

(March 16) Elizabeth Gibbons, Orlando's daughter, was baptized on this date.

(April 11) Pietro Pace, Italian organist and composer, died at Loreto (born 1559).

(May 17) William Camden founded a Chair of History at Oxford and the degree of Doctor of Music was conferred upon Orlando Gibbons by Oxford.

(May 18) Oxford conferred the degree of Doctor of Music on William Heyther. It is fairy certain that Gibbon's anthem "O clap your hands" was used for the exercises.

(May 22) Giovanni Boschetto Boschetti, Italian composer, died at Loreto (born c.1570).

(May 28) F. Pilkington was curate of St. Martin's at Chester on this date.

(June 13) Bateson had a private grace of the senate of the Master of Arts degree.

(June 22) Gagliano's "Il martirio di Sant' Agata" was performed at the palace of the Cardinal de' Medici.

(July 15) Nathaniel Giles was awarded the degree of Doctor of Music by Oxford.

(July 15) Hodemont resigned as Chapel Master because of a grievance.

(July 16) Pierre Maillard, Flemish musical scholar, died at Tournai (born 1550).

(August 30) Alessandro

(cont.) Stradivari, father of Antonio Stradivari, married Anna, the daughter of Leonardo Moroni.

(September 4) Jacob Hintze, German musical editor and composer, was born at Bernau near Berlin (died 1702, May 5).

(September 30) Johann Sebastiani, a German composer, was born at Weimar (died 1683, spring). He was an early and noted composer of Passions.

(October 21) John Wilson was recommended to the Lord Mayor as one of the "Servants of the City for Music and voice."

(November 15) Byrd's will carried this date.

(December 10) Jacomo Rapalini, a Mantuan, was appointed a singer at St. Mark's at a salary of eighty ducats.

(December 13) Johannes Campanus, a Czech humanist, died at Prague (born c.1572, June 24).

(January) Giovanni Ghizzolo became choirmaster at Sant' Antonio in Padua at this time.

(February) Gagliano during this month sent the score of his "Il Medoro" to Mantua, but it was not performed.

(March) Boschetti was made "maestro di cappella" at the Santa Casa of Loreto at this time, however, after only two months' service he died.

(March) Cifra returned to Rome at this time to become choirmaster at St. John Lateran.

(May) Eleuterio Guazzi, an

1622(cont.)

Italian musician, died at Parma or Venice (born 1597, February 22).

Henry Ainsworth, the English theologian, died at Amsterdam (birthdate unknown).

James Clifford, English divine, was born at Oxford (died 1698, September).

Giovanni Giacomo Gastoldi, Italian madrigalist, died at Venice (born c.1545 or c.1560). There is a discrepancy as to both birth and death dates on Gastoldi (See also 1609).

Raffaello Rontani, an Italian composer, died at Rome (birthdate unknown).

Friedrich Weissensee, German composer, died (born 1560).

Steffano Bernardi entered the service of the Archduke Karl Josef, Bishop of Breslau and Brixen at this time.

William Brade was reappointed at Gottorf this year.

Blas de Castro's name occurred this year as being recommended for the position of scrivener in the royal rent-office at Avila.

Crüger was appointed cantor at the church of St. Nicolaus in Berlin this year.

Henning Dedekind was preacher at Gebsee, Thuringia at this time.

Peacham included Dering in his list of excellent composers this year.

Doni entered the service of Cardinal Barberini and went with him to Rome at this time.

Effrem was at the grand-ducal court at Florence this year.

Giovanni Giacomo Gastoldi was maestro di cappella at the church of Santa Barbara, Mantua up to this time when he died. He was appointed to the position in 1581.

Gery (de) Ghersem this year converted a canonry of Mons into one at St. James' church, Brussels.

Heather was permitted to use Gibbons' anthem "Lift up your heads" for this degree at Oxford this year.

Vincenz Jelich, an Austrian composer, was at this time vicar, canon and instrumental musician to the Archduke Leopold at St. Mary's Zabern, Alsace.

Henry Lawes' portrait was painted and hung in the bishop's palace at Salisbury this year.

Marini entered the service of Ferdinando Gonzaga at Parma this year.

Francis Markham in his "Five Decades" of this year described drumming as an unnecessary study.

Carlo Milanezii was organist at Sant' Eufemia, Verona at this time.

Francesco Milleville was at this time Maestro di Cappella and organist at San Giorgio, Ferrara.

Guglielmo Miniscalchi, an

Italian composer and Augustinian Monk, was maestro di cappella of the Church of Sante Stefano at Venice at this time.

G. Olivieri was maestro di cappella at St. John Lateren, Rome this year.

Arthur Phillips this year became a clerk of New College, Oxford.

On the title page of the second edition of P. Philips' "Deliciae" of this year he was still referred to as canon of Soignies.

Tomkins this year ventured into publication of his own works.

Lazaro Valvaseni was an organist at Murano this year.

Loreto Vittori this year entered the Papal chapel as a singer (male soprano).

Johann Baptist von Weber was at this time made Freiherr by Ferdinand II.

"Amoenitatum Musicalium, Hortulus plantulis amoenissimis, etc.," a collection of dances and a few songs of various nations, was published this year in Germany.

John Attey's "First Booke of Ayres of Foure Parts, with Tablature for the Lute" was published this year and the school of lutenists started to fade. Up to this time almost thirty volumes of ayres had been published.

Banchieri's "Cantorini utile a novizzi e chierici" appeared this year.

The third edition of Banchieri's "L'organo suonarino, Op. XIII" and Op. "XXXXIII," including "Frutto salutifero alli R.P. sacerdoti per prepararsi alla celebratione della S. Messa privata e cantata" was issued this year.

Banchieri's secular vocal work "Vivezze di Flora . . . a 5 voci nello spinetto o chitarrone" was completed this year.

Brizeño's "Metodo mui facilissimo para aprender a tañer la guitarra a lo español . . . en el qual se hallaran cosas curiosas de romances y esquidillas . . ." was published this year by Ballard at Paris.

Castaldi's "Capricci" for two theorboes of different sizes was composed this year.

The "Concentus a 2-4" was published at this time in Germany.

Fabio Costantini's "L'Aurata Cintia" appeared at this time.

Croce's "Cantiones sacrae a 8 voci" was completed this year.

Crüger's "Meditationum musicarum Paradisus primus, order Erstes musikalisches Lust Gärtlein" was published this year at Frankfort.

The dedication of A. Diruta's "Messe concertate a 5 voci . . ." as well as the work itself appeared this year.

The second edition of G. Diruta's "Il Transilvano" was published this year by Vincenti at Venice.

Donati's "Concerti, ecclesiastici . . . D'Ign. D

maestro di cappella della Terra di Casal Maggiore." appeared this year.

Donati's "Messe a 4, 5 & 6 voci, parte da cappella e da concerto con il basso per l'organo . . ." was completed at this time.

Donati's "Motetti a 5 voci in concerto . . . Novamente ristampate & con diligentia corrette . . ." was written at this time.

Robert Fludd (Flud)'s "Monorchordum mundi symphoniacum" was published this year.

Franck wrote his "Laudes Dei vespertinae" for four to eight voices this year.

Gagliano's "Basso generalis sacrarum cantionum unis ad sex decantandarum vocibus" was published at this time.

Alessandro Grandi's "Madrigali concertati" for two to four voices (bk. II) was published this year at Venice.

Eleuterio Guazzi's "Spiritosi affetti" was published this year at Venice.

Vincenz Jelich this year composed "Parnassia Militia," songs for one to four voices as well as four ricercari for two cornets and trombone.

"An Apotheosis of Ignatius Loyolo" by Kapsberger was published this year.

Malachowski's "Motetto de Resurrectione Christi: Resurrexit Dominus omnipotens,"

written for two sopranos, two altos, two tenors, two basses, two violins, double bass, alto and tenor trombones and organ continuo, was published at this time.

S. Mareschall's "Melodiae suaves et concinnae Psalmorum aliquot atque Hymnorum Spiritualium" appeared at this time.

B. Marini's instrumental opu 5, "Scherzi e canzonette a 1, e 2 voci," was published this year at Parma.

Francis Markham's "Five Decades and Epistles of Warre" was published this year at London.

Milanuzii's "Ariose vaçliezze" books I and II were published. They were a collection of strophic arias for solo voice and continuo.

Milanuzii's "Litaniae della Madonna" for four to eight voices was published this year at Venice.

Milanuzii's "Messe e canzoni" for five voices was published this year at Venice.

G. Miniscalchi this year published a volume of concertato psalms and motets for two and three voices at Venice.

Monteverdi's "O bone Jesu" for two sopranos and contralto and "Sancta Maria" for the same were included in Donfried's "Promptuarium musicum" published this year at Strassbourg.

Nenna's "Responsoria 'a 5' for Matins of Holy Week" was published this year after his death.

1622(cont.)

The second edition of Philips' "Deliciae sacrae binis et ternis vocibus, cum basso continuo ad organum" was issued at this time.

Two motets by Philips for two voices with basso continuo were included in the "Promptuarium musicum" by Donfried.

Van den Hove's "Deliciae Musicae sive cantiones ad testudinis usum" published at Utrecht this year contained compositions for the lute by Jakób Polak.

Priuli's "Musiche concertate" for three to nine voices appeared this year.

Salomone Rossi's collection "Hashirim Asher Lishlomo" was published at Venice at this time.

Paul Schaeffer wrote a book of four-part dance tunes this year.

Scheidt paid a tribute to Venice in his "Concertus sacri" of this year.

Scheidt's "Ludorum musicorum prima et secunda pars" was published at this time.

"Follias" were included in the "Scherzo amorsi" composed by Giovanni Stefani this year.

"The Golden Garland of Prince delights" by Tomkins was published at this time.

Thomas Tomkins printed a collection of secular material this year.

Thomas Tomkins published his "Songs of 3. 4. 5. and 6. parts" (cont.) at this time. One of the selections was dedicated to Henry Molle.

Pietro Paolo Torre's collection of "Canzonette, madrigali et arie" was published this year at Venice.

Vincenzo Ugolini this year composed two books of eight and twelve part masses and motets.

Giovanni Valentini published "Musiche a 2 voci" this year.

Filippo Vitali's "Arie a 1, 2, 3 voci" (book 4) was published at Venice this year.

Zacconi's "Prattica dei musica" was published at this time.

Jonson's "Masque of Augurs" was produced this year.

Kapsberger's "Apotheosis of St. Ignatius of Loyola" was performed this year at the Jesuit College.

The famous Norwich Waits included at least two Tenor Cornetts.

Jean-Baptiste Poquelin (Molière), great comic dramatist of his age, was born (died 1673).

Henry Vaughan, English Cavalier, and later, religious poet, was born in Wales (died 1695).

George Wither's "Fair Virtue" was written this year.

The town of Erfurt had to pay 200,000 florins for the army of Duke Frederick of Altenburg.

Carel Fabritius, Dutch painter and follower of Rembrandt, was born (died 1654).

1622(cont.)
Willem Kalf, Dutch painter, was
born (died 1693 or 1695).

Frans Pourbus the Younger,
painter to King Henry IV, died
(birthdate unknown).

Charles Le Brun this year was
appointed first painter of the
French Academy. He set up the
Academy according to Poussin's
ideas.

(to 1623, August 30) Dowland was
abroad in the service of Philip
Julius, Duke of Wolgast, in
Pomerania during this period.

(to 1623) Peri during these
years was writing music for the
choirs of San Nicola at Pisa
where the court frequently ad-
journed.

(to 1624) B. Cosyn was organist
of Dulwich College at this time.

(to 1625) Dutch painting: Rubens,
"Maria de' Medici." The
painting was partly executed at
Antwerp but completed at Paris.

(to 1626) Donati was "maestro di
cappella" of the Terra di
Casalmaggiore during these
years.

(to 1627) Donfried's
"Promptuarium musicum" was pub-
lished during these years at
Strassbourg.

(to c.1627) The Bolognese
Accademia de' Floridi was held
at the house of Girolamo
Giacobbi during this period.

(to 1628) Alessandro Striggio,
son of the composer and a
friend of Monteverdi's, was the
secretary at the Gonzagas'

(cont.) court during this period.

(to 1630) Richard Gibbs was an
organist at Norwich Cathedral
during these years. He has been
confused with Orlando Gibbons.

c.1622
Baldassare Ferri entered the
service of the Bishop of Orvieto
as a chorister at this time.

(to 1623) Dutch painting: Van
Dyck, "Susanna and the Elders."

1623
(February 4) Francesco Cirillo,
an Italian singer and composer,
was born at Grumo Nevano near
Naples (date of death unknown).

(February 6) The first performance of a sinfonia in five part
writing, written for interpola-
tion in Cicognini's comedy "La
finta Mora;" music by Filippo
Vitali.

(April 27) Johann (Jan) Adam
Reinken, German organist and
composer, was born at
Wilshausen, Lower Alsace. He
was a pupil of Heinrich
Scheidemann and enjoyed so great
a reputation that Bach walked
from Lüneburg and Cöthen to
Hamburg many times to hear him
play (died 1722, November 24).
He was the first composer of
the "High Baroque."

(May 4) Asprilio Pacelli, an
Italian composer, died at
Warsaw (born c.1570).

(July 4) William Byrd, a major
English composer, probably died
at Stondon Massey Essex (born
probably at Lincolnshire, 1543).

(July 6) Jacopo Melani, an
Italian composer, was born at

212

1623(cont.)
Pistoia (died 1676).

(July 18) Upon the death on this
date of John Amery, a gentleman
of the Chapel Royal, "Ralphe
Amner, a basse from Winsore, was
sworn in his place."

(August 5) Pietro Antonio Cesti,
an Italian composer, was born
at Arezzo (died 1669, October
14).

(August 29) Orlando, the son of
Orlando Gibbons, was baptized
on this day.

(October 4) F. Pilkington was
curator at St. Martin's, Chester
at this time.

(November 29) Antoine Boesset's
title of "Surintendant de la
Musique du Roi et Maître de la
Musique de la Reine" appeared on
a document bearing this date.

(November 30) Thomas Weelkes,
English organist and composer,
died at London (birthdate unknown). He was prone to writing
with novel harmonic clashes.

(December 30) By letters patent
bearing this date Rev. John
Williams founded two fellowships
and four scholarships at St.
John's College, Cambridge. The
scholarships were reserved for
the "Bishop's Boys" from St.
Peter's, Westminster, and the
letters made it clear that the
scholars from St. Peter's might
include Westminster boys, if
sufficient Welsh or Lincolnshire
applicants did not appear.

(February) The Chapter Act
-Books recorded payments to
Bull of the sums of 12 "livres
d'Artois" (florins) on this date

(cont.) as well as in 1620,
February.

(March) Filipe de Magalhães, a
Portuguese composer, succeeded
F. Garro this month as master of
the royal chapel in Lisbon under
King Philip III.

(March) Giuseppe Giulio Cesare
Stradivari, son of Alessandro
Stradivari, was born (date of
death unknown).

(December) Giulio Oristagno, an
Italian organist and composer,
died at Palermo (born 1543).

(December) The Cathedral at
Chioggia burned down at this
time.

Marc' Antonio Cesti, Cavalli's
most famous contemporary and
coleader in the Venetian school
of opera, was born (died 1669).
He was choirmaster at Volterra,
at the court of Archduke
Ferdinand in Innsbruck, sang
tenor in the papal choir, was a
Franciscan Monk, and court conductor to Emperor Leopold I of
Austria. See August 5.

Philipp Dulichius, a German composer, died according to a respected source. Others give
his date of death as 1631,
March 25 (born 1562, December).

Orlando Gibbons, son of Orlando
and Elizabeth Gibbons, was born
(died 1650).

Mariana, writer of a treatise
attacking public amusements,
died (born 1536).

Giovanni Bernardino Nanini,
Italian composer who first held
the appointment of maestro di
cappella at the church of San

1623(cont.)

Luigi de'Francesi in 1599 and afterwards at that of San Lorenzo in Damaso, died at Rome (born c.1560). He was the brother of Giovanni Maria Nanini.

Since G. Olivieri ceased to hold the position as maestro di cappella, St. John Lateran, Rome this year, Fétis assumed that he died at this time.

John Parsons, an English organist and composer, died at London (birthdate unknown).

John Patten of Westminster, father-in-law of Orlando Gibbons, died (birthdate unknown).

Mogens Pederson, Danish singer, composer and pupil of Melchior Borchgrevinck, died (born c.1585).

John Playford, the Elder, younger son of John Playford of Norwich, was born at Norwich (died 1686, November).

Friedrich Emanuel Praetorius, a cantor, was born (died 1695).

Alvaro de Los Ríos, a Spanish composer, died (birthdate unknown).

Philip Rosseter, an English composer of songs with lute accompaniment, died (born c.1575).

Johann Heinrich Schmeltzer, a leading composer of the older generation who worked at Vienna, was born (died 1680).

"John Cooke, a basse from Lichfield" was sworn "pisteler" of the Chapel Royal in London this year.

John Daniel was sole executor of Samuel Daniel's will of this year.

Dowland was referred to as "Doctor Dowland" although there was no record of his having been awarded a doctor's degree either at Oxford, Cambridge, or Dublin.

Eredi was "maestro di cappella" of the cathedral at Ravenna at this time.

Carlo Fillago was appointed Grill's successor as organist at St. Marks this year.

Orlando Gibbons was appointed organist of Westminster Abbey this year succeeding John Parsons.

Hacket stated in his "Scrinia reserata" that in 1623 "the organ (in Westminster Abbey) was touch'd by the best finger of that Age Mr. Orlando Gibbons."

J. Herbst became Kapellmeister at Frankfort at this time.

When d'India left Turin this year Albini became even more active.

Tarquinio Merula, an Italian composer, was maestro di cappella at the church of Santa Maria at Bergamo at this time.

After Mogens Pederson's death this year Hans Nielsen was appointed vice-director of the royal chapel at Copenhagen.

Records of visitation of Laud in 1623 showed Peglinch homestead to be one of substance.

F. Pilkington became Chester Cathedral precentor this year

and held this position until his death.

C. Piochi was maestro di cappella of Amelio Cathedral at Umbria at this time.

Examples of the "Bergamasca" appeared in works by Rossi.

Paul Siefert was organist at St. Mary's, Danzig at this time.

While Dean of Westminster this year the Rev. John Williams purchased two fee farm rents issuing respectively out of manors of Sudbury and Great Stanmore in the county of Middlesex.

Agostini contributed a dialogue to G. Giamberti's "Poesie diverse" of this year.

Amat's scientific work "Fructus medicinae" was published this year at Lyons.

Banchieri's "La Banchierina, overo Cartello picciolo del canto figurato" was written this year.

Banchieri's stage work, "La barca da Venezia per Padova" with a libretto by Guarini (also called "La nuova mescolanza") was reprinted this year.

Adriana Baroni (born Basile) was imortalized in a book of verses, "Teatro delle glorie d'Adriana Baroni" issued this year.

Castaldi's "Primo mazzetto de fiori . . ." was published this year at Venice.

The second edition of Ceresini's "Messa et salmi" was issued at this time.

Donati's "Salmi boscarecci concertati a sei voci . . ." appeared at this date.

Donfried's "Der Tablatur für Orgel I^{ter}, II^{ter} Teil" was published this year at Hamburg.

Eredi published his vesper psalms this year.

Franck wrote his "Newes liebliches musikalisches Lustgärtlein" for five to eight voices this year.

The libretto for "Il Medoro" by Gagliano was published this year.

Gagliano's first book of "Varie musiche" was published at this time.

Giacobbi wrote the music to Mariscotti's "La selva de' mirti" this year.

Burkhardt Grossmann wrote his 116th Psalm at this time.

D'India published three of his laments this year.

Kapsberger this year published the last of his four books of "Villanelle" for voices, with chitarrone accompaniment.

Marini's concerted instrumental opus 6, "La lagrime d'Erminia in stile recitativo," was published this year at Parma by Possenti.

T. Merula's "Madrigals et altro musiche concertate a 1-5" was published at Venice this year.

Giovanni Antonio Merulo, an Italian singer and composer, wrote a book of madrigals for four voices with one instrumental Canzone. It was published this year at Venice.

Michael's Psalm CXVI for three to five voices was published this year posthumously at Jena. It contained contributions by fifteen composers, including music left by Michael and pieces by his sons Christian, Daniel and Tobias.

The third and fourth books of Milanuzii's "Ariose vaghezze" were published this year.

Milanuzii wrote a poem in praise of Giovanni Ghizzolo that was included in the latter's "Frutti d'amore" of this year.

Leo di Modena's essay on choral singing in the synagogue was published in Salomone Rossi's "Schirha-Schirim" of this year.

Monteverdi's "Lamento d'Arianna," text by Rinuccin was published at Venice by Gardano and edited by Magni.

Monteverdi's two "lettere amorosi" originally published in 1619 were reprinted this year.

Johann Nauwach's publication of this year "Arie passegiati" for solo voice showed the influence of Italian monody. It contained arias and madrigals.

The title page of P. Philips' collection of litanies of Loreto for from four to nine voices with bassus continuus for organ showed him as canon of Bethune. The book was published this year at Antwerp.

P. Philips' portrait appeared

(cont.) in Jacques Francquart's "Pompia funebris . . . Alberti Pii . . . veris imaginibus expressa" issued this year at Brussels.

Possenti's first book of madrigals, canzonets and arias was published at this time.

Quagliati's "La sfera armoniosa" for one and two voices and instruments appeared this year.

The first Psalter of Raban carried this date.

Schein's "Fontana d'Israel . . ." ("Israel's Brünnlein") was published this year at Leipzig by Adrio.

Schütz's Elegy on the Death of "Fürstin Frau Sophia, Herzogin zu Sachsen" was published at Freiberg at this time.

Schütz's "Historia der fröhlichen und siegreichen Anferstehung unsers einigen Erlösers und Seligmachers Jesu Christi" was published at Dresden this year.

Staden's sacred "Harmoniae variatae" for one to twelve voices was composed this year.

Jean Titelouzr's "Hymnes de l'Eglise pour toucher sur l'orgoe avec les fugues et recherches sur leur plain-chant" appeared this year.

Valerius collaborated in the anthology "zeeuwsche Nachtegael" published this year at Middleburg.

George Wither this year published his "Hymns & Songs of the Church" to widen the sphere of church music in public use. The book was a failure.

1623(cont.)

The term sonata as used in Rossi's third book of this year denoted "trio" sonatas or pieces for two melody instruments and a third instrument for the thoroughbass.

The Teatro della Sala, a wooden structure, burned to the ground this year.

William Camden, an English historian and close friend of William Heyther, died (born 1551).

John Daniel this year issued an edition of Samuel Daniel's poetical works, dedicating them to Prince Charles.

Mariana's poem "L'Adone" was published at this time.

Daniel Webster's "Devil's haro-Case" in which he mentioned "palaces & belvidears with musical water-works" at Naples was published this year.

Dutch painting: Van Dyck, "Cardinal Bentivoglio."

(and 1626) All that has survived of Filippo Albini's music is the two sets of "Musicali concenti" for one and two voices (1623 and 1626; and one item for four voices, in the former book).

(to 1626) Melchior Schild was organist at the principal church at Wolfenbüttel during these years.

(to 1628) Frescobaldi's "Primo libro delle canzoni a 1, 2, 3, 4 voci" was published at Rome during this period.

(to 1628) Staden's publication (cont.) "Hausmuski" appeared in four separate parts during this time.

(to December 1629) Milanuzii at this time was organist at Santo Stefano in Venice.

(to 1641) Francesco Colombini was organist at the cathedral of Massa del Principe during these years.

(to 1644) Hugh Davies, organist at Hereford and church composer, was active at this time.

(to 1644) The Papal reign of St. Urban VIII (born in Florence).

(to 1689) Giuseppe Giamberti wrote many important works both sacred and secular, published during this period.

c.1623

Manuel Rodrigues Coelho, a Portuguese composer, died (born 1583).

Henry Ferrabosco, singer, wind player and composer, was born at Greenwich (died c.1658).

Isaac Posch, an Austrian or German composer, died (birthdate unknown).

Marco Scacchi went to Poland to become a royal musician at this time.

At the Chapel Royal in Scotland out of sixteen canons, nine prebends and six choirboys only seven ever attended, and they only sang "the Common Tune of a psalm."

(to 1627) Dutch painting: Van Dyck, portrait of "Marchesa Geronima Spinola."

(January 31) Will Forster's
Virginal Book was issued on
this date. It included seventy
-eight compositions, about half
of which were by Byrd.

(March 2) Monteverdi wrote to
the Duke of Mantua discussing
the merits of various singers.

(April 8) Karl Lichtenstein
-Kastelkorn, a Moravian art
-patron, was born at Glatz
(died 1695, September 23).

(April 26) By a deed bearing
this date, the Rev. John
Williams declared that the
Dean and Chapter of Westminster
should hold the two fee farm
rents in trust for four scholars
of his own foundation
("Bishop's Boys"). The supposi-
tion that Henry Purcell was born
in Westminster was supported by
one of the stipulations of the
scholarship he was later to
enjoy as one of the "Biship's
Boys" at St. Peter's College,
Westminster. According to
Bishop William's deed if no
acceptable candidates could be
found from two other dioceses
then they could be accepted
from one of the Liberties of
Westminster.

(July 16) Silas Taylor, an
English antiquarian and com-
poser, was born at Harley,
Salop (died 1678, November 4).

(September 16) Berti was chosen
to succeed Paolo Giusto as
second organist of St. Mark's,
Venice at this time.

(November 6) P. Cornet's
"Courante 'Mandatemi da lui' adi
. . . " appeared at this date.

(December 12) Louis Constantin
on this day succeeded a friend,
Richomme, in the position of
"roy des violons."

(December 30) A letter was written by Schütz to Wilhelm Moser
concerning Schutz's opinion of
some music by Samuel Scheidt
(Tablatura Nova).

(April) Sigismondo d'India was
taken under the patronage of
Cardinal Maurice of Savoy, an
enlightened supporter of the
arts.

(December) Vincenzo Gallo, an
Italian composer, died in
Palermo (birthdate unknown).

Johann Georg Albinus, a hymn
composer, was born (died 1679).

Juan Aranies, a Spanish composer,
died some time after this date.

Giovanni Andrea (Angelini)
Bontempi, an Italian singer and
composer, was born at Perugia
(died 1705, June 1).

Casparini, an Italian organ
builder trained at Padua and the
man who built the organ at
Görlitz, was born (died 1706).

Gustaf Düben (the elder), an
organist and composer, was born
at Stockholm (died 1690,
December 19).

William King, an English composer, was born at Winchester
(died 1680, November 17).

Angelus Silesius (Johannes
Scheffler), a German writer on
mysticism, was born (died 1677).
His greatest work was "Der
Cherubinische Wandersmann."

Georgius Victorinus, a German composer, died at Munich (birth-date unknown).

Adrian Batten moved to St. Paul's Cathedral where he was vicar-choral and organist at this time.

The "Bishop's Boys" this year were the recipients of the four scholarships founded by the Rev. John Williams, Dean of Westminster.

Borlasca was "Kinzertmeister" at Munich at this time.

Caignet at this time was musician-in-ordinary of the King's chamber.

Gabriel Diaz appeared at Córdoba this year.

In the accounts for the year ending at Michaelmas of this year Dowland's name preceded that of Johnson.

Nicolas Formé this year received a benefice from King Louis XIII, the Abbey of Notre-Dame de Reclus, in the diocese of Troyes.

Leandro Gallerano became maestro di cappella at Sant' Antonio in Padua at this time.

Francis Hedgman left Cassel for Gottorp this year.

Jean Florent A'Kempis (under the name of Nicolas) was organist at the church of Sainte-Marie at Brussels at this time.

Francesco Lambardi this year took a leave from his position (cont.) as first organist at the royal chapel.

Stefano Landi was maestro di cappella at Santa Maria dei Monti at this time.

"Mr. Jan Leenders, musesijn," a viola da gamba player, learned to play the melodies of 150 psalms within the space of three days at the Hague this year.

Tarquinio Merula was church organist in Warsaw at this time.

Edward Millar was awarded the degree of Master of Arts this year by Edinboro University.

John Mundy was awarded the degree of Doctor of Music this year.

Hans Nielsen left his position of vice-director of royal chapel in Copenhagen at this time.

Up to this date there was hardly any important collection of madrigals that did not include some of B. Pallavicino's madrigals.

Peter Philips was mentioned as "Pietro Filippini" in a report on the restoration of the organ of the court chapel, according to which he approved of the work done by Mathieu Langhedul.

F. Pilkington this year spoke of his "now aged muse" in the preface of his "Second set of Madrigals."

João Soares Rebello, who taught music to King John IV, became a choirboy at the ducal chapel

chapel this year.

Thomas Selle was rector at Heide at this time.

Thomas Snodham, the printer, was working up to this time.

Giles Tomkins became organist of King's College, Cambridge this year. Conflicting sources say it was Thomas.

Agostin's first volume of masses was published this year by Robletti at Rome. The masses were composed for eight to twelve voices and the later volumes were issued in 1625, 1626, 1627, and 1628 respectively.

Cavaliere Anselmi of Treviso's settings of madrigal texts with music by different composers was published this year at Venice. The works were in two voices.

Juan Aranies' "Libro seguando de tonos y villancicos a una, dos, tres y cuatro voces, con la zifra de la guitarra española a la usanza romana" was published this year at Rome.

Carlo Milanuzzi this year published two of Berti's arias in his "Quarto scherzo delle ariose vaghezze" at Venice.

Although Caccini and Frescobaldi referred to strophic variations simply as "arie," Grandi's term cantata was quickly accepted in the collections of Berti, Turini, Rovetta, and Sances. The first two collections mentioned above appeared this year.

Boni's settings of de Ronsard's

(cont.) sonnets (1579) appeared in several editions up to this time.

Caignet composes "Les CL Pseaumes de David" this year and they appeared in an edited edition in 1626.

Cesare Crivellati was known by his "Discorsi musicali" published this year at Viterbo.

Crüger's "Synopsis musices" a method for thorough-bass was published this year at Berlin. A third edition appeared in 1634.

M. East published his sixth set of books at this time.

Franck wrote his "Newes musikalisches Opusculum" this year.

Frescobaldi's thematic transformations of "Capriccio sopra un soggetto" were published this year at Rome.

Daniel Friderici edited Thomas Morley's madrigals for three voices this year.

Stefano Landi's second book of madrigals for four and five voices was published at this time.

Stefano Landi's book os psalms was published this year.

Tarquinio Merula's "Madrigaletti a 3, lib 1" opus 4 was published this year at Venice.

Tarquinio Merula's "Madrigali a 4-8 voci, lib 1" opus 5 was published this year at Venice.

Tarquinio Merula's "Motetti e sonate concertati, a 2-5 voci, lib 1" opus 6 was published at Venice at this time.

Two songs by Miniscalchi were included in Milanuzii's "Quarto scherzo delle ariose vaghezze" issued this year.

Monteverdi's "Il Combattimento di Tancredi e Clorinda" (in the eighth madrigal book) was composed this year. The subject was taken from Tasso.

Monteverdi's "Ego flos campi" for alto and continuo and "Venite venite" for two sopranos and continuo and "Salve O Regina" for tenor and continuo were included in Calvi's collection published this year.

Morley's "Canzonets" appeared in a German translation this year at Rostock.

F. Pilkington's last work "The 2nd set of Madrigals and Pastorals of 3, 4, 5 & 6 parts . . ." was completed this year.

Giovanni Domenico Rognone -Taegio, an organist and composer, published a Requiem this year (See also 1605 and 1619).

Saracini's fifth and sixth books of madrigals and airs were published this year.

Saracini's "Le Quinte Musiche" was published this year at Venice.

Saracini's opera, "Le seste musiche" was composed at this time.

Scheidt's most important as well as influential work was the "Tabulatura Nova" of this

(cont.) year. It was a large collection of organ music which instituted the contrapuntal art of paraphrasing Protestant chorale melodies on the organ.

Schein's "Diletti pastorali" was published this year at Leipzig.

Hans Ulrich Steigleder, an organist and composer, published a work this year known as being the first specimen in Germany of copper-plate engraving for organ or clavier music. The engraving was done by his own hands - "Ricercar Tabulatura, Organis et Organoedis unice inserviens et maxime conducens adornata a J. U.S. . . . ejusdemque Autoris sumptibus et manibus propriis Aeri Cupreo insculpta excusa - Anno 1624."

Stobaeus' earliest publication was his "Cantiones sacra 5, 6, 7, 8 et 10 vocibus item aliquot Magnificat 5 et 6 vocibus adornatae" published this year at Frankfort.

Victorinus' "Philomela coelestis" appeared this year.

Frescobaldi wrote on broken chords in his "Capricci."

Monteverdi in his "Combattimento di Tancredi e Clorinda" indicated tremolo for bowed instruments.

Monteverdi's "Il Combattimento di Tancredi e Clorinda" was performed this year at Venice at the home of Girolamo Mocenigo.

A hundred years after the earliest attempts at a keyboard tablature in England, a similar notation appeared in Germany and was used there until this time

Engraving from the "Neues A B C Büchlein," by Lucas Kilian (1579-1637).

1624(cont.)
when modern scores first appeared.

At this time a unique, but inferior, type of ricercar for two or three voices with no text or continuo was used for didactic purposes such as vocalises for singers by Metallo published this year.

Andre Maugars translated Bacon's "Advancement of Learning" and it was published by P. Billaine this year at Paris.

"Count Mansfields Directions of Warre" was translated by W.G. this year and published.

Ferdinand II's reign over the imperial forces was relinquished to Wallenstein and Tilly this year.

Guarini, an Italian architect, was born (died 1683).

Poussin, a French painter, went to Rome this year.

(and 1625) Madrigals and motets by Arrigoni were included in printed collections of these years.

(to 1625) Christopher Gregory was at Gottorp during this period.

(to 1625) Remigio Romano published his collection of "canzonette" during these years.

(and 1627) Berti's two sets of "Cantade et arie" were published at Venice at these dates.

(to late 1627) Carissimi held professional appointments at Tivoli, first as a singer and

(cont.) then as an organist.

(to 1627) Robert Dallam built the organ of Durham Cathedral during these years and it remained in use until 1687.

(to 1628) Kaspar Kittel, a German composer, was sent to Italy by the Elector of Saxony to study during these years.

(to 1628) Marcin Mielecki, a Polish musician, was Praepositus of the Capella Rorantistarum for this period.

(to 1630) French architecture: Le Mercier, Louvre, Pavillon de l'Horloge (c.60' wide).

(to 1637) Monteverdi's "Gira il memico insidioso" and "Ardo avvampo" were written within this period.

c.1624
Thomas Este, English composer, died (born c.1560).

(to 1626) French painting: Poussin, "Echo and Narcissus."

1625
(January 7) Ruggiero Giovannelli, an Italian composer, died at Rome (born 1560).

(January 27) Adriaan Valerius, Dutch lawyer, poet, historian and musician, died at Veere (born 1575).

(February 2) F. Caccini's opera "La liberazione di Ruggiero dall' isola d'Alcina" was produced at Villa Poggio, Imperiale, near Florence.

(April 5) King James I's funeral was held on this date.

1625(cont.)

(April 19) Andreas Düben, cantor at St. Thomas', Leipzig, died at Leipzig (born 1558, May 27).

(May 1) King Charles I and Henrietta Maria of France were married at Paris. At the ceremony King Charles was represented by the Duke of Buckingham as his proxy.

(May 31) Orlando Gibbons and others were summoned to Canterbury to be present when King Charles I received his bride on her arrival from Paris.

(June 5) On this date at Canterbury (Whit-Sunday), Orlando Gibbons was seized with an apoplectic fit and died (born 1583). At the time of his death he held the position of organist at Westminster Abbey.

(June 5) After his father's death on this date, Christopher Gibbons, then just ten, was apparently adopted by his uncle Edward (Orlando's elder brother), who was in charge of music at Exeter Cathedral.

(June 6) Orlando Gibbons was buried in Canterbury Cathedral on this date.

(June 12) Orlando's sudden death caused great fear of the plague in court circles. John Chamberlain wrote to Sir Dudley Carleton on this date regarding his suspicion that Orlando had died of the plague. His suspicions were later deemed unfounded. Chamberlain in his letter described Gibbons as "the best hand in England."

(June 15) King Charles I and (cont.) his bride left Canterbury for London on this date.

(July 4) Cornelis Verdonck, the Flemish composer, died at Antwerp (born 1563). He was a pupil of Waelrant and a disciple of Lassus.

(July 19) Samuel Besler, the German composer, died at Breslau (born 1574, December 15).

(September 30) P. Cornet's "Fantasia 8 tuoni, 30 septembre 1625" appeared.

(November 3) Adam Gumpeltzhaimer, the German composer, died at Augsburg (born c.1559).

(December 24) Johann Rodolph Ahle, a church composer, was born at Mühlhausen in Thuringia (died 1673, July 9).

(November) Denis Caignet, French composer, died at Paris (birthdate unknown).

(December) John Daniel was a member of the royal company of musicians for the lutes at this time.

Giulio Cesare Arresti, an Italian composer, was born at Bologna (died 1701).

Bénigne de Bacilly, French theorist, singing teacher, and priest, was born at Lower Normandy (died 1692 or 1693).

Samuel Besler, writer of German texts for Passion music, died (See July 19).

(Dom) Pietro Cerone, an Italian priest, singer and musical theorist, died at Naples (born 1566).

1625(cont.)

Luiz de Christo, a Portuguese
organist and composer, was born
probably at Lisbon (died 1693,
September 7).

John Cooke, father of Henry
Cooke and a singer himself, died
(birthdate unknown).

Louis Couperin, a well-known
composer of the French harpsichord school, was born at
Chaumes-en-Brie (died 1661,
August 29).

Nicolas Gigault, French organist
and composer, was born, probably
at Paris (died c.1707).

Ruggiero Giovanelli, an Italian
madrigalist, died at Rome , possibly January 7 (born c.1560).

Pierre Guédron, French singer
and composer, died (born 1565).

Giovanni Legrenzi, an Italian
composer, was born at Clusone
near Bergamo(died 1690, May 26).

Giambattista Marini, Italian
composer, died (born 1569).

The Abbé Pierre Perrin, who
helped bring about the "première
comédie françoise en musique"
was born (died 1675). See 1620.

Enrico Radesca di Foggia, an
Italian composer, died at Turin
(birthdate unknown).

Thomas Urquhart, a Scottish
violin maker, was born (died
c.1680).

Magdalene Wildeck, Schütz' wife,
died (birthdate unknown).

John Adson was a member of the
English court band at this time.

William Brade became Director of
Music at Gottorf this year.

Girolamo Casati was organist at
Romanengo near Cremona at this
time.

T. Cima at this time was "maestro
di cappella" at the Roman
Seminary.

Bartolomé Del Cort was master of
the Chapel in Rome at this time.

Richard Deering was appointed
organist to Queen Henrietta
Maria after her marriage to
King Charles I this year.

Richard Deering's name appeared
this year as that of a "musician
for the lute and voice" to the
King.

G. Diruta was referred to as
organist at Chioggia on the
title-page of this year's edition of "Il Transilvano."

A. Düben (the elder) became organist this year at the German
church in Stockholm.

Erbach became cathedral organist this year at Augsburg.

Baldassare Ferri this year went
with Prince Ladislas of Poland
to the latter's father's court.

From this time on until the
civil war in England Thomas Ford
was one of the King's musicians.

Orlando Gibbons, as organist of
Westminster Abbey, officiated at
King James I's funeral this
year.

A bill for certain repairs to
the organ by Orlando Gibbons
this year was preserved in the

Muniment Room at Westminster.

Nathaniel Giles at this time
organist at St. George's Chapel,
Windsor, was granted special
leave of absence by the Windsor
Chapel to go to Canterbury on
order from King Charles I.

Johann Groh this year became
music director and organist of
the chapel of Rudolph von
Bünaw at Wesenstein.

James Harding was English court
musician among "The flutes" from
1581 until this date.

Hodemont this year was back at
St. Lambert's Cathedral with
the additional title of Horn
-Player to the Chapter.

Constantin Huygens at this time
became military secretary to
Prince Frederick Henry, a position he retained under King
William II and King William III
of the Netherlands until his
death.

Johann Klemm was appointed court
organist at Dresden this year.

King Charles I had in his pay
eight performers on the hautboys and sackbuts, six flutes,
six recorders, eleven violins,
six lutes, four viols, one
harp and fifteen "musicians for
the lute and voice" exclusive of
trumpeters, drummers and fifers.
Nicholas Lanier served as band
director at this time.

Nicholas Lanier this year was
sent to purchase pictures in
Italy by King Charles I.

Manoel Leitão de Avilez became
"maestro de capilla" at the

(cont.) Cathedral of Granada
this year.

Micheli returned to Rome as
maestro di cappella at the
Church of San Luigi de' Francesi
at this time.

John and David Morell, and
Clement Dixon this year formed
an ensemble with John Price I.

Angelo Notari, an Italian musician, was in King Charles' royal
service from this time forward.

T. Pilkington appeared as "sixth
conduct" at this time.

Heinrich Scheidemann was appointed organist at St.
Catherine's Church in Hamburg
this year.

Deeply affected by the untimely
death of his wife this year,
Schütz turned to the composition
of church music for the rest of
his life.

Thomas Selle was rector at
Wesselburen-Itzehoe at this
time.

Stadlmayr acted as "Kapellmeister"
to the Archduke Leopold at
Innsbruck at this time.

Daniel Taylor was a "singing
-man" at Westminster Abbey this
year.

John Tomkins was appointed a
Gentleman Extraordinary of the
Chapel Royal this year.

Thomas Tomkins this year composed music for King Charles I's
coronation.

Thomas Tomkins succeeded Richard
Marwood as precentor of

1625(cont.)
Gloucester Cathedral this year.

Agostini's second volume of masses was published this year by Robletti at Rome. The works are for eight to twelve voices.

G.B. Ala composed canzonets, madrigals and operas published at Milan this year and in 1617.

Banchieri's sacred vocal work "Misse a 5" appeared at this time.

Banchieri's sacred vocal work "Misse, salmi e litanie" for three voices was completed this year.

Banchieri's stage work "Il principiante fanciullo" containing works by Arcadelt, Lassus, Monteverdi, Pecci and others appeared this year.

Banchieri's stage work "La sampogna musicale" was completed at this time.

A solo motet by Berti was included in Leonardo Simonetti's "Ghirlanda sacra" published this year at Venice.

A variation of the air "Monicha" was written this year by Den Borren for the harpsichord.

Francesca Caccini's "La Liberazione di Ruggiero dall 'isola d'Alcina" was published at this time.

Cardoso's "Missae 4, 5 et 6 v" was issued at Lisbon this year.

Cruger's "Perceptae musicae practicae figuralis" was written this year.

Diruta's "Il Transilvano" was issued in this year and possibly 1626 (See also 1615).

Donati's "Concerti ecclesiastici . . . Opera V . . ." appeared at this time.

The second edition of Robert Fludd (Flud)'s "Monorchordum mundi symphoniacum" was published at this time.

Gagliano wrote his oratorio "La regina Sant' Orsola" this year.

Vincenzo de Grandis wrote his "Alcuni salmi et motetti" this year at Rome.

Johann Groh's "Trifolium sacrum musicale oder geistliches muskalisches Kleeblätlein . . ." was published at this time.

Hodemont this year published at Liege his "Armonica recreatione" containing twenty-one villanelle for three voices with continuo.

Leoni wrote a motet which appeared in a collective volume of this year.

Martinengo's monody "Regnum Mundi" was included in Simonetti's "Ghirlanda sacra" published at this time.

A motet for solo voice and continuo by Milanuzii was included in Simonetti's "Ghirlanda sacra."

Milanuzii's "Sacra cetra: afetti ecclesiastici" for two to five voices and some solo motets for bass voice were published this year at Venice.

"Follias" were included in the "secondo Scherzo delle Ariose vaghe" by Milanuzzi at this

time.

Guglielmo Miniscalchi this year
at Venice published his first
book of strophic "Arie" for solo
voice and continuo.

Monteverdi's "Ego dormio" for
soprano, bass and continuo was
included in Francesco Sammaruco's
"Sacri affetti" published this
year.

Monteverdi's "O quam pulchra"
for tenor and continuo, "Currite
populi" for tenor and continuo,
"Ecce sacrum paratum" for tenor
and continuo, and "Salve Regina"
for tenor and continuo were included in Simonett's collection
published this year at Venice.

Peri's festa, "La precedenza
delle dame" appeared this year.

A book of instrumental pieces
was composed by Peuerl at this
time.

The second edition of Philips'
collection of "Cantiones
sacrae" for eight voices with
addition of a bassus continuus
for organ was published this
year by Phalèse. Philips was
referred to on the title page
as canon of Bethune.

A cantata, "Ecco Filli" from a
song book "Accenti pietosi
d'Armillo" by Pelligrino
Possenti this year used a
strophic bass with great freedom.

Possenti this year published
his second book of madrigals,
canzonets and arias.

The Raban psalter of this year
increased the number of Common

(cont.) tunes to fifteen and
presented them in harmonized
forms, the earliest such to be
published in Scotland.

Schütz' "Cantiones sacrae
quatuor vocum, cum Basso ad
Organum" was published this year
at Freiberg. The works were
based on mystic Latin texts
more appropriate for Catholic
than for Lutheran Services.

Schütz' "De vitae fugacitate,
Aria quinque vocum supra Bassum
Continuom" was published this
year at Freiberg.

Schütz first scored for two
bassoon in 1619. He scored for
three in 1621 and five in this
year.

Leonardo Simonetti's "Ghirlanda
sacra" was published at this
time in Italy.

Staden published a collection of
dances, pavans, galliards,
courantes, etc. this year.

A church work by Staden,
"Kirchenmusik" - part I, for
two to fourteen voices, was
written this year.

Stadlmayr published "Musica
super cantum gregorianum" this
year.

Details concerning such dis-
tinguished Polish composers as
Waclaw of Szamotuly and Marcin
Leopolita were found in Szymon
Starowolski's "Scriptorum
Polonicorum Hekatontas" pub-
lished this year at Frankfort.

Tomkins composed coronation
anthems this year.

Vitali's Sacred songs for six

voices with "basso ad organum"
book I was published this year
at Venice.

Vitali's "Varie musiche" book 5
was published this year at
Venice.

C.T. Walliser published
"Ecclesiodae Novae" at this
time.

Some of W. Young's pieces were
included in Playford's "Musick's
Recreation on the Lyra Viol" of
this year.

Services in the church of the
Moritzkirche at Halle ceased at
this time.

The Raban Aberdeen Psalter was
the first published departure
from the homophonic psalmody
approved by the Kirk Assembly.

The organ mass in Germany was
eclipsed between the time of
Buchner (c.1540) and the first
quarter of the 17th-Century,
when Scheidt and Erbach were
active.

The "tattoo" dates from this
time as a drum call. It was a
musico-military ceremonial
practised in most armies at
about 10:00 pm, ending the
soldier's day.

"Akébar, Roi du Mogol," was produced at the palace of the
Bishop of Carpentras this year.

Violinists occasionally acted in
the ballets, for example this
year in the "Ballet des doubles
femmes."

D'India's sacred drama "Sant'
Eustachio" was performed this

(cont.) year in the apartments
of the Cardinal's palace.

In the London theatre a jigg up
to this time was the recognized
way of ending a more serious
theatrical entertainment and
jiggs were even performed between the acts of a tragedy or
history.

The jigg by this time had evolved
into either a more formal song
and dance act, or else a prose
farce.

Masque music flourished during
King Charles I's reign which
started at this time.

The accession to the throne of
King Charles I this year brought
about another revival of interest
in the Chapel Royal since he
attempted to push the Anglican
service on Scotland in 1627.

When Charles I became King there
were two drummers and two fifers
at the court.

John Flecher, English poet and
author of "The Maid's Tragedy,"
died (born 1579).

John Webster, poet and author of
many "tragedies of blood" such
as "The Spanish Tragedy," died
(born c.1580).

Draud's "Bibliotheca librorum
Germanicorum classica" was reprinted (See 1611) and his
"Bibliotheca exotica" appeared
this year.

King James I of England died
(birthdate unknown). He ruled
in Scotland as King James VI.

The citizens of Erfurt this
year gave 50,000 fl. to General

1625(cont.)
Merode to avoid the billeting of his army.

The town of Erfurt paid 60,000 fl. in war taxes to the Elector of Mainz at this time.

Paulus Potter, a Dutch painter, was born (died 1654).

(to 1626) Three books of motets and two books of psalms all by Brunetti were published by Alessandro Vincenti during these years at Venice.

(to 1628) Dutch painting: Frans Hals, "Gipsy Girl."

(and 1629) Banchieri's "Dialoghi, concentus et symphonie duae vocibus decantandae" was issued at both these dates.

(and 1629, 1649, 1682) The demand for spiritual continuo songs in the vernacular triggered a number of important Catholic collections embraced especially by the Jesuits. These included publications by the Austrian Prior Corner (Gross catholisch Gesangbuch," 1625), the Trutznachtigall (1629, published posthumously in 1649) by the Jesuit Friedrich von Spee and Kuen, Glettle, Laurentius von Schnüffi's ("Mirantisches Flötlein," 1682).

(to 1633) G. Voigtländer was a trumpeter at Lübeck during these years.

(and 1641, 1645) The modern trio setting with continuo only slowly became a part of the suite. It appeared in works by Peuerl (1625), Verdonk (1641), and Rosenmüller (1645).

(to 1649) The reign of King Charles I (House of Stuart) over England and Great Britain.

(to 1649) The formative period of English baroque music was concurrent with the reign of King Charles I.

(to 1650) Michelangelo Rossi, an Italian composer and pupil of Frescobaldi, was most active during this period.

(to 1661) Bonini's three published or manuscript treatises on religious matters appeared during these years.

c.1625
Giovanni Ghizzolo, an Italian composer, died at Novara (birthdate unknown).

Hans Jacob Christoffel von Grimmelshausen, among the first writers to assert the German baroque spirit, was born (died 1676).

Francesco Luccio, an Italian composer, was born at Venice (date of death unknown).

Daniel Speer, a German composer, was born (date of death unknown).

The theory that Cifra was in the service of the Archduke Charles of Austria at this time has been questioned.

Italian violinist Carlo Farina worked at Dresden for about ten years starting at this time.

Giles Farnaby's psalter; "The Psalmes of David to fower parts for viols and voyce;" with only the superius, having a dedication came down to us in manuscript from this time.

John Ward was among the most eminent of the later madrigalists active at this time.

William Foster's and Benjamin Cosyn's Virginal Books were written at this time.

The most important attempt at fusing the thorough-bass with the madrigal was made by Walter Porter, English composer active at this time.

Dutch painting: Frans Hals, "La Bohémienne" (oil on panel, 22 7/8" x 20 1/2").

Dutch painting: Jordaens, "Allegory of Fertility."

(to c.1632) Carlo Farina, an Italian violinist and composer, was employed at the Dresden court during this period.

(to c.1665) Séraphin Pinel, brother of Francois Pinel, lutenist, was active during these years.

1626

(January 1) Henry Lawes was sworn in as epistler of the Chapel Royal on this day.

(January 21) John Dowland, British composer, died at London (born 1652, December).

(March 31) Atto Melani, an Italian male soprano singer and brother of Jacopo, was born at Pistoia (died 1714).

(April 2) Edward Millar added seventy-five of the psalms in four parts in his own hand to James Pont's "Book of Psalmes," written by his father, Robert.

(April 3) Scanty evidence indicated that M. Peerson was almoner this year, according to the Deed Book of John Donne for this date. Even in 1633 when the buildings around St. Paul's were demolished before the cathedral was repaired and part of the Petty Canon's College bought for £240 "to house Mr. Peerson & his boys" he held the position.

(April 11) Paul Heinlein (Hainlen), German instrumentalist and composer, was born at Nürnberg (died 1686, August 6).

(April 26) Robert Dowland was appointed one of the lutenists to King Charles I to replace his father who had died.

(May 4) Jane Gibbons, daughter of Edward and Jane Gibbons, married Thomas Gale at Exeter Cathedral.

(May 21) Wolfgang (Karl) Briegel, a German organist and composer, was born at Nürnberg (died 1712, November 19).

(June 13) Nicholas Lanier was appointed Master of the Queen's music on this date.

(June 23) Cifra returned to his post at Loreto on this day.

(July 11) Nicholas Lanier was appointed Master of the King's Musick at a salary of £200 per year.

(July 13) Letters of administration were granted to the widow of Orlando Gibbons (Elizabeth) by Dean and Chapter of Westminster.

(July 30) A statement that Elizabeth's (widow of Orlando

1626(cont.)
Gibbons) will was proved on this date proved to be incorrect, for his widow outlived him considerably.

(August 11) Giovanni Cavaccio, the Italian instrumental composer, died at Bergamo (born c.1556).

(August 12) Giovanni Legrenzi, Italian composer born at Clusone near Bergamo, was baptised on this date.

(October 9) John Ferrabosco, an organist, wind player and composer, was baptised at Greenwich.

(October 11) Robert Dowland obtained a marriage licence for himself and Jane Smalley. They were to be married at St. Faith's Church.

(November 3) Henry Lawes became "clerk of the cheque" at the Chapel Royal in London.

(November 11) Nicolas Formé re-entered the Sainte-Chapelle, which he had left thirty-four years earlier.

(December 26) Johannes (Hans) Bach, Veit's younger son, died at Wechmar (born c.1580). He was a "Spielmann" and carpet-maker at Wechmar and was also known as a dancing master. He was a member of the second generation of the Bach family.

(January) James Harding (Jeames Harden), English flautist and composer, died at London (birthdate unknown).

(February) Bernardo Clavijo Del Castillo, a Spanish organist, harpsichordist and composer,

(cont.) died at Madrid (born c.1545).

(September) Carlo Felice Stradivari, son of Alessandro, was born (date of death unknown).

Francesca Caccini, the Italian singer and composer, died after this date, probably at Florence (born 1588, September 18).

John Coperario, the English viola da gambist, lutenist and composer, died at London this year or 1627 (born 1570).

Pieter Cornet, the organist active for many years at the Catholic court in Brussels, died (born 1593).

John Ferrabosco, organist, wind player and composer, was born at Greenwich (died 1682, October).

Giovanni Legrenzi, Italian violinist, was born (died 1690, May 26).

Charles Mouton, a French lutenist, was born (date of death unknown).

Daniel Norcome, lutenist, must have died prior to this date since his widow was buried this year (born 1576).

Juan Pablo Pujol, Spanish composer, died at Barcelona (born 1573).

Al-Shirwání, who gave brief descriptions of the art of music in his encyclopedia, died (birthdate unknown).

Francis Wiborowe, an English musician, died at Ely (birthdate unknown).

1626(cont.)

Heinrich Albert, German organist, went to Königsberg this year.

Albini referred to himself this year as "musico."

Christian Brade (William's son) left Gottorf at this time.

William Brade left Gottorf for Hamburg at this time.

C. Cocchi this year entered the Order of St. Francis in the service of Cardinal Dietrichstein at Olomouc in Moravia.

Coperario appeared (as lutenist and composer) to have been a member of the King's music for several years before this year when he was succeeded by Alphonso Ferrabosco the Younger as composer to the King.

B. Cosyn was employed at the Charterhouse at this time.

In Lomazzo's "Flores praestantissimorum virorum," published this year at Milan, Donati was referred to as "maestro di cappella" at Novera Cathedral.

Effrem was at Naples at this time.

Thomas Ford this year was appointed one of the musicians to King Charles I at £ 80 per year.

William Heather established the offices of Professor, Choragus and Coryphaeus this year at Oxford University. The first regular lectures in music followed.

John Hilton II was awarded the degree of Bachelor of Music from Trinity College at Cambridge.

Jan Hommel built an organ at St. Mark's Church in Cracow this year.

Giovanni Maggini prospered in his business of the manufacture of citharas, cellos, violas and violins and acquired an additional house and shop at this time.

Marini was "maestro della musica" to the Duke of Bavaria at Munich this year.

Domenico Mazzocchi frankly admitted in the preface to his opera "Catena d'Adone" of this year that he inserted arias "to break the tediousness of the recitative." He referred to them as "half-arias" and according to his words they relieved the "tedio del recitativo."

Conrad Neusiedler was mentioned this year as living at Augsburg and being employed as lutenist for the Stille Musica (private music) of the citizens.

A source recorded that this year at the Florentine court Puliaschi sang contralto, tenor and bass to the "chitarrone."

Stefanini was maestro di cappella at Modena Cathedral at this time.

Sigmund Gottlieb Staden, organist and composer, was sent at the expense of Nürnberg authorities to Berlin to receive instruction in the playing of the viola bastarda, a form of gamba. His teacher was Walter Rowe, the English instrumentalist in the

1626(cont.)
service of the Elector of
Brandenburg.

Tomkins was sworn in as gospeller
this year.

Nathaniel Tomkins came to
Worcester at this time.

Lazaro Valvasensi was an organist at Tolmezo, Friuli this year.

Agostini's third of five volumes
of masses was published this year
by Robletti at Rome (See also
1624, 1625, 1627 and 1628).

Anerio published litanies this
year.

Banchieri's literary work
"Armoniche conclusioni del suono
del organo . . ." was written
this year.

Banchieri's "Il virtuoso
ritrovato accademico (concerti a
1 & a 5)" was completed at this
time.

A guitar method by Luis de
Brizeño was published this year
at Paris.

Brunelli's "Fioretti spirituali
a più voci" appeared at this
time.

The fourth book of Buonamente's
compositions was published at
this time.

Seven books by Buonamente including sonatas, symphonies and
dances were published this year
by Vincenti at Venice. In the
dedication of the fifth book
(1629) the latter confessed that
he stole the compositions but
maintained that he was now returning them.

The sonatas by Buonamente published this year contain several
variations, not always identi-
fied as to their origin, as for
example "Cavaletto zoppo," which
as it turned out was based on
the "passamezzo antico."

Cerreto's "Due raggionamenti in
forma di dialogo" appeared this
year in manuscript only.

C. Cocchi's "Armonici concentus
. . ." was issued this year at
Venice.

Correa's "Facultad orgánica" of
this year was one of the most
important Spanish collections of
early baroque organ music. It
showed a strange mixture of
archaic as well as progressive
features.

Cortellini's masses were published this year by Vincenti.

Cortellini's "Messe concertate
a otto voci" was published this
year by Vincenti.

Francesco Costa wrote some monodic laments at this time.

Crüger's "Meditationum
musicarum Paradisus secundus"
was issued this year at Berlin.

Diruta's "Il Transilvano" was
possibly published this year
(See also 1615 and 1625).

The following works by Donati
appeared this year.

> "Concerti ecclesiastici . . .
> D'Ign. D. maestro di
> cappella della Terra di
> Casal maggiore . . ."
> "Litanie a 5, 6, 7 e 8, se
> piace, di Sig. D. Ignatio
> Donati Rosarium

1626(cont.)
Litaniarum B.V. Raccolta
di D. Lorenzo Calvo."
"Messe a 4, 5 & 6 voci . . .
Novamente in questa terza
impressione ristampati
. . ."
"Motetti a 5 voci in concerto
. . . Novamente in questa
terza impressione
ristampati e corretti
. . ."

Eccard's "Dreyssig geistliche
Lieder . . ." was reprinted this
year at Erfurt (See 1594 and
1609).

Eccard's "Odarum sacrarum" was
published this year at
Mülhausen.

Eccard's "XX Odae sacrae . . ."
was reprinted this year (See
1596).

Frescobaldi's "Capricci sopra
diversi soggetti" was published
at this time at Venice.

Gagliano wrote his oratorio
"Istoria di Iudit" this year.

Giovanni Battista da Gagliano's
"Motetti per concertare a 2,
3, 4, 5, 6 e 8 voci" was published at this time.

At this time a set of six-part
madrigals by Gesualdo was published posthumously by Muzio
Effrem.

Santino Girelli published his
second book of psalms this
year.

Alessandro Grandi's "Cantade et
arie," Book III, was published
this year at Venice.

J. H. Kapsberger published the

(cont.) third of his four books
of "Intavolatura di chitarrone"
at this time.

Marini's instrumental opus 8,
"Sonate, symphoni, canzoni pass
emezzi, baletti, corenti,
gagliardo, e ritornelli a 1-6
voci, per ogni sorte d'instrumente . . . con altre curiose e
moderne inventioni" was published this year at Venice.

D. Mazzocchi this year published
an opera "La catena d'Adone" as
well as a book of five-part
madrigals.

Tarquinio Merula's "Satiro e
Corsica, dialogo" was published
this year at Venice.

Giovanni Pasta's "Affetti
d'Erato" was issued at this
time at Venice.

D. Pecci's book of arias for one
to three voices, opus 2, appeared
this year.

Posch's "Musicalische Ehren-
und Tafelfreuden" was completed
at this time.

The second part of Schein's
"Musica Boscareccia . . ." was
published this year.

Schein's "Opella nova
Geistliche Konzerte . . . auff
jetzo gebraüchliche Italiänische
Invention" was reprinted this
year.

Schein's "Opella Nova, Ander
Theil Geistlicher Concerten" was
published at Leipzig at this
time.

Schein's "Studenten-Schmaus a 5"
was published this year at
Leipzig.

Sirena this year published a collection of church music, his first significant issue.

Staden's "Kirchenmusik," part II for one to seven voices with viols and other instruments, was written this year.

Titelouze's "Le Magnificat . . . suivant les huits tons . . ." was published at this time by Ballard.

Titelouze's "Missa quatuor vocum" was published by Ballard this year.

Valerius' "Nederlandtsche Gedenck-clanck" was published at this time.

A "Contrafagott" was listed this year in the inventory of the Barfüsser-kirche, at Frankfort.

One of the original patents for "taking up boys" was granted to Nathaniel Giles this year. This meant that boys from the Children of the Chapel Royal could not be taken for theatrical productions by force.

Briceños' collection of guitar music published at Paris this year included several sung chaconne accompaniments.

The melody of the Dutch national anthem first appeared this year.

D'India's polyphonic mass was performed this year at the Julian Chapel in Rome with great success.

Mazzochi's "La Catena d'Adone," taken from Marino's "La Prigione d'Adone," was produced

(cont.) at this time at Rome.

Thomas D'Urfey's "A Fool's Preferment," a rehash of Fletcher's "Noble Gentleman," was first performed this year.

The village of Wechmar, Germany, was "plagued with a terrible epidemic" at this time.

Sir Francis Bacon, English author and nobleman, died (born 1561).

Richard Cromwell, Lord Protector of England and Great Britain, was born (died 1712).

De Brosse, a French architect, died (born c.1555).

Jan Steen, a Dutch painter, was born (died 1679).

(to 1627) Castello's "Sonate concertate a 4, due parti" was published during these years.

(to 1628) Heinrich Albert started for Königsberg in 1626. Stobäus was at that time "Kapellmeister" there, but Albert was taken prisoner by the Swedes and did not reach his destination until 1628.

(and 1628) Further records of Richard Deering were found in court records of both these years.

(to 1629) Buonamente was an imperial court musician during these years.

(to 1629) Melchior Schild was court organist at Copenhagen during this period.

(and 1630) Heinrich Baryphonus' "Ars canendi" was published in

1626(cont.)
these years at Leipzig.

(to 1634) Giovanni Pasta was
organist at the church of Sant'
Alessandro in Colonna at
Bergamo for these eight years.

(February 2 to 1649) William
Gregory was a singer in the
Chapel Royal at London during
this period.

c.1626
Marcus Meiboom, a German or
Danish musical historian, was
born at Tønning, Slesvig
-Holstein (died 1710, February
15).

According to Lang, contemporary
documents indicate that musical
performances with a stage setting were given in Vienna as
early as this date.

Dutch painting: Adriaen Brouwer,
"The Smoker."

Charles Mouton, French lutenist,
was born (died c.1710).

(to 1633) Edward Tucker was organist at Salisbury Cathedral
during this period.

1627
(March 23) Ludovico Zacconi, the
Italian theorist, died at Pesaro
(born 1555, June 11).

(April 9) Johann Caspar von
Kerll, German organist and com-
poser, was born at Adorf,
Saxony (died 1693, February 13).
He was a pupil of Frescobaldi
and Carissimi.

(April 23) Schütz' opera "Dafne"
was produced at Torgau on this
date.

(May 1) Monteverdi wrote to
Striggio and agreed to write an
opera, but requested more time.

(May 7) Monteverdi sent Striggio
two librettos for approval; "La
Finta Pazza Licori" by Strozzi,
and "Narciso" by Rinuccini.

(May 15) Albert Chrostkowski,
jr., a Polish musician, was born
at Secemin (died 1670).

(May 22) Monteverdi wrote
Striggio, who had gout at the
time, and acknowledged receipt
of the libretto "La Finta Pazza
Licori."

(May 24) Monteverdi wrote
Striggio explaining that, since
the writer of the libretto was
still in Florence, he, the composer, could not start work on
"La Finta Pazza Licori."

(June 5) Monteverdi wrote to
Striggio to discuss prospective
changes in the libretto of "La
Finta Pazza Licori."

(June 13) Monteverdi wrote to
Striggio, praising a male singer
he had heard in Venice.

(June 19) Joan Gibbons (daughter
of Edward) was buried at Exeter
Cathedral on this day.

(June 20) Monteverdi wrote to
Striggio to inform him that "La
Finta Pazza Licori" had been
divided into five acts.

(July 3) Monteverdi wrote
Striggio complaining that he had
been afflicted with a severe
pain in his right eye.

(July 10) Monteverdi sent
Striggio the completed first
act of the opera "La Finta Pazza

Licori."

(July 24) Monteverdi wrote
Striggio, expressing a mild
displeasure with the bass chosen
to sing a major part in "La
Finta Pazza Licori."

(August 21) Jacques Maudit, a
French lutenist and composer,
died at Paris (born 1557,
September 16). He was most noted
for four-part chansons measurées.

(September 10) Monteverdi wrote
to the Marquis Enzio, accepting
the latter's commission to set
the music to an Intermezzo.

(September 10) Monteverdi's
opera "La Finta Pazza Licori,"
text by Strozzi, was completed
in manuscript form.

(September 10) Monteverdi sent
Striggio the balance of the completed "La Finta Pazza Licori."

(December 13) Monteverdi's opera
"Armida" and five intermedi and
a prologue was produced at
Parma. Texts were by Tasso and
Ascano Pio.

(December 18) Monteverdi wrote
to Striggio stating that his
son, Massimiliano, had been put
in prison for reading a for-
bidden book.

(July) William Heyther (Heather),
an English musician and scholar
died at Oxford (born c.1584).

Christoph Bernhard, a German
singer and composer, was born
at Danzig (died 1692, November
14).

Bishop Jacques-Bénigne Bossuet
was born (died 1704).

John Cooper, English composer
known as Giovanni Coperario,
died this year or 1626 (born
1570).

Joan Gibbons, daughter of
Edward and Jane Gibbons, died
(born 1602).

Louise Henriette of Brandenburg,
a hymn writer, was born (died
1667).

Thomas Middleton, writer of the
"Witch," originally credited to
R. Johnson II, died (born 1570).

Francesco Provenzale of Naples,
important opera composer and
founder of the Neapolitan school
of opera, was born at Naples
(died 1704, September).

Lodovico Grossi da Viadana, composer and an important figure in
the early history of the basso
continuo, died (born c.1564).

Agostini this year succeeded
Ugolini as "maestro di cappella"
at the Vatican Chapel.

Auxcousteaux was a singer at
the church of Noyon this year
according to one source.

Andrew Blackhall's son, Andrew,
was mentioned as having dis-
posed of the pension held in
behalf of the music school at
Musselburgh.

Christian Brade, William's son,
sailed for England this year.

Ceresini was at this time
maestro di cappella "della morte
in Ferrara."

C. Cocchi was "maestro di cappella" at Trieste Cathedral at
this time.

Donfried was rector of the school at Rottenburg on the Neckar this year and from this time forward director of music at St. Martin's Church there.

Carlo Farina, the violin virtuoso, had works printed in which playing in positions was required, as well as double stops, pizzicato, tremolo, col legno, and sul ponticello. These technical challenges have frequently been associated with later periods in music.

Alfonso Ferrabosco was made Composer of Music in Ordinary to the King of England this year with a salary of £40. He succeeded John Coperario who died this year.

Valentine Flood was in the service of the Elector of Brandenburg at this time.

Alessandro Grandi became maestro di cappella at Santa Maria Maggiore at Bergamo this year.

William Heyther this year founded "the music lecture" at Oxford and endowed it with £·17:6:8 per annum. The musical professorship at Oxford still rests on the "Heather Foundation."

C. Huygens this year married Susanne van Baerle of Amsterdam, who died ten years later leaving his a daughter and four sons.

Thomas Irishe was "Custos of the College of Vicars Choral of Exeter" this year.

Henry Loosemore became organist of King's College Chapel at this time.

Masotti, a publisher in Rome, invited Monteverdi to edit Arcadelt's madrigals for four voices this year.

Edward Millar this year taught at Blackfriars Wynd, Edinboro.

Francesco Milleville was organist at San Benedetto, Siena at this time.

Moritz this year resigned from leadership at Hesse-Cassel having lost the confidence of his Lutheran subjects through his Calvinistic policy.

R. Nicholson at this time became the first University professor of Music at Oxford under the William Heyther Foundation.

Peacham in his "Compleat Gentleman" published this year at London was most complimentary to Philips.

Pilkington at this time was still mentioned as "sixth conduct."

Schütz used a German libretto based on the Rinuccini text for his opera "Dafne."

S.G. Staden, the German organist and composer, received an appointment as one of the "Stadtpfeifer" of Nürnberg this year.

Usper was at this time principal of the great school of St. John the Evangelist at Venice.

Agostini's fourth of five volumes of masses was published this year by Robletti at Rome.

Monteverdi this year brought out an edition of Arcadelt's madrigals for four voices to be used in the teaching of composition to beginners.

Bodenschatz' "Geistliche Lieder und Psalmen" was issued this year at Leipzig.

Bodenschatz' "Manuale sacrum" was completed by this time.

Antoine Boesset's "Les Nymphes bocagères" appeared this year.

The preface to "Arie, scherzi e madrigali" published by Brunelli's pupil C.P. Bucchianti this year at Venice paid a tribute to the former.

Michelagnolo Capellini's oratorio, "Il lamento di S. Maria Vergine," appeared this year.

Ceresini's second book of madrigals, opus 4, was completed this year.

C. Cocchi's "Messe," for five voices was composed at this time.

Bishop Cosin this year added his translation of the hymn "Jam lucis orto sidere" to his "Collection of Private Devotions."

Dedekind's "Studentenleben, darinn allerlei akademische Studenten-Händel mit deutsch poetischen Farben entworfen, in fünf stimmen gesetzt von Musophilus Dedekind" was published this year by Johann Birckner at Erfurt.

Donati's "Motetti concertati a 5 & 6 voci . . . Opera VI. Novamente ristampata e corretta . . ." was published this year by Vincenti at Venice.

Donfried's "Viridarium musico-marianum a 2-4" was published this year in Germany.

Carlo Farinai this year wrote "Capriccio stravagante" (for violin). Niccolò Paganini probably was inspired by the work in his "Fandango Spagnuolo."

Fasolo's "Misticanza di vigna alla Bergamasca" was published this year at Rome.

Filmer's "French Court Ayres Englished" was published at this time.

Franck this year wrote his "Deliciae conviviales."

Frescobaldi's "Secondo libro di toccate . . . e partite d'intavolatura" was published this year at Rome. It included "Partite sopra Ciaccona (a chaconne)."

Frescobaldi's "Toccate . . . e partite d'intavolatura" was reprinted this year for the third time.

Santino Girelli's masses for five and eight voices, opus 3, was published this year.

John Hilton, II published his "Ayres, or Fa La's for Three Voices" at this time.

D'India this year published a volume of sacred music.

Vincenz Jelich this year composed six motets included in collective volumes.

Marin Mersenne's work "Traité de l'harmonie universelle" (of which he published an epitome in Latin) was printed this year.

Milanuzii's "Psalms" for two and
three voices was published this
year at Venice.

Miniscalchi's first book of
"Arie" was reprinted this year
at Venice.

Miniscalchi's second book of
strophic "Arie" for solo voice
and continuo was printed at this
time at Venice.

Nauwach's "Teutsche Villanellen"
for one to three voices and instruments was published this
year.

Posch composed "Harmonia
concertans," a book of sacred
songs for one to four voices,
in 1623. This year it was
edited by Widow.

Schein's "Cantional" was published this year at Leipzig.
The book, a major chorale book
of the Baroque, established the
organ accompaniment for the
chorale as a formal organ continuo.

The first German opera "Dafne"
was composed by Schütz at this
time. The text was translated
into German from Rinuccini and
adapted by Opitz.

The second edition of
Starowolski's work "Scriptorum
Polonicorum Hekatontas" was
published this year at Venice.

Usper at this time published
his "Vesper Psalms for the
whole year, opus 5."

Opera was imported to Germany
from Italy during this year.

Italian Opera was brought to

(cont.) Prague at this time.

Peri's "Dafne" was performed
this year at Torgau, Saxony.

Schütz' "Dafne" was performed
this year at Torgau for the
marriage of George II Landgrave
of Hesse to the sister of the
Elector of Saxony. It was the
first opera in Germany.

There were several "ports" in
the Straloch Lute Manuscript of
this year.

Sir Thomas Browne was awarded a
degree by Oxford.

Luis de Góngora, a Spanish poet,
died (born 1561).

Van Dyck returned to Antwerp
this year after studying for six
years in Italy.

Simon Vouet, the French painter,
returned to Paris this year with
an Italian wife. He had been
studying Veronese's art in
Venice.

(to 1629, January) Francesco
Manelli was maestro di cappella
at Tivoli Cathedral during these
years.

(to 1629) Rubens, the Dutch
painter, was involved in diplo-
matic missions to England,
Holland and Spain during this
period.

(to 1629) The Straloch lute
manuscripts were compiled at
this time.

(and 1654) Arcadelt determined
the purest type of the four
-part madrigal which was preserved through all changes af-
fecting the species up to 1627.

1627(cont.)
Monteverdi published a selection
and editions of the first book,
intended principally for the
practice of the classical "a
cappella" style, as late as
1654.

(to 1693) Italian opera remained popular during this period and grew to a high degree
of excellence under the court
conductor Johann Caspar Kerll.

c.1627
(January) Alphonso Marsh, sen.,
an English composer, was born
in London (died 1681, April 9).

Thomas Tomkins, English composer,
died at Gloucester (born c.1545).

1628
(January 3) Francesco Maria
Guaitoli, an Italian composer,
died at Carpi (born 1563).

(January 9) Monteverdi wrote
Striggio to thank him for his
aid to Massimiliano, the composer's imprisoned son. He also
expressed sorrow at the death
of Duke Vincenzo.

(January 21) Gregor Aichinger,
the German organist and composer,
died at Augsburg (born 1564).

(February 4) Monteverdi wrote
Striggio from Parma where re-
hearsals of the former's music
were being held.

(February 7) Alfonso Ferrabosco
III was given a salary for his
position as musician for the
Viols and Wind Instruments.

(February 7) Henry Ferrabosco
on this day began receiving a
salary for being the Musician
for the Voices and for the Wind

(cont.) Instruments.

(March 13) John Bull, English
organist, virginalist and composer, died at Antwerp (born
c.1562).

(March 15) Bull was buried on the
south side of Antwerp Cathedral.

(April 2) Constantin Christian
Dedekind, poet and composer, was
born probably at Reinsdorf,
Anhalt-Cöthen (died 1715,
September 2).

(April 7) Edward Gibbons' first
wife Jane was buried at Exeter
Cathedral.

(June 15) Orgas' "De Sancto
Martino: Deus noster" appeared.

(July 1) Monteverdi wrote to
Striggio asking his to help arrange the release of Massimiliano
from prison.

(July 5) Michael Cavendish,
English composer, died at London
(born c.1565).

(October 11) Ranuccio Farnese,
Duke of Parma, married Margherita
de' Medici.

(October 11) Gagliano's last
opera, "La Flora, overo Il natal
de' fiori," was performed at the
Pitti palace. Peri wrote the
part of Clori in the work.

(November 3) Francesco Maria
Melani, male soprano singer,
brother of Jacopo and Atto, was
born at Pistoia (date of death
unknown).

(November 3) A letter written by
Schütz to Elector Johann Georg
I of Saxony dealt with Schütz'
trip to Venice, and his thanks

to the Elector for continuing his salary while in Venice. He also mentioned buying some musical works in Venice.

(December 13) Monteverdi's "Mercurio e Marte" (Torneo) with libretto by Claudio Achillini, was produced for the first time at Parma.

(December 21) Samuel (Friedrich) Bockshorn, a Bohemian composer, was born at Žeržice near Mlada Boleslav (died 1665, November 12).

(March) Alfonso Ferrabosco, II, violist, singer and composer, died at Greenwich (born c.1575 or c.1580).

(April) Philips' first part of his "Paradisus sacris cantionibus consitus, una, duabus et tribus vocibus decantantis. Cum basso generali ad organum" was published at this time by Phalése at Antwerp.

(November) Paolo Quagliati, Italian keyboard performer and composer, died at Rome (born c.1560). Some sources give his date of death as 1630.

Jan Hommel, German-Polish organ builder, died at Lewoca, Slovakia (birthdate unknown).

Johann Jakob Löwe, a German composer, was born at Vienna (died 1703, September).

François de Malherbe, poet and theorist, died (born 1555).

The Duke of Mantua died (birthdate unknown).

Salomone Rossi, Hebreo madrigal

(cont.) composer, died (born c.1570 or 1587). His death has also been given by some as c.1628.

Giovanni Battista Stradivari, son of Alessandro, was born (date of death unknown).

Antonio Maria Abbatini was "maestro di cappella" at the church of Gesù at this time.

Steffano Bernardi's first important task was the arrangement of the festivities for the inauguration this year of the new cathedral at Salzburg.

Josias Broome and John Riley this year became Sergeant-Trumpeters of the Royal Household.

Dr. Richard Bushy was registered in the poor-rates book for St. Margaret's Parish, Westminister beginning this year, when he received permission to "proceed bachelors of arts" until his death.

J.B. Comes returned to Valencia at this time.

Dowland was said to have been a native of Westminster but the name did not appear in the parish registers before this year.

Erbach was appointed "Ratsherr" of Augsburg at this time.

Carlo Farina at this time was using imitations of the cries of various wild animals in his compositions.

Frescobaldi left his position at St. Peter's in Rome and went to Florence in the service of the

1628(cont.)
Grand Duke of Tuscany, Ferdinand (II), de' Medici.

Edward Gibbons, brother of Orlando, was one of the four Priest Vicars and in this year he was also Custos of the College (College of Vicars Choral of Exeter). Gibbons held the office of Custos intermittently but never permanently.

When Vincenzo Giustiniani reflected on his youth this year he complained that "in the present course of our age music is not much in use, not being practised in Rome by gentlemen, nor do they sing together with several voices as in past years, notwithstanding that it would provide the best possible means to unify and sustain evening parties."

Giustiniani remarked this year that the lute was no longer in use.

Michel Angelo Grancini was organist of San Sepolcro at Milan at this time.

John Hilton II was made parish clerk and organist of St. Margaret's, Westminster this year.

Sebastián López de Velasco was maestro di cappella to the Infanta Juana at this time. The position had at one time been held by Victoria.

When Thomas Lupo died this year Robert Johnson II aplied for his position of "composer to the lutes and voices."

Tarquino Merula was organist at Sant' Agata and master of the

(cont.) Cathedral at Cremona this year.

Orgas this year became praepositus at Capella Rorantistarum.

Pietro Paolo Sabbatini was maestro di cappella dell' Archiconfraternità della morte et oratione di Roma at this time.

Marco Scacchi became chief conductor of the royal chapel in Warsaw this year.

Schütz visited Monteverdi at Venice and thoroughly re-studied Italian music.

Thomas Tomkins was appointed successor to Alphonso Ferrabosco as composer in ordinary to King Charles I. The appointment was later revoked as it had been promised to Ferrabosco's son.

Vierdanck was sent to Vienna this year to study under Sansoni.

Agostini's last of five volumes of masses was published this year by Robletti at Rome (See also 1624, 1625, 1626, 1627). They were from eight to twelve voices.

Ardemanio's "Musica a più voci" was published this year at Milan.

Banchieri's literary work "Lettere armoniche" appeared at this time.

Banchieri's "La Prudenza giovenile" was reissued this year as "La Saviezza giovenile." It had originally been published in 1607 as "Il virtuoso ridotto tra signori e donne."

Orazio Benevoli wrote a fifty
-three part festival Mass for
the consecration of the
Cathedral of Salzburg. It used
two eight-part choruses with
soloists. The accompaniment was
for two organs as well as instruments and the score was almost a yard in size.

Cecchino's book of masses of
this year also included a set
of eight sonatas for various
instruments.

Domenico Crivellati this year
published a book of "Cantate
diverse" for one to three voices.

Donfried's "Corolla Musica
Missarum 37" was published in
Germany at this time.

Fasolo's "Il carro di Madame
Lucia" was published this year.

Franck wrote his "Cithera
ecclesiastica et scholastica"
for four voices at this time.

Franck this year composed his
"Evangelium paradisiacum" for
five voices.

Franck wrote his "Rosetulum
musicum" (concertos) this year.

Franck's "Sacri convivii musica
sacra" for four to six voices
was composed at this time.

Frescobaldi's "Secondo Libro di
toccate . . . e partite
d'intavolatura" was published
at Rome this year for the second
time.

Gagliano's last opera, "La Flora,
o vero Il natal de' fiori" was
published this year at Florence.

Girolamo Giacobbi this year
wrote his last work,
"Sanctissimae Deiparae Canticum."

A re-publication of Alessandro
Grandi's "Motetti a voce sola,"
with continuo, appeared this
year. The original publication
date is unknown.

A large quarto was written by
Gulielmus a Messaus, organist at
St. Walpurga, Antwerp during
this year. It contained ("inter
alia") thirty-eight organ and
virginal pieces by Bull.

Hizler's "Newe Musica" was completed this year.

Jelich this year composed his
"Arion I^{us}, sacred songs a 1-4
v. with organ," opus 2.

Jelich composed his "Arion II^{us},
psalms a 4v., a Magnificat,
Salve Regina," opus 3 this year.

Cesare de Judice wrote a book of
madrigals for two to four voices
at this time.

Stefano Landi's "Missa in
benedictione nuptiarum" for six
voices was published this year.

Giovanni Battista Locatello composed a book of madrigals this
year for two to seven voices.

S. López de Velasco published
masses, motets, psalms, etc.
this year.

Tarquinio Merula's "Concerti
spirituali . . . ., a 2-5 voci,
lit 2" was published at this
time at Venice.

Milanuzii's sixth book of "Ariose
vaghozze" was published this
year.

Milanuzii's "Psalms" for two and three parts was reprinted this year at Venice.

Milanuzii's "Salmi e vesperi" for two and three parts was published this year at Venice.

Monteverdi this year wrote incidental music for Tasso's "Aminta."

Monteverdi's "I cinque fratelle," a cycle of madrigals with words by Strozzi, was published this year.

Philips at this time issued the first part of his "Paradisus sacris cantionibus consitus, una, duabus et tribus vocibus decantantis. Cum basso generali ad organum."

Possenti's first book of madrigals, canzonets and arias was reprinted at this time.

Possenti's "Concentus armonici" (instrumental sonatas) was published this year.

The third part of Schein's "Musica Boscareccia . . ." was published at this time.

Schütz' "Psalmen Davids, in Teutsche Reimen gebrachte durch D. Cornelium Beckern . . ." was published this year at Freiberg. They were simple four-part harmonic settings of the German translation of the Psalter.

Staden's "Harmoniae novae" for three to twelve voices was composed this year.

Stadlmayr's "Hymni totius anni . . ." was published at this time.

Jan Turnowski this year published a "Cantionale" at Gdańsk (Danzig).

Ugolini this year composed a book of eight-part psalms and vespers with bass for the organ.

This year the first Dutch Reformed Church was organized in New York by French and Dutch settlers.

The Massachusetts Bay Colony, established this year, favored Ravenscroft's Psalter.

The term "drum-major" appeared this year for the first time.

Monteverdi's "Il Ballo delle' Ingrate" was performed at this time.

Monteverdi's "Torneo" was produced this year at Parma.

The consecration of Salzburg Cathedral took place at this time.

This year marked the first performance of an opera in Warsaw.

John Bunyan, theological and ethical thinker and writer, was born (died 1688).

(to 1629) Virgilio Mazzocchi was maestro di cappella this year at St. John Lateran in Rome.

(to 1629) Heinrich Schütz made a second journey to Italy during these years.

(to 1630) Carissimi became "maestro di cappella" at the church of Sant' Apollinare in Rome where he remained until his death.

1628(cont.)
(to 1631) John Stanley, the violist, was in Berlin during this period.

(to 1644) Printed works of Aloisi appeared during these years.

(to 1651) Polish composer Samuel Strokrocki during these years acted as organist at Warsaw.

(to 1657) Pietro Sabbatini's works were composed during this period.

c.1628
Jean d'Anglebert, a prominent composer of the French harpsichord school, was born at this time according to two sources. Another placed his birth at 1635 (died 1691).

Robert Cambert, French composer, was born at Paris (died 1677, February). He collaborated with Perrin in the composition of French operas.

According to an entry in the notebook of Dr. John Southcote published by The Catholic Record Society, the date of death for Peter Philips was c.1628. If this were true publications under Philips' name in 1630 and 1633 would have been posthumous and nothing indicated this on their title pages.

Jacob van Ruisdael, Dutch landscape artist, was born (died 1682).

Dutch painting: Adrian Brouwer, "The Smoker" (oil on panel 16 1/8" x 12 5/8").

1629
(January 6) Vincenzo Amato, an

(cont.) Italian composer, was born at Ciminna, Palermo (died 1670, July 29).

(January 12) Michael Vredman, a Flemish musician, died at Utrecht (born c.1564).

(January 27) Hieronymus Praetorius, German organist and composer, died at Hamburg (born 1560, August 10).

(February 28) Statius Olthoff, a German composer, died at Rostock (born 1555).

(March 13) Pierre Phalèse of the Dutch music publishing family, died at Antwerp

(April 20) Andrea Falconieri returned to the service of the Duke of Parma.

(July 5) Annibal (Hannibal) Orges, an Italian composer, died near Cracow (birthdate unknown).

(July 18) Matthew White was awarded the Bachelor and Doctor of Music degrees by Oxford.

(September 5) Domenico Allegri, the Italian composer, died at Rome (born c.1585).

(October 2) Antonio Cifra, the Italian composer, died at Loretto (born 1584).

(October 3) Paolo Agostini, Italian sacred composer, died at Rome (born 1593).

(November 29) Stefano Landi was on this day appointed a contralto singer at the Cappella Giulia, St. Peter's at Rome.

(December 6) Gregorio Allegri was appointed to fill a vacancy

1629(cont.)
among the singers in the
Apostolio chapel of Pope Urban
VIII.

(February) Girolamo Giacobbi,
Italian composer, died at
Bologna (born 1567, August).

(August) Mary Harvey (Lady
Dering), an English composer,
was born (died 1704).

Melchior Franck, the German composer, died (See 1639, June 1).

Christian Huygens, Dutch scien-
tist and second son of
Constantin Huygens, was born at
The Hague (died 1695, June 8).

Andrea Lambardi, brother of
Francesco Lambardi, sopranino
singer at the Santa Casa dell'
Annunziata, died at Naples
(birthdate unknown).

Giovanni Priuli (Prioli), an
Italian composer, died (birthdate unknown).

Jan Turnowski, Polish schoolmaster, died at Toruń (born
1567).

Wojciech Tylkowski, Polish musical theorist, was born at
Mazovia (died 1695, January 14).

Jan Willemszoon (Lossy), first
town musician and possibly organist at Haarlem, died (born
c.1545).

Agostini this year succeeded
Ugolini as Maestro at the
Vatican Chapel.

Castello was "maestro" of instrumental music at St. Mark's
in Venice at this time.

Eredi this year was "maestro di
cappella" at Ravenna.

Giuseppe Giamberti, an Italian
composer, was maestro di
cappella at the church of San
Giovanni Maggiore in Rome at
this time.

William Gosson, the first
"King's drum-major," died (birthdate unknown).

Adam Janecki this year after the
death of Father Annibal Orgas
became praepositus of the Chapel
of Roratists.

A certain Edward Kellie was this
year appointed Director of Music
to the Chapel Royal in Scotland.

After the death of Pierre
Phalese this year the business
was carried on by his daughters
Marie and Madeleine who were
inscribed in the registers of
the Guild of St. Luke as
"dochters Phalèse."

John Price I stayed at
Stuttgart until this time.

John Price I, his two brothers
-in-law, John and David Morell,
and John Dixon were appointed to
the "Kleine Kammermusik" at
Dresden this year.

When Lutheranism was suppressed
at Jauer in Silesia this year
and Catholic worship was re-
established, Profe was obliged
to return to Breslau, where he
became involved in mercantilistic
pursuits.

Melchior Schild became organist
for the Market Church at Hanover
this year.

Schütz during his stay in

Venice this year composed another opera, an Italian "comedy" that could be "acted singing." All that is known about it is through one of his letters.

Robert Tedder was at this time appointed "King's drum-major."

Nathaniel Tomkins was organist at Worcester Cathedral this year and was awarded the degree of Bachelor of Divinity by Balliol College, Oxford. He then became a canon.

The music for the first Spanish opera has been lost. It was set to Lope de Vega's "La Selva sin amor" this year. The composer may have been José Peyro.

J.J. Voss was presented by Laud to a canonry at Canterbury this year.

E. Widmann at this time referred to himself as imperial poet laureate.

Acheson's "The Military Garden" was published at this time.

Bellante's "Concerti accademici" published this year at Venice included mainly continuo madrigals for two to five voices with instruments.

Antoine Boesset's "French Court Ayres with their Ditties Englished" was published this year at London.

Bull's "Den lustelijcken Mey" (Laudes Vespertinae B. Mariae Virginis . . .") was published this year by Phalése at Antwerp.

Donati's "Madre de quatordeci figli . . ." was completed this

Donati's set of fifteen motets on the same bass appeared at this time.

Francesco Eredi's "L'Armida del Tasso . . . a 5 voci," opus 3, was published this year.

Robert Fludd (Flud)'s "Sophiae cum morioe certamen . . . and summum bonorum quod est verum magiae cabalae . . ." were both published at this time.

Franck this year wrote his "Prophetia evangelica" for four voices.

Melchior Franck completed his "Votiva columbae Sioniae suspiria" at this time.

Gibbons' "Examen Fluddanae Philosophiae . . ." was published this year and dedicated to Mersenne.

Grandi's "Cantade et arie," Book IV, was published this year at Venice.

A second of three books of motets with sinfonias by A. Grandi was published this year.

Grandi's "Salmi" for eight voices was issued at this time.

The English "ayre" drew on the "air de cour." The great popularity of the "ayre" was proven by many English editions, either in the original French as by Tessier in 1597 or in translation in Hilton's "French Court -Ayres with their ditties Englished" of this year.

The "polacca" and its "corrente" by Marini appeared this year.

1629(cont.)

They were composed for chamber ensemble in a trio setting and clearly showed melodic identity and rhythmic contrast in a varied couple typical of the time.

A sonata by Marini, published this year, had contrasting sections, the last of which was a canzona - like Allegro - and was repeated.

The Microcosmographie was written at this time.

Milanuzii's "Antifoni e litaniae" for one to four voices was published this year at Venice.

Milanuzii's "Messe concertate" for three voices was published this year at Venice.

An edition of Pevernage's "Laudes vespertinae B. Mariae Virginis" was published this year by Phalèse at Antwerp.

José Peyro composed music this year for Calderón's "El jardín de Falerina."

Two Christmas carols by Philips were included in Pevernage' "Laudes vespertinae B. Mariae Virginis."

Giovanni Rovetta, Monteverdi's assistant at St. Mark's, published his "Madrigali Concertati" this year.

Schütz' "Symphoniae sacrae" was published this year at Venice.

Jiří Třanovský this year at Brieg wrote "Odarum sacrarum sive Hymnorum . . . libri tres."

Francesco Turini published his "Mottetti a voce sola" this

(cont.) year.

Pietro Francesco Valentini's "con le sue Resolutioni in più di Duemilia Modi" was issued at this time.

Vitali's concerto, madrigals, "et altri generi di canta" for one, two, three, four, five and six voices were published by B. Magni this year at Venice.

Vitali's "Il terzo libro de madrigali a cinque voci" was published this year at Venice.

Giacinto Cornacchioli's opera "Diana schernita" was performed this year privately at the house of Count Hohenrechberg in Rome during the Carnival.

Lope de Vega's "La Selva sin Amor" was performed this year at Madrid.

The Musikkollegium Winterthur was founded this year.

John Milton's "Ode on the Morning of Christ's Nativity" was completed at this time.

Lope de Vega's "La Selva sin Amor." a pastorale, was completed this year and used for an opera text.

Pieter de Hooch, Dutch painter, was born (died c.1683).

Hendrik Terbrugghen, Netherlandish painter, died (born 1588).

Spanish painting: Francesco de Zurbarán,

"The Funeral of St. Bonaventure" (oil on canvas 8'2 3/4" x 7'2 5/8")

1629(cont.)
"The Heavenly Jerusalem"
"St. Peter Appearing To St.
   Peter Nolasco"

Czar Alexis I of Russia was born
(died 1676).

(and 1630) Donati was organist
at Lodi Cathedral during these
years.

(to 1633) Arizo was still a
singer in the royal chapel at
Madrid during this period.

(December to 1635) Carlo
Milanuzii was organist at Finale
di Modena at this time.

(to 1642) Men were considered
the best singers and the lute
(úd) and spiked viol (kamáncha)
were the most popular instruments at this time. These are
seen earlier in a painting of
musicians at the court of Sháh
Safí (active during these years)
to which a flute (náy) and
tambourine (da'ira) were added.

(to 1646) V. Mozzacchi was
maestro di cappella at St.
Peter's during these years.

(to 1652) Allegri sang in the
Sistine Choir during this period.

c.1629
Hendrick Jacobsz, Dutch violin
maker whose instruments resembled those of the Amati family,
was born at Amsterdam (died
1699, November 8).

Durual's "Travaux d'Ulysse" of
this year used a boat on the
stage at Paris.

1630
(January 18) Church authorities

(cont.) at Cracow appointed F.
Lilius conductor of the cathedral
choir, a position he retained
until his death.

(March 2) Thomas Bateson made
his will on this date.

(March 22) Richard Dering
(Deering), English organist and
composer, was buried at London.

(April 30) The Chapter Acts at
Christ Church, Dublin alluded to
the granting of a new lease on
Bateson's house and referred to
"the widdow Batson."

(May 25) Gery (de) Ghersem,
Flemish singer and composer,
died at Tournai (born c.1572).

(August 10) Lorenzo Ratti, an
Italian composer, died at
Perugia (birthdate unknown).
He was principally a motet com-
poser.

(November 15) Johann Kepler,
German astronomer and writer on
music theory, died at Ratisbon
(born 1571, December 27).

(November 19) Johann Hermann
Schein, a major German composer
of the Baroque Period, died at
Leipzig (born 1586, January 20).
He had held the position of can-
tor at the St. Thomas School.

(December 17) Gabriel Bataille,
a French lutenist, died at Paris
(born 1574 or 1575).

(March or April) Thomas
Bateson, the English composer,
died at Dublin (born c.1570).

(March) Pietro Benedetti on this
date was made a canon of the
Church of San Lorenzo at
Florence with the title of "S.

250

1630(cont.)
Amato Abate."

(March) Richard Deering (Dering),
English composer, died at
London (born c.1580).

(June) Giovanni Francesco Anerio,
Italian composer, died at Graz
or in Poland (born c.1567).

Hieronymus Amati, violin maker,
died (born c.1556).

John Banister, I, an English
violinist and composer, was
born (died London 1679, October
3). He was director of the
King's band and apparently the
first one to organize successful
public concerts.

Nicolas Antoine le Bègue, a
well-known composer of the
French harpsichord school, was
born (died 1702).

William Brade, English violinist
and composer, died at Hamburg
(born 1560).

John Daniel (Danyel), English
composer, died (born c.1565).

Sieur de L'Enclos, a French
lutenist, died in Paris (birthdate unknown).

Giovanni Battista Fontana,
Italian violinist and composer,
died at Padua (birthdate unknown). He was known for the
use of violinistic idioms in
his sonatas for solo violin and
continuo.

Alessandro Grandi, Italian composer, died at Bergamo (birthdate unknown).

Johann Nicolaus Hanff, a German
organist and composer, was born

(cont.) at Wechmar near
Mühlhausen, Thuringia (died
1706).

Otto Siegfried Harnisch, who
wrote texts in German for Passion
Music, died (birthdate unknown).

Fynes Moryson, who wrote the
"Itinerary," died (born 1566).

John Mundy, English organist and
composer, died at Windsor (born
c.1565).

Carlo Pallavicino, important
late 17th-Century opera composer,
was born at Brescia or Salo
(died 1688, January 26).

Paolo Quagliati, Italian madrigalist and organist at Santa
Maria Maggiore, died (born
c.1560).

Orazio Scaletta, an Italian composer, died at Padua (birthdate
unknown).

Sir William Stanley, the
Catholic adventurer to whom
Philips dedicated a book of
eight part madrigals in 1598,
died (born 1548).

William Stonard, English organist and composer, died at
Oxford (birthdate unknown).

Agazzari this year returned to
Siena where he became "maestro
di cappella" of the cathedral,
a position he held until his
death.

William Allen became the "King's
drum-major" this year.

Simone Arietto was currently a
violinist at the court of Savoy
at Turin.

1630(cont.)

William Brade's son Stephen was in Paris at this time.

Carissimi this year was appointed musical director of the Jesuit college of St. Apollinaire, for German students. It was here that he composed his long series of sacred histories and orator-ios.

Desquesnes was mentioned in the accounts for this year of Duke Ernest, Governor of the Netherlands.

The owner of a castle in Saxony bought six books of lute songs by Dowland and Jones at this time.

The citizens of Erfurt this year gave 50,000 pounds of bread and 7000 thalers to the Emperor's general, Tilly.

Jan Fabrycy, Polish composer and bass singer, this year became a member of the Capella Rorantistarum at Cracow. He was also known as Fabricius, Fabrycki, Fabrzycki and Zywiecensis.

Jacques Gaultier went to Holland and to Madrid this year.

George Herbert was ordained a priest at this time.

Hülphers belonged to a Thuringian family from Hilpershausen, Coburg. The family settled in Sweden this year.

Athanasius Kircher was a prof-essor at the Jesuit College at Würzburg where he taught Mathematics and Natural Philosophy at this time.

Kaspar Kittel was at this time a teacher of theorbo at Dresden.

Nicholas Lanier set Herrick's poem on the Birth of Prince Charles to music this year.

Du Mont was sent to Liège at this time to study organ and composition under Leonard de Hodimont and Lambert Pietkin.

Philips' name appeared without a title on the title page of the second and enlarged edition of the litanies released this year.

Two genealogical tables for Jean Rameau's wife, Claudine Demartinecourt, existed. The table of this year claimed that the group "go back to the Crusades."

Giles Tomkins this year was ap-pointed "Musician for the Virginalls" to King Charles I to succeed Richard Dering. He also made the chorister's house.

Ugolini this year composed a book of twelve-part vesper-psalms and motets, with a bass for the organ.

An enthusiastic audience at Rome this year welcomed the castrato Loreto Vittori when he sang Mazzocchi's "Lament of St. Magdalen."

Thomas Warwick was appointed or-ganist of the Chapel Royal in London at this time but soon left the position as his son was being knighted and becoming a Secretary of State.

Calvisius' "Melopoeia . . ." was published this year at Magdeburg.

1630(cont.)

A collection by Caroso was published at Rome as late as this year under the title "Raccolta di varij balli . . . nuouamente ritrouati negli scritti del sig. Fabritio Caroso."

Croce's "Laudate pueri" was included in a collection by Simonetti published at this time.

J. Crüger's "Synopsis musica," a book on ornaments, was published at Berlin this year.

A Diruta's "Sacrae modulationes Eremitici ordinis divorum . . ." and his "Sacri motetti a gloria di Giesù et ad honore di Maria a 1 & 2 voci . . ." both appeared at this time.

Donati's "Concerti ecclesiastici . . . D'Ign. D. maestro di cappella del Duomo di Lodi . . ." and his "Concerti ecclesiastici . . . Opera IV. Novamente ristampata . . ." were both published this year by Vincenti at Venice.

At this time Vincenti published Donati's "Fanfalughe," madrigals for two to five voices, and dedicated them to Milanuzii as one of the worthiest musicians of the time.

Dulichius' "Primus tomus Centuriae senarum vocum harmonias sacras audibus sanctissime Triados consecratas continentis. Stettini. Georg. Gretzschii. 1630" appeared.

Frescobaldi's "Primo libro, arie musicali" was published this year at Florence.

Gagliano's "Responsoria majoris

(cont.) hebdomadae quatuor paribus vocibus decantanda . . ." was published at this time.

Mass and "Salmi concertati" for three voices by Grandi was issued this year.

A book of motets for two to eight voices by Grandi was published this year. It was the last of six books, however, the date of the fifth was never found.

Hodemont this year published his "Sacri Concentus" for one to five voices with instruments and organ continuo at Liège.

The seventh book of Milanuzii's "Ariose vaghezze" was published this year.

Miniscalchi's third book of pleasant strophic "Arie" was published this year at Venice.

Peerson this year composed his "Mottects or Grave Chamber Musique" and it was published.

Staden published his "Hertzentrosta-Musica" this year as well as his "Musicalischer Freuden-und Andachtswecker oder geistliche Gesänglein" for four to six voices.

After this year composers developed the chamber cantata in several contrasting sections of recitative, arioso and aria, so that a strophic bass could rarely be used as the basis for a whole cantata.

The farce "The Singing Simpkin" was translated into German ("Pickelherring in the Box") in 1620. Similar farces were contained in Ayrer's collection

253

of 1618 and in the "Liebeskampf" of this year which provided a large repertory of popular theatre based on English models.

For the forty years prior to this date throughout most of Northern Europe amateur musicians were playing the same tunes, whether they were English, Dutch or German, and there remained little doubt that the jigg was the medium through which many of these tunes were disseminated.

By this time the madrigal had been for all intents and purposes discarded.

After this date the masque entered its declining period.

The oratorio form did not crystallize before this time and its beginning coincided with the appearance of bel-canto style.

After this year the terms Sonata and sinfonia were used more and more frequently to designate separate instrumental compositions.

At this time a reaction grew against considering the text to be the main unifying device in serious vocal composition.

An opera by Kapsberger was produced this year.

Lambardi's mascherata music for "Monte Parnaso" was performed this year at Naples. This was the initial attempt at opera in Naples.

Monteverdi's "La Delia e l'Ulisse," written with Manelli and an unknown librettist, was produced this year at Bologna.

Monteverdi's "Proserpina rapita" with text by Strozzi was produced this year at Venice.

"Les Noces de Vaugirard," a comic pastorale, was produced this year.

From this date forward the problem of form in opera moved to the foreground.

"ppp" appeared in music as early as this year.

The great epidemic this year in the Adriatic Republic lessened the enthusiasm for the arts as well as for amusements in general.

A plague struck Cremona this year and caused innumerable deaths while forcing all those who could to flee for safety.

Since their group numbered only about one thousand at Massachusetts Bay this year, the elders probably were able to hold congregational singing anywhere they thought appropriate.

More Puritans came to Boston than to Plymouth this year.

A great plague in Venice this year killed about half the population.

King Charles II (House of Stuart) of England was born (died 1685). He was the first "Restoration" King.

King John IV of Portugal this year succeeded to the dukedom of Bragança and took an interest in the choir.

At the end of this year Rubens, after the death of his first

1630(cont.)
wife, Isabella Brandt, married
Hélène Fourment, a sixteen year
old girl.

Velazquez, the Spanish painter,
went to Rome this year, on the
advice of Rubens, to study the
great masters.

(to 1631) Pietro Paolo Sabbatini
was maestro di cappella di S.
Luigi de'Francesi, Rome during
these years.

(to 1632) The organist and composer Delphin Strungk held
positions successively at the
principal church of Wolfenbüttel
during this period.

(to 1635) Chyliński held the
position of "Praefectus
musicorum" at the church of St.
Anthony at Padua at this time.

(to 1637) Monteverdi produced no
stage works during these years.

(to 1638) Antonio Maria
Abbatini's published works consisted in part of four books of
Psalms, three books of Masses,
and some Antifons for twenty
-four voices published at Rome
by Mascardi during these years
and in 1677.

(to 1639) Both the Pilgrims and
the Puritans considered the
achievements of Byrd, Morley,
and the rest to be the type of
frivolity and "popery" from
which they fled on the
"Mayflower," the "Arabella,"
and the other ships used for
the migration to the colonies
during these years.

(to 1639) Dutch painting: Frans
Hals, "Portrait of Willem van
Heythuryen" (18 5/10" x 14 4/5").

(to 1640) The "air de cour"
seemed to be in a decline during
this period.

(to 1640) Bel-canto style emerged
during these years.

(to 1642) Spanish painting:
Zurbarán, "St. Marina."

(to 1647) A. Diruta was organist
and "maestro di cappella" of
Sant' Agostino in Rome throughout these years.

(to 1648) Pedro Heredia was
choirmaster at St. Peters during
this period.

(to 1650) Books issued by the
Phalèse firm during these years
carried the imprint "Chez les
Héritiers de Pierre Phalèse."

(to 1661) Hendrik Liberti was
organist of Antwerp Cathedral
for all this time.

c.1630
Thomas Baltzar, a German violin-
ist and composer, was born at
Lübeck (died 1663).

Jan Cocx, a Flemish priest and
composer, was born at East
Flanders (died 1678, October
24).

Henning Dedekind, a composer,
died at Gebsee, Thuringia
(birthdate unknown).

John Goodgroome, an English organist and composer, was born
(died 1704, June 27).

Sigismondo d'India, an Italian
composer, died (born c.1562).

Szymon Jarzębski, Polish violinist at the royal court in Warsaw,
was born (died 1679).

Matthew Locke, English composer, was born at Exeter (died 1677, August). He became court composer to King Charles II and organist to Queen Catherine of Braganza. See c.1633.

Thomas Ravenscroft, Mus. Bac. and English composer, died (born c.1582). There is a valid question as to whether this man buried at Barnet was the composer. The alternate dates are birth - c.1590, death - c.1633.

Bernhard Smith, a German organ builder, was born (died 1708, February 20).

Giuseppe Felice Tosi, an organist and composer, was born at Bologna (date of death unknown).

One source mentioned a Louis Couperin at this time and described him as an organist at St. Gervais who also played viol and violin in the ballet music of the court. Couperin was also offered the sought-after post of Jouer de l'Epinette de la Chambre du Roi, but declined. He also was offered a position as one of the King's official organists. No other sources could be found to substantiate the claimed existence of a Louis Couperin at this time, however; an Armand-Louis and a Pierre-Louis were both 18th-Century members of the famous family.

John Hingston composed a "Fantasia for 2 cornetts and sackbut to the organ" at this time.

Edward Lowe became organist at Christ Church Cathedral, Oxford this year.

Biagio Marini was a genuine chamber music composer and certainly one of the first professional violin virtuosos from among the ranks of composers.

"The Marche before the battel" was included in the Fitzwilliam Virginal Book as "The Earle of Oxford's Marche" which celebrated "the fighting De Veres."

The Rowallan manuscript volume of lute music was compiled at this time.

The early baroque period came to an end this year. Its starting date was variously given at between c.1580 and c.1600.

The French courante at this time changed its character and became a danse très-grave in six beats. The time signatures vacillated from 3/2 to 6/4.

The second important school of opera was found in Rome at this time.

French painting: Baugin, "Wafers."

French painting: Poussin, "Midas and Bacchus;" "Tancred and Erminia;" "The Triumph of Flora" (oil on canvas 5'5" x 7' 10 7/8").

(to 1631) Dutch painting: Rubens, "Hélène Fourment" (She became his wife at this time).

(to c.1680) The middle baroque period is frequently given these dates.

(to c.1830) During this period the lower mordent has taken precedent over the upper.

(March 25) Philipp Dulichius, German composer, died at Stettin (born 1562, December). One source gives his death date as 1623.

(June 10) Filippo Vitali was appointed a singer in the papal choir.

(June 26) Vincenzo Albrici, an Italian composer, was born at Rome (died 1696, August 8).

(August 6) Juan Blas de Castro, Spanish madrigal composer, died at Madrid (born c.1560).

(September 7) Clemens Thieme, German instrumentalist and composer, was born in Gross-Dietmansdorf near Dresden (died 1668, March 27).

(October 4) Sebastian Scherer, German organist and composer, was baptized on this date at Ulm.

(October 18) Heinrich Müller, German ecclesiastic and hymnologist, was born at Lubeck (died 1675, September 17).

(November 25) F. Pilkington was made rector of Aldford (five miles south of Chester).

(December 15) Nicolas Formé made his will and made his sister the sole legatee.

(May) In an entry at this time Bateston is said to have died just a fortnight before the rent was to be paid, so that it is probable that the date was in the early part of March.

Scipione Cerreto, an Italian theorist and composer, died at (cont.) Naples (born 1551).

Gabriel Diaz, a Spanish composer, died after this date (born c.1590).

T. East's widow, Lucretia East, died (birthdate unknown).

Sebastian Scherer, a German organist and composer, was born at Ulm (died 1712, August 26).

In Warsaw at this time Jacopo Abbatis was still noted as a "man of great merit."

Heinrich Albert this year became organist at the old church in Königsberg.

Auxcousteaux occupied the position of "maître de musique" at the cathedral of Saint-Quentin at this time.

William Child was thought to have been awarded the degree of Bachelor of Music at Oxford this year, but the date on his exercise was 1639.

Gabriel Diaz was "capellár" in the church of Santa Inés at Córdoba up to this year.

Gabriel Diaz was one of the judges this year in a competition to elect a new "maestro de capilla" at Granada.

Engelmann was organist of St. Thomas Church, Leipzig at this time.

Gilles Hayne was appointed precentor at the collegiate church of St. John the Evangelist at Liege this year and held that position until his death.

Thomas Holmes became organist of

Winchester Cathedral this year and held the position until his death.

Randolph Jewett succeeded Thomas Bateson this year as organist of Christ Church Cathedral, Dublin. He was also appointed organist at St. Patrick's Cathedral.

Athanasius Kircher was driven from Germany by the Thirty Years' War.

Tobias Michael this year succeeded Schein as cantor and musical director of St. Thomas Church at Leipzig.

Monteverdi joined the priesthood this year.

John Mudd was organist of Peterborough Cathedral up to this year. He had held the position since 1583.

Wolfgang Schonsleder wrote under the pseudonym of Volupius Decorus. He treated one-sharp transposition as a regular alternative in his work "Architectonice musices."

John Stanley was at Cassel from this date forward.

Christoph Strauss, choir-master of St. Stephen's Cathedral in Vienna at this time, included trumpet fanfares in the mass.

"Den boek der gheestelijcke sangen . . . door eene, religieus van d'order van Sente François . . ." was published this year by Aertsens at Antwerp.

Cerreto's "Dialogo harmonico"

(cont.) appeared this year in manuscript.

Christoph Demantius composed a Lutheran motet Passion this year.

A. Diruta's "Messe concertate a 5 voci . . ." and his "Viridarium Marianum in quo Deiparae Virginis Letaniae, et Hymni 4, 5, 6 vocibus . . ." appeared this year.

Franck wrote his "Dulces mundani exilii deliciae" for one to eight voices at this time.

Klemme's "Tabulatura italica" this year was one of numerous collections that systematically used all twelve modes.

Mazzocchi's oratorio "Il martirio dei SS. Abbundio ed Abbundanzio" was produced this year at Rome.

Monteverdi's "Messa solennissima" was issued this year.

A third edition of Morley's canzonets was printed this year.

C.T. Padbrué's best known composition, "Kusjes" ("Little Kisses"), a series of songs for three or four voices, was translated from Latin and published this year in his native city.

The third edition of Philips' "Les Rosignols spirituels" was published this year by Veruliet.

Many organists and cantors followed the leadership of Schein, particularly Scheidt in his "Geistliche Conzerten" composed this year.

Heinrich Schütz's "Das ist je gewisslich wahr" was published

1631(cont.)

this year at Dresden. It was written in memory of Schein.

Stadlmayr published "Missae concertatae a 6 adjuncto choro secundo sive ripieni" this year.

Valentini's canon, "Nel nodo di Salomo a 96 voci" was published at this time.

"Nodus Salomonis" (Solomon's Knot), a famous canon by Valentini, was described by Kircher in this year in his "Musurgia universalis."

Vernizzi's "Angelici concentus" opus 3 was reprinted (See also 1606, 1611).

At intervals from this date forward Christ Church and St. Patrick's shared the services of the same organist.

Bertali's dramatic cantata for four voices, "Donna real" (first words, not the title), was sung at Vienna as early as this date.

Jonson's masque "Chloridia" was produced this year.

Sir Robert Bruce Cotton, the English literary noble, died (born 1571).

John Donne, renowned English metaphysical poet, died (born 1573).

Michael Drayton, Elizabethan poet and historian, died (born 1563).

John Dryden, a foremost English poet and writer of prose and drama, was born (died 1700).

Tilly and Gustavus met this

(cont.) year at the Battle of Breitenfeld.

The town of Magdeburg was destroyed at this time.

Brouwer, the painter, returned to Antwerp this year after spending time and achieving success in both Amsterdam and Haarlem. After this date not much was known about his activities.

(to 1632) A Thomas Mudd succeeded John Mudd as organist at Peterborough Cathedral for a period of about a year.

(to 1636) A Swedish garrison occupied the town of Erfurt, Germany, during these years.

(to 1638) Donati was "maestro di cappella" at Milan Cathedral during this period.

(to 1640) Scheidt's four books "Geistliche Concerten" were published during these years.

(to 1646) Herbst during this period was Kapellmeister at Nürnberg.

(to 1682) Italian architecture: Longhena, Santa Maria della Salute, Venice (c.200' x 155').

c.1631

Francois Couperin was born at Chaumes. He was a violinist, organist, teacher, and a pupil of Chambonnières, but never became as famous as his brothers. He lived at the parish of St. Louis en l'Ile (died c.1701). He was referred to as Sieur de Crouilly and one source recorded his date of death as 1703.

John Mudd, English organist and

c.1631(cont.)
composer, died at Peterborough
(birthdate unknown).

A "Gloria" composed this year by
Monteverdi, provided a brilliant
example of personal, nonliturgi-
cal musical treatment of a liturgical subject.

1632
(February 3) George Marson, an
English organist and composer,
died at Canterbury (born c.1573).

(February 23) Landi's second
opera "Il S. Alessio" was produced at this date at the
Palazzo Barberini.

(March 14) Landgrave Moritz of
Hesse-Cassel, German patron of
music and amateur composer,
died at Eschwege (born 1572,
May 25).

(March 20) Dallam this year made
an organ for the church of St.
Peter at York (the York
Cathedral organ).

(April 2) Georg Kaspar Wecker,
German organist and composer,
was born at Nürnberg (died 1695,
April 20).

(September 8) Leszczyński, a
widower, was joined at the monastery at Jasna Góra this year
by his son Aleksander.

(November 24) Jean Baptiste
Lully, Italian-French composer,
was born at Florence (died 1687,
March 22). The actual day of
his birth has also been given as
November 28 or 29. Lully's
position as an opera composer
and court musician was a pre
-eminent one.

(November 28) Sebastian Knüpfer,

(cont.) a German philologist and
musician, was born at Asch,
Voigtland (died 1676, October
10).

(December 4) C. Huygens on this
date was made a Chevalier de
l'ordre de Saint Michel by King
Louis XIII of France.

(December 17) Anthony Wood, an
English musical chronicler, was
born at Oxford (died 1695,
November 25).

(May) Schütz apparently resented
Price's privileged position at
the Dresden Court and at this
time wrote a strongly critical
letter concerning this.

Edward Gibbons, son of Murray
and Mary Gibbons, was baptised
(died 1637, May).

Johannes Bach, an Arnstadt musician, son of Caspar I and a
member of the second generation
of the Bach family, died (born
1602).

Melchior Borchgrevinck,
Netherlandish singer, organist
and composer, died at Copenhagen
(birthdate unknown).

Alessandro Ghivizzani, Italian
composer, died (born c.1572).

Giovanni Paolo Maggini, Italian
violin maker, died at Brescia
(born 1580 or 1581). He was a
pupil of da Salò.

Jan Bischoff by this time was
already a member of the Royal
Chapel in Warsaw.

William Child this year was appointed one of the organists of
the Chapel Royal at London.

Clifford was admitted as a chorister of Magdalen College this year. He remained there until 1642.

C. Cocchi was at this time "maestro di cappella" at San Francesco, Milan.

J.B. Comes was currently "maestro de capilla" at the Cathedral of Valencia.

Dallam (probably Thomas) was engaged to repair the organ at Magdalen College, Oxford in this year as well as in 1615 and 1637.

Amadio Freddi was maestro di cappella at Treviso Cathedral this year.

Nathaniel Giles was this year appointed one of the organists of St. George's Chapel, Windsor. His appointment was a joint one with William Child.

Henry Jaye, at Southwark, this year made a viol.

Monteverdi this year was ordained a priest of the church and retired from public activities.

Lambert Du Mont, Henry's brother, replaced the latter this year at the church at Maestricht.

C. Patiño was first heard of this year when he received a sum of money from King John IV of Portugal.

The real baroque style replaced the English madrigal this year in the works of such composers as Walter Porter, Monteverdi's pupil, as demonstrated in the former's "Madrigals and

(cont.) Ayres."

William Prynne this year wrote "Histriomastix" in which he attacked the contemporary stage.

John Wallis went up to Emmanuel College, Cambridge at this time.

C. Cocchi's "Ghirlanda sacra" was published this year at Milan.

Agostinho da Cruz at this time compiled his "Duas artes, huma de cantochão por estylo novo, outra de orgão com figuras muito curiosas, compostas no anno 1632" and dedicated it to King John IV of Portugal.

An important early Roman opera, "Sant' Alessio," was written this year by Stefano Landi. He wrote his own libretto.

Hendrik Liberti this year published a book of "Paduanes et galiardes."

Milanuzii's "Messe e canzoni" for five voices was reprinted this year at Venice.

Monteverdi's "Scherzi musicali cioè aria & madrigali . . ." was issued by Bartolommeo Magni this year.

Porter's "Madrigales and Ayres of two, three, foure and five voyces . . ." was published this year.

"Syntagma de origine Livonarum di Fridericus Menius," the first full account of Latvian songs and singing, was published at this time.

A musical drama, "Il ritorno di Angelica nell'Indie" by Tignali,

1632(cont.)

was produced at Rome. Tignali may be a misspelling of Tenaglia.

Tomkins' "When David Heard" was published this year.

Robletti this year published arias for one, two, and three voices by Vitali at Orvieto.

A Rudolfo Corelli was decapitated and mutilated and the "disjecta membra" thrown in front of his house. This act was because of his attempt, at the head of a band of rioters, to murder Mario Calcagnini, his overlord.

Landi's "Sant'Alessio" was performed this year in the new theater of the Palazzo Barberini. Sets were built by Bernini.

An attempt was made this year to introduce the Geneva tunes completed into England.

The Teatro Barberini opened this year with Landi's "Sant' Alessio."

Louis Bourdalove, a Jesuit father, was born (died 1704).

Thomas Dekker, English playwright, died (born c.1570).

King Gustavus Adolfus of Sweden died (born 1594). He was a staunch defender of his nation against the threat of Catholic domination.

The reign of Sigismundus III of Poland came to an end. He had ruled since 1587.

Tilly, in command of Ferdinand II's imperial forces, was de-

(cont.) feated at this time at Leipzig.

Jan Vermeer van Delft, the Dutch painter, was born (died 1675).

Sir Christopher Wren, English architect, was born (died 1723).

Brouwer was forced to pawn his property this year. His financial problems were said to result from use of alcohol and tobacco.

Van Dyck went back to England where he became most successful with the aristocracy and was appointed court painter to King Charles I.

Italian architecture: Borromini, the gallery at the Palazzo Spada in Rome (27' deep).

Italian painting: Rembrandt, "The Anatomy Lesson of Dr. Tulp" (66 3/4" x 85 1/4").

Colonial architecture: Smithfield, St. Luke's.

Dutch painting: Van Dyck, "Lord Philip Wharton."

(to 1633) S. Otto was succentor or assistant cantor at Freiberg and taught Andreas Hammerschmidt during these years.

(to 1636) John and Clement Dixon were still at Dresden at this time.

(to 1638) Monteverdi had no new publications whatsoever during this period.

(to 1648) The reign of King Ladislas IV over Poland, during which he established a permanent

1632(cont.)
Opera at Warsaw.

(to 1669) Kaspar Kittel held the post of instrumentalist and later court organist during these years.

(to 1819) In addition to Gluck's two there have been at least thirty other settings of "Iphigenia in Aulis" during this long period of years.

c.1632
Leandro Gallerano, an Italian composer, died, probably at Padua (birthdate unknown).

John Milton, who had acquired a considerable fortune by this time retired to Horton in Buckinghamshire.

Thomas Mudd, English organist and composer, died at Peterborough (born c.1560).

1633
(January 1) Michel de La Guerre was made organist at the Sainte -Chapelle in Paris, replacing LaGalle.

(January 24) Nathaniel Giles, English organist and composer, died at Windsor (born c.1550).

(February 23) Samuel Pepys, English amateur musician who wrote the famous diary, was born at London (died 1703, May 26).

(April 10) Werner Fabricius, German organist and composer, was born at Itzehoe, Holstein (died 1679, January 9).

(May 10) Jan Nowotarski, a Polish organist and Benedictine monk, died at Cracow (birthdate

(cont.) unknown).

(June 9) A. Draghi's "L'Oronisbe" was produced at Vienna. He wrote the libretto himself.

(June 19) Agostinho da Cruz, Portuguese instrumentalist and composer, died at Coimbra (born c.1590).

(July 12) Simon Besler, German composer, died at Breslau (born 1583, August 27).

(August 12) This date is given as the deathdate of Jacopo Peri, the opera composer. He died at Florence, but sources disagree as to the date (born 1561, August 20). Some sources give c.1615 as his date of death.

(August 24) Laurentius von Schnüffis, an Austrian singer and composer, was born in Schniffs, Vorarlberg (died 1702, January 7).

(September 17) Thomas Holmes was sworn a Gentleman of the Chapel Royal on this date.

(October 25) Jean Titelouze, French composer and organist, died at Roven (born 1563). His works for organ were dissonant and represented the last touch of Renaissance style. Here and there modern "concertato" mo-tives appeared, always in com-plementary rhythms.

(November 26) Johann Christoph Wagenseil, German historian and librarian, was born at Nürnberg (died 1708, October 9).

(October) Thomas Clifford, younger brother of James, was born (date of death unknown).

1633(cont.)

(October) Monteverdi wrote a letter to an unknown recipient thanking him for his praise and referring to his book "Prima Practica," a theoretical work.

Charles Emmanuel Borjon de Scellery, French lawyer and amateur musician, was born at Pont-de-Vaux, Bresse (died 1691, May 4).

Charles Couperin, son of Charles I, was born (died 1679). He was one of three of the eight children to become a professional musician (See 1638).

Amy Peerson, Martin's wife, died this year (birthdate unknown).

Peter Philips, English composer, died at Brussels (born c.1560).

Giles Tomkins, organist, was born at Salisbury (died 1725, July 24).

John Adson this year was sworn a musician-in-ordinary for the recorder and cornett.

Auxcousteaux was "maître des enfants" at the cathedral of Saint-Quentin at this time.

Caspar Bach I retired from his job as town piper and bought his own house.

Domenico Brunetti founded the Accademia dei Filaschisi this year.

This year Coelho finished his service at the Lisbon Royal Chapel.

P. Cornet received a pension at this time.

Correa left his position at the church of San Salvador this year.

A violin made by Jan Dankwart bore this date. It has been owned by the conductor of the Poznan Philharmonic Orchestra for many years.

An entry in the Parish Registers of Gateshead-on-Tyne this year read, "Paid the piper for playing to ye menders of ye high waies five severall daies, 3s. 4d. ."

A. Hammerschmidt was appointed organist in the service of the Count von Bünau this year. He published his first known composition, a Thanksgiving piece for eight voices.

Juan Hidalgo, a Spanish composer, was one of three harpists in the royal chapel at Madrid at this time.

Simon Ives, Henry and William Lawes were all engaged to write the music for Shirley's masque "The Triumph of Peace."

English documents indicated that Kellie was not appointed to the Scottish Chapel Royal until this year, but this was not true.

Kellie was in charge of music at the Scottish coronation ceremonies this year.

Althanasius Kircher went to the house of his order (Jesuit) at Avignon, then to Vienna, and finally to Rome where he stayed until his death in 1680.

Henry Lawes wrote music this year for Thomas Carew's masque, "Coelum Britannicum."

Francesco Manelli was at Rome
this year where his wife
Maddalena sang in several opera
performances.

Adam V. Michna was at this time
an organist at the Jesuit
College of Jindřichův Hradec.

C. Patiño was appointed to the
Spanish royal chapel this year,
succeeding Romero.

Martin Peerson remarried this
year.

Philips was still canon of
Soignies at this time.

Richard Portman this year succeeded Thomas Day as organist at
Westminster Abbey.

Profe was appointed organist to
the church of St. Elizabeth at
Breslau this year.

Mateo Romero retired this year
on a pension and was succeeded
by Patiño.

Hawkins quoted an advertisement
dated 1667 for two "chests of
viols" for sale, one made by
John Rose in 1598, the other by
Henry Smith this year.

Christoph Schultze was cantor
at Delitzsch at this time.

Schütz answered an invitation
from the King of Denmark to
visit Copenhagen this year.

Jean Titelouze this year applied
for permission to instruct a
successor (as organist at Rouen
Cathedral) because of his pre-
carious state of health. He
did not live long enough to
train a replacement, however.

John Tomkins went on a journey
with King Charles at this time.

Robert Tomkins was one of the
musicians in the household of
King Charles I this year.

G.J. Voss at this time became a
professor of history at
Amsterdam University.

Antonio Maria Abbatini's "Il
pianto di Rodomonte" was published this year at Orvieto.

Giovanni Battista Ala wrote
several motets included in the
"Luscina sacra" published this
year at Antwerp.

Bodenschatz' "Manuale sacrum"
was issued at Leipzig this year.

Antoine Boesset's "Les
Bacchanales" was completed at
this time.

Charles Butler's "The English
Grammar" was published at Oxford
this year and frequently thereafter.

Diruta's "Psalmi vespertini 3
vocibus qui in omnibus
Ecclesiae Solennitatibus
decantari solent, . . ." appeared at this time.

Donati's "Il secondo libro delle
messe da cappella a 4 et a 5
. . ." was completed this year.

Benedetto Ferrari wrote his
"Musiche varie a voce sola"
this year and it was published
at Venice.

Thomas Harper, the printer,
re-printed Ravenscroft's
"Psalms" in a second edition
which contained some settings
by Robert Palmer.

1633(cont.)

The second and third parts of Philips' "Paradisus" was reprinted this year by Phalèse.

William Prynne's "Histriomastix" was published this year at London. In it he denounced theatre and especially the masque. He referred to theatre music as "lust-provoking" and said it should be "unlawfull unto Christians."

Raban this year issued an extended version of his Psalter at Aberdeen. He became even more daring in this version.

Michel Angelo Rossi composed the opera, "Erminia sul Giordano" this year.

Staden published his "Geistlicher Music-Klang" at this time.

The beginning of Polish opera came this year with a "dramma per musica" titled "La fama reale, ovvero Il principe trionfanto Ladislao IV, monarcha della Polonia, re di Suezia." The composer was Piotr Elert and the first performance was at the royal court of Warsaw.

Michelangelo Rossi's "Erminia" was produced this year.

Felice Sances produced his "Cantade" at Venice at this time.

Violins came into use in the royal chapel at Madrid this year.

George Herbert, an English religious poet, died (born 1593).

George Herbert's "The Temple" was completed before he died

(cont.) this year.

King James II of England (House of Stuart), a Restoration King, was born (died 1701).

Willem van de Velde the Younger, Dutch painter, was born (died 1707).

Dutch painting: Hals, "Officers of the Kloveniers Arquebusiers at Haarlem." He painted eight huge official group portraits measuring from four to eight square meters.

Spanish painting: Zurbarán, "Lemons, Oranges and Rose."

(to 1636) G. Voigtländer was court trumpeter to Prince Friedrich III at Gottorf during these years.

(to 1637) B. Pekiel was organist of the royal chapel in Warsaw during this period.

(to 1640) The six parts of Johann Schop's "Neue Paduanen, Galliarden, Allemanden" were published at Hamburg over a period of seven years.

(to 1641) Schütz' stay at the Dresden court was interrupted at this time by the Thirty Years' War.

c.1633

Matthew Locke, the English composer, was born this year according to one major source (died 1677, August).

1634

(January 7) Adam Krieger, a German composer and poet, was born at Driesen Neumark, Prussia (died 1666, June 30). His compositions consisted of arias with his own texts, and songs for one to five voices with three or five part instrumental ritornelli between each verse. He was a pupil of Scheidt.

(February 3) Shirley's masque "The Triumph of Peace" was performed at court by the gentlemen of the four Inns of Court on Candlemas Day (Some sources maintain that at this time Candlemas was on February 2nd).

(February 18) Henry Lawes' music for Thomas Carew's masque "Coelum Britannicum" was performed at court.

(March 6) Bartolomeo Melani, singer, brother of Jacopo, Atto, etc., was born at Pistoia (date of death unknown).

(May 1) Frescobaldi was reinstated as organist at St. Peter's, Rome.

(June 24) Auxcousteaux entered the Sainte-Chapelle as clerk "haute-contre."

(September 5-6) The battle of Nördlingen took place.

(September 24) "Comus," a masque by John Milton, was performed on Michaelmas night, at Ludlow Castle.

(September 29) Henry Lawes performed the part of the Attendant Spirit in a production of Milton's masque "Comus" at Ludlow Castle.

(November 15) Johann Staden, German organist and composer, died at Nürnberg (born 1581).

(November 19) Paul Homberger, German composer, died at Ratisbon (born c.1560).

(April) Social and political troubles in Tuscany forced Frescobaldi to leave his position there and return to Rome.

(May or June) Jean Dufon, a Flemish singer and composer, died at Namur (born 1574).

(August and September) Three musical enthusiasts (a Captain, Lieutenant, and Ensign) toured England, inspecting organs.

(October) George Kirbye, English composer, died at Bury, St. Edmunds (born c.1565).

(October) Henry Lawes wrote five songs included in "Comus" presented in October 1634 and "Cupid to ye Knights Templars in a Maske at ye Middle Temple."

(October) Erasmus Widmann, German organist and composer, died (born 1572).

Melchior Bach, Arnstadt musician and son of Caspar I, member of the second generation of the Bach family, died (born 1603).

Adriano Banchieri, an important theorist and composer of sacred and secular vocal music, instrumental music, as well as madrigal comedies, died (born 1567).

Marc-Antoine Charpentier, French sacred composer, was born at Paris (died 1704, February 24). He was a pupil of Carissimi.

Robert Johnson II, English lutenist and composer, son of

John Johnson I, died at London (born c.1583).

Camillo Lambardi, tenor singer and composer, died at Naples (born 1560).

John Adson this year became a music teacher to the king at a salary of 20d. a day for life.

Hans Bach, the younger, married Martha this year.

Steffano Bernardi left Salzburg for unknown reasons, quite possibly because of ill-health since he died the following year.

Byrd's pedigree and coat-of-arms were recorded this year in the Heralds' Visitation of Essex.

Byrd's daughter, Rachel, married Edward Biggs this year.

Thomas, son of Byrd's son, Christopher, was recorded as living at Stondon Place at this time.

Robert Dallam this year built an organ for Jesus College at Cambridge.

Ebner was organist at St. Stephen's Cathedral, Vienna, starting this year.

Giles Farnaby's daughter married William Walters this year at St. Mary Magdalene, Bermondsey.

G.B. da Gagliano became a musician to the Grand Duke of Tuscany at Florence this year.

Thomas Gale at this time held

(cont.) the office of Custos at College of Vicars Choral of Exeter.

Edward Gibbons was the subject of formal protest on the part of two of the lay vicars this year. The complaints were that he was not in Holy Orders and his colleagues were dissatisfied because of his serious neglect of duties.

John Price I was in Copenhagen this year for the lavishly staged wedding celebrations of the Princess of Saxony.

Thomas Selle was cantor at Itzehoe this year.

Sigmund Gottlieb Staden became organist this year when his father died to the St. Lorenz Church. He succeeded Valentin Dretzel, who replaced the elder Staden as organist to St. Sebald Church.

Nicholas Tomkins was one of the Gentlemen of the Privy Chamber to King Charles I this year.

The pedigree of this year stated that Thomas Tomkins, first son of Thomas Tomkins, Sr. by his second marriage, died when his ship sank in 1591.

Giovanni Battista Ala wrote several motets included in "Pratum musicum" published this year at Antwerp.

Charles d'Ambleville wrote "Octonarium, seu canticum B.V. . . . ." this year at Paris.

Gerat Barry's "Militarie Discipline" of this year remarked that the "Drum mayor" was responsible for the provision of "dromes and phifes."

Berti was represented in
Alessandro Vincenti's edition of
"Arie diverse" published this
year at Venice.

Brassicanus wrote some of the
songs in Daniel Hizler's
"Musikalich figurirte Melodien
. . ." of this year.

Charles Butler was the author of
"The Feminine Monarchie; or a
treatise concerning Bees" reprinted this year at Oxford
(See also 1609 and 1619).

Crüger's "Synopsis musices," a
method for thorough-bass, was
published this year at Berlin
in a third edition (See also
1624).

Dering's "Cantiones sacrae" for
five voices was reprinted at
this time.

Donati's "Il primo libro de'
motetti a voce sola di Ign. D.
maestro di cappella nel Duomo
di Milano . . ." appeared this
year.

Eccard's "Geistliche Lieder
. . ." was reprinted at this
time.

Franck this year wrote his
"Psalm II" for four voices.

G.B. da Gagliano's "Psalmi
vespertini cum Litaniis
Beatissimae Virginis . . ."
was published at this time.

The five songs for Milton's
"Comus" by H. Lawes were typical
examples of early baroque continuo song.

Henry Lawes' compositions appear
in a manuscript volume belonging
to Dr. Cooper Smith, Rector of
Basingstoke.

Marini's opus 7, "Canto per le
musiche di camera concerti a
4-6 voci ed instromenti" was
published this year at Venice.

Marin Mersenne's musical
treatises "Les Préludes de
l'harmonie universelle" and
"Questions harmoniques" were
published this year.

Monteverdi's "Tre ariette" with
anonymous text was issued this
year by Vincenti at Venice.

Giovanni Pasta this year published a volume of solo arias at
Milan.

Giovanni Pasta this year published two books "Due Sorelle,
musica e poesia concertate" at
Venice.

Three volumes of five-part madrigals by Marco Scacchi were
published at this time.

Thomas Selle's "Deliciarum
Juvenilium Decas" was written
this year.

Johann Stobaeus published his
"Geistliche Lieder auf
gewöhnliche preussische Kirchen-
Melodeyen durchaus gerichtet und
mit fünff Stimmen componirt"
this year. It included 102
settings of choral tunes for
five voices. Half were by
Stobaeus and the balance by his
teacher, Eccard.

Lazaro Valvasensi at this time
wrote his "Secondo giardino
d'amorosi fiori" which contained
several secular songs including

1634(cont.)
early examples of the strophic
-bass cantata.

The first meeting of the French
Academy took place this year.

Under the "Schul-Ordnung" of
this year which was effective at
the time of J.S. Bach's appointment, the staff of the
Leipzig Thomasschule consisted
of a rector, an assistant rector,
a cantor and tertius. The group
was referred to as the
"superiores" and included four
junior masters for the lower
classes of non-foundation pupils.

The first chapter of operatic
history ended when Stéfano Landi,
a papal singer, performed his
own work, "Sant' Alessio,"produced this year.

Carew's masque "Coelum
Britannicum" was performed at
this time.

Landi's drama musicale "Il Sant'
Alessio," one of the highest
achievements of the Roman school
of opera, was produced this year
at the Palazzo Barbarini.

Routrov's "Hercule movrant" was
produced this year using theatrical staging machinery.

Masques were certainly extrava-
gantly mounted as was indicated
by the fact that it cost over
£ - 21,000 to produce Shirley's
"Triumph of Peace" at the Inns
of Court this year.

John Chapman, poet and transla-
tor, died (birthdate unknown).

Marie de La Fayette, French
novelist, was born (died 1693).

Sir Thomas Browne's "Religio
Medici" was written at this
time.

Wallenstein, a Jesuit trained
general, died (born 1583).

Ferdinand III succeeded
Wallenstein as generalissimo
this year.

Valentin de Boullongne, an
Italian painter, died (born
1591).

Jacques Callot, French painter,
died (born 1592).

Dutch painting: Rubens, "Quos
Ego" (19 1/4" x 25 1/4").

(to 1635) Part I of Tobias
Michael's chief work,
"Musikalische Salenlust," was
published this year. It contained thirty sacred pieces for
five voices in the madrigal
style.

(to 1635) Spanish painting:
Velásquez, "Surrender at Breda"
(10'1" x 12"). This painting
was an excellent evocation of
the legendary chivalry of noble
Spain.

(to 1635) Verdina was vice
-"Kapellmeister" at the Imperial
Chapel during this period.

(to 1637) Valentine Flood was
at Danzig during these years.

(to 1642) Jooris Willems during
this period worked at Ghent as
a cornett player and violin
maker.

(to 1656) Felicianus Suevus composed three books of masses and
a large amount of other church
music during this span of years.

c.1634

Dutch painting: Rembrandt, self
-portrait with his wife "Saskia"
(64" x 52").

Lazaro Valrasensi was an organist at Valvasone at this time.

(to 1636) F. Pilkington was
succeeded as rector of Aldford
by Joseph Bradwell during this
period.

1635

(January 28) Gottfried Vopelius,
German organist and composer,
was born near Zittau (died
1715, February 3).

(June 5) Philippe Quinault,
French dramatist, was baptised
at Paris (died 1688, November
26).

(July 6) Johannes Bach on this
day married Barbara Hoffmann of
Suhl. He had been apprenticed
to her father.

(August 7) Friedrich Spee,
German poet and probably compos-
er, died at Trier (born 1591,
February 25).

(September 18) Anna Schmied,
wife of Johannes Bach and
daughter of the Wechmar inn-
keeper, died (birthdate unknown).

(October 10) Hans Ulrich
Steigleder, German organist and
composer, died at Stuttgart
(born 1593, March).

(November 12) The Calendar of
State Papers for this year con-
tained a bill from Robert
Dallam bearing this date for
work done on Laud's organ at
Lambeth.

(December 1) Melchior Teschner,

(cont.) German church musician,
died at Oberpritschen, Posnania
(born 1584).

(December) Ranuccio Farnese, the
Duke of Parma, died (birthdate
unknown). At this time Andrea
Falconiere left his service for
Modena.

Girolamo (or Geronimo) Amati,
violin maker, died at Cremona
(born 1551).

Jean Henri d'Anglebert of the
French keyboard school, was
born at Paris. One source gives
his birthdate as 1630 (died
1691, April 23). He became
court clavicinist to King Louis
XIV.

Heinrich Bach, son of Caspar and
a member of the second generation of the Bach family, died
(birthdate unknown).

Steffano Bernardi, Italian
theorist and composer, died
(born c.1576).

Giuseppe Colombi, violinist and
composer who was attached to the
musical establishment at Modena,
was born (died 1694).

Scipione Dentice, an Italian
composer, died at Naples (born
c.1559).

Antonio Draghi, Italian sacred
composer, was born at Rimini
(died 1700, January 16). He
worked at Vienna and wrote 172
operas and 43 oratorios as well
as libretti for Leopold I.

Christian Erbach, German organist and composer, died at
Augsburg (born 1573).

Paul Esterházy, first member of

the family of barons to be
raised to the rank of prince of
the Holy Roman Empire and composer, was born (died 1713).

Daniel Hitzler, musical theorist,
died (born 1576).

Gottfried Wilhelm Sacer, a hymn
writer, was born (died 1699).

Philipp Jakob Spener, a hymn
writer, was born (died 1705).

Georg Weissel, a hymn writer,
died (born 1590).

Johannes Bach this year was appointed "Direktor der Raths
-Musikanten" at Erfurt and organist at the Prediger-Kirche
there.

Adrian Batten this year made a
transcript of some anthem music.

Robert Dallam built an organ for
Canterbury Cathedral at this
time.

Robert Dallam added pedals to
the organ at Jesus College,
Cambridge this year.

Erbach, Holtzner, Steigleder
and Kindermann helped maintain
the traditions of colorism in
their toccatas and canzonas
which drew strongly on Italian
models.

Examples of the Bergamasca occurred in works by Frescobaldi
at this time.

Richard Gibbs was organist at
Norwich Cathedral this year.

A. Hammerschmidt this year became organist at Freiberg.

Kellie was succeeded by Edward
Millar at this time.

William Lawes this year wrote
the music for Davenant's masque
"The Triumph of the Prince
d'Amour."

Alberto Lazari this year was a
Carmelite monk and maestro di
cappella and organist at the
parochial college of Massa
Lombarda.

King Charles I appointed Edward
Millar as Director of Music at
the Chapel Royal at this time.

M. de Nyert, a nobleman in the
suite of the Ambassador Créquy,
went to Rome this year and was
delighted by performances at the
Barberini opera.

Biagio Tomasi referred to himself this year as arch-presbyter
and vicar at Massa Fiscaglia
(Ferrara).

John Wilson was made one of the
King's musicians this year.

Five books of motets by Antonio
Maria Abbatini were published
by Grignani this year at Rome.

The Anthem Book of this year
gave information about the
Chapel Royal.

The development of the baroque
anthem was tied in with four
groups of composers. The first
group consisted of Porter, Child,
Portman, and the Lawes brothers
and their work was reflected in
the Anthem Book.

Arrigoni published vocal chamber
concertos this year at Venice.

Doni's "Compendio del trattato

de' generi e de' modi della
musica" was published this year
at Rome.

Theorists at this time asserted
that the accompanist should
adapt his style to that of the
ensemble, "le commune ed
ordinarie maniere del
sinfoneggiare" (Doni,"Comprendio
del Trattato di generi e di
modi").

Doni in his "Compendio del
trattato . . . " described
Borboni as "organista eccellente"
and praised some new organ
pipes he had made.

The "Fiori Musicali" by
Frescobaldi was written actually
for church services and played
both after the Credo and after
Communion. The work, opus 12,
was published this year at
Rome. Frescobaldi's approach
was contrapuntal and the work
was strict and severe. Bach
was greatly impressed with it
and copied it in its entirety.

Annibale Gregori's "Ariosi
concenti," opus 9, was published
posthumously this year in all
probability by the composer's
son Alberto.

Pedro Heredia's Madrigal "Passa
la vita all' abbassar d'un
ciglio" (sonnet by Pope Urban
VIII), 4 vo, in Giambattista
Doni's "Compendio . . ." was
published this year at Rome.

Pedro Heredia composed his
"Messa super cantu romano"
(four voices and organ) this
year.

Cesare de Judice wrote a book
of motets and madrigals at this

Lipparino composed motets this
year.

Marini's opus 9, "Madrigaletti
a 1-4 voci" was issued this
year at Venice.

The second book of Mersenne's
"De instrumentis harmonicis"
was published this year.

Marin Mersenne's musical
treatises "Harmonicorum libri
XII" and "De la nature des sous"
were published at this time.

The eighth book of Melanuzii's
"Ariose vaghezze" was issued
this year.

Edward Millar edited "Psalmes
of David . . . in Foure or More
parts, and some Psalmes in
Reports" this year at Edinboro,
the publisher was Andro Hart.

Scheidt's "Liebliche Krafft
-Blümlein" was published this
year.

"Arie a tre voci, etc." by
Vitali was published at Rome
this year by Paolo Massotti.

By this time verse anthem far
outnumbered full anthems. This
was obvious from the Anthem
Books of the period.

At this time a polyphonic version of the Scottish Psalter of
1564 was printed.

At this time concise chaconne
basses were the most frequent
type of recurring bass, both in
cantatas and motets.

The great madrigal art was extinct by this date.

273

1635(cont.)

The preface to Frescobaldi's "Fiori musicali" of this year discussed variations at some length.

Corneille's "Médée" was produced at this time with machinery.

In the years just before this date the fantastic subject matter of Roman opera prompted constant scenic changes and "divertissements" in both music and dance.

Under Richelieu's leadership France openly joined the enemies of the Emperor and of Spain.

This year the village of Wechmar, Germany, suffered its second major epidemic in ten years and more than 500 victims succumbed.

Philippe Quinault, poet and librettist, was born (died 1688).

Philipp Jakob Spener, writer of "Pia desideria," the program of Pietism, was born (died 1705).

Spanish playwright Lope de Vega died (born 1562, November 25).

The Cardinal Infante made a state entry into Antwerp at this time. Rubens supervised the entire decoration of the city.

(to 1636) Niccolò Fontei's "Bizzarie poetiche," based on poems by Giulio Strozzi, was published this year in two volumes.

(to 1640) Henry Molle, English composer, was Public Orator to Cambridge University during this period while Cosin was Master of Peterhouse.

(to 1674) Porta was succeeded as director of Cappella Antoniana in Padua during these years by Amadio Freddi, P. Bartolomeo Ratti, P.G. Belli, Alvise Balbi, G. Ghizzolo, Leandro Galleano, and Antonio della Tavola.

(to 1683) A William Pysing was a lay-clerk of Canterbury Cathedral for this long span of years.

c.1635

Myles O'Reilly, composer of Irish tunes "Limerick's Lamentation" and "Farewell to Lochaber," was born (date of death unknown).

Girolamo Casati was "maestro di cappella" at Como at this time.

This year when he was about twelve, Cirillo was sent to Rome to study music.

At this time a shoemaker named Francesco Draghi moved himself and his family from Pergola in the Marche, to Jesi, about twenty-five miles away. He was great-grandfather of Giovanni Battista Pergolesi.

Giovanni Battista Doni's "Trattato della musica scenica" was written at this time.

Thomas Warwick composed a song in forty parts which was performed before King Charles I this year.

French painting: Louis Le Nain, "The Pilgrims at Emmaus" (oil on canvas, 29 1/8" x 35 7/8").

Dutch painting: Rubens, "Country Fair" (oil on panel, 4'10 5/8" by 8'6 3/4").

c.1635(cont.)

Dutch painting: Van Dyck, "Portrait of Charles I of England" (oil on canvas, 8'11 1/8" x 6'11 1/2").

1636

(January 25) Edward Gibbons on this date or a year later was taxed for ship money, "over and above 13s. 4d. as a priest vicar of the Cathedral is taxed, at £ 6s. 8d. for his temporal estate."

(February 28) Murray Gibbons, son of Edward and Jane Gibbons, was buried at Exeter Cathedral.

(April 29) Esajas Reusner, a German lutenist and composer, was born at Löwenberg, Silesia. He was a pupil of his father and a child prodigy (died 1679, May 1).

(June 10) Antoine Barbé, French organist, died at Antwerp (born c.1573).

(September 12) Charles Coleman wrote the music for "The King and Queen's Entertainment at Richmond," a masque presented by Prince Charles on this date.

(November 6) Hans Bach died at an early age (birthdate unknown).

(December 22) Ferdinand III was elected "King" of the Holy Roman Empire on this date.

(December) Ferdinand II yielded his power, and Ferdinand III was crowned at this time.

Charles Louis Beauchamp, a dancing master, was born (died 1705).

Erhard Bodenschatz, German

(cont.) clergyman and music editor, died at Gross-Osterhausen near Querfurt (born at Lichtenberg, 1576). Other sources give his birth as c.1570 and death as 1638.

Georg Draud (Draudius), a German clergyman and scholar, died at Butzbach (born 1573, January 9).

Barbara Hoffmann, wife of Johann Bach, member of the third generation of the Bach family, died in childbirth (birthdate unknown).

Wincenty Lilius, Halian musician and publisher, died at Warsaw (birthdate unknown).

Giovanni Battista Spaccini, a colleague of Vecchi's, died (born 1588).

Johann Bach, member of the third generation of the Bach family, this year became organist at the Predigerkirche in Erfurt.

Francesco Bazzini returned to Bergamo this year.

Marco Bigongiari entered the "Cappella palatina" as a "musico" at this time.

Buonamente at this time was "maestro di cappella" at the Franciscan monastery of Assisi.

Correa this year sold some vocal compositions to the chapter at Jaén Cathedral.

Hammerschmidt, a suite composer, at this time was not as consistent with thematic unity as Schein.

Lanier was granted a charter this year and appointed Marshal of of the "Arte and Science of Musicke" in Westminster by the King.

The Lawes brothers this year collaborated on the music for Davenant's "Triumph of the Prince d'Amour."

Sir Charles Mallet this year referred to the Inceptors in Music having "white wavy damask capes," thus quoting the Laudian Code of 1636, Title VII Chapter V.

The Laudian Statutes of this year made certain provisions which are still in force at Oxford.

Francesco Manelli settled at Venice where his wife this year collected and edited his "Musiche varie." This is the only work by Manelli which has been preserved.

Milanuzii this year was appointed Maestro di cappella of the Cathedral at Camerino.

From this date forward Stadlmayr referred to himself as musical director to the Archduchess Claudia at Innsbruck.

Diedrich Steffkins, a violinist, succeeded Maurice Webster in the King's band this year.

Pierre Thierry, the organ builder, carried out important work on the organs at the Paris church of Saint-Gervais at this time.

Vitali was this year attached to the household of Cardinal Francesco Barberini.

Charles d'Ambleville wrote "Harmonia sacra" this year at Paris.

The sixth book of Buonamente's compositions was published at this time.

Charles Butler's "The Principles of Musick, in singing and setting: with the two-fold use thereof ('Ecclesiastical' and 'Civil')" was published this year at London.

Cardoso's "Missae de Beata Virgine Maria, 4, 5 et 6 v . . ." and his "Missae 4 et 6 v. liber secundus" were both published this year at Lisbon.

Donati's "Il secondo libro de' motetti a voce sola d'Ign. D. maestro di cappella del Duomo di Milano . . ." appeared at this time.

Donati's "Li vecchiarelli e perregrini concerti a 2, 3 & 4 voci . . ." was composed this year.

Donato's "Se pur ti quardo" "Livre VII des chansons à 4 parties" was reprinted at Antwerp (See also 1597, 1613 and 1620).

Nicolo Fontei this year composed his "Bizzarre poetiche" for Barbara Strozzi, a singer and composer.

Franck wrote his "Paradisus musicus" for four voices at this time.

Henry Lawes wrote "Come from the Dungeon" this year.

Henry Lawes this year wrote

"Dispairs Banquet, sung in The Pasions written by Mr. William Strood, presented by ye scollers of Ch. before both their Majestys, 1636."

Mauduit's "A Requiem for 5 voices" written for the funeral of the poet Ronsard was included in the seventh book of Mersenne's "Harmonie universelle."

Mersenne's "Harmonicorum instrumentorum libri IV" appeared this year.

Marin Mersenne's "Harmonie Universelle" written at this time was a most valuable source for musical thought during the early baroque in France. In it Father Mersenne remarked on the convincing expression used by Italian singers that might be confused with personal involvement. Mersenne, a friend of the eminent philosopher Descartes, published the book at Paris.

Mersenne this year wrote a work about the technique and music of the "lira da gamba."

Milanuzii's "Messe concertate" for three voices was reprinted this year at Venice.

Milanuzii's motets, litanies and a Mass for one to three parts, "Hortus Sacer Deliciarum" were published this year at Venice.

Milanuzii's "Psalms" for two to three voices was reprinted this year at Venice.

Henry Molle at this time wrote an Evening Service in D Major which was included in the Tudway Collection.

Martin Rinkart's "Nun danket alle Gott" was composed this year.

Antonio Savetta's "Salmi ariosi e brevi" for eight voices, opus 14, was published at this time.

Heinrich Schütz' "Musicalische Exequien . . . " was published this year at Dresden. It has been considered to be a forerunner of Brahms' German Requiem.

Heinrich Schütz' "Erster Theil Kleiner geistlichen concerten . . . " was published this year at Leipzig.

Thomas Selle's monodic collection "Monophonetica" was completed at this time.

Jiří Třanovský edited the hymnal "Cithara Sanctorum" published this year at Levoča.

Vitali this year composed his first of his two sacred works, "Hymni."

Vitali's "Hymnos Urbani VIII . . . in musicos modos ad templorum usum digestos" was published this year.

Hymn-singing in parts was established at Berne by this time.

The archlute was described by Mersenne in "Harmonie Universelle."

Detailed descriptions and illustrations of all the French bagpipes were provided in Mersenne's "Harmonie Universelle."

Mersenne writing this year and using a fine engraving to illustrate his text described a

1636(cont.)

large clavichord which in some
way could be considered rather
conservative design.

Mersenne this year described the
"cornet de poste" as a small
crescent-shaped bugle horn.

The Courtaut, an obsolete type
of woodwind instrument, was
pictured and described by
Mersenne in his writings this
year.

Mersenne asserted at this time
that the French fife differed
from the German one in that it
had a much shorter and narrower
bore, which resulted in a
sharper and more piercing tone.

By this time when Mersenne wrote
his "Harmonie Universelle" the
"musette" had been furnished
with the first keys used in the
production of semitones.

Mersenne in his "Harmonie
universelle" wrote with enthusiasm concerning "les 24 Violons
du Roy."

Mersenne was not familiar with
any family of single-reed instruments at this time.

Schlick's principal of laying
the groundwork for tuning was
included by Mersenne this year
in his "Harmonie universelle."

Mersenne showed stepwise ap-
pogiaturas in his writings of
this year.

The "ton de chambre" as computed
this year by Mersenne was as
follows: A=563 c.p.s., S=7˙3.

The "ton de chapelle" as computed this year by Mersenne was

(cont.) as follows: A=504 c.p.s.,
S=5˙3.

The Teatro Formagliari was at
this time opened to the public
in the palace of the same name.

The first institution of higher
education in the colonies was
founded this year at New Towne
(later called Cambridge) by a
grant of the Massachusetts Bay
Colony. Three years later after
a bequest from John Harvard the
college adopted the latter's
name.

Under King Philip III, the
Spanish Chapel this year was
united with the Flemish chapel
to form the royal chapel.

Nicolas Boileau, writer of "Art
Poétique" in 1674, was born
(died 1711).

Stephan Dedekind, pastor of
Reinsdorf, died (birthdate
unknown).

Giovanni Battista Aleotti, an
Italian architect, died (born
1546).

Dutch painting: Rubens,
"Landscape with Chateau of
Steen" (54" x 92 1/2").

(to 1637) Carlo Farina was employed by the Council of Danzig
during this period.

(to 1637) Marin Mersenne's
"Traité de L'harmonie universelle"
first appeared during these years.
The work was published at Paris
(See other entries for this year).

(to 1639) Schütz' "Kleine
geistliche Konzerte" were completed during these years.

1636(cont.)
(to 1640) Andrew Melville during this period was Patrick Davidson's assistant and successor at the sang school.

(to 1650) Michel Angelo Grancini was organist at the cathedral in Milan for these fourteen years.

(to 1651) These years represented Corneille's height of production and fame.

(to 1661) Francesco Foggia was maestro di cappella at the St. John Lateran church in Rome during this period.

1637
(January 1 to September 30) Froberger was in service at the court in Vienna.

(February 15) Emperor Ferdinand III came into power on this date.

(May 29) Jiří Třanovský, Bohemian-Slovak humanist, theologian and hymnologist, died at Liptovský Svätý Mikutáš (born 1592, March 27).

(June 9) Monteverdi on this day made a formal complaint to the Procurators at St. Mark's concerning Domenico Aldegati, a singer who had insulted the composer.

(June 16) Giovanni Paolo Colonna, an Italian composer, was born at Bologna (died 1695, November 28).

(June 22) Froberger received a grant of 200 florins from the Viennese court to be used for study with Frescobaldi in Italy.

(July 10) Heinrich Grimm,

(cont.) German composer, **died** at Brunswick (born c.1593).

(July 11) Johann Georg Ebeling, a German composer, was born at Lüneburg this year and was baptised on this day (died 1676).

(July 22) Letters of administration in the estate of Adrian Batten, late of St. Sepulchre's, London, were granted on this date by the Prerogative Court of Canterbury to John Gilbert, a clothier of the City of Salisbury. This was with the consent of Edward, John and William Batten, brothers of the deceased.

(August 1) Ebner was organist at the court chapel from this date forward.

(August 6) Ben Jonson, English poet and dramatist, died (born 1573). His association with the masque was important. His most renowned work was the play "Volpone."

(September 8) Robert Fludd (Flud), English physician and writer, died at London (born 1574).

(September 30 to 1641, April) Froberger studied with Frescobaldi at Rome during this period.

(November 5) The Ancient Society of College Youths, a society of bell-ringers, was founded on this date in London.

(December 7) Bernardo Pasquini, an Italian organist, harpsichordist and composer, was born at Massa Valdinievole, Florence (died 1710, November 21).

1637(cont.)

(December 27) Hieronymus Gradenthaler, a German organist and composer, was born at Ratisbon (died 1700, July 22).

(February) The first public opera-house in Italy, the Teatro di San Cassiano at Venice, opened with Manelli's "Andromeda," libretto by Benedetto Ferrari. The price of admission was four Venetian lire.

(April) Berti was receiving a salary of 180 ducats at this time.

(April) John Milton's wife, Sarah, died this year and his son Christopher with his family came to live with the poet.

(April) From this time until his death, John Price I was in the service of the emperor at Vienna.

(May) Edward Gibbons, son of Murray and Mary Gibbons, died. He was baptised in August of 1632.

Filippo Acciaiuoli, an Italian dramatist, theatrical manager and composer, was born at Rome (died 1700, February 7).

Nicol Bach, an Arnstadt musician and son of Caspar I, died. The former was a member of the second generation of the Bach family (born 1619).

Dietrich Buxtehude, renowned organist and composer, was born at Helsingor, Sweden. He is variously claimed by Denmark, Germany and Sweden. Franz Tunder was his father-in-law and he eventually succeeded him.

(cont.) Buxtehude could well be termed a precursor of Bach (died 1707, May 9).

Johann Georg Ebeling, a German composer, was born (died 1676).

Emilie Juliane of Schwarzburg-Rudolstadt, a hymn-writer, was born (died 1706).

The first Baron Guilford Francis North, English lawyer and amateur musician, was born at Kirtling, Cambridgeshire (died 1685, September 5).

Bernado Pasquini, an Italian composer and organist, was born at Tuscany (died 1710, November 2).

John Riley, a trumpeter, died at London (birthdate unknown).

Auxcousteaux became chaplain-in-ordinary of the Sainte-Chapelle in Paris this year.

Pierre Ballard, a printer, obtained a new patent this year. Fétis claimed the correct date to be 1639.

It was maintained that this year when it was discovered that Bevin was a papist he was dismissed from the Chapel Royal, but no evidence of this fact has been uncovered.

The "Elogio en la muerte de Juan Blas de Castro" of this year indicated that in about 1594, Juan Blas de Castro was "Músico Privado" to the Duke of Alba at Salamanca.

Cesti this year joined the Minorite friars under the name of Frate Antonio.

Richard Crashaw became a Fellow
at Cambridge at this time.

Dallam (probably Thomas) was
engaged to repair the organ at
Magdalen College, Oxford this
year as well as in 1615 and
1632.

Valentine Flood this year was
one of two English violists at
Danzig.

A Mr. Harris, the first of four
generations of organ builders
with that name, this year built
a double organ for Magdalen
College, Oxford.

Sometime prior to this date
Gilles Hayne was appointed
chapel master of the prince
-palatine, Wolfgang Wilhelm,
Duke of Neuburg.

Lanier provided settings for
Jonson's "Luminalia, or the
Festival of Light" this year.
The Queen and her ladies of the
court took part in the perfor-
mance.

Alberto Lazari was an academician at Cesena at this time.

Marco Marazzoli sang in the
papal chapel in Rome this year.

Giovanni Felice Sances this
year entered the imperial chapel
in Vienna as a singer.

Thomas Selle was cantor at the
Johanneum of Hamburg at this
time.

M. Weckmann received organ instruction from Jacob Praetorius
in Hamburg this year. The expense was borne by Elector
Johann Georg I.

Wolfgang Christoph Agricola
published a "Fasciculus
musicalis" for two voices this
year at Würzburg.

Adrian Batten's organ book in
Manuscript (Tenbury 791) which
contained a considerable amount
of 16th-century church music
compressed into organ score was
released this year. Portions of
it have survived.

Brasseur's "Sydera illustrium
Harmoniae scriptorum" was issued
this year at Mons.

Buonamente's seventh and final
book "Sonate, Sinfonie,
Gagliarde, Corrente, et Brandi"
was published this year by
Vincenti.

Gaspare Filippi composed his
"Concerti ecclesiastici . . ."
for one to five voices at this
time.

The first book of Frescobaldi's
"Toccate d'Intavolatura" was
published this year at Rome.
Included in the book was a
piece with amazing dissonance
in which the composer consistently alternated between chaconne
and passacaglia.

At this time Frescobaldi's
"Secondo libro di toccate . . .
e partite d'intavolatura" was
reprinted for the third time at
Rome.

Grandi's "messe concertate" for
eight voices was published this
year.

A book of motets with sinfonias
by Grandi was published this
year. It was the last of three
books.

A new edition of Hassler's "Kirchengesange . . ." with some additions by S.G. Staden was published at this time.

Father Athanasius Kircher's "Musurgia Universalis" was published at Rome this year. He was a German Jesuit priest.

Milton's "Comus," under the editorship of Lawes, was published this year, however, anonymously.

Henry Lawes at this time set the Psalmes of David to music.

Lipparino composed psalms for eight voices this year.

Tarquinio Merula's "Canzoni, overe Sonate concertate per chiesa, lit 2," opus 12, was published this year at Venice.

The term "sonata da camera" had by this time already been used by Merula in his "Sonate concertate da chiesa e da camera" published this year. The term was purely a functional one.

The trio sonata at this time was a form used by Belli, Bernardi, Buonamente, Frescobaldi, Ottavio Grandi, Merula, Possenti, Riccio, Turini, and Usper.

Tobias Michael's "Musikalische Seelenlust" (Part II) was published this year. It contained fifty pieces in one to six parts in concerto style for voices and instruments.

The "drummer major" was mentioned this year in Monro's "Monro His Expedition."

Michelangelo Rossi's oratorio "Erminia sul Giordano" was completed at this time and produced at Rome.

S.G. Staden issued a new edition of Hassler's "Kirchengesänge mit vier stimmen simpliciter gesetzt." In it he included eleven new chorale tunes and settings by his father (Johann Staden) and five by himself.

An offertory was written this year by Tomkins.

Manelli's opera "Andromeda," libretto by Ferrari, this year opened the first public theatre at Venice (San Cassiano).

"Il Falcone" by Mazzocchi was performed at the Barberini theater at this time.

Mersenne this year mentioned that certain woods, notably box, have long been preferred for instrument making. It may therefore be presumed that they gave especially good results in use. Older oboes preserved in museum collections show a surprising variety of material.

Marco Scacchi's oratorio "La Santa Cecilia" was performed this year at Warsaw.

About one generation after the first public opera house in Italy had opened the English initiated the earliest regular concert series.

The Moritzkirche at Halle was destroyed this year by fire.

Opera in three acts was unusual until the public performances at Venice starting at this time.

1637(cont.)

The theatre of San Cassiano was erected this year.

A permanent Opera in Warsaw was established by Ladislas IV.

King Charles I decided to force Episcopalianism on the people of Scotland. This included Land's Liturgy combined with his father's translation.

Hepburn's Regiment, The Royal Scots, had a drum major this year as they did later when they entered the British service in 1666.

When Murád IV captured Baghdad this year he took the renowned Persian musician Sháh Qulí as well as four other minstrels back to Stambúl to provide his court music.

Sir Thomas Browne became a physician in Norwich this year.

Benedetto Ferrari at this time wrote the libretto to the first opera ever performed in a public theater: "Andromeda" by Manelli.

The Archduke Ferdinand of Styria, later Emperor Ferdinand II, died (born 1578).

Dutch painting: Heda, "Still -life with Tobacco" (oil on panel 17 3/8" x 22").

(to 1638) Heinrich Schütz held a position at the court of Copenhagen during these years.

(and 1641) Vierdanck's "Erster Theil neuer Pavanen Gagliarden," "Ballette und Corrente" was published this year at Rostock and reprinted in 1641.

(to 1657) Emperor Ferdinand III, opera patron and composer, was at the imperial court of Vienna during these years.

(to 1657) Froberger served as an organist to the court of the emperor at Vienna during this period.

(to 1665) Bonlini gave the names of thirty-four operas which Cavalli produced at Venice during these years.

(to 1699) Eleven theatres for opera came into existence in Italy during these sixty-two years.

(to end 17th-Century) Venice produced 358 operas during this relatively short period.

(to 1740) Between the accession of Ferdinand III this year and the death of Charles VI in 1740, musical life at Vienna achieved its first great pinnacle.

c.1637

Adrian Batten, an English organist and composer, died at London (birthdate unknown).

(to c.1653) Gaspare Filippi, an Italian composer, was maestro di cappella at the Vicenza Cathedral at this time.

1638

(February 6) Ferrari and Manelli completed their second opera "La maga fulininata." It was dedicated to Viceconte Basilio Feilding.

(March 25) Thomas Holmes, English organist and composer, son of John Holmes, died at Winchester (birthdate unknown).

1638(cont.)

(April 7) Charles Couperin, violinist, organist, and probably composer, was born at Chaumes (died 1679). This date may have been April 8. See 1633.

(April 28) Piotr Krzesichleb, Polish ecclesiastic and musician, died at Mohilev (born 1552, July 26).

(May 6) Vincenzo Ugolini, Italian composer, died at Rome (born c.1570).

(May 28) Nicolas Formé, a French singer and composer, died at Paris (born 1567, April 26).

(September 1) Monteverdi dedicated his eighth book of madrigals to Ferdinand III.

(September 8) Mareschall's "Psalmen Davids" (thirty-five pieces) was published at Basel.

(September 23) Daniel Friderici (Friderich), German composer, died at Rostock (born 1584).

(September 27) John Tomkins, organist, died at London (born c.1586).

(October 3) Monteverdi hired two Roman singer-composers, Manelli and Ferrari, for the St. Mark's Choir at Venice.

(November 8) Johann Heinrich Alstedt (Alstedius), German theorist, died (born 1588).

(December 1) Arthur Phillips was appointed organist of Bristol Cathedral on this day.

(August) John Taverner of Norfolk, an English professor of music, died (born 1584).

(September) John Wilbye, English madrigal composer, died at Colchester (born 1573).

Sometime after this year Raffaela Aleotti, Italian composer and organist, died at Ferrara (born c.1570).

Antonio Amati, a violin maker from the famous family, died at Cremona (born 1550).

Giovanni Pietro Berti, Italian singer, organist and composer, died at Venice (birthdate unknown).

Erhart Bodenschatz, German composer, music editor and clergyman, died at Gross-Osterhausen (born 1576). See also c.1570 and 1636.

Pierre Bonnet-Bourdelot, French musical historian, was born at Paris (died 1708, December 19). He and his uncle collaborated on a music history.

Ignazio Donati, Italian composer, died at Milan (born c.1585).

Francis Pilkington, English madrigal composer, died (born c.1562).

Georg Quitschreiber, a Thuringian composer, died (born 1569).

Thomas Tomkins III was born (date of death unknown).

Heinrich Albert married Elisabeth Starke this year.

Raffaela Aleotti was still alive this year when Lorenzo Agnelli dedicated his second book of motets to her.

1638(cont.)

Fernando de Almeida became a
monk and was admitted to the
monastery of Thomar this year.

Cavalli this year succeeded
Berti as second organist at St.
Mark's, Venice.

John Cobb was sworn in as a
Gentleman of the Chapel Royal
at this time.

H. Du Mont went to France this
year.

Girolamo Fantini wrote his book
on trumpet technique at this
time.

According to Burney the term
"cantata" was first used by
Benedetto Ferrari this year.

Pierre Gaultier, French lutenist,
was at this time living at Rome.

Christopher Gibbons, son of
Orlando, the year became organist of Winchester Cathedral.

Dr. Richard Knight, a physician,
was this year appointed a
professor of music at Gresham
College in London.

Matthew Locke went to Exeter as
a chorister this year.

Marcin Mielczewski was a member
of the court band in Warsaw at
this time.

Milton this year sent home "a
chest or two of choice music
books" by Cifra.

J. Pilkington replaced Francis
Pilkington as minor canon of
Chester at the latter's death
this year. He had previously
been appointed a "conduct."

The Ottoman Sultan Murád IV this
year captured Baghdad but spared
the life of its most gifted musician Sháh Qúlé, who was re-
vered throughout Iraq and had
attracted the Sultan.

Agazzari's "La Musica
Ecclesiastica, dove si contiene
la vera deffinizione della
Musica come scienza non più
veduta e sua nobiltà" was published this year at Siena.

A book of motets for two to five
voices by Domenico Allegri was
published this year posthumously.

Szymon Berent published "Litaniae
de nomine Jesu" this year.

Ceresini's second book of motets
was completed at this time.

M. East this year published his
seventh set of books devoted
entirely to instrumental music.

A. Hammerschmidt this year completed his "Musicalische
Andachten" part I, with the sub
-title "Geistliche Concerten."
The work contained twenty-one
settings of German sacred works
for one to four voices.

Romualdo Honorio, an Italian
composer and monk of the
Calmaldolenses, this year composed "Concerti a doi tre e
quattro voci" with some psalms
in four and five parts.

"Arien und Kantaten" by Kittel
appeared this year. He was a
pupil of Schütz and the work
was a rather unsophisticated
attempt to use the virtuoso
technique of castrato singing
as a vocal exercise for German
choir boys. This marked the
first appearance of secular

1638(cont.)
cantatas for solo voice.

Pretentious settings of versified psalms were included in
Henry Lawes' music to Sandy's
paraphrases for one voice of
this year. He described them
as "set to new tunes for private
devotion."

Franceso Manelli this year wrote
his opera "La Maga fulminata"
for Venice.

The first indication of the
polarity between "concertato"
and a-cappella performance in
secular music was given in
Mazzocchi's madrigal book of
this year which contained both
continuo and a-cappella madrigals.

Mazzocchi at this time published
a set of "Dialoghi e sonetti."

Merula's "Curtio precipitato et
altri capricij. . . lit.2,"
opus 13, was published this year
at Venice.

Micheli's "Li salmi a quattro
voci" appeared this year at
Venice.

The music for Monteverdi's
opera "Il ballo delle ingrate"
was first issued this year in
his eighth madrigal book. The
full title was "Madrigali
guerrieri et amorosi con alcuni
opusculi in genere rappresentativo, che saranno per brevi
episodii fra in canti senza
gesto Libro ottavo." Included
also was the "Madrigali
Guerrieri et Amorosi" which
showed the fully developed
"Concertato" style of the mature
Monteverdi. The book was published by Scacchi.

George Sandys, a son of the
archbishop, published the complete Psalter this year.

A volume of four and five-part
masses by Marco Scacchi were
published this year.

Schütz at this time wrote a
ballet for the marriage of
Johann Georg II of Saxony.

Schütz's ballet "Orfeo e
Euridice" written this year was
lost.

B^b occurred first in a set of
variations for "fagotto" solo
with a continuo by Bartolomé de
Selma y Salaverde, published
this year at Venice.

De Selma's solo and trio sonatas for bassoon were printed
this year at Venice.

Stadlmayr this year published
"Odae sacrae . . . a 5 voc., et
totidem instr."

Victorinus' "Siren coelestis"
was published in an English
edition this year (See also
1616).

When King Charles I this year
renewed the charter of the
church of St. Mary, Manchester,
he provided for the musicians
and singing-boys.

Little on drums and fifes has
been preserved from English
sources except some exercised in
"Mars: his Triumph" published
this year.

Michel Angelo Rossi this year
wrote music for a play on the
subject of "Andromeda" and it
was performed.

1638(cont.)
Sir William Davenant this year
was appointed poet laureate of
England by King Charles I.

Milton went to Italy at this
time.

According to Milton, polyphonic
music was still popular this
year.

Milton, having been introduced
to Leonora Baroni this year by
Cardinal Barberini, wrote three
Latin poems in adulation.

Nicolas Malebranche, a priest,
was born this year (died 1715).

King Louis XIV the Great of
France (House of Bourbon) was
born (died 1715).

Christian Wilhelm, Margrave of
Bradenburg, was abducted at
this time.

Adriaen Brouwer, Flemish painter,
died (born 1605).

Meindert Hobbema, Dutch painter,
was born (died 1709).

Hercules Seghers, a Dutch
etcher, died (born 1589).

(to 1639) Niccolò Fontei published his "Melodiae sacrae,"
opus 3, in Venice during this
period.

(to 1639) French painting:
Poussin, "Arcadian Shepherds."

(to at least 1641) Borboni was
organist at St. John Lateran
during these years.

(to 1641) Matthew Locke was a
chorister at Exeter Cathedral
at this time.

(to 1642) Spanish painting:
Zurbarán, "St. Casilda." In
spirit of popular piety,
Zurbaran painted whole series of
female saints who were actually
Andalusian women in disguist.
The included peasants, society
women and heroines from comedies
by de Vega.

(to 1650) During this period the
leader of the north German
school was Heinrich Albert, a
cousin of Schütz whose "Arien"
were sung throughout Germany.

(to 1652 and 1655) The Gospel
dialogues "Musicalische
Andachten" (1638 to 1652), and
"Gespraeche über die Evangelia"
(1655) by Hammerschmidt were
imitated by many parochial musicians and composers in
Germany.

(to 1667) Italian architecture:
Borromini, "San Carlo alle
Quattro Fontane" (interior of
church, 52'6" x 34'; façade,
38' wide).

(to 1676) Albert's nine books of
songs were published during
these years.

c.1638
Richard Carlton, an English composer, died (born c.1558).

Bryne became organist of St.
Paul's Cathedral in London at
this time.

Dutch painting: Brouwer, "The
Smoker" (16 1/8" x 12 5/8").

Dutch painting: Van Dyck, "John
and Bernard Stuart."

Dutch painting: Jordaens, "The
King Drinks"(59 1/8" x 82 3/4").

c.1638(cont.)
Dutch painting: Jordaens,
"Twelfth Night."

1639
(January 24) Cavalli's opera "Le
nozze di Teti e di Peleo" was
produced at Venice in the Teatro
San Cassiano.

(February 27) Marco Marazzoli
produced the first comic opera,
one that he had written jointly
with Mazzocchi, "Chi soffre,
speri," at the Roman Palazzo
Barberini. The libretto was by
Guilio Rospigliosi, the future
Pope Clement IX.

(May 7) Auxcousteaux was temporarily in charge of the precentor-
ship of the Sainte-Chapelle at
Paris.

(June 1) Melchior Franck, German
composer, died at Coburg (born
1573).

(August 22) Mareschall's "Samuel
Marescallus Tornacensis
Flandricus, m. prop. scripsit
aetat. sua 85" for twenty-two
pieces was published.

(September 17) Jan Cocx became a
chorister at Saint-Bavon.

(October 1) Horatio da Parma was
praised by Maugars as one who
performed wonders on the viola da
gamba during the late 16th
-Century.

(October 27) Christaan van
Placker was admitted as a novice
by the Jesuits of Mechlin and
later became a humanities
teacher.

(November 7) William Cobbold,
English organist and composer,
died at Beccles (born 1560,

(cont.) January 5).

(December 21) Monteverdi's
"Adone" with libretto by Paolo
Vendramin was produced at the
Teatro S.S. Giovanni e Paolo in
Venice. Quite possibly some of
the music was by Manelli.

(February) "Armida," an opera
with both music and libretto by
Ferrari, was produced at Venice.

Andreas Hammerschmidt, central
German composer who was both
prolific and popular, was born
(died 1675).

Léonard de Hodemont (Hodiment),
Netherlandish composer, died at
Liege (born c.1575).

René Mézangeau, French lutenist
and composer, died (birthdate
unknown).

Richard Nicholson, English organist and composer, died
(birthdate unknown).

Johann Christoph Pezel (Petzold),
German violinist, trumpeter,
composer, was born at Calau,
Lusatia (died 1694, October 13).

Felicianus Suevus (Felix Schwab),
German composer, was born at
Altdorf Weingarten, Würtemberg
(date of death unknown).

Leonora Baroni was in Rome at
this time and was referred to by
various writers as the greatest
singer of her period.

William Child was thought to
have been awarded the degree of
Bachelor of Music at Oxford in
1631, but the date on his exercise was 1639.

William Davenant obtained a

patent for construction of the Dorset Garden Theatre (See also 1662).

Andrea Falconieri was appointed lutenist of the royal chapel at a salary of nineteen ducats a month.

Niccolò Fontei, Italian organist and composer, this year competed unsuccessfully with Cavalli for the post of second organist at St. Mark's in Venice.

A. Hammerschmidt left his position at Freiberg at this time and became organist at Zittau where he remained until his death.

Jewett was dismissed by the archbishop from the position as vicar-choral at St. Patrick's for not being in priest's orders.

Manuel Machado was still living at this time.

The great French violist Maugars heard the lira da gamba played at Rome this year. He also attended oratorical performances in the Congregation of the Holy Cross at Rome and further described a polychoral performance that he attended there. Finally he published an interesting report on the state of music in Italy in the first part of the century.

Mersenne states this year that the theorbo had single strings while the double-necked lute or theorbo-lute had them in pairs.

Merula resumed the position of maestro di cappella at Bergamo

(cont.) at this time.

Monteverdi, quite old by this time, with his student Cavalli became the leader of the Venetian opera school.

Immediately after Richard Nicolson's death this year A. Phillips succeeded him as organist of Magdalen College, Oxford as well as becoming a professor of music at the University.

Porter was appointed master of the choristers of Westminster Abbey at this time.

Jewett was succeeded in the position of organist of Christ Church, Dublin by Benjamin Rogers. Rogers stayed until 1641 when he returned to Windsor.

Juan Carles Amat this year wrote the earliest known treatise on the Spanish guitar, "Guitarra española, y vandola en dos maneras de guitarra, castellana y cathalana, de cinco órdenes . . . " It was published at Gerona and the latest edition of the work was dated Valencia 1758. A plagiarized version by Andres de Soto appeared in 1764.

Cavalli's "Le Nozze di Teti e Peleo" of this year united Monteverdian techniques with new features of the period.

William Child's "The First Set of Psalmes of III. Voyces" was published this year at London and reprinted in c.1650. The work was reissued as "Choise Musick to the Psalmes of David" in London in 1656.

V. Costazuti published a collection of verses "Applausi poetici alle glorie della signora Leonora Baroni" this year at Rome. The collection was reprinted in 1641.

Ferrari wrote "L'Armida" this year to his own poetry.

Three sets of "Cantiones sacrae" by Grandi were published at this time.

A. Hammerschmidt this year published two sets of dances, "Erster Fleiss, allerhand newer Paduanen, Galliarden, Balletten, Mascharaden, Arien, Concerten und Sarabanden" for viols.

The Leyden vocal manuscripts were compiled by this date.

Lobo's "Liber II" was published this year by B. Moretus.

The "Response faite à un curieux sur le sentiments de la musique d'Italie" by Maugars this year provided evidence that religious music as performed in Rome did not exclude dramatic effects, antiphonal grouping or direct allusions to the theater.

Experiments with comic opera began this year at Rome with "Chi soffre speri" by Mazzocchi and Marazzoli.

Merula's "Canzoni da suonare a tre," opus 9, and his "Concerto decimo quinto . . . Messi, salmi, . . . concertati, a 2-12" were both published this year at Venice.

Henry Molle wrote an Evening Service in F major, which was included in the Tudway Collection this year.

Both Hawkins and Burney referred

(cont.) to a collection of this year titled "Ayres and Madrigals for two, three, four and five voices, with a thorough bass for the organ or Theorbo Lute, the Italian way." This may well have been a second edition of Porter's earlier work.

Du Praissac's "Art of Warre" was Englished this year by J. Cruso.

Rovetta, a follower of Monteverdi, wrote a ceremonial mass at this time.

Schütz' "Anderer Theil kleiner geistlichen concerten . . ." was published this year at Dresden.

Schütz' "Kleine geistliche konzerte" was printed this year for the second time.

The text of Strozzi's "La Delia, ossia La sposa del sole" was set to music at this time either by Manelli or Paolo Sacrati.

Aria for 3 voices and other selections by Vitali were published at Rome this year by V. Bianchi.

Loreto Vittori's opera "Galatea" was produced at this time in the Palazzo Barberini in Rome, and the score was published.

The word "Opera" was used this year to mean literally a "work" (compare "opus") and was really a shortened form of the Italian "Opera in Musica" that is, a "Work of Music."

The center of Latin oratorio was at this time, according to Maugars, St. Marcello's at Rome.

Cavalli's "Le nozze di Teti e di Peleo" was produced this year at Venice.

1639(cont.)

Two operas written this year, Clavenet's "Le Ravissement de Prosperine" and J.B. Lhermitte's "La Chute de Phaeton," were produced with machinery.

Marazzoli's "Chi soffre, speri" was produced in Rome at this time.

At Venice this year the earliest opera buffa was composed, Marazzoli's "Chi soffre speri."

Francesco Sacrati's opera "Delia" was produced this year at Venice.

"La Galatea," a Roman opera by Loreto Vittori, was produced at this time at Rome.

The second edition of W. Barriffe's "Military Discipline, or the Young Artillery Man" was published this year.

"Lawes & ordinances of warre . . ." was issued this year by the Earl of Arundel and Surrey.

"The Souldiers Grammar" published this year at London mentioned that something similar to the office of drum-major general was in existence and that he was superior to the sergeant.

Robert Ward's "Animadversions of Warre" published this year included a lengthy description of "the Duty and Office of . . . the Drum Major of the Regiment."

France at this time was proud of the "tambour-major" as evidenced in de Praissac's "The Art of Warre."

"The Art of Warre" this year further asserted that "the drum-major must be lodged near the sergeant-major . . . or in his own lodging."

The existing text of the Mystery of Elche bore this year's date.

Thomas Carew, Cavalier poet, died (born c.1598).

Opitz, a German poet, died (born 1596).

Jean Racine, classical French tragedian, was born (died 1699).

John Milton set up a school in London this year.

John Milton's "Comus" was completed by this time.

Giovanni Battista Gaulli, Italian painter, was born (died 1709).

Maderna, the Italian architect who worked on St. Peter's, died (born 1556).

(to 1640) Monteverdi's opera "L'Adone" was produced during this period in Venice at the Carnival.

(to 1640) Schütz was employed at the court of Hanover at this time.

c.1639

Robert Creyghton, English clergyman and composer, was born at Cambridge (died 1734, February 17).

René Mesangeau, French lutenist and composer, died at Paris (birthdate unknown).

French painting: Claude Lorrain, "A Seaport at Sunset" (oil on canvas, 40 1/2 x 53 1/2").

c.1639(cont.)
Spanish painting: José Ribera, "Martyrdom of St. Bartholomew" (92 1/8" x 92 1/8").

1640

(January 21) The last masque before the civil war, Davenant's "Salmacida Spolia," was performed.

(January 23) "Il pastor regio," an opera with libretto by Ferrari, was produced at Venice.

(February 12) Michael Altenburg, German clergyman and church musician, died at Erfurt (born 1584, May 27).

(April 10) Agostino Agazzari, Italian composer, died at Siena (born 1578, December 2).

(June 9) Emperor Leopold I was born at Vienna (died 1705, May 5).

(July 9) Arthur Phillips was awarded the degree of Bachelor of Music by Magdalen College.

(August 3) John Bolt, English singer, virginalist and organist, died at Louvain (born 1564).

(August 25) Johann Christian Bach, son of Johann Bach, grandson of Johannes, and member of the fourth generation of the Bach family, was born (died 1682).

(November 7) Thomas Lawes, English musician, died at Salisbury (birthdate unknown).

(November 25) Giles Farnaby was buried at St. Giles, Cripplegate.

(December 3) Elizabeth

(cont.) Ferrabosco, singer, was baptized at Greenwich.

(November) Giles Farnaby, English composer, died at London (born c.1568).

(November) Nicolaus Adam Strungk, German violinist, organist and composer, was born at Brunswick (died 1700, September 23).

John Adson, English instrumentalist and composer, died probably at London (birthdate unknown).

Johann Altenburg, a hymn-writer, died (See February 12).

Elway Bevin, Welsh musician, died (born 1565).

Giulio Caccini, singer and early opera composer, died (born c.1558).

Thomas Connellan, an Irish composer of more than 700 airs, was born (date of death unknown).

Elizabeth Ferrabosco, singer, was born at Greenwich (date of death unknown).

Paul Flemming, a hymn-writer, died (born 1609).

Giovanni Domenico Freschi, Italian composer, was born at Vicenza (died 1690).

Salomo Liscow, a hymn-writer, was born (died 1689).

Paolo Lorenzani, an Italian composer, was born at Rome (died 1713, October 28).

Jacques Thomelin, French organist and composer, was born (died 1693).

Pavel Josef Vejvanovsky, an important Czech composer, was born (died 1694). He composed masses, requiems, a Te Deum, vespers, litanies, offertories and sonatas, as well as ballets and serenatas.

John Amner was awarded the Bachelor of Music degree by Oxford at this time.

Cavalli became second organist at St. Mark's this year.

A. Düben (the elder) this year became "hofkapellmeister" at the German church in Stockholm.

Henry Loosemore was awarded the Bachelor of Music degree by Cambridge this year.

Merula was maestro and organist of the Cathedral at Bergamo at this time.

H. Du Mont was currently organist at St. Paul's Church in Paris.

A change in Monteverdi's style, as noted by Doni this year, was obvious in his new style of recitative.

Nivers this year became organist at Paris church of Saint -Sulpice.

During the administration of Juan de Palafox y Mendoza, bishop after this date and later viceroy of Mexico, the annual expense for music reached 14,000 pesos, considered to be an astronomical figure. Standars of performance were apparently at the highest level.

G. Pinel married this year.

Johann Rosenmüller's name was inscribed in the matriculation book of the University of Leipzig, in spite of his parents' poverty.

Marco Scacchi criticized the psalms of Paul Siefert this year.

Sweelinck's contemporaries and successors numbered among them such names as the organists Kerckhoven, van Noordt and Padbrue.

Pietro della Valle this year maintained that the lyric drama appeared in Rome "upon a cart."

M. Weckmann was appointed organist and choirmaster to the electoral chapel in Dresden at this time.

Tomasz Wlodawski became a member of the royal chapel in Warsaw this year.

P. Ziani at this time was organist at San Salvador in Venice.

The first edition of the "Bay Psalm Book" was published this year at Cambridge, but without music.

James Bryson at Edinboro printed an edition of the Psalms this year.

Johann Crüger's "Newes vollkömliches Gesangbuch" was published this year at Berlin.

Doni's "Annotazioni sopra il compendio . . . ." was completed at this time.

J.B. Doni's "Traité de la Musique" appeared this year.

Niccolò Fontei published his "Compieta e litanie della Beata Vergine," opus 5, this year at Venice.

Denis Gauthier, the lutenist, wrote a tombeau this year for the organist Raquette.

Kapsberger published the fourth of his four books of "Intavolatura di chitarrone" this year.

Krzesichleb's Psalm Book containing a large number of anthems, hymns and religious songs was reprinted (See also 1601, 1603, 1620, and 1646).

S. Mareschall's collection of thirty-eight pieces on French and Italian motets appeared at this time.

Mazzochi this year published his "Musiche Sacre e Morali."

V. Mazzocchi published as opus 1 his "Sacrae flores" for two, three and four voices this year.

Merula's "Pegaso, salmi, motetti . . . , a 2-5, lib 3" opus 11 was published this year at Venice.

Monteverdi's opera "Il Ritorno d'Ulisse in Patria" was published at this time.

Monteverdi composed his "Selva morale e spirituale" this year. The Lamento d'Arianna was included (See also 1641).

"Audite mortales" by Pękiel was composed prior to this date.

"The Whole Booke of Psalmes Faithfully Translated into (cont.) English Metre" published this year at Cambridge, Massachusetts was the first book printed in New England.

Two volumes of four and five -part motets by Marco Scacchi were published this year.

An edition of Schütz's "Psalmen Davids . . ." was published this year at Güstrow. The original edition was issued at Freiberg in 1628.

Stadlmayr published "Salmi a 2 et 3 voc., cum 2 v.o. cornetti" this year.

The second edition of Turini's "Mottetti a voce sola" was issued at this time.

Doisi de Velasco published a treatise on the Spanish guitar, "Nuevo modo de cifra para tañer guitarra con variedad y perfección," this year at Naples.

Georg Weber this year published a sacred song book at Stockholm.

The overture to the ballet "Mademoiselle" this year was in two-part form, the first part slow, the second fast. It was the forerunner of the French overture which would appear shortly.

After this year an overture usually preceded the ballet, followed by a number of entrées including dances, instrumental numbers, and choruses. After this musicians of the King's band appeared in the production to prepare for the appearance of the King and other nobility in the final grand ballet at the end.

From this date forward laments were composed as independent dirges in memory of some renowned person.

Very few opera or cantata scores were printed for some time after this date.

The term "oratorio" was first used in its current meaning at this time.

Cavalli's opera "Gli amori d'Apollo e di Dafne" was produced at Venice this year at the Teatro San Cassiano during the Carnival.

The French this year used atmosphere-producing machinery on stage in Chapoton's "Descent d'Orphée aux Enfers."

This year saw a production of "Ballet de Mademoiselle," closer in form to opera than previous ballets because of its overture that had its origins in the association of pavan and galliard.

The great Franciscan organ at Vienna used A=458 c.p.s., S=3°8.

The texts in the Bay Psalm Book were hardly praiseworthy as poetry, and the translators of this year's edition even stated "If the verses are not always so smooth and elegant as some may desire or expect, let them consider that God's Altar needs not our pollishings."

The need for an updated psalm book, more easily available than the imported ones, was obvious at this time. The history of American music

(cont.) actually can be traced from this date forward.

The earliest reference to the tune "Turn again, Whittington" was in Shirley's "Constand Maid" written this year.

Three publications by the Stephen Daye press, which later became an "appendage of Harvard College," were issued to meet the basic needs of the colony at this time. They were "Oath of a Freeman,"an Almanac, and "The Whole Booke of Psalmes Faithfully Translated Into English Metre, Whereunto is Prefixed a Discourse Declaring Not only the Lawfulness, but the Necessity of the Heavenly Ordinance of Singing Scripture Psalms in Churches of God."

It has been pointed out by one source that there were no musical types in the colonies at this time.

New Englanders this year numbered nearly twenty thousand.

Robert Burton, eminent English author, died (born 1577).

William Wycherly, English writer, was born (died 1716).

Peter Paul Rubens, renowned Dutch painter, died (born 1577).

French painting: Claude Lorrain, "Marriage of Isaac and Rebecca."

Nicholas Poussin, French painter, this year returned to Paris after sixteen years in Rome and received a "splendid welcome."

(January to 1641, August) John Milton, his son Christopher, and the family moved to Reading during this period.

(to 1644) John Oker was organist of Gloucester Cathedral during these years according to one source.

(to 1645) Cesti lived in Rome during these years.

(to 1645) French painting: George De La Tour, "St. Joseph the Carpenter."

(to 1649) Salvatore Rosa's satiric opera "La musica, la poesia" was performed during these years. Its central theme dealt with the demoralizing influence of music.

(to 1649) Abendmusik at this time were musical evening performances of a semi-sacred nature. They were originated by Tunder at Lübeck and became so well-known that they were imitated in other towns in northern Germany, particularly Hamburg.

(to 1650) Benevoli's later works were written at Rome during this period for St. Peter's.

(to 1650) William Wake was organist of Exeter Cathedral during these years.

(to 1660) Many "carpe diem" men like Herrick and "Cavalier" poets like Abraham Cowley and Richard Lovelace retired from city life during this period of Puritan rule to write poetry.

(to 1679) Robert Ballard continued in his family's occupation of printing during this period.

c.1640

John Attey, English lutenist and composer, died at Ross (birthdate unknown).

Jean-Valentin de Bournonville, French organist and composer, died (born c.1580).

Cristoforo Caresana, Italian priest, singer, organist and composer, was born at Venice (died 1709, September 13).

Giovanni Battista Draghi, Italian harpsichordist and composer, was born (date of death unknown).

Gallot (first name unknown), French lutenist, was born, probably at Paris (died c.1691).

Charles (Carolus) Hacquart, gamba player and composer, was born at Bruges (died c.1730).

Johann Hieronymus Kapsberger, German composer and lutenist, died (birthdate unknown).

Samuel Mareschall, Flemish organist and composer, died at Basel (born 1554, May).

Sebastiano Moratelli, Italian composer, was born at Vicenza (died 1706, September).

Willem Swart, Dutch composer, died (born c.1575).

Pavel Josef Vejvanouský (Weywanowsky), Bohemian trumpeter and composer, was born at Hlučín, Bohemian Silesia, or Hukvaldy, Moravia (died 1694, June).

Christoph Bach at this time married Maria Magdalena Grabler of Prettin, a Saxon town. He was

c.1640(cont.)

a member of the third generation of the Bach family.

Doni at this time returned to Florence and settled down as professor at the University.

Chambonnières' "Pièces de Clavessin" was written at this time.

Henry Lawes' lament "Ariadne deserted" appeared.

As early as this time the Hofburg was the seat of an excellent operatic organization that had developed through the years.

Lully arranged for the production of Rossi's opera "Orfeo" at Paris. It enjoyed considerable success.

Orchestral overtures existed at this time.

John Ford, the English dramatist, died (born 1586).

Orazio Gentileschi, Italian painter, died (born 1563).

French painting: Louis Le Nain, "The Dairymaid's Family."

Spanish painting: Velasquez, "Three Musicians."

(or 1650) Dutch painting: Frans Hals, "Malle Babbe" (sorceress of Haarlem).

(to 1660) Early cantatas were often very long and their length was integral to their conception.

1641

(May 15) Filipe de Magalhães was

(cont.) pensioned by King John IV of Portugal.

(June 30) John Price took over his father's post at Vienna and remained there until his death.

(August 6) Henry Hinde, English organist and composer, died at Lichfield (birthdate unknown).

(October 6) Erasmo Marotta, Italian composer, died at Palermo (born c.1550).

(October 10) Wolfgang Kaspar (von Waldthurn) Printz, German theorist and composer, was born at Waldthurn, Palatinate (died 1717, October 13).

(December 1) Robert Dowland was replaced as "musician for the lutes and voices" by John Mercure.

(June) John Price I, English instrumentalist (tabor-pipe, cornett and viola bastarda), died at Vienna (birthdate unknown).

John Amner, English organist and composer, died at Ely (birthdate unknown).

Peter Bruhns, German musician, was born (died 1698).

Robert Dowland, English lutenist and composer, died probably at London (born c.1586).

Balthasar Moretus, printer, son of Jan Moretus, in the same trade, died (born 1574).

Wolfgang Caspar Printz, who wrote the first chronicle of music, was born (died 1717).

Charles Thierry, organ builder,

was born at Paris (date of death unknown).

Christoph Tietze, a hymn-writer, was born (died 1703).

Leonard Woodson, English organist and composer, died at Eton (birthdate unknown).

Heinrich Bach was summoned to Arnstadt where he was appointed organist and remained there until his death.

Rev. John Barnard was a minor canon at St. Paul's Cathedral in London in the reign of King Charles I and this year published the first collection of Cathedral music.

The Bassano family had settled in England and worked as court musicians until this date.

John Birchensha was in the service of the Earl of Kildare in Ireland until this year's rebellion when he settled in London.

Gasparo Casati was "maestro di cappella" at Novara Cathedral from this date forward.

Robert Dowland's name purportedly appeared this year in a list of "Musicians for the Waytes."

Jewett this year was restored to his post at St. Patrick's.

Daniel Norcome, violist, this year was still in service of the Archduke at Brussels.

B. Pekiel was appointed to the position of assistant conductor of the royal chapel in Warsaw at this time.

Pierre Pinel was a lutenist of whom little is known, except that he was alive this year.

G.B. Reghius undertook this year to publish music by Giovanni Battista Fontana at Venice.

Heinrich Scheidemann went to Lübeck to examine a new organ during this year.

Schütz returned to Dresden at this time in an attempt to re-organize the music.

Heinrich Schwemmer visited Nürnberg this year.

Selle was cantor, minor canon, and musical director at Hamburg Cathedral at this time.

Jacob Stainer this year began making violins.

Robert Tomkins was one of the King's musicians for lute, viols and voices at this time.

Tunder was recalled to Lübeck this year from Rome.

The Emperor presented Verdina with a gold medal during this year.

Thomas Warwick this year appeared as musician "for the Virginall."

John Wilson was on this year's list of His Majestys Servants of the Chamber in Ordinary.

Woodson resigned from his position as organist at Eton College this year.

John Barnard's "The First Book of Selected Church Musick . . . ." (Part-books only) was published

this year in England. It was
the earliest printed collection
of anthems. The book proved
that church composers of the
time were mostly from the old
school.

Severo Bonini, a composer who
wrote one of the earliest
histories of monody this year,
ended his work with a reference
to two "new swans": Luigi Rossi
at Rome and Cavalli at Venice.

Seven of Byrd's anthems were included in Barnard's "Selected
Church Music."

Cavalli's opera "Didone" appeared at this time.

Cazzati this year published his
opus 1, "Salmi e messa a 5
voci."

V. Costazuti published a collection of verses "Applausi
poetici alle glorie della
signora Leonora Baroni" in
1639 at Rome. The collection
was reprinted this year.

The following works by Donati
appeared this year:

"Ander Theil geistlicher
    Concerten"
"Dulcis amor Jesu" (for five
    voices)
"Erster Theil geistlicher
    Concerten, durch
    Ambrosium Profium"
"Paratum cor meum" (for five
    voices)

Gibbons' anthem, "Lift up your
heads" was not included in
Barnard's "Selected Church
Musick" but it was included in
Boyce's "Cathedral Music."

A. Hammerschmidt's "Musicalische
Andochten," part II, sub-titled
"Geistliche Madrigalien," and
containing thirty-four pieces,
was published this year.

Kircher's "Magnes, siue de arte
magnetica," which listed all the
songs and arias then in use to
cure a tarantula bite, was published this year at Rome.

Marini's opus 13, "Compositioni
varie per musica di camera, a
2-5 voci" was published at this
time at Venice.

Claudio Monteverdi's "Il
ritorno d'Ulisse in patria" was
revised and completed this year.

Monteverdi's "Selva morale e
spirituale" was published at
this time. His "Lamento d'
Arianna" was included.

Barnard this year printed a
Morning and Evening Service for
four and five parts by Morley.

Arthur Phillips composed music
at this time in several parts
for "The Requiem, or Liberty of
an Imprisoned Royalist!"

"Il Pio Enea," an anonymous
opera, was published this year.

Ambrosius Profius' "Geistliche
Concerten & Harmonien" was published at this time in Germany.

Rist's hymn-book "Himmlische
Lieder" was published this year.
Several selections included
were by Johann Schop.

Sacrati's opera "Finta pazza"
appeared at this time.

Stadlmayr this year published
"Psalmi integri a 4 voc.

concertantibus, quatuor allis accessoriis ad lib. accinendis cum 2 cornet, sive violin."

Anthems by Tomkins were published this year.

Fanictes for strings were written this year by Tomkins.

Vierdanck's "Ander Theil" appeared at this time.

Vitali's "Psalmi ad vesperas quinque vocibus cum basso ad organum si placet" was published this year by Vincenzo Bianchi at Rome.

Vitali wrote his second sacred work, "Salmi a 5 voci," this year while attached to the household of Cardinal Francesco Barberini.

Barnard this year printed John Ward's First Evening Service, "I will praise the Lord," and "Let God arise."

Barnard published Weelkes' "O Lord grant the king" this year.

For professional musicians the prorogation of the Parliament by King Charles II must have brought unpleasant memories of this year when most of their predecessors had been deprived of their livelihoods.

In Vienna, as early as this time, opera was performed which presented a near parallel to Hofmannsthal's "Ariadne auf Naxos" written for R. Strauss almost 300 years later. The libretto by F. Bonacossi was called "Ariadna abbandonata da Theseo e sposata dal dio Baccho."

Cavalli's opera "Didone" was produced this year at Venice at the Teatro San Cassiano, Carnival.

"La ninfa avara," an opera with libretto by Ferrari, was produced this year at Venice.

Monteverdi's "Le nozze di Eneo con Lavinia" (Giacomo Badoaro) was produced this year at Venice in Teatro SS. Giovanni e Paolo.

Monteverdi's "Il ritorno d'Ulisse in patria" (Badoaro) was produced this year at Venice, Teatro San Cassiano.

At the carnival this year Monteverdi's "La vittoria d'Amore," a ballet choreographed by Bernardo Morandi, was produced at Piacenza.

Sacrati's opera "La finta pazza," libretto: Giulio Strozzi, was produced at Venice this year.

Sir Thomas Browne married Dorothy Mileham at this time.

Abraham Cowley was expelled from Cambridge this year for satirizing the Puritans.

George Wither's "Hallelujah" was written at this time.

Marie Le Grange d'Arquiem (later Queen Maria Casimira of Poland) was born in France (date of death unknown).

Anthony Van Dyck, Dutch painter, died (born 1599).

Dutch painting: Jan Van Goyen, "The Two Oaks."

French painting: Louis Le Nain, "The Wagon."

1641(cont.)

Spanish painting: Ribera "St. Agnes with Angel." In this painting popular religiosity was dressed in exquisite delicacy and splendidly simple, but passionate, modesty.

(to 1642) Rist's "Himmlische Lieder" was published during these years.

(to 1644) Gasparo Casati's works were published during this period.

(April 1 to 1645, October)Johann Jacob Froberger was in service at the Viennese court during this period.

(to 1646) Profe published four large collections of "Geistliche Concertate und Harmonien a 1, 2, 3, 4, 5, 6, 7, etc., . . ." during these years.

(and 1649) Two collections, one printed in 1641 and the other in 1649, included a Mass for four voices by Monteverdi.

(to 1656) Vierdanck was organist at St. Mary's Church, Stralsund for these fourteen years.

(to 1677) Francis and Pieter Hemony of Zutphen and Amsterdam, carillon builders, were active at this time.

(to 1681) John Birchensha, violist and music theorist, was active during these years.

c.1641

Johann Wolfgang Franck, German opera composer, was born (date of death unknown).

Isabella Leonarda, Italian com-

(cont.) poser, was born at Novara (date of death unknown).

Cazzati was "maestro di cappella" at Sant' Andrea, Mantua at this time.

1642

(January 1) Cavalli's opera "Amore innamorato" was produced at Venice, Teatro San Moise.

(January 18) George Hudson, composer, was sworn in as musician to King Charles I, but did not take up his appointment until after the Restoration.

(January 30) Cavalli's opera "Narciso ed Ecco immortalati" was produced at Venice, Teatro SS. Giovanni e Paolo.

(February 10) Juan Carles Amat, Spanish (Catalan) apothecary and musical scholar, died at Monistrol (born 1572).

(February 24) Marco da Gagliano, Italian composer, died at Florence (born c.1575). He was an early associate of both Peri and Rinuccini.

(June 19) Samuel Scheidt wrote a letter to Duke August of Brunswick in which he asked him to accept some spiritual madrigals that Scheidt had written for the Duke's chapel.

(September 6) Georg Christoph Bach, cantor, son of Christoph, grandson of Johannes, and a member of the fourth generation of the Bach family, was born (died 1697, April 24).

(September 23) Giovanni Maria Bononcini, Italian composer, was baptised at Montecorone near Modena (died 1678, November 18).

(December 8) Johann Christoph Bach, Eisenach organist, son of Heinrich, grandson of Johannes, and a member of the fourth generation of the Bach family, was born (died 1703, March 31). "Wie bist du denn, o Gott" was to be one of his most celebrated works.

(February) Filippo Vitali was called back to Florence to succeed Gagliano as maestro di cappella to the duke of the Cathedral of San Lorenzo.

(April) Andrea Falconieri requested and was granted permission to leave his position at the royal chapel so that he might visit his wife at Modena.

(July) Francesco Lambardi, sopranello and tenor singer, and organist, died at Naples (born 1587).

(July) Schütz visited Dresden on a trip from Copenhagen.

(August) Row, the Minister of Carnock, remarked "this day also I gat four markis to buy a Psalme Book to our Kirk, according to the ordour in other congregations."

(Autumn) Monteverdi's "L'incoronazione di Poppea" (Giovanni Busenello) was produced at Venice, Teatro S.S. Giovanni e Paolo.

Alessandro Stradella, inventor of concerto grosso form and who wrote intermezze, oratorios etc., was born at Montefestino (died 1682, February 28).

Thomas Tomkins' wife Alice died (birthdate unknown).

Christoph Bach was at this time a member of the Erfurt "compagnie" of musicians under his brother Johannes.

T. Clifford was admitted chorister of Magdalen College, Oxford this year.

Jan Couchet this year became a member of the St. Lucas Guild.

Robert Dallam and his wife settled in Brittany this year and he built several notable organs in the Quimper district.

Prior to this date William Howes was a singer at St. George's Chapel, Windsor; after this time at Christ Church, Oxford.

Jewett was in Chester this year. He had been brought from Dublin in connection with some special services on the occasion of a visit from the king.

C. Melanuzii was maestro di cappella at Sant' Eufemia, Verona at this time.

Pasino was town organist of Lonato this year.

Johann Rosenmüller this year became collaborator and/or assistant Master at St. Thomas' School in Leipzig.

A Ruckers harpsichord bearing this date had two sets of jacks on one unison to create a difference in timbre.

Marcantonio Stradella, father of Alessandro Stradella, was governor of Vignola for Prince Boncompagni at this time.

Clemens Thieme, instrumentalist and composer, went to Copenhagen this year as choir-boy at the court chapel.

Sometime after this date Bonini wrote an important treatise on music: "Prima parte de discorsi e rigole sovra la musica."

Cavalli's opera "Egisto" was completed this year.

Cavalli's "La virtu de' strali d'Amore" appeared at this time.

The chorale "Preussische Festlieder" by Eccard were this year posthumously published.

Ferrari this year wrote a collection of solo cantatas (not under that name, however).

A. Hammerschmidt's "Musicalische Andachten," part III, sub. title "Geistliche Symphonien" containing thirty-one selections was written this year.

Herbst's theoretical work "Musica practica sive instructio pro Symphoniaces," published this year at Nürnberg, professed to be an instruction book for singers.

Romualdo Honorio composed a book of Masses this year in Venice.

Franceso Manelli wrote his opera "Alcate" this year for Venice.

Milanuzii's "Litaniae della Madonna" for four to eight voices was reprinted this year at Venice.

The libretto of Monteverdi's opera "L'incoronazione di

(cont.) Poppea" was printed this year at Venice (height only 5 1/2", previously 8 1/2").

Monteverdi's last opera, "L'incoronazione di Poppea," was completed this year.

C.T. Padbrue's "Nuptial Symphony" was published this year at Haarlem and Amsterdam.

Masses for four voices, opus 4, by Pasino appeared at this time.

Ranuccio Pico wrote his "Appendice de vari soggetti parmigiani" this year.

Luigi Rossi this year wrote his opera "Il Palazzo incantato" based on a libretto by Rospigliosi.

Thomas Selle, one of C.P.E. Bach's predecessors as cantor in Hamburg, this year wrote a St. John Passion "a 6 cum capella a 5" and a St. Matthew's Passion "in dialogo a 10."

Stadlmayr this year published "Missae concertatae a 10-12 instrum., cum 4 partibus pro secundo choro."

Two parts of "Preussische Fest-Lieder mit 5, 6, 8 Stimmen" appeared, twenty-one by Stobaeus and twenty-seven by his teacher Eccard.

Examples of the "Bergamasca" were found in works by Uccellini written this year.

Vallet's "Apollinus süsse Leyer . . ." for violin and bass, was published this year by Janssen at Amsterdam.

Vierdanck's "Erster Theil

geistlicher Concerten" appeared
this year.

Gabriel Voigtländer, a trumpeter,
in his "Allerhand Oden" of this
year added to the repertoire of
lower class German songs. The
volume was published at Sorø,
Denmark.

Since all theaters in England
were closed this year, dramatic
activity was non-existent. The
act was performed as a result of
a Parliamentary decision put
through by Puritan reformers.

The central German School of
Ahle, Kittel, Nauwach, Schein,
Neumark, Hammerschmidt
(Weltliche Oden), Krieger and
Dedekind was one of the most
important groups of composers
working at this time.

The Teatro dello Stallone was
founded this year at Padua.

Cavalli's "Egisto" was performed
this year at the Vienna opera
house.

Cavalli's "La virtù de strali
d'amore" was produced this year
at Venice, Teatro San Cassiano.

Niccolò Fontei's only opera,
"Sidonio e Dorisbe," was pro-
duced at the Teatro di San
Moisè in Venice this year.

Monteverdi's opera
"L'incoronazione di Poppea" was
produced this year at Venice.

Luigi Rossi's "Il palazzo
d'Atlante incantato" was produced this year at Rome.

Sacrati's opera "Bellerofonte"
was produced at this time at

(cont.) Venice.

The Puritan movement challenged
royalty by civil war that started
at this time.

Sir Isaac Newton was born (died
1727).

The trial and execution of
Archbishop William Laud and the
Earl of Strafford, the two men
appointed by King Charles I to
rule church and state, took
place this year.

John Milton married Mary Powell
at this time.

Robert Burton's "Religio Medici,"
an autobiography, was published
this year in England.

Thomas Fuller's "The Holy State
and the Profane State" was written at this time.

Cardinal Richelieu, protector of
the French crown and patron of
music, died (born 1585).

Rembrandt's first wife died this
year and left him a considerable
fortune.

Guido Reni, an Italian painter,
died (born 1575).

Poussin, French painter, returned
to Rome this year where he became Charles Le Brun's teacher.

French painting: Louis Le Nain,
"Peasants at Supper."

Dutch painting: Rembrandt, "The
Night Watch" (12'2" x 14'7").

(to 1643) A. Hammerschmidt's
"Weltliche Oden oder
Liebesgesänge" parts I and II,
secular pieces for one to three

1642(cont.)
voices with instrumental accompaniment, were completed during these years.

(to 1644) P.F. Buchner was musician to the "Palatino e
generale di Cracovia" at this
time.

(to 1644) Some works by Eccard
were given sacred words and included in the "Preussische
Festlieder" during this period.

(and 1644) The collection,
"Preussische Festlieder," written by Eccard and Stobäus, was
published by Stobäus in two
parts after Eccard's death.

(to 1644) Schütz lived in
Copenhagen at this time.

(to 1649) The English Civil War
took place during this period.

(to 1649) Masques were produced
privately throughout these
years.

(to 1650) Italian architecture:
Borromini, "Sant' Ivo," Rome
(maximum diameter c.85').

(to 1651) French architecture:
François Mansart, Maisons
-Laffitte, Chateau (c.235' by
117').

(to 1660) In England the
artistic achievements of the
Elizabethan and Jacobean ages
all but disappeared during this
period of Civil War and the
Commonwealth.

c.1641
Caspar Bach, musician and one of
the first of the Bach family,
died (born c.1570).

Benedictus a San Josepho, Dutch
organist and composer, was born
at Nijmegen (date of death unknown).

Pierre Gautier, French composer,
was born at Ciotat, Provence
(died 1697, September).

(to 1692) Thomas Shadwell was
noted mainly as the unfortunate
Mac Flecknoe in Dryden's satire.

1643
(January 1) "La finta savia,"
an opera, was produced. The
music was by Ferrari, Filiberto
Laurenzi, Arcangelo Crivelli and
Merula, the libretto by Strozzi.

(February 22 or 23) Gabriel
Voigtländer, German musician and
poet, died at Nyköbing (born
c.1596).

(March 1) Girolamo Frescobaldi,
Italian organist and composer,
died at Rome (born 1583,
September 9).

(April 20) Johann Christoph
Demantius, German composer, died
at Freiberg, Saxony (born 1567,
December 15).

(August 23) An ordinance for
abolishing superstitious monuments was passed by the Lords
and Commons assembled in
Parliament.

(October 25) Georg Ludwig
Agricola, German composer, was
born at Grossfurra, Thuringia
(died 1676, February 22).

(November 29) Claudio Monteverdi,
renowned Italian madrigal and
opera composer, died at Venice
(born 1567, May 14).

(December 8 or 9) Antoine

305

(Anthoine) Boesset (Sieur de Villedieu), French ballet and lute composer, died at Paris (born c.1585).

(December 30) "Il prencipe giardiniero," an opera with libretto by Ferrari, was produced at Venice.

(July) Pietro Verdina, an Italian singer and composer, died at Vienna (birthdate unknown).

(Autumn) Cavalli's opera "Egisto" was produced at Venice, Teatro San Cassiano.

Diego de Alvarado, Portuguese organist and composer of Basque origin, died at Lisbon (birthdate unknown).

According to his contemporary Gantez ("L'Entretien des musiciens," 1643) Auxcousteaux had been born in Picardy.

Giovanni Battista Buonamente, an Italian composer, died at Assisi (birthdate unknown).

Gasparo Casati, an Italian composer, died at Novara (birthdate unknown).

Juan Bautista Comes, Spanish composer, died at Valencia (born 1568).

Duarte Lobo, Portuguese composer, died (born c.1565 or c.1560).

Daniel Tailer, English composer, died at London (birthdate unknown).

William West, English singer and composer, died at London (birthdate unknown).

William Brewster, the Pilgrim father, prior to this date acquired a library of 323 books in English and 64 in Latin.

Child apparently retired to a small farm and devoted himself to compositon. The anthem "O Lord, grant the King a long life" was composed at this time.

Alessandro Costantini this year succeeded Frescobaldi at St. Peter's in Rome.

Since "The organs being prohibited," B. Cosyn was dismissed by the governors.

Dognazzi was "maestro di cappella" at this time.

In the introduction to a publication of this year Dognazzi claimed to have spent forty years in the service of the Gonzaga, Dukes of Mantua.

Baldassare Ferri this year was made a knoght of St. Mark's at Venice.

The chapter of Saint-Lambert at Liège made Gilles Hayne a canon this year. Recognition of a Requiem he had composed for the obsequies of Mari de' Medici was the basis for the act.

George Jeffries this year while a member of the Chapel Royal went to Oxford as joint organist to the king with John Wilson who was also a Gentleman of the Chapel.

S. Otto this year made an unsuccessful application for the position of cantor at Freiberg to succeed Demantius.

Mario Savioni entered the papal

chapel at Rome as a contralto
this year.

Christopher Simpson joined the
royalist army at this time.

B. Wardeński this year joined
the Royal Court at Warsaw as a
theorboist and lutenist.

J. Weichmann was cantor and organist at Wehlau at this time.

One of Walentyn Adamecki's
canons was included this year
in Scacchi's "Cribrum Musicum"
("Xenia apollinea").

Bellante wrote a song for two
voices included in Bettino's
"Concerti" issued this year.

Bigongiari this year set the
intermezzi "Gl' amori di Bacco"
to music for a comedy by
Francesco Sbarra.

One of Jan Bischoff's canons was
included by Marco Scacchi in
his "Cribrum musicum" published
this year at Venice.

Jean de Bordenave's "L'Estat
des églises collegiales et
cathedrales" was published this
year.

Cavalli's opera, "L'Egisto,"
was published this year and is
considered to be strongly influenced by Monteverdi.

As late as this time Clemens'
chansons were so popular that
some of them were reprinted by
Phalèse.

Dognazzi's "Musiche varie da
camera" appeared this year.

Eccard's "Geistliche u.

(cont.) tröstliche Lieder.
Michaelum Weyda" was composed
this year.

A canon by Elert was included
in Scacchi's "Cribrum musicum"
("Xenia Apollinea").

Giovanni Battista da Gagliano's
"Il secondo libro de' motetti a
sei et otto voci . . ." was
published this year.

Gantez's "Entretien des musiciens"
was published this year at
Auxerres.

A canon by Adam Gobiatus was
included in Scacchi's "Cribrum
musicum."

Herbst's principal theoretical
work was "Musica poetica sive
compendium melopoeticum . . ."
published this year at
Nürnberg. It purported to give
thorough instruction in harmony
and composition and was illustrated with numerous examples.

Jarzębski's only literary work,
"The Description of Warsaw,"
was published at Warsaw this
year and a canon inscribed "More
veterum" was included in
Scacchi's "Cribrum musicum"

One of Karezewski's canons was
included in Scacchi's "Cribrum
musicum."

A double canon in four parts by
Mielczewski was included in
Scacchi's "Cribrum musicum."

C.T. Padbrué's "'T Lof van Jubal"
("The Praise of Jubal") for
four, five and six voices was
published this year at Amsterdam.

Only one of Pękiel's works was
published during his lifetime.

It was a six-part triple canon included in Schacchi's "Cribrum musicum" this year.

Milanuzii's "Psalms" for two to three voices was reprinted this year at Venice.

"Follias" were included in Sabatini's "Dodici Chitarre Spostate" published at this time.

Marco Scacchi published his "Cribrum musicum ad triticum Syfertinum" this year at Venice.

Johann Schop's "Geistliche Concerte" was published at this time.

Thomas Selle this year wrote a second setting of St. John's narrative (Passion Music) "mit 6 Vocal-und 6 Instrumental stimmen sampt einer vocal -capella a 5 einfältigst pro choro remoto und dem Choro pro organo a 4 gesetzt in stylo recitativo" (oratorio).

A comprehensive collection of Staden's instrumental works was published posthumously this year. It contained not only dances, but pieces described as sonatas, symphonies, and canzonas.

Stadlmayr published "Missae IX voc. primo choro concert a 5 voc. secundo pleno cum symphoniis" this year.

A canon by Stokrocki was included in Scacchi's "Cribrum musicum."

Francesco Turini's "Messe a 4 e 5 voci a cappella" was published this year by Gardano.

Vierdanck's "Ander Theil geistlicher Concerten" and his "Geistliche Concerte" appeared this year.

One of B. Wardenski's canons was included in Schacchi's "Cribrum Musicum."

T. Wlodawski's "Cribrum Musicum" was published this year.

A dramatic type of Passion with non-liturgical insertions made its first appearance with Christian Flor, Sebastiani, Thomas Selle (St. John Passion, 1643) and also Schütz' pupil Johann Theile. It was carried further by Briegel, Kühnhausen, Meder and Pfleger.

This year or possibly a year later a "Quartfagott" was in the orchestra, used to accompany a song at a music festival held at Nürnberg.

Vienna's first great production of a music-drama this year was Cavalli's "Egisto."

The anonymous "comedia Sacra Philatea" was performed this year at Munich, a center for Jesuit drama.

Sacrati's opera "La Venere gelosa" was produced this year at Venice.

William Browne, pastoral English poet, died (born 1591).

Richard Crashaw this year relinquished his Fellowship at Cambridge, became a Catholic, and went to France.

Sir William Davenant, English poet, was knighted this year.

1643(cont.)

John Milton this year went to live with his son, the poet.

John Milton's "Doctrine and Discipline of Divorce" was completed at this time.

King Louis XIII of France (House of Bourbon) died (born 1601).

After this year the government of France was administered for the minor King Louis XIV by his mother, Anne of Austria, and Cardinal Mazarin, Richelieu's successor.

Papal troops this year seized the town of Vignola.

Jewett was organist of Chester Cathedral during these years.

(to 1645) Benevoli published several collections of motets and offertories during these years at Vienna.

(to 1645) C. Milanuzii was maestro di cappella and organist at San Mauro, Noventa di Piave, Lombardy during this period.

(to 1650) During this period Bontempi sang in the choir of St. Mark's, Venice.

(to 1672) R. Florido (first name unknown), Italian bass and composer, published many books of vocal compositions by contemporary masters during these twenty-nine years.

(to 1676) Jan Baltazar Karczewski, Polish violinist and composer, was a member of the court band in Warsaw during this period.

(to 1715) The reign of King (cont.) Louis XIV (House of Bourbon) over France.

(to 1715) The musical baroque in France reached its peak under the "Roi Soleil," King Louis XIV.

(to 1693) Petrobelli published his four books of motets, psalms, various church music, two books of "Scherzi amorosi" for two and three voices, chamber cantatas, etc. during this period.

c.1643

Giovanni Vincenzo Sarti, composer, was maestro di cappella at Forlì Cathedral at this time.

French painting: Louis Le Nain, "Peasant Family."

(to 1645) Stefano Filippini, composer, was at this time organist and maestro di cappella at Sant' Agostino.

1644

(January 5) Cavalli's opera "Deidamia" was produced at Venice, Teatro Novissimo.

(January 12) Jean Baptiste Boesset succeeded his father in the position of "Maître de la Musique du Roi" and that of "surintendant."

(January 14) Thomas Britton, who later operated a place of business which acted as a gathering place for noble-born amateurs and for some of the outstanding musicians of his time, was born at Rushden near Higham Ferrers (died 1714).

(January 24) In "The Actors Remonstrance," an anonymous tract, published in England on this date, the effect of the

309

closing of the theaters on the lives of stage musicians was described by the author.

(May 9) A second ordinance was passed by Lords and Commons assembled in Parliament "for the further demolishing of monuments of Idolatry & Superstition" in which the destruction of organs was enjoined.

(August 12) Heinrich Ignaz Franz von Biber, a Bohemian violinist and composer, was born at Wartenberg, Bohemia (died 1704, May 3).

(August 28) In the preface to the sixth section of his "Arien" Albert mentioned the centenary of Königsberg University on this date and stated that he had written a "Comödien-Musik" for the occasion. The work was later repeated at the Kurfürst Palace.

(September 4) Juan Cabanilles, Spanish organist and composer, was born at Algemesí (Valencia) (died 1712, April 29).

Lodovico Adimari, Italian operatic satirist, was born (date of death unknown).

Joannes Bannius, an author on musical subjects, died (born 1597).

Maria Caterina Calegari, Italian singer, organist and composer, was born at Bergamo (date of death unknown).

Tomaso Cecchino, Italian (Dalmatian) composer and maestro di capella, died at Lesina (born c.1580).

Antonio Stradivarius, greatest of the Italian violin makers, was born (died 1737, December 18).

Giovanni Battista Vitali, Italian violinist and composer, was born at Cremona (died 1692, October 12).

Johann Rodolph Ahle this year became organist at Erfurt.

Diedrich Becker went to Hamburg this year when he was married.

Christopher Gibbons, son of Orlando, joined the Royalist Army this year to fight in the Civil War.

Ives' son, Simon, was a student of Clare Hall, Cambridge at this time and probably died young. One of the pieces in "Musick's Recreation" is attributed to him.

José Marin was engaged as a tenor this year in the choir of the Convent of the Incarnation at Madrid.

M. Neri was first organist at St. Mark's, Venice at this time.

After losing both his positions because of the suppression of the choral service this year, Porter found a patron, Sir Edward Spencer.

This year when the Protectorate suppressed all choral services, Portman became a teacher and Playford listed him first among teachers "for Organ or Virginal."

Benjamin Rogers taught music at Windsor and its environs at this time.

Malachias Siebenhaar this year

was cantor at the town school at Magdeburg.

"Praxis pietatis melica," which included works by Crüger, was published this year and reissued in 1647.

Eccard's "Ander Theil . . ." appeared this year.

"Proserpina rapita," an opera with libretto by Ferrari, was published at this time.

Georg Philip Harsdörffer and Sigmund Staden composed a "spiritual Sylvan poem," Seelewig this year.

Florentino A'Kempis composed three symphonies this year. They were published at Antwerp and reprinted in 1647 and 1649 in enlarged editions.

Nicholas A'Kempis this year composed a book of eight-part masses and motets as well as "Symphoniae 1, 2, 3 violinorum" published this year at Antwerp.

Marini's opus 15, "Corona melodica ex diversis sacrae musices floribus concinnata, 2-6 voc. ac instrumentis" was published at this time at Antwerp.

M. Neri's book of "Sonate e canzone a 4," opus 1, to be played on sundry instruments in church or chamber was composed this year.

With musical assistance from Schop and others Rist this year published "Galathea, Sabbathische Seelenlust, Florabella" as well as other collections containing sacred

(cont.) and secular miniature songs in a popular style.

Scheidt's "LXX Symphonien auff Concerten manir . . ." was published this year at Leipzig.

Schein's "Musica Boscareccia . . ." was published this year in a new edition.

S.G. Staden this year published two collections titled "Seelenmusik" with two four-part settings of hymns with continuo. He provided new melodies to various hymnbooks of the time.

S.G. Staden this year composed the first German operatic work that was ever published. It was an allegorical "Singspiel" whose full title was "Das geistliche Waldgedicht oder Freudenspiel gennant Seelewig Gesengweiss auf italiänische Art gesetzet." The story was taken from "Frauenzimmer -Gesprächsspiele" by Harsdörffer.

Two parts of "Preussisch Fest -Lieder mit 5, 6, 8 Stimmen" appeared again, twenty-one by Stobaeus and twenty-seven by his teacher Eccard.

Dirck Janszoon Sweelinck this year published four of his compositions in an edition of the "Livre septième des chansons vulgaires."

The act this year which banned church organs in England led to the introduction of instrumental accompaniment.

Parliamentary suppression of the choral service took place at this time.

1644(cont.)

"Suppression of the organs" was considered at this time to be "Popish."

Cavalli's opera "Ormindo" was produced this year at Venice, Teatro San Cassiano.

Sacrati's opera "Proserpina rapita" was produced this year at Venice.

Sacrati's opera "Ulisse errante" was produced this year at Venice.

After the Ming dynasty ended this year official musical authorities of the new dynasty rejected the principle of equal temperament and in 1712 reverted to the original cyclic intonation derived from the twelve natural fifths of Ling Lun.

John Milton wrote his poem "Areopagitica" this year in defense of free speech.

The Battle of Marston Moor occurred this year. King Charles I's forces clashed with Parliament then under the direction of Sir Thomas Fairfax and Oliver Cromwell. The Parliamentary forces were victorious.

Marie Desmares Champmeslé, a French actress, was born (died 1698).

When English Puritans destroyed organs during the Civil War this year in order to abolish "Romish trappings" they also tried to stop taverns from buying them secondhand for profane use.

The power of the Barberini

(cont.) family was broken this year by the political revolution which followed the death of Pope Urban VIII. Cardinal Panfili was elected to the pontificate to replace him.

Gherardi, Italian Baroque architect, was born (died 1702).

Elisabeth Lämmerhirt, wife of J. Ambrosius, member of the fourth generation of the Bach family, and mother of Johann Sebastian, was born (died 1694, May 3).

François de Troy, a French painter, was born (died 1730).

Dutch painting: Van Ruisdael, "River."

(to 1655) The papal reign of St. Innocent X (born at Rome).

(to 1644) During these years singer and composer Barbara Strozzi published five books of cantatas, ariettas et duets, one book of madrigals for two to five voices and a book of sacred songs for solo voice and continuo.

(to 1912) The tenure of the Ch'ing Dynasty embraced this period.

c.1644

Bartolomeo Girolamo Laurenti, Italian violinist and composer, was born at Bologna (died 1726, January 18).

(to 1685) Thomas Cross engraved portraits during thse years.

1645

(January 3) Johannes Matthäus Bach, son of Heinrich, was born. He died as an infant (1646 or 1647).

1645(cont.)

(January 5) Pompeo Colonna's five act opera "Proserpina rapita" was performed at his palace.

(February 5) Cavalli's opera "Il Romolo e 'l Remo" was produced at Venice, Teatro SS. Giovanni e Paolo.

(February 9) Johann Aegidius Bach, Erfurt musician, son of Johann Bach, grandson of Johannes, member of the fourth generation of the Bach family, was born (died 1716 or 1717).

(February 22) Johann Ambrosius Bach, Eisenach musician, son of Christoph, grandson of Johannes, member of the fourth generation of the Bach family, was born at Erfurt (died 1695, January). He was the father of Johann Sebastian.

(March 1) Nicholas Lanier sent a letter which is published in Jonckbloet and Land's ("Musique et musiciens au XVIIIᵉ siècle."

(March 10) J. Wilson was awarded the degree of Doctor of Music by Oxford.

(March 29) Abraham Bach, son of Hans, the younger, was born (date of death unknown).

(April 8) John Evelyn was present at a performance on this date of Pompeo Colonna's "Proserpina rapita."

(April 16) Tobias Hume, English violinist and composer, an officer in the army and an excellent viola da gamba player, died (birthdate unknown).

(May 2) Lodovico Grossi de

(cont.) Viadana, Italian composer, died at Gualtieri o/Po (born c.1564).

(August 3) August Kühnel, German violinist and composer, was born at Delmenhorst (date of death unknown).

(September 28) At Michaelmas this year Edward Gibbons' name appears in the books of the Vicars Choral for the last time, another of the Priest Vicars was Custos.

(November 30) Andreas Werckmeister, German organist and composer, was born (died 1706, October 26). One major source gave his date of death as 1708. He was concerned with correct tuning.

(December 14) "La Finta Pazza," rather more a musical play than an opera, by Sacrati, with libretto by Strozzi, was performed on this date in the Petit Bourbon at Paris with elaborate stage machinery. Some of the recitatives had been replaced with dialogue.

(December 21) Johann Löhner, German organist and composer, was born (died 1705, April 2).

Johann Christoph Bach, Arnstadt town musician, son of Christoph, grandson of Johannes and member of the fourth generation of the Bach family, was born at Erfurt (died 1693, August 25).

Wojciech Debolecki, Polish composer and writer, died (born 1585). Some sources gave 1647 as his date of death.

Descoteaux, a famous French flutist, was born (died 1728). He was a musician of King Louis

XIV.

William Lawes, English composer and Gentleman of the Chapel Royal, was killed this year at Chester while fighting for the Royalists during the siege (born 1602).

André Maugars, French violist and politician, died (born 1580).

Georg Muffat, composer and organist, was born at Schlettstadt (died 1704, February 23).

Gottfried Vopelius, a German composer, was born (died 1715).

T. Clifford resigned this year as a chorister of Magdalen College, Oxford.

Benedetto Ferrari left Venice at this time and became the maestro di cappella at the ducal court of Modena.

Niccolò Fontei succeeded Simone Zavaglioli as chapel master at Verona Cathedral.

After this year there was another "chasme" until 1660 in the records of Edward Gibbons, so there was no record in the books of the Vicars to show when he died.

Marcin Mielczewski this year acted as conductor of the band for Prince Karol Ferdinand, Bishop of Plock.

Jacob Stainer, Austrian violin maker, this year married Margaret Holzhammer, by whom he had eight daughters and a son who died in infancy.

Marco Uccellini was master of instrumental music for the Duke of Modena at this time.

Della Porta's motets were published this year and in 1648 and 1651.

Donati's "Messe a 4, 5 & 6 voci. Parte da cappella e da concerto . . ." appeared at this time.

Giovanni Battista Fasolo's "Annuale" was published this year at Venice. It consisted of several organ pieces.

Gaspare Filippi published a motet at this time.

A volume of "Canzone sacre in musica" by Orazio Giaccio was published this year.

A. Hammerschmidt's "Dialogi oder Gespräche zwischen Gott und einer gläubigen Seele" (two parts) was written at this time.

Romualdo Honorio composed a book of Masses this year at Venice.

Kindermann's chief work "Harmonia organica in tabulaturam Germanicam composita . . ." was first published this year. The work was particularly important because it required the use of pedals.

Monteverdi's "Venite" for soprano and continuo was included in Casati's "Raccolta di motette" published by Gardano at Venice.

C.T. Padbrué's "T Lof van Jubal" for four, five and six voices was published this year at Amsterdam.

Portman this year published a book of meditations: "The

Soules Life, exercising itself in the sweet Fields of Divine Meditation, collected for the comfart thereof in these sad days of distraction." It was reissued by Playford in 1660.

Johann Rosenmüller this year published his first work, a set for instruments entitled "Paduanen, Alemanden, Couranten, Balleten, Sarabanden, mit 3 stimmen und ihrem Basso pro Organo."

Schein's "Cantional" appeared this year in a second edition, posthumously.

Schütz' "The Seven Last Words of Christ" was written this year.

Paul Siefert this year published a pamphlet, "Anticribatio musica ad avenam Scacchianam."

A sacred song book by Georg Weber was published this year at Stockholm.

Italian opera sung in Italian was introduced to Paris at this time.

Cavalli's "Doriclea" was pro- duced this year at Venice, Teatro San Cassiano.

Cavalli's opera "Titone" was produced this year at Venice, Teatro San Cassiano.

There was a solitary English musician at Weissenfels at this time.

Among the ten thousand Pilgrims and Puritans who had arrived by this time, one hundred and forty five were university graduates, giving "a higher

(cont.) percentage of educated men than any comparable commun- ity in Europe."

At the Battle of Naseby this year the forces of King Charles I and the Parliamentary forces of Cromwell and Fairfax did battle once more and again Cromwell and Fairfax were tri- umphant. This battle ended the military phase of the Civil War in England.

Jean de La Bruyère, writer of "Les Caractères," was born (died 1696).

Hugo Grotius, Dutch humorist and jurist, died (born 1583).

The authorship of John Milton's "Comus" was openly declared at this time.

Jules Hardouin Mansart, French architect, was born (died 1708).

Dutch painting: Carel Fabritius, self-portrait.

Dutch painting: Frans Hals, "Balthasar Coymans."

The reign of Czar Michael Romanov over Russia ended. It had started in 1613.

French painting: Nicholas Poussin, "Finding of Moses."

(to 1648) At this time Cesti lived at Volterra, where he was "maestro" at the seminary and "direttore della cappella" at the cathedral.

(to 1655) Spanish painting: Murillo, "The Beggar Boy" (oil on canvas 53 7/8 x 45 1/4").

(and 1656) Friedrich Spee wrote

1645(cont.)
"Güldenes Tugendbuch" at these
dates. The work included
twenty-eight songs.

(to 1662) Between these years
several Italian operas were
performed in Paris. The design-
ers and composers made extensive
use of elaborate machinery to
simulate floods, fires, flying
figures and other natural phenomena inside the plots of their
operas. The Italian operas performed in Paris during these
years served as models for
French composers in the use of
ballet, machinery and "pieces
en musique."

(to 1666) French architecture:
Mansart, Val de Grâce, Paris
(133' high).

(to 1676) The reign of Czar
Alexis I over Russia.

c.1645
Pietro Simone Agostini, Italian
composer, was born in Rome
(birthdate unknown).

Johann Anton Losy von Losymthal,
Bohemian lutenist, was born
(died 1721).

Carlo Milanuzii, Italian composer, died probably in
Lombardy (born c.1590).

Alessandro Stradella, great
Italian cantata composer, was
born according to a major
source (died 1682).

Antonio Stradivari, greatest
violin maker, was born (See
1644).

Charles Couperin this year followed his brother Louis to
Paris a few years after the

(cont.) latter and became a pupil
of Chambonnières.

Francesco Manelli went to Parma
at this time where he spent the
last years of his life in the
service of the Duke Ranuccio II.

French painting: Georges de la
Tour, "St. Joseph the Carpenter"
(38 1/2" x 28 1/2"). Another
source gave the measurements as
53 1/8" x 39 3/8".

1646
(February 23) Benevoli was transferred to Santa Maria Maggiore
on this date.

(March 18) Vincenzo de Grandis,
Italian singer and composer,
died at Rome (birthdate unknown).

(July 29) Johann Theile, German
violist, singer and composer,
was born at Naumburg, Saxony
(died 1724, June or 1728).

(September 11) Johann Stobaeus,
German composer and pupil of
Eccard, died at Königsberg
(born 1580, July 6).

(September 23) Christopher
Gibbons, English organist and
composer, son of Orlando, married Mary Kercher, daughter of
a canon.

(September 24) Duarte Lobo,
Portuguese composer, died at
Lisbon (born 1565, September).

(September 25) Johann Fischer,
German violinist and composer,
was born at Augsburg (died
c.1721). He was a pupil of
Lully.

(October 3) Virgilio Mazzocchi,
Italian composer, brother of
Domenico, died at Veia near

1646(cont.)
Civita Castellana (born 1597, July 22).

(November 7) Orazio Benevoli became "maestro di cappella" at the Vatican.

(November 15) A. Diruta's "Poesie heroiche morali e sacre poste in musica a 1, 2, 3, 4 & 5 voci . . ." was dedicated on this date at Rome.

(December 25) Harald Vallerius, Swedish mathematician, organist and composer, was born at Vallerstad (died 1716, March 8).

(February) Cavalli's opera "Egisto" was produced in the Palais Royal with a simple stage setting.

(February) Milton addressed a sonnet to Henry Lawes praising Lawes' musical talent.

Richard Hutchinson, English organist, died (birthdate unknown).

Rupert Mayr, an Austrian composer, was born (died 1712).

Pier Francesco Tosi, Italian singing-master and composer, was born at Bologna (died 1732, April).

Maria Elisabeth Wedemann, wife of Johann Christoph Bach, member of the fourth generation of the Bach family, was born (died 1705).

In Rome this year a company called the Accademia dei Febi Armonici was founded.

Johann Rudolph Ahle was appointed organist at Erfurt this

(cont.) year.

Johannes Matthäus Bach, son of Heinrich, died (born 1645, January 3). A possibility exists that he lived until 1647.

John Blow was the second child and younger son of Henry and Katherine Blow, who were this year married at Newark.

Marcantonio Cesti was "maestro di capella" in a Florentine church at this time.

Jan Couchet was mentioned this year in the accounts of Antwerp Cathedral as repairing and tuning the organs.

Thomas Gobert was appointed chaplain of the Sainte-Chapelle this year.

Paul Heinlen learned to play keyboard and all wind instruments and this year went to Italy for further study.

Jewett returned to Dublin this year and was appointed a vicar choral of Christ Church.

Nicholas Lanier begged Huygens to get him a passport to go to Holland at this time.

Lully, at this time fourteen, went to France as "garçon de chambre" and unofficial instructor to Mlle. d'Orleans. He was supposed to "keep company" with the nineteen-year-old Duchess of Montpelier, a leader of the fronde (opposition to King Louis XIV).

G. Pinel was lutenist of the French King's chamber this year.

Clemens Thieme returned to

Dresden from Copenhagen at this date and was appointed an instrumental player in the court chapel.

Thomas Tomkins was organist at Worcester Cathedral until this year when services in the cathedral were suspended after the siege of Worcester.

Giovanni Battista Vacchelli was organist of the town of Rubbiera at this time.

Vesi became chaplain at Padua Cathedral this year.

John Wilson at this time joined the household of Sir William Walter of Sarsden.

Byrd, Bull, Gibbons, all contributed to "Parthenia . . ." published in 1613 and reprinted this year as well as in 1651, 1655, and possibly 1659.

J.M. Corvinus' "Heptachordum Danicum" was published this year.

Donati's "Languet anima mea" for five voices and "Vierdter u. letzter Theil" were both completed at this time.

A. Hammerschmidt's "Musicalische Andachten," part IV, sub-title "Geistliche Motetten und Concerten," appeared this year. The work contained forty pieces.

Pedro Heredia published two masses with those of Floride de Silvestris a Barbarino this year at Rome (Bologna?).

Krzesichleb's Psalm Book, containing a large number of anthems, hymns, and religious

(cont.) songs was reprinted (See also 1601, 1603, 1620, 1640.

A composition by Scipione Lazarini, a three-part song, appeared this year in a collective volume.

Parran's "Traité de la musique" was published at this time.

An edition of "Parthenia," the first collection of virginal music in England, appeared this year.

An Almande and five Brandes by one Primrose were included in "T" Uitnement Cabinet" published this year at Amsterdam.

Profe's collection "Cunis solennibus Jesuli recens-nati sacra genethliaca" appeared at this time.

A complete edition of Staden's "Hausmusik" was published this year. It contained 118 short and comparatively simple pieces for three to four voices, or instruments ad libitum, and in a few cases obbligati.

Stadlmayr this year published "Apparatus musicus sacrarum cantorium 6-24 vocib. et instr."

A "Fancy" was written by Tomkins this year.

Giovanni Battista Vacchelli wrote his "Motetti concertati" at this time.

One of the first examples of French opera during the minority of King Louis XIV was "Akebar, roi de Mogol" by Abbé Mailly. It was performed at Carpentras in the presence of the Papal Legate, Cardinal Bichi.

1646(cont.)

An Italian opera company was brought to Paris this year and performed Cavalli's "Egisto."

Cavalli's opera "La prosperità infelice di Giulio Cesare dittatore" was produced this year at Venice, Teatro Novissimo.

Sir Thomas Browne's "Pseudodoxia Epidemica" was completed at this time.

Richard Crashaw's "Steps to the Temple" was written this year.

Edward Winslow wrote "Hypocrisie Unmasked" this year which described the departure from Leyden, saying that the congregation was greatly moved and sang Psalms.

Archduke Leopold Wilhelm came to the Southern Netherlands this year and developed great admiration for David Teniers. He brought his to Brussels and put him in charge of his gallery. The artist portrayed the gallery in a series of pictures of great documentary value.

French painting: Claude Lorrain, "Sea Port."

(to 1648) Eccard's "Cantionale sacrum" was published during these years in Botha. A later edition appeared between 1651 -1657.

(to 1649) Antonio Maria Abbatini was "maestro di cappella" at the church of San Lorenzo in Damaso during this period.

(to 1653) Islamic architecture: Pearl Mosque at Agra (court

(cont.) 150' x 150').

(to 1653) Rospigliosi served as papal legate in Madrid during thse seven years.

(to 1665) Thomas Gobert was master of the royal chapel in Paris at this time.

(to 1696) Four editions of Nivers' book: "La Gamme du si; nouvelle méthode pour apprendre à chanter sans muances" appeared during this period.

c.1646

Louis de Grigny, French organist, was born (died 1709).

B. Marine was at Düsseldorf at this time.

French painting: Eustache Le Sueur "The Death of Raymond Diocrès" (oil on canvas, 76 by 51 1/8").

1647

(March 2) Luigi Rossi's "Orfeo" was performed in Paris. Atto Melani sang the title role.

(May 10) Mateo Romero, Spanish or Flemish composer, died at Madrid (birthdate unknown). He was known as "Maestro Capitán."

(May 19) Jakob Scheiffelhut, German composer, was baptised at Augsburg.

(June 17) Major Robert Gibbons, possibly another son of Edward, became Governor of the Castle of Exeter.

(August 15) The Chioggia Cathedral was opened.

(September 12) Heinrich Albert's church music according to one source was confined to a "Te Deum" for three voices published on this date.

(October 18) Christian Clodius, a German music editor, was born at Neustadt near Stolpen (date of death unknown).

(December 1) Giovanni Battista Doni, Italian musical scholar, died at Florence (born 1594).

(December 20) Ann Gibbons, who married William Stocke at St. Margaret's, Westminster on this date, may have been Orlando's daughter of that name.

(December 31) Giovanni Maria Trabaci, organist and composer, died (born c.1580).

(March) John Milton, English composer, father of the poet, died at London (born c.1563).

(March, April, May) Luigi Rossi's opera "Orfeo," with libretto by Buti, was "sump- tuously" produced at the Palais Royal during these three months.

(October) Jacques Gaultier sent to his "quelques petites choses de nostre luth et quelques airs à chanter" to Constantin Huygens.

(December) Andrea Falconieri became maestro di cappella of the royal chapel at Naples.

Henry Aldrich, English scholar, architect and composer, was born at London, Westminster (died 1710, December 14).

Charles Butler, English agri- culturist, grammarian and mu- sical theorist, died (birthdate

(cont.) unknown).

Antoine Antoni Gallot, French lutenist, died at Wilno (birth- date unknown).

James Hart, English bass singer and composer, was born at York (died 1718, May 8).

Johann Heermann, hymn-writer, died (born 1585).

Pelham Humfrey, English composer who studied with Lully as a boy, was born (died 1674, July 19).

André Philidor, composer and windplayer, was born (died 1730, August 11). He was the son of Jean and known as "Philidor l'âiné."

Jakob Scheiffelhut, German com- poser, was born at Augsburg (died 1709, July 2).

The composer, Giovanni Maria Trabaci, died (See December 31).

Antonelli was mentioned by Florido as being at San Damaso in Rome this year.

Henry Blow II, son of Henry and Katherine Blow, was baptised this year.

Bontempi went to the Saxon court at Dresden this year or possibly 1650.

Cardoso this year was appointed vicar.

Cazzati at this time was "maestro di cappella" at the private chapel of the Duke of Sabionata at Bozolo.

Cenci in his madrigals of this year pleaded for a-cappella

singing.

John Cotton this year allowed that "any private Christian who hath a gifte to frame a spirituall song" might not only compose and sing it but might also perform the work on a musical instrument.

Gustaf Düben (the elder) was a member of the court chapel at this time.

Agostino Filippucci was at this time both priest and organist at San Giovanni in Monte, Bologna.

João Alvares Frovo (Frouvo) this year succeeded his teacher, Lobo, as choirmaster at Lisbon Cathedral.

Daniel Norcome, violist, was still in the service of the Archduke at Brussels this year.

Orazio Tarditti, organist and composer, was a Calmaldulian monk and abbot at Ravenna at this time.

Weichmann was this year appointed cantor and choir director at Königsberg.

A. Wood matriculated this year at Merton College.

Besides the musical academies at Bologna there were proper schools of music in this year and also in 1620 and 1700.

Wolfgang Christoph Agricola published a book of masses this year.

The second edition of the "Bay Psalm Book" was printed at this

Carissimi's only short opera, "L'amoro se passioni di Fileno," was published this year.

An important chorale book of the period: "Praxis Pietatis melica" (Practice of Piety in song) was edited and published this year by Crüger. The book had at least forty-six editions.

A. Diruta's "Il secondo libro de' salmi che si cantano ne' vesperi di tutto l'anno concertati a 4 voci . . ." appeared at this time.

Doni's "De praestantia musicae veteris" was published this year at Florence.

Niccolò Fontei published his "messa e salmi" opus 6 and "salmi brevi" opus 7 this year at Venice.

Jan Aleksander Gorczyn at Cracow this year published a handbook on music, "Tabulatura muzyki abo Zaprawa muzykalna . . . "

Florentino A'Kempis composed three symphonies in 1644. They were published at Antwerp and reprinted in this year and in 1649 in enlarged editions.

Vittorio Loreto at this time set to music "La pellegrina costante," an oratorio.

A.V. Michna this year published "Czech Music for the Virgin Mary" at Prague.

Several of Milanuzii's antiphons and litanies for one to four voices were issued this year posthumously at Venice.

A fourth edition of Philips'
"Les Rossignols spirituels"
(without Philips' name) appeared
this year at Cologne. It was
dedicated to Charles de Pas,
Abbot of Saint Armand.

Rossi's opera "Orfeo" was composed this year.

Scacchi's treatise "Breve
discorso sopra musica moderna"
and "Cantilena Quinque vocibus
et lachrymae sepulchrales ad
tumulum Johannis Slobaci" were
both published this year.

Schütz' "Symphoniarum sacrarum
secunda Pars . . ." was published this year at Dresden.

Tomkins' "Lord Canterbury" was
written at this time.

F. Vitali's "Libro quinto di
arie a tre voci" was published
this year by Landi at Florence.

G.J. Voss wrote his "De artis
poeticae natura ac
constitutione" at this time.

In the ballet "Les Rues de
Paris" this year the slow part
had a ponderous dotted rhythm,
the "rhythme saccad e" from the
Lullian overture, but the fast
movement did not yet have the
fugal texture that was to become typical.

Pierre Bayle, a liberal émigré
living in Holland and one of
the first to fight for freedom
of thought and conscience, was
born (died 1706).

Robert Herrick's "Noble Numbers"
was written this year.

Dutch painting: Paulus Potter,
"The Young Bull."

(to 1654) R. . . Florido (first
name unknown), Italian bass and
composer, was at the church of
Santo Spirito in Sassia at Rome
during this period.

c.1647
Goffredo Cappa, Italian violin
maker, was born (died 1717,
August 6).

Martino Pesenti, Italian composer, died at Venice (born c.1600).

As early as this date John Cotton
published a defense of singing.

Solomon Eccles was a teacher of
the virginals and viols from this
time forward.

French painting: Lorrain,
"Cleopatra Disembarking at
Taurus" (3' 10 3/4" x 5' 6 1/2").

1648
(January 7) M. East's will
carried this date.

(March 9) Caspar Bach, a
shepherd at Wechmar, was born
(date of death unknown).

(March 15) A book of posthumous
works by Martino Pesenti was
published.

(April 16) Matthaeus Loewenstern,
a German poet and composer, died
at Bernstadt (born 1594, April
20).

(April 27) Christoph Thomas
Walliser, German composer, died
at Strassbourg (born 1568,
April 17).

(May 9) M. East's will was
proved P.C.C. on this day.

(June 24) Thomas Salmon, English musical theorist, was born at London (died 1706, July).

(July 9) Arp Schnitger, a German organ builder, was born at Schmalenfleth (died 1718, July 24).

(July 12) Johann Stadlmayr, the German composer, died at Innsbruck (born 1560).

(July 16) Lorenzo Allegri, Italian lutenist and composer, died at Florence (born 1573).

(July 21) C. Huygens on this date wrote to Mlle. de La Barre and stated that in his house were "luths, tiorbes, violes, espinettes a vous divertir, quasi autant que toute la Suède vous en pourra fournir."

(August 6 or 9) Johann Michael Bach, Gehren organist, son of Heinrich, grandson of Johannes and member of the fourth genera- tion of the Bach family, was born (died 1694, May).

(September 1) Marin Mersenne, French theorist, died at Paris (born 1588, September 8).

(September 6) Johann Schelle, a German composer, was born at Geissing (died 1701, March 10).

(October 18) William King was admitted a clerk of Magdalen College, Oxford on this day.

(November 12) Thomas Ford, English lutenist and composer, made his will on this date. In it were mentioned Walter Porter, Wormall, Coggleshall, Drew, Evans and Cooke, all musicians.

(November 17) Thomas Ford, English lutenist and composer, was buried at St. Margaret's, Westminster.

(November) Thomas Ford, English lutenist and composer, died at London (born c.1580).

Pietro Degli Antonii, Italian composer, was born at Bologna (died 1720).

John Blow, English composer and organist, was born according to a major source. Others gave his birthdate as 1649 or c.1648 (died 1708).

Michael East (Easte), English composer, died probably at London (born c.1580).

Antonio Giannettini, an Italian composer, was born, probably at Fano (died c.1721, July 12).

Pedro Heredia, Spanish composer, died at Rome (birthdate unknown).

Ivan Lukačić, Dalmatian composer, died (birthdate unknown).

Johann Theile, pupil of Schütz and composer of "Adam and Eve," was born (See 1646, July 29).

Michael Wise, English counter- tenor, organist and composer, was born at Wiltshire (died 1687, August 24).

Jean Baptiste Boesset was en- nobled this year.

Edward Chilmead had lost his musical livelihood long before the Restoration, in fact at the time of the parliamentary visit- ation to Oxford this year.

T. Cima must have been awarded

1648(cont.)
the degree of L.L.D. prior to
this year.

Georg Dressel, a carpenter who
wrote a chronicle of important
events at Eisenach, was born
this year (died 1673).

Henry Lawes and his brother
William set choice psalms to
music at this time.

Michael Jacobi was cantor at the
town school of Kiel this year.

Jarzębski, who was held in
great esteem by his countrymen,
was this year installed "civium
iuratorum antiquae Varsoviae"
(among the members of the
patriciate of Warsaw).

Mersenne's spinet at this time
was tuned to: A=403 c.p.s.,
S=1˙4.

S. Otto was still living at
Schandau at this time.

Portman was still organist of
Westminster Abbey this year.

Giovanni Vincenzo Sarti this
year was maestro di cappella at
the Metropolitan Church in
Ravenna.

Sacchi at this time moved from
Warsaw to Italy.

Benedict Schultheiss' father,
Hieronymus, married this year
for the second time.

The "Geistliche Chormusik" or
"Musicalia ad Chorum Sacrum,"
dedicated to the city of Leipzig
and to the St. Thomas choir,
showed Schütz' conservative
traits.

After peace had come this year
Schütz helped to restore several
musical establishments which had
suffered during the war. He
gave advice, money and musical
assistance.

Archduke Ferdinand Charles became the patron for Austrian
violin maker Jacob Stainer this
year.

Orazio Tarditi was maestro di
cappella of Faenza Cathedral at
this time.

Vesi from this date forward was
"maestro di cappella" to
Giorgio Cornaro, Bishop of
Padua, Count of Piove, of Sacco,
etc.

Agricola published his
"Fasciculus variarum cantionum"
at this time. Motets were included in the work.

Ahle's published compositions
included "Compendium pro
tenellis" of this year. This
was a treatise on singing which
enjoyed three printings.

Ahle's "Geistliche Dialoge" appeared this year.

Bertali's cantata, for two
choruses of warriors and
"amoretti," "La pace trionfante"
was composed at this time.

Cardoso's "Livro de varios
motetes, Officio da Semana Santa
e outras cousas. . . ." was
published this year at Lisbon.

John Cobb's elegy on the death
of William Lawes was included in
"Choice Psalmes."

Works by Coperario were included
in the Amsterdam collection of

this year, "XX Koninkli, Ke
Fantasien on 3 Fiolen."

Johann Crüger's "Praxis
pietatis melica" was issued this
year in a third edition at
Berlin.

Dionigi this year published a
treatise on the "cantus firmus,"
"Li primi tuoni ovvero
introduzione nel canto fermo."
It appeared in an enlarged edition in 1667.

G. Dumanoir I this year wrote a
suite consisting of three five
-part airs and titled
"Charivaris."

Among lesser keyboard composers
of the Austrian school Wolfgang
Ebner was noted for a set of
thirty-six variations on a
theme by Emperor Ferdinand III
composed this year. The number
of variations corresponded to
the age of the composer.

Zahn gave a melody by Musophilus
Dedekind, "Gott vater aller
Gütigkeit," from the "Gothaer
Cantional" II of this year and
suggested that Musophilus might
well be Henning Dedekind.

An elegy by Hilton II on the
death of William Lawes, "Bound
by the neere conjunction of our
Soules," for three voices and
bass was included in Lawe's
"Choice Psalms."

S. Ives' elegy on the death of
W. Lawes, "Lament & mourn"
appeared in separate parts at
the end of "Choice Psalmes."

An elegy on the death of William
Lawes by Jenkins was included
at the end of "Choice Psalms."

"Choice Psalms" by the Lawes
brothers was published this
year.

Vittorio Loreto this year composed the music for "Il
sagrifizio d'Abrama," an oratorio.

A set of Psalms for double
chorus by Mazzocchi was published
this year posthumously.

A.V. Michna's "Officium
vespertinum" was published this
year at Prague.

S. Otto's important work,
"Kronen-Krönlein oder
Musicalischer Vorläuffer au ff
geistliche Concert-Madrigal
-Dialog-Symphon-Motetische
Manier mit 3, 4, 5, 6, 7, 8
Stim . . . ." was published at
this time at Freiberg.

Della Porta's motets were published this year and in 1645 and
1651.

Rosenmüller's "Kernsprüche" appeared this year.

Schütz' "Musicalia ad Chorum
sacrum" was published this year
at Dresden.

S.G. Staden this year published
an instruction book for singing.

Vernizzi's "Concerti Spirituali,"
opus 6 appeared at this time.

Georg Weber published four
books of songs at Danzig this
year.

John Wilson contributed to
"Choice Psalms."

After this year there was a
resurgence in the musical culture of Germany, which started

1648(cont.)

and culminated in Johann Sebastian Bach.

At this time "Concertato" style with instruments became important to the works of local Austrian composers such as Stadlmayr.

"Follias" were included in the "Galeria musicale . . . . compartita in diversi Scherzi di chitarriglia" by Stefano Pesori of Mantua, written this year.

Cavalli's opera "Torilda" was produced this year at Venice, Teatro San Cassiano.

"La vittoria d'Imeneo," an opera with libretto by Ferrari, was produced this year at Modena.

Sacrati's opera "L'isola d'Alcina" was produced this year at Venice.

Sacrati's opera "Semiramide" was produced this year at Venice.

The actors at the Théâtre du Marais this year improved upon Chapoton's "Descent d'Orphée aux Enfers," and titled it "La Grande Journée des Machines ou le Mariage d'Orphée et d' Eurydice," thus emphasizing the association of machinery and music.

D'Assoucy's poem "Le Jugement de Parîs" was written this year.

Robert Herrick's "Hesperides" appeared at this time.

This year marked the end of the Thirty Years War in Germany.

The Count of Ognatte was sent to Naples to suppress Masaniello's rising this year and remainēd

(cont.) there as viceroy.

The Emperor at this time took his court opera with him to both Prague and Pressburg.

French painter, Louis Le Nain died (born c.1593).

French painting: Mathieu Le Nain, "The Forge." This painting was completed prior to this date.

French painting: Poussin, "Landscape with the Burial of Phocion" (47" x 70 1/2").

(to 1668) The reign of King Jan Casimir over Poland.

(to 1686) J. Playford the elder opened his business in London as a bookseller and publisher this year in the Inner Temple "near the Church door." He did not live there.

c.1648

Robert Smith, an English composer, was born (died 1675, November 22).

1649

(January 5) Cavalli's opera "Giasone" was produced at Venice, Teatro San Cassiano.

(January 22) Pascal Colasse, French composer born at Rheims, was baptised on this day (died 1709, July 17).

(January 30) King Charles I's martyrdom was observed throughout England during the Restoration. King Charles II's purpose in conjuring up his father's ghost so frequently was probably based upon his need to remind everyone of this year's actions and to alert them against

1649(cont.)

the Whigs.

(February 14) Tomkins wrote his "Sad Pavan."

(February 23) John Blow, English composer, organist and royal musician, was baptised at Newark, Nottinghamshire.

(February 25) Johann Philipp (von) Krieger, German musician, was born at Nürnberg (died 1725, February 7).

(February 26) Girolamo Amati, violin maker, was born at Cremona (died 1740, February 27).

(March 19) Gerhard Johann Voss (Vossius), German scholar, died at Amsterdam (born c.1577).

(May 3) Johann Valentin Meder, German singer, conductor and composer, was born at Wasungen (died 1719, July).

(May 16) Szymon Berent, Polish composer, died at Brodnica (born 1585).

(May 23) Michel Farinel, French violinist, was baptised at Grenoble.

(June 5) William King was awarded the degree of Bachelor of Arts by Oxford.

(July 3) Francesco Sacrati was appointed maestro di cappella to the court of Modena.

(July 14) Pietro Benedetti died sometime after this date at Florence (birthdate unknown).

(September 30) A portrait of J. Hilton II from this year at

(cont.) the age of fifty has been preserved. The head was engraved for Hawkins' "History of Music."

(December 11) The preface to Monteverdi's "Messa a quattro voci et salmi, a 1, 2, 3, 4, 5, 6, 7 & 8 voci, concertate a parte da cappella & con le Letanie della B.V. . . . ." was published this year and edited by Vincenti at Venice.

(January) Cesti's first opera "Orontea" was produced at Venice, Teatro dei SS. Apostoli.

(April) Giovani Valentini, Italian organist and composer, died at Vienna (birthdate un-known).

(September) Ottavio Vernizzi, Italian organist and composer, died at Bologna (born c.1580).

(October) Giovanni Felice Sances became vice Kapellmeister of the imperial chapel at Vienna.

Giuseppe Antonio Bernabei, Italian composer, was born at Rome (died 1732, March 9).

John Blow, teacher of Purcell, organist of Westminster Abbey for two terms, and organist and composer in the Chapel Royal, was born (died 1708, October 1). A major source gave his birth as 1648.

Bellerofonte Castaldi, Italian theorbo player, guitarist, poet and composer, died (born 1581).

Pascal Colasse, a pupil of Lully, was born (died 1709).

Michel Farinel, French violinist, was born (date of death unknown).

Johann Valentin Meder, composer of Passion Music, was born (died 1719).

Ferdinand Tobias Richter, German organist and composer, was born at Würzburg (died 1711).

Martin Rinkart, a hymn-writer, died (born 1586).

Christoph Bernhard went to Italy this year to perfect his singing.

Antonio Bertali at this time succeeded Giovanni Valentini as court conductor at Vienna.

Bockshorn studied theology this year.

Carissimi was employed at St. Marcello in Rome after this date.

Marc-Antoine Charpentier, an ardent admirer of Carissimi, went to Rome this year to study painting. He was active in creating the Carissimi vogue in France.

Daniel Friderici this year reproached foolish conductors for "laying about with the baton that the chips fly."

Andreas Fromm, German composer, was cantor and professor at the Fürstliches Pädagogium in Stettin this year.

Bonifazio Graziani this year became maestro di cappella at the Jesuit church in Rome.

Paul Heinlen was appointed musician to the Nürnberg Town Council this year.

Neubauer as a suite composer at this time was not as concerned with thematic unity as Schein had been.

Juan de Padilla was chapel master at Puebla, Mexico when the cathedral was dedicated this year.

B. Pękiel was given Scacchi's post this year as principal conductor at the Royal Chapel in Warsaw.

G. Pinel was lute-master to the King of France at this time.

Edward Raban gave up his business of printing this year.

Marco Scacchi resigned this year as principal conductor of the Royal Chapel at Warsaw.

Heinrich Schwemmer sang at a musical festival at Nürnberg during this year.

Tomkins continued in service with the Chapel Royal until this year and the execution of King Charles I.

As far back as this time Uccellini, in Italy, had tried the sixth position.

John Wallis was appointed Savilian Professor of Geometry at Oxford this year.

Forkel gave this year as that of Johann Sebastian Bach's setting of "O wie selig seid ihr doch, ihr Frommen" (no. 152). It is not clear to what he had reference.

Szymon Berent published his "Litaniae de Beata Virgine Maria" at this time.

1649(cont.)

Francesco Cavalli's opera "Giasone" appeared at this time.

Crüger's "Geistliche Kirchen-Melodien über die von Herrn D. Luthero . . . auffgesetzte Gesänge und Psalmen" appeared this year at Leipzig.

Ferdinand III showed a respectable musical proficiency in the "Drama musicum" of this year.

Gaspare Filippi at this time published his "musiche" consisting of seventeed Italian songs, twelve madrigals, and nine sonatas.

The first attempt to change originally Catholic form into a Protestant type was made by Fromm in the "Actus musicus: De Divite et Lazaro," published this year at Stettin.

The first known German oratorio, "Vom reichen Mann und Lazarus," composed by Andreas Fromm, was published this year at Stettin.

Two of Hammerschmidt's most important works appeared this year, the third part of "Odes & Madrigals, sacred & secular, for 1-5 voices with continuo," and twenty Latin motets for one and two voices, with accompaniment.

The catalogue for the ducal library of John IV was printed at Lisbon this year by P. Craesbeeck.

John IV's "Defensa de la música moderna" (in Spanish) was published this year at Lisbon.

Florentino A'Kempis composed three symphonies in 1644. They

(cont.) were published at Antwerp and reprinted in this year, and in 1647 in enlarged editions.

Marini's opus 16, "Concerto terzo delle musiche da camera a 3-6 e piu voci," was published this year at Milan.

Micheli's "Vivit Deus" . . . Auctore R.M. rom. Opus sextum, a folio, was published this year at Rome by Grignani.

Arthur Phillips this year composed music for a poem by Dr. Pierce, "The Resurrection."

A volume of masses by P. Philips was published this year posthumously. It is identical with a book entered in a list of the musical library of John IV of Portugal this year, "Missas y salmos . . . a 8 & 9 . . . obras postumas."

Profe's supplement "Corollarium geistlicher Collectaneorum" appeared at this time.

Rotrou's "La Naissance d'Hercule" was written this year.

A famous book of songs "Trutznachtigall, oder Geistlich-poetisches Lustwäldlein," probably composed by Friederich Spee this year, has appeared in many editions since then.

Tomkins this year wrote "For these distracted Times."

Marco Uccellini at this time published sonatas or canzonas for violin solo and bass at Venice.

George Weber published three song books this year at Königsberg.

1649(cont.)

J. Weichmann at this time composed several books of motets, sacred & secular songs, two books of balletts, courants, allemandes, and sarabands in two parts.

Werner's collection of solo songs was published this year.

Up to this date the Thirty Years' War had stopped any intensive musical activity in Vienna, particularly costly operati productions.

Cavalli's opera "Euripo" was produced this year at Venice, Teatro San Moisè.

Cavalli's opera "Giasone" was produced this year at Venice.

Lucas von Bostel, a poet, was born (date of death unknown).

Richard Crashaw, English religious poet, died in Italy (born 1613).

The Independent Party of the English Parliament this year tried and executed King Charles I of England for treason.
Oliver Cromwell started his rule over England as Lord Protector.

At this time the King was executed, the monarcy abolished, and England became a republic. A Puritan movement dominated the country.

Juan Montañes, Spanish sculptor, died (born c.1580).

Dutch painting: Pieter Claesz, "Stillife with Fruit."

(to 1650) Francesco Luccio's two books of "motetti concertati"

(cont.) were published at this time.

(to 1652) Johann Kindermann at this time composed a large number of chorale tunes, harmonized for three voices, to the Nürnberg preacher Dilherr's "Evangelische Schlussreimen" and "Göttliche Liebesflamme."

(to 1652) Issac Voss was at the court of Christina of Sweden in Stockholm during this period.

(to 1653) The reign of the Council of State - Commonwealth over England and Great Britain.

(to 1660) Masques continued to be performed privately during these years.

(to 1660) English Commonwealth existed during this period.

(to 1660) Spanish painting: Velásquez, "Villa Medici Gardens" (18 7/8" x 16 1/2").

c.1649

Adam Jarzębski, Polish violinist and composer, died at Warsaw (born c.1590).

French painting: Poussin, "Polyphemus."

1650

(February 11) René Descartes, French philosopher and sometime music theorist, died at Stockholm (born 1596, March 31).

(February 20) Cavalli's opera "Orimonte" was produced at Venice, Teatro San Cassiano.

(April 26) Johannes Bach's son Johann Jakob was born. He was not a musician (date of death unknown).

1650(cont.)

(May 16) Gilles Hayne made his
will on this date and died at
the end of the month. He published masses and motets but
no trace remains of the thirty
-eight works purportedly used at
the Düsseldorf chapel.

(May 20) Francesco Sacrati,
Italian composer, died at
Modena (birthdate unknown).

(November 24) Manuel Cardoso,
Portuguese composer, died at
Lisbon (born 1571 March or 1569).

(February) D'Assoucy provided
incidental songs and choruses
for Corneille's "tragédie à
machines" "Andromède" produced
at the Palais du Petit Bourbon,
Paris at this time.

(May) Gilles Hayne (Egidius
Aegidius), Walloon composer,
died (birthdate unknown).

(Autumn) Cesti was singing at
Lucca at this time.

(November) "The English Dancing
Master" was entered at
Stationer's Hall.

John Abell, Scottish alto singer
and lutenist, was born in
Aberdeenshire (died 1724).

Ahle left a son, Johann Georg,
born this year. He received his
father's honors and was made
poet laureate by Emperor
Leopold I.

Giulio Cesare Ardemanio,
Italian organist and composer,
died at Milan (birthdate unknown).

Tommaso Bai, Italian singer
(tenor) and composer, was born

(cont.) at Crevalcuore near
Bologna (died 1714, December 22).

Jean Buterne, organist and composer, was born (died 1727).

Manuel Cardoso, Portuguese composer, died (See November 24).

Fabio Colonna, an Italian instrument maker, died at Naples
(born c.1567).

Johann Kaspar Ferdinand Fischer,
composer and later court
Kapellmeister at Baden, was
born (died 1746).

Orlando Gibbons, son of the
organist and composer of the
same name, died at Exeter (born
1623).

Johann Adam Gluck, grandfather
of the composer, was born in
Neustadt near Bohemia (date of
death unknown).

Joachim Neander, German composer, was born (died 1680).

Martin Peerson, English instrumental composer, died (born
c.1572).

Pierre Phalèse the younger died
at Antwerp and was buried in his
son's monastery. His children
erected a monument to his memory
this year in the church there.

André Raison, French organist,
was born (died 1720).

Johann Jacob Walther, German
violinist and composer, was
born at Witterda near Erfurt
(died c.1717).

Catharina Wedemann, wife of
Johann Michael Bach, member of
the fourth generation of the

Bach family, was born (died 1704).

Vincenzo Albrici was in the service of Queen Christina of Sweeden as director of her Italian opera-house until she abdicated this year.

The choruses for Corneille's "Andromède" have been attributed to Jean Baptiste Boesset.

Bontempi went to the Saxon court at Dresden in 1647 and possibly in this year.

Cazzati was "maestro di cappella" of the Accademia della Morte Ferrara at this time.

Cesti this year was at the court of the Medici at Florence.

Werner Fabricius, German composer and organist, went to the Leipzig University this year to study philosophy, theology and law.

João Alvares Frovo (Frouvo) became a clerk at the Treasury in Portugal this year.

Gouy replaced voices with viols this year.

A fine example of an English regal (small portable organ) bearing the initials I.L. and this date was preserved at the castle of Blair Atholl.

A. van Noordt was still known to have been organist at the Nieuwe Syts Capel (New Side Chapel) at this time.

Del Pane this year became a soprano singer in the imperial chapel at Vienna under

Sir W. Petty, Doctor of Medicine, was appointed professor of music at Gresham College in London at this time.

Salvator Rosa in a letter referred to Cesti as the "glory and splendour of the secular scene."

Pietro Paolo Sabbatini was professore di musica at this date.

Heinrich Schwemmer at this time became assistant master at the St. Laurence School in Nürnberg.

D'Assoucy this year wrote the words and music of a pastoral play, "Les Amours d'Apollon et Daphné." The work was probably never performed.

Brassicanus wrote some of the songs in "Harmonisches Chor-und Figuralgesangbuch . . ." published this year at Frankfort.

"Follias" were included in the "Quattro Wori della Chitarra spagnuola" by the academician Caliginoso before this date.

Bartolomeo Capello's "Sacra animorum" was published at this time.

Corneille's "Andromède" of this year was the earliest and most distinguished French opera.

Crüger's "Quaestiones musicae practicae" was published this year at Berlin.

Descartes' "Compendium musicae" of this year was one of the most remarkable books of this period.

"Follias" were included in "Il

1650(cont.)

Primo Libro di Canzone" of this
year by Andrea Falconieri.

Andrea Falconieri at this time
published his "Primo libro di
Canzoni, Sinfonie, Fantasie,
Capricci, Brandi, Correnti,
Gagliade, Alemane, Volte, per
Violini e Viole, overo altri
Strumenti a uno due e tre con
il Basso Continuo."

John Gamble published his "Ayres
and Dialogues to be sung to the
Theorbo Lute or Bass Viol" this
year.

Karel Guillet's "Institution
harmonique" was published at
this time.

A'Kempis' "Missae et Motetta"
for eight voices and continuo
was published this year at
Antwerp.

Kircher's "Musurgia universalis
sive ars magna consoni et
dissone" in two volumes was published this year at Rome.

Micheli's "Avviso inviato da me
R.M. ensieme con foglio reale
del canone musicale Fons
Signatus, alle famosi e
puritissimi sig. musici d'Italia
e de tutte gl'altri Regni . . ."
was published this year by
Grignani at Rome.

A canon in thirty-six parts
divided among nine choirs by
Micheli was included in
Kircher's "Musurgia universalis."

Micheli's "Canone musicale a
quattro voci, ad honore della
concettione della B.V.M.,
composto sopra le vocali di
nuovo, e curioso arlif icio
. . . Opera et inventione

(cont.) pellegrina de R.M. rom"
was published this year by
Grignani at Rome.

Micheli's "Le messe a quattro
voci" was published this year at
Rome.

A collection of Monteverdi's
containing psalms and a Mass was
printed this year posthumously.
His mass showed great contrast.

Thomas Harper this year printed
the first edition of "The
English Dancing Master" by John
Playford. It was dated 1651 but
published this year.

At this time a few works were
issued by the Phalèse company
and appeared in "Apud
Magdalenam Phalesium et
cohaeredes."

Scheidt this year wrote an important book, "Tabulaturbuch
hundert geistlicher Lieder und
Psalmen." It was the first
true book of organ accompaniments for congregational singing
in Protestant churches. It was
Scheidt's second and last book
for organ and was published at
Dresden.

The Cornettino was often required by Schütz in his works,
most particularly in No. 3 of
the third part of the "Symphoniae
sacrae" published this year.

Szymon Starowolski, the Polish
historian and ecclesiastic,
this year published his treatise
on accoustics "Musices practicae
erotemata" at Cracow.

G.J. Voss this year wrote "De
quatuor artibus popularibus
grammatica, gymnastica, musica
et graphica liber."

1650(cont.)

Italians in the northern countries such as Zamponi in Brussels ("Ulisse," 1650), Bontempi in Dresden ("Il Paride," 1662), Scacchi in Poland, Bertali and his successor Draghi in Vienna did not exceed in any way the average level of Italian opera production at their time.

A theory that Jubal, son of Cain, invented music appeared in the "Musurgia" by Kircher.

At about this time Locke and his contemporaries discovered the possibilities inherent in experimental harmonies of the early baroque recitative. They had by this time developed the elementary tonality of the middle baroque.

The use of a single time signature indicating a regular succession of harmonic and accentual patterns, set off by barlines at regular intervals gradually became more common at this time.

Girdlestone said "Supplementary harmony was unnecessary and the "basso continuo" was late in appearing in France, becoming common only after 1650."

The "isochronous" barline has become standard by this time following the lead of keyboard and lute music and early 17th-Century monodists.

The archlute was described by Kircher in "Musurgia."

The automatic hydraulic organ was introduced by Kircher in his "Musurgia universalis." It operated by hydraulic air com-

(cont.) pression.

The "Spillflöte" organ stop originated at this time.

The violin appeared in Playford's "English Dancing Master" of this year as was obvious by the use of the French violin clef.

Kircher's "Musurgia" fixed the upper limit or the range of the violin at the sixth position.

From this date forward in the British Foot Guards the Drum -Major was on the Legimental staff.

After this time France developed a national style which resisted Italian influence for more than a hundred years.

According to Girdlestone, "In Italy, the true forerunners of Lulli and Quinault were the composers of the Barberini opera in Rome before 1650, Mazzochi, Vittori and Landi."

Two productions of this year, Boyer's "Ulysse dans l'ile de Circé" and Corneille's "Andromède," combined the elements of music and machinery in their staging.

In d'Assoucy's "Amours d'Apollon et de Daphné" of this year spoken verses and sung arias alternated as in the oldest type of "ballet de cour."

D'Assoucy's "Les Amours d'Apollon et Daphné," an opéra comique, was produced this year.

D'Assoucy's opera "Andromède" was produced at Paris.

After this year more pastoral

plays were set to music, such as Perrin's "Issy Pastorale" with music by Cambert.

Cavalli's opera "Bradamante" was produced this year at Venice, Teatro SS. Giovanni e Paolo, Carnival.

Elton's "Compleat Body of the Art Military" was published this year.

D'Assoucy's poem "Ovide en belle humeur" appeared at this time.

Corneille's "Andromède" was written at this time.

The official Psalter of the Church of Scotland was approved this year.

Jeremy Taylor's "Holy Living" was written at this time.

Henry Vaughan's "Silex Scintillans" appeared this year.

A wedding was held this year by proxy at Turin for Adelaide of Saxony's marriage to the Elector of Bavaria.

French painting: Philippe de Champaigne, "Portrait of Arnauld d'Andilly" (oil on canvas, 35 7/8 x 28 3/8"). This picture is sometimes referred to as "Portrait of a Man."

(to 1652) Sir William Davenant was held prisoner in the Tower during these years.

(to 1652) Sir William Davenant's "Gondibert" was written at this time while he was in prison.

(to 1655) Chambonnières intro-duced the Couperins to Paris

(cont.) during these years.

(to 1655) Playford's musical works were printed by Thomas Harper during this period.

(to 1659) In undated petitions during these years Porter asked for commiseration.

(to 1659) Neapolitan opera grew from scores by Francesco Provenzale of Naples written during this period.

(to 1686) Playford was the most important music publisher in England for these thirty-six years.

(to 1689) Henry Herringman, an Englishman, worked as music printer "at the signe of The Bleu Anchor in the New Exchange" at this time.

(to 1728) Many editions of Playford's "The Dancing Master" were published during this lengthy period. It was a col-lection of airs for violin used for country dances, the tunes being popular ballad and other airs of the period.

(to 1750) Castrato singers flour-ished during this time which strangely was also called the "Golden Gap of Lutheran music."

(to 1750) Instrumental music written during this period, particularly that by Italians, is best judged by listening to it.

(to 1750) There was a tendency toward organ pitches as much as a whole tone lower during these years.

c.1650

Clamor Henrich Abel was born at Westphalia (date of death unknown).

P.S. Agostini, composer of "Il ratto delle Sabine" (The Rape of the Sabine Women), was born at this time (died c.1690).

Floriano (Aresti) Arresti, an Italian composer, was born at Bologna (died 1719).

Pietro Antonio Fiocco, composer and head of the Fiocco family of musicians, was born at Venice (died 1714, November 3).

Francis Forcer, an English composer, was born (died 1705).

Petronio Franceschini, an Italian composer, was born at Bologna (died 1681, January 25).

Bolognese composer Domenico Gabrieli was born (died 1690).

Giovanni Battista da Gagliano, Italian composer, died at Florence (born c.1585).

Teobaldo de' Gatti, Italian composer and Gamba player, was born at Florence (died 1717, August).

The Rev. Edward Gibbons, English composer and brother of Orlando Gibbons, died at Exeter according to one source (born c.1569). He became Priest Vicar and Succentor of Exeter Cathedral as a layman and also Master of the Choristers at King's College, Cambridge. A search for his will has proved abortive.

John Gostling, English bass singer, was born at East

(cont.) Malling, Kent (died 1733, July 17).

Johann Jeep, German composer, died at Ulm (born 1582).

Johann Hieronymus Kapsberger, who wrote the Apotheosis of St. Ignatius of Loyola, died at this time according to a major source.

Simon Pack, an English officer and amateur composer, was born (date of death unknown).

James (Jacques) Paisible (Peasable), French wind player, singer, and composer, was born in France (died 1721, August).

Jean Baptiste Prin, trumpet marine virtuoso, was born in England of French parentage (date of death unknown).

Daniel Roseingrave, an organist and composer, was born at London. He studied under John Blow and Henry Purcell (died 1727, May).

Pier Francesco Tost, singing teacher and author, was born (died 1730). Although Italian he worked mainly at London.

Thomas Tudway, English composer, was born at Windsor (died 1726, November 23).

Don Marco Uccellini, Italian violinist, was active at this time.

Antonio Veracini, an Italian violinist and composer, was born at Florence (date of death unknown).

Robert de Visée, French lutenist, singer and composer, was born (died c.1725).

c.1650(cont.)

Wolfgang Christoph Agricola lived at this time.

Bénigne de Bacilly went to Paris at this time where he was one of the first to study and write about production and cultivation of the human voice.

Cesti was an important figure in the history of mid 17th-Century music.

Michel de La Guerre was well known at this time as a composer of musical settings of poetry, motets, and organ works.

The village of Tadten, where Haydn's great-grandfather lived before he moved to Halnburg, was predominantly Hungarian.

Florentino A'Kempis was organist of St. Gudule at Brussels around this time.

At this time in spite of avowed xenophobia among musicians in England such as Locke and Playford, imitation of Corelli had brought on a flurry of English sonatas.

Lully developed the ground-bassed technique of the chaconne at this time.

Johann Sebastiani settled at Königsberg this year.

Chambonnières' dances were found in a manuscript of this time.

William Child's "The First Set of Psalmes of III Voyces" was published in London in 1639 and reprinted at this time. The work was reissued as "Choise Musick to the Psalmes of David" in London in 1656.

A few works by David De Koning appeared in "Apud Magdalenam Phalesium et cohaeredes.

Mico's three-part fantasy for viols appeared at this time.

German oratorio literature of the middle baroque was at first unimportant. It grew from school dramas such as the sacred "Nuremberg Acts" of this time in which Chorales, choruses, and songs alternated with spoken narration.

Germany was first conquered by the invasion of Italian art at this time.

By this date in Holland the bourgeoisie was in command of the field of art.

Composers had achieved new resources of harmony, color and form at this time.

Palestrina by now had become the supreme model for the conservative style.

Polyphonic singing was officially adopted by the Russian church during this period.

A new phase of the ballet began at this time. Benserade's poetry raised the "ballet de cour" to a refined literary art -form.

The sonata at this time was developing from the instrumental canzona by gradual separation and standardization.

At this date in the old German variation suite, the different dances of the suite were made up of variations of a main dance.

The first fugal section was frequently preceded by a chordal introduction. This feature became permanent in the church sonata, but the term "da chiesa" on the title-pages had up to this time no really formal significance. It simply affirmed the fact that the sonatas were church music.

Written indications of "crescendo" and "diminuendo" were found in Italy at this time.

The lack of signs for mordents in Scarlatti's works is most puzzling since they had been current in French, German, and English music since this date.

Tables for interpretation of ornaments existed at this time.

Before the establishment of a standing army at this time the drum major held a rank somewhat comparable to that of a present warrant officer.

Thomas Cross I may have cut some of the music of the few delicately engraved books of instrumental works which were issued at this time by John Playford, the elder.

The carissimi school wrote many Roman cantatas at this time.

Semi dramatic dialogues on sacred themes produced at this time were called "oratorios."

Carissimi's oratorio "Jephtha" was typical of oratorio's of the day.

Italian opera had by now taken the form it maintained with (cont.) little or no change for the next two centuries.

Venice retained its position as operatic capital of Italy from this time to the end of the century.

It has been claimed that the bassoon evolved from the pommer, however, both instruments were in use simultaneously until about this date.

The harpsichord at this time was provided with a regular arrangement of two eight-foot stops and one four-foot stop, or 8'8'4'.

Chambonnières' "Allemande la Rare" provided an example of French harpsichord style at this date.

Kettledrums at this time followed the trumpet into the orchestra both in German church music and in Italian opera.

"Les cromornes et les trompettes marines" appeared as a five-piece outfit at this time in France in the music of the Grande Écurie du Roy.

The Lira da gamba, a bowed string instrument, was in use this year.

In working on the "musette" Martin Hotteterre this year added a second chanter with six keys, which lay parallel to the first, and extended the scale upwards.

A seventh string was often added to the bass viol, at this time it was tuned to the player's convenience.

Even on the viol, the stick
(bow) was almost straight in
England at this date.

In England, consorts of viols
became increasingly popular and
remained in favor throughout
this time.

Dutch painting: Ter Borch, "The
Gallant" (oil on canvas 26 5/8
by 21 5/8").

Dutch painting: Frans Hals,
"Malle Babbe" (29 1/2" x 25").

French painting: Lorrain, "View
of the Campagna" (wash drawing).

French painting: Nicolas Poussin,
"Self-Portrait" (38 1/2" by
28 3/4").

Dutch painting: Rembrandt,
"Castle at Twilight."

(to 1659) A new king of religiosity appeared in Spain during
these years, trivial and fierce
in character. It resulted in
paintings of tortures, pictures
to shout meaning beyond any
possible mistake. Sometimes
images were princely, brilliantly
sumptuous, while at other times
the realism was almost sadistic.

(to 1660) Spanish painting:
Murillo, "Boy with Dog."

(to 1708) Giuseppe Torelli, who
lived at this time, provided the
model for instrumental music of
this century.

(to 1750) During this period of
the Baroque the harpsichord
rose to prominence especially in
France.

(to c.1799) A canon on the

(cont.) words "Non nobis Domine"
attributed to William Byrd was
popular for this long period.

1651
(January 20) Cavalli's opera
"Alessandro vincitor di se
stesso" was produced at the
Teatro SS. Giovanni e Paolo in
Venice.

(January 26) One of Scheidt's
letters written this year stated,
"I am astonished at the foolish
music written in these times."

(March 17) Maria Katharina Bach,
Daughter of Heinrich, was born
(died 1687).

(April 30) Barbara Maria Bach,
daughter of Christoph Bach, was
born (date of death unknown).

(May 17) Auxcousteaux at this
time was no longer in office,
but obtained a canonry at the
church of Sainte-Jacques-de
-l'Hôpital when he left Sainte
-Chapelle.

(June 12) Johann Georg Ahle,
German poet, organist, and composer, was baptised at
Mühlhausen, Thuringia (died
1706, December 2).

(July 2) Charles Coleman was
recommended for the degree of
Doctor of Music at Cambridge by
the committee appointed for the
reformation of the University
and was awarded the degree on
this day.

(October 6) Heinrich Albert,
German poet, organist and composer, died at Königsberg (born
1604, July 8). He was a cousin
of Schütz.

(October 10) Fétis gave this

date for Heinrich Albert's
death.

(October 22) Jacob Praetorius,
organist and composer, died at
Hamburg (born 1586, February 8).

(December 17) Ennemond Gaultier,
French lutenist, died at Villette,
Dauphiné (born c.1575).

(December 28) Johann Krieger,
German musician and younger
brother of Johann I, was born at
Nürnberg (died 1735, July 18).
Some confusion exists concerning
another composer with the same
name.

(September) Marcin Mielczewski,
a Polish composer, died at
Warsaw (birthdate unknown).

(Autumn) Cavalli's opera
"Calisto" was produced at the
Teatro Sant' Apollinare in
Venice.

(Autumn) Cesti's "Cesare amante"
was produced at the Teatro dei
SS. Giovanni e Paolo in Venice.

'Abd al-Jalíl, born 'Abd al
-Rahman, who defended the use of
the harp in Persian music, died
(birthdate unknown).

Katherine, daughter of Henry and
Katherine Blow, was baptised
this year.

John Bowman, English actor,
singer and composer, was born
(died 1739).

Christoph Herthum, husband of
Maria Catharina Bach, member of
the fourth generation of the
Bach family, was born (died
1710).

Johann Klemm, German organist
and composer, died (birthdate
unknown).

Jean Francois Lalouette, French
violinist, conductor and composer, was born at Paris (died
1728, August 31).

Volupius Musagetes (Wolfgang
Schoensleder), author on music,
died (born 1570).

William Turner, English composer,
was born at Oxford (died 1740,
January 13).

Bartlomiej Wardenski, a Polish
composer, died (birthdate unknown).

Several German composers, including Böddecker, this year used
the G string extensively as the
bass for their chords.

Playford's "Musical Banquet"
this year carried the canon
"Non nobis domine" on the title
page and mentioned Byrd as its
author.

Thomas Gobert became canon of
the Sainte-Chapelle this year.

Michael Jacobi was town cantor
at Lüneburg at this time.

King Louis XIV appeared this
year at the age of thirteen in
the court ballet "Masque de
Cassandre."

M.A. Muskiewicz became a substitute at the Capella Rorantistarum
this year.

Neri at this time was raised to
the rank of nobility by Emperor
Ferdinand II.

Georg Neumark was this year sec-

retary and librarian to the
ducal court at Weimar and became court poet for festival
occasions.

Pasino was maestro di cappella
at Salò at this time.

Michael Danican (Philidor) entered the Grande Ecurie of the
King Louis XIII's musicians
this year. He played oboe,
crumhorn and trumpet marine.

Johann Rosenmüller was organist
at St. Nicholas Church at this
time.

Wolfgang Christoph Agricola
this year composed a "Fasciculus
Musicalis" of masses, issued at
Cologne and Würzburg.

The book known as The Bay Psalm
Book (though this was not its
title) was published this year.

Byrd, Bull, Gibbons, all contributed to "Parthenia . . ."
published in 1613 and reprinted
this year as well as in 1646,
1655, and possibly 1659.

Cesti's opera "Cesare amante"
was written at this time.

Crüger's "Recreationes musicae,
das ist neue poetische
Amorösen" was published this
year at Leipzig.

Della Porta's motets were published this year and in 1645 and
1648.

Benedetto Ferrari's "Dafne in
alloro, introduzione di un
balleto" was published at
Vienna at this time.

Gaspare Filippi published his

(cont.) "Sacrae laudes" this
year.

Matthew Locke at this time wrote
his "Little Consort of Three
Parts."

T. Merula's "Canzoni da suonare
a 2-3, lit. 4" opus 17 was published this year at Venice.

Mielczewski's "Missa super O
gloriosa Domena" for six parts
carried this date.

Gaspare Casati's collection containing Monteverdi's "En
gratulemur hodie" for tenor,
two violins and continuo and
"Laudate Dominium" for bass and
continuo was published this year.

Monteverdi's "Messa a quattro
voci et salmi a una, due, tre,
quattro, cinque, sei, sette &
otto voci, concertali a parte da
cappella & con le Lelanie della
B.V. . . ." edited by A. Vincenti
was published at Venice this
year.

Neri's sonatas for three to
twelve instruments, opus 2, appeared at this time.

An edition of "Parthenia," the
first collection of virginal
music in England, appeared this
year.

Motets in two, three and four
concerted parts, opus 6, were
written this year by Pasino.

John Playford published "The
English Dancing Master," as
well as "Musick and Mirth" this
year. These were his first
printed works.

Playford's "Musical Banquet" appeared this year.

Sbarra's "Alessandro vincitor di
se stesso" was set this year by
Cavalli for production at
Venice.

Phillip von Zesen's "Jugend-und
Liebes-Flammen" was published
at this time.

In the ballet "Les Rues de Paris"
this year the slow part had a
ponderous dotted rhythm, the
"rhythme saccade" from the
Lullian overture, but the fast
movement did not yet have the
fugal texture that was to become typical.

Manual couplers dated back at
least as far as this year when
Geissler's organ at Lucerne was
completed.

Cavalli's opera "Armidoro" was
produced at the Teatro San
Cassiano in Venice.

Cavalli's opera "Oristeo" was
produced at the Teatro Sant'
Apollinare in Venice.

Cavalli's opera "Rosinda" was
produced at the Teatro Sant'
Apollinare in Venice.

Cesti's first successes at
Venice were "Orontea" and
"Cesare amante" produced this
year.

F. Luccio's "Gl' amori di
Alessandro Magno e di Rossane"
was produced at this time.

The first operatic performance
in Naples was apparently
Monteverdi's "Nerone" produced
this year by the Febi Armonici,
a company of Venetian singers.

The Count of Oynatte showed

(cont.) great interest in music
and this year ordered recon-
struction of the partially
destroyed Teatro San Bartolomeo
and also the conversion to a
theatre of one building in the
gardens of the royal palace.

The Teatro Malvezzi in Bologna
was opened this year.

King Louis XIV danced his first
ballet at this time.

Thomas Hobbes, the English
political theorist, this year
wrote his "Leviathan."

Jeremy Taylor's "Holy Dying"
appeared at this time.

Henry Vaughan's "Olor Iscanus"
was completed this year.

Emperor Maximilian of Bavaria
died (born 1573).

Cornelius de Vos, Flemish
painter, died (born c.1586).

American architecture: Saugus,
Scotch House (40' wide x 26'
high).

Spanish painting: Velásquez,
"Venus and Cupid" (48 1/4" by
69 3/4").

(July 1 to 1653, March 31)
Benedetto Ferrari served as
instrumentalist in the imperial
chapel at Vienna during this
period.

(to 1655) Juan de Padilla's
dated music in the Puebla
cathedral archives includes
Christmas villancicas with
Spanish text composed during
these years.

(to 1655) Schütz during this

1651(cont.)

period tried many times unsuccessfully to obtain his dismissal from the elector's service at Dresden.

(to 1657) Eccard's "Cantionale
sacrum" was published between
these dates (See also 1646).

(to 1658) J. Playford the elder
had business relations with
John Benson during these years.

(to 1663) Michael Jacobi was
cantor at the Johanneum of
Hamburg for these years. He
was a prolific song composer,
mostly using poems by Johann
von Rist as his texts.

(to 1677) F. Petrobelli was
maestro di cappella of Padua
Cathedral for these twenty-six
years.

(to 1698) Henrick Willems was
active as a violin maker at
Ghent during this period.

(to 1702) C.L. Day and E.B.
Murrie's "English song-books
1651-1702" appeared.

c.1651

Jean-Baptiste Anet, a French
violinist, was born (died 1710,
August 26).

Adam Gobiatus, Polish composer,
died (born c.1605).

Bernhard made a second trip to
Italy at this time.

Music enlivened the dying
pastoral play at this time.

1652

(January 28) Cavalli's opera
"Veremonda, l'amazzone di
Aragona" was produced at the

(cont.) Teatro SS. Giovanni e
Paolo in Venice.

(February 18) Gregorio Allegri,
singer, priest and composer,
died at Rome (born 1582 or
c.1580).

(May 14) Johann Philipp Förtsch,
German composer, was born at
Wertheim, Franconia (died 1732,
December 14).

(May 30) Madeleine (Magdelenam)
Phalèse died at the Sign of
King David (birthdate unknown).

(June 3) Madeleine (Magdalenam)
Phalèse was buried in the church
at her brother's monastery.

(July 24) Johann Weichmann,
German organist and composer,
died at Königsberg (born 1620,
January 9).

(July 28) Jörgen Friedrich
Hoyoul, German wind player and
composer, died at Copenhagen
(born c.1577).

(November 21) Jan Broscius
(Brozek), Polish mathematician
interested in accoustics, died
at Cracow (born 1585, November
1).

(September) Dirck Janszoon
Sweelinck, renowned Dutch organ-
ist and composer, died at
Amsterdam (born 1591, May).

Johann Krieger, German organ
composer, was born (died 1735
or 1736).

Szymon Lilius, royal organist
at Warsaw, died sometime after
this date (birthdate unknown).

John Price II, English instrumentalist, died at Vienna

1652(cont.)
(birthdate unknown).

Cesti's Innsbruck appointment
started this year.

Silvestro Durante was "maestro
di cappella" at the church of
Santa Maria Trastevere in Rome
at this time.

Froberger this year visited
Paris.

Michel Angelo Grancini became
maestro di cappella at the
cathedral in Milan at this
time.

William King was promoted to
a chaplaincy at Magdalen College
this year.

Lulli (Lully) entered the service of King Louis XIV at this
time.

Merula this year returned to
his position as maestro and organist at the Cathedral in
Cremona.

Salvator Rosa this year, in
writing about Cesti, stated "I
have news of our Padre Cesti,
who in Venice has become im-
mortal and is regarded as the
leading composer of the day."

Schütz this year wrote a letter
to Christian Reichbrodt begging
him to hire a poor Bass singer.

Quintilianus, the text of
Aristides "On Music" was edited
by Meibom in his "Antiquae
musicae auctores septem" II published this year.

One of Briegel's works alone,
for three and four instruments
published this year at Erfurt,

(cont.) contained ten each,
pavans, galliards, ballets and
courantes.

One of the first printings of
"Non nobis Domine" (usually attributed to Byrd) was in John
Hilton's "Catch as catch can,"
however, the composer's name
was omitted.

Cavalli's "Veramonda, l'Amazzone
di Aragona" was written this
year.

Catches by Child were included
in Hilton's "Catch as catch can."

William Cranford was represented
in Hilton's "Catch as catch can."

Dumont's "Cantica sacra" of this
year were one of the first
printed motet collections to use
basso continuo.

Hilton's "Catch that catch can,"
containing contributions by most
leading musicians, was issued in
many editions. It was referred
to also as "Catch as Catch Can."

John Hilton II published "Catch
That Catch Can, or A Choice
Collection of Catches Rounds &
Canons for 3 or 4 Voyces" at
London. It was printed by J.
Playford, the elder.

Some of Ives' instrumental works
were included in "Musick's
Recreation" this year.

John Jenkins' A boat, a boat"
and "Come pretty maidens" were
included in Hilton's "Catch
That Catch Can."

Several catches by Robert
Johnson appeared in "Catch that
Catch Can."

Robert Johnson II's "As I Walked Forth" was included in Playford's "Ayres & Dialogues" this year.

Henry Lawes' songs appeared this year in Playford's "Select Musical Ayres."

William Lawes' songs were included in "Catch that Catch Can."

Giovanni Antonio Leoni this year wrote "Sonate di violino a voce sola di . . . lib.1."

Matthew Locke wrote his "Duos for Two Bass Viols" at this time.

A book "The Lutes Apology for her Excellency" by Richard Mathew was printed this year by Thomas Harper for Lwewell Chapman at the Crowne in Popeshead Alley, London.

Meibomius' great work "Antiquae musicae auctores septem graece et latene" was published at Amsterdam this year by Elzevir. The date of his birth therefore must have been earlier than usually stated.

T. Merula's "Salmi et messa concertate a 3-4, lib. 3" opus 18 was published this year at Venice.

"Lessons" for viols were included in several of Playford's publications, such as "Banquet of Musick" and "Musick's Recreation on the Lyra Viol" both published this year.

The second edition of "The Dancing Master" was issued this year.

The first edition of Playford's "Select Musical Ayres and Dialogues" was published at this time.

J. Playford's "Musick's Recreation on the Lyra Viol" was published this year at London.

Several songs by William Webb were included in Playford's "Select musical ayres and Dialogues."

Georg Weber published a book of songs this year.

Pio Enea degli Obizzi this year built the Teatro degli Obizzi in his own house and held theatrical and musical spectacles and staged pastoral fables there.

Bertali's double-opera "Theti" and "Niobe" was produced this year at Mantua to celebrate the arrival of some archdukes.

Cavalli's opera "Eritrea" was produced at the Teatro Sant' Apollinare in Venice.

Cazzati's stage work "Il carnevale esigliato" was produced at the Teatro Obizzi in Padua.

Cazzati's stage work "I gridi di Cerere" was produced at the Teatro Obizzi in Padua.

Alfonso Ferrabosco II's death was incorrectly given as this year (see 1628).

Jan van Riebeeck founded the first Dutch settlement in South Africa at this time.

Inigo Jones, English theatrical architect, died (born 1573).

1652(cont.)

Jose de Ribera (known as Lo Spagnoletto), Spanish painter, died (born 1591). He was a great master of Caravaggesque school and portrayed eloquence in martyrs and saints, as well as ragged beggars and human freaks.

Georges de La Tour, French painter, died (born 1593).

Italian architecture: Borromini, "Sant' Agnesse" (work started on facade, c.160' wide).

Spanish painting: Ribera "The Clubfoot."

(to 1653) A. Hammerschmidt's "Musicalische Andachten" part V, sub-title "Chor-musik" contained thirty-one pieces for five and six voices in "Madrigal manier."

(to 1653) Three books by J. Playford, the elder, were published during these years.

(to 1653) Spanish painting: Velásquez, "Portrait of Queen Mariana" (oil on canvas 6'11 1/8" x 4'1 5/8").

(to 1653) Wilson's works appeared in Playford's "Select Musicall Ayres and Dialogues" published at this time.

(1653 and 1659) Several of Charles Coleman's songs were included in various editions of "Select Musicall Ayres and Dialogues" during these years.

(to 1654) Kircher's "Oedipus aegyptiacus" was written concerning music contained in Egyptian hieroglyphics.

(to 1685) During this period the

(cont.) works of Stefano Filippini were published and included two books of "concerti sacri" for two to five voices; two books of masses, three books of psalms and a book of motets.

(to 1686) Du Mont's five books of two to four part motets with instruments appeared during these years.

c.1652

Du Mont was appointed organist and harpsichordist at this time to the Duc d'Anjou, King Louis XIV's brother.

Nicolas Gigault became organist at the Paris church of Saint -Nicolas-des-Champs this year.

1653

(January 13) Arcangelo Corelli's father died (born 1593). He was also named Arcangelo.

(February 12) Giovanni Francesco Grossi ("Siface"), Italian male soprano, was born in Uzzanese Chiesina (died 1697, May 29).

(February 17) Arcangelo Corelli, Italian violinist and composer, was born at Fusignano, Imolo (died 1713, January 8). He was the first to fully realize tonality in instrumental music.

(February 23) Lulli's composition "Ballet de la Nuit" with 45 entrees, lasting thirteen hours was produced at the French court. It represented a major step in formulating French writing technique.

(March 26) Shirley's masque "Cupid and Death" with music by Matthew Locke and Christopher Gibbons was privately performed before the Portuguese ambassador.

1653(cont.)

(April 1) Filippo Vitali was presented to a canonry of the Cathedral of San Lorenzo and entitled Sant' Ambrogio.

(April 1) W. Young published his sonatas and dances in honor of Archduke Ferdinand, Earl of Innsbruck.

(April 10) Dorothea Maria Bach, daughter of Christoph Bach, was born (died 1679).

(April 14) Cavalli's "Le Nozze di Peleo e di Tetti" was presented in the Petit Bourbon.

(July 17) Johann Günther Bach, Arnstadt organist, son of Heinrich, grandson of Johannes, and member of the fourth generation of the Bach family, was born (died 1683, April 8).

(August 1) Manoel Correa, Portuguese composer, died at Saragossa (born c.1600).

(September 1) Johann Pachelbel, renowned German organist and composer, was baptised at Nürnberg (died 1706, March 6 or 7).

(September 3) Roger North, English lawyer, author and amateur musician, was born at Tostock, Suffolk (died 1734, March 1).

(November 26) Andreas Schmelzer, Austrian violinist and composer, was born at Vienna (died 1701, October 17).

(February) Benedetto Ferrari wrote the libretto to the opera "L'inganno d'amore" produced before the Diet at Ratisbon at this time.

(February) Johann Schultz, German organist and composer, died at Dannenberg, Brunswick (birthdate unknown).

(June) Cavalli's opera "Orione" was produced at the Teatro Regio in Milan.

(June) Matthias Klotz, violin maker, was born at Mittenwald (died 1743, August 16).

Walentyn Adamecki, Polish viola player, died at Warsaw (born 1599).

Johann Nikolaus Bach, Erfurt musician, son of Johann Bach, grandson of Johannes, and member of the fourth generation of the Bach family, was born (died 1682).

Tommaso Carapella, Italian composer, was born at Cerreto (died 1736, September 20).

Piotr Elert, Polish violinist and composer, died (born c.1599).

Sir Samuel Forbes of Foveran, Scottish historian who wrote on music, was born (died 1717).

Moreau, teacher of Clerambault, Dandrieu, and Montéclair, was born (died 1733).

Johann Pachelbel, great organist and composer, and leader in Protestant music, was born at Nürnberg (died 1706, March 6 or 7).

Carlo Francesco Pollarolo, Italian composer, was born at Brescia (died 1722). He was Antonio's father.

Edward Purcell, I, Gentleman Usher to King Charles II, was born at London (died 1717, June

2).

Luigi Rossi, important Roman
opera composer, died (born
1597 or 1598). He was also a
well known singer.

Filippo Vitali, Italian singer
and composer, died at Florence
(birthdate unknown).

Marc Antonio Ziani, Italian
composer, was born (died 1715,
January 22).

Caproli was called to Paris this
year along with a company of
singers to perform an opera at
the French court.

Cazzati was "maestro di cappella"
at Santa Maria Maggiore in
Bergamo at this time.

King Louis XIV's most famous
part from which he received his
nickname was Le Roi Soleil in
Lully's "Le Ballet de la nuit."
He danced the menuet.

Lully became a composer of royal
chamber music this year, succeeding Lazarin. The former
left the Duchess of Montpensier
to accept the appointment.

Marini was maestro to the
Accademia della Morte at Ferrara
at this time.

M.A. Miskiewicz this year was
promoted to the position of a
Roratist and shortly afterwards
became the Praepositus of the
chapel.

When the Count of Ognatte was
replaced this year as viceroy
the Febi Armonici lost their
chief patron among the nobility
and transferred their activities

(cont.) to the stage of the
Teatro San Bartolomeo.

J. Playford the elder was appointed clerk at Temple Church
this year. He married and subsequently lived at his place of
business in the Inner Temple.

Sebastian Scherer was town musician at Ulm this year.

The sonatas that Young composed
this year at Innsbruck were
written while he was in the
service of the Grand Duke
Ferdinand.

As late as this year the poet
Caspar Ziegler, with Schütz,
helped make an effort to bring
the madrigal into German poetry.

Abbatini's opera "Dal male il
bene" composed this year at
Rome was in collaboration with
Marazzoli. The latter wrote
the second act and Abbatini
wrote the first and third. The
work was produced this year at
the Palazzo Barberini at the
wedding of Maffeo Barberini and
Olympia Giustiniani. The libretto was by Giulio Rospigliosi.

D'Assoucy's only printed compositions at this time were
some "Airs a quatre parties"
published at Paris.

D'Assoucy's poem "Le
Ravissement de Proserpine" was
written this year.

Bigongiari this year collaborated with Sbarra in writing a
satirical opera, "La tirannide
del interese."

Some of Caesar's (William
Smegergill) songs were published
in "Select Musicall Ayres and

Dialogues" this year.

Cambefort's "Ballet de la Nuit" appeared this year.

A Manuscript music book containing cantatas ascribed to Cesti with an inscription by its owner dated at Uppsala this year has been preserved.

Some of E. Coleman's songs were included this year in "Select Musicall Ayres and Dialogues."

Coleman at this time composed the music for Shirley's "Contention of Ajax and Achilles."

Descartes' "Compendium musicae" was translated into English by Lord William Brounker and published anonymously this year.

Donati's Coloraturae "Concerten voce sola" : O admirablile commercium; O Fili Dei suavissime, for "canto" or "tenore" "Musica moderna prattica" were published this year by Herbst at Frankfort.

Eccard's works appeared in "Preussische Kirch-und Fest -Lieder" this year.

Eccard's and Stobaeus' books of songs were published at this time.

Gaspare Filippi published his vesper psalms and his masses this year. Both were for two choruses.

Herbst's manual for counterpoint and thorough bass "Arte practica et poetica" was published this year at Frankfort.

Nicholas Lanier's songs were included in "Select Musicall Ayres and Dialogues."

Henry Lawes' "Ayres and Dialogues for one, two and three Voyces" was published this year by T. Harper.

Several of William Lawes' songs and other vocal compositions were included in "Select Musicall Ayres and Dialogues."

Locke's music to Shirley's school masque, "Cupid and Death," was written this year.

Marini's opus 18, "Salmi per tutti le solennita dell'anno . . . ad 1-3 voci," was issued this year at Venice.

A.V. Michna published "The Czech Lute" this year at Prague.

Benjamin Rogers this year composed some airs in four parts for violins and organ, which were favorably received by Archduke Leopold.

Rospigliosi's "Dal Male il Bene," with music by Marazzoli and Abbatini, was compoeted and performed this year.

Christoph Schultze composed his Passion according to St. Luke at this time.

Shirley's masque, "Cupid and Death" showed strong influence of the French comedie-ballet.

"Florido concento di madrigali in musica a tre voci," published in Rome this year, included two of Antonio Francesco Tenaglia's madrigals, "Madonna udite" and "E cosi pur

349

languendo."

Georg Weber published a song book this year.

Chamber sonatas of this year by Young used two or three violins. Since they were composed on the Continent this fact is understandable.

Philipp von Zesen's "Jugend-und Liebes-Flammen" was published this year for the second time.

Munich, a locale enthusiastic about Italian art and Italian musicians, for many years welcomed opera at this time.

The Emperor at this time moved his court opera with him to Reichstag at Ratisbon.

"Arianna," which was produced this year at Rome, may have been written by Cirillo.

Bertali's "L'inganno d'amore" was performed this year at the Diet of Ratisbon.

Cavalli's opera "Helena rapita da Teseo" was produced this year at the Teatro SS. Giovanni e Paolo in Venice.

Cavalli's opera "Orione" was produced at this time at Milan.

Musical drama made its first appearance in Germany with Benedetto Ferrari's L'inganno d'Amore" produced this year at Ratisbon.

F. Luccio's "Pericle effeminato" was produced at this time.

"The Compleat Angler," an autobiographical account by Izaak

(cont.) Walton, was published at this time in England.

Simon Vlieger, Dutch artist, died (born 1601).

Dutch painting: Potter, "The White Horse" (oil on panel, 11 3/4 x 16 1/2").

(April 1 to 1657, October 30) Johann Jacob Froberger was employed at the court in Vienna during this period.

(to 1658) Oliver Cromwell, as Lord Protector of the Commonwealth, ruled England and Great Britain during these years.

(to 1658) Lully during these years tried to raise the Ballet de Cour to a higher level. Starting with the "Ballet de la nuit" and ending with the "Ballet d'Alcidiane" his influence started to spread.

(to 1672) The ballet composition period of Lully's career embraced these years.

(to 1679) Provenzale wrote eight operas for Naples during these years.

c.1653
Marco Antonio Ziani, Italian church composer who worked at Vienna, was born (died 1715).

"Gaultier le vieux" composed the "Tombeau" de Mésangeau at this time.

1654
(January 12) Cavalli's opera "Serse" ("Xerse") was produced at the Teatro SS. Giovanni e Paolo in Venice.

(January 30) Cavalli's "Ciro"

1654(cont.)
was produced at the Teatro SS.
Giovanni e Paolo in Venice.

(February 3) Cesti's "Alessandro
il vincitor di se stesso" was
produced at Lucca.

(February 17) Lully's ballet
"Les Proverbes" was performed.

(March 30) Samuel Scheidt,
German organist and composer,
died at Halle (born 1587). He
is considered to have been one
of the great masters of the
Baroque period.

(April 14) "Le nozze di Peleo e
di Theti" by Caproli was produced at the Petit Bourbon palace in Paris.

(April 14) Lully's "Les Nopces
de Pelée et de Thétis" was produced.

(May 1) Karel Guillet, Flemish
theorist and composer, died at
Bruges (birthdate unknown).

(July 5) Antonio Maria
Pacchioni, an Italian composer,
was born at Modena (died 1738,
July 16).

(July 25) Agostino Steffani,
Italian diplomat and important
opera composer of his time, was
born at Castelfranco (died 1728,
February 12).

(August 25) William King became
probationer-fellow of All
Souls' College on this date.

(September 7 or 8) Tomkins
wrote his last piece, a perpetual round.

(September 20) Hugh Sempill,
Scottish mathematician and

(cont.) writer, died (born 1596).

(November 5) Christian Liebe,
German organist and composer, was
born at Freiberg, Saxony (died
1708, September 3).

(November 30) Lully's "Le Temps"
was produced.

(December 15) Michel de la
Guerre's opera "Le Triomphe de
l'Amour sur les des bergers et
bergères" was rehearsed in public. It has been referred to
by some as the "first French
opera.

(December 29) Christian Heinrich
Aschenbrenner, German violinist
and composer, was born at
Altstettin (died 1732, December
13).

(June) Caproli returned to Rome
at this time.

(June) Cirillo at this time
married fifteen-year old
Caterina Senardi, a Roman girl.

(September) Vincenz Lübeck,
German organist and composer,
was born (died 1740, February
9).

Quirins Gerbrandt Blankenburg,
a Dutch organist, theorist and
composer, was born at Gouda
(died c.1740).

Vincenz Lübeck, North-German
organ music composer, was born
(See September).

Antonio Maria Pacchione,
Italian composer of church music
and oratorios who was attached
to the musical establishment at
Modena, was born (died 1738).

Pietro Francesco Valentini, mu-

351

sical scholar and composer, died
at Rome (born c.1585). He was
a pupil of Nanino.

Johann Rudolph Ahle was organist
at Blasiuskirche, Mühlhausen at
this time.

Christoph Bach (third generation)
was called to Arnstadt this year
to head the town musicians.

Girolamo Casati at this time was
"maestro di cappella" of the
Carmelite church at Pavia.

C.C. Dedekind was a member of
the Dresden court chapel from
this date forward.

Lully was appointed "compositeur
de la musique instrumentale" at
the French court this year at
the age of twenty-two.

Italian arias figured largely in
Lully's ballets starting at this
time.

B. Marini at this time was
maestro to the Church of Santa
Maria della Scala at Milan.

Nicola Melani, male soprano
singer and brother of Jacopo,
like Domenico sang at the
Saxon Court at Dresden this
year.

Del Pane was received into the
papal chapel in Rome at this
time.

Marco Uccellini this year became maestro di cappella at
Modena Cathedral.

A book of Heinrich Albert's
"Arien" published this year at
Königsberg contained a statement
to the effect that it had been

(cont.) "edited by the composer's
widow," however, the same book
included poems on events of
1655. Obviously the date was in
error.

Arcadelt's first book of madrigals for four voices was reprinted thirty-three times up to
this time.

The Philidor Collection (Vol.
VI) contained some of Boesset's
airs for the "Ballet du Temps"
of this year.

Bigongiari and Cesti this year
wrote new music for the Lucca
production of Sbarra's
"Alessandro vincitor di se
stesso."

Cambefort's "Ballet du Temps"
appeared this year.

Caprioli's "Nozze di Peleo e di
Teti" included numerous ballets
written by Benserade. This was
done to mollify the French
people.

"Serse" by Cavalli was produced
at Venice.

"Orontea, regina d'Egitto"
(libretto by Cicognini, originally set by Cesti in 1649) was
performed this year. It was
the earliest opera written for
Naples of which the score is
extant.

C.C. Dedekind's "J. Katzens
Aeltern-Spiegel aus desselben
Holländis-chem gehouchdeutschet
durch C.C.D. 1654" was published
this year at Dresden in eight
volumes.

Michel de La Guerre this year
published a "quarto" edition of
the libretto to "Le Triomphe de

l'Amour sur les bergers et bergères," originally written in one act.

John IV's "Respuesta a las dudas que se pusieron a la missa: Pamis quem ego dabo, Palestrina," a defense of Palestrina, was published this year at Lisbon.

Giovanni Legrenzi wrote some church sonatas at this time.

Lully composed his first ballet, "Le Temps," this year.

Marini's opus 20, "Vespri per tutte le festivita dell' anno, a 4 voci" was published this year at Venice.

A.V. Michna's "Sacra et Litaniae a 5, 6, 7, 8 vocum cum instrumentis" was published at Prague at this time.

John Playford, the elder's "Introduction to the Skill of Music" appeared at this time in London in the first of nineteen editions.

Rist's "Frommer und gottseliger Christen alltägliche Hausmusik" was published this year.

Uccellini's psalms for three to five concerted parts with instruments and litanies of the Holy Virgin, for five voices with instruments, opus 6, were issued this year at Venice.

The earliest notices of isolated performances of opera in Naples were from this date.

Other than performance of Cirillo's "Orontea" this year little is known about

(cont.) Neapolitan opera during the middle Baroque period.

Queen Christina of Sweden abdicated this year and after that the royal court employed opera companies for its entertainment, but only sporadically.

Experiments in opera comedy were carried on at Rome with "Dal mal il bene" by Abbatini and Marazzoli (libretto by Rospigliosi after Calderon).

When Cavalli's "Le Nozze di Peleo e di Teti" was given in Paris this year French artists played subordinate parts.

Cesti's opera "Alessandro vincitor de se stesso" was produced at Lucca this year.

F. Luccio's "Euridamante" was produced at this time.

Pietro Francesco Valentini's two favole, "La mitra" and "La trasformagione di Dafne," were produced at this time.

Playford's "Introduction" dealt with ornaments as follows: A single strobe a before note or lutenists letter means lower appaggiatura b over note after letter is a springer. He also referred to an ascending appogiatura as a "beat" and described a "back-fall shaked" as a fully prepared trill. He further showed an ascending trill and explained "double relish ornaments." For the viol or violin he had a graph of vibrato as repeated demisemi-quavers on the same note, but alternately a little higher and lower in their space.

John Dryden was awarded the

1654(cont.)
Bachelor of Arts degree from
Trinity College, Cambridge.

Carel Fabritius, a Dutch painter,
died (born 1622).

Paulus Potter, Dutch painter,
died (born 1625).

Dutch painting: Carel Fabritius,
"The Goldfinch" (13" x 8 5/8").

Dutch painting: Rembrandt,
"Bathsheba."

Dutch painting: Rembrandt, "Jan
Six" (44 1/2" x 40").

(and 1657) Bigongiari contributed cantatas for the festival
of the "Tasche" these years.

(June to 1665) Caproli returned
to Rome in June 1654 with letters of recommendation from
Cardinal Antonio Barberini.
Caprioli joined the latter's
household and remained there
during this period.

(to 1680) Domenico Melani,
Italian male soprano singer and
brother of Jacopo, sang at the
Saxon Court at Dresden during
these years.

(to 1722) Johann Adam Reinken
was Organist at Saint Catherine's
Church, Hamburg during this
period.

c.1654
Alsatian Sébastien de Brossard,
composer, conductor and priest,
was born (died 1730).

Jérôme de La Guerre, organist,
son or Michel de La Guerre, was
born at Paris (date of death
unknown).

The organ of Magdalen College
was moved from Oxford to Hampton
Court this year and Hingston was
appointed organist to the
Protector, Oliver Cromwell. The
latter enjoyed Hingston's singing of Dering's Latin motets.

1655
(January 15) Jean Baptiste
Farinel, French violinist and
composer, was born at Grenoble
(date of death unknown).

(January 18) Cavalli's opera
"Statira, principessa di Persia"
was produced at the Teatro SS.
Giovanni e Paolo in Venice.

(January 22) Michel de La
Guerre's opera "Le Triomphe de
l'Amour sur des bergers et
bergères" was performed before
the King at the Louvre in Paris.
The libretto was by Charles de
Beys. The work is interesting
for its unique treatment of
recitative.

(February 4) Lully's "Les
Plaisirs" was produced.

(February 18) Pietro Giovanni
Guarneri, Italian violin maker,
was born at Cremona (died 1720,
March 26).

(March 5) Weiland was appointed
court musician at Brunswick on
this date.

(April 1) Jan Couchet, harpsichord maker, probably died at
Antwerp on this day.

(April 3) Andrzej Nizankowski,
Polish organist, died at
Cracow (born c.1591).

(April 4) J. Couchet, harpsichord maker, was buried in
Antwerp Cathedral (birthdate

1655(cont.)

unknown).

(April 6) Constantin Huygens, Dutch physicist and natural philosopher, mentioned J. Couchet in a letter on this date to H. Du Mont, an organist in Paris.

(April 14) Johann Erasmus Kindermann, German organist and composer, died at Nürnberg (born 1616, March 29). He was a pupil of Staden and Cavalli.

(May 4) Bartolommeo di Francesco Cristofori, Italian harpsichord maker and recognised inventor of the pianoforte, was born at Padua (died 1731, January 27).

(May 30) Lully's "Les Bienvenus" was produced.

(July 30) Sigmund Gottlieb Staden (Theophil Staden), German organist and composer and son of Johann Staden, died at Nürnberg (born 1607).

(August 13) Johann Christoph Denner, German instrument maker, was born at Leipzig (died 1707, April 20).

(September 12) Sébastien de Brossard, French composer, was baptised (died 1730, August 10).

(September 15) Kaspar Förster, German singer and composer, left for Venice to join the war against the Turks.

(November 4) Cesti's "L'Argia" was produced at Innsbruck.

(December 1) Samuel Pepys married Elizabeth Marchant de Saint Michel at St. Margaret's,

(cont.) Westminster, on this date.

(January) Cavalli's opera "Erismena" was produced at the Teatro Sant' Apollinare in Venice.

(January) John Lawes, lay-vicar of Westminster Abbey, and brother of Henry Lawes, died at London (born c.1599).

(May) Rosenmüller's prospects of promotion were destroyed by an accusation against him of grave moral offense for which he was temporarily imprisoned. He escaped and went to Hamburg and then to Italy, where he taught for many years.

(July) When the Lord Protector agreed on field and garrison forces for Scotland at this time a drum-major was recognized in each of the infantry regiments.

Prior to this date Christoph Bach joined his younger brother Heinrich at Arnstadt. He died there while active as "gräflicher Hof- und Stadt-Musikus."

Jakob Bach, cantor, son of Wendel, grandson of Lips, and member of the fourth generation of the Bach family, was born (died 1718).

Heinrich Baryphonus, composer and theorist, died (born 1581).

Henry Blow, father of John Blow, the composer, died (birthdate unknown).

Richard Goodson, English organist and composer, was born (died 1718, January 13).

Biagio Marini, Brescian violinist, died according to one
source.   Others gave his death
date as 1665 (born c.1600).

Vivaldi's father, Giovanni
Battista, was born at Brescia
(date of death unknown).

Ahle was appointed a member of
the senate and afterwards burgomaster at Mühlhausen in
Thuringia.

Thomas Baltzar, German violinist
and composer, went to England
and stayed with Sir Anthony
Cope, of Hanwell, Oxon.

Bernhard returned to Dresden
and became vice-Kapellmeister.

King Jan Casimir dissolved the
Warsaw opera due to extensive
wars on Polish soil.

Cavalli used Da Capo in his
opera "Giasone."

P.E. Jan Couchet, harpsichord
maker, became master of the St.
Lucas Guild at this time.

Abraham Cowley this year was
arrested as a spy in London.

Kaspar Förster this year became
Kapellmeister of St. Mary's
church at Danzig.

Paul Heinlen became organist at
St. Egiduis, Nürnberg at this
time.

Nicholas Lanier journeyed between Flanders and England with
musical instruments this year.

Lully this year was appointed
director of a group of sixteen
violins referred to as the

(cont.) "petite bande."

Czar Alexis Michailovitch this
year appointed a commission of
fourteen members to revise the
texts of the chant books.

A. van Noordt transferred to the
Nieuwe Kirk this year.

Pekiel went to Cracow at this
time.

Dirk Pieterszon, Dutch music
editor, was still alive this
year.

Esaias Reusner was appointed
court lutenist at Brieg at this
time.

M. Weckmann accepted the organists position at St. James
Church in Hamburg.

Weiland this year was vice
Kapellmeister at Brunswick.

A. Wood was awarded the Master
of Arts degree at Merton this
year.

Bockshorn's "Opus musicum" for
one to eight voices with instruments appeared at this time.

Byrd, Bull, Gibbons, all contributed to "Parthenia . . ."
published in 1613 and reprinted
this year as well as in 1646,
1651 and possibly 1659.

Campan's treatise "A New Way of
making Fowre parts in Counter
-point . . ." was published
this year with annotations by
Christopher Simpson. The title
was "The Art of Setting or
Composing of Musick in Parts by
a most familiar and easie Rule."
A later edition appeared in
1664.

Cesti composed the opera "Argia" at this time.

C.C. Dedekind's "J. Frantzel, A et O Jesus! Zahen andächtige Buss-Gesänge . . . nicht nur wie zuvor mit bekannten sondern auch mit Herrn Const. Christ. Dedekindens . . . neu beige fügten Melodeyen herfür gegeben" was published this year at Leipzig.

The three known works of Mary Harvey's "The Lady Deering's Composing" appeared this year in H. Lawes' "Second Book of Select Ayres & Dialogues."

George Hudson's "Court Ayres" was published at this time.

S. Ives' instrumental works included pieces in Hudson's "Court Ayres."

Henry Lawes published his "Ayres and Dialogues for One, Two and Three Voyces" this year.

Giovanni Legrenzi wrote sonatas and masses at this time. The "La Cornara" sonata, opus 2, was of particular interest due to its chromaticism.

B. Marini's "Lacrime di Davide sparse nel Miserere concertato in diversi modi a 2-4 e pui voci" was published this year at Venice.

B. Marini's opus 22, "Per ogni sorte d'istromento musicale diversi gener di sonate da chiesa e da camera, a 2-4" was published this year at Venice.

Valentine Oldys, English chemist, who lived in Black Friars, London, contributed some pieces

(cont.) to Playford's "Court Ayres."

An edition of "Parthenia," the first collection of virginal music in England, was issued at this time.

The collection "Court Ayres" published by Playford this year brought together a repertory of over five-hundred dances. Practically every composer of the time was a contributor.

J. Playford the elder this year published an enlarged edition of his "Introduction to the Skill of Musik" at London. For many years it passed as the first.

Christopher Simpson's Annotations on Campian's "Art of Discant" were published this year.

Szymon Starowolski, Polish ecclesiastic and historian, published "Monumenta Sarmatiae" at Cracow at this time.

The theater San Samuele in Venice was built this year by Giovanni Grimani.

Cirillo's opera "Il ratto d'Elena" was performed at this time by the Febi Armonici at the Teatro San Bartolomeo.

Nicholas Lanier's song was sung at the Hague this year.

Playford in his "Introduction" discussed "a clear sound" as to expression and texture. He further described the "shaked beat" as a prepared and prolonged lower mordent, a compound ornament, and dealt with the "springer."

1655(cont.)

Ireen Christian of Sweden was abducted this year from her country because of her conversion to Catholicism. Her professed Catholicism was celebrated at Innsbruck with the performance of an opera by Pasquini.

Tristan L'Hermite, French poet and author, died (born 1601).

The Corporation of the Sons of the Clergy was founded at London this year.

Johann Georg II at this time became elector at Dresden.

Edward Winslow, one of the founders of New England, died (born 1595).

Eustache Lesueur, a French painter, died (born 1617).

Dutch painting (etching): Rembrandt, "Christ Presented to the People."

(to 1656) Hammerschmidt's "Musicalisches Gespräche über die Son - und Fest Evangelia" was published at this time in two parts and contained sixty -two pieces for four to seven voices with increased instrumental accompaniment.

(to 1661) Louis Couperin was the organist at St. Gervais during these years.

(to 1662) Johann Jakob Löwe was court director at Brunswick and Wolfenbüttel during this period.

(to 1667) The papal reign of St. Alexander VII.

(to 1674) Charles de Helfer,

(cont.) French composer, canon and master of the choir-boys at Soissons Cathedral, wrote several masses published during these years. Some of them appeared in various editions. "Missa pro defunctis" was included in La Borde's "Essai sur la musique," vespers and other church music.

(to 1682) Legrenzi's various collections, published during these years, were important in the development of the church sonata.

c.1655

Ruggiero Fedeli, Italian singer and composer, was born at Venice (died 1722).

Domenico Gabrieli, Italian composer and cellist, was born at Bologna (died 1690, July 10).

Henry Hall I, English organist and composer, was born at New Windsor (died 1707, March 30).

Jacob Kremberg, German composer, was born at Warsaw (date of death unknown).

Steffano Landi, a leading opera composer of the Roman school, died (born c.1590).

Carlo Ambrogio Lonati, Italian composer, was born at Milan (date of death unknown).

John Playford, the younger, printer, cousin of Henry and son of Matthew Playford, rector, was born at Stanmore Magna (died c.1685).

Richard Portman, English organist and composer, died, probably at London (birthdate unknown).

c.1655(cont.)
Pietro Torri, Italian organist
and composer, was born at
Peschiera, Verona (died 1737,
July 6).

By this time Bockshorn had
moved to Nürnberg where he was
director of music at the church
of the Trinity.

Cambert was organist of the
church of Saint-Honoré in Paris
from this date forward.

The most important work of
Denis Gaultier's "L'Illustre"
was a collection of suites, "La
Rhétorique des Dieux."

Dutch painting: Rembrandt,
"Beef Carcass" (28 1/2" x 20
1/2").

(to 1656) Dutch painting
(drawing): Rembrandt, "A Girl
Sleeping" (9 2/3" x 8").

1656
(January 10) Cavalli's opera
"Artemisia" was produced at the
Teatro SS. Giovanni e Paolo in
Venice.

(January 16) Lully's "Psyché et
la puissance de l'amour" was
performed.

(January 16) François Pinel appeared with his father, Germain,
and brother, Séraphin, in the
seventh entry of the "Ballet de
Psyché."

(January 31) The opera "La vita
umana, overo Il trionfo della
pieta" was produced at the
Palazzo Barberini in honour of
Queen Christina of Sweden. The
libretto was by Rospigliosi.

(February 14) Lully's "Les

(cont.) Galanteries du temps"
was performed.

(February 17) One of the last of
the collections of genuine virginal music was Elizabeth
Rogers "hir Virginal Booke"
which bore this date.

(February 27) Kerll entered the
service of the Bavarian elector
on this day. He was present at
the coronation of King Leopold
I and was invited to improvise
on a given theme in presence of
the court.

(February 29) A petition to
Cromwell's Council of State on
this date referred to Portman
as "recently deceased."

(March 4) Evelyn heard Thomas
Baltzar play on this date and
left an account of the event in
his diary.

(March 27) Caspar Bach's son was
born according to one source
(date of death unknown).

(March 31) Marin Marais, French
violist and composer, and pupil
of Lully was born at Paris (died
1728, August 15).

(April 27) Szymon Starowolski,
Polish ecclesiastic and historian, died at Cracow (born 1558).

(July 29) Andrea Falconieri,
Italian lutenist and composer,
died at Naples (born 1586).

(November 6) King John IV of
Portugal died (born 1604, March
19).

(February) Ferrari's opera "Gli
amori di Alessandro Magno e di
Rossane" was produced at
Bologna. The libretto was by

1656(cont.)
G.A. Cicognini.

(June) Thomas Tomkins, organist,
composer, and second son of
Thomas Tomkins and his first
wife, died at Martin Hussingtree
near Worcester (born 1572).

(September) Sir William
Davenant presented a semi-public
production, "The First Day's
Entertainment at Rutland House
by Declamations and Musick."
The music was by Locke, Colman,
H. Cooke, H. Lawes and Hudson.

(December) Jacopo Melani's opera
"Il podesta di Colognole" was
produced at the opening of the
Teatro della Pergola, in
Florence.

Artus (or Arthur) Auxcousteaux
(Hautcousteaux), French singer
and composer, died at Paris
(birthdate unknown).

Pierre Chabaneau de La Barre,
French composer, died (born
1592).

John Lenton, English violinist
and composer, was born at
London (date of death unknown).

Jean-Baptiste Moreau, French
composer, was born at Angers
(died 1733, August 24).

Georg (von) Reutter, composer,
choir director of St. Stephen's
and court organist, was born at
Vienna (died 1738).

Francesco Turin, a noted
Italian contrapuntist, died at
Brescia (born 1595).

Johann Westhoff, German violinist and composer, was born at
Dresden (died 1705, April).

Johann Rudolph Ahle was made a
member of the senate this year.

Diniz dos Anjos entered the
monastery at Belem at this time.

Lübeck violinist Baltzar through
his ability lowered the prestige
of the English violinists, Davis,
Mell, Paul Wheeler, Georg
Hudson, the elder John Banister,
and Stagins.

In Vienna, Bertali revived
"Theti."

Cirillo survived the catastrophic
plague epidemic at Naples.

Charles Coleman this year was
associated with Lawes, Locke,
Capt. Cooke, George Hudson and
his son Edward in the composition of the music for
Davenant's "First Day's
Entertainment at Rutland House
by Declamations and Musick."

The Duke of Mantua sent F.
Corbett to King Louis XIV this
year.

The elder Henry Purcell took
the role of Mustapha alternately
with Thomas Blagrave in
Davenant's production.

Oxford "weekly musical Meetings"
took place at the house of
"William Ellis, late organist of
St. John's College" at this
time.

Werner Fabricius, German organist and composer, this year was
appointed music director of St.
Paul's church at Leipzig.

John Forbes, Scottish music
publisher, began his business at
Aberdeen at this juncture.

Christopher Gibbons was in the orchestra for the performance of Davenant's "Siege of Rhodes."

Paul Heinlen this year became Kapellmeister at the Church of Our Lady, Nürnberg.

The performance of "The Siege of Rhodes" was under Puritan rule.

Lully broke with the custom of embellishments and begged King Louis XIV for permission to have an orchestra of his own, the sixteen (later to become twenty-one) "petits violons."

Jose Marin was mentioned this year as being one of three notorious highwaymen, imprisoned for robbery with violence.

L. Penna was maestro di cappella of Sant' Illario at Casale Monferrato at this time.

The elder Henry Purcell, who had married Elizabeth (surname unknown) some time before this year, was referred to only once in any known pre-Restoration document.

Malachias Siebenhaar was second preacher at St. Ulrich, Magdeburg this year.

Thomas Strutius, organist and composer, was organist at Holy Trinity, Danzig at this time.

Felicianus Suevus, the composer, was this year made priest and musical director at the monastery at Constance.

Tomkins' organ music was a late product of the old school of composition.

John Wilson attended weekly music meetings at Oxford where he this year became a music professor.

Albert's book of solo songs was published at this time.

Vincenzo Amato's published works this year comprised a volume of "Sacri concenti" for two to five voices and a second volume of "Messe (3) e salmi di vespro e di compieta" for four voices, both printed at Palermo by Bisagno.

Auxcousteaux this year set the French psalms of Godeau.

Blount's "Glossographia" appeared at this time.

In Cavalli's old fashioned canzonas it was obvious how composers had broken away from the even and inarticulate flow of older canzona themes to establish a new motivic type in which strong beats were articulated and emphasized rhythmically by characteristically long upbeat patterns.

Cavalli's "Musiche sacre" was published this year at Venice.

William Child's "The First Set of Psalmes of III. Voyces" was published in 1639 in London and reprinted in c.1650. The work was reissued as "Choise Musick to the Psalmes of David" in London this year.

Edward Coleman contributed music this year to the first part of Davenant's "The Siege of Rhodes."

Davenant's "Siege of Rhodes" was published this year as well as produced.

1656(cont.)

John Hilton II's "Love is the sun" and "When I first gazed" were published at this time.

H. Lawes contributed music to Davenant's "First Day's Entertainment of Musick at Rutland House."

Matthew Locke's "Little Consort of Three Parts" was published this year. It was a collection of suites, each containing four dances in constant order and bi-partite form.

Mielczewski's "Gaude Dei Benebrit" for five parts a cappella bore this date.

Successive editions of Statius Olthoff's "Psalmorum Davidis paraphrasis poetica Georgii Buchanan Scoti argumentis ac melodis explicata atque illustrata . . ." appeared up to this date.

"Elizabeth Rogers her Virginall Booke" was published this year and contained "Sir Thomas Fairfax's Marche," "The Scots Marche," and "Prince Rupert's Marche."

John Wilson's "Psalterium Carolinum" was published this year.

A theme such as that of the "grave" in the sonata in a major, No. 6, opus 5, was in the exact rhythm of themes found in the sonatas "La Strozza" and "La Varana" from opus 18 of cazzati which appeared at this time.

Benserade's ballet "Psyche" was produced this year.

Pre-Restoration re-opening of the English theatre occurred this year with "The Siege of Rhodes."

Marco Marazzoli's "Il Trionfo della pieta ossia la Vita humana" was produced this year at Rome.

An opera by Antonio Francesco Tenaglia was performed at the Carnival at the Palazzo this year at Rome. The title was unknown but may have been "Il qiudizio di Paride."

John Milton this year married Katherine Woodcock at St. Margaret's, Westminster.

Sir William Boteler or Butler of Biddenham, Bedfordshire, a prominent Parliamentarian, died (birthdate unknown).

King John (João) IV of Portugal, who founded a beautiful library in Lisbon, died (See Nov. 6).

Czar Theodore III of Russia was born (died 1682).

Robert de Cotte, French architect and decorator, was born (died 1735).

Dutch painter Jan van Goyen died (born 1596).

Nicolas de Largillière, French painter, was born (died 1746).

Dutch painting: Rembrandt, "The Anatomical Lesson of Dr. Deyman" (40" x 52").

Spanish painting: Velásquez, "Les Meninas" (10'5" x 9').

Spanish painting: Velásquez, "The Spinners" (c.7'3 3/8" by

1656(cont.)
9'5 3/4").

(to 1657) Italian architecture:
Cortona, "Santa Maria della
Pace" (51' wide).

(to 1657) The Tiratoio dell'
Arte della Lana in Florence,
one of the finest theatres in
Italy, was opened during this
season.

(to 1660) Pavel Joseph
Vejvarovský, Bohemian trumpeter
and composer, was educated at
the Jesuit College of Opava
during these years.

(to 1674) Johann Caspar Kerll
was Kapellmeister at Munich during this period.

c.1656
Spanish painting: Velásquez,
"Don Antonio El Ingles."

1657
(January 17) Lully's "L'Amour
malade" was produced.

(February 14) Lully's "Les
Plaisirs troublés" was performed.

(March 18) Giuseppe (Ottavio)
Pitoni, Italian composer, was
born at Rieti (died 1743,
February 1). He compiled a
history of the meastri di
cappella in Rome from 1500 -
1700.

(March 26) La Guerre's opera
"Le Triomphe de L'Amour sur des
berger et bergères" was produced with scenery and revived
at court.

(May 5) Jacques Philidor, ("le
cadet"), French musician,
brother of André, was born at
Paris (died 1708, May 27).

(May 5) Henry Playford, son of
John Playford the elder, was
born at London (died c.1709).

(June 26) Tobias Michael,
German composer of Flemish
descent and son of Roger, died
at Leipzig (born 1592, June 13).

(July 25) Philipp Heinrich
Erlebach, German composer, was
born at Esens, East Frisia
(died 1714, April 17).

(November 20) G. Dumanoir succeeded L. Constantin as "roi
des ménétriers."

(February) Kerll's opera
"Oronte" with libretto by
Alcani was produced at the open-
ing of the Munich opera-house.

(March) John Hilton II, English
composer, possibly son of John
Hilton I, died at London (born
1599).

(July) The office of Drum-Major
was wholly abolished.

(October) Louis Constantin,
French violinist and composer,
died at Paris (born c.1585).

(December) Michel (Richard) de
Lalande, French organist and
composer, was born at Paris
(died 1726, June 18).

Giovanni Battista Bassani,
Italian violinist, organist and
composer, was born at Padua
(died 1716, October 1).

Sampson Estwick, English divine
and composer, was born, probably
at London (died 1739, February
6).

The end of Emperor Ferdinand
III's reign at Vienna. He was

an opera patron and composer and
became Emperor in 1637.

Hájjí Khalífa gave only brief
descriptions of the art of music
in his encyclopedia this year.

Franciszek Lilius, choir conductor, died at Cracow (born
c.1600).

Sir William Mure of Rowallan,
compiler of lute collections,
died (born 1594).

Giuseppe Torelli, Italian violinist, born (See 1658, April 22).

According to Antoine Vidal,
"Bassani, born about 1657, was
then younger than Corelli and
we find it hard to believe that
he could have been sufficiently
precocious in his talent to
give lessons to a pupil like
himself."

Bigongiari collaborated with
Sbarra in composing "La corte"
at this time.

Bockshorn at this time was
"Kapellmeister" to the Duke of
Würtemberg at Stuttgart.

Cazzati became music director
of the church at Bologna and
established the Bologna School.

Louis Couperin's name appeared
among the performers in the
ballets "Amour malade" and
"Plaisirs troubles" this year.

A. Draghi's name appeared this
year in the cast of P.A.
Ziani's "Le fortune di Rodope
e di Damira."

William Gregory was one of the
signatories of the petition for

(cont.) a National College of
Music at this time.

William Howes, with Hingston,
signed the petition for a
National College of Music.

Nicholas Lanier travelled between Flanders and England with
musical instruments this year.

After the death of Lilius,
Pekiel became conductor of
Cathedral choir in Cracow and
stayed there until his death.

F. Pinel was elected "enseigneur
à Sa Majesté" this year.

Walter Porter referred to
Robert Johnson II this year as
a famous musician.

Hyacinthus Różycki was appointed
conductor of the royal chapel
in Warsaw, after Bartomiej
Pekiel's resignation and departure for Cracow. He
(Rozycki) remained there almost
until his death.

Heinrich Schütz this year sold
his house in Dresden and went
to live with his sister at
Weissenfels.

Giovanni Battista Vacchelli was
maestro di cappella at San
Francesco, Bologna at this time.

An octavo edition of Heinrich
Albert's collections was pub-
lished this year by A. Profe of
Leipzig.

A book of "Canzonette spirituali"
sung at the Oratorio was published this year.

C.C. Dedekind's "C.C. D. Churf.
Sächs. Hofmusici Aelbianische
Musen-Lust in 160 unterschied

1657(cont.)

licher berühmter Poeten
auserlesener, mit anmuthigen
Melodien beseelten Lust- Ehren-
Zucht' und Tugend-Liedern
bestehend" was published this
year at Dresden.

J. van der Elsts' "Notae
Augustinianae" appeared at this
time.

Mette Gjøe's "Tragica" was published this year.

A'Kempis' "Cantiones Natalitiae"
for five voices or instruments
was published this year at
Antwerp.

Adam Krieger's Arien was composed this year.

Giovanni Legrenzi composed
masses and psalms at this time.

Lully's ballet-opera "Amore
ammalati" was completed this
year.

Georg Neumark's chief work
"Musikalisch-oietischer
Lustwald," a collection of
sacred and secular songs, was
published this year at Jena.

Della Porta's "Salmi da
cappella" was published at this
time.

Porter this year published his
"Motetts of Two Voyces for
Treble or Tenor and Bass with
the Continued Bass or Score.
To be performed to an Organ,
Harpsycon, Lute or Bass-viol."

Schütz' "Zwölf geistliche
Gesänge a 4" was published this
year at Dresden.

John Wilson this year published

(cont.) his "Psalterium
Cardinum: The Devotions of His
Sacred Majesty in his Solitude
& sufferings."

The Council in Erfurt at this
time added a balcony to the City
Hall, for the purpose of musical
performance by the Erfurt band.

Berti's Italian play "Amore
malato" of this year included
ballets by Lully, who also
played the part of Scaramouche.

There is some evidence that
Lully used the oboe in "L'Amour
malade" prior to Cambert's
"Pomone" (1671, Paris).

Melani's "La Tancia" was produced
this year at Florence. This may
be the same as Moniglia.

Andrea Moniglia's "La Tancia
overo il Podest'a di Colognole"
was produced this year at
Florence (See Melani's "La
Tancia.").

Zani's opera "Le fortune di
Rodope e di Damira" was produced
this year at Venice.

King Frederick I of Prussia was
born. He was Elector of
Brandenburg (1688-1701) as
Frederick III (died 1713).

Jacques Autreau, French painter,
was born at Paris but turned
playwright without deserting
his former art, at the age of
sixty (date of death unknown).

Franz Snyders, Flemish painter,
died (born 1579).

Joseph Vivien, French painter,
was born (died 1734).

Dutch painting: Rembrandt,

1657(cont.)
"Portrait of a Rabbi."

Dutch painting: Pieter Jansz
Saenredam, "The Old Town Hall of
Amsterdam."

(and 1658, 1663, 1665) Ahle's
"Thuringischer Lustgarten," a
series of church compositions,
was published at these years.

(to 1658) Bartolomeo Melani sang
in the Munich court chapel at
the this time but was arrested
in the latter year for political
intrigue.

(to 1660) French architecture:
Le Vau, Vaux-le-Vicomte,
Château (235' x 125').

(to 1666) Italian architecture:
Bernini, Throne of St. Peter,
aspe of St. Peter's Rome.

(to 1667) Krieger's "Arien" was
written during these years for
solo voice or small solo ensembles and five-part
ritornelli. As continuo lieder
they were near perfection.

(to 1771) Cazzati was "maestro
di cappella" at San Petronio,
Bologna during this period.

(to 1675 or 1676) Gracián Babán
was "maestro de capilla" at the
Cathedral at Valencia at this
time.

(to 1676) Sebastian Knüpfer was
Cantor at St. Thomas in Leipzig
during this period. He was
also general director of the
town music, having succeeded
Michael in the former position.

c.1657
Gaetano Greco, Italian composer,
was born at Naples (died c.1728).

1658
(January 21) Cavalli's opera
"Antioco" was produced at the
Teatro San Cassiano in Venice.

(February 14) Boesset wrote the
music for the balle,
"Alcidiane" performed on this
date.

(February 14) Lully's "Alcidiane"
was produced. It is assumed
that although the date of performance was the same this was
not the same work as Boesset's
with the same title.

(April 22) Giuseppe Torelli,
Italian violinist and composer,
was born at Verona (died 1709,
February 8 or 1716). Sources
disagree on these dates.

(May 5) Pietro Scarlatti, father
of Alessandro, married Eleonora
D'Amato at Palermo.

(June 18) Cavalli's opera
"Hipermestra" was produced at
the Teatro della Perfola in
Florence.

(July 22) From this date forward,
the coronation day of Leopold I,
Kerll's great reputation started.

(July 24) Violinist Baltzar
impressed Anthony Wood with his
playing according to the latter's
diary.

(August 11) Antoine de Cousu,
French singer and theorist,
died at Saint-Quentin (birthdate
unknown).

(August 28) Kerll's opera
"Applausi festivi" was produced.

(September 3) Evelyn on this
date recorded that Henry Purcell
the younger was born a year, or

slightly more after "Died that
archrebel Oliver Cromwell
. . . . . "

(December 1) Marin de La Gueme,
organist and brother of Jérôme,
was born at Pans (died 1704,
July 16).

(January) Cesti was in Rome at
this time and shortly afterward
moved to Tuscany.

(February) Ferrari's opera
"Erosilda" was performed at
Modena. The libretto was by
Carlo Vigarani.

(March) Werner Fabricius, organist and composer, tried to get
the position of cantor at St.
Thomas' church in Leipzig. He
was not elected.

Artus Auxcousteaux, a master of
church music, died according to
one source (born c.1590).

Hájjí Khalífa, Turkish author,
died according to one source
(birthdate unknown).

Henry Purcell, probably the
greatest of all English composers, was born at London according to some sources (died 1695,
November 21).

Edward Raban, an English music
printer, died (birthdate unknown).

Jan Bischoff was still a member
of the royal chapel in Warsaw
at this time.

Caresan this year became a
singer in the royal chapel at
Naples.

Sir Aston Cockain, Baronet

(cont.) wrote on Thomas
Pilkington in his "Choice Poems
of several sorts . . ." published this year at London.

A. Draghi went to Vienna where
he spent the remainder of his
life.

Werner Fabricius was this year
appointed organist at St.
Nichol's church in Leipzig.

Michel de La Guerre at this
time became "Receveru Général
du temporel de la Sainte
-Chapelle" and was given free
quarters in the precincts of
the Palace in Paris for himself and his family.

Paul Heinlen this year became
organist at St. Sebald's
Cathedral, Nürnberg. He composed a large number of sacred
songs and texts by contemporary
poets, as well as some church
music.

Nicholas Lanier journied between Flanders and England with
musical instruments this year.

Playford the elder's credit for
the invention of the "new ty'd
note" this year was in error.

Records now available showed
the elder Henry Purcell as
dwelling in a house that had
been occupied up to this time
by either William Crane or
Captain Hickes.

Possibly the elder Purcell did
not appear in "Siege of Rhodes"
until this year. There is
still uncertainty as to the
actual date of the first performance according to one
source.

1658(cont.)

The prosecution this year of "Thomas Smith at the Music-house at Blue Bell by the postern gate of London Wall" was for having "one puncheon of compounded & unadulterated unwholesome drink fit to have the head beaten out." It has been suggested that it should have been for "having countenanced unwholesome music probably far worse than the drink if the truth were known."

Jacob Stainer, Austrian violin-maker received by diploma this year the title of "Hofgeigen-macher" to the archduke.

A. Werckmeister attended school in Benningen at this time.

Bockshorn's "Geistliche Concerten" appeared this year.

Charles Coleman contributed the musical definitions to Phillips' "New World of Words" of this year.

Cousu this year wrote "La Musique universelle," one of the earliest works dealing with hidden fifths and octaves.

C.C. Dedekind's "J. Katzens Aeltern-Spiegel aus desselben Holländis-chem gehouchdeutschet durch C.C.D. 1654" was published this year. (See also 1654 and 1665).

Hammerschmidt's "Fest-Buss-und Dank-Lieder," thirty-two hymns for five voices and five instrumental parts ad libitum a-peared at this time.

This year's edition of Hilton's "Catch that Catch Can" still did not give Byrd's name as composer

(cont.) of the canon "Non nobis domine."

Henry Lawes published his "First Book of Ayres and Dialogues for One, Two and Three Voyces" this year.

In the suites by Johann Jakob Loewe this year the introductions were called "sinfonie."

Micheli's "Li responsori a cinque voci" was issued this year at Rome.

In this year's "Brief Introduction to the Skill of Musick" Playford gave some instructions for the violin but he was mainly concerned with the viol.

Thomas Strutius, organist and composer, published a Sonata for eight instruments this year.

J. Wilson's music appeared in Playford's revised edition of "Catch that Catch Can."

Davenant's "The Cruelty of the Spaniards in Peru, expressed by instrumental & vocal music, & the art of perspective in scenes" was produced at this time.

Davenant's play "The History of Sir Francis Drake" was produced this year at London. Matthew Locke wrote the incidental music.

F. Luccio's "Medoro" was produced at this time.

Richard Lovelace, English Cavalier poet, died (born 1618).

Christian Henrich Postel, German librettist, was born (died 1705).

368

1658(cont.)
Sir Thomas Browne's "The Garden of Cyprus" was completed this year.

Oliver Cromwell, Lord Protector of England, died and the Puritans tried to continue their rule under Cromwell's son, Richard (born 1599).

Dutch painting: Pieter de Hooch, "Interior with Card Players" (30" x 26 1/2").

(and 1659) According to a major source Lully "deliberately set the Italian style against the French in the prologue to the ballet 'Alcidiane' (1658), and, similarly, in the 'Ballet de la Raillerie' (1659) he composed an amusing dialogue between Italian and French music in which he cleverly contrasted the simple syllabic style of the Italian canzonetta with the subtle turns of the French air."

(to 1659) The reign of Richard Cromwell as Lord Protector of England and Great Britain under the Commonwealth.

(to 1664) The technique of the ballet was established on a new basis during this period. Vocal and instrumental sections were now treated as a unity.

(to 1669) Matthias Kelz, German composer, was at Augsburg at this time where he probably composed his "Primitiae musicales" and "Epidigma harmoniae novae," two books of sonatas and dance movements for one or two violins and viola da gamba.

(to 1670) Italian architecture: Bernini, "Sant'Andrea al

(cont.) Quirinale," Rome (c.115' x 100').

(to 1671) Maurizio Cazzati was maestro di cappella at the church of San Petronio at Bologna for this period.

(to 1671) Lully composed about thirty ballets during these years.

(to 1679) William Godbid printed music published by John Playford during this period.

(to 1705) Emperor Leopold I ruled at the imperial court at Vienna during these years. He was both an opera patron and composer.

c.1658
Richard Dering, English sacred composer, died (born c.1570).

Henry Ferrabosco, singer, wind instrumentalist and composer, died at Jamaica (born c.1623).

M. Locke's "The History of Sir Francis Drake" was produced at this time.

Dutch painting: Jan Vermeer, "View of Delft."

1659
(January 24) Lully's "Oedipe" was produced.

(February 19) Lully's "La Raillerie" was performed.

(February 21) According to Pepys' diary a musical evening in which a Purcell took part occurred on this date or a year later. Whether this referred to Henry or to Thomas, or to some other member of the family cannot be decided on the evidence at present available.

(August 1) Antoine Moque, Netherlands organist, carillonist and composer, was born at Ostende (died 1723, August 23).

(August 6) Gustaf Düben, the younger, composer, was born at Stockhold (died 1726, December 5).

(September 10) A definite date of birth for the elder Purcell's third son, Henry, is not possible to establish, however, Sietz' choice of this date is worth considering.

(November 20) The fact that Henry Purcell was born before this date is reasonably safe to assume from the inscription on his memorial at Westminster Abbey.

(November 30) Walter Porter, English singer and composer, died at London and was buried on this day (born 1595). He was a pupil of Monteverdi.

(December 26) Cavalli's opera "Elena" was produced at the Teatro San Cassiano in Venice.

(January) Cesti was in Rome again by this time.

(April) Pierre Perrin and Robert Cambert at this time produced "La Première Comédie Française en Musique Représentée en France: Pastorale, etc." at Issy near Paris in M. de La Haye's house. The latter was the King's goldsmith. The work was later produced before the King at Vincennes. The work represented a compromise between French and

(cont.) Italian style.

(June) The statement that Henry Purcell must have been born some time after June of this year is a frequent one, but not documentable.

(July) Queen Christina of Sweden settled in Italy at this time at the Palazzo Riario at Trestevere. Here she had a household of servants, writers and musicians.

(August) Cesti was in Rome again at this time.

(December) Cesti at this time accepted an appointment to the papal choir.

Jeremiah Clark, English composer, was born (died 1707). He has now been credited with the composition of the most famous "Purcell voluntary."

Élisabeth Jacquet de La Guerre, French composer, was born at Paris (died 1729, June 27).

T. Pestel, madrigal writer, died (born 1584).

Francesco Antonio Mamiliano Pistocchi, singing teacher and composer who founded a school in Bologna, was born (died 1726).

Henry Purcell II, English composer and organist, was born at London (died 1695, November 21). Sources disagree on Purcell's death between 1658 and 1659.

Alessandro Scarlatti, considered to be the founder of the Neapolitan School of composer, and a great creative genius, was born at Piapani, Sicily (died

1725).

One of Baltzar's suites for strings carried this year's date and referred to him as "Mr. Baltzar, commonly called the Swede."

Tentative experiments in French opera were begun by Robert Cambert, the French composer.

A pupil of Cazzati, G.C. Arresti, this year attacked his teacher, on a theoretical question, in his "Dialogo tra un maestro e un discepolo desideroso d'approfitare nel contrapunto."

T. Cima entered his name as a candidate for the position of "maestro di cappella" at the Cathedral of Orvieto, but was unsuccessful.

G.P. Colonna was elected organist of San Petronio, Bologna this year.

G.P. Colonna had already become famous as a composer by this time.

Louis Couperin's name appeared among those of the performers in the "Ballet de la Raillerie" this year.

The division viol music in Christopher Simpson's "Division Violist" was apparently by Daniel the violist.

Giovanni Battista Fasolo, Italian composer, was this year "maestro di cappella" to the Archbishop of Monreale near Palermo.

Antonio Melani was in the ser-

(cont.) vice of the Archduke Ferdinand Karl of Austria this year.

The "Ménestrandise," a musicians' guild or trade union, founded in 1321, was formally sanctioned by the King at this time.

Perrin claimed priority over La Guerre in the invention of the "comédie francoise en musique."

André Philidor this year succeeded his uncle, Michael, as fifth player of the oboe, crumhorn etc. in the Grande Écurie.

Jean Philidor became a fifer in the Grande Écurie this year and at the time of his death he had become first player of the crumhorn and trumpet marine as well as an oboist and drummer.

Séraphin Pinel inherited his father's position this year.

From this date forward the elder Henry Purcell's family lived in one of the houses on the south side of the Great Almonry, a residential area just south of Tothill Street a few yards west of Westminster Abbey. Almost certainly they had moved there with their infant son born this year.

Simpson taught the seventh position on all strings of the viola da gamba by this time.

Count Corzio di Salabue this year stated that Antonio Stradivarius was already working and inserting his own labels.

Bertali's "Il re Gilidoro" appeared at this time.

Bockshorn's "Theatrum musicum" was written this year.

Brassicanus this year wrote some of the songs included in Erhardi's song-book.

M.C. Calegari's first book of "Motetti a voce sola" appeared at Bergamo at this time.

Comenius compiled and edited the famous "Kancionál" (Hymnal) this year at Amsterdam.

Richard Elton in his "The compleat Body of the Art Military" of this year described the qualifications for the office of drum-major.

Erhardi's "Harmonisches Chorund Figuralgesangbuch" was published this year at Frankfort. It included thirty-five settings for five voices by Herbst, as well as several other compositions.

Giovanni Battista Fasolo's "Arie spirituali, morali e indifferenti" was published this year at Palermo.

Jean Francois Ferrel wrote a small pamphlet this year at Paris: "A savoir que les maistres de dance, qui sont de vrays maistres larrons à l'endroit des violins de France, n'ont pas royale commission d'incorporrer ès leur compagnie les organistes et austres musiciens, comme aussy de leur faire paîer redevance, démonstré par J.F. Ferrel, practicien de musique a Paris, natif de l'Anjou."

John Gamble published his "Ayres and Dialogues for one, (cont.) two and three voices" this year.

Lewis Grabu composed his opera "Ariadne, or the Marriage of Bacchus" at this time. The libretto was by Pierre Perrin.

Johnson's "As I walk forth" was included in Playford's "Ayres & Dialogues."

Nicholas Lanier's songs and several other pieces were included in "Select Musicall Ayres and Dialogues."

Henry Lawe's songs were included in "Select Musical Ayres and Dialogues."

William Lawe's songs and several other vocal compositons were included in "Select Musicall Ayres and Dialogues."

A concerto by Mielezewski, "Deus in nomine tuo," for bass solo, two violins, bassoon and organ was included in a collection, "Jesu hilf" published this year by J. Havemann at Berlin.

Heinrich Muiller published this year "Geistliche Salen-Musik" which contained about two hundred hymns for which 126 tunes with figured bass were provided.

A. van Noordt published his "Tablatuurboeck van Psalmen en fantasijen waarvan de psalmen door verscheijden versen verandert zijn soo in de superius, tenor als bassus met 2,3 en 4 part" this year. It was the first Dutch work for keyboard to be printed in Holland.

Another edition of "Parthenia" appeared this year.

The "Memoirs of Sanuel Sainthill" printed in "The Gentleman's Magazine" this year gave the earlies revue of "Marylebone Gardens," a famous place of entertainment.

Schmelzer's chamber music included a set of twelve trio sonatas written this year.

Christopher Simpson's book "The Division-Violist: or, an Introduction to the Playing Upon a Ground" was published this year at London. It was an instruction book for viols and violin. Other editions appeared in 1665 and 1712.

Wilson's music was included in Playford's "Select Ayres & Dialouges."

Discussion about the characteristics and merits of French and Italian music, singers and accompanists, have provided a literature that lasts over a century, however, polemics did not break out until this year.

Lully inserted many Italian arias in his early ballets. In one of these, "Le Ballet de la Raillerie" of this year there was a dialogue between French and Italian music in which each disputant sang in his own language and to his own style of music. After this Italian arias did not figure in Lully's ballets.

Boesset wrote the music this year for "La Mort d'Adonis," with text by Perrin. Some of the arias were sung at court.

Cesti's "Venere cacciatrice" was produced at Innsbruck this year.

Simpson in his "Division Violist" asked for a "full and clear sound" and also said "We play loud or soft, according to our fancy, or the number of the music . . . sometime . . . in one and the same note." He discussed ornamentation at great length referring to an ascending appogiatura as a "beat," describint "a shaked beat" as a compound ornament (prepared and prolonged lower mordent), describing a "double relish ornament," describing a "springer" and dealing with tremolo in bowed instruments. He also stated that a single rising stroke before a note or lutenist's letter meant a long appoggiatura whereas a single rising stroke over a note or after a letter indicated a "springer."

John Dryden composed "Heroic Stanzas" dated this year as a tribute to the memory of Oliver Cromwell.

Sebastiano Ricci, Italian painter, was born (died 1734).

Hyacinthe Rigaud, French painter, was born (died 1743).

Dutch painting: Willem Kalf, "Still Life" (30" x 23").

Dutch painting: Rembrandt did one of his many self portraits.

(and 1660, 1664) Bockshorn's "Geistliche Harmonien" was published at these dates.

(December 21 to 1662, February) Cesti was a member of the papal choir in Rome during this period according to many sources.

(to 1669) The renowned diary of S. Pepys embraced these years.

1659(cont.)

(to 1669) Mario Savioni was maestro di cappella at the papal chapel in Rome during this period.

(to 1677) Carlo Grossi during these years wrote four operas for Venice: "Romilad," "Artaserse," "Giocasta," and "Nicomede."

c.1659

Michel Danican died at Paris (birthdate unknown). King Louis XIII bestowed the name Philidor on the family and they were known as Philidor.

1660

(January 21) The Mitre concerts were mentioned by Pepys in his entries for this date.

(February 13) Johann Sigismund Kusser, Austro-Hungarian composer, was baptised at Bratislaua (died 1727, November).

(February 18) The Mitre concerts were mentioned by Pepys in his entries for this date.

(February 21) The name of "Pursell" is first found in Pepys' Diary under this date where its bearer was referred to as "Master of Musique." Pepys mentioned a meeting with "Mr. Lock & Pursell . . . " (Pursell, the elder).

(March 21) Fernando de Almeida, Portuguese composer, died at Thomas (born c.1618).

(April 6) Johann Kuhnau, German organist, composer and author on music, was born at Geising, Saxony (died 1722, June 5).

(May 1) After Cromwell's death all dictatorships weakened and shortly Parliament restored the monarchy in England.

(May 2) Alessandro Scarlatti renowned composer, was born at Palermo (died 1725, October 24). Souces are not in total agreement as to this date as may be noted from alternate entry.

(July 5) Benjamin Rogers composed a "Hymnus Eucharisticus" in four parts, to a text by Dr. Nathaniel Ingelo. It was performed for King Charles II on this date. The composer became organist at Eaton College.

(August 15) A. Werckmeister joined the school at Nordhauser.

(November 17) A warrant was issued "to admit Christopher Gibbons, musician upon the Virginalls" to Chapel Royal at London.

(November 22) Cavalli's "Serse," with libretto by Minato, was produced in the gallery of the Louvre. Lully wrote the overture.

(December 4) André Campra, French composer of Italian descent, was born at Aix-en-Provence (died 1744, June 29).

(December 5) Juan Hidalgo's "Celos aun del ayre matan" was produced at the Buen Ritiro palace at Madrid. This was the earliest Spanish opera of which the music is partially extant.

(June) Gervase Price became Sergeant-Trumpeter of the Royal Household.

(November) George Hudson was

374

appointed Composer to King
Charles II.

Luis de Aranda, Spanish organist,
died some time before this date
(birthdate unknown).

Francesco Bazzini, Italian organist, theorbist and composer,
died at Bergamo (born 1600).

André Campra, French opera composer, was born. Specific date
given by one source. See Dec. 4.

Johann Sigismund Cousser, German
opera composer, was born (died
1727).

Henri-Denis Dupont, Walloon
theologian, organist and composer, was born at Liege (died
1727, September 1).

Johann Joseph Fux, Austrian
organist and composer, was born
in Hirtenfeld, Styria (died
1741, February 14).

Samuel Hafenreffer, author on
music, died (born 1587).

Stephen Jeffries, English organist and composer, was born
(died 1712).

Adam Janecki, Polish ecclesiastic
and musician, died at Cracow
(birthdate unknown).

J. Kuhnau, born this year, was
considered Bach's predecessor
at Leipzig (See 1660, April 6).

Biagio Marini, Italian violinist,
died according to a major source
(birthdate unknown).

Gaspard Le Roux, French clavecinist and composer, was born
(died 1710).

M.H. Schacht, compiler of a
musical dictionary, was born
(died 1700).

Thomas Warwick, English organist
and composer, died at London
(birthdate unknown).

Christian Witt, German composer,
was born at Altenburg (died 1716,
April 13).

Sir Thomas Baynes, Doctor of
Medicine, was this year appointed
professor of music at Gresham
College in London.

Briegel was "Kapellmeister" to
the Duke of Saxe-Gotha at this
time.

Cavalli arrived in Paris this
year having been summoned by
Cardinal Mazarin. He had composed about thirty operas and
was considered to be the foremost operatic composer of the
peninsula. "Cavalli" may have
been misread for "Corelli" which
would account for a mistaken
idea of a trip to Paris by
Corelli.

William Child at this time was
appointed Gentleman of the
Chapel Royal and one of the
King's private musicians.

James Cob became a member of the
Chapel Royal this year.

Raphael Courteville resumed his
place in the Chapel Royal when
it was re-established at this
time.

Kaspar Förster became
Kapellmeister at Copenhagen this
year for the second time.

Christopher Gibbons this year
became organist of the Chapel

Royal, private organist to King
Charles II, and organist at
Westminster Abbey.

John Goodgroome was appointed a
Gentleman of the Chapel Royal
at this time.

Harris' double organ was restored
to Magdalen College, Oxford this
year after Cromwell had taken it
down and moved it to Hampton
Court where it was installed in
the great gallery.

The London firm of W.E. Hill &
Sons was referred to in Pepys'
Diary this year. Hill & Sons
were violin makers, dealers and
repairers doing a business at
140 New Bond St. who held a
position of recognized authority
on all matters relating to the
violin.

John Hingston was appointed a
musician for the viol in the
King's private music, this year,
replacing Alfonso Ferrabosco.

Pelham Humfrey became a member
of the first set of children of
the re-established Chapel Royal
at London this year under Henry
Cooke.

Jewett was almoner at St. Paul's
Cathedral, London at this time.

Henry Lawes was reinstated in
his court appointments this year
as a result of the Restoration.

Edward Lowe became an organist
at the Chapel Royal at this
time.

Lully's overture to the ballet
insertions in Cavalli's "Serse"
of this year was probably the
first example of the fully de-

(cont.) veloped French overture
with the second part in fugal
texture and triple meter.

Lully's works were most important
in establishing the national
French style after this date.

The church of Lüneberg employed
six instrumentalists at this
time.

A. Marsh I this year was appointed a Gentleman of the
Chapel Royal by King Charles II.

At the Restoration this year
John Mawgridge became "King's
drum-major."

Alessandro Melani was maestro di
cappella at San Petromio,
Bologna at this time.

Francesco Maria Melani sang the
part of Amastris in Cavalli's
"Serse" at its Paris production
this year.

Juan de Padilla this year returned
to Spain where he acted as chapel
master in the wealthy Zamora
convent at San Pablo.

When the Chapel Royal was re-
established this year Henry
Purcell was appointed one of the
Gentlemen.

The elder Henry Purcell's appointment as musician-in-ordinary
for lutes and voices was retroactive to this year from 1662.

Thomas Purcell was appointed a
Gentleman of the Chapel Royal
this year.

An Italian company was established at Paris this year with
"Scaramouche" (Dominique) who
performed with Moliere's company

at the Palais-Royal until 1673.

As far back as this date Schmelzer was referred to as "most famous and almost the most distinguished violinist in all of Europe.

Laurentius von Schnüffis received an engagement at the Innsbruck court Theatre at this time.

Bernhard Smith this year went to England with two nephews.

Nicolaus Adam Strunsk, violinist, composer and organist, this year was appointed 1st violinist at the Wolfenbüttel court chapel.

M. Wise was appointed a child of the Chapel Royal in London at this time.

Bertali's "La magia delusa" was completed this year.

Bockshorn's "Jubilus Bernhardi" appeared at this time.

Bockshorn this year composed two "Lieder von dem Leyden und Tode Jesu."

Bockshorn's three-part sonatas were written at this time.

Bontempi's "Nova quatuor vocibus componendi methodus" was published this year at Dresden and dedicated to Schütz.

Cavalli's "Ercole amante" was composed at this time.

In celebration of the return of the monarchy this year William Child wrote a five-part full anthem, "O praise ye the Lord."

Crüger's "Rechter Weg zur Singekunst" was issued this year at Berlin.

Vol. I of the Philidor Collection of this year contained a suite "pour les cromornes" by Degrignis.

Ferrari's "Le ali d'amore," an introduction, and "La gara degli elementi," an introduction to a tournament, were published this year at Parma.

Nicolas Fleury's instruction book "Méthode pour apprendre facilement à toucher le théorbe sur la basse continue" was published this year at Paris.

Giovanni Domenico Freschi this year published a mass with a collection of psalms.

Juan Hidalgo's opera "Celos aun del aire matan" was composed at this time.

John Jenkins this year at London published twelve sonatas for "two Violins and a Base with a Thorough Base for the Organ or Theorbo." This composition heralded the arrival of the Italian trio sonata in England.

"Arca Musarithmica," a mechanical device for composing music, was described and illustrated by Kircher in his "Musurgia universalis" published this year at Rome.

Giovanni Legrenzi composed motets at this time.

Emperor Leopold I this year wrote an oratorio "Il sacrificio d'Abramo."

Portman in 1645 published a book

of meditations: "The Soules Life, exercising itself in the sweet Fields of Divine Meditation, collected for the comfort thereof in these sad days of distraction." It was reissued in this year by Playford.

Roberday's "Fugues et Caprices" appeared at this time.

Mario Savioni wrote his "Concerti morali e spirituali" this year.

Uccellini this year published his "Canto dell'ozio regio, opera di musica."

Vesi at this time composed "Le mascherate . . ." for two to four voices, with two violins ad lib., opus 5.

J. Wilson published his "Cheerful Ayres" this year.

From this date forward two main classes of sonatas became clearly distinguishable, the sonata da chiesa (the church sonata) and the sonata da camera (chamber sonata).

The Italian players, at the instigation of Cardinal Mazarin, founded a permanent Parisian group this year.

King Charles II this year established in imitation of Louis XIV a group of twenty-four performers on violins, tenors, and basses, popularly known as the "four & twenty fiddlers."

The Restoration of choral service took place at this time.

After the Restoration of the monarch theaters opened again (cont.) and the modern stage replaced the old Shakespearean theater. Drama, however, first reappeared under the mantle of music.

In England Italian operas were produced at court this year.

Cavalli's "La pazzio in trono, ovvero Caligola delirante" was produced this year at the Teatro Sant' Apollinare in Venice.

Kerll's opera "Ardelia" was produced this year.

The design of the flute was altered at this time. A hole was bored midway between the open end and the first hole. It was covered by a closed key, and was operated with the little finger of the right hand.

Daniel Defoe, journalist and political agent, was born (died 1731). Most of his life a social and financial outcast, he started his career studying for the ministry. Later he tried the hosiery trade and failed. He was arrested for sedition in his tract "The Shortest Way with the Dissenters" and spent five months in prison. After his release he became a journalist and Whig secret agent. When he was sixty he wrote "Robinson Crusoe." He was ultimately the author of over 400 publications.

Sir William Davenant managed his own theatre this year.

John Bunyan was arrested this year under Restoration rule for Baptist preaching.

John Dryden wrote "Astraea Redux" this year and dedicated

it to the restored monarchy.

John Milton's "Ready and Easy Way to Establish a Commonwealth" appeared at this time.

Sir Edmund Waller obtained a seat in Parliament this year.

King George I was born (House of Hanover), died 1727.

The British Army, weary of Puritan rule by this time, invited the Prince of Wales to emerge from exile and resume the monarchy as King Charles II which he did.

When King Charles II returned from exile in France this year he showed a strong partiality to everything French, including music.

The Royal Society for Improving Natural Knowledge was founded this year.

Le Mercier, a French architect, died (born 1590).

Prandtauer, a German Baroque Architect, was born (died 1726).

Diego Rodriguez de Silva y Velásquez, major Spanish painter, died (born 1599).

French painting: Charles Le Brun, "Chancellor Séguier in the Train of Queen Maria Theresa at Her Entry into Paris, August 26, 1660." (oil on canvas, 9' 8 1/8" x 11' 5 3/4").

Dutch painting: Rembrandt, "Self-Portrait at the Easel" (44" x 34").

(to 1661) Davis Mell and George

(cont.) Hudson were Masters of the King's Music responsible for the band during these years.

(to 1662) Daniele Castrovillari had three of his operas produced during this period.

(to 1663) West this year said that Oker was reappointed to the organist's post of Wells during these years.

(to 1664) The pages of the Westminster Abbey Precentor's Book and Treasurer's Accounts for these years have entries for various receipts, disbursements, and other transactions connected with the elder Purcell's official duties.

(to 1664) French painting: Nicolas Poussin, "Summer" (c.46 7/16" x 63").

(to 1666 or 1667) John Jenkins during this period lived with the family of Lord North and taught music to his sons.

(to 1669) A. Draghi wrote about a dozen librettos during these nine years.

(to 1669) Lully provided music for several of Moliere's comedies during this period.

(to 1669) Samuel Pepys' Diary included these years.

(to 1670) Italian writers described Palestrina and Lassus as "gli antichi" during this decade. Their music was considered archaic, written solely in the stylus gravis.

(to 1682) George Loosemore was organist of Trinity College during these years.

(to 1685) Masques were performed privately during these early years of the Restoration under King Charles II.

(to 1685) The reign of King Charles II (House of Stuart) over England and Great Britain.

(to 1700) This period of forty years was the second period of English 17th-Century history, characterized by secular reaction to the Puritanical austerities of the period 1600-1660, and a restoration of the monarchy under King Charles II of England.

(to 1750) One or two oratorios were performed each year at Vienna during this period.

(to 1799) Many old Greek melodies were recopied in new manuscripts during these years, however, frequently with too much elaboration as a result of Turkish influence as well as other factors.

(to 1800) Once the Comédie -Italienne was established in Paris during these years about 22 theaters or theatrical groups existed which produced musical works, including the Opéra, Opéra-Comique and their mutations.

c.1660

John Abell, celebrate singer (alto) and lutenist, was born (date of death unknown).

Attilio Ariosti, a Dominican monk and an opera composer, was born (date of death unknown).

Johann Philipp Bendeler, a German theorist, was born at Riethnordhausen near Erfurt

(cont.) (died 1708).

Bartolomeo Bernardi, Italian violinist and composer, was born at Bologna (died 1732, May).

Antonio Borosini, Italian singer, was born at Venice (died after 1711).

Gottfried Finger, Moravian composer, was born at Olomoue (date of death unknown).

Angelo Maria Fiore, Italian composer and cellist, was born at Milan (died 1723, June 4).

Johann Caspar Ferdinand Fischer, German Kapellmeister to Markgraf Ludwig of Baden at Schloss Schlackenwerth in Bohemia, was born according to Forkel (died c.1738). Other sources gave his lifespan as c.1665 to 1746, March 27).

Alexandre Philidor, French musician and brother of Jacques, was born at Paris (date of death unknown).

Daniel Purcell, organist and composer, was born at London (died 1717, December 12).

Gaspard Le Roux, French harpsichordist and composer, was born at Paris (died c.1707).

Giulo Taglietti, Italian composer, was born at Brescia (date of death unknown).

S. Eccles embraced the tenets of Quakerism at this time.

C. Haward this year designed the English spinet.

Thomas Tudway, the composer, was admitted as a chorister of the

c.1660(cont.)
Chapel Royal at London at this time.

A house near the Thames owned by Jane Vaux was opened this year as a place for public entertainment.

Christoph Bernhard's "Tractatus compositiones augmentatus" was written at this time. It was a manuscript treatise which discussed an embellishment figure he referred to as "quaesitio notae" ("searching note").

Giacomo Carissimi wrote "Jepthe" this year according to one source.

Ferrari's "Sansone" written about this time showed a sharp dramatic characterization in both aria and recitative.

Kaspar Förster's Latin dialogues "David De Divite, Holofernes" written this year were influenced to a great degree by Carissimi's concise choral style.

The trombone at this time kept the flat stay on the bell joint but had tubular ones on the slide.

Dutch painting: Van Ruisdael, "Jewish Cemetery" (56" x 74 1/4").

Dutch painting: Van Ruisdael, "A View of Haarlem."

Spanish painting: Velásquez, "Infanta Margarita of Austria."

Dutch painting: Vermeer, "The Little Street in Delft" (21 3/4" x 17").

(to 1670) The "Tablature Book

(cont.) of Löcse," containing Magyar and Polish dance tunes, was published during this period.

(to 1671) Cossoni during these years was first organist at San Petronio, Bologna.

(to 1680) French architecture: The Palace of Versailles.

1661
(January 18) Pekiel's "Missa brevis" was performed on this date.

(February 16) The elder Purcell was installed singing-man and master of the choristers at Westminster Abbey.

(February 19) Lully's "L'Impatience" was produced.

(March 4) Pekiel's "Missa secunda" was performed.

(March 9) Cardinal Mazarin of France died (born 1602).

(April 19) M.C. Calegari joined the Order of St. Benedict at the convent of Santa Margherita, Milan, and took the name of Cornelia.

(April 23) The coronation of King Charles II took place on this date, St. George's Day. Both Blow and Child were present.

(May 7) Juan de Padilla was appointed chapel master at Zamora Cathedral.

(May 30) From the beginning of the Restoration period there was apparently a great deal of confusion as to proper disposition of funds brought in by ticket sales at coronations. This was already obvious at King Charles

381

II's coronation.

(May 31) The word "band" first appeared in a manuscript order on this date. The order stated that "the King's band of violins shall take instructions from Hudson and Mell."

(June 6) Giacomo Antonio Perti, Italian composer, was born at Bologna (died 1756, April 10).

(June 9) Bertali's "Il Ciro crescente" was performed as intermezzi between the acts of Guarini's "Il pastor fido" at Laxenburg Palace.

(June 28) The first Duke's Theatre was opened under Davenant's management.

(July 1) Clifford was appointed tenth minor canon of St. Paul's Cathedral at London.

(July 2) Pepys attended the Duke's Theatre and saw the second part of "The Siege of Rhodes."

(July 8) Melani's opera "Ercole in Tebe" was produced at the Teatro della Pergola in Florence.

(July 30) Lully's "Les Saisons" was performed.

(August 29) Louis Couperin, violinist, organist and composer, died at Paris according to a major source (born 1626).

(September 2) Georg Böhm, German organist and composer, was born at Hohenkirchen near Ohrdruf, Thuringia (died 1733, May 18).

(September 5) Jean-Baptiste

(cont.) Henri d'Anglebert, French organist, was born at Paris (died 1735, December).

(September 12) Christoph Bach, son of Johannes and grandson of Veit, member of the third generation of the Bach family, died at Arnstadt (born 1613, April 19).

(September 29) At Michaelmas (this date) the elder Purcell was retroactively paid £7.10s for three-quarters as Master of the Choristers.

(October 6) Maria Magdalena Grabler, of Prettin, Saxony, widow of Christoph Bach, died (born 1614).

(October 25) Pepys called at Hunts' about his lute, which was almost finished. He had a new neck for double strings installed.

(December 19) Pepys frequently attended services at Westminster Abbey because of his enthusiasm for music and on this date he was allowed to sing in the choir.

(December 27) Ambrosius Profe (Profius), German organist, composer, and musical editor, died at Breslau (born 1589, February 12).

(February) Christopher Gibbons (son of Orlando) petitioned the King at this time "for a letter fo the Dean & Chapter of Winchester Cathedral to obtain his his tenant right in virtue of his marriage . . ."

(April) A warrant was granted this month by Reverand Dean to the Chanter and the rest of the choir for the erection of scaffolds in the Churchyard for His Majesty's Coronation to be held on St. George's Day.

(April) Jean-Féry Rébel, French harpsichordist, violinist, conductor, and composer, was born at Paris (died 1747, January 2).

Cristoforo Besozzi, oboist and bassoonist, was born at Milan (died 1725, October 22).

Jean de Cambefort, French composer of the "ballet de cour," died (born 1605).

Pompeo Colonna, Prince of Gallicano, Italian amateur poet and musician, died at Rome (birthdate unknown).

Louis Couperin died at the height of his fortune at the age of thirty-five (born 1626). Sources do not agree on this date.

Johann Rudolph Ahle was made a burgomaster this year.

Leone Allacci became "custode" of the Vatican Library at this time.

D'Anglebert this year became organist to the Duke of Orleans.

Ashmole described the processional hymn sung at the Installation of the Knights of the Garter this year.

Christoph Bach applied for a position as musician in the city of Naumburg but died before the issue was decided.

Baltzar was appointed conductor of the King's celebrated band of twenty-four violins at this time.

An inventory of this year referred to selected church music by Barnard.

In "The Virgin's Pattern," the life of Susanna Perwich among famous musicians of the time, Albertus Bryne was described as "that famous velvet-fingered organist."

Letters of this year showed that Cesti wished to return to Innsbruck and tried to persuade Rosa to go with him.

Bishop Cosin's version of the "Veni Creator" was adopted in the Prayer Book this year.

Charles Couperin inherited the position of organist at St. Gervais from his brother Louis and married this same year.

Dallam worked on the organ of New College, Oxford this year while his two sons Thomas and Toussaint stayed in France and continued to construct organs there.

Kaspar Förster this year left his post as Kapellmeister at Copenhagen and went to Dresden.

Roger Hill was sworn a Gentleman of the Chapel Royal this year.

S. Ives was installed as eighth minor prebendary of St. Paul's at this time.

Jewett this year was minor canon and junior cardinal at St. Paul's, London.

Henry Lawes lived next door to the Purcells in the Great Almonry this year but moved into the Dean's yard before his death the following year.

Antimo Liberati this year became a singer in the papal chapel.

After the death of Cardinal Mazarin this year Lully made a complete reversal and became an ardent supporter of French music.

Lully this year was appointed "Superintendent" of the King's music and thus gained control of the "grande bande." He became a French citizen at the end of the year and changed the spelling of his name from Lulli to Lully.

Davis Mell succeeded Lanier as Master of the King's Band at the time of the Restoration.

Molière this year introduced a comedy-ballet with a play. He referred to it as a play "sewn on a ballet."

Shortly after the F. Pistocchi family moved to Bologna this year his great progress in music was recognized and he was made a member of the Accademia dei Filarmonici before the publication of his "Cappricci puerile . . . sopra un basso d'un balletto."

A. Poglietti became organist to the court chapel in Vienna at this time and remained in the position until his death.

Thomas Purcell was lay-vicar of Westminster Abbey as well as copyist this year.

Johann Sebastiani at this time was appointed cantor to a

(cont.) cathedral at Königsberg.

Issac Staggins, the English musician, played at the coronation festivities this year at Westminster Hall.

Tenaglia's opera "Clearco" used Da Capo.

Giles Tomkins was appointed organist at Worcester Cathedral this year.

Wilson's professorship at Oxford terminated at this time.

W. Young this year was appointed court violinist as well as flutist.

Bertali's "Gli amori di Apollo con Clizia" was completed this year.

Cambert's "Ariane" was composed at this time.

A few tunes were ample for many sets of words, especially in John Eliot's versification for the Indians of this year. The title of the work was "Wame Ketoohomae Unketoohomaongash David."

La Guerre set a short collection of verses by various authors to music this year as well as an edition of the libretto (in quarto) of the opera "Le Triomphe de l'Amour sur des bergers et bergères."

"The Pleasant Companion, or New Lessons for the Flagelet," by Greeting, was published this year.

Some of S. Ives' instrumental works were included in "Musick's Recreation."

Locke's "Music for His Majesties Sagbutts and Cornets" was issued this year.

Edward Lowe this year published his "Short Directions for the Performance of Cathedral Service."

Lully's "Ballet de l'Impatience" was composed this year.

A.V. Michna's "The Music of the Holy Year" was published this year at Prague.

"Patrem rotulatum" #1 by Pekiel was completed this year.

An enlarged edition of Schütz' "Psalmen Davids . . ." was published this year at Dresden. Its original publication was in 1628 at Freiberg.

Schütz wrote the Passion according to St. Matthew at this time.

Somaize's "Grand Dictionnaire de Prétieuses" was published this year.

A year after the success of Cavalli's "Xerxes" in Parish the death of Cardinal Mazarin brought on a violent reaction against Italian music which the Cardinal had supported.

An Italian theatre was established on a permanent basis this year at Paris.

Cesti's "Dori, ovvero La schiava fedele" was produced this year at the Teatro dei Sorgenti in Florence as well as in many other parts of Italy.

Kerll's opera "Erinto" was produced at this time.

Tenaglia's opera "Clearco" was produced this year at Rome.

The coronation ceremonies this year included the first performance of "Zadok the priest" by H. Lawes.

Thomas Fuller, English author, died (born 1608).

John Milton lived at Petty France at least until this year.

John Dryden wrote his "Panegyric on the Restoration" dated this year and dedicated it to a restored monarchy.

Thomas Fuller's "History of the Worthies of England" appeared this year.

Jan Aleksander Gorczyn, Polish journalist, engraver and editor, this year founded the first Polish periodical, "Merkuriusz Polski."

Pieter Claesz, Dutch painter, died (born 1597).

(and 1662, 1663, 1669) References to the curtall in the Lord Chamberlain's Records appeared in these years.

(to 1663) Thomas Baltzar was Master of the King's band during these years.

(to 1664) Records available for this period showed the elder Purcell as living in a house occupied either by William Crance or by Captain Hickes.

(to 1674) Theodore Steffkins' (violinist) name appeared intermittently in the English court records during this period.

1661(cont.)

(and 1675) Among Giulio Cesare Arresti's works were cantatas for solo voice and three oratorios performed at private houses in Bologna during both these years.

(to 1676) David Standish during this period was organist at Peterborough Cathedral.

(to 1677) John Foster was organist at the Durham Cathedral at this time.

(to 1679) Charles Couperin was the organist at St. Gervais during these years.

(to 1681) August Kühnel was a member of the court chapel at Zeitz during this period.

(to 1681) Petzold lived in Leipzig during these years with one interruption in 1672.

(to 1756) French architecture: Versailles Palace (1903' long).

c.1661

Jean-Baptiste Anet, French violinist and composer, was born (died 1755, August 14).

1662

(January 1) At this time King Charles II had not only doubled his musical establishment, but almost doubled his choirman's salaries, raising them from 40 to 70 per annum. This obviously affected the Purcell family fortunes.

(January 21) E. Coleman on this date succeeded Lanier in the royal band.

(January 24) Marco Marazzoli, Italian singer, harpist and

(cont.) composer, died at Rome (date of death unknown).

(February 7) Cavalli's opera "Ercole amante" was produced at the Tuileries in Paris. The libretto was by Buti who had been Rossi's librettist for "Orfeo." Interludes were composed by Lully. The performance was in honor of the marriage of King Louis XIV but met with only indifferent success.

(February 7) Lully's "Hercule amoureux" produced on this date was actually identical with Cavalli's "Ercole amante" (See entry above).

(February 20) Charles Couperin married Marie Guérin on this date.

(February 23) Johann Crüger, German composer, died at Berlin (born 1598, April 9).

(March 13) Katherine Purcell (H. Purcell's sister) was baptised on this date and therefore must have been twenty-nine when she married rather than twenty-two as sometimes reported.

(May 3) John Banister, I on this date was appointed leader of the king's band.

(May 13) Henry Purcell the younger was hardly old enough to have been affected by the excitement at attending the arrival of Catharine of Broganza on this date.

(July 1) Simon Ives, English organist and composer, died at London (born 1600, July 20).

(August 8) Thomas Purcell was appointed, jointly with Pelham

1662(cont.)

Humfrey, Composer in Ordinary
for the Violins to His Majesty.
He shared the position at the
start with Pelham Humfrey.

(August 14) Dom Regio Cesti's
"Serenata" was produced at
Florence. The work for voices
and orchestra had passages
treated in the French style in
which a concertino consisting
of two violins and bass was de-
tached from the concerto grosso
in which the viols were foremost.

(September 10) Joseph Campra,
double-bass player, was baptised
at Aix (died 1744, March 31).

(September 26) Kerll's opera
"Antiopa giustificata" was produced on this date.

(October 21) Henry Lawes,
English composer, singer and
instrumentalist, died at London
(born 1596, January 5).

(October 22) J. Wilson on this
date was sworn in as a
Gentleman of the Chapel Royal.

(November 10) Thomas Purcell
was appointed to the Private
Music for lutes and voices.

(November 13) Juan de Padilla
was appointed chapel master at
the primatial cathedral of
Toledo, at an annual salary of
200 ducats.

(November 15) Henry Purcell,
the elder, shared an appointment as musician-in-ordinary for
lutes and voices with Angelo
Notari, the retroactive warrant
bearing this date was retroactive to 1660.

(November 15) Thomas Purcell

(cont.) received the outright
position of composer-in-ordinary
for the violins in place of
the deceased Henry Lawes.
Another source placed this as
November 29.

(November 18) Boretti's opera
"Zenobia" was performed on this
date at the Vienna court.

(February) The ecclesiastical
authorities released Cesti following the intervention of
Emperor Leopold I.

(March) Pękiel's "De
Resurrectione Domini" was performed on this date.

(March) "Missa Paschalis" by
Pękiel was heard at this time.

(May) Cesti's "La magnanimita
d'Alessandro" was produced at
this time at Innsbruck.

(October) Henry Lawes lived
next door to the Purcell's in
Westminster at this time.
After Lawes' death the house
was occupied by Mr. Swettenham.

André Cardinal Destouches, a
French composer who started his
career as a soldier, was born
(died 1749).

Andreas Düben, the elder, musician and composer, died at
Stockholm (born c.1590).

Mary Gibbons (née Kercher),
wife of Christopher, died and
was buried at Westminster Abbey
(birthdate unknown).

Christian Keimann, hymn writer,
died (born 1607).

Thomas Preston, II, English organist, was born (died 1730).

1662(cont.)

Anne-Renée Rébel, singer and
sister of Jean-Féry Rébel, was
born at Paris (died 1722). At
the age of eleven, she appeared
in court ballets and ultimately
became one of the finest singers
at court.

Vincenzo Albrici was appointed
"Capellmeister" to the Saxon
court at Dresden this year.

Henry Aldrich at this time became a student at Christ Church,
Oxford.

Cavalli was called to Paris for
the Peace of the Pyrenees. This
was where he produced "Ercole
amante."

Cirillo revised and added to
Cavalli's "Alessandro vincitor
di se stesso" and Ferrari's
"Principe giardiniere" when both
works were revived at the royal
palace this year.

H. Cooke at this time became assistant to the Corporation of
Musicians.

Robert Creighton held the Greek
professorship at Cambridge this
year.

William Davenant obtained a
patent for construction of the
Dorset Garden Theatre (See also
1639).

J.G. Ebeling was director of
music at the St. Nicholas Church
of Berlin at this time.

John Ferrabosco this year was
appointed organist at Ely
Cathedral.

Johann Jacob Froberger went to
London at this time and was

(cont.) robbed twice en route.

Thomas Greeting at this time was
made a musician in ordinary
(without fee) in the King's
private music.

William Lawes this year received
most favorable treatment in
Fuller's "Worthies of England."

Edward Lowe this year became
professor of music at Oxford.

A third member of the "Mudd"
family was organist this year
at Lincoln Cathedral.

Pepys, in describing Christmas
Day in the Chapel Royal this
year, remarked, "The sermon
done, a good anthem followed
with vialls, and the King came
down to receive the Sacrament."

Pierre Phalese celebrated the
jubilee of his entrance into
religion at this time.

From this date forward G.
Pitoni attended Pompeo Natale's
music school in Rome.

Up to this time Mr. and Mrs.
Playford, the elder, lived at
the Inner Temple, after which
she opened a boarding school and
they lived there.

From this time on the elder
Purcell, with his fellow
Gentlemen of the Chapel Royal,
found his economic plight somewhat easier due to a general
increase in all salaries, from
40 to 70 per annum.

Robert Tomkins was one of the
King's musicians this year.

A. Werckmeister entered the
Gymnasium at Quedlinburg at

at this time.

Aguilera's "Psalmos" in four volumes was issued this year at Saragossa.

John Banister contributed to this year's "Courtly Masquing Ayres" by Playford.

Bockshorn's "Raptus Proserpinae," a dramatic cantata, appeared at this time.

Bontempi's opera "Paride" was published this year at Dresden with both German and Italian words.

Stephen Bulkley this year compiled and printed a collection of words of anthems used at York.

"Celos aun del aire matan" by Calderón was completed this year.

Cambert's "Adonis" appeared at this time.

Cavalli's opera "Ercole Amante" was published this year at Paris.

A book of "Anthems to be sung . . . in the Cathedral Church of the Holy and Undivided Trinity in Dublin" by Clifford was printed this year.

Some of Coleman's instrumental compositions were included in "Courtly Masquing Ayres."

C.C. Dedekind's "Geistliche Erstlinge in einstimmigen Concerten gesetzt" was published this year by Seyfert in Dresden.

Dering's "Cantica Sacra" for

(cont.) two and three voices was published at this time in London.

John Forbes published at Aberdeen his "Cantus, Songs and Fancies, for Three, Four or Five Parts, both apt for Voices and Viols," this year. It was the first book of secular music ever printed in Scotland.

João Alvares Frovo (Frouvo)'s "Discursos sobre a perfeiçam de Diathesaron" was published at this time in Lisbon by A. Craesbeck.

John Gamble this year wrote the music to the songs in John Tatham's "Aqua Triumphalis."

A. Hammerschmidt's "Kirchen- und Tafel-Musik 1,2,3 Vocal und 4,5,6 instrumental-stimmen enthalten" completed this year contained twenty-two pieces.

Hidalgo this year wrote the music for Calderon's play "Siquis y Cupido, o sea Ni amor se libra de amor," as well as for a play by Juan Velez "Los celos hacen estrellas."

Jenkins' "The Lady Katherine Audley's Bells" first appeared in Playford's "Courtly Masquing Ayres."

The words to five anthems by Jewitt were included in "Anthems to be sung in the Cathedral Church of the Holy & United Trinity in Dublin."

Kircher's "Musurgia universalis . . . " was translated into German by Andreas Hirsch this year (Hall, Suabia) and contained valuable information on the nature of sound and the theory of composition.

1662(cont.)
W. Lawes' instrumental music was included in "Courtly Masquing Ayres."

Locke's "Courtly Masquing Ayres" "for violins (or viols) and thoroughbass" was published at this time by Playford.

The collection "Court Ayres" published by Playford this year brought together a repertory of over five-hundred dances. Practically every composer of the time was a contributor.

Ensemble suites of the middle baroque period included a collection by Schmelzer.

The first British standing army was established this year.

The "Halfway Covenant" of this year tried to infuse new life into an orthodoxy threatened by changing circumstances.

The newly established band of violins penetrated the Chapel Royal by playing "ritornelli."

Opera was introduced this year at the Catholic capital of Protestant Saxony.

Several Italian operas were performed in Paris from 1645 to this date.

Bontempi's opera, "Il Paride" was produced this year at Dresden and Venice.

Davenant's "Law against Lovers" was produced this year and contained some songs by Alphonso Marsh, I.

Richard Bentley, English linguist, was born (died 1742).

Pascal, French philosopher, died (birthdate unknown).

Queen Mary II, House of Stuart, was born (died 1694). She ruled jointly with King William III.

The Royal Society of London was incorporated this year by Charter of King Charles II.

Pöppelmann, German Baroque Architect, was born (died 1736).

Francisco de Zurbaran, Spanish painter, died (born 1598).

French painting: Philippe de Champaigne, "Mother Catherine Arnauld and Sister Catherine of St. Susanna" (65" x 90").

(to 1664) A Richard Browne was organist at Worcester Cathedral during this period.

(to 1667) Ercole Bernabei was chapel master at San Giovanni in Laterano during these years.

(to 1699) Devereux Clothier, an old drummer in ordinary of the royal household, was active at this time.

(to 1741) The town of Eisenach was the capital of a miniature duchy belonging to the estate of the Prince of Weimar during these many years.

c.1662
Henri Desmarets, French composer, was born at Paris (died 1741, September 7).

John Shore, English trumpeter and lutenist, was born at London (died 1752, November 20).

"The Old Troop, or Monsr. Raggou" by John Lacy was produced this

c.1662(cont.)
year. A "Mr. Morgan" wrote the music.

1663

(January 8) Lully's "Les Arts" was produced.

(January 27) Juan de Padilla was chapel master of Zamora Cathedral up to this date. He had started in the position on May 7, 1661.

(April 2) Johann Jullus Weiland, German conductor and composer, died (birthdate unknown).

(July 1) Franz Xavier Murschhauser, German theorist and composer, was baptised at Zabern (died 1738, January 6).

(July 2) King Charles II addressed the Vice-Chancellor of Oxford recommending Christopher Gibbons be admitted to the degree of Doctor of Music. . .

(July 2) Thomas Selle, German composer, died at Hamburg (born 1599, March 23). He was a predecessor to C.P.E. Bach at Hamburg.

(July 4) H. Purcell probably received more than the £ 30 Hingeston had received on this date and on other such occasions for attendance at Windsor in his official capacity as "Keeper of the Organs."

(July 8, 13) William Child was awarded the Doctor of Music degree by Oxford. His exercise was an anthem which was performed at St. Mary's Church on July 13.

(July 27) Thomas Baltzar's name appeared on the Register as

(cont.) "Mr. Thomas Balsart" one of the violins in the King's Service, July 27, 1663."

(August 7) W. Wake was sworn in as a Gentleman of the Chapel Royal on this date.

(August 20) William Gregory, English singer and composer, died at London (birthdate unknown).

(August 20) Old accounts bearing this date provided a general description of the workshop that was to be H. Purcell's as keeper and repairer of "His Majesty's organs."

(October 3) Lully's "Les Nopces de village" was produced.

(October 14) Lully's "L'Impromptu de Versailles" was produced at Versailles on this date, at the Palais Royal on November 4 and at the Louvre on January 29, 1664.

(November 19) Friedrich Wilhelm Zachau, German organist and composer, was born at Halle (died 1712, August 14). He was Handel's teacher.

(November 20) Pirro Albergati, Conte Capacelli, Italian amateur composer, was born at Bologna (died 1735, June 22).

(November 22) Pepys in his diary recorded his attendance at the Chapel Royal on this date.

(December 5) Severo Bonini, Italian composer and writer on music, died at Florence (born 1582).

(December 21) Evelyn in his diary mentioned his visit to the

1663(cont.)
Chapel Royal at this time.

(December 21) Henry Purcell on this date succeeded Signor Angelo as one of the King's Band of Music.

(August) Pepys was again in communication with Hunt, seeing first a "Viall" which he was considering purchasing.

(October) Andrea Adami di Bolsena, Italian musical scholar, was born at Bolsena (died 1742, July 22).

Correa de Arraujo, Spanish organ composer, died (birthdate unknown).

Thomas Baltzar, German violinist and composer, died probably at London (born c.1630).

Giovanni Lorenzo Gregori, Italian violinist and composer, was born at Lucca (died 1745, January).

Cotton Mather, occasional writer on music who observed that congregational singing had "degenerated into an odd noise," was born (died 1728).

Franz Xavier Anton Murschhauser, German theorist and composer, was born probably at Zabern (died 1738, January 6).

John Oker, English organist and composer, died (birthdate unknown).

Joseph Purcell, another brother of Henry Purcell's, was born (date of death unknown). This fact is not well-documented.

Heinrich Scheidemann, German

(cont.) organist and composer, died at Hamburg (born c.1596).

Bartolommeo Albrici this year resigned as organist at the Saxon court church at Dresden.

State Papers this year stated: "1663, Mr. Banister appointed to be chief of His Majesty's violins."

A document in the State Archives for the Tyrol at Innsbruck states that by this year Cesti had been in service as "maestro di cappella" to the Archduke Ferdinand of Austria for about twelve years.

Child's portrait, painted this year, was presented by him to the Music School at Oxford.

Clifford this year wrote that it was customary to sing four anthems on a Sunday "in fully appointed choirs."

In a list of the "Choralisten" of this year C.C. Dedekind's name appeared among the basses.

At the age of eight this year Denner moved with his family from Leipzig to Nürnberg.

Gustaf Düben, the elder, was organist of the German church at Stockholm at this time.

Du Mont became chapel master to the King this year.

Ebner was "Kapellmeister" at St. Stephen's from this date forward.

At the request of King Charles II, Christopher Gibbons was awarded the Doctor of Music degree at Oxford this year.

1663(cont.)

William Holder this year was awarded the degree of Doctor of Divinity and was elected F.R.S. He was active as a composer during his life.

Michel Lambert was music master of the children at the royal chapel at this time.

John Oker was awarded the degree of Bachelor of Music by Oxford this year.

Canon Rene Ouvrard, choirmaster of the Sainte-Chapelle in Paris, began working this year on a "guerre en musique" taken from the story of the Maccabees.

Cruciano Draghi Pergolese married Maddalena Cerquetta at this time and his eldest son, Francesco Andrea (born at Jesi on November 14, 1683) was G.B. Pergolesi the composer.

Johann Sebastiani this year became Kapellmeister at the electoral palace church, in Königsberg.

Clemens Thieme at this time went to the court of Zeitz on recommendation of Schütz and became successively Konzertmeister and director of the chapel.

M. Wise this year became Lay Clerk at St. George's Chapel, Windsor.

Gottfried Aich's "Fructus ecclesiastici, a 3,4,5 voc. 2 vel 3 instr. cum 2 choro" was published this year at Augsburg.

Giulio Cesare Arresti published two masses this year at Venice.

Arrigoni at this time published at Venice a book of psalms ("Salmi") which also contained a Magnificat.

John Banister's four songs for Katherine Philips' ("the matchless Orinda's") tragedy "Pompey" were composed this year.

Banister's career as a composer for the stage apparently started this year with the "instrumental, vocal and recitative musick" to Sir Robert Stapylton's comedy "The Slighted Maid."

Bertali's oratorio "Maria Magdalena" appeared at this time.

An indication of Blow's early promise was obvious with the inclusion of the words of three of his anthems this year in Clifford's "Divine Services and Anthems."

Cazzati published his "Risposta alle oppositioni . . . " at this time.

R. Cesti's motet "Beatus vir" was included in a collection published at Venice this year.

Clifford at this time published a collection of texts of anthems.

C.C. Dedekind's "Die doppelte Sangzälle worinnen XXIV. Davidische Psalmsprüche in einstimmiger Partitur nach allen Sachtmannischen und heutiger Capell-Manier enthalten" was published this year by Christian Kirchner at Leipzig.

Eccard's works appeared in

1663(cont.)

"Christlich . . . Gesangbuch"
published this year at Erfurt.

One of Eccard's melodies was
included this year in
"Passionale melicum. Martino
Jane" published at Görlitz.

A. Hammerschmidt's "XVII Missae
sacrae 5 ad 12 usque vocibus et
instrumentis" appeared at this
time. The masses included only
a Kyrie and a Gloria.

Knüpfer's "Lustige Madrigale" of
this year finally created a
demand for the German continuo
madrigal.

Lanier composed a New Year's
song this year.

Legrenzi published a sonata for
six instruments at Venice at
this time. He concurrently
wrote church sonatas.

Sir William Leighton's words for
an anthem were included this
year in Clifford's collection.

The words of an anthem by Henry
Molle were included in Clifford's
Collection.

"Montrose' March" was included
in "Musickes Hand-maide . . ."

Keyboard pieces by John Moss
were included in "Musicke's
Hand-maide . . ."

An anthem by "Mudd" was included
in Clifford's Collection.

"Musicke's Hand-maide Presenting
New and Pleasant Lessons for the
Virginals or Harpsycon" was pub-
lished at London this year by
"Honest John" Playford. The
work was printed from engraved

(cont.) copper plates.

Poglietti this year wrote "Aria
bizzara del rossignolo" according
to a respected source.

Several of Wigthorpe's songs were
included in Clifford's Collection.

The fifes and trumpets which had
provided the martial music of
the "Companies des mouquetaires"
in the French army were replaced
by hautbois and shortly afterwards the number was established
as four for each company.

The most important institutions
for the cultivation of music in
the reformed regions of
Switzerland during the 17th
Century were the Collegia
musica, the one in Berne was
started this year.

The first theatre at Drury Lane
was built by the "King's Company"
at this time.

Draghi's opera "Achille in
Sciro" was produced this year at
Vienna.

Locke's "Macbeth" was produced
at this time.

Davenant this year wrote
"Playhouse to be Let."

John Dryden's "The Rival Ladies"
and "The Wild Gallant" were
both completed at this time.

Sorel's novel "Fancion" was
published this year.

Abbé Pellegrin was born at
Marseilles (died 1745). He
came from a family of magistrates.

(to 1664) Wilson's anthem
"Hearken God" was included in

Clifford's "Services & Anthems"
at this time.

(and 1665) C.C. Dedekind's
"Davidische geheime Musik
-Kammer, darinnen XXX.
Psalmsprüche enthalten" was
published this year at Dresden
by Seyfert. Another edition
was published by Caspar Wächter
at Frankfort in 1665.

(to 1665) Thomas Fenell was a
singer in London at Westminster
Abbey during this period.

(to 1665) J. Playford, the
elder, carried on business with
Zachariah Watkins during these
years.

(to 1666) John Banister was
Master of the King's band during
this period.

(to 1666) Italian architecture:
Bernini, "Scala Regia" for the
Vatican (200' deep).

(to 1669) Johann Krieger was
pupil and assistant to the organist Johann Schröder in
Copenhagen at this time.

(to 1674) Provenzale during
these years was music teacher at
the Conservatorio Santa Maria
di Loreto at Naples.

c.1663
G.M. Pagliardi was maestro di
cappella to church of Gesù di
Genova, Rome at this time.

John Rogers, English lutenist,
died at London (birthdate unknown). He had been attached
to the household of King
Charles II and lived in London.

Dutch painting: Vermeer,

(cont.) "Woman at the Window."

1664
(January 29) Lully's "Le
Mariage forcé" was produced on
this date. Molière collaborated
in this work which had an overture and various dances, including some for Egyptians and
Spaniards. There was no attempt
to characterize these, but some
dances, "nervous" music, was provided for a scene in which a
musician conjured up demons.

(February 9) Cavalli's opera
"Scipione Africano" was produced
at the Teatro SS. Giovanni e
Paolo in Venice.

(February 15) Lully's "Les
Amours desguisés" was produced.

(March 3) Ralph Amner, English
singer, died at Windsor (birthdate unknown).

(March 15) Georg Oesterreich,
German composer, was born at
Magdeburg (died 1735, June 6).

(April 8) Ceremonies were held
on this date at Windsor to
solemnize the installation of
Prince George of Denmark as a
"knight companion of the Order
of the Garter." He had been
elected to the order at the
beginning of the year.

(April 8) Thomas Salmon was
admitted as a commoner of
Trinity College, Oxford.

(May 8) Lully's "Les Plaisirs
de l'isle enchantée" was produced.

(May 8) Lully's (and Molière's)
"La Princesse d'Élide" was produced in the open air on this
date. The work, a musical pastoral play with interludes (music

1664(cont.)

by Lully) and an "Air des Valets de Chiens et de Chasseurs avec des Ars de Chasse" with the horn figures in all probability played by strings.

(June 15) Bonifazio Graziani, Italian composer, died at Rome (born 1605).

(July 9) Charles Coleman, violist and composer, died at London prior to this date (birthdate unknown).

(August 3) Claude Jean Baptiste Boesset (Seigneur de Launay), French composer, was baptised (date of death unknown).

(August 4) Louis de Lully, a French composer, was born (died 1736).

(August 11) Henry Purcell, I, actor, composer, died at London according to some major sources (birthdate unknown).

(August 13) Henry Purcell, I was buried in the east cloister of Westminster Abbey.

(September 9) Johann Christoph Petz, German composer, was born at München (died 1716, September).

(October 5) The arched viol, a sostinente keyboard instrument, was seen by Pepys at a music meeting at the Post Office in London on this date.

(October 5) After the administration of the elder Purcell's estate on this date, the year ended with great mourning over his sudden demise.

(November 3) The work that H. Purcell was required to do as

(cont.) tuner and repairer of His Majesty's instruments was learned from Hingeston's old accounts such as one for this date that stated that he repaired the organs, harpsichords, pedals and other instruments.

(November 18) Bertali's operetta "Pazzo Amor" was composed for the birthday of Empress Eleonora.

(November 28) John Goodgroome became musician in Ordinary to the King on this date succeeding the late Henry Purcell.

(November 28) Angelo Notari, Italian composer, died (birthdate unknown).

(December 10) William King was appointed successor to Pickhaver as organist of New College.

(December 24) From the titles and benefits for this date Purcell's widow received thirteen shillings as the regular share for a "singing-man."

(December 24) A. Werckmeister on this date became organist at Hasselfelde, Brunswick.

(April) the Court prepared for its annual summer stay at Windsor, closing earlier than usual this year, according to Luttrell's entry for this date as well as various notices in London newspapers.

(August) Some time after this date, when the elder Purcell died, Christopher Gibbons moved into the building at Westminster.

Nicolas Bernier, French composer, was born at Mantes (died 1734, September 5).

Richard Browne, English organist
and composer, died at Worcester
(birthdate unknown).

Edward Finch, English ecclesiastic and composer, was born
(died 1738, February 14).

Pablo Nasarre, blind Spanish
organist and theorist, was born
(died 1724). He took Holy
Orders and later became organist
at Saragossa.

Germain Pinel, lutenist and possible son of Pierre, died
(birthdate unknown). According
to La Laurencie, a great number
of pieces attributed to his son
Francois were really by him.

Johann Christoph Schmidt,
German organist and composer,
was born at Hohenstein (died
1728, April 13).

Alstedt's "Elementale musicum"
was translated into English this
year by John Birchensha.

D'Anglebert this year succeeded
his master Chambonnieres as
clavecinist to King Louis XIV.

Christoph Bernhard was appointed
cantor at Hamburg this year.

John Blow's voice broke at this
time.

Donato Calvi this year referred
to M.C. Calegari as a famous
singer and composer.

Giovanni Pasta was mentioned by
P. Donato Calvis in his "Scena
letteraria de gli scrittori
bergamaschi" written this year.

Repairs to King Charles II's
"organs, pedalls, harpsichords
(cont.) & other instruments"
occurred as early as this year
in his "Privy Purse Expenses."

The well-known work of this year
by the Rev. James Clifford,
Minor Canon of St. Paul's gave
as the "Common Tunes" for chant-
ing the English Psalter, etc.,
correct versions of each of the
eight Gregorian tones for the
Psalms.

H. Cooke was in excellent voice
at this time.

Silvestro Durante was "maestro
di cappella" at the church of
"nella Consolazione" this year.

R. . . Florido (first name unknown), Italian bass and composer,
was at Giacomo degl' Incurabili
at this time.

Pelham Humfrey left the choir
this year and was sent abroad by
King Charles II to pursue his
studies.

Allusions to a "music room" were
found as late as this date in
Killigrew's "Parson's Wedding."

In collaboration with Molière,
Lulli this year began writing
"comédie-ballet" plays with
ballet "entrées" as interludes.

M. Neri was made court organist
of the Elector of Cologne at
this time.

Pasquini was organist to the
City of Rome at the Ara Coeli
from this date forward.

All trace of Séraphin Pinel was
lost by this year.

When he was five years old this
year young Purcell may have oc-

casionally gone to the Abbey or
to Whitehall with his father or
his uncle (Thomas).

Sebastian Scherer at this time
was second organist at the
Cathedral at Ulm.

Issac Staggins, English violinist
and oboeist, was given permission
this year to play outside the
court at His Majesty's Theatre.

Giovanni Battista Vacchelli at
this time was a member of the
Accademia della Morte of Modena
under the name of "Il
Naufragante."

M. Weckmann this year became
aquainted with Düken, the
Swedish chapel master.

Birchensha first became known
as the editor of a work this
year, "Templum Musicum: or the
Musical Synopsis of . . .
Alstedius" published at London.

Campian's treatise "A New Way
of making Fowre parts in
Counter-point . . . " was published this year with annotations by Christopher Simpson.
The title was "The Art of
Setting or Composing of Musick
in Parts by a most familiar and
easie Rule." An earlier edition appeared in 1655.

Clifford's "Collection" was published this year in a second
edition.

Dedekind's "Gottes stäte Liebe
. . . wegen der . . . Fru Annen
Sibyllen . . . des Herrn Paul
Hofmanns . . . Ehe-Liebsten
. . . 1664" appeared at this
time.

G. Dumanoir, I this year wrote
a pamphlet "Le Mariage de la
musique avec la danse."

John Geeres composed three
anthems this year.

The anthem written this year by
Gibbons for his admission to the
doctorate of music (at the Act
of 1664 in St. Mary's Church)
was included in the "Act-Music"
in the Bodleian Catalogue.

An anthem by Henry Hinde was
included in Clifford's "Divine
Services."

Five anthems by Humfrey were
included in Clifford's "Divine
Services."

Four of Jewett's anthems were
included in Clifford's Anthem
Book.

Robert King composed many songs
included this year in "Choice
Ayres, Songs and Dialogues."

Henry Lawes' words to several
of his anthems appeared in
Clifford's "Divine Services and
Anthems."

Legrenzi this year composed his
first opera "Achille in Sciro."

Edward Lowe published his second
edition of "Short Directions for
the Performance of Cathedral
Service" this year (See also
1661).

Molière and Lully's "Le Mariage
force" of this year was the
first of the "comédies-ballets"
which achieved their climax in
"Le Bourgeois gentilhomme" of
1670.

Lully's motet "Miserere" was

composed this year.

M. Neri's book of motets for two and three voices appeared at this time.

The Durham choirbooks of this year contained works by Henry Palmer.

Pękiel's "Missa" and "Patrem Rotulatum #2" both appeared at this time.

Porter's "Divine Hymns" of this year published by Playford may be identical with "The Psalms of George Sandys set to Music for two Voyces with a thorough -bass for the Organ" published c.1671.

Schmelzer's chamber music included "Sonatae unarum fidium" of this year.

Schütz' oratorio, "Historia der Freuden- und Gnaden-reichen Gehurt Gottes und Marien Sohnes, Jesu Christi . . ." was published this year at Dresden.

The only surviving music by the violinist Theodore Steffkins was a manuscript suite of this year for unaccompanied bass viol.

"Follias" were included this year in the "selva di varie Composizioni d'Intavolatura per cimbalo ed organo" by Bernard Storace.

Thomas Strutius, the organist at Danzig at this time, produced a setting of St. Matthew's text but the manuscript has not survived.

Records of Christ Church state

(cont.) that Tomkins' "Music De Sacra" was written this year.

Giovanni Battista Vacchelli wrote a "Motetti a voce sola" Book 1 Op 2 at this time.

Five editions of Voigtländer's "Oden und Lieder" had appeared by this date.

In the matter of whether or not the Corelli descended from Coriolanus, Zabarella, the author of a "Corelio" published at Padua this year, having to trace back the origins of the powerful house of Corer of Venice, connected it to the Corelli of Rome, for whom he contrived "descent in direct line through the Kings of Paphlagonia from Japhet, son of Noah."

The city of Erfurt was the object of heavy bombardment this year.

Vincenzo Amato produced the opera "Isaura" this year at Palermo.

Four of Cazzati's oratorios were sung this year at Bologna, "Il Caino condannato," "Celeste aiute a chi ben fà, non manca," "Il diluvio," "Il zelante difeso."

Dryden wrote his play "The Indian Queen" this year.

According to Nathaniel Hodges the plague in England broke out this year at the end of the summer in Westminster.

Karl Lichtenstein- Kastelkorn was elected Prince-Bishop of Olomouc (Moravia) at this time.

Francisco de Zurbarán, Spanish painter, died (born 1598).

Dutch painting: Frans Hals,
"Governors of the Old Men's
Almshouse."

Dutch painting: Frans Hals,
"Women Governors of the Old
Men's Almshouse" (67" x 98").
This is not the same picture as
the above entry.

(and 1665) C.C. Dedekind's
"Süsser Mandel-Kärnen erstes
und zweites Pfund von
ausgekärneten Salomonischen
Liebes-Worten in XV. Gesängen
mit Vohr- Zwischen- und Nach
-Spielen auf violinen
zubereitet" was published this
year at Dresden by Seyfert and
in another edition in 1665 by
Caspar Wächter at Frankfurt.

(to 1666) Heinrich Müller wrote
his "Geistliche Erquick-Stunden"
at this time.

(to 1667) Bartolommeo Albrici
went to England with his brother
Vincenzo during this period.
They jointly held the position
of composer to King Charles II.

(September 29 to 1667, September) John Hingeston, keeper and
repairer of His Majesty's organs
was paid £ III.4s.bd. for services during this period.

(to 1671) Lully entered into
collaboration with Molière and
during these years produced
many "comédies-ballets" including "Le Mariage Forcé," "La
Princesse d'Elide," "L'Amour
Médecin," "Le Sicilien," "Le
Ballet des Muses," "Le Grotte
de Versailles," "George Dandin,"
"Les Amans Magnifiques,"
"Monsieur de Pourceaugnac," "Le
Bourgeois Gentilhomme," and,
finally, "Psyché," written in

(cont.) collaboration with
Corneille and Quinault.

(to 1672) Denis Gaultier during
these years composed his collection of compositions entitled
"La Rhétorique des dieux . . ."

(to 1674) Bernhard was cantor
at Hamburg during this decade.

(to 1676) Racine's career spanned
these years.

(to 1678) Johann Kaspar Horn
this year published a large
number of allemandes, courantes,
etc. for viols, both with and
without wind instruments.

(to 1714, January 22) Louis
Hotteterre was a flutist at the
French court.

c.1664
Grzegorz Gerwazy Gorczycki,
Polish composer, was born (died
1734, April 30).

Johann Schop, German instrumentalist and composer, died
(birthdate unknown).

"Club Anthem" was the familiar
name by which an anthem composed
jointly by John Blow, Pelham
Humfrey and William Turner this
year was known. They were all
three choristers at the Chapel
Royal when they composed the
work.

Giovanni Legrenzi was maestro
di capella of the church of the
Spirito Santo at Ferrara at this
time.

Dutch painting: Vermeer, "The
Lace-Maker."

1665
(January 20) Domenico

1665(cont.)
Mazzocchi, Italian composer,
died at Rome (born 1592,
November 2).

(January 26) Cavalli's opera
"Mutio Scevola" was produced at
the Teatro San Salvatore in
Venice.

(January 26) Lully's "La
Naissance de Vénus" was produced.

(February 12) Wolfgang Ebner,
German organist and composer,
died at Vienna (born c.1610).

(March 20) Biagio Marini,
Italian violinist and composer
and possibly a pupil of
Monteverdi, died at Venice
(born c.1595 or c.1600 or 1597).

(March 31) Lewis Grabu was appointed composer to the King's
Musick in England.

(April 14) On this date the
English started the unpopular
war against the Dutch and by
the end of the month the plague
had claimed the first of its
victims in London.

(May 17) Quite possibly Humfrey,
Blow and John Blundeville had
been released from active duty
at the Chapel Royal by this
date because of the plague.

(May 28) Pepys, who went to the
Chapel Royal on this date, reported that he heard little music presumably because everyone
had left London because of the
plague.

(May 31) Robert Dallam, English
organ builder, died at Oxford
(born 1602).

(July 3) Werner Fabricius,

(cont.) German organist and composer, was married on this date.

(July 12) Pepys recorded on this
date that a solemn day of fast-
ing had been ordained for "this
Wednesday & the first Wednesday
of every month during the visitation" (of the plague).

(August 6) Jean-Baptiste de
Lully, French composer, was
born (died 1701, June 9).

(August 22) Rosa reported to
his friend Ricciardi that Cesti
planned to move himself and his
whole troop of singers to the
imperial court in Vienna under
most favorable terms.

(August 28) Johann Christian
Bach married Anna Margaretha
Schmidt, daughter of a town
musician.

(September 15) Lully's "L'Amour
médecin" was produced in five
days. Moliere provided the
text and Lully included a
chaconne for the solemn entry of
four doctors, a highly comical
touch.

(September 16) Pierre Thierry,
French organ builder, died at
Paris (born 1605).

(October 31) Pepys made an entry
concerning Mrs. Coleman's singing.

(November 12) Samuel (Friedrich)
Bockshorn, Bohemian composer,
died at Stuttgart (born 1628,
December 21).

(November 21) Pierre Jean
Burette, medical man and writer
on musical subjects, was born
at Paris (died 1747, May 19).

1665(cont.)

(June) By this date the number "visited" by the plague had increased to 470 a week.

(July) George Hudson joined John Banister's royal band of violins at this time.

Clamor Heinrich Abel, German violist, was born in Westphalia (date of death unknown).

Giuseppe (Antonio Vincenzo) Aldrovandini, Italian composer, was born at Bologna (died 1701, February 8).

Miguel Ambiela, Spanish secular priest and composer, was born at Aragon (died 1733, March 23).

John Bishop, English organist and composer, was born (died 1737, December 19).

Nikolaus Bruhns, North-German composer and organist, was born at Schwabstädt, Slesvig (died 1697). He was a pupil of Buxtehude.

Nicholas Laniere, masque composer and scenic designer, died (born 1588). See 1666, February.

Biagio Marini, Italian composer, died (born c.1595). See March 20.

Richard Mico, English composer who wrote both fantasies and pavans for the viols, died prior to this year (birthdate unknown).

Don Francisco Valls (Valle), Spanish composer and choirmaster at the Barcelona Cathedral, was born (died 1747 or 1745).

Filippo Acciaiuoli settled in

(cont.) Rome after this date.

Vincenzo Amato became "maestro di cappella" at Palermo Cathedral this year and retained the position until his death.

Johann Christian Bach settled at Eisenach prior to this date after he married.

Johann Christoph Bach (fourth generation) at this time became the organist at Eisenach.

Cavalli became first organist at St. Mark's this year.

Duponchel was "maestro di cappella" this year at the basilica of the Twelve Apostles in Rome.

Elizabeth Farnaby (possibly the former wife of Richard Farnaby) married Joseph Tison at Stepney this year.

Baldassare Ferri entered the service of Emperor Ferdinand III at this time.

From this time forward records showed that Christopher Gibbons occupied the house in Great Almonry South in which the Purcells had lived up to the time of the death of Purcell the elder.

Lewis Grabu, French composer, moved to England this year.

August Kühnel visited France this year to acquaint himself with the art of French viola da gamba players.

George Loosemore was awarded the degree of Bachelor of Music by Cambridge this year.

1665(cont.)

John Loosemore built the organ at Exeter Cathedral at this time.

G.M. Pagliardi this year was "maestro di cappella" to the church of Santi Apollinare at Rome.

C. Pollarolo this year became a chorister at St. Mark's in Venice.

Printz was appointed cantor at Sorau at this time.

After the elder Purcell's death his wife Elizabeth must have moved to Tothill Street South, her address for the poor-rates from this time to her death.

Schmelyer accompanied the Emperor to Innsbruck this year.

Laurentius von Schnüffis entered a religious order and some time after this year was made a poet laureate by Emperor Leopold I.

J.G. Stanley was a member of the Duke of Slesvig's court band at this time.

Nicolaus Adam Strungk this year joined the court chapel of Elector Johann Friedrich of Hanover.

Pavel Josef Vejvanovský, bohemian trumpeter and composer, this year completed his musical studies in Vienna, probably under Schmelger, and joined the chapel of the Prince-Bishop K Lichtenstein-Kastellkorn at Kroměříz.

The "Lyra Viol" by W. Addison appeared this year.

Saint Aelred wrote "De abusu musices" published this year at Paris in the "Bibliotheca Concinatoria."

Giulio Cesare Arresti this year published twelve sonatas for two violins and cello.

Bertali's "Alcindo" (with a prologue by Draghi) was completed this year.

Bernhard's "Geistliche Harmonica" was published this year at Dresden.

Bertali's oratorio "La Strage degl' innocenti" appeared at this time.

Except for fragments of "Pomone" and "Les Peines et les plaisirs de l'amour," the only music by Cambert that has survived is a collection of "Airs à boire" for two and three voices (published this year) and a "Trio italien burlesque."

"The Dancing Master" was published this year, containing "The Dragoons March."

C.C. Dedekind's "Aelbanians wertester Hirtenknabe Filareto" was published this year at Dresden.

C.C. Dedekind's "Darinnen 175 der besten Dicht-Meistern anmuthige Zucht-und Tugend -Lieder unter anständige Arien gelegt" was published this year by George Heinrich Froman at Leipzig.

C.C. Dedekind's "Davidisches Harfen-Spiel d. i . der ganze Psalter, in neue Lieder, nach denen evangelischen Kirchenmelodien abgefasst, und

1665(cont.)

mit eigenen wohlklingenden
Gesangweisen versehen" was pub-
lished this year by Caspar
Wächter at Frankfort.

C.C. Dedekind's "J. Katzens
Aeltern-Spiegel aus desselben
Holländischem gehoochdeutschet
durch C.C.D. 1654" was published this year. (See also
1654, 1658).

Duponchel's "Psalmi vespertini
una cum Latiniis B.M.V." was
issued at this time in Rome.

Edward Elys' "Dia Poemata" was
published this year.

Agostino Filippucci this year
published a mass, five psalms
and a Magnificat, opus 1, all
in five parts with instruments.

Kindermann's chief work "Harmonia
organica in tabulaturam
Germanicam composita . . ." was
reprinted this year.

Lanier composed a New Year's
song at this time.

Legrenzi this year composed the
opera "Zenobia e Radamisto."

P.G. Schott's "Schola
steganographia" was written
this year.

Heinrich Schütz' "Christmas
Oratorio" was composed at this
time.

Schütz' "The Passion According
to St. Matthew" appeared this
year.

Christopher Simpson's "The
Principles of Practicle Musick"
was published this year at
London.

A second edition of Simpson's
"The Division Violist" was published at this time at London.

Jean-Jacques Souhaitty's
"Nouvelle Méthode pour apprendre
le plain-chant et la musique"
was published this year.

The influence of the plague upon
the Church was made obvious from
an entry this year in the
Westminster Abbey Precentor's
Book,"In the year 1665 by reason
of God's visitation by the
plague of pestilence, no wax
lights or tallow candles were
used in the church but the service was daily performed by
daylight . . . ."

Giovanni Giacomo Arrigoni's
opera "Gli amori di Alessandro
e di Rossane" was dedicated to
Emperor Leopold I and was produced probably at this time in
Vienna.

Cazzati's oratorio "Il transito
di S. Giuseppe" was sung this
year at Bologna.

The opera "Il principe generoso"
was produced this year at the
imperial court in Vienna. It
was by Remigio Cesti, not by
Pietro Antonio, as had previously
been supposed.

Antonio Draghi's "Alcindo" and
"Cloridia" were both produced
at this time in Vienna.

Kerll's opera "L'amor della
patria superiore al ogn' altro"
was produced this year.

A production of Lully's "Petit
Ballet de Fontainebleau" occurred at this time.

Giulio Riva's "Adelaida regia

404

1665(cont.)
principessa di Susa" was produced this year at Munich.

Lady Grizel Baillie, author
and/or poetess, was born (died
1746).

La Rochefoucauld's "Maximes"
was published at this time.

Queen Anne, House of Stuart,
was born (died 1714).

Nicolas Poussin, French painter,
died (born 1594). His style was
highly intellectual with color
subordinated to the drawing
line. He spent most of his life
in Rome.

Pieter Jansz Saenredam, French
painter, died (born 1597).

(to 1666) Heinrich Schütz wrote
the "Historia des Leidens und
Sterbens unseres Herrn und
Hey Landes Jesu Christi" and
Passions after the German versions of Matthew, Luke and John
during this period.

(to 1669) Dutch painting: Van
Ruisdael, "The Mill Near Wijk
Bij Duurste De."

(to 1670) Chardin showed that
the Indian "víná" was in use
in Persia as the kingira during
these years. Its use elsewhere
was referred to by Al-Jáhiz
(d.896) and by Al-Jurjání
(c.1375), although in the works
of the former it was called
(probably erroneously)
"kinkila." Chardin also asserted
that the systematist theory of
Safí al-Dín, as discussed by
Abu'l-Uafa'b. Sa'íd was still
in use at this time.

(to 1673) Johann Wolfgang Franck

(cont.) was employed during
these years at the court of the
Margrave of Ansbach, both as
court musician and as "Kammer
-Registratur-Adjunkt."

(to 1675) Spanish painting:
Murillo, "Girl with her Duèna."

(to 1676) Thomas Fenell was a
violinist in the King's Band
of Music during this period.

(to 1690) Angelo Grancino built
violins during these years.
His business was carried on by
his son and grandsons.

(to 1694) Pavel Josef
Vejvanovsky during these years
worked at the chapel of the
Prince-Bishop K. Lichtenstein
-Kastellkorn at Kroměříž, first
as a field-trumpeter, and later
taking over the leadership of
the chapel after Biber's departure. He also directed the
choir at St. Mauritius collegiate church until his death.

(to 1700) The reign of King
Charles II over Spain.

c.1665
Giuseppe Antonio Vincenzo
Aldovrandini, Italian composer,
was born at Bologna (date of
death unknown).

Damian, Polish composer, was
born (died 1729, April 18).

Johann Caspar Ferdinand Fischer,
German composer, was born (died
1746, March 27). Forkel placed
his dates as c.1660 to c.1738.

Carlo Luigi Pietro Grua,
Italian composer, was born at
Florence (date of death un-
known).

c.1665(cont.)

Pietro Torri, Italian organist and composer, was born at Peschiera, Verona (died 1737, July 6).

Tommaso Antonio Vitali, composer and violinist and son of Giovanni Battista Vitali, was born at Bologna (died c.1740 or c.1747).

A paper on Birchensha's "Grand Scale" with his exposition of the same was preserved in the British Museum.

Dutch painting: Rembrandt, "The Jewish Bride."

Dutch painting: Vermeer, "Girl with a Turban," "The Lacemaker" (oil on canvas 9 1/2" x 8 1/4"), "The Studio."

(to 1670) Dutch painting: Vermeer, "The Artist in His Studio"(52" by 44").

1666

(January 9) Lully's "Le Triomphe de Bacchus dans les Indes" was produced.

(January 16) Antonio Sartorio's opera "Seleuco" was produced at the Teatro San Salvatore.

(January 26) Johann Andreas Herbst, German theorist and composer, died at Frankfort (born 1588).

(February 13) Cesti's "Tito" was produced at the Teatro dei SS. Giovanni e Paolo in Venice.

(February 20) Cavalli's opera "Pompeo Magno" was produced at the Teatro San Salvatore in Venice.

(April 25) Johann Heinrich Buttstett (Buttstädt), German organist and composer, was born at Bindersleben near Erfurt (died 1727, December 1).

(May 6) Paul Siefert, German organist and composer, died at Danzig (born 1586).

(May 25) Issac Staggins, the violinist and oboist, was at this time a member of the "twenty-four violins" appointed to serve under John Bannister. In this date he received an additional appointment as tenor oboist.

(May 28) T. Purcell supplicated for arrears of payment.

(June 2) Paris Francesco Alghisi, Italian composer, was born at Brescia (died 1743, March 29).

(June 13) Johann Jakot Heidegger, Swiss operatic manager and librettist, was born at Zurich (died 1749, September 4).

(June 30) Adam Krieger, German composer, died at Dresden (born 1634, January 7). He was a poet as well as composer.

(July 8) Heinrich Lorenz Hurlebusch, German organist and composer and father of Conrad, was born at Hanover (date of death unknown).

(July 12) Cesti's "Nettuno e Flora festegglanti" was produced at Vienna.

(July 25) The naval victory of the British occurred on "St. James, his Day." James, Duke of York, was credited with the victory.

(August 6) A definition of

1666(cont.)
"tone" appeared in Pepys' Diary.

(August 20) "Le Jaloux invisible," a three-act comedy by Guillaume Marcoureau de Brécourt, was performed at Paris at the Hôtel de Bourgogne.

(September 2) During the night before this the Great Fire broke out in Pudding Lane, London. St. Paul's Cathedral was destroyed.

(October 10) London citizens held a feast day on this date to celebrate the end of the Great Fire and a happier atmosphere spread over England.

(October 16) Jan Cocx succeeded Gaspard Boest as master of the children and musical director at Antwerp Cathedral.

(October 18) On this date Evelyn reported that King Charles II had adopted the new "unfrenchified" dress he referred to as "Persian."

(November 5) Attilio Ariosti, Italian violinist and composer, was born at Bologna (died c.1740).

(November 15) For a special birthday treat for Queen Catherine on this date the King preferred her over his "misses."

(November 20) London citizens observed a general thanksgiving on this date for the end of the plague.

(November 25) Giuseppe Guarneri, Italian violin maker, was born at Cremona (died c.1740).

(December 2) Lully's "Les Muses"

(cont.) was produced.

(December 5) Francesco Scarlatti, violinist and composer, was born at Palermo (died c.1741).

(January) Francesco Della Porta, Italian organist and composer, died at Milan (born c.1590).

(February) Nicholas Lanier, singer, composer and painter, died at London (born 1588).

(November) Louis Grabu was appointed Master of the Queen's music.

Georg Bronner, German composer, was born at Holsatia (died 1724).

Alphonse d'Ève, Flemish composer, was born at Brussels (died 1727).

Jean-Noël Marchand, French lutenist and brother of Jean-Baptist, was born at Paris (died 1710, May 31).

Francesco della Porta, organist and church composer, died (born c.1590). See January.

Benjamin Schütz, younger brother of Heinrich, died (born 1596).

James Shirley, masque writer, died (born 1596).

Henry Aldrich was awarded the degree of Bachelor of Arts this year.

Benedictus a San Josepho referred to himself at this time as "Frater ordinis F.F. beatiss. Virg. Mariae de Monte Carmelo."

Bontempi this year was appointed "Kapellmeister" as coadjutor to

1666(cont.)

Schütz, but then gave up this position after a year and devoted himself to architecture, science, etc.

Bryne became organist of Westminster at this time.

William Bull was appointed Trumpeter Extraordinary to King Charles II this year.

Cambert at this time was appointed superintendent of music to dowager Queen, Anne of Austria.

The Accademia dei Filarmonici was founded this year at Bologna by Count Vincenzo Maria Carrati. This institution absorbed all the earlier academies and rose to great fame.

Marc' Antonio Cesti went to Vienna this year for "Pomo d'Oro."

From Crescimbeni, his colleague at the Accademia dei Arcadi, it was ascertained that Corelli began his violin studies at Bologna this year when he was thirteen years old.

Abraham Couchet became a member of the St. Lucas Guild this year.

Jozef Couchet became master of the St. Lucas Guild at this time.

S. Eccles' generally vague attitude at this time implied a deranged intellect.

Louis Grabu, a Frenchman, was this year appointed Master of the King's Music, the highest official musical post in

(cont.) England. He succeeded John Banister.

Lewis Gruber became master of English Chamber Musick at this time, succeeding Lanier.

Thomas Harris of New Sarum this year agreed to build an organ for Worcester Cathedral.

Jacob Hintze at this time became court musician to the Elector of Brandenburg at Berlin.

Nicolas Hotteterre probably entered the royal music as oboist this year. There remains a possibility, however, that the appointment was a year later.

During his absence at this time Humfrey was appointed royal lutenist.

Jewett was appointed organist, master to the Choristers and lay-vicar of Winchester Cathedral this year.

King Louis XIV at this date founded the Academie de France.

Antonio Stradivari was making violins this year in which he affixed his own labels.

Giovanni Vitali this year became "sonatore" or "musico di violone da brazzo" at the church of San Petronio at Bologna.

Abbatini's opera "Ione" was published this year at Vienna.

Leone Allacci's "Drammaturgia," a catalogue of Italian musical dramas produced up to this time, was and is indispensable in the study of the history of Italian opera. The work was published at Rome.

Bertali's "Cibele ed Atti" appeared at this time.

The Philidor Collection (Vol.
VI) contained some of Boesset's
airs for the "Triomphes de
Bacchus" of this year.

G.M. Bononcini's Op. 1 "I primi
frutti del giardino musicale,"
for two violins and continuo,"
was published this year at
Venice.

Cavalli's "Pompeo" was completed
at this time.

C.C. Dedekind's "Belebte oder
Ruchbare Myrrhen-Blätter das
sind zweistimmig beseelte
heilige Leidens-Lieder" was published this year by Seyfert at
Dresden.

A second edition of Forbes'
"Cantus, Songs and Fancies, for
Three, Four, or Five Parts, both
apt for Voices and Viols" was
published at this time at
Aberdeen. It was published
again in 1682.

An anonymous opera "Il Germondo"
was published this year.

Jacob Hintze this year edited
the twelfth edition of Crüger's
"Praxis pietatis" and added to
it sixty-five hymns to the
Epistles by himself. "Giet
dich zufrieden" and "Alle
Menschen müssen sterben" have
achieved the greatest success.

King John IV's "Defensa de la
música moderna" was translated
into Italian this year and published at Venice.

Cesare de Judice wrote a
"Requiem" at this time on the

(cont.) death of King Philip IV.

"Lashley's March" was included
in "Musick's Delight on the
Cithern."

M. Locke's "Musick's Delight on
the Cithern" was published this
year.

Schütz' three Passions according
to St. Mathew, St. Mark and St.
John were all completed by this
time.

G.B. Vitali's earliest work as
a pupil of Maurizio Cazzati
(for counterpoint), "Correnti e
balletti da camera a due violini
col suo basso continuo per
spinetta o violone da G.B.
Vitali" opus 1, was published
this year.

King Charles II resolved this
year that he would install
French music at the English
court.

Canon René Ouvrard was dismayed
this year when the French King,
at Lulli's instigation, dis-
banded his troupe of Italian
singers.

One of the lieder reappeared
this year as a procession-song
at the Feast of the Ascension.

St. Paul's in London had one of
the organs that escaped destruction or removal as a result of
Parliament's ordinance against
monuments of idolatry and superstition, however, it was a
victim of the great fire at this
time.

Boretti's "Zenobia" was revived
this year at Venice.

Cesti's Pomo d'Oro was performed

1666(cont.)
in Vienna at this time.

C. Pallavicino's opera
"Demetrio" ("Aureliano"), with
libretto by Giacomo Dell'Angelo
was produced this year at the
Teatro San Moisé in Venice.

John Bunyan's "Grace Abounding
to the Chief of Sinners" was
written this year.

John Dryden's "Annos Mirabilis"
appeared at this time.

Major events marked this year in
England. Newton published his
law of gravitation, a plague
continued, and the war with the
Dutch turned badly for the
English.

Czar Ivan V of Russia was born
(died 1696).

Guercino, an Italian painter,
died (born 1591).

Franz Hals, Dutch portrait
painter, died (born c.1580).

François Mansart, French architect, died (born 1598).

Vanbrugh, English architect,
was born (died 1726).

English architecture: Sir
Christopher Wren, city play for
the rebuilding of London.

(to 1667 and 1669) J.G. Ebeling
published "Pauli Gerhardi
geistliche Andachten, bestehend
in 120 Liedern mit 4 Singstimmen,
2 Violinen und Generalbass" at
Berlin at this time. A reduc-
tion of the work into two parts
appeared in 1669.

(to 1669) Marcantonio Cesti

(cont.) held the position of
assistant conductor at the
Imperial Court of Vienna during
these years.

(to 1670) Corelli was at Bologna
during this period after which
all trace of him is lost for
some time.

(to 1672) Louis Grabu was
Master of the King's Band during
these years.

(to 1675) Antonio Sartorio, the
composer, was Kapellmeister at
the court of Hanover during this
period.

(to c.1676) C.C. Dedekind was
"Konzertmeister" at the Dresden
court chapel for this decade.

(to 1678) From 1666 to the year
of his death (1678) G.M.
Bononcini published a quite considerable amount of both instrumental and vocal music.

(to 1680) Stradivari made his
violin, "Sellière" sometime
during these years.

(to 1737) During this period
Antonio Stradivari made 1,116
instruments including 540 violins, 12 violas, 50 violoncellos
and possibly over 100 more.

c.1666
Buns' earliest work, a collection of masses, litanies and
motets in four, five and six
parts with instrumental accompaniment, was published at this
time by Phalèse at Antwerp.

(to c.1681) The French flageolet,
a primitive form of recorder,
enjoyed some popularity in
England during this period until
the actual recorder replaced it.

(January 5) Lully's "Pastorale comique" was produced.

(January 24) Bertali's "La contesa dell' aria e dell' acqua" (a ballet on horseback) appeared.

(January 29) Hingeston's accounts for this date asserted that he was paid for repairing the organs at Hampton Court, St. James, and Whitehall. This indicated Purcell's duties as keeper and repairer of His Majesty's organs. Conceivably this date could have been one year later to the day.

(January 30) Kerll's opera "Atlanta" was produced.

(February 5) Johann Gottfried Reiche, German trumpeter, was born at Weissenfels (died 1734, October 6).

(February 10) Lully's "Pastorale comique" was produced again on this date (See January 5).

(February 10) Lully's "Le Sicilien, ou l'Amour peintre" was produced.

(February 12) The earliest mention of G.B. Draghi was found in Pepys' Diary entry for this date.

(February 20) Pepys in his Diary in the entry for this date stated: "They talk how the King's violin, Banister, is mad that a Frenchman is come to be chief of some part of the King's musique."

(March 14) By this date Banister's disgrace was completed by an order from the Lord Chamberlain which gave Grabu his

(cont.) position as leader of the select band of twelve violins.

(April 12) Johann Ambrosius Bach was appointed a member of the Erfurt "compagnie" of musicians under his uncle Johannes.

(May 7) Johann Jacob Froberger, German organist, harpsichordist and composer, died at Héricourt, near Montbéliard (born 1616, May 19).

(May 28) Melchior Schild, German organist and composer, died at Hanover (born 1593).

(June 9) Cesti's "Semiramide" was produced at Vienna and later revived in 1674 as "La schiava fortunata."

(July 12) Cesti's "La Germania esultante" was produced at Vienna, Favorita.

(July 16) A. Werckmeister's first marriage occurred on this date.

(July 28) Young Purcell on this date probably heard the "strange, bold sermon of Dr. Creeton" in the Chapel Royal.

(August 3) Evelyn made reference to Birchensha at this time.

(August 21) Pepys' Diary for this date stated that Blow "with a fellow-chorister named Loggings came to sing with his boy, Tom Edwards, and in spite of their evident musical skill made very unpleasant sounds with their broken voices."

(August 31) Johann Rist, German poet and composer, died at Webel a/Elbe (born 1607, March

8).

(September 23) Jean-Louis de Lully, French composer, was born (died 1688, December 28).

(October 1) Louis Grabu produced an "English Song upon Peace" at the court of King Charles II.

(October 1) Several favorable developments culminated in an excellent concert at Whitehall given on this date.

(October 26) Humfrey was back in England and on this date was sworn as a Gentleman of the Chapel Royal.

(November 1) Pepys on this date referred to a certain anthem as "a good piece of musique," but then criticized it with the statement, "but still I cannot call the Anthem anything but instrumental musique with the voice, for nothing is made of the words at all."

(November 5) Franz Tunder, German organist and composer, died at Lübeck (born 1614). The majority, but not all of the sources agree on this year.

(November 6) Kerll's opera "Le prentensioni del sole" was produced.

(November 7) Davenant's and Dryden's version of "the Tempest" with incidental music by Humfrey and Banister opened at the first Duke's theatre.

(November 15) By this date Pepys' distaste for Humfrey had grown to an active dislike, principally due to the latter's complete lack of respect for

(cont.) the Establishment and particularly for his denigration of Grabu. Pepys' entry in his diary on this date read, "'little Pelham Humphreys (Humfrey) lately returned from France,' his coxcombry and his musical frecocity, has become famous by frequent quotation."

(December 4) Michel (Pinolet) de Montéclair, French composer, was baptised at Andelot Haute-Marne (died 1737, September 27).

(April) This year when he was approaching his eighth birthday Purcell possibly took part as a chorister in the gala ceremonies for the Order of the Garter. The celebration was held on the anniversary of King Charles II's coronation.

(August) London was excited with the news of the fall of Clarendon on this date and with the establishment of the Cabal which was important in furthering the cause of Catholicism in England for the next few years.

(September) Francesco Manelli, Italian singer and composer, died at Parma (born 1595).

(October) Young Pelham Humfrey returned from France at this time.

Jean Claude Gillier, French composer, was born at Paris (died 1737, May 30).

Louise Henriette of Brandenburg, a hymn-writer, died (born 1627).

Antonio Lotti, Venetian opera composer, teacher of Galuppi and ultimately conductor at San Marco, was born (died 1740,

January 5).

Biagio Marini, Italian composer
and probably a pupil of the composer Fontana, died according to
a major source (born 1597).

Cardinal Pietro Ottoboni, an
Italian composer, was born (died
1740).

John Christopher Pepusch,
German composer, was born at
Berlin (died 1752, July 20).
He lived in England for many
years where he arranged melodies
for Gay's "Beggar's opera."

Johann Christoph Bach this year
married Maria Elisabeth
Wedemann, daughter of the town
clerk at Arnstadt.

Banister's loss of status and
salary at Court this year un-
doubtedly influenced his decision
to perform a regular series of
concerts at Whitehall in 1672.

Antonio de Belem, Portuguese
composer, was made prior of his
order at this time.

Caproli, with G.E. Barnabei,
was at this time appointed co
-chapel master of the French
church at Rome, San Luigi dei
Francesi.

Caresana became organist at the
royal chapel of Naples this
year.

Cesti in his ensembles used
alternate singing as seen in
his trio from "Semiramide"
written at this time.

A comic aria from "Le Disgrazie"
of this year showed a typical
motto beginning and also the

(cont.) lively and precise
rhythms of Cesti's comic and
popular style.

Jacques Cordier's name was included this year on the list of
the deceased French queen's
officers.

G.B. Draghi arrived in England
at this time.

Thomas Greeting, flageolet
player and teacher, was teaching
at London this year.

Hawkins quoted an advertisement,
dated this year, for two "chests
of viols" for sale, one made by
John Rose in 1598, the other by
Henry Smith in 1633.

From this date forward
Alessandro Melani was maestro
di cappella at Santa Maria
Maggiore, Rome.

Nivers this year became organist
to the King and music master of
the Queen in Paris.

Ouvrard this year completed his
work on a "guerre en musique"
taken from the story of the
Maccabees.

F. Pinel at this time succeeded
Claude Tissu as "ordinaire de
la musique de la chambre du roi
pour le théorbe."

A Count von Tattenbach in all
probability an emissary from the
court of Bavaria heard Agostino
Steffani as a boy singer at St.
Mark's in Venice this year. He
was pleased by his voice and
intelligence and took him to
Munich.

Antonio Stradivarius married
Francesca Feraboschi at this

time.

Nicholas Stratford, later to be Bishop of Chester, went to Manchester this year as warden and revitalised the music at the Church of St. Mary.

Vacchelli was maestro di cappella at Pesaro at this time.

A "C. Venturini" was engaged this year as a bass singer at the court of Hanover.

Vitali was a member of the Bologna Accademia de' Filaschisi and Accademia de' Filarmonici from this time forward.

M. Weckmann this year presented three of his works to Elector Johann Georg II.

Le Bègue's "Livre d'Orgue" appeared at this time.

Benserade's ballet "Les Muses" was completed this year.

Boesset at this time composed "Paroles de musique pour le concert de chambre de la musique de la reine."

Bononcini's opus 2 "Sonate da camera e da ballo" for two violins and continuo of this year survived in an unpublished manuscript at Modena.

Boretti composed his opera "Alessandro amante" at this time.

Cesti's "Il Pomo d'Oro" was written at this time for production at Vienna.

"Des Durchleuchtig Hochgebohrnen Fürsten, Herrn

(cont.) Friedrich Wilhelms, des jungern Herzogs zu Sachsen eilften Gebuhrts-Tag, 1667, mit einem Singe-Spiele . . . von C.C. Dedekinden, K.g.P. und K.S.C." was published in quarto at Dresden.

Dionigi in 1648 published a treatise on the "cantus firmus," "Li primi tuoni ovvero introduzione nel canto fermo." It appeared this year in an enlarged edition.

S. Eccles this year published his "A Musick-Lector, or, The Art of Musick . . . "

In Hilton's "Catch that Catch Can," published this year by Playford, a catch appeared instead of an Epitaph on Ralph Amner of Windsor, known as the Bull Speaker. The music was composed by Dr. William Child. This edition of the Hilton work had extensive additions and the second title of "The Musical Companion" as well as a second part containing "Dialogues, Glees, Ayres & Ballads," etc.

This year's edition of Hilton's "Catch as Catch Can" contained a piece by de Hodemont.

"Neue Arien" (New Airs) was published this year by Adam Krieger of Dresden. Another edition was issued in 1676.

Some of Lanier's songs were included in "The Musical Companion."

Zygmunt Lauxmin this year published his treatise entitled "Ars et praxis musicae" at Wilno.

Legrenzi composed masses and psalms at this time.

Lully's "Ballet de Flore" appeared this year.

Pistocchi at this time issued his "Cappricci puerile . . . sopra un basso d'un balletto."

Placker this year published at Antwerp a collection of the words of Flemish sacred songs, "Evangelische Leeuwerck ofte."

The three-part song, "Sweet tyranness, I now resign my heart," included in Playford's "Musical Companion" of this year was probably by Purcell.

Esajas Reusner's imaginative suites "Deliciae testudinis" composed at this time often started with a stylized prelude or sonatina.

Rosenmüller's "Sonate da camera" appeared this year.

Christopher Simpson's "Compendium" was published at this time as an enlarged edition of his "The Principles of Practicle Musick."

Jean-Jacques Souhaitty's "Nouveaux Éléments du chant . . ." was published this year.

Marco Uccellini's "Sinfonici concerti, brievie facili" was published at this time.

Giovanni Battista Vacchelli this year wrote his "Sacri concerti."

Vitali's "Balletti, correnti alla Francese, gagliarde e brando per ballare. Balletti,

(cont.) correnti e sinfonie da camera a quatro stromenti" was published this year by Giacomo Monti at Bologna.

Vitali wrote his sonatas, opus 2, at this time, "Sonate a due violini col suo basso per l'organo di G.B.V. Musico di Violone da Brazzo . . . & accademico filachese," and they were published by Monti at Bologna.

G.B. Vitali published trio sonatas this year which actually more or less established the sonata da chiesa form.

Wilson's music was included in Playford's "The Musical Companion."

Some of M. Wise's works were included in "The Musical Companion."

The original fount of music type cut by Peter Walpergen for Dr. Fell was used in the "Yattendon Hymnal published this year. Some sources, however, claim it was issued in 1683.

Musicians were placed in their modern position in front of the stage by Davenant for Dryden's adaptation of "The Tempest" this year.

"Follias" were included in the "arie per il balletto a cavallo" by Schmelzer at this time.

By the end of this year the French vogue had reached its peak.

Cazzati's oratorio "Sisara" was sung this year at Bologna.

1667(cont.)

No less than four new works by Cesti were heard in Vienna during this season.

Cesti's "Le disgrazie d'amore" was produced this year at Vienna.

"Il Pomo D'oro," an opera in five acts with prologue, by Cesti and libretto by F. Sbarra was produced at this time in Vienna. The work was performed at the wedding of Emperor Leopold I.

"Secret Love, or The Maiden Queen" by Dryden was produced this year. "Mr. Morgan" wrote the music.

The plague and fire in London caused temporary suspension of theatrical production, however, a production of Davenant and Dryden's adaption of Shakespeare's "Tempest" started the re-opening of the theaters.

C. Pallavicino's opera "Il tiranno umiliato dall'amore, overo Il Meraspe" with libretto by G. Faustini was produced this year at the Teatro dei S.S. Giovanni e Paolo in Venice.

Allaci recorded the fact that a real pasticcio was performed at Naples this year under the title of "Amor non a legge," with music by several different composers whose names were not recorded.

Antonio Saltorio's operas "La prosperità di Elio Seiano" and "La caduta di Elio Seiano" were produced at this time, probably at Venice.

"Le Sicilien" was produced this

(cont.) year. According to La Grange, the singers were concealed in boxes with grilles, while the actors mimed.

Abraham Cowley, essayist, Cavalier poet, and prose writer, died (born 1618).

Jonathan Swift, British satirist, was born (died 1745).

Jeremy Taylor, chaplain to King Charles I and master of "sacred rhetoric," died (born 1613).

George Wither, a lyric poet, died (born 1588).

John Dryden's opera made from "The Tempest" (Shakespeare) with collaboration by Davenant appeared at this time.

John Milton completed "Paradise Lost" at this time. It was a poetic work in great contrast with the air of frivolity which pervaded most Restoration literature.

Boffrand, French architect, was born (died 1754).

Borromini, Italian Baroque architect, died (born 1599).

Alonso Cano, architect and painter to King Philip IV, died (born 1601).

Italian architecture: Bernini's colonnades completed for St. Peter's at Rome (breadth of ellipse, 780').

King Louis XIV paid a visit to Royal Gobelin manufacturing to show his interest in what would now be referred to as "the standard of French design."

1667(cont.)

(to 1668) Cesti used bassoons in his productions of "Il pomo d'oro" during these years.

(to 1669) The papal reign of St. Clement IX (born at Pistoia). He was also a composer.

(to 1672) Ercole Bernabei was chapel master at San Luigi dei Francesi (jointly with Caprioli) during this period.

(and 1673, 1675, 1680, 1682, 1683) Thomas Greeting's "The Pleasant Companio: or New Lessons and Instructions For the Flagelet" was published at London in this year and other editions appeared at the other years. It was supposedly first published in 1661 with the above title coming from the 1675 edition.

(to 1673) Carlo Pallavicino was at Dresden during these years first as vice-Kapellmeister and then as Kapellmeister to Johann Georg II of Saxony.

(to 1674) French architecture: Perrault, The Louvre in Paris (East front, 570' long x 90' high).

(to 1677) Johann Melchior Gletle, Swiss composer, was Kapellmeister at Augsburg Cathedral during this period.

(to 1690) Italian architecture: Guarini: Sma Sindone, Turin.

c.1667

Gaetano Greco at the age of ten years entered the Naples Conservatorio dei Poveri di Gesò at this time.

1668

(January 18) Lully's "Le Carnaval" was produced.

(February 27) A famous passage in Pepeys' diary on this date made reference to "wind-musique when the angel comes down."

(March 5) Francesco Gasparini, Italian composer, was born at Camaiore, near Lucca (died 1727, March 22).

(March 27) Clemens Thieme, German instrumentalist and composer, died at Zeitz (born 1631, September 7).

(April 8) Johann Ambrosius Bach (twin) married Elisabeth, daughter of Valentin Lämmerhirt.

(May 7) Pepys mentioned "Marylebone Gardens" in his "Diary" entry at this time.

(June 3) Miskiewicz's "Jesu dulcis memoria" for mixed chorus appeared on this date.

(July 15) Pepys paid £5 to Haward for a spinet.

(July 18) Lully's "George Dandin" was produced.

(September 22) Juan Cabanilles, Spanish organist and composer, was ordained a priest.

(November 10) François Couperin, son of Charles, renowned clavecinist, organist, and composer, was born at Paris (died 1733, September 12). He has been ranked as the "outstanding figure of French instrumental music" and the greatest French clavecinist.

(December 3) Kaspar Kasimir

417

1668(cont.)
Schweizelsperg, German composer, was born (date of death unknown).

(February) Acciaiuoli's "Il girello" was first produced in Rome at the Palazzo Colonna in Borgo.

(April) Buxtehude acquired the position of organist at St. Mary's church (Marienkirche) of Lübeck, one of the best and most lucrative appointments in Germany.

(April) Giles Tomkins, English organist and composer, died at Salisbury (birthdate unknown).

(May) William Holder, after achieving success in teaching a deaf mute to speak, wrote a paper on the subject in "Philosophical Transactions."

(August) Giovanni Rovetta, Italian singer and composer, died at Venice (birthdate unknown).

(September) Rosa heard that Cesti intended returning to Venice to live.

(October) John Gostling, an English singer, was admitted to St. John's College at Cambridge. He was eighteen years old at the time.

(November) Apollonio Apolloni visited Rosa in Rome and brought good news concerning Cesti, their mutual friend, who was at this time in Tuscany.

Johann Jakob Bach, son of J. Christian and grandson of Johann, a member of the fifth generation of the Bach family, was born (died 1692). He was an

(cont.) Eisenach musician.

Albertus Bryne (Bryan, Brian), English organist and composer, died at London (birthdate unknown).

John Eccles, English composer, was born at London (died 1735, January 12).

Apostolo Zeno, an "Italian" literary man, was born at Venice (died 1750). He came from an honorable Venetian family and was widely versed in literature and archaeology. Together with Metastasio he attempted to revolutionize operatic libretti. As a member of the Hapsburg court he brought the influence of French classicism to bear on operatic drama.

Attilio Ariosti, Italian violinist and composer, became a Servite monk at this time.

Giulio Cesare Arresti this year became "maestro di cappella" of San Salvatore, at Bologna.

Georg Christoph Bach at this time proceeded to Themar near Meiningen to accept the position of cantor.

Maria Katharina Bach this year married Christoph Herthum, organist at Ebeleben, near Sondershausen, later at Arnstadt.

Diedrich Becker was "Ratsviolist" (violist to the Senate) this year.

Angelo Berardi was "maestro di cappella" at the cathedral of Viterbo at this time.

Blow's first position was succeeding Albertus Bryne as organist of Westminster Abbey. His appointment dated from Michaelmas this year and the annual salary was £10.

Bononcini joined the Accademia Filarmonica at this time and shortly thereafter returned to Modena, where his two sons were born.

Bryne in all probability retained his position at Westminster until Blow's appointment this year.

Cavalli this year became "maestro di cappella" at St. Mark's.

G. Dumanoir at this time was "roi des ménétriers" in the Confrérie de Saint-Julien.

J.G. Ebeling was professor of music at the Caroline "Gymnasius" at Stettin this year.

John Forbes joined his father this year in the latter's music publishing business in Scotland.

The two positions were joined in the entry for Hingeston as both "Tuner & Repairer of the Wind Instruments & Organs by patent under the Broad Seal, £60" recorded in Treasury of the Chambers Office accounts for this year.

J. Pachelbel went to Ratisbon to the "Gymnasium poeticum" at this time or possibly one year later.

According to Poullet at this time a tuba ductilis was in use (cont.) in Persian music and the English trumpet was also known to the country.

This year was rather uneventful for musicians at King Charles II's Court. As far as the records show nothing of importance occurred within even the Purcell family.

Sebastian Scherer was director of music at Ulm at this time.

Thomas Strutius this year was organist at St. Mary's in Danzig.

M. Wise was appointed organist and master of the choristers of Salisbury Cathedral at this time.

Bénigne de Bacilly's book, "Remarques curieuses sur l'art de bien chanter . . ." was published at this time, first only under his initials "B.d.B."

Banister this year wrote songs for Sedley's "Mulberry Garden" and Davenant's "The Man's the Master."

Diedrich Becker this year published his "Musicalische Frülings-Früchte (sic)" apparently a set of ensemble suites.

Boretti's opera "Eliogabalo" appeared at this time.

La Bruyère's "Caractères" was published this year.

Joh. Crüger's "Praxis pietatis" was published this year at Frankfort.

Poisson's French edition of Descartes' "Compendium musicae" appeared at this time.

1668(cont.)

Diruta's "Davidicae modulationes et Litaniae B. Mariae Virginis 3 vocibus concinendae, una cum Basso ad organum . . ." was completed this year.

Agostino Filipucci this year published a book of masses for four voices, opus 2.

William Godbid printed "Musica Deo Sacra" this year.

William King this year published at Oxford "Poems of Mr. Cowley (The Mistress) and others, composed into Songs and Ayres, with a Thorough Basse to the Theorbo, Harpesicon, or Basse Violl."

G. Mazzaferrata composed madrigals for two to three voices at this time.

Mario Savioni wrote some madrigals for five voices this year.

Fabian Stedman this year published his "Tintinnalogia."

Most of Tomkins' sacred compositions were included in "Musica Deo Sacra" this year. The collection was printed twelve years after Tomkins' death.

Uccellini's "Compositioni armoniche" for violin and other instruments in four and five parts was published this year at Antwerp.

Vitali's "Acunes à deux violons avecq. la basse continue pour les espinettes ou basse Violon" was published this year by P. Phalese in "Livre cinquieme du recueil des danses, ballets allemandes, brandes etc."

Vitali's "Ballette, correnti, gighe, allemande e sarabande a violino e violone o spinetta con il secondo violino a beneplacito" was published this year by Monti.

Another late appearance of the crumhorn was reported from Breslau at this time.

Treatises at this time described the character of each instrument, the musette as guileless and rustic, the German flute as tender and sad, the hautboy as merry and suitable to rustic revels, with a tender yet martial tone.

The musical movement, "musette," was decreed too simple to be included in productions before sophisticated town audiences. It did not correspond to any dance form, but was defined by orchestration and a characteristic bass.

Cazzati's oratorios "Giuditta" and "Psiche deificata" were both sung at Bologna this year.

Davenant's "The Unfortunate Lovers" was revived this year and contained some songs by A. Marsh, I.

Dryden's "An Evening's Love" was produced at this time and included some songs by A. Marsh, I.

The Febi Armonici reappeared at Naples this year and performed a new opera, "L'amor della patria," by an unknown composer who possibly may have been Cirillo.

Kerll's opera "I colori geniali" was produced this year or in

1668(cont.)

1669.

Lully's "La Grotte de Versailles" was produced at this time.

Czar Alexis Michailovitch this year appointed a second commission of six to revise the texts of the chant books. The commission was headed by Alexander Mesenetz.

Tomkins this year set the following pitches: A=474 c.p.s., S=4°3.

Sir William Davenant, the English poet, died (born 1606).

John Dryden's "Essay of Dramatic Poesy" was completed at this time.

Lucas von Hildebrandt, an Austrian architect, was born (died 1745).

(to 1672) Silvestro Durante was "maestro di cappella" at Santa Maria Trastevere during these years.

(to 1675) C. Piochi during this period was "maestro di cappella" at Siena Cathedral.

(to 1677) Jean François Lalouette during these years was first a violinist and then a conductor at the Opera.

(to 1688) Thomas Tollet, an Irish composer, was one of the Dublin city musicians during this period.

(to 1720) Francesco Ruggieri, Italian violin maker, made instruments during the period embracing these years.

c.1668

Catherine Shore, English singer, was born at London (died c.1730).

Dutch painting: Rembrandt, "Family Portrait" (50" x 66 1/2").

1669

(January 6) Johann Valentin Bach, cantor, son of Georg Christoph, grandson of Christoph and a member of the fifth generation of the Bach family, was born (died 1720, August 12).

(January 19) Leone Allacci, Italian musical scholar of Greek parentage, died at Rome (born 1586).

(January 25) A letter written by Salvator Rosa bearing this date mentioned Acciaiuoli and Alessandro Melani as the author and composer respectively of "L'empio punito."

(January 30) "Missa pulcherrima ad instar Praenestini" by Pekiel appeared on this date.

(January 31) Cesti's "Genserico," his last opera, was produced at the Teatro dei SS. Giovanni e Paolo in Venice.

(February 2) Louis Marchand, French organist and composer, was born at Lyons (died 1732, February 17).

(February 13) Lully's "Flore" was produced.

(February 17) Acciaiuoli's "L'empio punito" with music by Alessandro Melani appeared on this date.

(March 23) Philipp Friedrich Buchner, German composer, died at Würzburg (born 1614, September

10).

(April 1) Antonio Bertali,
Italian composer, died at Vienna
(born 1605, March).

(June 3) On this date when
Purcell was ten years old, Grand
Duke Cosimo III of Tuscany saw
a comedy-ballet in London based
on the score of "Psyche." He
attended a special performance
at Drury Lane for this event.

(June 9) Giovanni Felice Sances'
opera "Apollo deluso" was produced at Vienna.

(June 28) Cambert and Perrin
obtained a royal patent to perform "académies d'opéra ou
représentations en musique et
en langue françoise sur le pied
de celles d'Italie." The patent
was issued for a period of
twelve years by King Louis XIV
and included the Marquis de
Sourdéac as a recipient with the
other two men.

(August 29) Edward Coleman,
English singer, lutenist, viol-
ist and composer, died at
Greenwich (birthdate unknown).
He set to music several school
plays or masques by Shirley.

(October 1) Giovanni Felice
Sances became Kapellmeister of
the imperial chapel at Vienna.

(October 6) Lully's "Monsieur de
Pourceaugnac" was produced.

(October 10) Johann Nicolaus
Bach, Jena organist, son of J.
Christoph, grandson of Heinrich
and member of the fifth generation of the Bach family, was
born at Eisenach (died 1753,
November 4).

(October 14) Marc'Antonio Cesti,
the Italian composer, died at
Florence or Vienna (born 1623,
August 5). The source that
gave his place of death as
Florence referred to him as
Pietro Antonio Cesti. See 1618.

(October 17) Johann Nicolaus
Bach (fifth generation), son of
J. Christoph, was christened.

(January) Blow rejoined the
King's service as "a musician for
the virginals."

Carlo Draghi, later court organist at Vienna, was born (died
1711).

Hebenstreit, German dulcimer
player, first a dancing-master
and violinist, was born at
Eisleben (died 1750, November
15).

Singer Maddalena Musi, nicknamed
Mignatta, was born (died 1751).

Hieronymus Schultheiss, father
of the organist Benedict, died
(born 1600).

Christopher Simpson, English
gambist, theorist and composer,
died (birthdate unknown).

Abdias Treu, author on music,
died (born 1597).

Since the foundation of the
Academie de Musique this year
its relations with the Government have frequently been altered but never completely interrupted.

Henry Aldrich was awarded the
degree of Master of Arts this
year at Christ Church, Oxford.

Jakob Bach (fourth generation)

was sent to the Eisenach Latin
school this year.

Johann Nikolaus Bach, German
organist, travelled in Italy at
this time.

Bockshorn's "Theatrum musicum"
appeared.

Bontempi went to Italy this year.

H. Cooke left London for
Hampton Court at this time.

F. Corbett this year was in
Paris again.

Corelli's division of the sonata
into four movements was not an
innovation since many before
him had made this division. It
appeared frequently in works by
G.B. Vitali in the collections
of this year.

Baldassare Ferri this year made
a trip to London to sing.

Agostino Filippucci at this
time was president of the
Accademia dei Filarmonici in
Monte, Bologna.

John Jackson held the office of
"Instructor in Musick" at Ely
Cathedral for three months of
this year.

King Louis XIV this year appeared in the ballet "Flora."

Richard Meares, I this year
indicated that he was making
viols, lutes, etc. as early as
this.

Johann Micheal Nicolai was a
chamber musician at the court
of Württemberg at this time.

Del Pane this year became choir
-master at the papal chapel.

L. Penna entered the Carmelite
Order at Mantua prior to this
date.

Colbert supported Perrin's efforts to create a national opera
and procured the royal patent
for him that gave Perrin the exclusive right to operatic performances.

Jacques Philidor entered the
Grande Écurie this year as fifer
and afterwards was promoted to
the oboe, crumhorn and trumpet
marine, succeeding his father.

As a chorister at the Chapel
Royal after this year, Purcell
sang the traditional anthems by
Tallis and Byrd.

Jacob Stainer, the Austrian
violin maker, was imprisoned this
year and forced to renounce
Lutheranism of which he was
suspected.

William Turner was sworn in as
a Gentleman of the Chapel Royal
this year.

Pietro Andrea Ziani at this
time became second organist at
St. Mark's in Venice.

Banister wrote songs for
Shadwell's "Royal Shepherdess"
this year.

Pękiel Bartlomiej composed his
"Missa Pulcherrima ad instar
Praenestini" at this time.

Bernabei's book of madrigals for
three voices, "Concerto
madrigalesco," appeared this
year at Rome.

Bernhard's setting of the Latin hymn "Prudentia Prudentiana" was issued this year at Hamburg.

Boesset composed two books of "Airs" in three or four parts this year published by Ballard and reprinted in 1671.

Bononcini's opus 3 "Varij fiori" for two to four instruments with continuo was published this year at Bologna.

The works of Denis Gaultier included the "Pièces de luth" published this year and the "Rhétorique des Dieux" which was not printed during his lifetime, but has survived in an impressive manuscript.

William Holder published his "Elements of Speech" this year.

George Hudson's "Musick's Recreation on the Viol, Lyraway" was published at this time.

Numerous catches and rounds by Ives were included in Playford's "Select Ayres & Dialogues."

Johnson's "As I Walk Forth" was included in "The Treasury of Musick."

Kerll's sacred works, a book of "Sacrae cantiones" for one to five voices with organ, was published this year in addition to two books of masses.

Lanier's songs were included in "The Treasury of Music."

H. Lawes' songs appeared in "The Treasury of Musick."

W. Lawes' songs appeared in "The Treasury of Musick."

Songs by A. Marsh, I were included in "The Treasury of Musick."

"Musicke's Recreation on the Viol" published this year contained seventeen dances by John Moss.

John M. Nicolai composed "Erster Theil geistlicher Harmonien" (sacred songs for three voices with two violins) this year.

Giovanni Domenico Partenio's opera "Genserico" was written at this time.

"Cantilena de Passione Domini gratiarum actoria" by A. Paszkiewicz appeared this year.

Petzold's "Musica vespertina lipsica" was written at this time.

Giovanni Pittoni this year wrote his "Intavolatura di tiorba," twelve sonatas for solo theorbo with harpsichord continuo.

Lawes' "The Treasury of Musick" published this year included works by William Tomkins.

Wojcieh Tylkowski this year published his "Philosophia curiosa."

Marco Uccellini's "Sinfonie boscarecie" for solo violin and bass with addition of two other violins, opus 8, was published at this time at Antwerp.

Vitali's opus 5 sonatas were first printed this year. Vitali, a pupil of Cazzati, started writing trio sonatas during this period.

Wilson's music was included in

"The Treasury of Musick."

The Sheldonian Theatre was built this year.

Operas in Paris at this time began to be performed at a theatre established by Perrin under authority of the King.

Cavalli's opera "Coriolano" was produced at the Teatro Ducale in Piacenza.

Cazzati's oratorio "La vittoria di San Filippo Neri" was sung this year at Bologna.

Kerll's opera "I colori geniale" was produced this year or possibly in 1668.

Lully's "La Jeunesse" was produced at this time.

Petz' opera "Trajano imperatore romano" was performed this year at Bonn.

Cortona, Italian architect, died (born 1596).

Herman Hals, Dutch painter, died (born 1611).

Rembrandt van Rijn, celebrated Dutch painter, died (born 1606).

Dutch painting: Vermeer, "The Geographer."

(to 1670) John Dryden's "Tyrannic Love," and "Conquest of Granada" appeared during these years.

(to c.1680) During this period P.S. Agostini wrote six operas for Genoa, Milan and Venice.

(to 1686) During these years

(cont.) Petzold published collections chiefly composed of instrumental music.

(to 1711) Italian domination of the Viennese court began with Bertali and continued with Sances, Pietro Ziani, Pederzuoli and most of all A. Draghi, who during the second half of the century was music director at the Viennese court.

c.1669
Michel Angelo Grancini, Italian organist and composer, died (born c.1600).

L. Penna became maestro of the Carmelite Church at Parma at this times.

Johann Kuhnau was entered in "Kreuzschule" at Dresden at this time. He became a regular Ratsdiscantist and obtained regular instruction in music.

Dutch painting: Rembrandt, "Return of the Prodigal Son" (103 1/8" x 80 5/8").

1670
(January 20) J. Melani's opera "Girello" was produced at the Teatro Cocomero in Florence (It is not certain that Melani was the composer but it is certain that the music is not by Pistocchi, to whom it has frequently been credited).

(February 4) Lully's "Les Amants magnfiques," a musical pastoral by Molière, was produced.

(February 6) Francesco Stradivarius, son of Antonio Stradivarius, was born (died 1670, February). The child lived only about a week.

1670(cont.)

(March 21) The Chapel Royal was in chaos while enlargements were being made and new fittings were hung on this date. By authority of a warrant Captain Cooke, Master of the Children, was given new curtains for the music room. Conceivably this could have all occurred one year later.

(April 23 or 27) Loreto Vittori, Italian male soprano singer and composer, died at Rome (born 1604, January 16).

(April 24) Christian Ludwig Boxberg, German composer, was born at Sondershausen (died 1729).

(July 6 and 12) On these dates orders were issued to alleviate some of the dire economic conditions surrounding the children of the Chapel Royal.

(July 18) Giovanni Bononcini, Italian composer, was born at Modena (died 1755 or 1747).

(July 29) Vincenzo Amato, Italian composer, died at Palermo (born 1629, January 6).

(October 8) Cambert and Perrin with the Marquis de Sourdéac as producer and with Beauchamps as ballet-master recruited singers in the province of Languedoc and on this date rented the Salle du Jeu de Paume "de la Bouteille" for a period of five years.

(October 10) J. Christoph Bach complained to the Eisenach authorities about his extremely low salary, a hardship suffered by all organist at this time.

(October 14) Lully's "Le

(cont.) Bourgeois gentilhomme" was produced. His collaborator was Molière.

(November 15) Jan Amos Comenius, Czech educational reformer and hymnologist, died at Naarden near Amsterdam (born 1592, March 28).

(December 22) Giovanni Felice Sances' opera "Aristomene Messenio" was produced at Vienna.

(February) Francesco Stradivarius, son of Antonio Stradivarius, died according to many sources (See February 6).

(May) The showing of effigies or "monuments" provided a profitable source of income for Westminster Abbey. Although there seem to be no extant records after the reign of King Charles II, the accounts of this month showed that the sums were considerable.

(June) At this time Captain Cooke had found it necessary to submit a petition to King Charles II concerning the desperate economic conditions of the Children of the Chapel Royal. As a chorister Purcell was directly affected by the lack of funds.

Jan Bischoff, Polish composer, died at Warsaw (birthdate unknown).

Louis De Caix D'Hervelois, French violinist and composer, was born at Paris (died 1760).

Antonio Caldara, Italian composer, was born at Venice (died 1736, December 28). He was a pupil of Legrenzi.

(Don) Pompeo Canniciari, Italian

composer, was born at Rome (died
1744, December 29).

Turlough Carolan, Irish harper
and composer, was born near
Nobber, County Meath (died 1738,
March 25).

Jacques Champion de
Chambonnières, French harpsichordist and organist, died
(born 1602). His death has also
been given as c.1672. He was
chamber harpsichordist to King
Louis XIV.

Albert Chrostkowski, Polish musician, died at Warsaw (born
1627, May 15).

Louis Fuzelier, French librettist, was born (date of death
unknown).

Matteo Gofriller, a violin
maker, was born (died 1742).

David Kellner, German organist,
lutenist, carillonist and composer, was born at Leipzig (died
1748, April 6).

Henry Loosemore, English organist, died at Cambridge (birthdate unknown).

Theodoric Pedrini, Italian(?)
musician and priest, was born
(died 1745). He taught the
Chinese emperor's sons and also
built harpsichords and organs
and composed violin sonatas
under the name "Nipredi."

Bartlomiej Pekiel, Polish organist, conductor and composer,
died at Cracow (birthdate unknown).

Philibert (Philbert), a French
flutist, was born (date of

(cont.) death unknown).

Georg Ludwig Agricola became
"Kapellmeister" at Gotha this
year.

Beaumavielle was brought from
Toulouse to Paris by Perrin
this year to sing in "Pomone"
(Cambert) produced in 1671.

Briegel was appointed
"Kapellmeister" to the Landgrave
of Hesse-Darmstadt. He remained
there until his death.

Jose Cabanillas, Spanish organist and composer, this year was
appointed to the cathedral of
Urgell in the Pyrenees. He remained there until his death.

H. Cooke became Marshal of the
Corporation of Musicians this
year.

The "old violinist Giambattista
Bassini" took Corelli as a
pupil toward the end of this
year according to one source.

Corelli's progress was so rapid
this year that the Accademia
Filarmonica, already well-known,
accepted Corelli as a student
although he was only seventeen
years of age.

Rev. Dr. Robert Creyghton, the
composer, was at this time
Bishop of Bath and Wells.

Jacques Danican played at court
this year. He also composed
marches, dance music, etc. and
enjoyed special favors from
King Louis XIV.

James Hart was a singer in York
Minster until this year when he
was appointed a Gentleman of
the Chapel Royal and lay-vicar

of Westminster Abbey.

Johann Krieger was appointed
chamber organist at Bayreuth
this year.

F. Pistocchi at this time was
a chorister at San Petronio,
but must have been dismissed
shortly afterwards.

T. Pleasants became organist and
master of the choristers at
Norwich Cathedral this year.

Charles Purcell studied as a
"Bishop's Boy" at St. Peter's
College, Westminster from this
date forward.

In the Westminster Abbey
Treasurer's Account for
Michaelmas of this year Charles
Purcell's name was listed among
the "Bishop's Boys" who were
recipients of the four scholar-
ships founded by the Reverend
Williams, Dean of Westminster.

At this time when he was fourteen Purcell had as yet shown
no trace of creative talent
other than one piece he wrote
this year for the King's birthday.

Berthold Spirido, a German composer, was at the monastery of
St. Theodor near Bamberg from
this date forward.

Thomas Tudway at this time became organist of King's College
chapel at Cambridge.

Issac Voss was awarded the degree
of D.C.L. this year by Oxford.

Werckmeister at this time refused a position offered to
him at Elluch.

Thomas Wilson this year played
the organ at Ripon Minster.

Banister at this time wrote
songs for Dryden's "The Conquest
of Granada" and Aphra Behn's
"The Forc'd Marriage."

Boretti's opera "Marcello in
Siracusa" appeared this year.

Cazzati this year published a
sonata for solo violin and continuo.

In France, after the publication
this year of Chambonnières'
harpsichord pieces, an independent school of harpsichord
playing flourished simultaneously with the specific productions of French organists.

Chambonnières' "Pieçès de
Clavessin" was published at this
time.

Jan Cocx this year composed a
solemn Mass dedicated to the
cathedral chapter at Antwerp.

C.C. Dedekind's "Davidischer
Harfenschall mit schönen
Melodeien gezieret" was published this year at Frankfort
by B.C. Wust.

C.C. Dedekind arranged the
words for the sacred musical
drama "Freudenund Trauerspiel
über die Geburt Jesu" published
this year at Dresden in eight
volumes.

C.C. Dedekind's "Geschwinder und
seliger Abschied, der . . .
Frauen Annen Margareth . . .
Metzner am 8 Wintermonats, 1670
. . . am 15 beerdigt" appeared
at this time.

Draghi this year set the lib-

1670(cont.)
retto "La risa di Democrito" by
Minato.

Henry Purcell this year wrote
his first occasional work for
King Charles II, "Address of the
children of the Chapel Royal to
the King, & their master,
Captain Cooke, on His Majesty's
birthday, A.D. 1670, composed
by Master Purcell, one of the
Children of the said Chapel."

Henry Herringman this year published the fourth edition of
Carew's Masque, "with The songs
set to Musick by Mr. Henry
Lawes."

Legrenzi composed motets at this
time.

Matthew Locke this year com-
posed the music for a revival of
Shakespeare's "Tempest" in
England.

Johann Löhner's "Geistliche
Sing-Stunde" was published at
this time.

Lully's "Amant magnifique" and
"Bourgeois Gentilhomme" were
both completed this year.

Chamber Sonatas by Rosenmüller
were published at this date.

Marco Silvani's "Canzonette per
camera a voce sola" published
this year at Bologna included
Pallavicino's "La speranza" in
three movements.

Berthold Spirido at this time
wrote his most important work
"Neue bis dato unbekannte
Unterweisung." It gave in-
stuctions in the art of composition as well as in playing
organs and spinets.

Two editions of Vitali's
"Correnti e balletti da camera
. . ." were published this year
at Venice.

The "polished and effortless
elegance of the French dance
suite" had drawn attention of
the musical world by this time
and musicians had adopted it
at an international level.

"Follias" appeared this year
in the "Pièces de luth
composées . . . par Jacques de
Gallot avec les Folies d'Espagne
enrichi es de plusiers beaux
couplets" (Ecorcheville collection, 1670-1680).

Up to this time only very few
examples of sonatas for solo
instruments were found in works
by Marini, Giovanni Battista
Fontana, Martino Pesenti,
Uccellini, and a few other
isolated composers.

In the chapel at San Petronio
this year three violins, an
alto viol, two tenor viols,
two theorboes and a bass viol
were found as well as trombones.

After this date, the most common instrumentation for both
church and chamber sonatas
were two Violin parts with
Continuo. This was known as
the trio sonata.

Renatus Harris at this time
introduced the fourniture stop
on the organ he built at the
Church of St. Sepulchre,
Holborn, London.

Examples of the viola d'amore
existed as early as this year.

Chambonnières in his "Pièces"
this year used broken chords,

429

1670(cont.)
twin ornaments, trills and
showed English virginal strokes.

National French opera was finally
achieved under the patronage of
King Louis XIV.

Cesti's opera "Argia" was written
and produced this year at the
Teatro dei Rinnovati, in Siena.

Dryden's "The Conquest of
Granada" was produced at this
time and contained some songs by
A. Marsh, I.

Lully's "Les Jeux pythiens" was
produced this year.

An opera "Ermengarda regina de'
Longobardi" was supposed to be
composed by Cesti, but the music was written by Antonio
Sartorio and produced this year
at Venice.

William Congreve, English writer,
was born (died 1729).

Dryden wrote "The Conquest of
Granada" at this time.

Molière's "Le Bourgeois
gentilhomme" was completed this
year (music by Lully).

The Treaty of Dover was signed
this year.

At this time a charter was
granted the Hudson's Bay
Company.

Jacob van Ruisdael, the Dutch
painter, died (born c.1600).

Le Vau, the French architect,
died (born 1612).

(to 1671) Bockshorn's "Neue
angestimmte . . . Tafel-Music"

(cont.) appeared this year.

(to 1671) Nicholas Staggins was
appointed musician in ordinary
for the violin starting at
Michaelmas 1670 by a warrant of
December, 1671.

(to 1675) Dutch painting: Van
Ruisdael, "The Burst of
Sunlight" (oil on canvas
32 5/8 x 38 5/8").

(to 1676) The papal reign of
St. Clement X.

(and 1676) Dedekind was considered to be particularly
successful in providing the
words for sacred musical
dramas, such as "Neue geistliche
Schauspiele, bequemt zur Musik"
published at Dresden in eight
volumes on these dates.

(to 1679) John Birchensha was
still living in London and
teachine viol during these
years.

(to 1696) Most of the instruments made by M. Klotz fall between these dates. They were
well built, following a model
by Stainer, but were poorly
varnished.

c.1670
A son was born to Johann
Ambrosius Bach. He died very
young (date of death unknown).

Giuseppe Boniventi, Italian
composer, was born at Venice
(date of death unknown).

Francois Bouvard, a French composer, was born at Paris (died
after 1756).

Giovanni Maria Casini, Italian
organist and composer, was

c.1670(cont.)
born at Florence (died c.1715).

Thomas Clayton, an English composer, was born (died c.1730).
He became a member of the King's
band and later travelled to
Italy from whence he brought
back music which he adapted to
English words for an opera libretto, "Arsinoë, Queen of
Cyprus."

Henry Eccles, English violinist,
was born at London (died 1742).

John Goldwin, English organist
and composer, was born (died
1719, November 7).

Lacoste, a French composer, was
born (died after 1757). He was
accused of plagiarism and too
close imitation of Campara's
style.

Richard Leveridge, English bass
singer and composer, was born
at London (died 1758, March 22).

Antonio Literes, Spanish organist and composer, was born near
Madrid (died 1747, January 18).

Jean-Baptiste Marchand, French
lutenist and violinist, was
born at Paris (date of death
unknown).

Orazio Tarditi, Italian organist and composer, died at
Faenza (birthdate unknown).

Benedetto Vinacesi, Italian
composer, was born at Brescia
(died 1719).

Jean Baptiste Volumier, Flemish
violinist, dulcimer player and
composer, was born in Spain
(died 1728, October 7).

De Brossard studied philosophy
and theology at Caen, Normandy
at this time.

Johann Löhner settled in Nürnberg
as organist this year.

Charpentier's pastorale "Le
Sort d'Andromède" appeared at
this time.

Jan Cocx published a collection
of eight-part church music this
year.

At this time the Guthrie viola
da braccio manuscripts were compiled.

The suite at this time still
followed the pattern set by
Froberger and Locke with the
gigue appearing somewhere in the
middle of the work.

Friedrich Chrisian Bressand, the
poet, was born (died c.1699).

1671
(January 17) Molière's "Psyché"
was produced at Paris with music
by Lully. Corneille also collaborated in the mechanical
spectacle which had Venus
descending "dans une grande
machine" in the prologue.

(February 17) Johann Christoph
Bach succeeded his father in
the position as court musician
to Count Ludwig Günther of
Schwarzburg-Arnstadt.

(February 19) Charles Hubert
Gervais, French composer, was
born at Paris (died 1744, January 15).

(March 3) The new opera-house
in Paris (Académie Royale de
Musique) opened its doors with
a performance of "Pomone" by

1671(cont.)

Perrin and Cambert. The opera
("pastorale") had five acts and a
prologue and was enthusiasti-
cally received.

(March 21) Azzolino Bernardino
Della Ciaia, Italian organist,
composer and amateur organ
builder, was born at Siena (died
1755, January).

(March 24) Johann Christoph's
daughter Maria Sophie Bach was
born on this date or the same
day in 1674 (date of death unknown).

(May 12) Erdmann Neumeister, a
composer, librettist and violent
opponent of Pietism, was born
(died 1756).

(May 23) On this date a decree
awarded more money to Captain
Cooke, Master of the Children
of His Majesty's Chapel Royal.
The additional sum was for all
his duties such as teaching the
children music, for their
nurses and for traveling to re-
cruit other boys for the group.

(June 8) Tommaso Albinoni,
Italian composer, was born at
Venice (died 1750, January 17).

(June 16) Johann Christoph Bach,
Ohrdruf organist, son of
Ambrosius, grandson of Christoph
and a member of the fifth gener-
ation of the Bach family, was
born at Erfurt (died 1721,
February 22). He studied with
Pachelbel.

(June 18) Johann Christoph Bach
was christened at Eisenach.

(September 1) F. Pinel resigned
in favour of Laurent Dupré as
"ordinaire de la musique de la

(cont.) chambre du roi pour le
théorbe."

(November 9) On this date
D'Avenant's company opened the
new theater at Dorset Garden.

(December 2) Lully's "Le
Comtesse d'Escarbagnas" was produced.

(December 21) William Young,
English musician, died at
London (birthdate unknown).

(February) Nicolas de Grigny,
French composer and organist,
was born at Rheims (died 1703,
November 30).

(May) At the end of this month
Captain Cooke took all his
charges, the Children of the
Chapel Royal, to Windsor for a
fortnight. Purcell was a member
of the group.

(October) Johann Ambrosius Bach
succeeded his cousin Johann
Christian at Eisenach.

Azzolino Della Ciaia, Italian
composer, was born at Siena
(died 1755).

Antoine Forqueray, great violinist and composer, was born (died
1745, June 28).

Pierre Phalèse, son of Pierre
Phalese, the younger, and an
Augustinian monk at Antwerp,
died (born 1594).

Walter Rowe, II, violist, composer, and son of Walter Rowe,I,
died (birthdate unknown). He
taught viol to Princesses Louise
Charlotte and Hedwig Sophia.

Vincenzo Albrici returned to
Dresden this year and resumed

his former position.

A literary quarrel between
Giulio Cesare Arresti and
Maurizio Cazzati, his chapel
master, resulted in the latter
losing his position.

Johann Aegidius Bach at this
time was a viola-player in his
father's group of musicians at
Erfurt.

Johann Ambrosius Bach (twin)
settled this year at Eisenach as
Town Musician.

Johann Christoph Bach (twin) was
appointed "Hofmusikus" at this
time at Arnstadt.

Jakob Bach this year left the
Eisenach Latin School after
being found guilty of a theft.

Shadwell, in "The Humorist" published this year, stated
"Birkenshaw is a rare fellow,
give him his due; for he can
teach men to compose that are
deaf, dumb, and blind."

Bononcini played violin in the
court orchestra this year,
probably at Modena.

Bontempi was back at Dresden by
this time.

King Charles II at this time
indicated that the chapel within
the palace at Holyroodhouse,
Scotland did not please him.

Some music historians claimed
that Corelli was in Rome as
early as this year.

Duponchel was organist to
Cardinal Bicchi at Osimo this
year.

Eccles this year accompanied
George Fox to the West Indies and
organized Quakerism there.

John Ferrabosco was awarded the
degree of Bachelor of Music this
year by Cambridge.

Molière and Lully joined forces
for a period of collaboration
that lasted up to this time.

John Mawgridge was appointed to
the King's music this year.

J. Pachelbel went to Vienna this
year or in 1672.

A suite by Poglietti, "Sopra la
ribellione di Ungheria" referred
to this year's rebellion when
an attempt to remove Hungary
from Hapsburg rule was made.

F. Passarini at this time was a
Franciscan monk and "maestro di
cappella" at the church of San
Francesco, Bologna.

G.A. Perti this year began to
study music with his uncle,
Lorenzo Perti, a priest at San
Petronio, Bologna.

Playford in an attempt to restore
Church music after the
Restoration this year introduced
a hymn for Good Friday as well
as "six divine songs for one
voice to the organ."

Sebastian Scherer was organist
of the Cathedral at Ulm at this
time.

Schmelzer this year was promoted
Imperial Vice-Kapellmeister.
From 1665 to this date it had
been his duty to provide all the
appropriate music for operas
performed at the court and also
for all the manifold court

festivities.

Vitali's "Balletti, correnti, gighe . . ." was published this year. In the preface Marino Silvani referred to Vitali's violin playing as "eccellente nell'arte del suono" and added other praise, "it is not only those who hear him who admire 'le sue prodigiose virtu' but also those who examine his compositions, worthy of the highest praise."

J. Westhoff this year taught languages to the Saxon princes.

Pietro Iacomo Batti's "Vita del V. Servo di Dio Gio: Giovenale Ancina" was published this year at Rome.

The second edition of Bacilly's "Remarques curieuses sur l'art de bien chanter . . ." appeared at this time.

Banister wrote songs this year for Crowne's "Juliana" and possibly also for a revival of Tuke's "Adventures of Five Hours."

Boesset composed two books of "Airs" in three or four parts. One published in 1669 by Ballard and reprinted in this year.

Bononcini's opus 4 "Aire, correnti, sarabande, gighe & allemande" for violin & "violone" (or "spinetta") was published this year at Bologna and reprinted in 1674.

Bononcini's opus 5 "Sinfonia, allemande, correnti e sarabande" in five to six parts with continuo was published this year at Bologna.

Boretti's operas "Ercole in Tebe" and "Dario in Babilonia" were completed this year.

Cavalli's opera "Scipione" was written for the opening of the Torre di Nona opera house in Rome.

"Psalm Tunes" was published at Aberdeen this year by John Forbes.

Hammerschmidt's "Sechsstimmige Fest- und Zeit-Andachten" contained thirty-eight settings.

Humfrey this year wrote songs for Crowne's "History of Charles the Eighth of France" and Wycherley's "Love in a Wood." Both were plays.

Lully's "tragédie-ballet Psyché" was completed at this time.

Moss' "Lessons for the Base-Viol" was published this year.

J. Playford the elder this year edited "Psalms & Hymns in Solemn Musick of Foure Parts on the Common Tunes to the Psalms in Metre: used in Parish Churches."

Provenzale's "Lo Schiavo di sua moglie" was composed at this time.

Vitali's oratorio "Agar" was composed this year.

A later edition of Vitali's "Sonate a due violini . . ." was issued this year at Venice.

The division of the sonata into four movements also appeared in works by Vitali in his collections this year.

1671(cont.)
The new Theatre in Dorset
Gardens opened with opera as the
main attraction.

The first Roman opera house
opened this year, the Tors di
Nona. One major source incorrectly gave Venice as its location. Prior to this operas had
been performed only in private
homes.

Bontempi and M.G. Peranda's
"Apollo und Daphne" was given
this year at Dresden.

"Pomone" by Cambert and Perrin
was first performed this year
at the Hôtel de Nevers. The
opera had 145 performances in
Paris and marked the first use
of oboe probably in addition to
the bassoon.

Locke's "The Empress of Morocco"
was produced at this time.

Minato's "Iphide Greca" with
music by Partenio, Freschi and
Sartorio, was performed this
year at the Teatro dei Saloni.

Sartorio's opera "Selevco" was
produced this year at Milan.

Nicholas Staggins' "How unhappy
a lover" (Dryden, "Conquest of
Granada") was first performed
at this time.

Milton this year wrote "Paradise
Regained" and "Samson Agonistes"
and both were published.

King Louis XIV visited the Duke
of Condé at Chantilly this year.

(to 1672) The "Philosophical
Transactions" of this year contained references to "the
judicious and extraordinary

(cont.) skilful musician Mr.
John Birchensha."

(to 1677) An Albertus Bryne was
organist and fourth fellow of
Dulwich College during this
period.

(to 1679) Berthold Spirido's
"Neue bis dato unbekannte
Unterweisung" parts ii-iv appeared separately during these
years as "Nova instructio pro
pulsandis organis spinetis,
manuchordis."

(to 1680) Thomas Farmer was a
member of the King's band in
England during this period.

(to 1683) French sculpture:
Pierre Puget, "Milo de Crotona."

(to 1683) English architecture:
Wren, St Mary-le-Bow, London
(total height 223').

(and 1686, 1694) Giulio Cesare
Arresti, one of the founders
of the Bolognese Accademia
Filarmonica, was president at
these times.

(to 1700) William Hall was a
member of the King's band during this period.

(to 1700) Andreas Schmelzer was
violinist at the Court Chapel
in Vienna for these twenty-nine
years.

(to 1712) The English music
printer, John Heptinstall, was
established in Londong during
this period.

c.1671
Johann Christian Bach at this
time returned to Erfurt to
assume his father's position
as "Direktor der Raths

c.1671(cont.)
-Musikanten."

At this time Corelli was a violinist at the theater of Tor di Nona according to some sources.

Dutch painting: Vermeer, "Lady Standing Before a Virginal."

1672

(January 10) On this date Thomas Purcell and Pelham Humfrey were appointed composers, as assistants to George Hudson, by this time old and infirm, to come in ordinary with fee "upon death or other avoidance."

(January 21) Giuseppe Antonio Silvani, Italian composer, was born at Bologna (date of death unknown).

(March 13) On or about this date Cambert's opera patent was taken and given to Lully and Cambert's career in Paris was terminated. Lully, on the other hand, became highly influential in the field of dramatic music in France. The patent gave Lully a complete monopoly over opera and restricted the use of music in theatrical productions other than Lully's. Finally, it awarded all proceeds from his music to himself or his heirs.

(March 17) Colonna's oratorio "Il trionfo della fede" was performed at Bologna.

(March 21) Carlo Pallavicino's son, Stefano Benedetto, was born at Salò (date of death unknown). He was his father's last librettist and wrote a "Discorso della musica" on his

(cont.) own.

(June 11) Francesco Antonio Bonporti, Italian composer, was baptised at Trento on this date (died 1749, December 19).

(June 17) Orazio Benevoli, Italian composer, died at Rome (born 1605, April 19).

(July 8) Molière's "La Mariage force, comédie-ballet en 3 actes," originally set to music by Lully, was revived at the Palais-Royal, with music by Charpentier.

(July 13) Henry Cooke (Captain Cooke), English bass singer, choirmaster and composer, died at Hampton Court (born c.1616).

(July 15) Pelham Humfrey was appointed successor to Cooke as Master of the Children, thereby becoming Purcell's teacher.

(July 17) H. Cooke was buried in the east cloister of Westminster Abbey.

(August 3) Robert Smith became a musician in ordinary in England.

(August 8) Humfrey held a patent (jointly with Thomas Purcell) as "Composer in Ordinary for The Violins of His Majesty."

(September 26) Thomas Gobert, French composer, died at Paris (birthdate unknown).

(October 31) Kerll's opera "Amor tiranno, ovvero Regnero innamorato" was produced.

(November 6) Heinrich Schütz, great German Baroque composer, died at Dresden (born 1585, (October 8).

(November 15) Lully opened the Académie de Musique in Paris.

(November 15) Lully's "Les Festes de l'Amour et de Bacchus" was produced.

(December 14) Antonio Saltorio's opera "Orfeo" was produced at the Teatro San Salvatore.

(December 26 to 30) Advertisements appeared in the "London Gazette" during this period for the first of the concert series founded by John Banister. This was probably one of the first professional chamber music concerts in Europe to be supported by box-office receipts.

(December 30) The first of Banister's concert series took place on this date at his house called the "Music School."

(January) Denis Gaultier, French lutenist and composer, died at Paris (born 1597).

(February) Ralph Dallam began building the organ at Greenwich Church.

(April) Cardinal André Destouches, French composer, was born at Paris (died 1749, February 3).

(June) Alessandro Scarlatti, with his sisters Anna Maria and Melchiorra, went to Rome to stay with relatives.

Carlo Agostino Badia, Italian composer, was born at Venice (died 1738, September 23).

Orazio Benevoli, Italian composer, died (born 1605).
See June 17.

Jacques Champion de Chambonnieres, French organist, harpsichordist and composer, died (born 1602). His death has also been given as 1670.

Anthony Walkeley, English organist and composer, was born at Wells (died 1718, January 16).

In a letter written this year d'Assoucy proposed to Molière that he write the music for Molière's forthcoming "Malade imaginaire."

Giuseppe Antonio Bernabei this year succeeded his father as chapel master at the church of San Luigi dei Francesi in Rome.

Borjon, in a famous plate published with his "Traité de la musette" this year, illustrated a "bass oboe" which apparently was equipped with an apparatus to "improve the dispositon of the primary holes."

H. Cooke this year resigned from his position as Marshal of the Corporation of Musicians "by reason of sickness."

George Dallam lived in Purple Lane at this time.

S. Eccles was in New England this year.

Vincenzo de Grandis, Italian composer, this year was "maestro di cappella" at the church of Gesù in Rome.

Hack was a court musician at Munich at this time.

Wiilliam Holder was at this time appointed a canon of St. Paul's and later became a sub-dean in the Chapel Royal.

1672(cont.)

Nicolas Hotteterre was oboist in the king's musketeers this year.

Giovanni Legrenzi was director of the Conservatorio dei Mendicanti at this time.

At forty years of age this year Lully wrote his first opera in Paris. Corelli had just arrived there and had given him the idea for the French overture. This information was according to Piero Maroncelli.

Lully intrigued against Cavalli this year, "how could the young Corelli, in 1672, have provoked his thunderbolts - a violinist of 19 years, quite unknown in France, who had published nothing and had no aspiration towards opera?"

Lully obtained an exclusive privilege of founding an "Académie Royale de Musique." The resulting school of opera was centered at the Palais Royal. The opera house was set up on the Rue de Vaugirard.

Thomas Mace invented a lute this year which had fifty strings.

Italian violinist Nicola Matteis settled in England this year where (London) he created a sensation introducing the works of Italian violin composers.

Cardinal Mazarin was already dead eleven years by this time when Corelli was said to have been in France attending "the improvements which they were making in music under the influence of Cardinal Mazarin" according to a noted music historian.

Alessandro Melani was "maestro di cappella" at San Luigi de' Francesi, Rome from this year forward.

Paganini's first violin, which he had as a child, was made this year by Hieronymus Amati.

F. Passarini was "maestro di cappella" in his own Franciscan monastery at this time.

Petzold entered an Augustinian Monastery in Prague this year but left soon after to become a Protestant.

Long before this date J. Playford, the elder, had issued a few musical works printed from engraved copperplates but he himself never engraved on copper as had been incorrectly asserted.

If the theory that this year's "Macbeth" music is by Purcell is valid he must have written it when he was fourteen years old.

T. Purcell, with Humfrey, was this year made Master of the King's Band of Music. After that the former also had the title "Master of the Choristers."

The trumpet aria from Sartorio's "Adelaide" of this year greatly resembled a "French" type beginning by Purcell.

Johann Schelle was cantor at Eilenburg at this time.

At the time that the Scarlatti household at Palermo was broken up this year there may have been Scarlatti relatives already living in Naples.

Venn in his "Military and

Maritime Discipline" regarded
the drum-major as indispensable.

Banister wrote songs this year
for Wycherley's "The Gentleman
Dancing-Master."

Birchensha was responsible for
the publishing of Thomas
Salmon's "An Essay to the
Advancement of Musick" this year
at London.

Bononcini's opus 6 "Sonate,"
for two violins and continuo,
was published this year at
Venice. It was reprinted at
Bologna, in 1674 and 1677.

Bontempi's German opera "Die in
Lorbeer verwandelte Daphne"
was written this year with
Marco Giuseppe Peranda.

Boretti's opera "Claudio Cesare"
appeared at this time.

Borjon's "Traité de la musette
avec une nouvelle méthode pour
apprendre de soy-même à jouer
de cet instrument facilement et
en peu de temps" was published
this year at Lyons.

De Brossard composed his
"Pièces de luth" at Normandy
from this year forward.

This year Cambert followed his
first operatic success with the
"Pastorale héroique des Peines
et des Plaisirs de l'Amour."

A Manuscript music book containing cantatas ascribed to
Cesti with an inscription by
its owners date at Rome this
year has been preserved.

Works by Child were included in
Playford's "Musical Companion."

Some of E. Coleman's compositions were included in
Playford's "Musical Companion."

G.P Colonna's "L'alloro trionfato"
was completed this year.

Davie's "Ancient Rites and
Monuments of the Monastical and
Cathedral Church of Durham" was
published at this time.

C.C. Dedekind's "C.C.D.'s
Kuhrfürstl. Sächs. bestallten
deutschen Concert-Meisters
sonderbahrer Seelen-Freude,
oder kleinerer geistlichen
Concerten, Erster Theil" was
published this year by Seyfert
at Dresden.

Thomas Farmer this year wrote
his adaptation of Ravenscroft's
"The Citizen Turn'd Gentleman."

Gaultier wrote his "Pièces de
luth recueillies et écrites à
caen et autres lieux ès années"
at this time.

Numerous catches and rounds by
Ives were included in Playford's
"Musical Companion."

Lully's ballet "Le Triomphe de
L'amour" was published this
year.

Lully with Quinalt this year
wrote the "Pastorale Des Fêtes
de l'Amour et de Bacchus."

Molière's last "comédie-ballet,"
"Le Malade Imaginaire" was set
to music by Charpentier after
Molière broke with Lulli at this
time.

Lorenzo Penna's "Albori musicali"
was published this year at
Bologna.

1672(cont.)

J. Playford, the elder, repub-
lished Hilton's "Catch that
Catch can" this year under the
second title given it in 1667,
"The Musical Companion."

Poglietti this year in a suite
of abstract dance movements
pictured the history of the
Hungarian rebellion.

Guitar-books by Ruiz de Ribayaz
were published at this time.

Thomas Salmon's "An Essay to the
Advancement of Musick, by cast-
ing away the perplexity of different Cliffs, and uniting all
sorts of Musick in one universal
character." was published this
year by J. Carr.

W.A. Sartorio's opera "Adelaide"
was composed at this time.

Mario Savioni this year wrote
his "Madrigali e concerti" for
three voices.

Johann Sebastiani's
"Parnassblumen" was published
this year at Hamburg.

Johann Sebastiani this year
deliberately included in his St.
Matthew's Passion a number of
chorales as descant solos with
strings and continuo accompaniment "zur Erweckung mehrer
Devotion" in the congregation.

Alessandro Stradella wrote a
prologue for this year's revival
of Cesti's "La Dori" in Rome.

Venn's "Art of Drilling" appeared at this time.

The oratorio, "Gefte," was composed this year by Vitali.

The Privy Council this year declared that the Abbey Church
should be "the Chapel Royal in
all times coming." The reference
was to Scotland.

Bononcini this year was the first
to state unequivocally that the
lower figure of a time-signature
denoted the unit of time and the
upper showed how many of these
units made up a bar.

Salmon's attempt at this time to
reform the clefs by the introduction of a single universal
clef met with little support and
considerable attack.

The first theatre at Drury Lane
burned down this year.

The first commercial concert was
attempted in England at this
time.

Cambert's opera "Les Peines et
les plaisirs de l'amour" was
produced this year at the Paris
Opera.

Charpentier this year provided
new music for a revival of
"Andromède" at the Comédie
-Francaise.

"Epsom Wells" was first produced
at Dorset Gardens this year.

Lully's opera "Les Festes de
l'Amour et de Bacchus" was produced this year at Paris.

Sartorio's "L'Adelaide" was published this year at Venice.

A Passion oratorio by Sebastiani
was produced this year at
Königsberg. There was no trace
of plainsong and German music
from this time on never included
any.

Nicholas Staggins' "How pleasant
is mutual love" (Shadwell,
"Epsom Wells") was first performed this year.

Staggins' "Whilst Alexis
pressed" (Dryden, "Marriage à
la Mode") was first performed at
this time.

The catatas "L'alloro trionfante"
by Vitali and Giovanni Paolo,
and "Il trionfo della fede" with
music by F. Pratichista as well
as an overture by Vitali were
performed this year at the
Accademia degli Unanimi of
Bologna.

Joseph Addison, great English
essayist, was born (died 1719).

Richard Steele, English writer
and poet, was born (died 1729).

Dryden's "Marriage à la Mode"
appeared at this time.

The Declaration of Indulgence
was issued this year.

Czar Peter, the Great of Russia
was born (died 1725). He
created a new Russia, awakening
the country from its lethargy.

French architecture: Blondel,
Porte St. Denis, Paris (81'
high).

Dutch painting: Pieter de Hooch,
"Lady with Maid on a Roof"
(29" x 24 5/8").

(to 1673) "The Musical Companion
in two books" by Playford was
written at this time.

(and 1673) As early as in the
Passions by Sebastiani (1672)
and Theile (1673) chorales were

(cont.) included at strategic
spots alternating with arias.
This arrangement set the pattern
for the Passions of the Bach
type.

(to 1674) Ercole Bernabei was
chapel master at San Pietro in
Vaticano during this period.

(and 1674, 1685, 1691) G.P.
Colonna was elected principal of
the Accademia Filarmonica at
these years.

(to 1674) Thomas Purcell was
Master of the King's Band during
this period.

(to 1677) Johann Krieger II during these years was court organist at Bayreuth, succeeding his
brother there.

(to 1678) John Banister, the
excellent violinist who had been
conductor of the King's Private
Band, arranged performances of
music in London during this period. They were held in a rented
room "over against the George
Tavern in White Friars" with "a
large raised box for the musicians, whose modesty required
curtains." This description was
provided by a contemporary of
the times.

(to 1679) English architecture:
Wren, St. Stephen's Walbrook,
London (82'6" x 75').

(to 1686) Lully's series of
French operas and ballets during
these years uses overtures.

(to 1686) Quinalt wrote twenty
pieces (verses) for Lully. He
substituted for Italian recitativo secco with a kind of accompanied recitative.

1672(cont.)
(to 1807) In Paris during these
years a special singing-school
existed at the Opéra.

(to 1825) Critiques on music
were printed at this time at
Paris in the "Mercure de France."

c.1672
Thomas Eccles, English violinist, was born at London (date of
death unknown).

Georg Kaspar Schürmann, German
singer, conductor and composer,
was born at Hanover (died 1751,
February 25).

In his consort for four viols
written this year Locke combined
three dances with an opening
fantasia. In the latter he
carried the style of the fancy
even farther than Jenkins had.

Nicola Matteis, violinist, composer and father of Nicolas,
went to England at this time.

(to 1695) J. Carr, the English
publisher, was in business during this period.

1673
(January 14) Antonio Giannettini
entered the Cappella di San
Marco as a bass singer.

(January 17) A royal warrant
from the Lord Chamberlain's
office that accompanied the
dismissal of Henry Hall came
down. Henry Hall was Henry
Purcell's schoolmate and fellow
chorister in the Chapel Royal.

(February 10) Charpentier's "Le
Malade imaginaire, comédie
-ballet en 3 actes" was produced
at the Palais-Royal, in Paris.

(February 22) John Wilson, Mus.
Doc., died at Winchester (born
1594, April 5).

(March 1) Kaspar Förster,
German singer and composer,
died at Oliva near Danzig (born
1617).

(March 4) Johann Balthasar Bach,
son of J. Ambrosius, member of
the fifth generation of the
Bach family, and brother of J.
Sebastian, was born at
Eisenach (died 1691, April).

(March 25) The responsibilities
given to Edward Purcell as early
as this date were not those
that would have been assigned
to as young a man as Edward,
Henry's son, who was not yet
seventeen years old.

(April 16) Lindau in his
"Geschichte Dresdens," 1862
mentioned the Kapellmeister
Pallavicino as being present at
a private celebration of Mass
at the French Embassy at
Dresden.

(April 27) Lully's "Cadmus et
Hermione" was produced at
Paris.

(May 12) Issac Voss was appointed by King Charles II to
a vacant prebend at St. George's
Chapel of Windsor.

(May 13) Johannes Bach, the
eldest son of Johannes Bach,
died at Erfurt (born 1604,
November 26). He was director
of the Town Musicians and organist of the Prediger-Kirche, at
Erfurt. He was the "sire" of
the Erfurt branch of the family.

(May 23) Young became musician
in ordinary to the King.

1673(cont.)

(June 10) Henry Purcell, the younger, was appointed as another assistant to Hingeston on this date. Apparently there was too much for one person with one assistant to take care of. The duties of Hingeston were to keep the royal instruments in good repair.

(July 9) Johann Rudolph Ahle, German organist and composer, died at Mühlhausen (born 1625, December 24).

(July 13) One source gave this date as that of H. Cooke's death, but more evidence points to the same date a year earlier (see 1672).

(July 15) One source gave this as the date of Pelham Humfrey's succession to the position of Master of the Children of His Majesty's Chapel Royal. More evidence indicated the same date a year earlier as accurate (see 1672).

(August 2) Ralph Dallam's will carried this date.

(August 28) Andreas Düben, the younger, composer, was born at Stockholm (died 1738, August 23).

(September 13) Hercule Bréhy (known also as Pierre), Netherlandish composer and organist, was born at Brussels and baptised on this date (died 1737, February 28).

(September 19) Ralph Dallam's will was proved (probated) on this date.

(December 17) On this date by warrant Henry Purcell was dis-

(cont.) missed from the choristers of the Chapel Royal because his voice had changed. He was to receive a yearly stipend after his dismissal of £30.

(April) Nicolini, real name Nicola Grimaldi, Italian male contralto singer, was born at Naples (died 1732, January 1).

(May) Johann Valentin Eckelt, German organist and composer, was born at Werningshausen near Erfurt (died 1732, December 18).

(August) Edward Purcell was at this time employed at court, as a gentleman usher, daily waiter, and assistant. On this date a warrant granted him 100 marks per annum.

(September) Cambert arrived in London.

(Autumn) Carlo Pallavicino had returned to Venice, where his operas were restarted at the theatres there.

(December) Juan de Padilla protracted an illness and died at Toledo (born c.1610).

Johann Christoph Bach, son of J. Christian, grandson of Johann, member of the fifth generation of the Bach family and Gehren Cantor, was born (died 1727).

Jeremiah Clarke,I, English organist, was born (died 1707, December 1). There is considerable disagreement as to his birthdate. Some give it as 1674 and some as earlier than this year.

Ralph Dallam, English organ maker, died at Greenwich (birthdate unknown). His date of death has also been given as 1672.

Gottfried Grünewald, German composer, was born at Eibau, Lusatia (died 1739, December 19).

Reinhard Keiser, German scholar of the Leipzig Thomasschule and respected and important opera composer, was born (died 1739).

John Weaver, English dancing-master, was born at Shrewsbury (died 1760).

Filippo Acciaiuoli directed the Teatro di Torre di Nona ("Tordinona") in Rome at this time.

Johann Michael Bach (fourth generation) moved from Arnstadt to Gehren this year. He was both organist and parish clerk at Gehren.

John Banister's concerts in England were continued this year.

Brevi was at this time organist and afterwards "maestro di cappella" at Bergamo Cathedral.

From this date until his death Cazzati was in the service of the Duchess Anna Isabella di Gonzaga at Mantua.

A. Draghi this year was appointed intendant of the court theatre at Vienna.

G. Dumanoir, II, became involved in a long dispute with Lully over a privilege accorded (cont.) to the latter to train orchestra musicians. The case was decided by law this year in Lully's favor.

Ruggiero Fedeli, singer and composer, entered the chapel of St. Mark's in Venice this year as a bass singer.

Petronio Franceschini, one of the founders of the Accademia Filarmonica, was their president during this year.

Richard Hart this year became a musician in ordinary, replacing Robert Smith.

Johann Krieger this year went to Italy and studied with Rosenmüller, Rovetta and various other teachers.

John Leverett wrote home from Boston at this time to the effect that there was "not a Musician in the Colony."

At the death of Madeleine Phalèse in 1652 her sister Marie de Mayer undertook the management of the firm, which she continued until this year or perhaps a year later.

Pitoni this year became "maestro di cappella" at Terra di Rotondo and later at Assisi, where he began to score Palestrina's works, a practice he later recommended to his pupils as the best way of studying style.

J. Playford, the elder took part this year in the Salmon and Locke controversy, by addressing a letter to the former, "by way of Confutation of his Essay . . ." which was printed with Locke's "Present Practice of Musick vindicated."

According to one source Henry Purcell's activities were vague up to this year when the first extant record bearing his name appeared.

"The Tempest" first appeared this year, but there was no evidence of any of Purcell's music being written prior to 1695.

Thomas Purcell was appointed Marshal of the Corporation of Musicians this year replacing Henry Cooke who had resigned by reason of illness. This fact has been given as occurring in 1672 as well.

Thomas Purcell this year assumed the responsibility for annual payments to the King's musicians.

An engraving showing the river front of the Dorset Garden Theatre was prefixed to Elkanah Settle's "Empress of Morocco."

At the beginning of this year Agostino Steffani moved to Rome and began to compose assiduously.

Johann Theile this year accepted the invitation of Duke Christian Albert of Holstein to be his court Kapellmeister at Gottorp.

James White, Dallam's partner, finished building the Greenwich organ.

The Accoltuhus this year at Brzeg published a collection of 647 hymns and songs, "The Perfect Polish Hymn-Book."

Aschenbrenner's best-known work "Gast- und Hochzeit-freude, bestehend in Sonaten, Präludien, Allemanden, Couranten, Balletten,

(cont.) Arien, Sarabanden, mit drei, vier und fünf Stimmen, nebst dem basso continuo" was completed this year.

John Banister this year contributed to Locke's "Melothesia."

Banister's best known contribution to dramatic music was four of the six "Ariels Songs" for Shadwell's adaptation this year of "The Tempest."

G.M. Bononcini's opus 7, "Ariette, correnti, gighe, allemande e sarabande," in two to four parts, was published at Bologna this year and reprinted in 1677.

G.M. Bononcini's opus 8, "Musico -prattico che brevemente dimostra il modo di giungere alla perfetta cognizione di tutte quelle cose che concorrono alla composizione de i canti . . ." was published this year at Bologna and reprinted in 1688. The work was of a theoretical nature.

Bontempi with Peranda this year composed the German opera "Jupiter und Io."

Boretti's opera "Domitiano" appeared at this time.

Prior to this date Boretti composed several operas in addition to "Zenobia."

Buononcini published his "Musico prattico" at Bologna this year and in 1688.

Charpentier this year composed the music for Molière's "Malade Imaginaire."

Jan Cocx may have been the composer of the "Ferculum musicum" for one to four voices and instruments published this year at Antwerp.

C.C. Dedekind's "C.C.D.'s Musikalischer Jahrgang und Vesper-Gesang von dreien Theilen darinnen CXX., auf Sonn-Fest- und Apostel-Taage, geschiklich auserlesene, zur Sänger-Übung, nach rechter Capell-Manier gesetzte Deutsche Concerten durchgehends mit zweien Discanten befindlich" was published this year by Paul August Hamann at Dresden.

J.W. Franck wrote his "Glückwünschendes Jagdballet" this year for the court of the Margrave of Ansbach.

Freschi at this time published a mass with a collection of psalms.

Locke's "Melothesia" of this year included a courant for harpsichord by William Hall.

Several of Roger Hill's songs were included in "Musical Companion."

Humfrey's song "I pass all my time in a shady old grove" was included in Playford's "Choice Songs."

Jumilhac this year wrote "La Science et la pratique du plain-chant . . . . The work distinguished him as a musical theorist and an authority on plainsong.

A. Kircher's "Phonurgia Nova Sive Conjugium Mechanico -physicum Artis" appeared this year.

Locke this year composed the music for a revival of Shakespeare's "Macbeth" in England.

Locke's "Melothesia or Certain General Rules for Playing upon a continued-Bass" was published this year by J. Carr at London.

Locke wrote music this year for the masque "Orpheus and Euridice," an intermezzo included in Settle's "Empress of Morocco."

Locke at this time composed some of the music for "Psyche" an adaptation by Shadwell of the "Tragi-Comedy-Ballet" of the same name by Molière, Quinault and Corneille, with music by Lully (1671). Locke subtitled the work "The English Opera."

Löhner's "Poetischer Andacht -Klang" was published this year.

Lully's "Cadmus et Hermione" appeared at this time.

Keyboard pieces by John Moss were included in "Melothesia."

Penna at this time composed masses and other church music as well as French correnti in four parts.

In the second edition of Placker's "Evangelische Leeuwerck ofte" this year the date was changed by hand to 1673 on a great number of copies.

Playford's "Choice Songs and Ayres" was published this year.

Theile this year published his

1673(cont.)

"Passio Domini nostri Jeou Christi sei Matthaeum" at Lübeck and dedicated the work to Duke Christian Albert of Slesvig -Holstein.

Voss this year anonymously published his "De poematum canu et viribus rythmi," a treatise on the alliance of poetry and music.

An edition of G.B. Vitali's "Balletti correnti, gighe . . ." was published this year by Monte.

Kircher in his "Phonurgia" referred to a new quilled instrument.

Locke in his "Melothesia" called an ascending appoggiatura a "Fore-fall" and referred to the double stroke ornament as a "shake."

A French troupe gave operas in London at this time.

The company at the first Duke's theatre this year moved to Dorset Garden in the Strand.

Bazzani's opera: "L'inganno trionfato, overo La disperata speranza ravvivata ne' successi di Giacopo Quinto di Scozia e Maddalena di Francia" was performed this year at the private theatre of Count Sissa at Parma, in celebration of his son's wedding.

Buxtehude started the "Abendmusiken" this year at Lübeck.

Davenant's adaptation of Shakespeare's "Macbeth," with music by Locke, was produced

(cont.) this year at the Dorset Garden Theatre.

Duffett's "The Spanish Rogue" was produced at this time and contained several songs by A. Marsh, I.

M. Locke's "Psyche" was produced this year.

From this date forward Lully produced an opera almost yearly, or, as he called it, a "tragédie lyrique."

Marco Uccellini's "Le nari d'Enca" was performed at this time.

Molière, the renowned French playwright, died (born 1622). He was refused Christian burial.

William Wycherly, in imitation of Molière on the continent, wrote sophisticated marital comedies. His "The Country Wife" was written this year.

The "Test Act" was passed at this time.

(and 1674) Vitali was "maestro di cappella del santissimo Rosario di Bologna" at the church of San Petronio at Bologna during these years. The title was indicated on his works written while he was there.

(to 1678) Many reviews appeared in the "London Gazette" during these years that indicated that Banister's public concerts continued until near the period of his death.

(to 1679) At this time J.W. Franck was at the court of the Margrave of Ansbach, directing both court music and theatrical performances.

(to 1685) Charpentier's con-
nection with the Théâtre
-Francais continued after
Molière's death this year until
1685, the year of "Venus et
Adonis."

(to 1686) Lully, at his school
of opera, during this period
produced his famous series of
operas; twelve of them in collaboration with Quinault, and
three with Campistron and Thomas
Corneille, Pierre's brother.

(to 1687) These years are considered to be the opera composition period of Lully's career.

(to 1691) Heinrich Müller's
"Geistliche Erquick-Stunden"
contained devotions which were
set in verse and had tunes in
the form of spiritual arias by
several Nürnberg poets and musicians, members of the Pegnitz
-Blumen-Genossenschaft. They
were published under the title
"Poetischer Andacht-Klang" during these years.

(to 1701) Provenzale taught music at the Conservatorio dei
Turchini, Naples for these
twenty-eight years.

c.1673
Francois Duval, French violinist
and composer, was born (died
1728, January 27).

Charpentier's pastorale "Les
Arts florissans" appeared at
this time.

1674
(January 5) On this date Evelyn
reported seeing "an Italian opera
in music, the first that had

(cont.) been in England."

(January 9) Reinhard Keiser,
German composer, was born at
Teuchern, near Weissenfels
(died 1739, September 12). His
birthdate has also been given
as 1673.

(January 12) Giacomo Carissimi,
Italian composer, died at Rome
(born 1605).

(January 15) On this date
Draghi's dances were performed
in a production of Shadwell's
adaptation of Shakespeare's
"The Tempest."

(January 19) Lully's "Alceste,
ou Le Triomphe d'Alcide" was
produced at Paris. Sources
give both Versailles and Lully's
"Academie" as the location of
the performance. Perhaps there
were two this season.

(January 22) Hans Jensen
Buxtehude, Danish organist,
died (born 1602).

(February 4) On this date an
advertisement in the London
Gazette mentioned "A rare
Concert of four Trumpets Marine,
never heard of before in
England."

(February 22) Johann Augustin
Kobelais, German composer, was
born at Wählitz near Halle
(died 1731, August 17).

(February 22) John Wilson, composer, singer, violinist, composer and musician-in-ordinary
to the King in the Private
Music, died (born 1595, April
5).

(February 24) Matthias
Weckmann, German organist and

composer, died at Hamburg (born 1619). One source gave his birth as 1621.

(March 2) Roger Hill, English composer, died at London (birthdate unknown).

(March 15 or 16) John Blow was a Gentleman of the Chapel Royal from this date forward.

(March 24) Johann Christoph's daughter Maria Sophie Bach was born on this date or the same day in 1671 (date of death unknown).

(March 25) Catterina Stradivarius, daughter of Antonio Stradivarius, was born (died 1748, June 17).

(March 27) A warrant on this date decreed that Grabu assist with the production of Cambert's "Ariane, ou le Marige de Bacchus."

(March 30) Cambert and Perrin's "Ariane, ou le Mariage de Bacchus" ran a month after its opening on this date at the Theatre Royal in Bridges Street at London. The opera was sung in French although a translation was made available for readers, the first of its kind.

(April 9) Lewis Grabu's opera "Ariadne, or the Marriage of Bacchus" was produced at the Drury Lane Theatre.

(May 16) Boys belonging to His Majesty's Chapel Royal sang in "The Tempest" with songs by Reggio. The order for this was handed down on this date.

(June 9) Johann Aegidius Bach

(cont.) married Susanna Schmidt.

(July 4) On this date twelve additional violinists were ordered to report to Cambert at Whitehall for the royal entertainment to be presented at Windsor on July 11.

(July 14) Pelham Humfrey, English composer, died at Windsor (born 1647).

(July 17) Humfrey was buried in the cloisters of Westminster Abbey.

(July 23) John Blow became master of the Children of the Chapel Royal.

(August 2) Philip, Duke of Orleans, French amateur musician, nephew of Louis XIV and Regent of France 1715-1723, was born at Saint-Cloud (died 1723, December 2).

(August 27) Johann Christoph Bach, who taught clavier in Erfurt, Rotterdam and England, was born (died c.1730) See 1673.

(September 29) A warrant for a new felt hat for Purcell arrived at Michaelmas this year reminding him of his time as a chorister.

(November 1) Colonna became "maestro di cappella" of San Petronio, Bologna.

(November 19) Nicola Matteis on this date was described in Evelyn's "Diary" as a rare violinist "whom I never heard mortal man exceed on that instrument."

(December 1) Vitali was appointed assistant "maestro di cappella" to Duke Francesco II of Modena.

1674(cont.)

(December 2) On this date Evelyn reported hearing Signor Francisco play the harpsichord.

(April) Pietro Reggio had contributed to Shadwell's original production of Shakespeare's "The Tempest."

(May) At this time another performance of "The Tempest" included songs by Pietro Reggio.

(July) Cambert's "Pomone" was revived at the theatre in Whitehall in French altered by Grabu. It was the first performance abroad.

(July) A. Wood's "Historia et Antiquitates Universitatis Oxoniensis" was published.

(September) At St. Paul's Covent Garden, John Blow married Elizabeth, daughter of Edward Braddock, Gentleman of the Chapel Royal and Master of the Children of Westminster Abbey.

(September) William Holder was a fellow student of Purcell's at about this time. He was a former chorister and probably the son of the Canon of St. Paul's and may have been the composer of the service and the two anthems preserved in the Tudway manuscripts.

Tommaso Albinoni, renowned Italian violinist and composer, was born (died 1745).

Michel de La Barre, French flutist and composer, was born at Paris (died c.1744).

Jean-Laurent Le Cerf, French theorist, was born (died 1707). He wrote "comparaison de la

(cont.) musique italienne et de la musique française."

Friedrich Niedt, German lawyer and writer on music, was born at Jena (died c.1717).

Theodore Steffkins, English violinist, died (birthdate unknown).

D'Anglebert this year at thirteen years of age inherited the position of "Ordinaire de la Musique" from his father.

Bernabei succeeded Johann Kaspar Kerl this year as Kapellmeister at Munich.

John Blow succeeded Pelham Humfrey in two of the latter's positions this year, a week after Humfrey was buried. The positions were Master of the Children of the Chapel Royal and composer in the King's Private Music.

F. Corbett was in London at this time.

Robert Creyghton was appointed canon residentiary and precentor of Wells Cathedral this year.

Henry Eccles was a violinist in the King's Masque at this time.

Eisenhut at this time was "canonicus regularis" at St. George's, Augsburg.

Henry Hall this year succeeded Theodore Coleby as organist of Exeter Cathedral.

John Jackson this year was appointed nominally a vicar -choral, but in actual fact organist at Wells Cathedral.

Kerll left Munich at this time
and went to Vienna where he
gave lessons at what was then
high prices.

John Mawgridge's livery-garb
this year cost approximately
£ 52.

J.V. Meder this year became
cantor at Reval College, probably in Copenhagen.

J. Pachelbel was a pupil of
Kerll's in Vienna this year and
apparently acted as Kerll's assistant as organist of the imperial chapel.

At about this time James Paisible
joined the King's Band of Musick.
His name appeared in Staggins'
list of instrumentalists who
played for the masque "Calisto"
as an "Hoboye" player.

F. Pistocchi's father applied
for his son's readmission to the
choir at San Petronio this year.

At the beginning of this year
Thomas Purcell succeeded John
Wilson as musician-in-ordinary
to the King in the Private
Music.

Francesco Santarini, the im-
presario at the Teatro San
Moise at this time, reduced the
admission price from four
Venetian lire to a quarter-ducat.

Staggins abruptly achieved
prominence this year when he was
appointed Master of the King's
Music to succeed Grabu. One
source lists him as Master of
the Queen's Music.

Werckmeister this year refused
a position offered him at

(cont.) Elbingerode.

J. Westhoff at this time became
a chamber musician at Dresden.

The "Art Poétique" was published
this year and was well-received
throughout Europe.

Bononcini's opus 6 "Sonate" for
two violins and continuo was
reprinted at Bologna in this
year and in 1677. It was originally published at Venice in
1672.

Cambert was probably the composer of a "Ballet et musique
pour le divertissement du roy
de la Grande-Bretagne" whose
libretto was printed "Dans la
Savoye par Thomas Nieucombe"
this year.

Colonna's "Le contese di Pallade
e Venere sopra il bando d'Amore"
appeared at this time.

Dering's "Cantica sacra" for two
voices was published this year
at London.

Eisenhut composed his "Hymni
ariosi" at this time.

Petronio Franceschini's intermezzi for Pagliardi's opera
"Caligula delirante" were published this year at Bologna.

Charles Hacquart's "Cantiones
sacrae" was published this year
at Amsterdam.

James Hart's best-known song
"Adieu to the pleasures and
follies of love," written for
Shadwell's operatic adaptation
of "The Tempest," was published
this year as one of the six
"Ariel's Songs."

Jeffries at this time contributed a motet "Erit gloria Domini" to Dering's "Cantica sacra."

Scipione Lazarini this year wrote two books of motets, opus 1 and 2.

Locke's "6 Latin Hymns and 1 English Anthem" was published at this time.

Locke's music for Shadwell's adaptation of "The Tempest" this year was published.

Lully's opera "Alceste" with libretto by Quinault was composed this year.

G. Mazzaferrata this year composed twelve sonatas for two violins with a "bassetto viola" ad lib.

Pierre Phalèse's "Thesaurus Musicus Continens Selectissima Alberti Ripae Valentini Bacfarci et Aliorum . . ." was published this year at Louvain.

Gaspar Sanz, guitarist, this year published his "Instrucción de música sobre la guitarra española" at Saragossa.

Steffani published his first work this year, "Psalmodia vespertina volans 8 plenis vocibus concinenda ab Augost. Steffana in lucem edita aetatis suae anno 19 Monachii 1674."

The Bernese cornettis and musical director Sultzberger produce a three-part song-book as early as this date.

Harald Vallerius, Swedish mathematician, organist and composer, this year wrote a treatise (cont.) "Physico musica de sono."

An edition entitled "Vitali maestro di capella del Santissimo Rosario di Bologna & Accademico filaschise" was published this year. It contained "balletti, correnti alla francese . . ."

Wise's "I charge you o daughters" was included in Dering's "Cantica sacra."

The Gentlemen of the Chapel Royal as a group this year petitioned for £ 877.7s., owed to them since the summer of 1674, when they had gone to Windsor.

"Follias" were included in the "Instrucción de Musica" by Gaspar Sanz.

In the masque "Calisto" the oboe apparently reached England again under Cambert's influence.

Cesti's "Semiramide" was revived as "La schiava fortunata" this year (See also 1667).

Lully's "Psyché" this year was probably the first French opera to include bassoons.

Locke's version of "The Tempest" was produced at this time.

Shadwell's adaption of Shakespeare's "Tempest" was produced this year at the Dorset Garden Theatre.

Shadwell's "Psyche" "treating the musical element more dispersedly and picturesquely" was produced as a free adaptation of Molière's "Psyche" for Locke.

1674(cont.)
Robert Herrick, English Cavalier
poet, died (born 1591). He was
the leader of a group of "carpe
diem" poets in London.

John Milton, eminent English
poet, died (born 1608).

Dryden's opera taken from
Milton's "Paradise Lost" appeared this year.

Wycherly's "The Plain Dealer"
was written at this time.

Jan Sobieski this year became
King of Poland.

Philippe de Champaigne, French
painter, died (born 1602).

Dutch painting: Jan Steen,
"Celebration in a Tavern" (oil
on canvas, 46 1/2 x 63 3/8").

English architecture: Wren,
Drury Lane Theater.

(and 1675) Ercole Bernabei was
quite possibly the composer of
four dramatic works performed
at the electoral court at
Munich during these years.

(to 1675) C.C. Dedekind's
"Königs Davids göldnes Kleinod,
oder hundert und neunzehender
Psalm, nach eigener Abteilung,
in zwei und zwanzig Stukken,
mit dreien Concertirenden
Singe- dreien Instrumental-
und vier ausvöllenden Capell
-Stimmen, componiret von C.C.D.
der Zeit Kurf. Sächs. bestelltem
deutschen Concertmeister" was
published this year by Hamann
at Dresden.

(and 1676 to 1677, 1687) Clamor
Heinrich Abel's "Erstlinge
musikalischer Blumen" first ap-

(cont.) peared in three volumes
at Frankfort (1674 and 1676 to
1677). Later they were combined
under the title of "Drei Opera
musica" published at Braunschweig
in 1687.

(to 1678) Kusser arrived from
Brunswick to assist Reinken at
the Hamburg German Opera during
this period.

(to 1700) Staggins was Master of
the King's band during these
years.

(to 1706) Pedro Ardanaz was musical director at Toledo
Cathedral during this period.

(to 1710) Henry Eccles during
these years was a member of the
King's Band.

(to 1710) Charles Hacquart composed ten Sonatas for three and
four string instruments during
these years.

(to 1720) John Reading II, an
English organist and composer,
was organist of Chichester
Cathedral during these forty-six
years. His dates of birth and
death are not known.

c.1674
Between this year and 1678 Johann
Bach, successor to J. Seb. Bach
as organist at Mühlhausen, was
born (died 1730). He married
but had no children.

John Barrett, English composer,
was born (died c.1735).

1675
(January 3) Johann Jonas Bach,
son of J. Ambrosius, member of
the fifth generation of the
Bach family, and brother of J.
Sebastian, was born at Eisenach

(died 1685).

(January 12) Lully's "Thesée" was produced at Saint-Germain.

(January 29) Staggins replaced Grabu as Master of the King's Music.

(February 27) John Gostling, English bass, was married.

(March 1) Steffani was appointed court organist at Munich.

(March 9) Thomas Purcell was not listed among the nine musicians who accompanied King Charles II to Newmarket for nineteen days starting on this date.

(March 16) Petronio Franceschini was appointed cellist in the chapel at San Petronio, Bologna.

(March 17) "Circé, tragédie, précédée d'un prologue, par M. Corneille de l'Isle" with music of the intermèdes by Charpentier was produced at the Théâtre de Guénégaud in Paris.

(April 2) Johann Christoph Bach, son of Johann Aegidius, was born but died young (date of death unknown).

(May 27) Purcell's name did not appear in the warrant of this date for musicians employed by Staggins for the "masque at Whitehall" notwithstanding a large group of performers who were assembled for the event.

(June 12) Shadwell's "The Libertine," a tragi-comic version of the Don Juan legend, was first produced at Dorset Garden on this date.

(June 18) Antonio Maria Bononcini (Marc' Antonio), composer, was born at Modena (died 1726, July 8).

(June 26) From this date to the end of the summer King Charles II retired to Windsor, accompanied by his musical retinue.

(July 3) Randolph Jewett, Irish or English organist and composer, died at Winchester (born c.1603).

(July 12) Evaristo (Felice) Dall' Abaco, Italian violinist and composer, was born at Verona (died 1742, July 12).

(August 15) Purcell and Hingeston did not go to Windsor with King Charles II until this date, the rest of the group had been there since the beginning of the summer.

(September 17) Heinrich Müller, German ecclesiastic and hymnologist, died at Rostock (born 1631, October 18).

(October 24) According to one source Christopher Gibbons was buried at the cloisters of Westminster Abbey on this date. Other sources have his date of death as October 20, 1676.

(November 8) Andreas Hammerschmidt, Austro-Bohemian organist and composer, died at Zittau (born 1612 or 1639).

(November 17) "L'Inconnu, comédie en 5 actes de M. Corneille de l'Isle et de M. Visé; mêlées d'ornemens de musique de Charpentier" was produced at the Théâtre de Guenegaud in Paris.

1675(cont.)

(November 22) Robert Smith,
English composer, died at
London (born c.1648).

(December 28) Raphael
Courteville, Gentleman of the
Chapel Royal, died probably at
London (birthdate unknown).

(February) Shadwell's "Psyche"
with music by Draghi and Locke
was produced at the Dorset
Garden Theatre.

(February) Staggins' court
masque, "Calisto, or the Chaste
Nymph" was performed at
Whitehall.

(February) Issac Staggins,
Nicholas' father, played for the
masque "Calisto" with his son,
the composer.

(April) "Siface" was admitted to
the papal chapel at Rome this
month.

(November) John Forbes,
Scottish music printer and publisher, died at Aberdeen (birthdate unknown).

Thomas Davidson, master of the
Music School in Scotland, died
(birthdate unknown).

Johann Khuen, German composer
and beneficiary of St. Peter's
at Munich who wrote many sacred
songs, died at Munich (birthdate
unknown).

Michel de La Barre, French
flutist, was born (died 1743).

Hedwig Lämmerhirt, second wife
of Johann Bach (third generation), died (birthdate unknown).

Anthony Van Noordt, Dutch or-

(cont.) ganist, died at
Amsterdam (birthdate unknown).

Abbé Pierre Perrin, founder of
the Académie Royale de Musique
and active man in the creation
of French opera and the "première
comédie francoise en musique,"
died (born 1620 or 1625).

Antonio Vivaldi, renowned
Italian composer, was born at
Venice (died 1741, July 28).
One isolated source gave his
birth as 1669.

Domenico Zipoli, Italian organist and composer, has been incorrectly assigned this birthdate. Actually he was a Tuscan
born in 1688 (died 1726, January
2).

Johann Michael Bach (fourth
generation) married Katharina
Wiedemann of Arnstadt this year.

Angelo Berardi was "maestro di
cappella" at the cathedral of
Tivoli at this time.

After his father's death this
year Georg Böhm was sent to the
Latin school at Goldbach.

Bruges had a carillon at this
time.

Cametti discovered the name of
Arcangelo Corelli as the third
of four violinists serving the
Church of St. Louis of France
this year at Rome. His pay was
one and one half écus. This
then proved Corelli's presence
in Rome.

Clifford this year was advance
to the sixth minor canonry.

As early as this year Colasse
was on friendly terms with Lully.

The preclassical German school used the following Corelli techniques after this date: arpeggios like those in the first sonata of opus 5 (allegro), chains of sixths as in the second (allegro), rapid figures in thirds as in the third (first allegro).

Baldassare Ferri this year at the age of sixty-five was given permission to retire to his native country.

Agostino Filippucci this year was president of the Accademia dei Filarmonici at Monte, Bologna.

De Grandis became chapel master to the Duke of Brunswick at this time.

Gaetano Greco this year was a student-teacher of the violin at the Naples "Conservatorio dei Poveri di Gesù."

An opera with libretto based on the subject of King Philip's War in New England written this year by F.S. Hyde was mentioned by Hipsher, but no information was included.

Jérôme de La Guerre this year was admitted as a substitute for the "recette du temporal de la Sainte-Chapelle."

Matteis' spectacular rise and the popularity enjoyed at the time by Italian musicians in London prefaced Grabu's decline early this year.

Georg Muffat was organist of Strasbourg Cathedral until this time.

F. Pistocchi began a career as an operatic singer this year.

Purcell became an apprentice to Hingeston and learned quickly. This year he was paid £2 for tuning the organ at Westminster Abbey, apparently on his own.

Bernard Smith built the organ for St. Margaret's, Westminster at this time.

The Duchy of Holstein at Gottorp was invaded and occupied by the troops of the Danish King this year and Kapellmeister Theile and the Duke of Holstein had to seek refuge at Hamburg.

This year or possibly a year later Harald Valierius, the Swedish mathematician, organist and composer, was appointed "director musices" ("rector cantus") at the University of Uppsala.

Vopelius at this time became cantor at the church of St. Nicholas at Leipzig.

Werckmeister accepted a position as court organist at Quedlinburg this year.

Biber at this time composed fifteen violin sonatas representing episodes in the life of Christ. These were known as the "Mystery Sonatas."

Some of Isaac Blackwell's songs were included in Playford's "Choice Ayres."

Bononcini's "Trattenimenti musicali" for three to four instruments, opus 9 was published this year at Bologna.

Cavalli's vespers for eight

voices was published at this
time.

Charpentier this year composed
the "intermedes" for "Circé."

A manuscript collection of keyboard pieces in the
Bibliothèque Nationale bearing
this date and assembled for
"Instruction und unterricht,"
included a number of women's
names in the titles of the
pieces. All the selections are
called "canzona."

Draghi's "Psyche" music and
Locke's songs were published
this year.

J.G. Ebeling's "Archaeologiae
Orphicae sive antiquitates
musicae" was published this
year at Stettin.

J.W. Franck wrote his opera
"Die unvergleichliche Andromeda"
for the court of the Margrave of
Ansbach at this time.

Hymn-books with settings for
four voices based on Goudimel's
psalter were produced this year
at Berne as the "Transponierte
Psalmenbuch" of Sultzberger.

Hieronymus Gradenthaler this
year wrote a book of sonatas for
violin solo and four-stringed
instruments.

Some of Roger Hill's songs were
included in H. Lawes' "Select
Ayres."

Humfrey's music for Dryden's "The
Indian Emperor" was heard this
year after the composer's death.

Giovanni Legrenzi at this time
composed the opera "Eteocle e

(cont.) Polinice."

Legrenzi's opera, "Eteocle e
Polinice," was published this
year.

Locke this year composed music
for Shadwell's adaptation of
the comedy-ballet "Psyche" by
Moliere and Lully. It was
called "The English opera or
the Vocal Musicke in Psyche."
Ths music was published with
Locke's music to "The Tempest"
under the above title.

Paolo Lorenzani's "Sacri
concerti" and "Scelta di
motetti sacri" were both published at this time.

The Louis de France vocal manuscripts were compiled this
year.

Lully's "Thésée" was composed
this year.

Psalms were frequently published
at this time in amusing editions
with flower pictures and emblems
such as in the "Lust und
Artzeney-Garten."

Johann Nicolai this year at
Augsburg wrote twelve sonatas,
partly for two violins and a
viola da gamba, and partly for
two violins and bassoon.

Del Pane's "Motetti" for two
to five voices, opus 2 was published this year at Rome.

Del Pane's "Sagri concerti" for
two to six voices, opus 3 appeared this year.

Petzold's "Musicalische
Seelenerquickungen" appeared at
this time.

Playford's "Choice Ayres" was published this year.

One source gave this date for Purcell's opera "Dido and Aeneas."

Purcell's song "When Thirsis did the splendid eye" was published this year.

Johann Sebastiani's second collection of "Parnassblumen" was published this year at Hamburg.

Some of William Turner's songs were included in Shadwell's "The Libertine."

Pierre Gussanville questioned the usual practice of attributing the reform of Gregorian Chant to Pope Gregory I.

The founding of the musical society "Accademia dei Filarmonici" at Bologna was given as this date by a major musicologist but it appears to have been considerably earlier.

Antonio Giannettini's first opera, "Medea in Atene," was produced this year at Venice. It was the greatest success of any of his works.

Dal Gaudio's opera "Almerico in Cipro" was produced this year at Venice.

Legrenzi's "Eteocle e Polinice" was produced this year at Venice.

Locke's music for "Psyche" was heard this year at London.

Pallavicini's opera "Diocleziano" with libretto by Matteo Noris was produced this

(cont.) year at the Teatro dei SS. Giovanni e Paolo at Venice.

C. Pallavicini's opera "Enea in Italia" with libretto by G. Francesco Busani was produced this year at the Teatro dei SS. Giovanni e Paolo in Venice.

"Psyche" by Shadwell this year in a production listed a "Mr. Morgan" as having written the music.

Uccellini's opera "Li eventi di Filandro ed Edessa" was performed this year at the Collegio dei Nobili in Parma.

John Dryden's "Aurengzebe" was written at this time.

Philipp Jakob Spener this year wrote "Pia desideria" which became the doctrine for Pietism.

Jacopo Amiconi, Italian painter, was born at Venice (died 1752).

Gerard Dou, Dutch painter, died (born 1613).

Sir James Thornhill, British decorator and exponent of the late Baroque, was born (died 1734).

Jan Vermeer van Delft, Dutch painter, died (born 1632).

(to 1682) Louis de France was master of the Music School at Aberdeen during these years.

(to 1684) Many of Damascene's songs were included in "Choice Ayres and Songs" during this period.

(and 1690, 1702) "Preussisches Kirchen-Schul- u. Hans -Gesangbuch" published at these

1675(cont.)
dates contained melodies by
Eccard.

(to 1710) English architecture:
Wren, St. Paul's (London),(514'
by 250', total height 366').

c.1675
Tomasso Albinoni, Italian composer and violinist, was born
at Venice according to one
source. Others give his date
of birth as 1671, June 8 (died
1750, January 17).

Johann Friedrich Bach, who succeeded Johann Sebastian at
Mühlhausen, was born (died 1730).

Giovanni Antonio Boretti,
Italian composer, died at
Venice (birthdate unknown).

John Church, English composer,
was born at Windsor (died 1741,
January 6).

Michel Angelo Gasparini,
Italian contralto singer and
composer, was born at Lucca
(died 1732).

Tomaso Redi, Italian composer,
was born at Siena. He was
maestro di cappella at the
Santa Casa di Loretto in Rome
for forty years and was a mass
composer (died 1738, July 20).

Cabanilles was considered to be
the greatest Spanish organist
of this time. His compositions
tended to be "old-fashioned" but
as an organist he served as a
leader and model for subsequent
members of the Spanish school.

This period in Bologna was dominated by Colonna and his pupils, including Bononcini and
Predieri. Their work was done

(cont.) at the Chapel of San
Petronio.

Teobaldo de' Gatti at this time
went to Paris, where he joined
the orchestra at the Paris
Académie Royale de Musique.

Jacques Hotteterre of the most
famous of a noted family of
woodwind makers and players was
active at this time at the
French court.

G.M. Pagliardi was "maestro di
cappella" to the Duke of
Tuscany at this time.

Philidor was the name assumed by
a celebrated family of musicians
which flourished at the French
court at this date. The true
name of the family was Danican.

John Playford was England's
most prolific theorist, composer
and publisher at this time.

Antonio Veracini lived at
Florence during this period.

Thomas Greeting this year published a book of instruction for
playing the flageolot.

In all probability Fabian
Stedman's method of Change
-Ringing was composed at this
time.

Technical invention took prece-
dence over musical matters at
this time. The need was obvious
in all areas for unification of
technique and to some degree for
stabilization. An example was
needed that would force recognition by all innovators a "chel
d'école."

Hemony at this time maintained
that a good bell "must be so

459

c.1675(cont.)

proportioned that its partial tones contain three octaves, two fifths, a minor third and a major third."

The oboe first appeared at the French court at this time.

The Spanish organ did not have a pedal keyboard and was still restricted to the simple bass of one diatonic octave, just as in the previous century.

The viola d'amore was apparently introduced during this period.

The unloading of the string (violin) was introduced in France by Sainte-Colombe at this time.

The sonata developed from the instrumental canzona and around this time there were two clearly defined types of the Baroque Sonata, the sonata da chiesa (church sonata) and the sonata da camera (chamber sonata). Both were composed for small instrumental groups.

At this time in England, the Italian schools of music held unchallenged leadership in the musical world.

Lima was an important center of musical activity at this time.

About 400 new operas were produced in Vienna during the fifty years surrounding this date.

The struggle between Orthodoxy and Pietism which had begun in the second half of the century continued throughout this period and actually overshadowed Bach's importance.

At this time in England the following sign 𝄢 was a variant of 𝄢 and was interpreted as a) trill, b) 1/2 shake, c) mordent.

English painting: Sir Peter Lely, "Nell Gwynn" (47 1/2" by 38").

Italian painting: Medina, "The Cabal."

(to c.1699) Johann Wilhelm Haas, German brass instrument maker, was active during these years.

(to c.1699) The Italian one-movement canzona concertata developed into the concerto in its modern form during this period.

(to c.1699) At this time Italian style was the principal foundation for German composers.

(to c.1699) Opera became the backbone of musical life in Berlin at this time when it first developed a foothold there during these years.

(to c.1699) German clavichords during this period encompassed a range of four octaves.

(to c.1725) At this time in England act-tunes were composed especially for every play.

(to c.1799) Signs of articulation were not uncommon during this period.

(to c.1799) This was the prime period of spinet manufacture. The most renowned 17th-Century makers were Keene, Player, Haward, and the Hitchcocks, Thomas and John. In the early 18th-Century Slade, Mahoon and Baker were the best known men

c.1675(cont.)
in the field.

1676
(January 6) Wise became a
Gentleman of the Chapel Royal.

(January 10) Lully's "Atys" was
produced at Saint-Germain.

(January 14) (Pietro) Francesco
Cavalli, Italian composer, died
at Venice (born 1602, February
14). He was also an organist
at St. Mark's and eventually
succeeded Monteverdi.

(January 19) John Weldon,
English organist and composer,
was born at Chichester (died
1736, May 7).

(February 22) Georg Ludwig
Agricola, German composer, died
at Gotha (born 1643, October
25).

(March 16) By this date Locke
had gained enough control over
the Chapel Royal band (which he
directed during Staggins' leave
of absence for study in Italy)
so that his invitation to "some
of the gentlemen of His Majesty's
Music" was effective.

(April 19) Pasquini's first
opera "La donna ancore è fedele"
with libretto by Domenico
Filippo Contini was produced
at the Palazzo Colonna in Rome.

(April 21) William Howes,
English singer, instrumentalist
and composer, died at Windsor
(birthdate unknown).

(April 25) A. Marsh, II was
admitted a Gentleman of the
Chapel Royal.

(May 17) Joachim Gigault, French

(cont.) organist, was born at
Paris (died 1765, March).

(July 5) On this date Elizabeth
Purcell made an application to
the Vestry of Westminster Abbey
requesting some allowance be
granted for her lodgings.

(October 17) Christopher Gibbons,
Orlando's son, left a
"nuncupative" will bearing this
approximate date.

(October 20) Christopher Gibbons,
English composer, son of Orlando,
died at London (born 1615). One
source gave his burial date as
October 24, 1675. He was buried
at the Abbey Cloisters.

(October 24) Louis-Thomas
Bourgeois, French singer and
composer, was born at Fontaine
-l'Évêqué, Hainault (died 1750,
January).

(November 18) Durfey's play "The
Fool Turn'd Critick" was performed at Drury Lane.

(November 23) Johann Bernhard
Bach, Eisenach organist, son of
J. Egidius, grandson of Johann
Bach, member of the fifth gener-
ation of the Bach family, was
born at Erfurt (died 1749,
June 11).

(December 19) Louis Nicolas
Clérambault, French composer,
clavecinist and organist, was
born at Paris (died 1749,
October 26).

(October) A payment was made at
this time when troops were being
raised for service in Virginia:
"Drummers impressed by Drum
-Major-General John Mawgridge
for the occasion-15."

1676(cont.)

Johann Christoph Bach, clavier
teacher, son of J. Christoph,
grandson of Heinrich, member of
the fifth generation of the
Bach family, was born (date of
death unknown). This is in conflict with another source, see
August 27, 1674.

John Blow's son Henry died
(birthdate unknown).

Adam Horacy Casparini, Polish
organ builder, was born at
Wroclaw (died 1745).

Juan Cererols, a Spanish composer, died (born 1618).

Joachim Düben, father of Karl
Vilhelm Düben, Swedish-German
musician, was born (died 1730).

Johann Georg Ebeling, German
composer, died at Stettin
(born 1637, July 11).

Paul Gerhardt, the principal
hymnist of the century, died
(born 1607).

Ernst Christian Hesse, German
violinist and composer, was
born at Grossgottern,
Thuringia (died 1762, May 16).

Sebastian Knüpfer, German philologist and musician, died at
Leipzig (born 1632, November
28).

Jacopo Melani, Italian composer,
died at Pistoia (born 1623,
July 6).

Adam Václav Michna, Czech composer and poet, died at
Jindřichův Hradec, Bohemia
(born c.1600).

Somis, a pupil of Corelli, was

(cont.) born (died 1763).

Degli Antonii was president of
the Accademia dei Filaschisi
this year.

Jakob Bach (fourth generation)
at this time became a teacher
in a Thuringian village, Thal.

Buns became superior of the
monastery at Boxmeer this year
or a year later.

Dering was included this year
in Mace's list of excellent
composers.

Duponchel at this time was
organist at the Cathedral in
Osimo.

Domenico Gabrieli became a member of the Accademia Filarmonica
in Bologna this year.

Carlo Grossi this year became
a singer at St. Mark's Venice.

Charles Hacquart attended the
negotiations for the Peace of
Nijmegen at this time.

Henry Jaye, an instrument maker,
was listed this year by Mace as
one of the best viol makers.

William Lawes' name was mentioned this year in Mace's list
of eminent composers of fantasies.

Leibnitz at this time went to
live at the court of Hanover
and with the Duchess Sophia
raised the intellectual standard
of the court to a high level.

Christian Liebe, German organist and composer, went to
Leipzig this year.

Pitoni moved to Rieti at this time.

Purcell received payment for work as a copyist at Westminster Abbey this year and in 1688.

Johann Schelle at this time succeeded Knüpfer as cantor at St. Thomas' Church and School in Leipzig.

Bernhard Smith became organist at St. Margaret's, Westminster this year.

According to Pitoni, chapel master at St. Peter's in Rome at this time, Stradella considered the oratorio "S. Giovanni Battista" to be his best work.

Theile was an unsuccessful candidate this year for the St. Thomas cantorate at Leipzig.

Vallerius this year became organist of the cathedral at Uppsala.

Volume II of Abel's "Erstlinge Musikalischer Blumen" was published this year at Frankfort.

Four airs by Arne were found in a collective album of this year according to Eitner.

Johann Christoph Bach's (fourth generation) motet "Der Gerechte" was written this year.

Charles Davenant's opera "Circe" with music by Banister was composed at this time.

Aphra Behn's "Abdelazar" was published this year.

Biber's "Sonatae tam aris quam

(cont.) aulis servientes" was published this year at Salzburg.

Charpentier's "Airs de la comédie de Circé" was issued this year by Ballard.

Dedekind arranged the words for the sacred musical drama "Musik bequemten Schauspielen angewendet" and it was published this year at Dresden in eight volumes.

Duponchel's "Messe a 3, 4, e 5 voci concertate con Vio. e ripieni a beneplacito" opus 3 was published this year at Rome and in a later edition at Venice in 1685.

Etherege in his "Man of Mode" this year referred to "French hautboys."

Petronio Franceschini's opera "Oronte di Menfi" was published at this time.

D. Francesco Frederici this year wrote two oratorios, "Santa Cristina" and "Santa Caterina di Siena" for the Congregation of Oratorians.

Gradenthaler's tutor for elementary harmony and singing and a book of sonatas for violin and four-stringed instruments were both published this year.

"Neue Arien" (New Airs) was published in 1667 by Adam Krieger of Dresden and a later edition appeared this year.

Legrenzi at this time composed the opera "Germanico sol Reno."

Thomas Mace' "Musick's Monument" was published this year at London.

Songs composed by A. Marsh, I were included in "Choice Ayres & Dialogues."

Mazzaferrata this year composed "Salmi concertati" for three to four voices.

Playford's "Choice Ayres, Songs and Dialogues" was published this year.

A song by Purcell was included in the new edition this year of Book I of Playford's "Choice Ayres."

The "Papist" of "Jesuit" plot was commemorated in a political catch written this year by Purcell. The composition has been assigned to this year on the basis of a sub-title in "A Choice Compendium" published by J.H., "A catch made in time of Parliament, 1676."

Savioni at this time wrote several motets for solo voice.

Shadwell's "The Virtuoso" was published this year.

Stradella this year wrote the music to "S. Giovanni Battista."

Some of Turner's songs were included in Durfey's "Madame Fickle" published at this time.

A collection of twelve sonatas for violin by Johann Jakob Walther was published this year under the title "Scherzi."

A catalogue at St. Michael's library printed this year revealed that not only well-known large collections of choral works were on hand but also printed works by Ahle,

(cont.) Hammerschmidt, Scheidt, as well as those by a number of other composers.

The office of drum-major general was in existence this year at the latest.

Mace characterized the saraband in his Musick's Monument as "more toyish, and lighter than Corantes." He also provided the best contemporary description of the substance and spirit of the consort of viols at its highest point of development. In the matter of phrasing he asked for "a kind of Cessation, or standing still, sometimes Longer, and sometimes Shorter, according to the nature, or Requiring of the Humour of the Musick." Concerning interpretation he remarked "Liberty (and very often . . .) to Break Time; sometimes Faster, and sometimes Slower, as we perceive the Nature of the Thing Requires." In the matter of expression and/or texture he suggested "a Handsom-Smooth -Sweet-Smart- Clear-Stroak; or else Play not at all." His feelings were that "in Musick, may any Humour, Conceit or Passion (never so various) be Exprest." The section on ornamentation covered the "ascending appoggiatura, half-fall ("ever from a half- note beneath"), the ascending slide "whole-fall," the prolonged lower mordent in terms of lute technique, the double relish ornament, the springer, a single rising stroke a) before the note or lutenists letter meant lower appoggiatura b) over the note or after the letter meant a springer and finally he described a genuinely unprepared trill, begun on its main note.

Banister this year wrote the
music for Duffett's masque
"Beauties Triumph," "presented
by the scholars of Mr. Jeffery
Bannister, and Mr. James Hart,
at their new boarding-school
for young ladies and gentle-
women, kept in that house which
was formerly Sir Arthur Georges,
at Chelsey." Josiah Priest was
involved with the work.

Davenant's "Circe" with
Banister's music was produced
at the Dorset Garden theatre
this year.

Aphra Behn's "Abdelazer" was
performed this year for the
first time.

Colonna's oratorio "La morte di
sant' Antonio di Padova" was
performed at Bologna.

Pasquini's opera "La donna
ancor è fedele" was produced
this year at Rome.

The following works by
Staggins received their first
performance this year: "As
Amoret with Phyllis sat" (words
by Scrope, in Etheredge, "The
Man of Mode"), "How severe is
fate" (Lee, "Gloriana"), "Let
business no longer" (Lee,
"Gloriana"), and "When first
Amintas" (Etheredge, "The Man
of Mode").

Prince Franz Leopold Rákoczy of
Transylvania was born (died
1735).

Pope Clement X this year was
succeeded by Pope Innocent XI.

American architecture: Bacon's
Castle, Virginia (c.48' x 40').

(or 1679) Marguerite-Louise
Couperin, soprano and harpsichordist, was born at Paris
(died 1728).

(to 1682) The reign of Czar
Theodore III over Russia.

(to 1684) Numerous songs by
Humfrey were included in "Choice
Ayres, Songs & Dialogues" during
these years.

(to 1685) Antonio Sartorio was
maestro di cappella at St.
Mark's in Venice during this
period.

(to 1686) Antonio Giannettini
at this time was second organist
at the Cappella di San Marco.

(to 1686) Petz during these
years was a singer and violinist
in the chapel of St. Peter's at
Munich.

(and 1688) Collections by Johann
Jakob Walther were published
this year and in 1688 and were
of the highest quality.

(to 1689) The Papal reign of St.
Innocent XI.

(to 1699) The chamber organ's
use and status during these
years were described in Mace's
"Musick's Monument."

(to 1713) A "Mr. Bryan" was
organist at Allhallow's, Barking,
till his death in 1713. He may
have been Albertus Bryne.

(to 1716) English architecture:
Wren, Greenwich, Royal Hospital
(150' high).

(to 1718) Degli Antonii was
president of the Accademia dei
Filarmonici sixteen times during

1676(cont.)
this period.

c.1676
Johann Michael Bach, an organ builder, was born (date of death unknown).

Jacques de Bournonville, French composer, was born at Amiens (died 1758).

Nicolas Racot de Grandval, French composer and harpsichordist, was born at Paris (died 1753, November 16).

After Torelli's death the center of concerto composition moved from Bologna to Venice where Antonio Vivaldi, a Legrenzi pupil, sparked the upward trend of the solo concerto.

(to c.1685) Purcell's anthems mostly belonged to the early period (to c.1685). Most of his stage works were written during the last six years of his life.

1677
(January 5) Lully's "Isis" was produced at his school of opera.

(January 16) Érrard Titon du Tillet, French author, was born at Paris (died 1762, November 26).

(French 13) Although this was a difficult time for musicians Purcell on this date received the benefits of a warrant for more clothing.

(February 26) Nicola Fago ("Il Tarantino"), Italian composer and teacher, was born at Taranto (died 1745, February 18).

(April 20) John Foster, English

(cont.) composer, died at Durham (birthdate unknown).

(May 22) His Majesty's musicians resisted performing for his birthday celebration as was made obvious by a warrant issued on this date requiring all musicians to appear for practice.

(May 25) Alessandro Stradivarius, son of Antonio Stradivarius, was born (died 1732, June 26).

(May 27) Maria Salome Bach, daughter of Johann Ambrosius, was born (date of death unknown). She married a man named Wiegand.

(May 29) For the celebration of King Charles' birthday on this date the French complement turned out in full array and performed Paisible's music for Madame de la Roche-Guilhen's comedy-ballet, "Rare-en-tout."

(August 6) Giovanni Battista Vivaldi, Antonio's father, married Camilla Calicchio.

(September 10) Henry Purcell succeeded Matthew Locke as composer-in-ordinary to the violins on this date.

(September 13) On this date Purcell finished writing the table of contents for a series of anthems which he had previously scored, presumably for his own purposes. The scores would have been of little use for practical performance.

(September 27) Giovanni Clari, Italian composer, was born at Pisa (died 1754, May 16).

(October 29) Charles d'Assoucy, French poet, musician and adventurer, died at Paris (born

1677(cont.)
1605, October 16).

(December 10) John Blow was
awarded the degree of Doctor of
Music by the Dean and Chapter
of Canterbury.

(February) Robert Cambert, first
French opera composer, died at
London (born c.1628).

(April) The "Mercure galant"
published an "éloge fun e bre"
for Cambert.

(May) Banister's last work for
the stage, the music for
Davenant's "Circe" was performed
at Dorset Gardens Theatre.

(August) Matthew Locke, English
composer, died at London (born
c.1630). See c.1633.

(August) The accounts of musicians for the church of Saint
-Louis-des-Français at Rome for
this month do not mention
Corelli.

Johann Michael Albani, Austrian
violin maker (real name Alban),
was born at Bozen (died 1730,
March 27).

Johann Ludwig Bach, conductor,
son of Jakob, grandson of
Wendel, member of the fifth
generation of the Bach family,
was born (died 1731 or 1741).

Maria Salome Bach, daughter of
J. Ambrosius, member of the
fifth generation of the Bach
family, was born (date of death
unknown).

Maurizio Cazzati, Italian composer, died at Mantua (born
c.1620).

Hymn-writer Johann Franck died
(born 1618).

John Reading III, English organist and composer, was born
(died 1764, September 2).

Angelus Silesius (Johannes
Scheffler) died (born 1624).
He was a writer on German
mysticism, his greatest work,
"Der Cherubinische Wandersmann."

The Bachs at Arnstadt this year
petitioned to have Heinrich
Gräser, who had been ridiculing
them, forced to apologize publicly.

Johann Ambrosius Bach became
part of the new band of Prince
Johann Georg I this year.

As early as this year Bassani
was organist and "maestro di
cappella" of the Confraternità
della Morte at Finale di Modena.

Bassani at this time market the
courante "largo."

Giuseppe Antonio Bernabei this
year followed his father to
Munich as assistant chapel
master, and was appointed
chapel master after Ercole's
death in 1688.

According to the register of
Lambeth degrees, the only
vacancy which Blow could possibly have filled prior to this
date was that created by the
death of Christopher Gibbons.

Buns became Superior of the
monastery at Boxmeer in this
year or perhaps a year earlier.

Fischer's categorical statement
that Bononcini published his
first concerti grossi in this

year has dubious value since a list of published works by Bononcini does not include any set of concerti grossi.

William Bull was appointed Trumpeter in Ordinary this year.

A collection of eight-part church music by Cocx was mentioned in an inventory of printed music made this year for the church of St. James.

Lully this year procured a position for Colasse as "batteur de mesure" (Conductor) at the Académie Royale de Musique.

When Locke died this year Draghi succeeded him as organist to King Charles II's queen, Catherine of Braganza.

Estwick was awarded the degree of Bachelor of Arts this year.

Ruggiero Fedeli, singer and composer, at this time left his position at the chapel of St. Mark's in Venice.

Thomas Fenell became vicar -choral of St. Patrick's Cathedral at Dublin this year.

Giovanni Domenico Freschi this year became house composer at the new Teatro di Sant' Angelo at Venice.

Ann, Elizabeth and Mary Gibbons, daughters of Christopher and Elizabeth, were all living at this time.

Élisabeth Jacquet de La Guerre's compositions were announced at this time by her "Mercure de France."

Kerll became organist at St. Stephen's Cathedral this year.

Krieger at this time returned to Bayreuth by way of Vienna where he was ennobled by the Emperor Leopold I.

After this year Antoine Moqué remained an adult singer in the parish church choir of Ostend.

J. Pachelbel was appointed court organist at Eisenach this year.

Pitoni presently became "maestro di cappella" of the Collegio di San Marco in Rome, where his works for two and three choirs were premiered.

In the famous frost scene in Purcell's "King Arthur" he pictured the extreme cold with an instrumental and vocal tremolo. The idea came from Lully who introduced the same effect in the frost scene of "Isis" this year. It was in the chorus of the "Trembleurs."

Purcell was paid £ 2 at Michaelmas this year for his de facto position of organ-tuner and copyist at Westminster Abbey.

A. Scarlatti's knighthood apparently was of little value as it had little significance at the time.

Jacob Stainer, Austrian violin maker, made two fine instruments for the monastery of St. Georgenburg this year.

Fabian Stedman was a member of the "Ancient Society of College Youths" at this time and dedicated his "Campanalogia" published this year to the group.

Antonio Maria Abbatini's published works consisted in part of four books of Psalms, three books of Masses, and some Antifons for twenty-four voices published at Rome by Mascardi this year.

Volume III of Abel's "Erstlinge Musikalischer Blumen" was published this year at Frankfort.

An autobiography, "Les Aventures de M. d'Assoucy" was first published this year at the time of his death.

Bassani's "Balletti, correnti gighe e sarabande" appeared this year. The balletto provided a significant example of chromaticism.

N.A. Le Bègue's "Pieces de clavecin" were published this year at Paris.

When Prince William married Princess Mary Stuart this year Blankenburg wrote "La Double Harmonie d'une musique qui a fait deux en tournant le papier et prouve comment deux font un et un fait deux." It was in invertible counterpoint as well as reversible form and was published at Amsterdan in 1733.

G.M. Bononcini's opus 7 "Ariette, correnti, gighe, allemande e sarabande," in two to four parts, was reprinted this year.

Bononcini this year wrote a "dramma da camera" for the Modenese court, "I primi voli dell' aquila austriaca dal soglio imperiale alla gloria." It provided a rare example of a 17th-Century chamber opera. Only the libretto, however, is (cont.) extant.

Bononcini's opus 6 "Sonate," for two violins and continuo, was reprinted at Bologna this year (See also 1672, 1674).

Henry Bowman's "Songs for 2 & 3 Voyces" was published this year and in 1678, 1679 and 1683.

Briegel's hymn-book for Darmstadt appeared this year.

Buns' "Musica montana" was published this year by Lucas de Potter.

A. Campra composed the motet "Deus noster refugium et virtus" at this time.

J. Carr this year published "Tripla Concordia."

Thomas Farmer wrote his adaptation to Otway's "The Cheats of Scapin" this year.

Petronio Franceschi's opera "Arsinoe" was published at this time.

Francisco's "Easie Lessons on the Guittar" was published this year by J. Carr.

Freschi this year composed his opera "Helena rapita da Paride" for the Teatro di Sant' Angelo at Venice.

G.P. Harsdorfer's "Deliciae physicomathematicae" was published this year at Nürnberg.

Kerll's sacred play "Pia et fortis mulier" appeared at this time.

Jean Francois Lalouette composed intermèdes for a private per-

1677(cont.)

formance this year in Paris of a comedy by Desbrosses and Verneuil.

Legrenzi wrote church sonatas at this time.

Legrenzi composed the opera "Totila" this year.

Lully's "Te Deum" which used strings, drums and trumpets, was completed at this time.

G. Mazzaferrata this year composed solo chamber cantatas.

Baron North I's anonymously published "A Philosophical Essay on Musick" appeared this year. It included some strange observations on the phenomena of sound.

James Paisible at this time wrote music for the French comédie meslée de musique "Rare en tout," a literary work by Mlle de La Roche-Guilhen, who otherwise was known only as a novelist.

Del Pane this year edited Abbatini's antiphons for twelve bass and twelve tenor voices.

Playford published his "Whole Book of Psalms" this year and it became the standard edition of Sternhold and Hopkins. The collection had twenty editions.

Poglietti at this time wrote a series of variations, "Aria Allemagna con alcuni Variazoni." It was a birthday present for the Austrian Empress, Eleonora Madalena Theresa.

The chronograms on the title

(cont.) -page of the "Aria bizzara del rossignolo by Poglietti proved that it was written this year.

Hawkins suggested this year as the latest possible date for the composition of Purcell's "Dido and Aeneas."

Purcell this year composed an elegy on the death of Matthew Locke which was included in Book II of the "Choice Ayres" in 1679.

Reggio's "A Treatise to sing well any Song whatsoever" was published this year by Carr.

Vitali's "Balletti, correnti, gighe . . ." was published this year by Monti in a new edition.

Two editions of Vitali's "Correnti, balletti da camera . . ." were published this year again at Venice.

Vitali's "Salmi concertati a due, tre, quattro e cinque voci, con stromenti consecrati all" was published this year by Monti.

An edition of Vitali's "Sonate a due, tre, quattro e cinque stromenti" was published this year by Monti.

Dr. John Wallis' "On The Trembling of Consonant Strings, a New Musical Discovery" was published this year in "Philosophical Transactions" of the Royal Society of London.

Cambert's "Pomone" (libretto by Perrin) was performed this year at the tennis court at Hôtel de Guénégaud.

1677(cont.)

Colonna's oratorio "Sansone" was performed this year at Bologna.

Legrenzi's "Totila" was produced at this time at Venice.

Ravenscroft's "The English Lawyer" had its first production this year.

Uccellini's "Il Giove d'Elide fulminato" was performed at this time.

Vitali's "Opera quinta" also called "Sonatas" appeared this year at Bologna.

Thomas Symmes, Harvard-trained minister, was born (died 1725).

Evaristo Baschenis, Italian painter, died (born 1617).

Federico Bencovitch, Dalmatian painter influenced by Piazzetta, was born (died 1753).

Guillaume Coustou, French sculptor, was born (died 1746).

Pieter de Hooch, Dutch painter, died according to one source.

Mathieu Le Nain, French painter, died (born c.1607).

(to 1678) Bononcini's opus 10 and 13 "Cantate de camera" for solo voice, in two volumes, was published at this time at Bologna.

(to 1678) Johann Pachelbel, organist and composer, was in the court orchestra at Eisenach during these years.

(to 1680, February) Jacob Kremberg entered and remained in the service of the Administrator (cont.) of Saxony as a chamber musician during this period.

(to 1681) Christian Heinrich Aschenbrenner during these years was the first violinist at the ducal chapel of Zeitz.

(to 1688) Francesco Foggia was "maestro di cappella" at the Santa Maria Maggiore in Rome for this eleven year period.

(to 1690) William Standish (son of David) was organist at Peterborough Cathedral during these years.

(to 1692) Kerll was Court organist at Vienna for these fifteen years.

(to 1693) Buns composed at least four important collections of church music during this time.

(to 1700) William Bull was Trumpeter-in-ordinary to the King of England at this time. He was also in business as a trumpet maker who also produced hearing-horns, powder flasks and "wind gunes."

(to 1704) William Williams, the English composer, was active during this period.

c.1677

Jean Baptiste Morin, French composer, was born at Orléans (died 1745).

Johann Georg Reinhard, Austrian organist and composer, was born. He composed three cantatas for the Austrian court: "La piú bella," "L'eroe immortale" and "Il giudizio di Enone" (died 1742, November 6).

Tommaso Scarlatti, Italian

(Sicilian) tenor, was born at
Palermo (died 1760, August 1).

Bridget Tomkins, the composer's
wife, died (born 1570).

1678

(January 2) The first performance of an original German
opera took place in Hamburg on
this date. The opera was
Johann Theile's "Adam und Eva."
The theatre was established by
Reinken in the "Gänsemarkt" of
the free Hansa city and the
opera was founded by senators
and citizens with an altruistic
interest in the arts.

(January 15) The parliamentary
session at this time referred
to in Purcell's political catch
may well have been that which
began on this date.

(February 3) The "Ballet von
Zusammenkunft und Wirckung
derer VII. Planeten," danced and
sung on this date at Dresden,
could well have been by
Bernhard rather than Schütz.

(February 8) According to a
letter written by Thomas Purcell
Purcell at this time was composing for John Gostling. It
read: "This is for Mr. John
Gostling, chanter of the choir
of Canterbury Cathedral.
London the 8th of February,
1678/9."

(March 4) Antonio Vivaldi,
Italian master of the concerti,
was born (died 1741, July).
There is considerable disagreement as to this date and many
sources tend to compromise with
c.1675.

(March 26) Jérôme de La Guerre

(cont.) replaced Michel de la
Guerre at Sainte-Chapelle as
"recette de temporel de la
Sainte-Chapelle."

(April 12) Alessandro Scarlatti
and Antonia Anzalone were married in Rome.

(April 19) Lully's "Psyché" was
produced with libretto written
by Corneille taken from the
"Psyche" story.

(May 16) Andreas Silbermann,
German organ, clavichord and
piano builder, was born at
Kleinbobritzsch (died 1734,
March 16).

(May 30) Hans (?) Bach's wife,
Dorothea, died (birthdate unknown).

(June 7) Johann Caspar Bach,
son of Johann Aegidius, was
born (died young).

(June 25) Louis Grabu suffered
great hardship due to the
court's penurius attitude. A
letter on this date from Henry
Savile to the Earl of Rochester
described Grabu's situation as
doubly hard since Nicholas
Staggins apparently lost no
time in assuming full control.

(August 12) On this date
Christopher Kirkby warned the
king of a "Popish Plot" to
murder him and pub his brother
on the throne.

(August 14 to September 26)
Daniel and Thomas Purcell attended the King at Windsor for
these forty-four days.

(September 20) Christine
Dorothea Bach, daughter of
Johann Christoph, was born

1678(cont.)
(date of death unknown).

(September 27 and 28) On these
dates Oates and a fellow con-
spirator, Israel Tonge, were
summoned to appear before the
Privy Council. Tonge produced
a mysterious bundle of papers
purporting to give details of
the plot against the King's
life.

(October 14) Purcell may have
learned a great deal from
Jenkins, who, apparently because
of a terminal illness, was replaced at Court by John Moss on
this date.

(October 21) After Titus Oates
had aroused Parliament on this
date the "Popish Plot" was
underway.

(October 21) In all probability
the parliamentary meeting referred to in Purcell's political
catch this year was the one
held on this date when Oates
and Tonge were summoned to appear in order to substantiate
the story they were spreading.

(October 24) Jan Cocx, Flemish
priest and composer, died at
Antwerp (born c.1630).

(October 27) John Jenkins,
English composer and musician,
died at Kimberly, Norfold (born
1592).

(November 4) Silas Taylor,
English antiquarian and composer, died at Harwich (born
1624, July 16).

(November 12) King Charles
postponed the Yorkshire Feast
which was to have been held on
this date because of the pol-

(cont.) itical unrest at the
time.

(November 18) On this day
Banister moved his concerts to
the Music School in Essex
Buildings in the Strand.

(November 18) Giovanni Maria
Bononcini, Italian composer,
died at Modena (born 1642).

(November 22) Banister on this
date at his new home, the Music
School in Essex Buildings in
the Strand, produced what may
have been a forerunner of the
annual concert in honor of St.
Cecilia, patron saint of music.

(November 25) Josiah Priest in
the "London Gazette" on this
date announced his intention to
move his school from Liecester
Fields to Chelsea.

(December 7) On this date there
appeared "an order from the
king and council prohibiting
His Majesty's subjects to resort
to the chapels of Her Majesty
or foreign ministers where the
Romish warship is celebrated,
under severest of penalties."

(December 30) William Croft,
English organist and composer,
was baptised at Nether
Ettington, Warwickshire (died
1727, August 14).

(January) Charpentier's "Les
Amours d'Acis et de Galatée,"
opera "repré sentée chéz M. de
Rians, procureur du roi, au
Châtelet" was produced at
Paris.

(January) Grabu's opera "Timon
of Athens" with libretto by
Shadwell was produced at Dorset
Gardens.

(January) At this time when Shadwell first started to alter the play "Timon," to suit Restoration palates, he called on Grabu, rather than an English composer, to add the music to Shapespeare's English dramatic poetry.

(Ma6) Pachelbel at this time went to Erfurt as organist of the Predigerkirche.

(c.June) Durfey's "Squire Oldsapp" was produced at Dorset Gardens.

Jacques Aubert, French composer, was born according to one source (died 1753).

Jean Hotteterre, one of a French family of players of the hurdy-gurdy and later of wind instruments, died (birthdate unknown).

Filippo Juvarra, Italian architect and scenic designer, was born at Messina (date of death unknown).

Thomas Strutius, German organist and composer, died at Danzig (birthdate unknown).

John Watts, English bookseller and printer, was born (died 1763, September).

It is not sure whether Johann Christoph Bach succeeded Pachelbel this year as court organist although it has been so stated.

Pierre de la Barre, organist and lutenist to King Louis XIII deliberately composed in an Italian manner and was so successful that when a trio of his

(cont.) was posthumously printed in the "Mercure Galant" this year it was mistaken for a composition by Luigi Rossi.

Bassani became "maestro di cappella" to the Duke of Mirandola probably no later than this year.

John Blow acquired his lease in the Great Sanctuary at Westminster as early as this year when he was also granted a lease at Atkins Alley.

Georg Böhn entered the "Gymnasium" at Gotha this year.

Thomas Britton at this time established weekly concerts and formed a club for the practice of music. The concerts featured Italian music.

Brossard's vocal composition appeared this year in the "Mercure galant" under the anagram of Robsard des Fontaines.

For the next two years King Charles II had trouble with kinds of myth-making other than the plots.

Corelli was listed as second violinist this year in the accounts of the church of Saint-Louis-des-Français at Rome.

John Moss succeeded Jenkins in the King's private music this year.

Pachelbel, at this time, moved from Eisenach to Erfurt.

S. Pack, the amateur composer, received his first commission as a captain this year.

Until this year Charles Purcell
had been studying as a "Bishop's
Boy" at St. Peter's College,
Westminster. He was referred to
in the records as "Carolo
Pursell."

It is reasonably sure that
Purcell spent at least the first
part of this year as a "Bishop's
Boy" although the reason is not
clear. He was nineteen by this
time and had achieved some
degree of prominence.

The Westminster Abbey Treasurer's
Accounts for this year provided
the earliest extant records with
information concerning Purcell's
schooling.

Reinken, who succeeded
Scheidemann, founded the Hamburg
Opera this year.

"Siface" this year sang in
Cavalli's opera "Scipione
Africano" in Venice.

The Corporation of the Sons of
the Clergy was incorporated this
year by a charter from King
Charles II.

Nicolaus Adam Strungk was appointed director of music at
Hamburg this year.

G.B. Viviani at this time made
some alterations in Cavalli's
"Scipione Africano" for its
revival.

Two minor compositions of
Banister's in two parts were
included in some "Lessons for
Viols or Violins" added to a
small volume, "New Ayres and
Dialogues" published this year.

G.A. Bernabei wrote "Alvilda in

(cont.) Abo" at this time.

This year at Oxford Henry
Bowman published a small folio
volume "Songs for one, two and
three voyces to the Thorow-Bass.
With some Short Simphonies.
Collected out of some of the
Select Poems of the incomparable
Mr. Cowley, and others, and
composed by Henry Bowman,
Philo-Musicus." A second edition
appeared in 1679.

Bononcini's opus 12 "Arie e
correnti," for two violins and
"violone" was published this
year at Bologna.

Bononcini's opus 11 "Madrigali"
for five voices was published
this year at Bologna.

Henry Bowman's "songs for 2 & 3
voyces" was published in 1677
and reissued in this year and
in 1679 and 1683.

Buns' "Completoriale melos
musicum" was published this year
by Lucas de Potter.

Gerolamo Cantone's "Armonia
Gregoriana" was published at
this time at Turin.

Charpentier's "Airs sérieux et
à boire" was published this
year in the "Nouveau Mercure
galant."

Colonna's "Pelope e Ippodamia"
appeared at this time.

Du Cange's "Glossarium ad
scriptores mediae et infimae
latinitatis" was issued this
year at Paris.

Thomas Farmer this year wrote
songs for Tate's "Brutus of
Alba" and Aphra Behn's "Sir

Patient Fancy."

J.W. Franck wrote his opera "Der verliebte Föbus" this year for the court of the Margrave of Ansbach.

Giovanni Domenico Freschi wrote his "Tullia Superba" at this time for the Teatro Sant' Angelo at Venice.

The first Dutch opera, "De triomfeerende Min" was written by Hacquart this year for Amsterdam and the Hague. Dirk Buysero wrote the text.

Jenkins' "Mitter Rant" was included in Playford's "Musick's Handmaid."

Lully and Corneille wrote an opera this year with the libretto taken from the "Psyche."

G. Mazzaferrata's "12 Sonatas . . ." was published at this time.

Petzold's "Deliciae musicales, oder Lustmusik" appeared at this time.

Playford's collection "Musick's Handmaid" of this year included the best harpsichord music of the period, including that of Purcell.

"Honest John" Playford re-edited his "Musick's Handmaid . . . Lessons for Virginals or Harpsycon" this year and with the second part published both jointly in collaboration with his son Henry.

Provenzale's opera "Difendere l'offensore, o vero La stellidaura vendicata" and "La

(cont.) Stellidaura vendicata" were both completed this year.

Purcell this year composed his earliest anthem "Lord, who can tell" (Psalm xix, 12-14).

Several of Purcell's songs were published this year. "Cease O my sad soul," "I saw that you were grown so high," "More love or more disdain I crave," "Sweet be no longer sad," "Sweet tyranness, I now resign," "When I a lover pale do see."

The third edition of Simpson's "The Principles of Practicle Musick" was published this year at London.

Theile wrote his opera "Orontes" this year at Hamburg.

An edition of G.B. Vitali's "Balletti, correnti, gighe . . ." was published this year by Monti.

The winter season of this year brought several important developments in the English public concert tradition.

The first British military band appeared at this time.

Coventry Waits had a double curtall this year.

The Horse Grenadiers adopted the oboe this year.

It is most probably that infantry regiments still continued at this time to use the drum-major unofficially.

This year sixteen drummers were added to the Coldstream Guards.

The drum-major was mentioned at

this time in "The Art of War at Present Practised in France.

One hundred and thirty comedies were performed this year in private houses at Rome.

Bassani's first oratorio was performed this year at Mirandola.

Cavalli's opera "Scipione Aericano" was produced in Venice this season.

Colonna's oratorio "Santa Teodora" was performed this year at Bologna.

C. Pallavicino's opera "Vespasiano" with libretto by Giulio Cesare Corradi was produced this year at the Teatro San Giovanni Crisostomo, Carnival in Venice.

"Timon of Athens" for which Purcell wrote some masques was produced this year.

Alessandro Stradella this year composed the music for the opera "La forza dell'amor paterno" which was performed at Genoa in this year's Carnival.

Nicolaus Adam Strungk's opera "Der unglücklich-fallende Sejanus" with libretto by Christoph Richter was produced this year at Hamburg.

Theile's "Adam und Eva" the first singspiel ever publically performed in German had its premiere in Hamburg (see 1678, January 2).

Theile's German opera "Orontes" was produced this year at Hamburg.

Barthold Feind, German poet, was born (died 1721).

John Bunyan wrote "Pilgrim's Progress" this year.

Dryden's "All For Love" appeared at this time.

Tates' play "Brutus of Alba" was published this year.

Jacob Jordaens, Flemish painter, died (born 1593).

Juvara, an Italian Baroque architect, was born (died 1736).

Spanish painting: Murillo, "Immaculate Conception" (107 7/8" x 74 3/4").

(to 1679) Locke's "Musick's Handmaid" was published during these years by Playford.

(to 1680) Georg Oesterreich studied at the School of St. Thomas in Leipzig during these years.

(to 1681) Johann Krieger II was court conductor to the Count of Reuss at Greiz during this period.

(to 1684) French architecture: J.H. Mansart (architect) and Le Brun (decorator), Versailles Palace, Hall of Mirrors (240' x 34' x 43' high).

(to 1685) Strungk wrote six operas for the Hamburg opera house during these seven years.

(to 1687) Buxtehudes's "Abendmusiken" were written during this period.

1678(cont.)

(to 1691) Bernabei wrote fourteen operas and other dramatic
works for the Munich court during these thirteen years.

(to c.1696) During this,
Scarlatti's early period which
began with "Gli equivoci" and
ended with "Pirro e Demetrio,"
concise aria forms were characteristic of his work.

(to 1710) Bassani wrote nine or
ten oratorios during these
years.

(to 1738) The Hamburg Public
Opera House was the first in
Europe, outside Venice, where
German composers could combine
Italian and French sources with
their own work to create an
original, national form. The
first operas performed there
were on religious subjects influenced by school drama.

c.1678

Georg Muffat became organist to
the Bishop of Salzburg at this
time.

Georg Christian Schemelli,
German musician and hymnologist,
was born at Herzberg (date of
death unknown).

1679

(January 3) Pietro Filippo
Scarlatti, Italian organist,
was born at Rome (died 1750,
February 22).

(January 6) On this date Corelli
conducted the orchestra of the
Teatro Capranica for the
première of a work by his friend
Pasquini, "Dove è amore è
pietà."

(January 9) Werner Fabricius,

(cont.) German organist and
composer, died at Leipzig (born
1633, April 10).

(January 24) King Charles II
dissolved Parliament.

(January 27) Alessandro
Scarlatti was commissioned to
write a Latin oratorio for the
following Lent.

(January 31) Lully's "Bellérophon"
was produced in Paris.

(February 8) A letter bearing
this date written by Thomas
Purcell to John Gostling referred
to Gostling's exceptionally low
notes.

(February 14) Georg Freidrich
Kauffmann, German organist and
composer who composed an oratorio,
four cantatas and miscellaneous
organ pieces, was born at
Ostermondra, Merseburg (died
1735, March).

(February 18) On this date the
following "Order directed to
Mr. Nicholas Staggins, Master of
His Majesty's music, that His
Majesty's four & twenty violins
should attend His Majesty every
night that a play is acted at
court" was issued by the Lord
Chamberlain. Purcell as composer to the King's violins was
obviously affected by the document.

(February 25) John Gostling,
bass singer, was sworn a
Gentleman Extraordinary of the
Chapel Royal.

(February 28) William Tucker,
English clergyman and composer,
died at London (birthdate unknown).

(March 4) The Duke of York left England on this day.

(March 15) Johann Christian Bach, son of Georg Christoph, grandson of Lips, was born (died 1707, June 16).

(March 16) Colonna's oratorio "Salomone amante" was performed at Bologna.

(March 24) Michel L'Affilard was appointed to the Sainte-Chapelle in Paris.

(April 5) Louis Sanquin, Comte de Livre, was born (date of death unknown).

(April 10) On this date an order was issued to pay for "impressing and furnishing 16 drummers for the eight companies added to the Coldstream Guards in 1678."

(April 27) On this date the House of Commons voted against the Duke of York for "recusancy."

(May 23) Banister had been given a pass and six months' leave of absence on this date, probably to study foreign musical styles.

(May 26) Though defeat seemed inevitable, King Charles II stayed at the helm until this date when he found it expedient "to prorogue both Houses."

(June 3) A letter addressed by Corelli from Rome on this date to Count Fabrizio Laderchi offered an unpublished sonata especially composed for the Count. This proved that Corelli's stay in Rome was extended. The sonata was for vio-lins and lute or two violins.

(June 11) Johann Christian Bach married Anna Dorothea Peter.

(June 28) John Ferrabosco married Anne Burton at the Holy Trinity Church, Ely.

(August 23) Great concern swept England when King Charles II's life was in danger on this date after an attack of "ague." This showed the popular confidence he had hoped for.

(September 8) Jean Philidor, member of the French family of musicians née Danican whose name Philidor was given them by Louis XIII, died at Paris (born c.1620). He was an instrumentalist and composer of dance music.

(September 29) At Michaelmas this year Blow left his position of organist at Westminster Abbey and was succeeded by his pupil, Purcell.

(October 3) John Banister I, English violinist and composer, died at London (born 1630).

(October 16) Jan Zelenka (Johann Dismas Zelenka), Bohemian composer, was born (died 1745, December 23). He became court composer at Dresden.

(November 11) Pallavicino's opera "Le amazoni nell'isole fortunate" with libretto by G. Maria Piccioli was produced at Venice at Piazzola near Padua.

(November 13) Michel de La Guerre, French organist and composer, died at Pans (born c.1605).

1679(cont.)

(November 20) Evelyn in his
diary on this date wrote that he
heard a "Viola d'Amore" played
by a German and spoke of its
"sweetness and novelty."

(November 24) Giovanni Felice
Sances, Italian tenor and composer, died at Vienna (born
c.1600).

(January) J.W. Franck killed
one of his court musicians,
Johann Ulbrecht in a jealous
rage and fled to Hamburg to
escape punishment.

(February) A. Scarlatti's opera
"Gli equivoci nel sembiante" was
produced at Rome in the Teatro
Capranica. The libretto was by
Contini. Scarlatti conducted
the performance himself.

(March) Antonio Borosini entered
the chapel of St. Mark's,
Venice, now under Cavalli's
successor, Natale Monferrato.

(April) Later this month the
new Parliament voted on an Act
of Attainder against Danby.

(June) Toward the end of this
month King Charles II apparently
felt that the situation was well
enough under control for him to
order his musicians to Windsor
on the last day of the month.

(August) Corelli's disappearance
from the lists of Saint-Louis
-des Français at the beginning
of this month may indicate that
one of his trips to Germany took
place during this summer.

(August) "I will love Thee, O
Lord" was a topical work by
Purcell, referring to King
Charles II's predicament at this

(cont.) time.

(October) Mrs. Playford, the
wife of the publisher, died
(birthdate unknown).

Johann Georg Albinus, the hymn-
writer, died (born 1624).

Dorothea Maria Bach, daughter
of Christoph and J. Ambrosius'
sister (fourth generation),
died (born 1653, April 10).

Pietro Castrucci, Italian violinist, conductor and composer,
was born at Rome (died 1752,
February 29).

Charles Couperin, violinist,
organist and composer, died at
Paris (born 1638, April 17 or
1633). See April 7 or 8.

William Godbid, printer, with
whom John Playford, the younger,
studied printing, died (birthdate unknown).

Musgrave Heighington, English
organist and composer, was
born at Durham (died 1774).

Eva Hoffmann, wife of Heinrich
Bach (third generation), died
(born 1616).

Szymon Jarzębski, Polish violinist at the royal court in
Warsaw, died at Warsaw (born
c.1630).

Francesco Mancini, Italian
composer, was born at Naples
(died 1739, June 11).

Esajas Reusner, German lute
composer, died (born 1636).

Domenico Sarro, Italian composer, was born at Trani,
Naples (died 1744).

1679(cont.)
Gotthard Wagner, German composer, was born at Erding (died
1739).

Christian von Wolff, German
philosopher, was born (died
1754). He brought the doctrines
of Leibnitz to public attention.

John Abell this year was sworn
a "gentleman extraordinary" of
the Chapel Royal.

Paul Agricola, vice
-"Capellmeister" to the
Elector Philipp Wilhelm at
Neuberg-on-Danube, had two of
his operas performed there this
year.

A catastrophic plague raged in
Vienna this year. Lieber
Augustin, Viennese minstrel,
was rescued from the plague
pit.

In speaking of Aranjuez this
year Mme. d'Aulnoy wrote
" . . . when we arrived, I
believed myself in some en-
chanted Palace."

Johann Christoph Bach was
described this year as
"wohlverordneter Organist bey
denen Kirchen alhier" at
Eisenach.

J. Christoph Bach complained
again this year to the authorities in Eisenach about his
monetary problems. This time
he even advised them how to
solve the problems.

Johann Christoph Bach (twin)
married Martha Elizabeth
Eisentraut at this time.

Campra is supposed to have
filled the position of "maître

(cont.) de musique" in the
cathedral at Toulon this year.

After this date Charpentier was
placed in charge of the composition of music performed at
the Dauphin's private mass.

At the age of eleven this year
François Couperin inherited the
position of organist at Saint
-Gervais from his father,
Charles, who died.

Edward Finch was awarded the
degree of Master of Arts this
year.

John Playford, the younger,
this year entered into partnership with William Godbid's
widow, Anne.

Grabu retired from England to
France this year.

"Siface," or Giovanni Francesco
Grossi, as he was officially
listed, was a member of the
papal choir until this year
when he entered the service of
the Duke of Modena. He found
Vitali there still serving as
assistant chapel-master.

Jérôme de la Guerre took charge
of the organ at Sainte-Chapelle
this year, replacing Michel de
La Guerre who had died.

Through the influence of
Constantijn Huygens Charles
Hacquart was invited to enter
the service of the Prince of
Orange at this time.

By the beginning of this year
the meddling of King Louis
XIV's agents added to the pro-
liferation of "Popish plots."
A complicated web of intrigue
pervaded the English court.

481

1679(cont.)

Sebastiano Moratelli this year entered the service of the Elector-Palatine Philip William, then living at Düsseldorf.

Simon Pack's Christian name was often wrongly given as Henry but was plainly indicated this year as Simon Pack in Playford's "Choice Ayres & Songs."

Purcell's appointment this year as organist at Westminster Abbey ended his apprenticeship, although he continued as Hingeston's assistant instrument-keeper and instrument-repairer until the latter's death in 1683.

Purcell early this year was composing sacred music for Gostling, the renowned bass, then chanter at Canterbury Cathedral.

A "Lexikon" of 1792 described a certain Nikol Rosenkron who went to Nürnberg this year and gained a reputation as a "Fagott"-player.

Alessandro Scarlatti's debut in Rome this year was marred by a scandel concerning his sister.

Georg Caspar Schürmann went to Wolfenbüttel at this time in response to an invitation from the Duke of Braunschweig.

Sebastiani retired this year with a pension from the electoral palace church.

William Shore became a King's Trumpeter-in-Ordinary this year.

"Siface" sang in Pallavicini's "Nerone" at Venice this season.

Antonio Stradivarius was working on his ornamental violin known as the "Hellier Strad" this year.

G.F. Tosi this year was president of the Academia dei Filarmonia.

Thomas Tudway was appointed instructor of the choristers at King's College at Christmas of this year.

J. Westhoff visited Sweden at this time.

P.S. Agostini's opera "Adelinda" appeared this year.

Johann Michael Bach this year composed his "Nun hab ich überwunden" for double chorus and continuo in G major.

J.S. Bach's Chorale, "O Gott, du frommer Gott," was taken from a tune of this date.

A third edition of Bacilly's "Remarques curieuses sur l'art de bien chanter . . ." was issued at this time.

One of Banister's songs was included in the second book of "Choice Ayres and Songs."

G.A. Bernabei this year wrote "Enea in Italia."

Blow set an ode for the celebration of New Year's Day this year to music.

Blow wrote songs at this time for Tate's "The Loyal General."

Two madrigals by Boretti were included this year in Playford's "Scelta di canzonette."

Henry Bowman's "songs for 2 & 3 voyces" was re-issued this year (See also 1677, 1678 and 1683).

A second edition of Henry Bowman's small folio volume "Songs for one, two and three voyces to the Thorow-Bass. With some Short Simphonies. Collected out of some of the Select Poems of the incomparable Mr. Cowley, and others, and composed by Henry Bowman, Philo-Musicus." appeared (See also 1678).

Briegel's secular vocal work "Musikalisches Tafel-Confect" was published this year at Frankfort.

Two of Caproli's cantatas were included in Playford's "Scelta di canzonette italiane di diversi autori."

James Cob composed songs and catches, included in Playford's "Choyce Ayres."

Farmer this year wrote songs for Dryden's "Troilus and Cressida," Durfey's "The Virtuous Wife" and Lee's "Caesar Borgia."

Petronio Franceschini's opera "Apollo in Tessaglia" was published this year.

Petronio Franceschini's oratorio "La vittima generosa" was published at this time.

J.W. Franck wrote his opera "Die drey Töchter Cecrops" this year for the court of the Margrave of Ansbach.

Freschi wrote his operas "Circe" and "Sardanapolo" this year for the Teatro Sant'Angelo at Venice.

Gaultier this year wrote his "Livre de musique pour le lut."

Godbid and Playford's "Scelta di canzonette" published this year contained Albrici's songs "Di Cupido" and "Ninfe vezzose."

Some of Roger Hill's songs were included in Playford's "Choice Ayres."

Emperor Leopold's oratorio "Die Erlösung des menschlichen Geschlechts" of this year, one of a very few oratorios in German, was significant becase of the "individual tone of the music."

Perrine this year published a "Livre de musique pour le lut."

Perti's opera "Atide" written with G.F. Todi and D. Degli Antonio appeared at this time.

"L'Amour vainqueur," a pastoral by Anne Philidor, was written this year.

Playford selected the songs for "Choice Ayres & Songs" published this year from songs that had been included since the first revision in 1676.

Playford published his "Dancing Master" this year.

Provenzale's "Candaule" appeared at this time.

Four of Purcell's light, amorous lyrics were included in Playford's second book of "Choice Ayres & Songs" this year. They were "Since the pox," "Amintas to My grief," "Scarce had the rising sun," and "I resolve against cringing."

1679(cont.)

Purcell's song "What hope for us remains now he is gone" was published at this time.

This year marked the publication of Scarlatti's "Il Consiglio Dell' Ombra" at Naples and of "Gli Equivoici Nel Sembiante Ovvero L'Errore Innocente" at Bologna, Ravenna and Rome.

Jean-Jacques Souhaitty's "Essai du chant d'église par la nouvelle méthode des nombres" was published this year.

Theile's oratorio "Michal und David" appeared at this time.

The "Sala de' Signori Capranica," an opera house, opened this year in Rome.

Bazzani's opera "Ottone in Italia" was performed this year at the Collegio dei Nobili, in Parma.

Colonna's oratorio "San Basilio" was performed this year at Bologna.

"Andromeda und Perseus" by Corneille was performed this year in Germany.

Four of J.W. Franck's operas were performed this year at Hamburg: "Michal," "Andromeda und Perseus," "Die macchabäische mutter," "Don Pedro."

Johann Löhner's "Die triumphirende Treue" was produced this year.

Pallavicino's arie e canzoni with two violins and continuo from "L'Adalinda" was performed this year at Florence from

(cont.) manuscript.

Pallavicino's "Il Nerone" was performed at this time using an unusually large orchestra at the Teatro San Giovanni Crisostomo in Venice. The libretto was by Corradi.

Pasquini's opera "Dov'é amore e pieta" was produced this year at the opening of the Sala de' Signori Capranica opera house in Rome.

Anne Philidor's pastorale "L'Amour vainqueur" was produced at court this season.

Pistocchi's "Leandro" ("Amori fatali") was performed this year by puppets at Venice.

Alessandro Scarlatti's first opera was produced at the Collegio Clementino this year.

Thomas Hobbes, English political theorist and writer, died (born 1588).

Dryden's "Oedipus" (with Nathaniel Lee) and his alteration of "Troilus and Cressida" were both completed this year.

Kiyomasu, Japanese painter, was born (died 1763).

Jan Steen, Dutch painter, died (born 1626).

J.F. de Troy, French painter, was born (died 1752).

(to 1680) The Hibernian Catch Club at Dublin was founded this year by the vicars-choral of St. Patrick's and Christ Church Cathedrals.

(to 1681) Corelli's second

1679(cont.)
disappearance from records covered these two years.

(to 1681) Daniel Roseingrave was
organist at Gloucester Cathedral
during this period.

(to 1683) Alexandre Philidor
played the bass crumhorn and the
trumpet marine in the royal
band for these four years.

(to 1685) Michel de La Lande at
this time was the organist at
St. Gervais.

(to 1686) J.W. Franck during
these years wrote thirteen operas
for the Hamburg opera house.

(to 1688) John Abell was gen-
erously patronised by royalty
and during these years received
"bounty money" totaling £740.

(to 1688) T. Greenhill engraved
music during these years.

(to 1692) Sybrandus van Noordt
was organist at Oude Kerk at
Amsterdam during these years.
He was probably a son of
Jacabus van Noordt.

(to 1695) Domenico Scarlatti
(1685) was the sixth of ten
children born to Alessandro
Scarlatti and Antonio Anzalone
during these years.

(to 1699) John Hudgebut, the music publisher, worked in London
and employed Heptinstall and
others to print his publications
during this period. He was the
author of a rare work, a copy of
which has survived.

c.1679
Agostino Filippucci, Italian
organist and composer, died at

(cont.) Bologna (birthdate unknown).

Nicola (Francesco) Haym,
Italian composer and man of
letters of German extraction,
was born at Rome (died 1729,
August 11).

Pallavicini's oratorio "Il
trionfo della castità" written
at this time was dedicated to
Cardinal Ottoboni.

Purcell's anthem "They that go
down to the sea in ships" was
written this year.

(to 1680) About this time
Purcell set a text, which fit no
liturgical occasion, included by
the Anglican calender as well as
the date when King Charles I's
martyrdom was memorialized.

(to 1680) Purcell's verse anthem
"Who hath believed our report?"
was composed at this time.

(and 1685, 1687, 1688) Nicola
Matteis' "Ayrs for the Violin"
were published at these years.

1680
(January 6) Johann Georg Bach,
son of Johann Aegidius, was born
but died young (date of death
unknown).

(January 26) Johanna Juditha
Bach, daughter of Johann
Ambrosius, was born (died c.1707).

(February 3) Lully's "Proserpine"
was produced in France.

(February 6) Robert King was appointed a member of the royal
band.

(February 6) A. Scarlatti's
opera "L'honestà ne gli amori"

was produced at Rome, Palazzo Bernini. The libretto was by Felice Parnasso and the work was published at this date.

(March 11, July 26 and December 9) In a letter written by Playford in which he described his latest book of songs he referred to the collection of "songs set by Signior Pietro Reggio" that were advertised in the "London Gazette" on these dates.

(March 20) Emanuele d'Astorga, Italian amateur composer, was born at Augusta, Sicily (died 1757).

(April 3-7) Playford, the elder advertised the lease of his Islington house in "The True News, or Mercurius Anglicus" during these days.

(April 19) The English court moved to Windsor for the summer on this date.

(May 14) Barbara Katharina Bach, daughter of Johann Christoph (twin), was born (date of death unknown).

(June 8) King Charles II declared publicly on this date that he had never married Lucy Walters (this, then, placed the royal seal on Monmouth's bastardy).

(June 10) Purcell celebrated Corpus Christi on this date by completing the first of the four-part fantasias, this one in his favorite key, G minor.

(August 9) Antoine Moqué went to Louvain as a novice of the Oratorians, but he lived at Bruges as organist of the church

(cont.) of St. Donat.

(August 24) A. Scarlatti's second son was born (died 1684).

(September 8) Baldassare Ferri, Italian male soprano singer, died at Perugia (born 1610, December 9).

(September 9) Purcell's first professional composition in large vocal and instrumental form was the ode composed as a welcome to King Charles II who returned from Whitehall on this date. Its title was "Welcome Viceregent of the mighty King."

(September 13) Cesare de Judice, Italian composer, died at Palermo (born 1607, January 28).

(September 24) Aleksander Wladyslaw Leszczyński, Polish composer, died at Czestochowa (born 1616).

(October 1) Kerll was appointed court organist on this date.

(November 2) Playford's "Choice Ayres & Songs . . . . third book, 1681 . . . . sung at Court & at Public Theatres" was ready for publication.

(November 3) The Elector, Maximilian Emanuel issued a decree on this date that accorded to the "honorable priest, court & chamber musician, & organist Steffani" (Agostino Steffani) a gift of 1200 florins for "certain reasons & favours."

(November 14) Charpentier's "Les Fous divertissans, Comédie en 3 actes, avec trois divertissements, par M. Raymond Poisson" was produced on this

1680(cont.)
date at the Paris Théâtre de
Guénégaud.

(November 17) William King,
English composer, died at
Oxford (born 1624).

(November 18) Jean Baptiste
Loeillet, Flemish composer, was
born at Ghent (died 1730, July
19).

(November 28) Athanasius
Kircher, German scholar and
musical theorist, died at Rome
(born 1602, May 2).

(December 11 or December 14) On
this date Tate's adaptation of
Shakespeare's "Richard II" (with
at least one song by H. Purcell,
as well as possibly instrumental
music) opened at the Theatre
Royal, Drury Lane. "Retir'd
from any mortal's sight" was
the title of the song. On the
latter date the production was
suppressed for political reasons.

(December 16) Playford's "Choice
Ayres & Songs . . . . third
book, 1681 . . . sung at Court
& Public Theatres" was not advertised in the "London Gazette"
until this date.

(December 20) Nicolas Couperin,
organist and (?) composer, was
born at Paris (died 1748, July
25).

(December 23) J. von Krieger was
court conductor at Weissenfels,
a post he retained until his
death.

(January) The office of Drum
-Major was restored but only to
the Foot Guards.

(May) The "Mercure galant" was

(cont.) published.

(June) Early this month Purcell
found himself with considerable
free time and was able to solve
numerous musical problems of
quite considerable complexity
within the twenty days that it
took for him to produce the
first twenty-seven of his four
-part fantasias. By the end of
the week following June 10
Purcell had finished five more
fantasias and by the end of the
month two or three more.

(August) Purcell wrote two more
fantasias at the end of the summer.

(September) Purcell's wedding
day must have been about this
time.

(October) Nathaniel Lee's
"Theodosius" ("The Force of
Love") was produced at Dorset
Garden at least as early as
this date and published with
Purcell's music shortly after-
wards.

Antonio Maria Abbatini, Italian
composer, died at Tiferno (born
c.1598).

Berthold Heinrich Brockes, a
Hamburg senator who created a
form favored by all European
composers, was born (died 1747).

Henrique Carlos Correa,
Portuguese composer, was born
at Lisbon (died c.1747).

Petronio Franceschini, Italian
cellist, died (birthdate unknown).

Francesco Geminiani, Italian
violin virtuoso, composer,
pedagogue, and essayist, was

487

1680(cont.)
born according to one source
(died 1762). December 4, 1687
is the generally accepted date
of birth.

William Howard, Viscount
Stafford's funeral was held
this year (birthdate unknown).

Joachim Neander, German composer, died (born 1650).

Matteo Palotta, Neopolitan musician who worked at the imperial court in Vienna, was
born (died 1758, March 28).

Antonio Pollarolo (Polaroli),
Italian composer, was born at
Venice (died 1746, May 4).

Giuseppe Porsile, Italian composer, was born at Naples (died
1750, May 29).

Johann Heinrich Schmelzer,
church composer and virtuoso
violinist who worked at Vienna,
died (born 1623).

Antonio Vivaldi, eminent
Italian composer, was born (died
1743). Sources do not agree on
this year of birth.

Manuel Zumaya, Mexican composer,
was born (died 1740).

John Abell was admitted "in
ordinary" to the Chapel Royal.
A year before he was sworn a
"gentleman extraordinary."

Blow's miniature opera "Venus
and Adonis" probably written
before King Charles II's death
and certainly after this date
was an important forerunner of
Purcell's "Dido and Aeneas."

Bontempi this year returned to

(cont.) Perugia.

William Bull at this time
moved his workshop from "The
Trumpet and Horn" in Salisbury
Street near the Strand to the
lower end of the Haymarket,
toward the Pall Mall end.

On the day before his birthday
King James II had urged the
prosecution of one Henry
Cornish (former Whig sheriff)
who had persecuted Papist
plotters this year. James was
satisfied to see the man con-
victed, on flimsy evidence, and
to be drawn and quartered ten
days later.

Charpentier, who had gone to
Rome as a painter and returned
as a musician, composed cantatas
in the Italian style from this
year forward. They were for
private concerts of the
Princesse de Guise.

It was surprising that Corelli
was not influenced by the many
examples of tripartite construction (allegro, adagio,
allegro) which concertos by
Stradella, Taglietti, and
particularly Torelli provided
starting at this time.

Cummings mentioned an ode this
year by Purcell "to welcome the
Duke of York on his return from
Scotland."

Henri-Denis Dupont wished to
succeed Guillaume de Lexhy as
organist at the Cathedral of
Saint-Lambert at Liège, but
lost out to a man named
Gottire.

Eccles was prosecuted this
year at Barbadoes for seditious
words.

Estwick was awarded the degree
of Master of Arts this year.

Förtsch at this time became
Theile's successor as court composer to Duke Christian Albert.

Johann Joseph Fux matriculated
this year at Graz University.

W. Lawes' influence on Purcell's
fantasies was evident.

The "Mercure Galant" of this
year mentioned concerts which
were given at Dijon at M. de
Malteste's residence.

Domenico Melani returned to
Italy at this time as agent for
the elector.

Merula held a court appointment
at Florence at one time prior to
this year.

Until late this year Playford,
the elder lived at his
Islington house. He then moved
to a private house in Arundel
St., near the Thames Side "the
lower end over against the
George" (some references in
1686 give "over against the
Blue (or Blew) Ball").

Preston of York this year repaired the organ at Magdalen
College, Oxford.

Josias Priest moved to Chelsea
at this time.

Kaspar Printz, the composer,
claimed he met Corelli at
Munich this year.

Apparently the accountant at
Westminster entered Charles
Purcell's name again this year
and then either discovered his

(cont.) error or made a last
-minute change. He crossed the
name Charles off the vellum and
replaced it with "Henrico"
(later "Henrici" and even
"Henri"), who continued to be
named up to this time.

Purcell, as a matter of record,
continued to receive the annual
stipend up to and including
Michaelmas this year. At that
time he may have been totally
disqualified by marriage.

Purcell must have profited from
his intense concentration on
the fantasias this summer since
his professional effort on a
large vocal and instrumental
scale, the ode to welcome
Charles back to Whitehall
"Welcome, Viceregent," appeared
almost at once.

Purcell's creative surge was as
great this year as fifteen
years later.

Although Purcell lived in St.
Ann's Lane for a brief period
after his marriage this year or
a year later, he certainly was
not born in the house in St.
Ann's Lane so frequently
described as his birthplace.

Purcell was eventually buried
under the organ of Westminster
Abbey which he started playing
this year.

The carefully composed fantasias
that Purcell wrote this year
revealed beyond equivocation
that by this time he had finished his apprenticeship and
had entered into the beginning
period of his great works.

At this time the long series of
dramas in which Purcell's music

played so important a part
started.

Scarlatti served Queen Cristina
of Sweden as "maestro di
cappella" from this year forward.

Anna Maria Scarlatti sang this
year in Venice at the Teatro S.
Giovanni Crisostimo.

Daniel Speer, the German composer, was cantor at Göppingen
at this time.

Agostino Steffani, composer,
was this year ordained a priest
with the title of "Abbate of
Lepsing."

Antonio Stradivarius and his
wife at this time left their
home at the Casa del Pescatore
in the parish of San Matteo.
They moved to a house they had
purchased in the Piazza San
Picenardi.

Tudway retained his position
as instructor of the choristers
at King's College until midsummer of this year.

Visee this year played on the
guitar and theorbo for the
Dauphin.

Susanna Barbara Wedemann, Maria
Barbara Bach's aunt, this year
married Johann Gottfried
Bellstedt.

Westhoff returned to Dresden
at this time.

P.S. Agostini's opera "Il
ratto delle Sabine" was published this year at Venice.

Johann Christoph Bach this

(cont.) year composed a motet
using an augmented sixth chord.

G.A. Bernabei at this time
wrote a new prologue for Cesti's
"Dori."

Ercole Bernabei's "Il litigio
del cielo e della terra" appeared this year.

Duron's "Venir el amor al mundo"
was written at this time.

Thomas Farmer this year wrote
a song for Otway's "The
Souldier's Fortune."

Freschi's "Berenice Vendicata"
was published this year.

Denis Gaultier's "Pieces de
luth en musique par le Sr.
Perrine" was published this
year at Paris.

This year marked the publica-
tion at Amsterdam of
Hacquart's music for Buysero's
"De triomfeerende Min."

Hidalgo at this time wrote incidental music for Calderón's
last comedy, "Hado y divisa, de
Leonido y de Marfisa."

G. Mazzaferrata composed canzonets and cantatas this year.

Otway's "The Orphan" was published at this time.

Dryden's "Spanish Fryar," a
play with music by S. Pack, appeared this year.

This year saw the publication
of Behn's play "Rover" with
music by S. Pack.

Pallavicino's "Messalina" was
completed at this time.

Perrine this year published a collection of "Pièces de luth en musique, avec des règles pour le toucher parfaitement." He arranged Gaultier's lute music in ordinary keyboard notation, usable for both lute and harpsichord.

Purcell's fantasias composed this year have been ranked as "masterworks" equal to the better-known "Dido & Aeneas" and "Hail, bright Cecilia."

Purcell's connection with the stage was definitely established this year with his composition of a masque scene as well as numerous act-songs for Lee's "Theodosius." Prior to this work, however, there is no evidence of Purcell having any connection with the theatre in any capacity.

Reggio's "Songs set by Signior Pietro Reggio" were published this year at London.

Scarlatti's "Gli Equivoici Nel Sembiante Ovvero L'Errore Innocente" was published this year at Monte Filottramo.

A St. John's Passion, an oratorio by Scarlatti, was published at this time.

The "Synopsis of Vocal Musick" was published this year.

Theile this year completed his oratorio "Esther."

A second edition of Wojcieh Tylkowski's "Philosophia curiosa" appeared at this time.

Editions of Vitali's "Balletti correnti alla francese" and (cont.) "Correnti e balletti da camera . . . ." were both published this year at Bologna by Monti.

M. Wise this year co-authored "The Wiltshire Ballad."

The Concerto first appeared in music this year as a new orchestral form.

"Follias" were included this year in the "Pièces de luth composées . . . . par Jacques de Gallot avec les Folies d'Espagne enrichies de plusiers beaux couplets" (Ecorcheville collection).

Marc-Antoine Charpentier at this time affixed the description "Jurieux et emporté" to the notes F and Bb.

Saint-Lamber in his "Traité" of this year depicted the "springer" ornament.

The Teatro Malvezzi was restored at this time.

Bazzani's opera "Il pedante di Tarsia" was performed this year at Bologna.

Operas by J.W. Franck given this year at Hamburg included "Aeneae . . . Ankunfft in Italien," "Die drey Töchter Cecrops," "Alceste," and "Jodelet."

Freschi's opera "Berenice" was first performed at this time at Padua.

Pallavicini's opera "Messalina" with libretto by Piccioli was produced this year at the Teatro Vendramino di San Salvatore in Venice.

1680(cont.)

Perti conducted his "Missa solennis" for solo voices, chorus, orchestra this year at San Petronio.

Quinault's "Alceste" was produced this year in Germany.

Scarlatti's "Gli Equivoci" was performed this year at Naples.

Scarlatti's "Miserere" for SATB; SSATB was performed at this time.

Scarlatti's "Passio secundum Johannem" was sung this year.

Strungk's operas "Die drei Töchter Cecrops," "Esther," and "Doris" were produced this year at Hamburg.

Acciaiuoli's "Damira placata" with music by Marco Antonio Ziani was performed this year by puppets at Venice on a provisional stage at the Carnival.

Bunyan's "The Life and Death of Mr. Badman" was written at this time.

Thomas Otway this year wrote "The Orphan."

Gianlorenzo Bernini, Italian Baroque sculptor and architect, died (born 1598).

Briseux, French architect, was born at Baume-les-Dames in Franche-Comté (died 1754).

Sir Peter Lely, English painter, died (born 1618).

During this time Purcell was not recorded as being a resident of St. Margaret's Parish,

(cont.) Westminster.

(to 1683) Henry Purcell wrote sixteen fantasies during this period as well as twenty-two trio sonatas of which one was a chaconne.

(to 1684) Maciej Wronowicz was chorus master at Wloclawek Cathedral during these years.

(to 1685) Blow at this time composed his only dramatic work "Venus and Adonis."

(to 1685) Chrysander stated that Corelli during these years spent some time with Farinelli at Hanover.

(to 1685) Scarlatti's "Diana ed Endimione" was sung at this time.

(to 1686) Playford in association with his father during these years published "near the Temple Church" and also issued a few works in his own name from the same address.

(to 1687) Domenico Gabrieli played cello for these eight years in the orchestra of San Petronio at Bologna.

(to 1688) Charpentier acted as composer and musical director to the Princesse de Guise during this period.

(to 1690) Johann Michael Bach, the organ-builder who settled at Stockholm, was born sometime during these years, according to Forkel.

(to 1700) About 150 operas were performed at Venice during these years, averaging about seven per year.

1680(cont.)
(to 1710) Stephen Jeffries in
this period was appointed organist of Gloucester Cathedral.

c.1680
Francesco Bernardi ("Senesino"),
male mezzo-soprano, was born at
Siena (died c.1750). He sang
in Handel's opera troupe.

T. Bertin de la Dové, French
composer, was born at Paris
(died 1745).

Claude Denis, French theorist,
was born (died c.1752).

Michael Festing, English violinist and composer, was born,
probably in Germany (died 1752,
July 24).

Johann Ernst Galliard, German
oboist and composer, was born
at Celle (died 1749).

Barnabas Gunn, English organist
and composer, was born at
Birmingham (died 1753, February
6).

John Isham (originally Isum),
English organist and composer,
was born (died 1726, June).

Jean Baptiste Stuck, French
composer of German descent, was
born at Florence (died 1755,
December 9).

Jean Baptiste Farinel was
Konzertmeister to the Elector of
Hanover this year.

G.B. Viviani according to Fétis
lived in Innsbruck at this time.

"Follias" were included in a
manuscript of this year by the
lutenist Béthune.

Charpentier's pastorale "Le
Retour du printems, idylle sur
la convalescence du roi" appeared at this time.

The "Codex Vietórisz," a collection of virginal transcrip-
tions in German tablature by
various hands, was collected
this year.

Purcell's fantasias for viols
written at this time have been
considered the best of the
contrapuntal fantasias for
strings without continuo.

The following works by Purcell
were published at this time:
verse anthem, "Behold now,
praise the Lord," catch, "Here's
that will challenge," and the
verse anthem, "Out of the deep."

Stradella at this time distinguished between a concertino
and a concerto grosso in his
operas and oratorios and in his
"Sinfonie a più instrumenti."

Sacred music, solo and choral,
was abundant in France during
this period.

After pre-tonal experiments of
the early baroque and the introduction of rudimentary tonality
in Italy at about this time the
turning point in the use of
harmony occurred.

At this time Italian influence,
especially in sacred music, was
strengthened by the presence of
Lorenzani and several Italian
singers in Paris singing in the
royal choir.

William Claesz, Dutch painter,
died (born 1594).

(to 1682) During these years the

c.1680(cont.)
following works by Purcell appeared (either anthems or verse anthems).

"Blessed is he whose unrighteousness is forgiven" (verse anthem).
"Bow down Thine ear" (verse anthem).
"Hear me, O Lord, and that soon" (verse anthem).
"Hear my prayer" (anthem).
"I will given thanks unto the Lord" (verse anthem).
"Lord, how long wilt Thou be angry?" (anthem).
"Man that is born of woman" (anthem).
"O God, Thou art my God" (anthem).
"O God, Thou hast cast us out" (anthem).
"O Lord, God of hosts" (anthem).
"O Lord, Thou art my God" (verse anthem).
"Remember not, Lord, our offences" (anthem).
"Save me, O God" (?).

(to 1685) Scarlatti's "Diana ed Endimione" was performed during this period.

(to c.1730) The late baroque period is generally placed at this time.

1681
(January 7) Count Ludwig Günther dismissed all his musicians.

(January 20) Francesco Bartolomeo Conti, Italian theorbist and composer, was born at Florence (died 1731, July 20).

(January 21) Lully's "Le Triomphe de l'Amour" was produced and was the first perfor-

(cont.) mance of its kind with women dancers.

(January 25) Petronio Franceschini, Italian composer, died at Venice (born c.1650).

(January 26) On this date a Richard Robinso was appointed instrument-keeper to replace Henry Brockwell who gave up the position for undisclosed reasons.

(January 27) King Charles II sent John Abell to Italy to study. After his return Evelyn described meeting him (January 27, 1681-1682).

(January 30) On this date the court and the royal family commemorated the martyrdom of King Charles II's father.

(February 11) A Francis Purcell was admitted as groom-in-ordinary to King Charles II. He was Thomas Purcell's son and Henry's first cousin.

(February 15) Michel Forqueray, French organist, was born at Paris (died 1757).

(February 23 and 25) "La Pierre philosophale," a comedy in three acts by Corneille and Visé; and airs de danse and divertissements by Charpentier, were performed at the Théâtre de Guénégaud in Paris.

(March 13) Perti was elected a member of the Accademia Filarmonica.

(March 14) Georg Philipp Telemann, German composer, was born at Magdeburg, Saxony (died 1767, June 25).

(March 21) Monmouth rode into Oxford over Magdalen Bridge on the morning of this day when Parliament opened. His men were armed with "Protestant flails."

(March 28) Sir Constantin Huygens, Dutch poet and musician, died at the Hague (born 1596, September 4).

(April 9) Alphonso Marsh I, English composer, died at London (born c.1627, January).

(April 11) Anne Philidor, French musician, composer and conductor, and son of André, was born at Paris (died 1728, October 8).

(April 11 to 14) J. Playford, the elder, advertised the lease of his Islington house in "Smith's Protestant Intelligence" on these dates.

(May 15) T. Purcell of St. Martin's Parish granted power of attorney to his son Matthew to receive his salary as a Gentleman of the Chapel Royal.

(June 4) Krieger's first dramatic work, the serenata "Die drey Charites," was produced at Halle.

(June 4) Thomas Purcell made his will on this date. He was probably facing problems raised by his illness and was inclined to look to the future and take care of his relatives.

(June 8) On this date a Mr. Purcell received £37.10s from secret service funds. This was probably Edward, Thomas' son, who for some time now had held an important position at court as a gentleman usher Daily

(cont.) Waiter.

(July 6) Alessandro Stradella composed his "Il barcheggio" for a wedding ceremony on this date.

(July 8) Georg Neumark, German hymn composer, died at Weimar (born 1621, March 16).

(July 9) Baptismal registers at All Hollows the Less revealed that one Henry, son of Henry and Frances Purcell, was baptised there on this date (died 1681, July 18).

(July 18) If Henry Purcell, the musician, was the father of the child who died on this date his marriage probably took place a year earlier than the accepted date of 1681.

(July 22) Charpentier's "Endimion, tragédie" was produced at Paris.

(August 22) Pierre Philidor, French musician and son of Jacques, was born at Paris (died 1731, September 1).

(September 8) At the time of Stephen College's execution King Charles II left at 5 a.m. to relax at New Market "for some time," as was observed by Luttrell in his entry for this date.

(September 28) Johann Mattheson, German theorist, organist, harpsichordist, singer and composer, was born at Hamburg (died 1764, April 17).

(October 20) Nathaniel Tomkins, English organist, died at Martin Hussingtree near Worcester (born 1599).

(October 22) Benedetto Ferrari,
Italian composer and librettist,
died at Modena (born 1597).
His was the first opera troupe
to come to Venice.

(November 15) Shortly after
Catherine of Braganza's birthday
celebrated on this date the
court Whig factions arose.

(November 17) Dryden's "Absalom
& Achitophel" appeared anonymously on this date and was re-
published the following month.

(November 17) At the anniversary
of Queen Elizabeth's acession
on this date Parliamentarians
paraded all day in London's
streets. That night they held
a great Protestant celebration,
all in preparation for
Shaftesbury's trial, held a
week later.

(November 29) Johann Nikolaus
Bach married Sabina Katharina
Burgolt.

(December 23) Scarlatti's third
son, Alessandro Raimondo, was
born at Rome (date of death
unknown).

(January) King Charles II on
this date gave orders for the
prorogation of a "fiery, eager
and high-flying Parliament" and
had them carried out a week
later. They were ordered to
reassemble at Oxford, a Tory
stronghold, on January 21.

(February) Henry Aldrich was
installed a Canon of Christ
Church this month.

(March) Francesco Corbetta
(Francisque Corbett), Italian
guitarist, died at Paris (born

(cont.) c.1620). He was a
favorite of King Louis XIV.

(April) This month King Charles
II was active in further negotiations with King Louis XIV.
He was also concerned with
affairs of the Navy and his departure for Hampton Court for
the summer.

(May) Henry Aldrich was awarded
the degree of Bachelor and
Doctor of Divinity at Christ
Church.

(July) The probable date of the
appearance of Purcell's "I will
love Thee, O Lord" has been
given as between July 1681 and
the end of the year.

(August) At the beginning of
this month, if not earlier,
Purcell was working on a welcome ode of major importance.

(August and September) During
these months Purcell surely
added to his musical responsibilities at the Church Court
and Chamber, several in connection with the theater.

Gabriel da Annunciacão,
Portuguese composer, was born
at Ovar (died 1747).

Gluck's father, Alexander
Johannes Gluck, was born at
Neustadt (date of death unknown).

John Loosemore, English organist, died (birthdate unknown).

Alessandro Poglietti, Italian
composer, died at Venice
(birthdate unknown).

Carlo Ricciotti, Italian composer, was born (died 1756,
July).

Christoph Runge, German composer, died (born 1619).

Giuseppe Valentini, Italian composer, was born at Rome (date of death unknown).

Vincenzo Albrici this year became organist at St. Thomas' Church at Leipzig.

Johann Christoph Bach (fourth generation) was dismissed from his duties at Arnstadt at this time.

An "Eisteddfod" was held this year at Bewpyr Castle under the auspices of Sir Richard Bassett.

Angelo Berardi was "maestro di cappella" at the cathedral of Spoleto at this time. He was also a teacher.

In A. Berardi's "Ragionamenti musicali" Caproli is referred to as one of the best cantata composers of his time.

Campra was "maître de musique" at Arles this year.

Undisputable evidence placed Corelli at Rome at this time.

C.C. Dedekind was a member of the Elbische Schwanen-Orden this year and took a pseudonym of Concord, usually written "Con Cor D" or "Con Cor Den" as in the volume of poems "1681 Jahres ausgegäben von Con Cor Den."

Pietro Antonio Fiocco at this time helped to found a private school of music in Brussels.

William Fischer, a notary, took the test at Edinburgh this year.

(cont.) His name appeared written in early Scottish church manuscript.

Grew at this time mentioned "a dancing-master's kit," and since dancing-master's instruments would naturally be smaller than others, the name gradually was reserved for them only, as viol or violin was reserved for the larger sizes.

Giovanni Legrenzi became vice-"maestro di capella" at St. Marks' this year.

Emperor Leopold was so delighted with Biber that he ennobled him this year by granting him the prefix "von."

Rev. William Perry at this time was appointed professor of music at Gresham College.

Purcell's autograph copies of works by the older masters from this year proved that he continued to study them after he had started to compose.

The thesis that Purcell had a great deal of extra time to devote to composition during the first part of this year was supported by records revealing that King Charles II and others at Court were preoccupied with political affairs throughout this period.

It is possible that a compatriot of Purcell returning from Italy this year may have showed him an original copy of Corelli's Opus I.

Thomas Tudway was awarded the degree of Bachelor of Music this year by Cambridge.

1681(cont.)

Leonard Woodson II became a Gentleman of the Chapel Royal this year.

Mario Albioso published his "Selva di canzoni siciliani" this year at Palermo.

The fourth edition of Bacilly's "Remarques curieuses sur l'art de bien chanter . . ." appeared at this time.

John Banister this year published his "The Most Pleasant Companion" which dealt with the recorder.

Biber's six sonatas for violin with figured bass were published this year at Salzburg.

Biber's eight solo sonatas which were composed and published at this time combined various national influences as did Froberger's.

Biber's Sonata in C minor for violin and figured bass was published this year.

The text of Blow's New Year's Ode for this year, "Great Sir, the joy of all our hearts," showed the King's position as favorably as possible and dealt more upon foreign affairs than domestic.

Blow at this time wrote songs for Lee's "The Princess of Cleve."

Caresana's most famous work was his "Solfeggi" published this year at Naples.

"A Choice Compendium" was published by "J.H." at this time.

G.P. Colonna's "Motetti," opus 3; "Motetti sacri," opus 2; and "Salmi brevi," opus 1 were all published this year at Bologna.

Corelli's "XII suonate a tre, due violini e violoncello, col basso per l'organo," opus 1, was published this year at Rome and dedicated to Queen Christina of Sweden.

Dedekind at this time arranged the words for the sacred musical drama "Altes und neues in geistlichen Singspielen vorgestellt" and it was published in eight volumes at Dresden.

Thomas Dinely's "Voyage Through the Kingdom of Ireland" was published this year. In it he commented on the Irish predilection for the bagpipe and Irish harp.

Freschi this year wrote his opera "Pompeo Magno in Cilicia." It was for the Teatro Sant' Angelo at Venice.

Lully's ballet "Triomphe de l'Amour" appeared at this time.

Mielczewski's "Missa Rorate de Beata Virgine Maria" for four parts and continuo carried this date.

Perti's opera "Oreste" was written this year.

Three of the songs from "Theodosius" were included in Playford's "Choice Ayres & Songs . . . . . third book, 1681 . . . . sung at Court & at Public Theatres."

The oboe at this time made a tentative first appearance in

1681(cont.)
a Purcell score, "Swifter, Isis."

Purcell's compositions of this
year included: "Blow up the
trumpet in Sion," music for "The
History of King Richard II,"
music for "Sir Barnaby Whigg,
or No Wit like a Woman's," and
a welcome-song for King Charles
II, "Swifter, Isis, swifter
flow."

The following songs by Purcell
were published this year:
"Amintor, heedless of his
flocks," "How I sigh when I
think," "I take no pleasure in
the sun's bright beams,"
"Pastora's beauties when un-
blown," "Since one poor view
has drawn my heart," "When her
languishing eyes said 'love.'"

Benedict Schultheiss' "Heiliger
Sonntags-Handel und Kirch
-Wandel . . . durch Sigmund von
Birken" was published at this
time at Nürnberg.

Steffani's first stage work appeared this year, "Marco
Aurelio, Dramma posto in Musica
da D Agostino Steffani, Direttor
della Musica di Camera di S.A.S.
etc. di Bavaria, l'anno 1681."

Stradella's works this year included "La Forza del Amore
paterno."

Vitali's opus 10 "Inni sacri
per tutto l'anno a voce sola
con cinque stromenti" was published this year at Modena.

Werckmeister published his
"Orgelprobe" ("organ-rehearsal")
this year.

Colonna's oratorio "Il transito
di San Giuseppe" was performed

(cont.) this year at Modena.

Pietro Antonio Fiocco's opera
"Alceste" was performed at this
time at Hanover.

Petronio Franceschini's opera
"Dionisio" with second and
third acts by partenio was given
this year at Venice.

Operas by Johann Wolfgang
Franck published this year at
Hamburg were "Semele;"
"Hannibal;" and "Charitine."

Acciaiuoli's "Ulisse in
Feaccia" with music by Antonio
del Gaudio was performed this
year by puppets.

The performance at Versailles
of "Nicandro e Fileno," a
pastoral by Lorenzani (a pupil
of Benevoli), represented a
final but unsuccessful attempt
to replace French opera, now
so firmly entrenched at the
French court.

Melani's opera "Il carceriere
di se medesimo" was produced
this year at Florence.

A. Scarlatti's opera "Tutto il
mal non vien per nocere" was
produced this year at Rome's
Accademici uniti. The libretto
was by Totis.

Steffani's opera "Marco Aurelio"
was produced at this time at
Munich.

Calderon, the Spanish poet who
wrote "El jardin de Falerina,
died (born c.1600).

Dryden's "The Spanish Friar"
appeared at this time.

This year ended as it had begun

1681(cont.)
with political strife.

Gerard Ter Borch, Dutch painter,
died (born 1617).

Justus Suttermans, Flemish
painter, died (born 1597). He
was a favorite painter of the
Medici family.

American architecture: Hingham,
Old Ship Meeting House.

(to 1683) Since H. Purcell's
twenty-two trio-sonatas were
written between 1680 to 1683,
one may assume that during this
period he devoted considerable
time to them.

(to 1684) J. Playford, the
elder had business relations
with John Carr during these
years.

(to 1688) Cataldo Amodei,
choirmaster at the church of
San Paolo Maggiore, was at this
time at the Conservatorio di
Sant' Onofrio at Naples.

(and 1689, 1707) Corelli's
works included four sets of trio
sonatas, equally divided among
church sonatas (opus 1, 1681
and opus 3, 1689) and chamber
sonatas (opus 2 and opus 4),
as well as a set of solo sonatas
(opus 5, 1707). There were a
dozen sonatas in each group.

(to 1729) James Hawkins was
organist at Ely Cathedral during
this period.

(to 1735) Johann Krieger, II
lived at Zittau as municipal
musical director and organist
during these years.

Kuhnau this year wrote a motet

(cont.) for the town council
election. Its quality secured
him the position of cantor with
a sufficiently high salary so
that he could afford to continue
his studies.

Purcell married one Frances
(? Peters) at this time.

Purcell's song "Beneath a dark,
a melancholy grove" was published this year.

"I will love Thee, O Lord" by
Purcell has been assumed by
some to refer to King Charles
II personified as King David
and his situation with Absalom
(Monmouth). This interpretation of the Psalm was further
underscored by a contemporary
paraphrase of Psalm iii, published at this time.

1682
(January 29) João Alvares Frovo
(Frouvo), Portuguese writer on
music theory, died at Lisbon
(born 1602, November 16).

(January 30) After the Tories
had finished their observance
of the martyrdom of King
Charles I on this date, the
Whigs replied by offering "an
indignity" to the picture of
the Duke of York at the
Guildhall.

(February 9) Johann Jakob Bach,
brother of J.S. Bach, son of J.
Ambrosius and member of the
fifth generation of the Bach
family, was born at Eisenach
(died c.1722).

(February 11) Johann Jakob
Bach was christened at Eisenach.

(February 14) A. Werckmeister
married for the second time.

1682(cont.)

(February 28) Alessandro Stradella, renowned Italian singer, violinist and composer, died at Genoa (born 1642).

(March 27) Lukasz Chojnacki, Polish musician, died at Ląd (birthdate unknown).

(April 16) Jean Joseph Mouret, French composer, was born at Avignon (died 1738, December 22).

(April 18) Lully's "Persée" was produced at Paris.

(April 21) (Dom) Pierre-Benoit de Jumilhac, French theorist, died at Saint-Germain des Prés (born c.1611).

(May 17) On this date Purcell travelled to Windsor with sixteen other musicians.

(May 26 to 30) The "Impartial Protestant Mercury" during these days noted that the King's birthday was "kept very solemnly by all the lovers of the King."

(May 27 and 29) Purcell probably wrote "What shall be done in behalf of the man" (3rd ode commissioned by the court) to celebrate the return of James, Duke of York, from Scotland on May 27 and for King Charles II's birthday on the 29th he wrote "The summer's absence unconcerned we bear."

(June 19) On this date John Moore, Lord Mayor of London, confirmed his choice of candidates for the two offices of London Sheriffs in the traditional manner.

(June 24) Maitland gave a true and impartial account of the

(cont.) Proceedings of the Common-Hall of the City of London at Guildhall for electing Sheriffs, however, during the elections unruly demonstrations and serious irregularities aborted the issue of Whigs vs. Tories in the election of London Sheriffs.

(July 11) Edward Lowe, English organist and composer, died at Oxford (born c.1610).

(July 11) Purcell found himself up for an appointment as organist of His Majesty's Chapel Royal, as was indicated by the entry in the "Chequebook" for this date.

(July 14) Purcell was appointed organist of the Chapel Royal.

(July 22) Damascene secured letters of denization in England.

(July 31) Thomas Purcell, Henry's uncle, died at London (birthdate unknown). He had been as a father to Henry.

(August 2) Purcell's second son, John Baptista Purcell, was baptised. A different source gave this date as August 9 (buried 1682, October 17).

(August 2) T. Purcell was buried in the cloisters of Westminster Abbey.

(August 6) Josias Bauchier was appointed to fill Thomas Purcell's place as Gentleman of the Chapel Royal.

(August 31) Johann Nikolaus Bach, surgeon, son of J. Günther, member of the fifth generation of the Bach family, was born (date of death unknown).

1682(cont.)

(September 10) This date was the fifth anniversary of the elder Henry Purcell's appointment as composer-in-ordinary to the King.

(September 10) If H. Purcell was married in September, this would provide further explanation of the somewhat cryptic entry in the Fitzwilliam Museum autograph, "God bless Mr. Henry Purcell 1682 September the 10th." It could have been written on his wedding anniversary.

(September 16) Purcell was sworn in as organist of His Majesty's Chapel Royal on this date.

(September 30) Quite possibly Purcell composed a work for this occasion of the inauguration of the Lord Mayor and it (a catch) was first performed on this date.

(October 17) Purcell's son John Baptista was buried (born 1682, August 2 or 9).

(October 21) King Charles II's return from Newmarket on this date was supposedly celebrated by Purcell's setting of the ode "The summer's absence unconcerned we bear," however, the welcome song was purportedly used on the occasion of the King's birthday on May 29.

(October 22) Pietro Antonio Fiocco married Jeanne de Latere of Brussels.

(October 29) The text to Purcell's anthem "Blow up the trumpet" (Joel ii. 15-17) was the correct one for the twentieth Sunday after Trinity, which this

(cont.) year coincided with the Lord Mayor's celebrations on this date.

(October 29) A number of "songs said to have been written for the inauguration of the Lord Mayor, Sir Wm. Pritchard, on October 29, 1682" actually amounted to one catch. A number of Purcell's song-tunes were, however, revived on this occasion.

(November 5) In view of close political victories, King Charles II kept a close watch on all activities. He forbade all bonfires, public fireworks and festivals for Guy Fawkes Day this year.

(November 17) King Charles II forbade all bonfires, public fireworks and festivals for Queen Elizabeth's Accession Day this year.

(November 17) John Goodwin succeeded Thomas Purcell in the Private Music.

(December 18) Wendel Bach, probably a farmer at Wolfsbehringen, near Gotha, son of Lips and grandson of Veit, member of the third generation of the Bach family, died (born 1619).

(December 27) Elizabeth Ball, Christopher Gibbons' widow, was buried at Westminster Abbey. She was Gibbons' second wife.

(December 30) Pergolesi's mother was born.

(August) Corelli was again at the Church of Saint-Louis-des -Francais, this time as the head of ten violinists.

(September) The treasurers of the two Honorable Societies of the Inner and Middle Temple in England had conversations with Smith concerning the construction of an organ for their church. A contest for the best organ was on between Smith or Harris.

(autumn) Antonio Sartorio's opera "Orfeo" was performed at Naples.

(October) Caresana produced the dramatic cantata "Il sospetto."

(October) John Ferrabosco, organist, wind player and composer, died at London (born 1626).

(November) From this time forward Johann Günther Bach was associated with his father as organist.

Johann Christian Bach, Erfurt musician, son of Johann Bach, grandson of Johannes and member of the fourth generation of the Bach family, died at Erfurt (born 1640, August 2).

Johann Friedrich Bach, organist, son of J. Christoph, grandson of Heinrich and member of the fifth generation of the Bach family, was born (died 1730).

Johann Jakob Bach, Stockholm court musician, son of J. Ambrosius, grandson of Christoph and member of the fifth generation of the Bach family, was born (died 1722).

Johann Nikolaus Bach, Erfurt musician, son of Johann Bach, grandson of Johannes and member of the fourth generation of the

(cont.) Bach family, died of the plague (born 1653).

Cervetto (Giacomo Basevi or Bassevi, called Cervetto the Elder), Italian violoncellist and composer, was born (died 1783, January 14).

Francesco Bartolommeo Conti, an Italian composer associated with the Josephine Theater, was born according to a major source who gave his death as 1732. The generally recognized dates were 1681, January 20 to 1731, July 20.

Jean François Dandrieu (d'Andrieu), French organist, harpsichordist and composer, was born at Paris (died 1738, January 17).

Theodor Christlieb Reinhold, German composer, was born (died 1755, March 26).

John Robinson, English organist, was born at London. He was a chorister of the Chapel Royal in London under Blow and became organist of the churches of St. Lawrence and St. Magnus, London Bridge (died 1762, April 30).

Vincenzo Albrici relinquished his position at St. Thomas' Church in Leipzig to become director of music at St. Augustine's Church in Prague.

J. Christoph Bach (fourth generation) was appointed both court and town musician at Arnstadt by Count Anton Günther.

Johann Günther Bach was deputy organist at Arnstadt at this time.

1682(cont.)

Johann Günther Bach this year married Anna Margaretha, daughter of Bürgermeister Krül, of Arnstadt.

Heinrich Bach (third generation) petitioned the Consistory to appoint his son Johann Günther (fourth generation) as his assistant.

King Charles II may have been encouraged by the sentiments voiced by the anonymous poet who wrote the text for Blow's New Year's ode for this year, "Arise, great monarch, arise."

John Blow from this date forward lived in the Great Sanctuary at Westminster where he had a lease and paid the Poor Rate regularly from this year until his death.

Blow and Purcell were associated from this year on in their capacities as two of the three organists of the Chapel Royal.

Clifford became senior canon this year.

As early as this year, according to his pupil Georg Muffat, Corelli's concertos were already being played in Rome. They were the earliest known examples of the concerto grosso.

Queen Christina of Sweden held musical festivities and it was probably at such an affair that Muffat this year heard Corelli's concertos which impressed him so greatly.

Muffat maintained that Corelli started to write his opus VI this year at Rome.

The Chapelle Royale, for which most of Couperin's church music was written, was built at this time.

A. Draghi was this year appointed director of the imperial chapel at Vienna.

Richard Goodson this year succeeded Edward Lowe as organist of Christ Church in Oxford, Professor of Music at the University and organist of New College, Oxford.

Kahnau this year moved to Leipzig where he remained until his death.

Johann Löwe became organist at Lüneburg this year.

Andreas Moser relied on Muffat's "Armonico tributo" of this year as a basis for denying the existence at that time of the great prototypes of Corelli which Muffat had invoked.

Purcell at this time moved into new quarters in Great St. Anne's Lane. His name was listed, with the annotation, "new arrival," 24th on the roster of names for that sheet in the St. Margaret's poor-rates for this year.

Henry Purcell apparently lived in St. Margaret's Parish, Westminster at the time of John Baptista's birth which was recorded in the Westminster Abbey accounts for that year.

Alessandro Scarlatti this year became "Maestro di Cappella" at the Royal Chapel in Naples.

Mathias Shore became a King's Trumpeter-in-Ordinary at this

1682(cont.)

time.

Nicholas Staggins was awarded
the degree of Doctor of Music
by Cambridge this year although
he did not perform the customary
exercise at the time.

Albergati's opus 1 "Balletti,
correnti . . . " for one or two
parts appeared this year.

Blow at this time wrote songs
for Durfey's "The Royalist."

Blow's series of royal "Welcome"
songs began this year with
"Great Sir, the joy of all our
hearts."

Colonna's opus 4 "Litanie con
le quattro antifone della B.
Virgine" was published this year
at Bologna.

The 1701 collection by Corelli
stated that numbers 2, 4, 5,
and 11 were composed at Rome
at this time.

Cousser's "Composition de
Musique suivant la méthode
Françoise" appeared this year.

G.B. Draghi this year contributed
songs to Aphra Behn's comedy
"The City-Heiress."

The last edition of John Forbes'
"Cantus, Songs and Fancies, for
Three, Four or Five Parts, both
apt for Voices and Viols" was
published this year. Prior
editions had appeared in 1662
and 1666.

Freschi's operas "Giulio Cesare
trionfante" and "Olimpia
vendicata" were composed this
year for the Teatro Sant'
Angelo in Venice.

An edition of Thomas Greeting's
book on flageolot playing was
printed this year.

A trumpet sonata composed this
year by Grossi, a composer of
the Bologna school, revealed
how early concerto style appeared in works of this category.

Vopelius' "Gesangbuch" contains
seven four-part settings of
Hymn-Tunes done by
Hammerschmidt.

J.S. Kusser this year published
at Stuttgart his "Composition
de Musique suivant la méthode
française, contenant six
Ouvertures de Théâtre
accompagnées de plusieurs Airs."

Locke's "The Pleasant Companion"
was published this year.

Johann Löhner's "Auserlesene
Kirch- und Tafel-Masic" was
published at this time.

Lully's "Persée" was completed
at this time.

Menestrier published his "Des
ballets anciens et modernes
selon les règles du theâtre"
this year. On German court
festivals he wrote, "On fait en
Allegmagne de ces Festins
d'appareil, particulièrement le
Carnaval, où les Princes, les
Seigneurs et les Dames se
déguisent en Hôteliers et
Hôtelières, en Valets et
Servantes d'hôtelleries ce
qu'on nomme Virtschafft."

Georg Muffat's "Armonico
tributo" (sonate di camera) was
published this year at
Salzburg. The work was a tribute
to Corelli as well as Lully.

Durfey's play "Injured Princess" this year had music by Pack.

Aphra Behn's play "False Count" this year had music by Pack.

"A Chorographical Description of the County of West-Meath" was written at this time by Sir Henry Piers.

A second edition of Placker's "Evangelische Leeuwerck ofte" (a collection of words of Flemish songs, first edition published in 1667) with a fifth section and the music for each song added appeared this year in two volumes.

Purcell's anthem "In the midst of Life" was written prior to this year.

The third edition of "Songs and Fancies," the only book of Scottish secular music of this century, was published at this time.

Robert de Visée's "Livre de Guittarre" was published this year at Paris in its first edition. The work was dedicated to the King of France. The author admitted imitating Lully's rhythmic dance style but avoided including "follias" because they had become too commonplace.

De Visée's Suite III Prelude (possibly for guitar) was written at this time.

A later edition of Vitali's "Sonate a duo Violini . . ." was published this year at Venice.

Vitali's "Varie partite del passo a mezzo, ciaccona, capricci e (cont.) passagalli a 3 : due violini e violone ò spinetta" was published this year by Gasparo Ferri.

Gottfried Vopelius' "Neu Leipziger Gesangbuch" was published this year at Leipzig. It contained 100 hymns by Schein as well as other tunes.

Walther's "Passion" appeared anonymously in Vopelius' Leipzig hymn book and was in use there until 1721.

Italians at this time still wrote sonatas in five or six movements and at this time the German Westhoff published one which carried ten tempo markings and nine separate movements (Adagio conunadoke Maniera, Allegro, Adagio, Allegro overo un poco presto, Adagio, Aria adagio assai. La guerra (allegro), Aria tutto adagio, Vivace (c), Vivace (6/4)).

Corelli's concerti were performed at Rome at this time with as many as one hundred and fifty musicians in the orchestra.

The King's and Duke's Companies were united this year and usually performed at Drury Lane.

Italian opera came to Portugal at this time.

Acciaiuoli's "Chi è cagion del suo mal pianga se stesso" with music probably by himself ("poesia d'Ovidio, e musica d'Orfeo") was performed this year at the Palazzo Colonna in Rome.

Eccles this year wrote music for Behn's "The City Heiress"

and Otway's "Venice Preserved."
Both were produced at the Dorset
Garden Theatre.

Johann Wolfgang Franck's operas
"Diocletianus" and "Attila" were
both performed this year at
Hamburg.

Johann Löhner's "Abraham" was
produced this year.

Pallavicini's opera "Il re
infante" with libretto by Noris
was produced this year at the
Teatro San Giovanni Crisostomo
in Venice.

Pistocchi's "Girello" was performed by puppets this year at
Venice.

"The Libertine," Shadwell's
tragi-comic version of the Don
Juan legend, was revived this
season at Dorset Garden.

Sir Thomas Browne, English
physician and author, died (born
1605).

Bunyan's "The Holy War" was
written at this time.

Dryden's "Mac Flecknoe" appeared
this year.

Thomas Otway's "Venice Preserved"
was written this year.

The rigged elections, riots,
false ballots and political
conniving all contributed to
making the elections this year
the bitterest of all contests
between Whigs and Tories.

King James II had by this time
already been satirized in a
pamphlet as "Julian the
Apostate."

Throughout this summer the
loyal party (Tory) gradually
gained the upper hand.

Gibbs, an English architect, was
born (died 1754).

Longhena, an Italian architect,
died (born 1598).

Claude Gellée, the French
painter known as Claude Lorrain,
died (born 1600).

Bartolomé Esteban Murillo,
Spanish painter, died (born
1617).

Jacob Isaacksz Van Ruisdael,
Dutch painter, died (born
c.1628).

Bassani lived at Bologna this
year where he was made
"principe" of the Accademia dei
Filarmonici. He had already
been a member.

(to 1683) Purcell's verse
anthem "I was glad when they
said" appeared at this time.

(to 1685) J.W. Franck was music
director at the Hamburg
Cathedral during these years.

(to 1689) The reign of Czar
Ivan V over Russia. He was
deposed in 1689 by Peter I (the
Great) and died in 1696. Until
1689 they ruled jointly.

(to 1692) Daniel Roseingrave
was organist at Winchester
Cathedral during this period.

(to 1694) J.S. Kusser was
Chapel Master at Wolfebüttel
during these years.

(to 1708) Corelli during these
twenty-six years participated

1682(cont.)

at the festival of Saint Louis
as director of the small
orchestra.

(to 1718) Richard Goodson,
senior was Professor of Music at
Oxford during this period.

(to 1725) The reign of Czar
Peter I (the Great) over Russia.
He ruled jointly with Ivan until
1689 when the latter was deposed
(died 1725).

c.1682

Domenico Gizzi, Italian male
soprano and teacher, was born at
Arpino (died 1758 or later).

George Loosemore, English organist, died at Cambridge (birthdate unknown).

Jakob Scheiffelhut was musical
director at St. Anne's,
Augsburg this year.

The English idiom was predominant
in Blow's "Venus and Adonis"
written this year for one of
King Charles II's mistresses.

Johann Casper Fischer's "Le
Journal de Printemps consistant
en Airs et Balets à 5 parties et
les Trompettes à plaisir" appeared at this time.

Purcell's verse anthem "Let mine
eyes run down with tears" was
written this year.

(to 1685) Purcell wrote music
for "The Double Marriage" during
these years.

(to 1685) During this period
Purcell wrote the following
verse-anthems:

"Awake, put on thy strength"

(cont.)

"In Thee, O Lord, do I put
my trust"
"It is a good thing to give
thanks"
"I will give thanks unto Thee,
O Lord"
"The Lord is my light"
"My heart is fixed"
"O praise God in His holiness"
"Praise the Lord, O my soul"
"Rejoice in the Lord alway"
(The "Bell" anthem)
"Unto Thee I will cry"
"Why do the heathen?"

(and 1686) "The Delightful
Companion; or Choice New
Lessons for the Recorder or
Flute" was published by John
Playford in c.1682 at London.
A second edition appeared in
1686.

1683

(January 9) Lully's "Phaéton"
was produced at Versailles in
Paris.

(January 13) Christoph Graupner,
German composer, was born at
Hartmannsdorf, near Saxony
(died 1760, May 10).

(January 14) Gottfried
Silbermann, German organ,
clavichord and piano maker, was
born at Kleinbobritzsch (died
1753, August 4). He established
a school of organ building and
also invented the "Cembal
d'amore."

(January 16) Jacques Adrien
Boutmy, organist, was born at
Ghent (died 1719, September 6).

(January 25) A. Scarlatti's
opera "Pompeo" with libretto by
Minato was produced at the
Teatro Colonna in Rome.

1683(cont.)

(February 4) On this date
Purcell took the sacrament in
public according to the usage
of the Church of England. He
did this before witnesses
which was required by statute.
Those present were Moses Snow,
Robert Tanner, Bartholomew
Wormall, and Giles Borrowdell.

(February 11) Solomon Eccles,
musician and shoemaker, died
at London (born 1618).

(March 23) The Rye House Plot
was thwarted on this date. It
would have caused officials to
investigate Purcell's taking of
the sacrament according to the
Church of England more closely.

(April 8) Johann Günther Bach,
Arnstadt organist, son of
Heinrich, grandson of Johannes
and member of the fourth generation of the Bach family,
died (born 1653, July 17).

(April 10) Flaminia Scarlatti,
Alessandro's daughter, was born
at Rome (date of death unknown).

(April 16) Moses Snow and
Robert Tanner were summoned to
appear at court in Westminster
Hall on this date to testify
under oath that they had seen
Purcell take the sacrament and
had also seen the minister and
churchwarden sign the document.

(April 17) Johann David
Heinichen, German composer and
theorist, was born at Krössuln
near Weissenfels (died 1729,
July 15).

(April 21) Vincenzo de Grandis
left his position at the court
of Modena.

(May 24 to 28) Purcell advertised his first instrumental
publication in the "London
Gazette" during this period.

(June 11) On this date a further
notice appeared in the "London
Gazette, H. Purcell's first
instrumental publication, ad-
vising subscribers to go to
Purcell's house or send an order
on paper and the money would be
collected later (See previous
entry).

(July 28) The marriage ceremony
of Prince George of Denmark and
the Lady Anne, with the Bishop
of London presiding, took place
at St. James', Piccadilly on
this day. Certainly, London's
"beau-monde" turned out "tutti
quanti" to the event and
Purcell's music was a major
part of the event, thus placing
him in a favorable light.

(August 2) John Lenton was appointed musician for the violin
to King Charles II.

(August 5 or 8) Johann Ernst
Bach, Arnstadt organist, son
of J. Christoph, grandson of
Christoph and member of the
fifth generation of the Bach
family, was born. Forkel gave
the earlier date and Spitta and
others the later (died 1739,
March 21).

(August 24) Meinrad Spiess,
German priest and composer, was
born at Honsolgen, Suabia (died
1761, July 12).

(August 28) Christoph Schultze,
German composer, died at
Delitzsch (born 1606, December).

(September 2) Michel Philidor,
French musician and son of

1683(cont.)

André, was born at Versailles (date of death unknown). He was a drummer in the King's band and was Lalande's godson.

(September 25) Jean Philippe Rameau, "France's foremost composer of the eighteenth century," was born at Dijon, Burgundy. He was christened at the church of St. Etienne. Rameau was the leader in the development of clavecin technique and the major theorist of his time (died 1764, September 12).

(October 20) King Charles II returned from Newmarket and he and his court went into mourning for the death of King Alphonso 6th of Portugal, Her Majesty's brother.

(October 29) Purcell advertised in the "London Gazette" that "subscribers requirements having been met, further copies of the 'sonatas of III Parts' by Henry Purcell are to be sold by J. Playford, J. Carr and H. Rogers."

(November 11) Johann Georg Bach, son of Georg Christoph, was born (died 1713, March 13).

(November 14) Pergolesi's father was born (date of death unknown).

(November 21 or 22) Nothing in Purcell's description of "Laudate Ceciliam" indicated that the piece was performed on these dates which had been judged to be the case.

(November 22) By this date Purcell had composed two, or possibly three, odes to St. Cecilia. He had finished two of the works, "Laudate Ceciliam" and "Welcome to all the

(cont.) pleasures" in time to rehearse them for the festivities on this date.

(December 17) Official notice came down from the Lord Chamberlain's office for the first time on this date appointing "Henry Purcell to be organ-maker & keeper etc, in the place of Mr. Hingeston, deceased."

(December 23) Scarlatti's opera "Psiche, o vero Amore innamorato" with libretto by Totis was produced at the Palazzo Reale in Naples.

(February) By the beginning of this month the political situation had quieted enough for Monmouth to be released on bail, in spite of his overt insubordination and complicity in various Whig activities.

(February) Purcell at this time had been noticed by the authorities of Westminster Abbey, perhaps because of his recent appointment as Lowe's successor.

(February) Eight new songs by Henry Purcell were included in the fourth book of "choice Ayres & Songs to Sing to the Theorbo-lute or Bass-viol." The collection was listed in the Term catalogue for this month and in all probability was in the press for the usual six months or more.

(Spring) Johann Sebastiani, German Passion composer, died at Königsberg (born 1622, September 30).

(June) Although a precise date for the completion of engraving and annotation of the frontis-

piece to Purcell's "sonnata's of
III. Parts" is lacking, evidence
provided by the portrait shows
only that is was struck not
later than this month and possibly as much as a month earlier.

(October) Blow's wife died in
childbirth and many of the musicians at Court were actually
in mourning, although it was
not official (birthdate unknown).

(December) John Hingston, English
organist, violinist and composer,
died at London (Westminster)
(birthdate unknown).

Johann Nicolaus Bach, son of J.
Ambrosius, brother of J.
Sebastian and member of the
fifth generation of the Bach
family, was born at Eisenach
(date of death unknown).

Salomon Bendeler (Bendler),
German bass singer, was born at
Quedlinburg (died c.1724).

William Broderip, English organist, was born (died 1726,
January 31).

Fétis and Pietrucci in their
respective memoirs both stated
incorrectly that this was the
date of Cristofori's birth.

Haydn's great-grandfather,
Caspar Haydn, and his wife were
killed when the town of Hainburg
was captured by the Turks.

Hingeston, instrument-keeper and
repairer at Westminster Abbey,
died (birthdate unknown).

Domenico Montagnana, Italian
violin maker, was born (died
1756).

Carlos Patiño, Spanish composer,
died at Madrid (birthdate unknown).

Jakob Stainer, Austrian violin
maker, died (born 1621, July 14).

Paul de Villesavoye, French
composer, was born at Paris
(died 1760, May 28).

It has been stated that Calista
was one of the "most fam'd
Italian Masters" whom Purcell
took as a model for his own
sonatas written this year.

Campra this year was "maître de
musique" at Toulouse.

Charpentier competed this year
for one of the four positions
as "sous-maître de chapelle,"
Lelande secured one of the
openings; but illness forced
him to withdraw.

The name of Jeremiah Clarke
with this date was carved in
the stone arcade of the north
aisle of St. George's Chapel.

The office of Surintendant
della Chapelle Royale was
divided this year among four
people, each of whom was required to direct the music for
only three months of each year.
With Lully's influence Colasse
secured the second of these
positions.

Thomas Cross began to engrave
this year and soon created a
revolution in English music
publishing.

Cross' name appeared as the
music engraver on Purcell's
"Sonnata's of III. Parts" this
year.

Adam Drese, a viola da gamba player, this year became conductor of the court orchestra at Arnstadt.

Domenico Gabrieli was president of the Accademia Filarmonica in Bologna this year.

Grabu at this time returned to England from his retirement in France.

Matthias Klotz returned to Mittenwald this year from Cremona and immediately began to instruct the impoverished people of the town in violin-making.

Louis Laguerre, Jean's father, went to England this year.

Michel Lalande served as surintendant de la chapelle royale at this time.

Louis Marchand showed such precocious skill at the organ at this time that he was appointed organist of Nevers Cathedral. He was fourteen years old.

Perti went to Venice this year.

According to one source a "Te Deum" by Perti was sung under the composer's direction in Vienna, at the end of the Turkish siege this year. This had to be a mistake since Perti had not yet made a name for himself and was hardly known except at Bologna.

Jacques Philidor was admitted to the Chapel of Grand Écurie this year.

After Godbid's death Playford, (cont.) the younger and Godbid's widow Anne printed musical works published by the elder Playford, Henry Playford, Joseph Hindmarsh and others until this date.

Purcell this year classed "adagio" as in speed "a middle movement."

Purcell had to pass the Test Act of 1683 in regard to his religious standing. There is some doubt as to whether he may have been a Catholic secretly or openly.

Purcell became composer to the court under King Charles II.

After the title of "Laudate Ceciliam" on folio 190(rev.) Purcell added the description: "A Latin song made upon St. Cecilia, whose day is commemerated yearly by all Musicians, made in the year 1683."

The idea that young Henry Purcell was born in June was based on the engraved frontispiece to the "Sonata's of III. Parts" of 1683, where it was noted that Purcell was twenty-four at the time of the engraving.

Purcell was possibly inspired by Corelli's works in his twelve trio sonatas written this year.

Probably events such as the celebration of King Charles II's birthday in 1677 created Purcell's dislike for the "levity & balladry of our neighbours" (France) which he mentioned in his preface to the trio-sonatas at this time.

1683(cont.)

Purcell felt justified in deprecating himself as late as this year when he wrote about himself in the preface to the trio-sonatas. He felt that his education was inadequate.

"Accounts for liveries for musicians" ending at Michaelmas this year showed that three positions held by Thomas Purcell were still vacant.

Bernhard Smith at this time built the organ at Durham Cathedral.

Thomas Tomkins, senior sold his estate in Cornwall this year and came to Gloucestershire.

The pedigree this year stated that "Thomas died unmarried" (Tomkins).

Tosi was organist of the church of San Petronio at Bologna.

The original fount of music type cut by Peter Walpergen for Dr. Fell in 1667 was used in the "Yattendon Hymnal" published that year. Some sources, however, claim it was issued in 1683.

Albergati's "Sonatas for two violins and bass, opus 2 was written this year.

Blow and Tudway both provided verse anthems "on ye Thanksgiving for ye discovery of ye Rye House Conspiracy" at this time.

Blow this year composed the Anthem "We will rejoice in Thy salvation"(Ryehouse Plot).

Henry Bowman's "Songs for i & 3 voyces" was reissued in this year (See also 1677, 1678, and 1679).

Buns' "Encomia sacra" was published this year by Arnold van Eynden of Utrecht.

Caproli's oratorio "Davide prevaricante, e poi pentito" appeared this year.

C.C. Dedekind's "C.C.D.'s Singende Sonn- und Fest-Tags Ahndachten" was published this year by Michael Günther at Dresden.

Duponchel's "Domine probasti" for four voices was included in "Salmi vespertini di Caifaleri."

Durfey's "New Collection of Songs and Poems" appeared this year.

"Musikalischer Vorschmack" issued at this time contained four melodies by Eccard.

Eisenhut this year composed "Sacer concentus."

Thomas Farmer wrote a song for Lee's "Constantine the Great" at this time.

Freschi this year wrote his opera "Silla" for the Teatro di Sant' Angelo in Venice.

D. Gabrieli published the operas "Il Gige in Lidia" and "Cleobulo" this year at Bologna.

Gasparo Gaspardini's "Sonate a tre, 2 voci e violencino, con il B. per l'organo," opus 1 was published this year at

Bologna.

Richard Hunt's "The Genteel Companion for the Recorder," in eight volumes, was published at this time.

Kaspar Kittel this year composed arias and cantatas for one, two, three and four voices with continuo, opus 1.

Michel Lalande this year composed a cantata "Le Concert d'Esculape."

Legrenzi composed the opera "Quistino" in Venice this year.

Legrenzi this year composed the opera "I due Cesari." It was mentioned in the Paris "Mercure galant."

Lully's "Phaéton" was completed at this time.

Pachelbel wrote "Musikalische Sterbens-Gedancken" this year.

Otway's play "Atheist" was this year set to music by Pack.

Pack's setting of "Tell me, Thyris, tell your anguish" was issued, as a musical appendix, with the 1683 quarto of Dryden and Lee's tragedy "The Duke of Geise." His name was not given, however. Later, quartos omitted the music.

"Marzio Coriolano," an opera by Perti with libretto by Frencasco Valsini (anagram of Francesco Silvani), appeared at this time.

Purcell's anthem "I will sing unto the Lord" was written prior to this date.

Purcell's catch "Young John the gardener" was published this year.

Purcell's Morning and Evening service in Bb ma. was composed prior to this date.

Purcell's ode for St. Cecilia's Day "Welcome to all the pleasures" was composed this year.

Purcell this year composed an ode for the Marriage of Prince George of Denmark to Princess Anne "From hardy climes."

The first of Purcell's odes for St. Cecilia's Day was composed this year. It may have been "Laudate Ceciliam."

Purcell's "Sonata in F Major" appeared at this time.

Carr and Playford this year at London published Purcell's "Sonnata's of III. Parts." These were his first Italianate sonatas and were written for two violins and bass. One of the sonatas was a chaconne. He wrote a second set in 1697.

A number of the eight songs by Purcell that Playford published in the fourth book of "Choice Ayres & Songs" were probably composed during this year.

All of the seven songs by Purcell in Playford's fifth book of "Choice Ayres & Songs" were definitely composed this year, if not earlier.

The following songs by Purcell were published this year:

"From silent shades"
"Let each gallant heart"

"Rashly I swore I would
disown"
"She loves and She confesses
too"
"She who my poor heart
possesses"
"When Strephon found his
passion vain"

Purcell's sacred song "Sleep,
Adam" appeared at this time.

By this time Purcell had composed the following verse
anthems:

"Blessed be the Lord, my
strength"
"Let God arise"
"Lord, who can tell?"
"My beloved spake"
"O Lord our Governor"
"Thou knowest, Lord, the
secrets of our hearts"

Purcell's welcome-song for
Charles II "Fly, bold rebellion"
was written this year.

Humphry Salter this year wrote
"The Genteel Companion; Being
exact Directions for the
Recorder." It contained a
minuet.

"Agar et Ismaele," an oratorio
by Scarlatti, was published
this year. "It was a step
closer to the Italian overture
type."

Scarlatti's opera "Il Pompeo"
was published this year at Rome.
It was his first attempt at
"opera seria."

Part V of Berthold Spirido's
work "Neue bis dato unbekannte
Unterweisung" appeared separately
this year as "Musikalische
Erzgruben."

A. Steffani this year wrote
some "Sonate da camera" for two
violins, viola and bass.

Sir James Turner's "Pallas
Armata" was published at this
time. The "colonel-drumm" was
mentioned in the work.

Vitali's "Balletti, correnti, e
capricci per camera a due
violini e violone" was published
this year by Stampa del Gardano
at Venice.

An edition of Vitali's "Sonate
a due, tre, quattro, e cinque
stromenti" was published this
year by Giacomo Monti.

A body of people known as "The
Musical Society" held the first
of a series of annual celebrations this year at London.

Bernhardt Smith this year suggested A=474 c.p.s., S-4·3.

Concerts were being organized
in England at this time by
Sadler. Italian music was the
principle attraction.

Johann Wolfgang Franck's opera
"Vespasianus" was performed
this year at Hamburg.

Pallavicino's opera "Bassiano
overo Il maggior impossible"
with libretto by Noris was
produced this year at the
Teatro dei SS. Giovani e Paolo.

Pallavicino's opera "Carlo, re
d'Italia" with libretto by
Noris was produced this year
at the Teatro San Giovanni
Crisostomo in Venice.

A "degenerate" version of the
most famous of all jiggs
"Pickelhering" was performed at

this time at Dresden.

Scarlatti's oratorio "Agar et Ismaele esiliati" was produced this year at Rome.

Strungk's operas "Theseus," "Semiramis" and "Floretto" were produced this year at Hamburg.

Izaak Walton, English writer, died (born 1593).

Edward Young, English poet, was born at Upham, in Hampshire (died 1765).

Dryden wrote his opera "King Arthur" this year or the next to be performed using some of the stage machinery planned for the 1685 production of his "Albion & Albanius."

Dryden's "Riligio Laici" was written this year.

Jean Baptiste Colbert, Cardinal Mazarin's successor, died (born 1619).

King George II of England (House of Hanover) was born (died 1760).

The Turkish seige of Vienna took place at this time.

Guarini, Italian architect, died (born 1624).

(to 1684) Johann Christoph Bach, son of Johann Christoph II, member of the sixth generation, attended the Eisenach Latin school at this time.

(to 1684) Brossard occupied a position at Notre-Dame during these years.

(anc 1684) Domenico Scarlatti's opera "Il Giustino" had a libretto that was a revision of a drama by Beregani that had been performed in Venice in 1683 and in Naples in 1684, music by Legrenzi.

(to 1686) Johann Georg Conradi was conductor at Ansbach during this period.

(to 1690) Christian Heinrich Aschenbrenner was first violinist at the Merseburg ducal chapel during these years.

(to 1692) The Blaikie viola da gamba manuscripts were compiled at this time.

(to 1692) The mediocrity of all the music written for celebrations between these years was put to shame by Purcell who revealed the progress he had made in mastering old techniques and developing new ones in these nine years.

(to 1706) Flavio Carlo Lanciano during these years wrote ten Latin oratorios for the archiconfraternity, "del Crocifisso."

(to 1708) Michel L'Affilard during this period was a tenor singer in the choir of King Louis XIV, with a salary of 900 livres.

(to 1717) Lotti produced eighteen successful operas in Venice during these thirty-four years.

(to 1733) Thomas Cross, junior, the printer, worked with great skill and artistic success during this period.

c.1683

Filippo Amadei, Italian cellist and composer, was born at Reggio (date of death unknown).

Carlo Bergonzi, Italian violin maker, was born at Cremona (died 1747).

Gasparo Gaspardini, Italian composer, was maestro di cappella at Verona Cathedral.

Jean François Lépine, senior, French organ builder, was born (died 1762, October 21).

Pieter de Hooch, Dutch painter, died (born 1629).

Ribera, Spanish architect, was born (died 1742).

(to c.1708 to 1710) Thomas Cross signed himself as "junior" during these years and sometimes in the very earliest part of his career.

1684

(January 18) "Amadis de Gaule," an opera in five acts by Lully with libretto by Philippe Quinault, was produced at the Opéra in Paris.

(February 12) Pietro Ziani, Italian organist and composer, died at Naples (born 1620).

(February 16) Bohuslav Matěj Černohorský, Bohemian composer, was born at Nymburk, Bohemia (died 1742, July 1).

(February 16) Purcell's salary as "keeper of the organs" may have been part of the £60 per annum he was allotted on this date.

(February 17) Scarlatti was ap-

(cont.) pointed "maestro di cappella" to the Viceroy at Naples. He was chosen over several native Neapolitan musicians.

(February 17) Francesco Scarlatti was appointed a violinist of the Royal Chapel at Naples.

(March 31) Francesco Durante, Italian composer, was born at Frattamaggiore near Naples (died 1755, August 13).

(April 6) Cristina Scarlatti, Alessandro's daughter, was born at Rome (date of death unknown).

(May 8) Henri Dumont, Walloon organist and composer, died at Paris (born 1610).

(May 26) To satisfy his "frenchify'd" appetites King Charles II sent for the prince's players of France, who went directly to Windsor after their arrival in England on this date.

(July 2) The King appointed Nicholas Staggins first Professor of Music at Cambridge.

(August 12) Nicolo Amati, Italian violin maker, died at Cremona (born 1596, September 3). He made what was considered the "ideal Cremona violin."

(August 24) Johann Aegidius Bach married Juditha Katharina Syring.

(September 18) Johann Gottfried Walther, German composer and lexicographer, was born at Erfurt (died 1748, March 23).

(September 25) The King and Duke of York left on a small

1684(cont.)
expedition for "political fence
-mending." They travelled from
Winchester to London and when
they arrived on this date were
greeted by Purcell's setting of
Thomas Flatman's ode "From those
serene & rapturous joys."

(October 20) Maria Barbara Bach,
first wife of Johann Sebastian
Bach, daughter of J. Michael
Bach, granddaughter of Heinrich,
J. Sebastian's great-uncle, and
member of the fifth generation
of the Bach family, was born
(died 1720, July).

(November 4) Sebastian Scherer
was appointed organist of St.
Thomas' Church, at Strasbourg.

(November 10) Purcell was surely
involved somehow in elaborate
preparations for the Queen's
birthday, which began on this
date.

(November 15) Luttrell described
Her Majesty's birthday at
Whitehall on this date as being
celebrated with fireworks and a
great ball.

(November 21 and 22) During the
week after the Queen's celebration Purcell was probably involved in the preparations for
the St. Cecilia's Day celebrations for the evening of the
21st and the day of the 22nd.

(December 11) The Prince's
players from France must have
had very little effect on the
English stage since they de-
parted on this date after a
very brief theatrical season at
Whitehall.

(December 28) Pallavicino's
opera "Massimo Puppieno" with

(cont.) libretto by Aurelio
Aureli was produced at the
Teatro dei SS. Giovanni e Paolo
in Venice.

(February) Scarlatti became
"maestro di cappella" at the
Royal Chapel in Rome.

(February) A revival of
Scarlatti's "Pompeo" took place
at the Teatro San Bartolomeo.

(April) J. Ambrosius Bach requested permission to leave
Eisenach to accept a position
at Erfurt, but it was not
granted. The Burgomeister and
the Council of Eisenach both
refused the request.

(May) By this time Smith and
Harris had each built an organ
for the church of Honorable
Societies of the Inner and
Middle Temple in England.

(December) Issac Staggins,
English oboe and violin player,
died at London (birthdate unknown).

Michel von Beethoven was born
at Mechlin (date of death unknown).

As a matter of interest, with
the old way of reckoning time,
Handel's birth would be this
year, however, 1685 is quite
universally accepted.

Gottlieb Hayne, Berlin organist,
was born (died c.1758).

Johannes Olearius, German hymn
-writer, died (born 1611).

Johann Rosenmüller, German composer, died (born 1619). He
was particularly known for his
chamber sonatas and was con-

sidered to be a strong German
rival of Lully.

Scarlatti's second son died
(born 1680, August 24).

Floriano Arresti this year became a member of the Accademia
Filarmonica of Bologna.

G.B. Bassani at this time was
elected "maestro di cappella" of
the Accademia della Morte at
Ferrara. In 1688 he became
"maestro" at the cathedral.

One source revealed a Cornelius
van Beethoven who lived at
Mechlin and could have been the
father of Michael Beethoven born
this year.

Vincenzo Bernabei was appointed
court organist at Munich this
year.

Blow and Purcell both supported
"Father" Smith in his contest
this year with Renatus Harris at
the Temple Church.

Georg Böhm at this time entered
the University of Jena.

J.H. Buttstett's first appointment was to the Reglerkirche
this year.

By this beginning of this year
King Charles II finally was in
a position to enjoy the results
of his political victory.

According to one source Corelli
remained at Hanover this year
with a friend, Farinelli, a
reputable violinist from whom
he may have "borrowed" the idea
of variations on the famous
theme of "Folies d'Espagne"
published this year by Playford

(cont.) as "Faronnell's Ground."

Johann Heinrich Ernesti was
rector of the Thomasschule from
this date forward.

Thomas Farmer, English composer,
graduated from Cambridge at this
time.

Francis Forcer this year was one
of the four stewards of the St.
Cecilia's Day festivities.

Freschi at this time wrote his
opera "L'incoronatione di
Dario" for the Teatro di Sant'
Angelo at Venice.

Toward the end of spring this
year the contest between the
organ-builders approached its
decisive phase. Renatus Harris
asked the Benchers of the Inner
Temple for permission to arrange
a public hearing of his organ
in the Temple Church.

Kerll resigned his position as
court organist and returned to
Munich this year.

J. Kuhnau succeeded Kühnel at
this time as organist at St.
Thomas' at Leipzig.

Lalande was given a wife, Anne
Rébel, by the King this year.

Christian Liebe this year was
organist at Frauenstein and
afterwards became rector there.

John Moss left the King's
private music at this date.

Henry Playford this year was
granted control of his father's
publishing business along with
Richard Carr.

John Playford, the elder bade

1684(cont.)
farewell to the public in his
"Choice Ayres," Book V.

When the court returned to
Vienna this year A. Poglietti's
widow was allowed a pension of
18 florins monthly, until her
remarriage.

Purcell and Blow both took part
in the famous organ competition
at the Temple Church this year.

Purcell moved from Great St.
Ann's Lane to Bowling Alley
East just before the last
quarter of this year. This was
obvious since he paid only
three-quarters of his yearly
rent.

The St. Cecilia's day celebration for this year did not hold
the interest of the previous
year when Purcell's music was
a feature.

Early this year Purcell prepared another composition for
publication. This one contained
a preface written by him to his
"Musical Entertainment,"
"Welcome to all the Pleasures,"
which was performed the previous November in honor of St.
Cecilia.

At the end of this summer
Purcell was busy writing another
welcome ode for King Charles
II's return from Windsor to
Whitehall.

Scarlatti left Rome where he
had recently produced several
operas.

Francesco Scarlatti this year
became a violinist in the royal
band at Naples.

Bernhard Smith and Renatus
Harris each built an organ in
the church of the Societies of
the Temple at this time.

Since Staggins had not performed
the usual exercise upon receiving his Doctor of Music
from Cambridge he felt obliged
to do so and to have the fact
and its consequence announced
in the London Gazette: "Dr.
Nicholas Staggins, who was some
time since admitted to the
degree of Dr. of music, being
desirous to perform his exercise upon the first opportunity
for the said degree, has
acquitted himself so much to
the satisfaction of the whole
University this Commencement,
that by solemn vote they have
constituted and appointed him
to be a public professor of
music there."

The professorship at the
University of Cambridge dated
from this year when Staggins,
master of the King's band, was
appointed to the position, apparently through court influence.

This year Antonio Stradivarius
was making larger-built instruments with a varnish of a
deeper color and as on the
"Long Strads" it gave a rich
hue of amber and light red.

Alexandre Thierry this year
built the organ at Saint
-Germain-en-Laye castle.

Vitali became "maestro di
cappella" to Duke Francesco II
of Modena this year.

Zachau this year was elected
organist of Our Lady's Church
at Halle.

Blankenburg's most famous work was "Onderwijzinge hoemen alle de Toonen en halve Toonen, die meest gebruijckelijck zijn, op de Handt-Fluijt zal konnen t'eenemael zuijver Blaezen" published at Amsterdam by P. Matthijsz. It was reprinted in 1871.

Blow's most important Ode for St. Cecilia's Day, "Begin the Song," was composed this year.

In Blow's "Venus and Adonis" of this year there was singing throughout.

Boesset's "Fruits d'automne" was published this year by Ballard.

August Boetius at this time wrote his "Merkwürdige und Auserlesene Geschichte von der beruhmten Landgraffschalft Thüringen," while at Gotha.

Colonna's opus 5, "Messe piene" was published this year at Bologna.

G.B. Draghi contributed songs to Nahum Tate's farce "A Duke and No Duke."

J.P. Förtsch this year wrote his first and second operas: "Croesus" and "Das unmöglichste Ding."

Domenico Gabrieli's "Balletti gighe, correnti e sarabande," opus 1 was published at this time.

Grabu's "Pastoralle. A Pastoral in French beginning with an Overture and some Aires for Violins, ..." was issued this year at London.

Johann Krieger II's "Neue musicalische Ergetzlechkeit," containing three parts, sacred, "political" and theatrical songs in score, was published this year at Frankfort and Leipzig.

Legrenzi this year composed his last opera, "Pertinance."

Lully's opera "Amadis" was composed at this time.

Southerne's play "Disappointment" with music by Pack appeared this year.

Purcell's vocal duet "When gay Philander left the plain" was published at this time.

The following songs by Purcell were published this year:

"A thousand several ways I tried"
"Beware, poor shepherd's"
"He himself courts his own ruin"
"In Chloris all soft charms agree"
"Let us, kind Lesbia, give away"
"Through mournful shades and solitary groves"

Purcell's welcome-song for King Charles II, "From those serene and rapturous joys," was written this year.

Gaspar Sanz this year wrote a treatise on the Spanish guitar.

Scarlatti's "Il Pompeo" was published this year at Naples.

Jakob Scheiffelhut at this time wrote his "Musicalischer Gemüts-Ergötzungen erstes Werck."

Christopher Simpson's "Division

Violin" was published this year
containing pieces by Davis Mell.

Strungk's selection of opera
airs was published this year at
Hamburg, "Ein hundert auserlesene
Arien zweyer Hamburgischen
Operen, Semiramis und Esther"
Mit beigefügten Ritornellen.

The number of parts, four or
less, was exceeded in such works
as the "Varie Sonate," opus 11
by Vitali this year. It had
three violin parts, two viola
parts, a violone and figured
bass and was published by Ferri
at Modena.

The first great performance of
the "Ancient Society of College
Youths" was recorded in the
books of the society and took
place at St. Saviour's,
Southwark.

In the British service it was
mentioned in an indent for arms
and accoutrements this year that
there was a request for "one
drum for the drum-major."

"Follias" were included this
year in the "Division Violin" by
Playford under the title of
"Faronell's Division on a Ground."

"Psyché," set to music by Lully,
was revived this year with music
by Charpentier.

J.W. Franck's opera "Semiramis"
was performed this year at
Hamburg.

An oratorio by Mazzaferrata was
performed at Siena this season.

Pallavicino's opera "Licinio
imperatore" with libretto by
Noris was performed this year at

(cont.) the Teatro San Giovanni
Crisostomo in Venice.

Pallavicino's opera "Ricimero,
re de'Vandali" was performed
this year at the Teatro San
Giovanni Crisostomo in Venice.

Pollarolo's opera "Roderico" was
performed this year at Brescia,
Milan, Naples, Rome and Verona.

Pierre Corneille, classical
French tragedian, died according
to several sources (born 1606).

Adriaen Van Ostade, Dutch painter, died (born 1610).

Jean Antoine Watteau, renowned
Flemish painter who lived in
Paris, was born (died 1721).

(to 1685) During this year
Purcell moved from Great St.
Ann's Lane to Bowling Alley East,
as was obvious from entries in
the St. Margaret's, Westminster
Churchwardens' Accounts for
1684 and 1685.

(to 1685) Thierry restored the
organs built by his father at
Saint-Gervais during these
years.

(to 1685) Westhoff toured Europe
as a violinist and visited
England at this time.

(to 1690) Johann Förtsch during
these years wrote twelve opera
for the Hamburg opera house.

(to 1690) Förtsch was house
composer to the Hamburg Opera,
providing almost the whole repertory during this period.

(to 1690) Antonio Stradivari at
this time principally tried to
avoid the defects of other

1684(cont.)

makers, in the meantime trying
new methods for himself.

(to 1698) The elder Biber's
name was mentioned during this
time in connection with about a
dozen plays performed at
Salzburg University.

(to 1700) Antonio Stradivarius'
work at this time showed the
progress of those experiments
which were to culminate in perfection of form and balance.
His greatest changes in crafts-
manship took place during these
years.

(to 1702) Scarlatti at this time
was settled in Naples and mon-
opolized the stage at St.
Bartolomeo.

(to 1730) André Philidor was
librarian of the King's musical
library where he founded an excellent collection of dance
tunes, divertissements, operas
by Lully and other works of interest from the reign of King
Henri III to the end of the
17th-Century.

c.1684

François Dagincour(t)
(d'Agincour), French composer,
was born at Rouen (died 1758,
June 18).

Alessandro Marcello, Italian
philosopher, mathematician and
composer, was born at Venice
(died c.1750).

Charpentier this year was appointed "maître de musique" to
the Jesuits of the Maison
-professe in Paris.

Blow's opera "Venus and Adonis"
was produced at London.

Queen Catherine I of Russia
was born (died 1727).